Self Study Notes

For

The Kitáb-i-Íqán

The Book of Certitude

Volume I

Sohrab Kourosh

First Edition: December 2016

ISBN: 978-0-692-81182-5

Kourosh Publishing
701 Thomas Ct.
Southlake, Texas, 76092
USA

Contents

Preface i
A Note on Transliteration v
References to the Bible vii
References to the Qur'án vii
Introduction to the Kitáb-i-Íqán ix
Historical Background and Scriptural Significance ix
The immediate circumstances surrounding the revelation of the Kitáb-i-Íqán xii
Part One 1
Paragraph No. 1 1
Paragraph No. 2 9
Paragraph No. 3 21
Paragraph No. 4 28
Paragraph No. 5 29
Paragraph No. 6 39
Paragraph No. 7 44
Paragraph No. 8 51
Paragraph No. 9 55
Paragraph No. 10 55
Paragraph No. 11 56
Paragraph No. 12 71
Paragraph No. 13 90
Paragraph No. 14 96
Paragraph No. 15 101
Paragraph No. 16 103
Paragraph No. 17 113

Contents

Paragraph No. 18 125
Paragraph No. 19 129
Paragraph No. 20 136
Paragraph No. 21 146
Paragraph No. 22 146
Paragraph No. 23 157
Paragraph No. 24 163
Paragraph No. 25 183
Paragraph No. 26 189
Paragraph No. 27 199
Paragraph No. 28 203
Paragraph No. 29 210
Paragraph No. 30 212
Paragraph No. 31 214
Paragraph No. 32 216
Paragraph No. 33 219
Paragraph No. 34 221
Paragraph No. 35 224
Paragraph No. 36 225
Paragraph No. 37 226
Paragraph No. 38 228
Paragraph No. 39 233
Paragraph No. 40 234
Paragraph No. 41 240
Paragraph No. 42 242
Paragraph No. 43 245
Paragraph No. 44 248
Paragraph No. 45 250
Paragraph No. 46 251
Paragraph No. 47 257
Paragraph No. 48 265
Paragraph No. 49 270

Contents

Paragraph No. 50 271
Paragraph No. 51 272
Paragraph No. 52 273
Paragraph No. 53 276
Paragraph No. 54 276
Paragraph No. 55 287
Paragraph No. 56 292
Paragraph No. 57 297
Paragraph No. 58 306
Paragraph No. 59 307
Paragraph No. 60 315
Paragraph No. 61 316
Paragraph No. 62 318
Paragraph No. 63 319
Paragraph No. 64 322
Paragraph No. 65 329
Paragraph No. 66 334
Paragraph No. 67 340
Paragraph No. 68 342
Paragraph No. 69 344
Paragraph No. 70 350
Paragraph No. 71 357
Paragraph No. 72 359
Paragraph No. 73 373
Paragraph No. 74 374
Paragraph No. 75 384
Paragraph No. 76 389
Paragraph No. 77 396
Paragraph No. 78 397
Paragraph No. 79 400
Paragraph No. 80 408
Paragraph No. 81 419

Contents

Paragraph No. 82 420
Paragraph No. 83 425
Paragraph No. 84 432
Paragraph No. 85 434
Paragraph No. 86 439
Paragraph No. 87 443
Paragraph No. 88 444
Paragraph No. 89 445
Paragraph No. 90 449
Paragraph No. 91 453
Paragraph No. 92 456
Paragraph No. 93 462
Paragraph No. 94 467
Paragraph No. 95 468
Paragraph No. 96 468
Paragraph No. 97 469
Paragraph No. 98 471
Paragraph No. 99 474
Paragraph No. 100 479
Paragraph No. 101 483
Appendix I 495
Appendix II 531
Appendix III 555
Appendix IV 563
Appendix V 571
Bibliography 575
Index 585

The Íqán is the most important book written on the spiritual significance of the Cause. I do not believe any person can consider himself well versed in the teachings unless he has studied it thoroughly.

(Shoghi Effendi, The Light of Divine Guidance v I, p. 37)

Preface

This is not a commentary on the Kitáb-i-Íqán (the Book of Certitude). Nor is it an exegetical work. This is a compilation of notes prepared by myself and other members of my family during our studies of the Kitáb-i-Íqán, as well as notes from handouts I prepared for study sessions and deepening classes on this Book over the last twenty-five years.

As Bahá'u'lláh stated:

> . . . in every age, the reading of the scriptures and holy books is for no other purpose except to enable the reader to apprehend their meaning and unravel their innermost mysteries. Otherwise reading, without understanding, is of no abiding profit unto man.
> (The Kitáb-i-Íqán, ¶185)

The study of the Kitáb-i-Íqán can take place on several levels. On one level a person can read the Book and benefit greatly without referring to any other books or materials. However, in light of Shoghi Effendi's statement regarding the importance of the Kitáb-i-Íqán, "the book is so important that the most minute detail is worthy of consideration,"[1] its study at deeper levels becomes imperative.

Considering the fact that in the course of exposition and interpretation of the theological and religious concepts, Bahá'u'lláh employs many theological, philosophical, and religious terms, and makes reference to other sacred scriptures as well as historical events, the study of the Kitáb-i-Íqán at deeper levels can be greatly aided by the study or review of the additional source materials.

In compiling these "Self Study Notes," an effort was made to furnish, in the same volume, information that might not be readily available to all readers at the time of their reading of the Book. It is hoped that the availability of the necessary information will eliminate interruptions in the process of study and thus contribute to a more enriched understanding of the concepts and a more enjoyable and rewarding study experience.

The Self Study Notes for the Book of Certitude are compiled in two volumes. Thus, the Notes in this first volume include the definition of

---

[1] Quoted in the book "George Townshend", p. 73.

mystical terms, the historical or scriptural basis for certain spiritual concepts, and either the full text of the scriptural verses quoted or the summarized original sources to which Bahá'u'lláh refers in the first part of the Book of Certitude (paragraphs 1–101).

In some cases, works by historical or religious scholars that provide the background for understanding the many references to the spiritual themes or events of the past cited by Bahá'u'lláh, have been quoted. Also included are references to Bahá'u'lláh's other Writings, as well as the Writings of the Báb, 'Abdú'l-Bahá, and Shoghi Effendi, which will help to clarify certain passages or assist in understanding the concepts presented in the Book.

Study of the Kitáb-i-Íqán at deeper levels requires the study of complimentary materials, an effort has been made here to maintain a balance in this process whereby sufficient information is provided to facilitate understanding, but detailed analysis of the subject matter or collateral sources that might divert the reader's attention from the Sacred Text or cause boredom have been avoided. Additional materials on a few subjects have been provided in appendices for those readers who wish to have more information on those subjects.

This book was originally prepared in a format in which the full text of the Book of Certitude was presented accompanied by annotations in the form of footnotes. However, in compliance with the instructions and guidance provided by the department of the Secretariat of The Universal House of Justice, an alternative format was selected for the book.[2]

---

[2] In their letter to the present author, The Department of the Secretariat of The Universal House of Justice provided the following guidance regarding the format of the Book:

> With regard to the format of your study guide, . . . it would not be proper to publish a full-text edition of a Bahá'í Sacred Text incorporating a study guide. By the same token, it would not be proper to publish a study guide incorporating a full-text edition of the Sacred Text. A format should be chosen which does not include the entire text and in which the explanations are not in the form of annotations keyed to the text.
> (Letter dated 24 April 2014, on file with this author)
>
> In stating that the House of Justice feels it is important to distinguish clearly between the Sacred Texts themselves and study guides or commentaries written upon them, it is meant that the Sacred Text itself should not be printed in full within, or as an appendix to, a study guide.
> (Letter dated 22 March 2015, on file with this author)

In recent print editions of the Book of Certitude, the paragraphs are numbered. This book has been prepared with a special format in which utilizing the paragraph numbers, sentences or phrases from each paragraph are quoted under that paragraph number. These are assigned a sequential Note number and comments are provided under that Note number.

Every effort has been made to minimize the impact of personal interpretation of the Sacred Text, and if, of necessity, an explanation borders on interpretation, it is requested that it be regarded solely as the author's individual interpretation, which lacks any authority.[3]

In preparing this compilation of notes, 'Abdu'l-Ḥamíd Ishráq-<u>Kh</u>ávari's four volumes of compendium to the Kitáb-i-Íqán ("Qámus-i-Íqán," written in Persian), Adib Taherzadeh's four volumes of *The Revelation of Bahá'u'lláh*, and Hooper Dunbar's *A companion to the Study of the Kitáb-i-Íqán*, have been used and quoted. I am grateful to Mr. Dunbar and to the late Mr. Taherzadeh for their permission to use their work and am indebted to a number of other Bahá'í scholars who are named in the footnotes, notes, and appendices, whose work sheds light on many important and difficult subjects. However, in quoting or referencing the materials from the books, papers, articles, and presentations of these scholars, care has been taken to follow the guidance of the Universal House of Justice that the authority of the Revealed Word be upheld.[4]

---

[3] Regarding personal interpretation, The Universal House of Justice states:

> The existence of authoritative interpretations does not preclude the individual from engaging in the study of the Teachings and thereby arriving at a personal interpretation or understanding. A clear distinction is, however, drawn in the Bahá'í Writings between authoritative interpretation and the understanding that each individual arrives at from a study of its Teachings. Individual interpretations based on a person's understanding of the Teachings constitute the fruit of man's rational power and may well contribute to a greater comprehension of the Faith. Such views, nevertheless, lack authority.
> (Kitáb-i-Aqdas, Notes, pp. 221– 22)

[4] Regarding the presentation of personal ideas, The Universal House of Justice states:

> In presenting their personal ideas, individuals are cautioned not to discard the authority of the revealed words, not to deny or contend with the authoritative interpretation, and not to engage in controversy; rather they should offer their thoughts as a contribution to knowledge, making it clear that their views are merely their own.
> (Kitáb-i-Aqdas, Notes, p. 222)

I am also indebted to my wife, Dr. Elham Kourosh, and my other family members for their help and encouragement in preparing this book, especially Dr. Emitis Hosoda, Dr. Atoosa Kourosh, Ms. Artemis Kourosh, Dr. Arianne Shadi Kourosh, and Mrs. Naseem Kourosh for their valuable contributions and editorial endeavors.

I dedicate this book to the memory of my late teacher and a great scholar of the Faith, Mr. Ishráq-Khávari, for his tireless work in writing books, providing information and insight, and encouraging the study of the Sacred Texts.

Any comments, corrections, or additions to these notes are welcomed and will be considered for inclusion in the future editions with appreciation and gratitude.

Sohrab Kourosh

A Note on Transliteration

Based on the following guidance from the Guardian and the Universal House of Justice, Arabic and Persian terms, names, and words are presented in accordance with the transliteration system adopted by Guardian.

> Particularly regarding the transliteration of Oriental terms, he would urge you to exercise the minutest care.
> (Shoghí Effendí, *Extracts from the USBN,* January 30, 1930)

> Shoghi Effendi has given the proper transliteration of the Eastern terms and wants you to abide by them, keeping every dash, point, accent or inverted comma.
> (Shoghi Effendi, *Extracts from the USBN*, N. 46. November 1930)

> Adherence to "the system of transliteration which the Guardian has supplied" will avoid confusion in future, and insure in this matter a uniformity which is greatly needed at present in all Bahá'í literature.
> (Shoghi Effendi, *Directives from the Guardian*, p. 79)

> There is no doubt that transliteration is irksome and often confusing, but what the average person does not realize is that through transliteration the exact word is nailed down and those who are familiar with the system know immediately what the original word was because they can reconstruct it in Arabic or Persian. For scholars and critics of the Faith this accuracy is very important. It also serves the purpose of doing away with multiple and confusing spellings of the same word."
> (Rúḥíyyih Rabbaní, *The Priceless Pearl*, p. 205)

> Regarding the transliteration of Persian and Arabic words the House of Justice requests that the method adopted by the beloved Guardian, and which is described in the various volumes of 'The Bahá'í World', be followed, as it permits all languages which use the Roman alphabet to transliterate such terms in the same way throughout the Bahá'í world.
> (From a letter written on behalf of the Universal House of Justice to the National Spiritual Assembly of Panama, July 16, 1979, in *Lights of Guidance*, p. 107)

Based on the above guidance, most of the Persian and Arabic terms in this text are presented in accordance with the system of transliteration which the Guardian has supplied. (See *The Bahá'í World*, Vol. IV (1930–1932), pp. 314–316; *The Dawn-Breakers*, Appendix, p. 673.) However, some terms or names, such as Islám, Islámic, Baghdád, Irán and Shoghí Effendí, which are commonly used in English without diacritical marks, appear without diacritical marks, and terms that appear without diacritical marks in texts quoted from other sources have not been altered.

For some words that have been transliterated differently by different authors (such as:Shí'ah, Shí'i, and Shí'ih or Surih, Súrah and Sura, etc.), the form that has been used by Shoghí Effendí (such as Shí'ah or Súrah) has been selected for use in this book. However, where a word in different transliteration form appears in a text that is quoted from other sources, it is not altered.

References to the Bible

Among the English translations of the Bible, the King James Version of the Bible occupies the most prominent position.

> Shoghi Effendi himself uses the King James Version of the Bible, both because it is an authoritative one and in beautiful English.
> (From a letter dated 28 October 1949 to an individual believer)

In this book the King James Version of the Bible is used for citations from both The Old Testament and The New Testament.

The Biblical citations from the King James Version are referenced as:

(The Book in the King James Version. The Chapter No.: the Verse No.)

Such as:

(Matthew 13:43)

References to the Qur'án

Among the English translations of the Qur'án, Sale's and Rodwell's are two of the more well known and prominent translations. Shoghi Effendi commented on these translations:

> Sale's translation is the most scholarly we have, but Rodwell's version is more literary, and hence easier for reading.
> (From a letter dated 23 November 1934 to an individual believer)

In this book, unless otherwise noted, the translation of John Meadows Rodwell (first published in 1867, published in Everyman's Library in 1909 and reissued is 1992) is used for Qur'ánic quotations. In the Rodwell translation the súrahs (chapters) of the Qur'án are arranged chronologically and their numbers differ from the original Arabic. In citations from the Qur'án the súrahs have been numbered according to the original numbering, but the verse numbers are those in Rodwell's translation which sometimes differ from the original Arabic numbering.

The Qur'án citations from the Rodwell's translation are referenced as:
(The Qur'án súrah No.:verse No.)

When referencing the Qur'án citations from the other translations, the name of translator is mentioned such as:

(The Qur'án, N. J. Dawood tr, súrah No.:verse No.)

Introduction to the Kitáb-i-Íqán

Historical Background and Scriptural Significance:

The Kitáb-i-Íqán has great prominence among the Writings of Bahá'u'lláh. Its significance is emphasized in the Writings of the Central Figures[5] of the Faith as well as the writings of Shoghi Effendi:

Bahá'u'lláh called it the lord of the books, and in His last major Writing, the Epistle to the Son of the Wolf, states:

> Briefly, there hath been revealed in the Kitáb-i-Íqán (Book of Certitude) concerning the Presence and Revelation of God that which will suffice the fair-minded.[6]

In the Kitáb-i-Íqán, He states:

> All the Scriptures and the mysteries thereof are condensed into this brief account. So much so that were a person to ponder it a while in his heart, he would discover from all that hath been said the mysteries of the Words of God, and would apprehend the meaning of whatever hath been manifested by that ideal King.[7]

In the introduction to the first English translation of the Kitáb-i-Íqán in 1904, 'Abdú'l-Bahá wrote:

> O' Thou who are athirst for the water of life this manifest book is the fountainhead of the water of eternal life. Drink so much as thou art able from the fountain of the living water. O' thou who art seeking after the knowledge of God! Immerse thyself in the ocean of the explanation of the Beauty of the Merciful, so that thou mayest gather from its depths the pearls of the wisdom of God.[8]

---

[5] Bahá'u'lláh, the Báb, and 'Abdú'l-Bahá.

[6] Bahá'u'lláh, Epistle to the Son of the Wolf, p. 118.

[7] Bahá'u'lláh, The Kitáb-i-Íqán, ¶ 266.

[8] 'Abdú'l-Bahá's statement on the frontispiece of the first English translation of the Kitáb-i-Íqán, titled: *The Book of Assurance.* Translated by Ali-Kuli Khan Nabílu'd-Dawlih and Howard MacNutt. Published in New York for the Bahá'í Publishing Society by Bretano's, 1924.

Shoghi Effendi described the place and significance of this book in a summary of its themes in *God Passes By*:

1. The place of the Kitáb-i-Íqán in Bahá'í Literature:

   - "Foremost among the priceless treasures cast forth from the billowing ocean of Bahá'u'lláh's Revelation ranks the Kitáb-i-Íqán (Book of Certitude), revealed in the space of two days and two nights . . . it was written in fulfillment of the prophecy of the Báb, Who had specifically stated that the Promised One would complete the text of the unfinished Persian Bayán"

   - ". . . this Book, setting forth the Grand Redemptive scheme of God, occupies a position unequaled by any work in the entire range of Bahá'í literature, except the Kitáb-i-Aqdas, Bahá'u'lláh's Most Holy Book."

   - "Revealed on the eve of the declaration of His Mission, it proffered to mankind the 'Choice Sealed Wine,[9] whose seal is of musk,' and broke the 'seals' of the 'Book' referred to by Daniel."[10] [11]

   - "Well may it be claimed that of all the books revealed by the Author of the Bahá'í Revelation, this Book alone,

---

[9] This phrase is a reference to the verses in the Qur'án in which the righteous are promised to have the "Choice sealed wine" in Paradise:

> Surely, among delights shall the righteous dwell! Seated on bridal couches they will gaze around; Thou shalt mark in their faces the brightness of delight; Choice sealed wine shall be given them to quaff, The seal of musk. For this let those pant who pant for bliss.
> (The Qur'án 83:22–28)

[10] Shoghi Effendi, *God Passes By*, pp. 138–39.

[11] Daniel Chapter 12 (the last chapter of Daniel's prophetic dream of the future):

> And I heard, but I understood not: then said I, O my Lord, what shall be the end of these things? And he said, 'Go thy way, Daniel: for the words are closed up and sealed till the time of the end'.
> (Daniel, 12:8)

by sweeping away the age-long barriers that have so insurmountably separated the great religions of the world, has laid down a broad and unassailable foundation for the complete and permanent reconciliation of their followers."[12]

2. The style of the Kitáb-i-Íqán:

- "A model of Persian prose, of a style at once original, chaste and vigorous, and remarkably lucid, both cogent in argument and matchless in irresistible eloquence."[13]

3. The major themes of the Kitáb-i-Íqán:[14]

- ". . . proclaims unequivocally the existence of a personal God, unknowable, inaccessible, the source of all Revelation, eternal, omniscient, omnipresent and almighty;"
- "Asserts the relativity of religious truth and the continuity of Divine Revelation;"
- "Affirms the unity of the of the Prophets, the universality of their Message, the identity of their fundamental teachings, the sanctity of their scriptures, and the twofold character of their stations;"
- "Denounces the blindness and the perversity of the divines and the doctors of every age;"
- "Cites and elucidates the allegorical passages of the New-Testament, the abstruse verses of the Qur'án, and the cryptic Muḥammadan traditions which have bred those age-long misunderstandings, doubts and animosities that have sundered and kept apart the followers of the world's leading religious systems;"

[12] Shoghi Effendi, *God Passes By*, pp. 138–39.

[13] Shoghi Effendi, *God Passes By*, p. 138.

[14] Ibid., p. 138.

- "Enumerates the essential prerequisites for the attainment by every true seeker of the object of his quest;"
- "Demonstrates the validity, sublimity and significance of the Báb's Revelation;"
- "Acclaims the heroism and detachment of His disciples;"
- "Foreshadows, and prophesies the world-wide triumph of the Revelation promised to the people of the Bayán,"

The Kitáb-i-Íqán was revealed in Baghdád, the capital of Iraq, which was a part of the Ottoman Empire in 1862, approximately one year before Bahá'u'lláh's public declaration in the Garden of Riḍván. At the time of the revelation of the Kitáb-i-Íqán the Bábí Faith was in a state of flux. Mírzá Yaḥyá[15] (Azal), the half-brother of Bahá'u'lláh and the figurative head of the Bábí Faith at the time, was hiding in disguise in Iraq for fear of his own life. He did not have the knowledge and the leadership ability to manage and lead the Bábí community.

Bahá'u'lláh had to take over the leadership of the Bábí community to rescue it from total disarray and disintegration. The Kitáb-i-Íqán was revealed during this time of turmoil. It is assumed that the Kitáb-i-Íqán fulfilled the dual purpose of proving the truth of the Báb's claim and also of preparing the ground for Bahá'u'lláh's own public declaration.

The immediate circumstances surrounding the revelation of the Kitáb-i-Íqán:

The following is paraphrased from *The Revelation of Bahá'u'lláh* by Adib Taherzadeh, Vol. I, pp. 152–63:

His Holiness the Báb had three maternal uncles. His second uncle, Mírzá Siyyid 'Alí, also known as Khál-i-A'ẓam (the Greatest Uncle), who was the uncle who raised him after the passing of his father, was the only one

[15] The "Arch-Breaker of the Covenant of the Báb," *God Passes By*, pp. 28, 90, 112–15, 233.

of His uncles to have embraced His Cause at the time of His Martyrdom. Aware of the special qualities that the Báb possessed since earliest childhood, Ḥájí Mírzá Siyyid 'Alí was the first to embrace the Cause of the Báb in Shíráz after the Letters of the Living and was himself martyred few months before the Blessed Báb as one of the Seven Martyrs of Ṭihrán[16]

[16] Ḥájí Mírzá Siyyid 'Alí, surnamed Khál-i-A'ẓam (Literally, "The Greatest Uncle."), the Báb's maternal uncle, and one of the leading merchants of Shíráz. It was this same uncle into whose custody the Báb, after the death of His father, was entrusted, and who, on his Nephew's return from His pilgrimage to Hijáz and His arrest by Husayn Khán, assumed undivided responsibility for Him by pledging his word in writing. It was he who surrounded Him, while under his care, with unfailing solicitude, who served Him with such devotion, and who acted as intermediary between Him and the hosts of His followers who flocked to Shíráz to see Him. His only child, a Siyyid Javád, died in infancy. Towards the middle of the year 1265 A.H. (1848–9 A.D.), this same Ḥájí Mírzá Siyyid 'Alí left Shíráz and visited the Báb in the castle of Chihríq. From thence he went to Ṭihrán and, though having no special occupation, remained in that city until the outbreak of the sedition which brought about eventually his martyrdom.

Though his friends appealed to him to escape the turmoil that was fast approaching, he refused to heed their counsel and faced, until his last hour, with complete resignation, the persecution to which he was subjected. A considerable number among the more affluent merchants of his acquaintance offered to pay his ransom, an offer which he rejected. Finally he was brought before the Amír-Niẓám. "The Chief Magistrate of this realm," the Grand Vazír informed him, "is loth to inflict the slightest injury upon the Prophet's descendants. Eminent merchants of Shíráz and Ṭihrán are willing, nay eager, to pay your ransom. The Maliku't-Tujjár has even interceded in your behalf. A word of recantation from you is sufficient to set you free and ensure your return, with honours, to your native city. I pledge my word that, should you be willing to acquiesce, the remaining days of your life will be spent with honour and dignity under the sheltering shadow of your sovereign." "Your Excellency," boldly replied Ḥájí Mírzá Siyyid 'Alí, "if others before me, who quaffed joyously the cup of martyrdom, have chosen to reject an appeal such as the one you now make to me, know of a certainty that I am no less eager to decline such a request. My repudiation of the truths enshrined in this Revelation would be tantamount to a rejection of all the Revelations that have preceded it. To refuse to acknowledge the Mission of the Siyyid-i-Báb would be to apostatise from the Faith of my forefathers and to deny the Divine character of the Message which Muḥammad, Jesus, Moses, and all the Prophets of the past have revealed. God knows that whatever I have heard and read concerning the sayings and doings of those Messengers, I have been privileged to witness the same from this Youth, this beloved Kinsman of mine, from His earliest boyhood to this, the thirtieth year of His life. Everything in Him reminds me of His illustrious Ancestor and of the imáms of His Faith whose lives our recorded traditions have portrayed. I only request of you that you allow me to be the first to lay down my life in the path of my beloved Kinsman."

The Amír was stupefied by such an answer. In a frenzy of despair, and without uttering a word, he motioned that he be taken out and beheaded. As the victim was being conducted to his death, he was heard, several times, to repeat these words of Ḥáfiẓ: "Great is my gratitude to Thee, O my God, for having granted so bountifully all I have asked of Thee."

The Báb's eldest uncle, Ḥájí Mírzá Siyyid Muḥammad, had great respect for his Nephew's integrity and spirituality. He wrote a letter to the Báb's mother after the Báb visited him upon returning from pilgrimage, and attested to the following:

> "His eminence Jináb-i-Hájí[17] has safely arrived and I am pleased to spend my time in His presence. . . . Truly, His bountiful soul is the

---

"Hear me, O people," he cried to the multitude that pressed around him; "I have offered myself up as a willing sacrifice in the path of the Cause of God. The entire province of Fárs, as well as 'Iráq, beyond the confines of Persia, will readily testify to my uprightness of conduct, to my sincere piety and noble lineage. For over a thousand years, you have prayed and prayed again that the promised Qá'im be made manifest. At the mention of His name, how often have you cried, from the depths of your hearts: 'Hasten, O God, His coming; remove every barrier that stands in the way of His appearance!' And now that He is come, you have driven Him to a hopeless exile in a remote and sequestered corner of Ádhirbáyján and have risen to exterminate His companions. Were I to invoke the malediction of God upon you, I am certain that His avenging wrath would grievously afflict you. Such is not, however, my prayer. With my last breath, I pray that the Almighty may wipe away the stain of your guilt and enable you to awaken from the sleep of heedlessness."

"He took off his turban, and, raising his face towards heaven, exclaimed, 'O God, Thou art witness of how they are slaying the son of Thy most honourable Prophet without fault on his part.' Then he turned to the executioner and recited this verse: 'How long shall grief of separation from Him slay me? Cut off my head that Love may bestow on me a head.'" (Mathnaví, Book 6, p. 649, 1, 2; ed. 'Alá'u'd-Dawlih.) (*A Traveller's Narrative,* Note B, p. 174.)

These words stirred his executioner to his very depths. Pretending that the sword he had been holding in readiness in his hands required to be resharpened, he hastily went away, determined never to return again. "When I was appointed to this service," he was heard to complain, weeping bitterly the while, "they undertook to deliver into my hands only those who had been convicted of murder and highway robbery. I am now ordered by them to shed the blood of one no less holy than the Imám Músáy-i-Káẓim himself!" (The Seventh Imám). Shortly after, he departed for Khurásán and there sought to earn his livelihood as a porter and crier. To the believers of that province, he recounted the tale of that tragedy, and expressed his repentance of the act which he had been compelled to perpetrate. Every time he recalled that incident, every time the name of Ḥájí Mírzá Siyyid 'Alí was mentioned to him, tears which he could not repress flowed from his eyes, tears that were a witness to the affection which that holy man had instilled into his heart."
(Shoghi Effendi, *The Dawn-Breakers*, Chapter XXI, p. 446)

[17] Ḥájí is the title of a person who has completed the rite of pilgrimage to Mecca (called Ḥáj). This pilgrimage is enjoined on all Muslims who are able to undertake it. Jináb is a courtesy title (His Honor).

> source of felicity for the people of this world, and the next. He brings honor to us all . . ."[18]

Yet, despite His admiration for the Báb, Ḥájí Mírzá Siyyid Muḥammad did not recognize the station of the Báb for many years. He was heartbroken when his brother was martyred and did not understand the reason why he did not accept the intercession of the influential merchants who were trying so hard to save his life.

Although he was a devoted and practicing Muslim, and their family was known for their piety and charity, after they were identified with the Cause of the Báb and his brother was killed for following and supporting the Báb, the whole family experienced hardship and he and his youngest brother were subject to discriminatory treatment by their business associates and other merchants. For several years he did not want to discuss this subject with anyone. However, once when engaged in a series of discussions with Áqá Mírzá Núru'd-Dín,[19] a close relative of the Báb,

---

[18] Adib Taherzadeh, *The Revelation of Bahá'u'lláh,* Vol. I, p. 153.

[19] Áqá Mírzá Áqá-i-Afnán (Núru'd-Dín), "His mother was a sister of Khadíjih Bigum, the wife of the Báb, and Áqá Mírzá Áqá was born two years before His Declaration. In a Tablet to His wife revealed in the prison of Máh-Kú, the Báb assures her that when Áqá Mírzá Áqá reaches the age of maturity, he will be her helper and protector. These prophetic words of the Báb were fulfilled, for Áqá Mírzá Áqá dedicated his life to the service of his beloved aunt whom he revered and served with unbounded devotion. Khadíjih Bigum lovingly taught him the Faith and at the age of thirteen Áqá Mírzá Áqá recognized the truth of the Mission of the Báb.

Soon after His Declaration near Baghdád, Bahá'u'lláh sent Nabíl-i-A'ẓam to Persia to announce the momentous news to the Bábís. Nabíl went to the home of Áqá Mírzá Áqá and announced the joyful tidings to the believers in Shíráz. Áqá Mírzá Áqá immediately gave his allegiance to Bahá'u'lláh and considered himself a humble servant at His threshold. On one occasion the wife of the Báb, who was seated behind a curtain, heard Nabíl inform the friends that the Blessed Beauty was the Promised One of the Bayán, 'Him Whom God shall make Manifest'. No sooner did that noble woman hear this announcement than she put her forehead to the ground in adoration of her newly-found Lord and is reported to have whispered to her nephew: 'Offer at His sacred threshold my most humble devotion.' Thus the bonds of love and adoration which had united these two became strengthened through their immediate response to the Cause they had both spontaneously espoused.

From the early days Áqá Mírzá Áqá became the recipient of many favours and bounties from Bahá'u'lláh. The custodianship of the House of the Báb, which was conferred upon the wife of the Báb and her sister, also included him and his descendants. In 1879 Áqá

Ḥájí Mírzá Siyyid Muḥammad was forced to reconsider his position. During the discussion, Ḥájí Mírzá Siyyid Muḥammad intimated that he could simply not believe that His own Nephew was the promised one of Islam. In reply, Áqá Mírzá Núru'd-Dín compared Ḥájí Mírzá Siyyid Muḥammad to Abú'-La'hab,[20] the uncle of Muḥammad. Ḥájí Mírzá Siyyid Muḥammad was understandably shaken by the comparison and asked Áqá Mírzá Núru'd-Dín what he should do to convince himself of the validity of the Báb's claim. Áqá Mírzá Núru'd-Dín suggested that he go on pilgrimage to Iraq and while there, visit his sister, the mother of the Báb, who had been living there since the martyrdom of her Son, and then go to Ba<u>gh</u>dád in order to attain the presence of Bahá'u'lláh and ask his questions of Him.

Inspired by this encounter, Ḥájí Mírzá Siyyid Muḥammad, who lived in <u>Sh</u>íráz, wrote to his youngest brother, Ḥájí Mírzá Ḥasan-'Alí, who lived in Yazd, and asked him to accompany him on pilgrimage. He agreed to join him. It was not until they reached Ba<u>gh</u>dád that Ḥájí Mírzá Siyyid Muḥammad revealed to his brother the real purpose of the visit. The younger brother became angry, and although younger in age, he spoke harshly to him and said he did not want to hear about the Faith and left.

Mírzá Áqá moved to India and established a trading business in Bombay. A few years later, in 1887, he travelled to Egypt and Beirut where he stayed for some time in the home of his maternal uncle Ḥájí Mírzá Siyyid Ḥasan, known as Afnán-i-Kabír (the Great Afnán). In Beirut he and his eldest son Áqá Siyyid Áqá received permission to visit Bahá'u'lláh. They both attained His presence for the first time on the anniversary of the Báb's Declaration which that year coincided with 20 January 1888. Bahá'u'lláh bestowed unbounded blessings upon them. He is reported to have honoured them by ordering His servant to place a fur-lined overcoat on the shoulders of each as they were sitting in His presence. With Bahá'u'lláh's approval Áqá Mírzá Áqá and his eldest son proceeded to Port Said and established a business there. Each year he was permitted to go to the Holy Land where he attained the presence of Bahá'u'lláh."
(Adib Taherzadeh, *The Revelation of Baha'u'llah,* Vol. 4, p. 328)

Lawḥ-i-Dunyá (The Tablet of the World) was revealed in 1891 in honour of Áqá Mírzá Áqá-i-Afnán, when he was in the presence of Bahá'u'lláh.

[20] Abú'-La'hab, (the name means the "father of flame") was one of the uncles of Muḥammad who refused to acknowledge the prophethood of Muḥammad and was one of his staunchest opponents. The Súrah of Al-La'hab, the Súrah (Chapter) 111 of the Qur'án is in reference to him. For a brief history of Islam and the life of Muḥammad, see Footnote 20 in Appendix I.

Mírzá Áqá Ján,[21] described the events that followed in a (Tablet) addressed to Shaykh 'Abdu'l-Majíd-i-Shírází.[22] According to the Tablet, Ḥájí Siyyid Javá'd-i-Karbilá'í[23] went to Bahá'u'lláh and informed Him that the Báb's two uncles were in Baghdád. Bahá'u'lláh instructed him to bring them to His presence. The next day, Ḥájí Siyyid Javá'd, arrived with Ḥájí Mírzá Siyyid Muḥammad.

While in Bahá'u'lláh's presence, the Báb's eldest uncle was overwhelmed by His utterances and in the end beseeched Bahá'u'lláh to help him to see the truth of the Báb's Message, bearing in mind that certain Islamic traditions[24] were not, in his view, fulfilled by his Nephew.[25] Bahá'u'lláh readily consented to help him and bade him to return with a list of the questions which puzzled him. The Báb's uncle then returned with four

---

[21] Mírzá Áqá Ján, the amanuensis of Bahá'u'lláh for forty years, *God Passes By* p. 115.

[22] Shaykh 'Abdu'l-Majíd-i-Shírází was one of the early believers (see *The Revelation of Bahá'u'lláh*, Vol. I, p. 154).

[23] Ḥájí Siyyid Javád-i-Karbilá'í was one of the prominent believers at the time of Bahá'u'lláh in Baghdad.
(see the *The Revelation of Bahá'u'lláh* vol.1 p.155)

[24] Islamic traditions: The religion of Islam is supported by two pillars, one is the Qur'án and the other is Sunnah, the words and deeds (living example) of the Prophet Muḥammad, which were heard or observed by His close followers and were recorded for posterity. Customarily, the word Tradition (Ḥadíth) is used in reference to the words or sayings of the Prophet (the verbal part of Sunnah). The followers of the Shí'ah sect of Islam hold that the words and deeds of the Imáms (the descendants of the Prophet Muḥammad through His daughter Fátimih) form a corpus that is complementary to the Prophetic Sunnah and Traditions. For further details on the Qur'án and Islamic Traditions see Appendix I.

[25] The followers of many religions are expecting some special events to take place that signify the time of the end, coinciding with the coming or return of their promised one. The most common events and signs are:
First: The rolling up of the heavens.
Second: The sun will be darkened.
Third: The moon shall not give her light.
Fourth: The stars shall fall from heaven.
Fifth: The dead shall arise from their tombs.
Sixth: Ferocious animals will make peace with grazing animals.
Seventh: They will share the same pasture and food. (from *The Brilliant Proof*, pp. 31–32)

categories of questions all dealing with the coming of the Qá'im.[26] The questions have been preserved in the papers of the Afnán family.[27]
The questions he asked were the following:[28]

- *The Day of Resurrection:*[29] Is there to be a corporeal resurrection? The world is utterly filled with injustice.[30] How are the just to be requited and the unjust punished?"
- *The Twelfth Imám was born at a certain time and lives on*[31]. There are traditions all supporting this belief. How can this be explained?"

---

[26] Qá'im (one of the stations claimed by the Báb), the word means "He who ariseth" or "the one that is standing." It is the title of the promised one of Islam whose advent coincides with the Day of Resurrection. Bahá'u'lláh states "When the Qá'im ariseth, that day is the Day of resurrection," The Kitáb-i-Íqán, ¶152.

[27] Afnán (Literally means "twigs") are the family of the Báb (cousins, uncles etc.) who became believers. They chose Afnán as their family name (an allusion to the Báb being the main trunk of the tree, and they being the twigs).

[28] Quoted from H. M. Balyuzi, *Bahá'u'lláh, The King of Glory*. Oxford: George Ronald, 1980. pp. 164–65.

[29] The Islamic concept of the Day of Resurrection is very similar to this concept in Judaism, Christianity, and Zoroastrianism. In general they believe that the advent of the promised one of Islam, the Mahdí (literally meaning the Guided One for Sunnis) or Qá'im (literally meaning the Standing One or the Rising One for the Shí'ahs) is coincidental with the Day of Resurrection. In that day all the dead will rise from their graves in their physical bodies and will be present in the plane of resurrection. They will all be judged by the weight of their good deeds. All have to pass over a bridge (called Ṣerat) that spans Hell and connects the plane of judgment to Heaven (Paradise). This bridge is narrower than a hair, sharper than a blade, and longer than any conceivable measure. The people of the right (those whose good deeds overweigh their bad deeds), will have no trouble passing over the bridge. The more righteous a person the faster he/she passes over the bridge. Those whose bad deeds are heavier will fall from the bridge into Hell. The majority of Muslims believe in corporeal resurrection and physical Heaven and Hell. For more details see Appendix I.

[30] The Muslims believe that their promised one (Mahdí or Qá'im) will come with worldly power and authority, will establish justice and punish the unjust (Justice and equity will fill the world, in the same manner that injustice and inequity has filled it up). They believe that he will establish the ascendancy of Islam and Muslims over all other religions and people and will kill the nonbelievers (in Shí'ah belief, even the non-Shí'ah Muslims). For more details see Appendix I.

---

[31] The followers of the <u>Sh</u>í'ah sect of Islam believe that an authentic and reliable Tradition from the Prophet Muḥammad states: "I leave two things of value amidst you in trust which if you hold on to, you will never go astray: the Qur'án and the members of my household. These will never be separated until the Day of Judgment." They believe that the "members of my household" means Imám 'Alí Ibn-i-Abíṭáleb (the cousin and son-in-law of the Prophet) and 'Alí's male descendants (those who were accepted by the <u>Sh</u>í'ahs as Imáms, the inspired religious leaders, (their number differs, i.e., four or six or eleven according to different sects)). The main sect of <u>Sh</u>í'ah Islam (who accept twelve Imáms, 'Alí and eleven of his descendants) accept the authority of those whom they call the "Fourteen Sinless or Inerrant,"—the Prophet Muḥammad, Imám 'Alí, his wife Fátimih, the daughter of the Prophet, and their accepted male descendants or Imáms. The "Twelfth Imám" is believed to be the promised one of Islam, also called Qá'im (the one that is standing) and Mahdí (the guided one). The <u>Sh</u>í'ah believe that he is the son of the Eleventh Imám, Ḥasan al-'Askarí, who was known not to have a son. There are several stories about the identity of his mother and his miraculous birth. Some stories hold that his mother was a slave girl named Rayḥáneh or Ṣaqíl or a Byzantine slave-girl who was bought by the Tenth Imám, 'Alí al-Hádí, for his son the Eleventh Imám, Ḥasan al-'Askarí. In some versions of story, the girl was a princess, the daughter of a Byzantine Emperor, who was informed in a vision that she would be the mother of the Mahdí. The Twelfth Imám is believed to have been born in 255 AH/868 AD (or in some stories five years later, close to the date of the death of the Eleventh Imám on 260 AH/ 873 AD) in Sámarrá, in Iraq. He was given the same name as the Prophet, Abu'l-Qásim Muḥammad. The miraculous and extraordinary story of his birth originated from an unknown woman who was a relative of the Eleventh Imám. She said that she visited the Eleventh Imám's house one day and did not see any signs of pregnancy in the Imám's wife, but when she was leaving in the afternoon, the Imám asked her to stay because his wife was going to give birth to his son. That night the Imám's wife gave birth to a boy, who at the moment of birth prostrated and prayed by reciting a few Qur'ánic verses. This lady related that when she went back to the Imám's house for another visit a few weeks later, she saw a five- or six-year-old boy playing in the yard. She asked the boy who he was and the boy told her that he was the child that was born few weeks ago and when she expressed surprise, the boy said that we (Imáms) grow at an extraordinary rate.
(For more details see Moojan Momen, *An Introduction to Shi'i Islam*, pp. 160–61)

"The usual miraculous accounts of his talking from the womb, etc . . . may be passed over to the only occasion on which he is said to have made a public appearance. This was in 260/874 when the Eleventh Imam died, it appears that none of the Shi'ih notables knew of the birth of Muḥammad [the "Twelfth Imam"] and so they went to the Eleventh Imam's brother, Ja'far, assuming that he was now the Imam, Ja'far seemed prepared to take on this mantel and entered the house of the deceased Imam in order to lead the funeral prayers. At this juncture a young boy came forward and said: 'Uncle, stand back! For it is more fitting for me to lead the prayers for my father than for you.' After the funeral, Ja'far was asked about the boy and said that he did not know who the boy was. For this reason, Ja'far has been vilified by generations of Shi'is as *Kadhdhāb*, the liar. The boy was seen no more and Shi'is tradition states that from that year he went into occultation. At Sámarrá, beside the gold-domed Shrine of the Imáms 'Alí al-Hádí and Ḥasan al-'Askarí is a mosque under which there is a cave. The end of one of the rooms of the cave is partitioned off by a gate which is called Báb al-Ghayba (Gate of the

- *Interpretation of the Holy Texts.*[32] This Cause does not seem to conform to the beliefs held throughout the years. One cannot ignore the literal meaning of the Holy Texts and Scriptures. How can this be explained?

- *Certain events, according to the traditions that have come down from the Imáms, must occur before the advent of the Qá'im.*[33] Some of these are mentioned.

Occultation) and was built on the instructions of the Caliph an-Nāṣir in 606/1209. The area behind the gate is called Ḥujrat al-Ghayba (Chamber of the Occultation) and in the corner of this is a well, the Bi'r al-Ghayba (Well of the Occultation) down which the Imam Mahdí is said to have disappeared. Shi'is gather in the rooms of the cave and pray for his return."
(Moojan Momen, *An Introduction to Shi'i Islam*, p. 161)

Shí'ahs believe that the Twelfth Imám, who was born in 255 AH/868 AD, is still alive and continues to be in occultation. He is believed to be residing in two invisible cities called Jábulsá and Jábulqáá, and will appear at the end of the time prior to the day of resurrection, in which time he will kill all the nonbelievers and establish the rule of Shí'ah Islam over the world. In the mind of a Shí'ah, the Báb Who was born in Shíráz in 1819 could not be the Qá'im who was born almost one thousand years earlier and was to come out of occultation. For more details see Appendix I.

[32] There are many references in the Shí'ah holy traditions regarding signs and events that appear before or at the time of the advent of the Qá'im. Among them are the rising of the sun from the west and the appearance of a star the size of the moon from the east. Several of the enemies of the Shí'ahs who died many centuries ago will return to fight against him, among them is Dajjál (the one-eyed disciple of Satan), and many other signs and event. The Qá'im will kill so many of his enemies with his sword that their blood will flow like a river that reaches the knees of his horse. He is expected to promote Islam and establish the rule of the Qur'án. Contrary to these expectations, the Báb established a new religion and revealed a new Holy Book.
(For more details about this subject see *An Introduction to Shi'i Islam*, pp. 161–71, quoted in Appendix I).

[33] As mentioned in footnote no. 30 above, the Shí'ahs believed that the "Twelfth Imám, did not die but has been concealed by God from the eyes of men. His life has been miraculously prolonged until the day when he will manifest himself again by God's permission. . . . he is still in control of the affairs of men and is the Lord of The Age *(Ṣáḥib az-Zamán)*. . . . The Hidden Imám was popularly believed to be resident in the far-off cities of Jábulsá and Jábulqá and in former times books were written about persons who had succeeded in traveling to these places. Less has been made of this particular tradition in recent times when modern geographical knowledge permeated the Shí'ah masses and it became generally realized that no such places existed."

"The Hidden Imam, the Imam Mahdí, is in occultation awaiting the time that God has decreed for his return. This return is envisaged as occurring shortly before the final Day

> But none of these has happened. How can this be explained?"

In answer to these questions, Bahá'u'lláh, within the span of two days and two nights, revealed what is known today as the Kitáb-i-Íqán[34] but was in the early days referred to as Risálíy-i-Khál (Epistle to the Uncle). The original copy/manuscript of the Book was written in the hand of 'Abdú'l-Bahá, who was eighteen years of age at that time. A few corrections and the following paragraph near the end of the book were written by Bahá'u'lláh Himself:

> Amidst them all, We stand, life in hand, wholly resigned to His will; That perchance through God's loving kindness and His grace, this revealed and manifest Letter may lay down His life as a sacrifice in the path of the Primal Point,[35] the most exalted Word. By Him at Whose bidding the Spirit hath spoken, but for this yearning of Our soul, We would not, for one moment have tarried any longer in this city. "Sufficient Witness is God unto Us."[36]

In this book, Bahá'u'lláh addresses the issues and expectations common among the believers of all religions that become obstacles and veils that prevent them from recognizing the promised one of their religion (the new Manifestation of God), whom they await and for whose advent they pray. Bahá'u'lláh does not validate the Shí'ah stories regarding the birth of the

---

of Judgment. The Hidden Imam will then return as the Mahdí with a company of his chosen ones and there will also return his enemies led by one-eyed Dajjál and the Sufyānī. The Imam Mahdí will lead the forces of righteousness against the forces of evil in one final apocalyptic battle in which the enemies of the Imam will be defeated." (Momen, *An Introduction to Shi'i Islam*, pp. 165–66)

[34] Some scholars think that for a book of this size (almost 200 pages in Persian) to be revealed and transcribed within the span of two days and two nights, the same procedure used in the later instances of revelation, in which Bahá'u'lláh chanted or spoke the revealed words and His amanuensis copied the revelation in the form of the "revelation writings" (khaṭṭ-i-tanzíl خط تنزيل), might have been adopted. The text was subsequently transcribed from the revelation writings. For additional information see (Symbol & Secret, Qur'an Commentary in Bahá'u'lláh's Kitáb-i-Íqán, p. 8) and for a sample of the "revelation writings" see (Adib Taherzadeh, *The Revelation of Bahá'u'lláh,* Vol.1, p. 110.)

[35] The "Primal Point", from which have been generated all created things, is one of the titles of the Báb. He is also called His Holiness the Exalted One.

[36] Bahá'u'lláh, The Kitáb-i-Íqán, ¶279.

Twelfth Imám and the occultation stories about him by discussing the particulars of those tales.

The Kitáb-i-Íqán dispelled every doubt that Ḥájí Mírzá Siyyid Muḥammad had harbored. He became a devout believer, and at the end of his life he acknowledged his belief in the twin Manifestations of the Báb and Bahá'u'lláh in his will and testament. The remainder of the Báb's family, as was prophesied by the Báb Himself, including his youngest uncle, Ḥájí Mírzá Siyyid Ḥasan-'Alí, eventually embraced the Faith.

The original manuscript of the Kitáb-i-Íqán was presented to Shoghi Effendi in 1948 by Fátimih-Khánum-i-Afnán, the great-granddaughter of Ḥájí Mírzá Siyyid Muḥammad. It was placed in the International Archives Building[37] at Bahá'í World Center on Mount Carmel in Haifa, Israel.

The Kitáb-i-Íqán was revealed by Bahá'u'lláh in Persian (Fársi). It was first published in Persian in Bombay, India in the early 1880s and was again published among a group of the Writings of Bahá'u'lláh in 1890.[38] It was first translated into English by 'Alí-Kuli Khán, Nabilu'd-Dawlih, assisted by Howard MacNutt, and published under the title "The Book of Assurance" in New York by George V. Blackburn, Co., in 1904. It was later retranslated into English by Shoghi Effendi as "The Kitáb-i-Íqán: The Book of Certitude" and first published in 1931 by The National Spiritual Assembly of the Bahá'ís of the United States of America.

The following letter, written by Shoghi Effendi to the National Assembly through his secretary, refers to this translation:

> As the Íqán is the most important book wherein Bahá'u'lláh explains the basic beliefs of the faith, he thought a proper rendering of it would infinitely enhance the teaching work in the West. He hopes that this new rendering will be an improvement on the previous one, but he fully admits that it is far from perfect, far from the original itself. Shoghi Effendi has given the proper transliteration of the Eastern terms and wants you to abide by

---

[37] An account of this presentation can be found in *Shoghi Effendi: Recollections* by Hugo Giachery on p. 149. More details are presented in Appendix I.

[38] H. M. Balyuzi, *Bahá'u'lláh:The King of Glory*, p. 165, and Shoghi Effendi, letter dated February 9, 1930, *Unfolding Destiny*, p. 424.

them, keeping every dash, point, accent or inverted comma. To help you in this, he has also on a separate sheet written these in their proper form. He wishes you further not to include the introduction that exists in the last edition, for he does not think it worthwhile and enlightening. Drop also the glossary that exists at the end of the last edition and form a glossary using the definitions that he has sent to be put in the forthcoming Bahá'í World. As Shoghi Effendi has been emphasizing the need of submitting all publications to the Reviewing Committee, he wants to be the first to abide by that rule, though he hopes that they will not make unnecessary delay. In Germany they have translated the 'Íqán from the last translation and they are waiting for Shoghi Effendi's rendering to make the necessary alterations and publish their own. The proceeds of the sale of the book Shoghi Effendi wishes to go to the American National Assembly in an unlabeled form. This is a gift of his own personal labors that he wishes to present that body and he wishes it to be considered as a token of appreciation for the help they have rendered him in carrying on his arduous task.
(Signed) RUHI AFNAN.

Unable to find a good typist, I have had to do the work myself, and I trust that the proofreaders will find it easy to go over and will not mind the type errors which I have tried to correct. I would especially urge you to adhere to the transliteration which I have adopted. The correct title is, I feel, 'The Kitáb-i-'Íqán,' the sub-title 'The Book of Certitude.' May it help the friends to approach a step further, and obtain a clearer idea of the fundamental teachings set forth by Bahá'u'lláh.
(Signed) SHOGHI.
(Shoghi Effendi, *Extracts from the USBN*)[39]

The English translation is divided into two parts:

- Part I: Proofs of all previous Manifestations

  The major themes of this part are:[40]

---

[39] Following Shoghi Effendi's instruction, in this "Self Study Notes," the Book is Refered to as the Kitáb-i-Íqán.

[40] See Taherzadeh, *Revelation of Bahá'u'lláh* vol.1, pp. 162–175.

Reasons for man's opposition to the prophets
Signs of the return of Christ
Interpretation of symbolic terms found in sacred books of the past

- Part II: Proofs of the Báb's mission:

The major themes of this part are:[41]

The sovereignty of the Manifestations of God
The meaning of Life, Death, and Resurrection
The veil of knowledge and the requirements of the true seeker
Specific proofs of the Báb's divine origin
Anticipation of His own Revelation

A second edition of "The Kitáb-i-Íqán: The Book of Certitude" with an introduction and index was published in 1950. The book has been subsequently printed more than fifteen times. This Self Study Notes is based on the 2003 edition in which the paragraphs are numbered.

---

[41] Taherzadeh, *Revelation of Bahá'u'lláh*, vol. 1, pp. 175–97.

PART ONE

IN THE NAME OF OUR LORD THE EXALTED, THE MOST HIGH.[1]

1. "In the Name of Our Lord the Exalted, the Most High" is a translation of the Arabic "Bismih Rabin al 'Ali'u'l-A'lá." This invocation of the name of God, contains also two references to His Holiness the Báb, whose given name was Siyyid 'Alí Muḥammad. 'Alí in Arabic means the Exalted; He is also referred to in the Writings of the Faith and among the Persian believers as *Ḥazrat-i-A'lá* ("His Holiness the Most High"). These titles of the Báb are also mentioned in other Writings of Bahá'u'lláh in juxtaposition to His own title Abhá ("the Most Glorious"), such as in one of the Fast prayers:

> Thou seest me, O my God, holding to Thy Name, the Most Holy, the Most Luminous, the Most Mighty, the Most Great, the Most Exalted, the Most Glorious . . ."
> (Bahá'u'lláh, *Prayers and Meditations*, p. 288)

Paragraph No. 1:

shores of the ocean of true understanding[2]

2. The Arabic word translated by Shoghi Effendi as "True Understanding" is *"'Irfán."* In both Persian and Arabic there are several words for *knowledge* and *understanding*, such as "Ilm" which is the knowledge possessed by men such as mathematics and other sciences. *'Irfán,* "true understanding," however, is a spiritual or divinely assisted knowledge—not a knowledge that can be acquired through books. *'Irfán* comes from the root word *"'arafa"* which means to know or recognize. There is an Islamic tradition that states: "Whoever knows (*'arafa*) his own self, he will verily know (*'arafa*) his God." *Irfán* is this type of knowledge and has a much wider meaning than the word *'Ilm.* It is a state of complete understanding that involves both the intellectual faculties and the heart of a person. In this special application, the word

'Irfán (true understanding) describes the state of deep awareness and recognition of truth.

> The Revelation of Bahá'u'lláh confers a new capacity on those whose hearts are touched by its light and enables them to acquire a knowledge which is not dependent on learning. This knowledge is referred to in Islam as "a light which God casteth into the hearts of whomsoever He willeth.
> (Adib Taherzadeh, *Revelation of Bahá'u'lláh*, Vol. 1, p. 43)

Bahá'u'lláh describes it in these words:

> It is this kind of knowledge which is and hath ever been praiseworthy, and not the limited knowledge that hath sprung forth from veiled and obscured minds. This limited knowledge they even stealthily borrow from one another, and vainly pride themselves therein!
> (Bahá'u'lláh, The Kitáb-i-Íqán, ¶48)

Again He states:

> Not, however, until thou consumest with the flame of utter detachment those veils of idle learning, that are current amongst men, canst thou behold the resplendent morn of true knowledge. . . .
>
> The heart must needs therefore be cleansed from the idle sayings of men, and sanctified from every earthly affection, so that it may discover the hidden meaning of divine inspiration, and become the treasury of the mysteries of divine knowledge.
> (Bahá'u'lláh, The Kitáb-i-Íqán, ¶ 75, 77)

As mentioned above, another meaning of *'Irfán* is recognition. Shoghi Effendi translates *'Irfán* in the first verse of the Kitáb-i-Aqdas as recognition:

> The first duty prescribed by God for His servants is the recognition of Him Who is the Dayspring of His Revelation and the Fountain of His laws,
> (Bahá'u'lláh, The Kitáb-i-Aqdas, ¶1)

A third meaning of the word *'Irfán* is to describe the school of thought which is translated in English as "Mysticism." "Mystical" and "Mysticism" are translations of the Arabic and Persian words 'Irfání and 'Irfán. The Webster Dictionary definitions of Mysticism and Mystical are:

Mysticism:

> 1 : the mystical union or direct communion with ultimate reality reported by mystics.
>
> 2 : a theory of mystical knowledge: the doctrine or belief that direct knowledge of God, of spiritual truth, of ultimate reality, or comparable matters is attainable through immediate intuition, insight, or illumination, and in a way differing from ordinary sense perception or ratiocination. Any theory postulating or based on the possibility of direct and intuitive acquisition of ineffable knowledge or power.

Mystical:

> 1: having a spiritual meaning, existence, reality, or comparable value that is neither apparent to the senses nor obvious to the intelligence: relating to such a value; Symbolical; Anagogic (the church is the mystical body of Christ) or (the mystical interpretation of Scriptures)
>
> 2: resulting from, or manifesting an individual's direct or intimate knowledge of or communion with God (as through contemplation, vision, an inner light); concerned with or relating to such experience, derived immediately rather than mediately: based upon intuition, insight, or similar subjective experience; remote from ordinary human knowledge or comprehension."
>
> (Merriam-Webster Online Dictionary 2010 last viewed 4/3/2015, see, the site: http://www.merriam-webster.com)

Considering the above definitions, a significant number of the Writings of Bahá'u'lláh are mystical writings, and this is due to the mystical nature of revelation. Shoghi Effendi explains:

> The Bahá'í Faith, like all other Divine religions, is thus fundamentally mystic in character. Its chief goal is the development of the individual and society, through the acquisition of spiritual virtues and powers.
> (Shoghi Effendi, in *Compilation of Compilations*, Vol. 2, p. 238)

Defining true mysticism, he states:

> We liken God to the Sun, which gives us all our life. So the Spirit of God reaches us through the Souls of the Manifestations. We must learn to commune with Their Souls, and this is what the Martyrs seemed to have done, and what brought them such ecstacy of joy that life became nothing. This is the true mysticism, and the secret, inner meaning of life which humanity has at present, drifted so far from.
> (Shoghi Effendi, *The Unfolding Destiny of the British Bahá'í Community*, p. 406)

Additional materials on this subject are presented in Appendix II.

except he be detached[3]

3. In the Sacred Writings of the Bahá'í Faith, detachment is considered a necessary condition for spiritual progress that enables us to overcome the barriers that prevent us from reaching the shores of the ocean of true understanding. Detachment is highly praised and recommended in the Bahá'í Faith that has been precisely defined by the Central Figures of the Faith to prevent misunderstanding.

> At one time this sublime Word was heard from the Tongue of Him Who is the Possessor of all being and the Lord of the throne on high and of earth below—exalted is the glory of His utterance:
>
> Piety and detachment are even as two most great luminaries of the heaven of teaching. Blessed the one who hath attained unto this supreme station, this habitation of transcendent holiness and sublimity.
> (Bahá'u'lláh, *Tablets of Bahá'u'lláh*, p. 253)

The three barriers between God and man delineated by Bahá'u'lláh in a Tablet cited by Adib Taherzadeh are:

> In another Tablet (*Ma'idih-i-Ásmáni,* vol. VIII, p. 26) Bahá'u'lláh states that there are three barriers between God and believers to pass beyond them so that they may be enabled to attain His presence. The first one . . . is attachment to the mortal world. The second attachment to the next world and all that is destined for man in the life hereafter. And the third is attachment to the "Kingdom of Names".
> (Adib Taherzadeh, *The Revelation of Bahá'u'lláh,* Vol. 2, page 35)

Additional materials on this subject are presented in Appendix II.

enter thus the tabernacle[4]

4. Tabernacle: signifies a place where God is present. According to the Book of Exodus (in which for the first time in religious writings a tabernacle was described) a tabernacle was a portable sanctuary that was carried by the Israelites during their journey through the Sinai wilderness after their exodus from Egypt. It was a structure built to the exact material and fabrication specifications and measurements given to Moses by the Lord (Exodus, Chapters: 25–31).[42] It was the place where the Lord was present and told the children of Israel He would meet them there. Inside it were two chambers. One was a holy place containing holy bread (shew bread) and candlesticks. The other chamber contained the Holy of Holies and the Ark of the Covenant. The Ark contained the law given to Moses at Sinai. The first place was the accessible part of the Tabernacle, but it could only be entered by the high priest of Israel on the Day of Atonement.

> 25,1 And the LORD spoke unto Moses, saying: 25,2 'Speak unto the children of Israel, that they take for Me an offering; of every man whose heart maketh him willing ye shall take My offering. 25,3 And this is the offering which ye shall take of them: gold, and silver, and brass; 25,4 and

[42] All Biblical references are from the King James Version.

blue, and purple, and scarlet, and fine linen, and goats' hair; 25,5 and rams' skins dyed red, and sealskins, and acacia-wood; 25,6 oil for the light, spices for the anointing oil, and for the sweet incense; 25,7 onyx stones, and stones to be set, for the ephod, and for the breastplate. 25,8 And let them make Me a sanctuary, that I may dwell among them. 25,9 According to all that I show thee, the pattern of the tabernacle, and the pattern of all the furniture thereof, even so shall ye make it. 25,10 And they shall make an ark of acacia-wood: two cubits and a half shall be the length thereof, and a cubit and a half the breadth thereof, and a cubit and a half the height thereof. 25,11 And thou shalt overlay it with pure gold, within and without shalt thou overlay it, and shalt make upon it a crown of gold round about, . . . And thou shalt put the ark-cover above upon the ark; and in the ark thou shalt put the testimony that I shall give thee. 25,22 And there I will meet with thee, and I will speak with thee from above the ark-cover, from between the two cherubim which are upon the ark of the testimony, of all things which I will give thee in commandment unto the children of Israel, . . . 28,1 And bring thou near unto thee Aaron thy brother, and his sons with him, from among the children of Israel, that they may minister unto Me in the priest's office, even Aaron, Nadab and Abihu, Eleazar and Ithamar, Aaron's sons. 28,2 And thou shalt make holy garments for Aaron thy brother, for splendour and for beauty. 28,3 And thou shalt speak unto all that are wise-hearted, whom I have filled with the spirit of wisdom, that they make Aaron's garments to sanctify him, that he may minister unto Me in the priest's office. 28,4 And these are the garments which they shall make: a breastplate, and an ephod, and a robe, and a tunic of chequer work, a mitre, and a girdle;. . . 28,15 And thou shalt make a breastplate of judgment, the work of the skilful workman; like the work of the ephod thou shalt make it: of gold, of blue, and purple, and scarlet, and fine twined linen, shalt thou make it. 28,16 Four-square it shall be and double: a span shall be the length thereof, and a span the breadth thereof. 28,17 And thou shalt set in it settings of stones, four rows of stones: a row of carnelian, topaz, and smaragd shall be the first row; 28,18 and the second row a carbuncle, a sapphire,

> and an emerald; 28,19 and the third row a jacinth, an agate, and an amethyst; 28,20 and the fourth row a beryl, and an onyx, and a jasper; they shall be inclosed in gold in their settings. 28,21 And the stones shall be according to the names of the children of Israel, twelve, . . . 28,30 And thou shalt put in the breastplate of judgment the Urim and the Thummim; and they shall be upon Aaron's heart, when he goeth in before the LORD; and Aaron shall bear the judgment of the children of Israel upon his heart before the LORD continually, . . . 29,42 It shall be a continual burnt-offering throughout your generations at the door of the tent of meeting before the LORD, where I will meet with you, to speak there unto thee. 29,43 And there I will meet with the children of Israel; and [the Tent] shall be sanctified by My glory.

In the New Testament story of the transfiguration of Christ, Peter wanted to build three tabernacles to honor Jesus, Moses, and Elijah respectively:

> And after six days Jesus taketh Peter, James, and John his brother, and bringeth them up into an high mountain apart, And was transfigured before them: and his face did shine as the sun, and his raiment was white as the light.
> And, behold, there appeared unto them Moses and Elias talking with him.
> Then answered Peter, and said unto Jesus, Lord, it is good for us to be here: if thou wilt, let us make here three tabernacles; one for thee, and one for Moses, and one for Elias.
> (Matthew 17:1–4)

which, according to the dispensations[5] of the Providence

5. Dispensation: "the divine ordering of the affairs of the world." (Random House Webster's Dictionary)

   In the Bahá'í Writings the word "Dispensation" generally refers to the divine Revelation or in some cases to a religion.

> Indeed, if any living creature were to pause to meditate he would undoubtedly realize that these verses are not the work of man, but are solely to be ascribed unto God, the One, the Peerless, Who causeth them to flow forth from the tongue of whomsoever He willeth, and hath not revealed nor will He reveal them save through the Focal Point of God's Primal Will. He it is, through Whose dispensations divine Messengers are raised up and heavenly Books are sent down.
> (The Báb, *Selections from the Writings of the Báb,* p. 135)
>
> At no time, in no Dispensation, have the Prophets of God escaped the blasphemy of their enemies,
> (Bahá'u'lláh, *Gleanings from the Writings of Bahá'u'lláh*, p. 57)
>
> Consider the Dispensation of Jesus Christ.
> (Bahá'u'lláh, *Gleanings from the Writings of Bahá'u'lláh*, p. 83)
>
> Every discerning observer will recognize that in the Dispensation of the Qur'án both the Book and the Cause of Jesus were confirmed.
> (Bahá'u'lláh, *Gleanings from the Writings of Bahá'u'lláh*, p. 21)
>
> . . . the Law of the Mosaic Dispensation,
> (Bahá'u'lláh, *Gleanings from the Writings of Bahá'u'lláh*, p. 22)

hath been raised in the firmament of the Bayán.[6]

6. "Raised in the firmament of the Bayán": Bayán means utterance. The mother Book of the Báb's dispensation was called the Bayán. There are two Bayáns: one in Persian and the other in Arabic. The Persian Bayán was to have nineteen váḥids (parts or units), each having nineteen chapters. However, it was only completed to the tenth chapter of the ninth váḥid by the Báb. Regarding this Book Shoghi Effendi states:

> Within the walls of that same fortress [Máh-Kú] the Bayán (Exposition)—that monumental repository of the laws and precepts of the new Dispensation and the treasury enshrining most of the Báb's references and tributes to, as

> well as His warning regarding, "Him Whom God will make manifest"—was revealed. Peerless among the doctrinal works of the Founder of the Bábí Dispensation; consisting of nine váḥids (Unities) of nineteen chapters each, except the last váḥid comprising only ten chapters; not to be confounded with the smaller and less weighty Arabic Bayán, revealed during the same period.
> (Shoghi Effendi, *God Passes By*, p. 24)

The Báb prophesized that the Bayán would be completed by the Promised One. The Kitáb-i-Íqán serves as fulfillment of this prophecy and is considered to be the completion of the váḥids of the Persian Bayán:

> It was written in fulfillment of the prophecy of the Báb, Who had specifically stated that the Promised One [The one whom God will make manifest] would complete the text of the unfinished Persian Bayán . . .
> (Shoghi Effendi, *God Passes By* p.138)

The Bábí religion is therefore called the Dispensation of the Bayán. Bahá'u'lláh in many of His Writings and specifically in the Kitáb-i-Íqán (pp. 44–68), explains that the firmament (heaven) described in the Scriptures symbolizes a religion or dispensation. Therefore, the Firmament of the Bayán is the religion of the Bayán. Thus it seems that the tabernacle raised in the firmament of the Bayán signifies the Báb and His own Revelation, which is the Tabernacle, and whoever attains to the station of faith in Him enters the Tabernacle that has been raised in the dispensation of Bayán, and attains the presence of God in the religion of the Bayán.

Paragraph No. 2:

they that tread the path of faith[7]

7. "They that tread" is the translation of *sálekin* (plural of sálik). In Islamic mystical literature, Sálik is the word used to connote one who on his quest for God, gives up self and passion—in other words, one who treads the path of faith. Suluk (treading the path) is the action of the sálik—it is the motion in an inward direction

towards the essence of one's own being and thus towards God. The process that takes place is a war that rages within one's self—a war waged against the ego and against the self and passion. A famous mystic named Láhíjí said that Suluk is going from bondage and multiplicity towards freedom and unity. In mysticism, once the sálik reaches the station of knowing himself, he is then able to see within it the reality of his own essence—the divine reality reflected in human soul. Bahá'u'lláh makes reference to this in the Hidden Words:

> O Son of Spirit.
> I created thee rich, why dost thou bring thyself down to poverty? Noble I made thee, wherewith dost thou abase thyself? Out of the essence of knowledge I gave thee being, why seekest thou enlightenment from anyone beside Me? Out of the clay of love I molded thee, how dost thou busy thyself with another? Turn thy sight unto thyself, that thou mayest find Me standing within thee, mighty, powerful, and self-subsisting.
> (Bahá'u'lláh, The Hidden Words, Arabic, no. 13)

Contrary to the general belief among mystics that those who tread the path of faith can reach God, Bahá'u'lláh teaches that God is Exalted and Unknowable and that the highest level of knowledge man can attain is the knowledge of the Manifestation of God.

> So perfect and comprehensive is His creation that no mind nor heart, however keen or pure, can ever grasp the nature of the most insignificant of his creatures; much less fathom the mystery of Him Who is the Daystar of Truth, Who is the invisible and unknowable Essence. The conception of the devoutest of mystics, the attainments of the most accomplished amongst men, the highest praise which human pen or tongue can render are all the products of man's finite mind and are conditioned by its limitations. Ten thousand Prophets, each a Moses are thunderstruck upon the Sinai of their search at His forbidding voice, "Thou shalt never behold Me!" whilst a myriad Messengers, each as great as Jesus, stand dismayed upon their heavenly thrones by the interdiction, "Mine essence thou shalt never apprehend!" From time immemorial He hath been veiled in the ineffable

> sanctity of His exalted Self, and will everlastingly continue to be wrapped in the impenetrable mystery of His unknowable Essence. Every attempt to attain an understanding of His inaccessible Reality hath ended in complete bewilderment, and every effort to approach His exalted Self and envisage His Essence hath resulted in hopelessness and failure. How bewildering to me, insignificant as I am, is the attempt to fathom the depths of His knowledge! How futile my efforts to visualize the magnitude of the power inherent in Thy handiwork—the revelation of Thy creative power! How can mine eye which hath no faculty to perceive itself, claim to have discerned Thine essence, and how can mine heart, already powerless to apprehend the significance of its own potentialities, pretend to comprehend Thy nature?
> (Bahá'u'lláh, *Gleanings from the Writings of Bahá'u'lláh*, p.62)

In the Seven Valleys, Bahá'u'lláh outlines the various stages a seeker on such a path would traverse. The valleys include the valleys of search, love, knowledge, unity, contentment, wonderment, and true poverty and absolute nothingness. Bahá'u'lláh in the valley of true poverty, and absolute nothingness explains that this valley is the state of "dying from self and the living in God." He then defines what dying from self means. The meaning of dying from self (*fanáyih az nafs*) and living in God is explained by Bahá'u'lláh in a tablet called the *Tablet of Shaykh-i-Fání. Fání* means someone who has attained to *faná* (dying of self).

> O Shaykh, O thou who hast surrendered thy will to God! By self-surrender[43] and perpetual union with God is meant that men should merge their will wholly in the Will of God, and regard their desires as utter nothingness beside His Purpose. Whatsoever the Creator commandeth His creatures to observe, the same must they diligently, and with the utmost joy and eagerness, arise and fulfill. They should in no wise allow their fancy to obscure their judgment, neither should they regard their own imaginings as the voice of the Eternal. In the Prayer of Fasting We have revealed: "Should Thy Will decree that out of Thy

[43] The term *fanáyih az nafs* is translated here by Shoghi Effendi as "self-surrender."

> mouth these words proceed and be addressed unto them, 'Observe, for My Beauty's sake, the fast, O people, and set no limit to its duration,' I swear by the majesty of Thy glory, that every one of them will faithfully observe it, will abstain from whatsoever will violate Thy law, and will continue to do so until they yield up their souls unto Thee." In this consisteth the complete surrender of one's will to the Will of God. Meditate on this, that thou mayest drink in the waters of everlasting life which flow through the words of the Lord of all mankind, and mayest testify that the one true God hath ever been immeasurably exalted above His creatures. He, verily, is the Incomparable, the Ever-Abiding, the Omniscient, the All-Wise. The station of absolute self-surrender transcendeth, and will ever remain exalted above, every other station.
> (*Gleanings from the Writings of Bahá'u'lláh*, pp. 337–38)

He also explained elsewhere:

> In this station, this most exalted habitation, this journey of utter self-effacement, the wayfarer forgetteth his soul, spirit, body, and very being, immerseth himself in the sea of nothingness, and liveth on earth as one unworthy of mention. Nor will one find any sign of his existence, for he hath vanished from the realm of the visible and attained unto the heights of self-abnegation.
> (*Gems of Divine Mysteries*, p. 70)

Bahá'u'lláh also defines "the life in God" or immortal life as:

> Know then that "life" hath a twofold meaning. The first pertaineth to the appearance of man in an elemental body . . . . This life cometh to an end with physical death, which is a God-ordained and inescapable reality. That life, however, which is mentioned in the Books of the Prophets and the Chosen Ones of God is the life of knowledge; that is to say, the servant's recognition of the sign of the splendours wherewith He Who is the Source of all splendour hath Himself invested him, and his certitude of attaining unto the presence of God through the Manifestations of His Cause. This is that blessed and everlasting life that perisheth not: whosoever is quickened thereby shall never

> die, but will endure as long as His Lord and Creator will endure.
> (*Gems of Divine Mysteries,* pp. 47–48)

The Path of Faith in this Dispensation is defined by Bahá'u'lláh in the opening words of His Most Holy Book:

> The first duty prescribed by God for His servants is the recognition of Him Who is the Dayspring of His Revelation and the Fountain of His laws, who representeth the Godhead in both the Kingdom of His Cause and the world of creation. Whoso achieveth unto this duty hath attained unto all good; and whoso is deprived thereof hath gone astray, though he be the author of every righteous deed. It behooveth everyone who reacheth this sublime station, this summit of transcendent glory, to observe every ordinance of Him who is the Desire of the world. These twin duties are inseparable. Neither is acceptable without the other. Thus hath it been decreed by Him who is the source of Divine inspiration.
> (Bahá'u'lláh, The Kitáb-i-Aqdas, ¶1)

they that thirst for the wine of certitude[8]

8. The wine mentioned in the Sacred Writings is an allegory for the words of God and divine Revelation. Jesus compared His new Revelation to new wine and His new religion to a new bottle:

> Then came to him the disciples of John, saying, Why do we and the Pharisees fast oft, but thy disciples fast not? And Jesus said unto them, Can the children of the bridechamber mourn, as long as the bridegroom is with them? but the days will come, when the bridegroom shall be taken from them, and then shall they fast. No man putteth a piece of new cloth unto an old garment, for that which is put in to fill it up taketh from the garment, and the rent is made worse. Neither do men put new wine into old bottles: else the bottles break, and the wine runneth out, and the bottles perish: but they put new wine into new bottles, and both are preserved.
> (Matthew 9:15–17)

> O SON OF DUST!
> Turn not away thine eyes from the matchless wine of the immortal Beloved, and open them not to foul and mortal dregs. Take from the hands of the divine Cup-bearer the chalice of immortal life, that all wisdom may be thine, and that thou mayest hearken unto the mystic voice calling from the realm of the invisible. Cry aloud, ye that are of low aim! Wherefore have ye turned away from My holy and immortal wine unto evanescent water?
> (Bahá'u'lláh, The Hidden Words, Persian, no. 62)

> The wine mentioned in the Tablets has undoubtedly a spiritual meaning for in the book of Aqdas we are definitely forbidden to take not only wine, but every thing that deranges the mind. In poetry as a whole wine is taken to have a different connotation than the ordinary intoxicating liquid. We see it thus used by the Persian Poets such as Sa'dí and 'Umar Khayám and Ḥafiz to mean that element which nears man to his divine beloved, which makes him forget his material self so as better to seek his spiritual desires. It is very necessary to tell the children what this wine means so that they may not confuse it with the ordinary wine.
> (Shoghi Effendi, *The Light of Divine Guidance,* vol. II, p. 6)

their minds from vain imaginings[9]

9. These vain imaginings is a translation of "subaḥát-i-Jalál," which literally means the veils of glory. Vain imaginings are like veils of glory that gradually, are wrapped around the person of the Manifestation of God. These vain imaginings cause the followers to attribute extraordinary characteristics to their prophets and think that their physical life and appearance was different from that of the ordinary people. These are the imaginary veils that like clouds prevent clear view. Bahá'u'lláh further in the book explains this:

> Consider how men for generations have been blindly imitating their fathers, and have been trained according to such ways and manners as have been laid down by the dictates of their Faith. Were these men, wherefore, to discover suddenly that a man that hath been living in their

> midst, Who, with respect to every human limitation, hath been their equal, had risen to abolish every established principle imposed by their Faith-principles by which for centuries they have been disciplined, and every opposer and denier of which they have come to regard as infidel, profligate and wicked,—they would of a certainty be veiled and hindered from acknowledging His truth.
> (Bahá'u'lláh, The Kitáb-i-Íqán, ¶81)

> And when he was come into his own country, he taught them in their synagogue, insomuch that they were astonished, and said, Whence hath this man this wisdom, and these mighty works? Is not this the carpenter's son? is not his mother called Mary? and his brethren, James, and Joseph, and Simon, and Judas? And his sisters, are they not all with us? Whence then hath this man all these things? And they were offended in him. But Jesus said unto them, A prophet is not without honour, save in his own country, and in his own house. And he did not many mighty works there because of their unbelief.
> (Matthew 13:54–58)

Thus, when the "vain imagining" or the "veils of glory" surround a person or a situation, they prevent us from seeing properly and become an obstacle to understanding. These vain imaginings prevent the inner eye from seeing clearly especially when it concerns the Prophets or Manifestations. Although all Manifestations of God were spiritually different and superior to normal human beings, They occupied an ordinary physical human frame. But Their followers glorified Their physical nature to the point that Their physical lives were made to appear superhuman. The vain imagining and veils of glory which in the minds of Jews were wrapped around the person of their expected Messiah caused the countrymen of Jesus to reject Him, because they imagined that a carpenter Whom they already knew and whose brothers and sisters were living among them could not be a prophet and did not match the image they had for their Messiah, which was to come with worldly power and authority.

Another example of this is that the same Jesus Whom to Jews looked like a simple and ordinary man, in turn, as a result of the vain imagining in the minds of His followers, was wrapped in the veils of Glory. Some Christians (especially the Catholics) believe that the above verses Matt. 13:54–58 and those in Mark 6:3 ("Is not this the carpenter, the Son of Mary, the Brother of James, and Joseph, and of Juda, and Simon? and are not his sisters here with us? And they were offended at him"), which state that Jesus had brothers and sisters are not true and reliable, because they negate the Church's teachings on the physical divinity of Jesus, and are contradictory to the teaching of the Church regarding the perpetual virginity of Mary. The Catholic Church teaches that the most ancient creeds call Mary "aei-parthenos," which means "Ever-virgin," and postulates that God closed Mary's womb after she gave birth to Jesus, and that she did not have any other children and remained ever a virgin. Having brothers and sisters makes Jesus similar and equal to Moses and this cannot be because in their minds Jesus was divine whereas Moses was a man. There has been a traditional divergence of views between Catholics and other Christians based on different interpretations of the same verse.

In some cases, such as in the case of Muḥammad, attributing superhuman qualities to the Prophet was in direct conflict with verses of the Qur'án and utterances of Muḥammad Himself, Who claimed he was just a man like others but had received Revelation.

> Say: I am only a man like you. It is revealed to me that your God is one God: go straight then to Him, and implore his pardon.
> (The Qur'án 41:5)

For instance, there was a legend about Muḥammad that claimed that he did not have a shadow. Therefore, when the Báb declared His mission, many Muslims, including His own uncle, who had fantastical ideas about the physical reality of the Manifestation of God or the promised Qá'im (in this case, Muḥammad and the Twelfth Imám) did not recognize Him because physically He appeared the same as any human being.

their heart[10] from worldly affections[11]

10. The heart is the center of human consciousness, the interface of the soul and the mind, the place of 'Irfán, inner spiritual knowledge,

and true understanding. In all sacred writings the heart is the place of the divine presence. Bahá'u'lláh states:

> It is incumbent on these servants that they cleanse the heart—which is the wellspring of divine treasures—from every marking, and that they turn away from imitation, which is following the traces of their forefathers and sires, and shut the door of friendliness and enmity upon all the people of the earth.
> (Bahá'u'lláh, The Seven Valleys, p. 5)

> O SON OF BEING!
> Thy heart is My home; sanctify it for My descent. Thy spirit is My place of revelation; cleanse it for My manifestation.
> (Bahá'u'lláh , The Hidden Words, Arabic, no. 59)

In the Kitáb-i-Aqdas, addressing the kings of the earth, He stated:

> By the righteousness of God! It is not Our wish to lay hands on your kingdoms. Our mission is to seize and possess the hearts of men. Upon them the eyes of Bahá are fastened.
> (Bahá'u'lláh, The Kitáb-i-Aqdas, ¶83)

> That the heart is the throne, in which the Revelation of God the All-Merciful is centered, is attested by the holy utterances which We have formerly revealed. Among them is this saying: 'Earth and heaven cannot contain Me; what can alone contain Me is the heart of him that believeth in Me, and is faithful to My Cause.'* How often hath the human heart, which is the recipient of the light of God and the seat of the revelation of the All-Merciful, erred from Him Who is the Source of that light and the Well Spring of that revelation.
> (Bahá'u'lláh, *Gleanings from the Writings of Bahá'u'lláh*, pp. 185–86)

* This tradition "Earth and Heaven cannot contain Me, but the heart of My faithful servant containeth Me" is one of the two Islamic holy traditions for which very detailed commentaries have

been revealed by the pen of 'Abdú'l-Bahá. The other one is the holy tradition of the Hidden Treasure.

11. There are many stories regarding the people who realized the divine nature and could see the spiritual ascendancy of the Manifestations of God, such as Jesus, the Báb, and Bahá'u'lláh, but worldly affections prevented them from confessing their faith or joining the ranks of the followers of the new Manifestation. Examples of the worldly affections are attachment to wealth and worldly power, concern for the disapproval of family members and other people, or fear of losing the position of religious or civil leadership:

> And, behold, one came and said unto him, Good Master, what good thing shall I do, that I may have eternal life? And he said unto him, Why callest thou me good? there is none good but one, that is, God: but if thou wilt enter into life, keep the commandments. He saith unto him, Which? Jesus said, Thou shalt do no murder, Thou shalt not commit adultery, Thou shalt not steal, Thou shalt not bear false witness, Honour thy father and thy mother: and, Thou shalt love thy neighbour as thyself. The young man saith unto him, All these things have I kept from my youth up: what lack I yet? Jesus said unto him, If thou wilt be perfect, go and sell that thou hast, and give to the poor, and thou shalt have treasure in heaven: and come and follow me. But when the young man heard that saying, he went away sorrowful: for he had great possessions.
> (Matthew 19:16–22)

Writing about the time of Bahá'u'lláh in Baghdád, and the famous people who visited Him during those days, H. M. Balyuzi states:

> Another who sought out Bahá'u'lláh in those days was Mírzá Muḥammad-Ḥusayn-i-Kirmání, known as Mírzá Muḥiṭ, he who had vied for the leadership of the Shaykhí movement after Siyyid Káẓim's death. This was the man who had been overwhelmed when the Báb challenged him with a declaration of His Mission by the Ka'bah at Mecca, and in answer to whose questions, the Báb revealed the *Ṣaḥifiy-i-Baynu'l-Ḥaramayn*. But despite this, Mírzá Muḥiṭ

had turned away from the Báb and had lived on in Karbilá until, more than two decades later, he now sought a secret meeting with Bahá'u'lláh.

Nabíl writes:

Nearing the end of his days, whilst residing in 'Iraq, he, feigning submission to Bahá'u'lláh, expressed, through one of the Persian princes who dwelt in Ba<u>gh</u>dád, a desire to meet Him. He requested that his proposed interview be regarded as strictly confidential. "Tell him," was Bahá'u'lláh's reply, "that in the days of My retirement in the mountain of Sulaymáníyyih, I, in a certain ode which I composed, set forth the essential requirements from every wayfarer who treads the path of search in his quest of Truth. Share with him this verse from that ode:
'If thine aim be to cherish thy life, approach not our court; but if sacrifice be thy heart's desire, come and let others come with thee. For such is the way of Faith, if in thy heart thou seekest reunion with Bahá; shouldst thou refuse to tread this path, why trouble us? Begone!' If he is willing, he will openly and unreservedly hasten to meet Me; if not, I refuse to see him." Bahá'u'lláh's unequivocal answer disconcerted Mírzá Muḥiṭ. Unable to resist and unwilling to comply, he departed for his home in Karbilá the very day he received that message. As soon as he arrived, he sickened, and, three days later, he died.
(H. M. Balyuzi, *Bahá'u'lláh: The King of Glory*, p. 152)

These two lines are from the ode (ghazál) *titled* "Sáqí az <u>gh</u>ayb-i-ba<u>gh</u>á" (O Cupbearer from the unseen immortal realm) which was revealed by Bahá'u'lláh during the period in which He lived in Sulaymáníyyih. For more details regarding this Ode and this author's provisional translation of it in its entirety see Appendix II.

the effulgent glories[12]

12. Effulgent is a translation of the word "tajalíyát." The dictionary meaning of the word effulgent is: diffusing a flood of resplendent light, radiant (Webster's New International Dictionary: Second

Edition, 1946). The use of this word serves to indicate, in harmony with the Bahá'í teachings, that man is able to attain to the knowledge of the attributes of his Creator—in other words, to know the resplendent light or attributes of his creator, in contrast to the Súfí idea of being able to know the essence of the Creator.

become the recipients of a grace[13] that is infinite

13. According to Webster's New International Dictionary: Second Edition, the ecclesiastic definition of grace is:

> a. Graciousness shown by God to man; especially divine favor unmerited by man; the mercy of God as distinguished from his justice.
> b. In theology, a free gift from God to man for his regeneration and sanctification; an impetus and influence emanating from God and operative for the spiritual well-being of the recipient.

Standard for the true understanding[14]

14. Throughout the religious history the words and deeds of the leaders of religions and their understanding and interpretation of the sacred scriptures were accepted as standard and followed by the believers of the previous dispensations. The differing understanding and interpretations of these mortal men have been the cause of sectarian divisions in all religions and opposition to every Manifestation of God. Bahá'u'lláh states that the standard is the Book of God itself, rather than the understanding of the "divines" of the age:

> Say: O leaders of religion! Weigh not the book of God with such standards and sciences as are current amongst you, for the book itself is the unerring balance established amongst men. In this most perfect balance whatsoever the peoples and kindreds of the earth possess must be weighed, while the measure of its weight should be tested according to its own standard, did ye but know it.
> (Bahá'u'lláh, The Kitáb-i-Aqdas, ¶99)

Paragraph No. 3:

awaited the advent of the Manifestations of God.[15]

15. "Manifestation of God": This term is used for the first time in sacred scriptures by the Báb, and used here again by Bahá'u'lláh in the opening paragraphs of the Kitáb-i-Íqán. It is used to refer to all major prophets of the past as well as the Báb and Bahá'u'lláh. In the holy books and scriptures of the past, those who revealed and promoted the word of God were referred to as prophets. Jesus chose the designation of "The Son of man" for Himself, and Muḥammad referred to Himself as "the Messenger of God"; these appellations distinguished them from the minor prophets. In this Dispensation they are referred to as the Manifestations, because they are not known only as the revealers of the Word, but they also manifest the attributes of God.

> From the foregoing passages and allusions it hath been made indubitably clear that in the kingdoms of earth and heaven there must needs be manifested a Being, an Essence Who shall act as a Manifestation and Vehicle for the transmission of the grace of the Divinity Itself, the Sovereign Lord of all.
>
> The Person of the Manifestation hath ever been the representative and mouthpiece of God. He, in truth, is the Day Spring of God's most excellent Titles, and the Dawning-Place of His exalted Attributes. If any be set up by His side as peers, if they be regarded as identical with His Person, how can it, then, be maintained that the Divine Being is One and Incomparable, that His Essence is indivisible and peerless? Meditate on that which We have, through the power of truth, revealed unto thee, and be thou of them that comprehend its meaning.
> (Bahá'u'lláh, *Gleanings from the Writings of Bahá'u'lláh*, p. 67)

Bahá'u'lláh defines the station of the Manifestation of God in the first paragraph of the Kitáb-i-Aqdas:

> The first duty prescribed by God for His servants is the recognition of Him Who is the Dayspring of His Revelation

> and the Fountain of His laws, who representeth the Godhead in both the Kingdom of His Cause and the world of creation.
> (Bahá'u'lláh, The Kitáb-i-Aqdas, ¶1)

Sanctified persons of His chosen Ones.[16]

16. Sanctified Persons of His chosen Ones: The word "person" is the translation of the Arabic word "Haykal," which is translated elsewhere by Shoghi Effendi, as "Temple." The Báb also referred to the difference between those "chosen" to be "The Manifestation of God" and the remainder of humankind. In His Tablet to Muḥammad Sháh, He states:

    > The substance wherewith God hath created Me is not the clay out of which others have been formed. He hath conferred upon Me that which the worldly-wise can never comprehend, nor the faithful discover.
    > (The Báb, *Selections from the Writings of the Báb*, p. 11)

how frequently have they prayed that the breeze of divine mercy might blow, and the promised Beauty step forth from behind the veil of concealment, and be made manifest to all the world.[17]

17. Every Manifestation of God has predicted or prophesied the return of Himself or the appearance of the Promised One, and Their followers pray for the return or the coming of the Promised One. The Jews expected the coming of the Messiah. The Christians pray in the only prayer revealed by Christ: "Thy Kingdom Come, Thy Will be Done . . ." longing for His return. The Muslims were expecting the twin Manifestations of the Qá'im and Imám Ḥusayn (for Shí'ah) or Mahdí and of Jesus Christ (for Sunnis). (see footnotes 22–25 of Introduction)

and the light of the Unseen[18] **did shine above the horizon of celestial might**

18. The word "Unseen" is a reference to God. In Islamic and Bahá'í Scriptures, God is referred to as "The Exalted Unapproachable

Unknowable Unseen." God cannot be seen by humans, not even the Prophets and Messengers of God.

In the same context the Qur'án states:

> And when Moses came at our set time and His Lord spake with him, He said, "O Lord! Shew Thyself to me, that I may look upon thee." He said "Thou shalt <u>not</u> see Me; but look towards the mount, and if it abide firm in its place, then thou shalt see Me." And when God manifested himself to the mountain it turned to dust and Moses fell in a swoon.
> (The Qur'án 7:139)

However, according to Bahá'u'lláh, so great is the station of this Day, that if a simple believer sincerely beseeches God "Show Thyself to me," he will hear from the kingdom of utterance the voice: "Behold, you will see me," which is seeing the Manifestation of God standing within him (see Note No. 6, above).

and turned away from His face—the face of God Himself.[19]

19. Bahá'u'lláh states that the Manifestation of God is the face of God that humanity can see. The Gospels attest to both the revelation of the Face of God and the turning away from the face of God.

The *New Testament* records the instance of the revelation of the face of God: Similar versions of the story of transfiguration of Christ are detailed in Matthew 17:1–9, Mark 9: 2–10, and Luke 9:2–36. The following is the story according to Matthew:

> And after six days Jesus taketh Peter, James, and John his brother, and bringeth them up into an high mountain apart, And was transfigured before them: and his face did shine as the sun, and his raiment was white as the light. And, behold, there appeared unto them Moses and Elias talking with him.
> (Matthew 17: 1–3)

Apparently, before the transfiguration, or seeing in the Face of Christ the Face of God, the three disciples did not recognize the greatness of His Station. They simply could not imagine that the

Man before them had the same station as Moses Who reflected the light of Countenance of God in His face:

> And it came to pass, when Moses came down from mount Sinai with the two tables of testimony in Moses' hand, when he came down from the mount, that Moses wist not that the skin of his face shone while he talked with him. And when Aaron and all the children of Israel saw Moses, behold, the skin of his face shone; and they were afraid to come nigh him. And Moses called unto them; and Aaron and all the rulers of the congregation returned unto him: and Moses talked with them. And afterward all the children of Israel came nigh: and he gave them in commandment all that the LORD had spoken with him in mount Sinai. And till Moses had done speaking with them, he put a vail on his face. But when Moses went in before the LORD to speak with him, he took the vail off, until he came out. And he came out, and spake unto the children of Israel that which he was commanded. And the children of Israel saw the face of Moses, that the skin of Moses' face shone: and Moses put the vail upon his face again, until he went in to speak with him.
> (Exodus 34:29–35)

Moses was also given the following high praise at His death in the *Torah*:

> And there arose not a prophet since in Israel like unto Moses, whom the LORD knew face to face.
> (Deuteronomy 34:10)

Elias or Elijah was the mightiest prophet of Israel. He appeared between the time of Moses and Jesus and performed miracles similar to both. He parted the waters of the River Jordan in order to cross it (II Kings 2:8); he brought a dead person back to life (I Kings 17:17–22); he caused heavenly fire to come from heaven and consume his sacrifice offering (II Kings 10:12), and he also conversed with God (3 Kings 19:9–15). According to the Old Testament, Elijah was taken to heaven in his corporeal body (4 Kings 2:8–11) and was to return to Earth at the time of the coming of the Messiah (Malachi 4:5): "Behold I will send you Elijah before the coming of the great and dreadful day of the Lord." This is the reason that people asked Jesus about the coming of Elijah, and Jesus said that John the Baptist was Elijah (Matthew 11:13–15): "For all the prophets and the law prophesied until John. And if ye will receive it, this is Elias which was to come. He that hath ears to hear, let him hear."

Moses and Elijah are the two pillars of Judaism. Moses represents the Law (as law giver), and Elijah represents the Prophets.

At the time of Christ, the stations of Moses and Elijah were so high in the sight of the Jews that they could never see the reality of Jesus or even put Him at the same level as those two prophets. The experience of seeing the transfiguration of Christ for the three disciples who saw the light of God in His face, and Moses and Elijah standing at His sides was transformative. At that point they saw Him as equal to Elias and Moses.

> And, behold, there appeared unto them Moses and Elias talking with him. Then answered Peter, and said unto Jesus, Lord, it is good for us to be here: if thou wilt, let us make here three tabernacles; one for thee, and one for Moses, and one for Elias.
> (Matthew 17:3–5)

The word 'tabernacle' is also of significance here because in the Old Testament, the tabernacle is equated with the Holy of Holies where God is present (see Note No. 4, above). At this point the disciples realized that Jesus was the Christ, and being aware of the prophecy that Elijah should descend from heaven before the coming of Christ, asked:

> And his disciples asked him, saying, Why then say the scribes that Elias must first come? And Jesus answered and said unto them, Elias truly shall first come, and restore all things. But I say unto you, That Elias is come already, and they knew him not, but have done unto him whatsoever they listed. Likewise shall also the Son of man suffer of them. Then the disciples understood that he spake unto them of John the Baptist.
> (Matthew 17:11–13)

In the New Testament, Jesus explains the station of Godhead to His Disciples:

> If ye had known me, ye should have known my Father also: and from henceforth ye know him, and have seen him [because they saw the face of Christ, that is the face of God]*. Phillip saith unto him, Lord, shew us the Father, and it sufficeth us. Jesus saith unto him. Have I been so long time with you, and yet hast thou not known me, Phillip? He that hath seen me hath seen the Father, and how sayest thou then, Shew us the Father? Believest thou not that I am in the Father and Father in me? The words that I speak unto you I speak not of myself: but the Father that dweleth in me, he doeth the works. Believe me that I am in the Father, and the Father in me . . .
> (John 14:5–20)

* The text in brackets is by this author.

Regarding His own Revelation, Bahá'u'lláh states:

> O ye that inhabit the heavens and the earth! There hath appeared what hath never previously appeared. He Who, from everlasting, had concealed His Face from the sight of creation is now come." From the whispering breeze that wafteth amidst its branches there cometh the cry: "He Who is the sovereign Lord of all is made manifest. The Kingdom is God's," while from its streaming waters can be heard the murmur: "All eyes are gladdened, for He Whom none hath beheld, Whose secret no one hath discovered, hath lifted the veil of glory, and uncovered the countenance of Beauty.
> (Bahá'u'lláh, *Gleanings from the Writings of Bahá'u'lláh*, p. 30)

> O ye leaders of religion . . . ! Who is the man amongst you that can rival Me in vision or insight? Where is he to be found that dareth to claim to be My equal in utterance or wisdom? No, by My Lord, the All-Merciful! All on the earth shall pass away; and this is the face of your Lord, the Almighty, the Well-Beloved.
> (Bahá'u'lláh, Epistle to the Son of the Wolf, p. 128)

Denial of the Face of God:

While the apostles were slow to recognize the Station of Christ, it was the leadership of the Jewish community, the Pharisees and the chief priests and elders who not only did not recognize His station, but spat upon and slapped the Face of God that the apostles had witnessed upon the mountaintop.

They denied the Messiah for Whom the Jews had been praying for at least a thousand years. The following account of the arraignment of Christ before the Pharisees is from Matthew:

> And they that had laid hold on Jesus led him away to Caiaphas the high priest, where the scribes and the elders were assembled. But Peter followed him afar off unto the high priest's palace, and went in, and sat with the servants, to see the end. Now the chief priests, and elders, and all the council, sought false witness against Jesus, to put him to death; But found none: yea, though many false witnesses came, yet found they none. At the last came two false witnesses, And said, This fellow said, I am able to destroy the temple of God, and to build it in three days. And the high priest arose, and said unto him, Answerest thou nothing? what is it which these witness against thee? But Jesus held his peace. And the high priest answered and said unto him, I adjure thee by the living God, that thou tell us whether thou be the Christ, the Son of God. Jesus saith unto him, Thou hast said: nevertheless I say unto you, Hereafter shall ye see the Son of man sitting on the right hand of power, and coming in the clouds of heaven. Then the high priest rent his clothes, saying, He hath spoken blasphemy; what further need have we of witnesses? behold, now ye have heard his blasphemy. What think ye? They answered and said, He is guilty of death. Then did they spit in his face, and buffeted him; and others smote him with the palms of their hands, Saying, Prophesy unto us, thou Christ, Who is he that smote thee?
> (Matthew 26:58–68)

Paragraph No. 4:

Ponder[20] for a moment

20. The word ponder is repeated many times in the Kitáb-i-Íqán. Bahá'u'lláh explains a spiritual concept and then invites the reader to ponder in order to internalize the concept. Here He asks the reader to ponder the reasons for the denial of the Manifestations of God by the very people who longed for Their appearance. The story of the arraignment of Christ before the Pharisees and His eventual crucifixion is one example of this phenomenon. The people of our time imagine Christ with a halo around His Head and with an irresistible spiritual countenance. However, His ordinary human appearance prevented the people of His time from recognizing His Station. The Jews were awaiting a Messiah who would come with physical and military power and worldly glory and authority, and who would possess a kingdom and might. They were expecting to hear a heavenly sound and a host of angels, and Elijah descending in his corporal body from heaven announcing His appearance. However, none of these things happened literally in the material world. The high priest of Israel therefore saw no problem in slapping the ordinary looking carpenter's son who claimed such a high station. The people around him considered, what may seem to Christians today as a deplorable act, an act of faith on the part of the Pharisees.

Thus it hath been revealed: O the misery of men! No Messenger cometh unto them but they laugh Him to scorn (Qur'án 36:30).[21]

21. Bahá'u'lláh often laments the plight of the other Manifestations of God and identifies His own suffering with Their suffering:

> Praise be to Thee, O Lord My God, for the wondrous revelations of Thy inscrutable decree and the manifold woes and trials Thou hast destined for Myself. At one time Thou didst deliver me into the hands of Nimrod; at another Thou hast allowed Pharaoh's rod to persecute Me. Thou, alone, canst estimate, through Thine all-encompassing knowledge and the operation of Thy Will, the incalculable afflictions I have suffered at their hands. Again Thou didst

cast Me into the prison-cell of the ungodly, for no reason except that I was moved to whisper into the ears of the well-favored denizens of Thy Kingdom an intimation of the vision with which Thou hadst, through Thy knowledge, inspired Me, and revealed to Me its meaning through the potency of Thy might. And again Thou didst decree that I be beheaded by the sword of the infidel. Again I was crucified for having unveiled to men's eyes the hidden gems of Thy glorious unity, for having revealed to them the wondrous signs of Thy sovereign and everlasting power. How bitter the humiliations heaped upon Me, in a subsequent age, on the plain of Karbílá! How lonely did I feel amidst thy people! To what a state of helplessness I was reduced in that land! Unsatisfied with such indignities, My persecutors decapitated Me, and, carrying aloft My head from land to land paraded it before the gaze of the unbelieving multitude, and deposited on the seats of the perverse and faithless. In a later age, I was suspended, and My breast was made a target to the darts of the malicious cruelty of My foes. My limbs were riddled with bullets, and My body was torn asunder. Finally, behold how, in this Day, My treacherous enemies have leagued themselves against Me, and are continually plotting to instill the venom of hate and malice into the souls of Thy servants. With all their might they are scheming to accomplish this purpose. Grievous as is my plight. O God, My Well-Beloved, I render thanks unto Thee, and My spirit is grateful for whatsoever hath befallen me in the path of thy good-pleasure.
(Bahá'u'lláh, *Gleanings from the Writings of Bahá'u'lláh*, pp. 88–90)

Paragraph No. 5:

To them that are possessed of true understanding and insight the Súrah of Húd surely sufficeth.[22]

22. The Súrah of Húd (pronounced Hood) is the eleventh chapter of the Qur'án [revealed in Mecca, except for one verse]. Bahá'u'lláh makes mention of this chapter very early on in the discussion because its theme and stories can put the seeker in the proper state

of mind to consider the points that He subsequently elucidates. In the Súrah of Húd, the story of other prophets, their sufferings, and the denial by their contemporaries are told.

There are four prophets who are mentioned in the Qur'án but not in the Old Testament. The four are Húd, Ṣáliḥ, Shu'aib, and of course, Muḥammad Himself. However, there is another prophet, Abraham, who although he is mentioned in the Old Testament, is attached to a somewhat different story than the Abraham of the Qur'án. These are the five prophets that (according to the Qur'án) were sent to the peoples of Arabia.

Some commentators of Qur'án believe that Húd was a descendant of Adam through His father Ham, who was a son of Noah. Húd came to a tribe called Áud. Áud was the grandson of Arám who was the grandson of Noah, and it is possible that he is the same person as Eber in the Old Testament.

When Húd came to the Áud, descendants of Adam, they denied Him. He told them that God would raise others in their stead. According to the Qur'án, God destroyed Áud with a fierce wind and storm that continued for eight days and nights.

The significance of the Súrah of Húd is that in this chapter, Muḥammad details the stories of many Prophets of God, who looked like ordinary people, and thus when they were attempting to teach people, were not accepted but instead persecuted. This scenario is the same as that of the Báb and the people of His time. Even His uncle could not accept Him as the Qá'im because He looked like an ordinary person.

The major themes of the Súrah of Húd are:

1. The prophets looked like ordinary people. They did not demonstrate any supernatural powers or characteristics.
2. Their major goal was to teach people; they did not perform any supernatural act.
3. They were opposed by people who wished to follow and continue the ways of their forefathers and did not want to listen to them.

4. They were persecuted by people and were subject to a lot of indignities.

There is an Islamic tradition relating that a believer who had not seen Muḥammad in a few months saw Him in a mosque and was amazed at how much He had aged. When he asked the Prophet about this, Muḥammad replied that it was the revelation of the Súrah of Húd and its sister Súrahs that had aged Him. Rodwell relates the following story:

> In later life, as Muhammad was entering the mosque, a disciple said, "Ah, Thou for Whom I would sacrifice father and mother, white hairs are hastening upon Thee!" And the Prophet raised up His beard with His hand and gazed at it; and the disciple's eyes filled with tears. "Yes," said Muhammad, "(the Súrih of) Húd and its sisters have hastened my white hairs."
> (Rodwell, Qur'án, 225–226 n.)

The verse in the Súrah of Húd that caused Him to age is the verse that commands Him to be steadfast and perform the duties of the Messenger of God. That verse is as follows:

> And truly thy Lord will repay every one according to their works! for he is well aware of what they do.
> Go straight on then as thou hast been commanded, and he who hath turned to God with thee, and let him transgress no more. He beholdeth what ye do.
> (The Qur'án 11:113–114)

Commentators on the Qur'án state that there were no revealed verses in the Qur'án that were harder for Muḥammad and affected Him more than two specific verses—one of them being the above verse in the Súrah of Húd, and the other one being in the Súrah of Al 'An'am (The Cattle). The story contends that Muḥammad asked God to relieve Him from the persecution and suffering He was enduring at the hands of His enemies, but He received the following revelation:

> We know too well that what they say grieves you. It is not you that they are disbelieving; the evil-doers deny God's own revelations. Other apostles have been denied before

> you. But they patiently bore with disbelief and persecution until Our help came down to them: for non can change the decrees of God. You have already heard of those apostles. If you find their aversion hard to bear, seek if you can a chasm in the earth or a ladder to the sky by which you may bring them a sign. Had God pleased He would have given them guidance, one and all. Do not be foolish then.
> (The Qur'án 6:33–35)

This means that God gave Him no choice but to endure the problems and sufferings. The revelation of this verse in which God tells Muḥammad that he must withstand the trials and indignities heaped upon him, as they were heaped on the Prophets in the Súrah of Húd, is what caused Him to age fast. There are more references to Húd in other chapters of the Qur'án, but they are brief mentions.

Examine the wondrous behavior of the Prophets, and recall the defamations and denials uttered by the children of negation and falsehood.[23]

23. The reference made to the children of negation might have several levels of meaning. On the most basic level it refers to those who break the Greater Covenant with God by not recognizing His Manifestation, as well as to those who break the Lesser Covenant by not following the chosen successor of the Manifestation.

    These are the people Jesus referred to as the generation of vipers.

    > O generation of vipers, how can ye, being evil, speak good things? for out of the abundance of the heart the mouth speaketh.
    > (Matthew 12:34)

    > And he began to teach them, that the Son of man must suffer many things, and be rejected of the elders, and of the chief priests, and scribes, and be killed.
    > (Mark 8:31)

perchance you may cause the bird of the human heart to wing its flight away from the abode of heedlessness and doubt. [24]

24. The heart is the interface of the soul or spirit and the mind of humans, it is the center of man's consciousness, his "inmost reality." It is the place that God can be present (See Note No. 10, above).

This concept is reiterated repeatedly in the Hidden Words.

> O SON OF DUST!
> All that is in heaven and earth I have ordained for thee except the human heart, which I have made the habitation of My beauty and glory; yet thou didst give My home and dwelling to another than Me; and whenever the manifestation of My holiness sought His own abode, a stranger found He there, and, homeless, hastened to the sanctuary of the Beloved. Notwithstanding I have concealed Thy secret and desired not thy shame.
> (Bahá'u'lláh, The Hidden Words, Persian, no. 27)

The heart is also presented allegorically as a bird. The human heart is able to operate in the physical realm as well as soar in the spiritual realm just as a bird moves on the land as well as being able to soar in the air.

> O SON OF SPIRIT!
> The bird seeketh its nest; the nightingale the charm of the rose; whilst those birds, the hearts of men, content with transient dust, have strayed far from their eternal nest, and with eyes turned towards the slough of heedlessness are bereft of the glory of the divine presence. Alas! How strange and pitiful; for a mere cupful, they have turned away from the billowing seas of the Most High, and remained far from the most effulgent horizon.
> (Bahá'u'lláh, The Hidden Words, Persian, no. 2)

The abode of heedlessness is a state of being in which the people are unaware of their own spiritual condition. Complacent and satisfied with the ritualistic aspects of their Faith, they do not feel a need for spiritual growth. Bahá'u'lláh describes the condition of those who are in the abode of heedlessness in the following term:

> O YE THAT ARE LYING AS DEAD ON THE COUCH OF HEEDLESSNESS!
> Ages have passed and your precious lives are well-nigh ended, yet not a single breath of purity hath reached Our court of holiness from you. Though immersed in the ocean of misbelief, yet with your lips ye profess the one true faith of God. Him whom I abhor ye have loved, and of My foe ye have made a friend. Notwithstanding, ye walk on My earth complacent and self-satisfied, heedless that My earth is weary of you and everything within it shunneth you. Were ye but to open your eyes, ye would, in truth, prefer a myriad griefs unto this joy, and would count death itself better than this life.
> (Bahá'u'lláh, The Hidden Words, Persian, no. 20)

and partake of the fruit of the tree of divine knowledge.[25]

25. In the Writings of Bahá'u'lláh, the Manifestation of God is referred to as "Divine Tree" or "Divine Lote Tree."

Such is the share of the pure in heart of the bread that hath descended from the realms of eternity and holiness.[26]

26. There are many references to the "bread that hath descended from the realms of eternity and holiness" or the "bread of heaven" in past Dispensations as well as in the Bahá'í Writings:

    The "bread of heaven", called 'manna,' first appears in the Book of Exodus in the Old Testament:

> And they took their journey from Elim, and all the congregation of the children of Israel came unto the wilderness of Sin, which is between Elim and Sinai, on the fifteenth day of the second month after their departing out of the land of Egypt. And the whole congregation of the children of Israel murmured against Moses and Aaron in the wilderness: And the children of Israel said unto them, Would to God we had died by the hand of the LORD in the

land of Egypt, when we sat by the flesh pots, and when we did eat bread to the full; for ye have brought us forth into this wilderness, to kill this whole assembly with hunger. Then said the LORD unto Moses, Behold, I will rain bread from heaven for you; and the people shall go out and gather a certain rate every day, that I may prove them, whether they will walk in my law, or no. And it shall come to pass, that on the sixth day they shall prepare that which they bring in; and it shall be twice as much as they gather daily. And Moses and Aaron said unto all the children of Israel, At even, then ye shall know that the LORD hath brought you out from the land of Egypt:
And in the morning, then ye shall see the glory of the LORD; for that he heareth your murmurings against the LORD: and what are we, that ye murmur against us? And Moses said, This shall be, when the LORD shall give you in the evening flesh to eat, and in the morning bread to the full; for that the LORD heareth your murmurings which ye murmur against him: and what are we? your murmurings are not against us, but against the LORD. And Moses spake unto Aaron, Say unto all the congregation of the children of Israel, Come near before the LORD: for he hath heard your murmurings. And it came to pass, as Aaron spake unto the whole congregation of the children of Israel, that they looked toward the wilderness, and, behold, the glory of the LORD appeared in the cloud. And the LORD spake unto Moses, saying, I have heard the murmurings of the children of Israel: speak unto them, saying, At even ye shall eat flesh, and in the morning ye shall be filled with bread; and ye shall know that I am the LORD your God. And it came to pass, that at even the quails came up, and covered the camp: and in the morning the dew lay round about the host. And when the dew that lay was gone up, behold, upon the face of the wilderness there lay a small round thing, as small as the hoar frost on the ground. And when the children of Israel saw it, they said one to another, It is manna: for they wist not what it was. And Moses said unto them, This is the bread which the LORD hath given you to eat. This is the thing which the LORD hath commanded, Gather of it every man according to his eating, an omen for every man, according to the number of your persons; take

> ye every man for them which are in his tents. And the children of Israel did so, and gathered, some more, some less.
> (Exodus 16:1–17)

There are also references to "bread" in the New Testament. In the Gospel of John 6:26–59, Jesus explains the meaning of the "bread of heaven" referred to in the Old Testament, when a crowd of Jews who had witnessed Him feed a multitude of thousands with five barley loaves and two small fishes, detailed in John 6:5–12, approach him:

> Jesus answered them and said, Verily, verily, I say unto you, Ye seek me, not because ye saw the miracles, but because ye did eat of the loaves, and were filled. Labor not for the meat which perisheth, but for that meat which endureth unto everlasting life, which the Son of man shall give unto you: for him hath God the Father sealed. Then said they unto him, What shall we do, that we might work the works of God? Jesus answered and said unto them, This is the work of God, that ye believe on him whom he hath sent. They said therefore unto him, What sign showest thou then, that we may see, and believe thee? what dost thou work? Our fathers did eat manna in the desert; as it is written, He gave them bread from heaven to eat. Then Jesus said unto them, Verily, verily, I say unto you, Moses gave you not that bread from heaven; but my Father giveth you the true bread from heaven. For the bread of God is he which cometh down from heaven, and giveth life unto the world. Then said they unto him, Lord, evermore give us this bread. And Jesus said unto them, I am the bread of life: he that cometh to me shall never hunger; and he that believeth on me shall never thirst. But I said unto you, That ye also have seen me, and believe not. All that the Father giveth me shall come to me; and him that cometh to me I will in no wise cast out. For I came down from heaven, not to do mine own will, but the will of him that sent me. And this is the Father's will which hath sent me, that of all which he hath given me I should lose nothing, but should raise it up again at the last day. And this is the will of him that sent me, that every one which seeth the Son, and

believeth on him, may have everlasting life: and I will raise him up at the last day. The Jews then murmured at him, because he said, I am the bread which came down from heaven. And they said, Is not this Jesus, the son of Joseph, whose father and mother we know? how is it then that he saith, I came down from heaven? Jesus therefore answered and said unto them, Murmur not among yourselves. No man can come to me, except the Father which hath sent me draw him: and I will raise him up at the last day. It is written in the prophets, And they shall be all taught of God. Every man therefore that hath heard, and hath learned of the Father, cometh unto me. Not that any man hath seen the Father, save he which is of God, he hath seen the Father. Verily, verily, I say unto you, He that believeth on me hath everlasting life. I am that bread of life. Your fathers did eat manna in the wilderness, and are dead. This is the bread which cometh down from heaven, that a man may eat thereof, and not die. I am the living bread which came down from heaven: if any man eat of this bread, he shall live for ever: and the bread that I will give is my flesh, which I will give for the life of the world. The Jews therefore strove among themselves, saying, How can this man give us his flesh to eat? Then Jesus said unto them, Verily, verily, I say unto you, Except ye eat the flesh of the Son of man, and drink his blood, ye have no life in you. Whoso eateth my flesh, and drinketh my blood, hath eternal life; and I will raise him up at the last day. For my flesh is meat indeed, and my blood is drink indeed. He that eateth my flesh, and drinketh my blood, dwelleth in me, and I in him. As the living Father hath sent me, and I live by the Father: so he that eateth me, even he shall live by me. This is that bread which came down from heaven: not as your fathers did eat manna, and are dead: he that eateth of this bread shall live for ever. These things said he in the synagogue, as he taught in Capernaum.
(John 6:26–59)

In this Revelation, Bahá'u'lláh gives a clear explanation of the "bread of heaven":

> Know thou that, according to what thy Lord, the Lord of all men, hath decreed in His Book, these favors vouchsafed by Him unto mankind have been, and will ever remain, limitless in their range. First and foremost among these gifts that the Almighty hath conferred upon man is the gift of understanding. . . . Next in rank is the power of vision, the chief instrument whereby his understanding can function. . . .
>
> These gifts are inherent in man himself. That which is preeminent above all other gifts, is incorruptible in nature, and pertaineth to God Himself, is the gift of Divine Revelation. Every bounty conferred by the creator, be it material or spiritual, is subservient unto this. It is, in its essence, and will ever so remain, the Bread that cometh down from Heaven. It is God's supreme testimony, the clearest evidence of His truth, the sign of His consummate bounty, the token of His all-encompassing mercy, the proof of His most loving providence, the symbol of His most perfect grace. He hath, indeed, partaken of this highest gift of God who hath recognized His Manifestation in this Day.
> (Bahá'u'lláh, *Gleanings from the Writings of Bahá'u'lláh*, p. 195)

In the Tablet of the Temple, He states:

> Glorified is He Who sendeth down His verses to those who comprehend. Glorified is He Who speaketh forth from the Kingdom of His Revelation, and Who remaineth unknown to all save His honored servants. Glorified is He Who quickeneth whomsoever He willeth by virtue of His word "Be," and it is! Glorified is He Who causeth whomsoever He willeth to ascend unto the heaven of grace, and sendeth down therefrom whatsoever He desireth according to a prescribed measure. . . .
>
> Through them the believers in the Divine Unity have turned towards Him Who is the Object of the adoration of the entire creation, and by them the hearts of the righteous have found rest and composure, could ye but know it! Through them the earth hath been established, the clouds have rained down

> their bounty, and the bread of knowledge hath descended from the heaven of grace, could ye but perceive it!
> (Bahá'u'lláh, *The Summons of the Lord of Hosts*, pp. 3, 7)

'Abdu'l-Bahá states:

> The gates of the Kingdom are opened wide, and every favoured soul is seated at the banquet table of the Lord, receiving his portion of that heavenly feast. Praised be God, thou too art present at this table, taking thy share of the bountiful food of heaven. Thou art serving the Kingdom, and art well acquainted with the sweet savours of the Abhá Paradise.
>
> Then strive thou with all thy might to guide the people, and eat thou of the bread that hath come down from heaven. For this is the meaning of Christ's words: 'I am the living bread which came down from . . . he that eateth of this bread shall live forever.
> ('Abdu'l-Bahá, *Selections from the Writings of 'Abdu'l-Bahá*, p. 57)

Paragraph No. 6:

a brief mention will be made in this Tablet of divers accounts relative to the Prophets of God.[27]

27. Both the Old Testament and the Qur'án use the medium of storytelling to transmit spiritual ideas and to educate people. Many of the stories in the Qur'án are about the same prophets or persons mentioned in the Old Testament. However, in spite of some similarities, there are significant differences in the personalities and activities of the main characters, and in the outcomes and moral conclusions of the stories. In the Kitáb-i-Íqán, whenever there is a reference to those stories, Bahá'u'lláh refers to the Qur'ánic versions.

    As mentioned above, while both books convey ideas in the form of stories, these stories are often different in their messages and in the way they portray the unfoldment of the Divine Plan. To further clarify this point, the accounts of the story of Adam and Eve as related in the Qur'án and the Old Testament are presented here.

The story in the Qur'án is found in the Súrah of Al-A'ráf (Súrah of Heights). In this Qur'ánic version, Satan is the one who deceives Adam and Eve to disobey God. The story also provides the background and reason for Satan's actions. It is explained that Eblis (another name for Satan)—in his opposition to the plan of God—deceived Adam and Eve and encouraged them to eat the forbidden fruit—a sign of disobedience to God—which led to their banishment from Paradise:

> We created you; then fashioned you; then said we to the angels, "Prostrate yourselves unto Adam: and they prostrated them all in worship, save Eblis: He was not among those who prostrated themselves. To him said God: "What hath hindered thee from prostrating thyself in worship at my bidding?" He said, "Nobler am I than he: me hast thou created of fire; of clay hast thou created him."
> He said, "Get thee down hence: Paradise is no place for thy pride: Get thee gone then; one of the despised shalt thou be." He said, "Respite me till the day when mankind shall be raised from the dead." He said, "One of the respited shalt thou be." He said, "Now, for that thou hast caused me to err, surely in thy straight path will I lay wait for them:
>
> Then I will surely come upon them from before, and from behind, and from their right hand, and from their left, and thou shalt not find the greater part of them to be thankful." He said, "Go forth from it, a scorned, a banished one! Whoever of them shall follow thee, I will surely fill hell with you, one and all. And, O Adam! dwell thou and thy wife in Paradise, and eat ye whence ye will, but to this tree approach not, lest ye become of the unjust doers." Then Satan whispered them to shew them their nakedness, which had been hidden from them both. And he said, "This tree hath your Lord forbidden you, only lest ye should become angels, or lest ye should become immortals." And he sware to them both, "Verily I am unto you one who counselleth aright." So he beguiled them by deceits: and when they had tasted of the tree, their nakedness appeared to them, and they began to sew together upon themselves the leaves of the garden. And their Lord called to them, "Did I not forbid

> you this tree, and did I not say to you, 'Verily, Satan is your declared enemy.'"
>
> They said, "O our Lord! With ourselves have we dealt unjustly: if thou forgive us not and have pity on us, we shall surely be of those who perish." He said, "Get ye down, the one of you an enemy to the other; and on earth shall be your dwelling, and your provision for a season."
> He said, "On it shall ye live, and on it shall ye die, and from it shall ye be taken forth."
> (The Qur'án 7:10–23)

The Genesis story gives no explicit reason. It does not explain how and why the serpent knows about the forbidden fruit. While the serpent encourages Eve, there is no indication that the serpent is indeed Satan:

> And the LORD God caused a deep sleep to fall upon Adam, and he slept: and he took one of his ribs, and closed up the flesh instead thereof; And the rib, which the LORD God had taken from man, made he a woman, and brought her unto the man. And Adam said, This is now bone of my bones, and flesh of my flesh: she shall be called Woman, because she was taken out of Man. Therefore shall a man leave his father and his mother, and shall cleave unto his wife: and they shall be one flesh. And they were both naked, the man and his wife, and were not ashamed.
> (Genesis 2:21–25)
>
> Now the serpent was more subtil than any beast of the field which the LORD God had made. And he said unto the woman, Yea, hath God said, Ye shall not eat of every tree of the garden? And the woman said unto the serpent, We may eat of the fruit of the trees of the garden: But of the fruit of the tree which is in the midst of the garden, God hath said, Ye shall not eat of it, neither shall ye touch it, lest ye die. And the serpent said unto the woman, Ye shall not surely die: For God doth know that in the day ye eat thereof, then your eyes shall be opened, and ye shall be as gods, knowing good and evil. And when the woman saw that the tree was good for food, and that it was pleasant to the eyes, and a tree to be desired to make one wise, she

took of the fruit thereof, and did eat, and gave also unto her husband with her; and he did eat. And the eyes of them both were opened, and they knew that they were naked; and they sewed fig leaves together, and made themselves aprons. And they heard the voice of the LORD God walking in the garden in the cool of the day: and Adam and his wife hid themselves from the presence of the LORD God amongst the trees of the garden. And the LORD God called unto Adam, and said unto him, Where art thou? And he said, I heard thy voice in the garden, and I was afraid, because I was naked; and I hid myself. And he said, Who told thee that thou wast naked? Hast thou eaten of the tree, whereof I commanded thee that thou shouldest not eat? And the man said, The woman whom thou gavest to be with me, she gave me of the tree, and I did eat. And the LORD God said unto the woman, What is this that thou hast done? And the woman said, The serpent beguiled me, and I did eat. And the LORD God said unto the serpent, Because thou hast done this, thou art cursed above all cattle, and above every beast of the field; upon thy belly shalt thou go, and dust shalt thou eat all the days of thy life: And I will put enmity between thee and the woman, and between thy seed and her seed; it shall bruise thy head, and thou shalt bruise his heel. Unto the woman he said, I will greatly multiply thy sorrow and thy conception; in sorrow thou shalt bring forth children; and thy desire shall be to thy husband, and he shall rule over thee. And unto Adam he said, Because thou hast hearkened unto the voice of thy wife, and hast eaten of the tree, of which I commanded thee, saying, Thou shalt not eat of it: cursed is the ground for thy sake; in sorrow shalt thou eat of it all the days of thy life; Thorns also and thistles shall it bring forth to thee; and thou shalt eat the herb of the field; In the sweat of thy face shalt thou eat bread, till thou return unto the ground; for out of it wast thou taken: for dust thou art, and unto dust shalt thou return. And Adam called his wife's name Eve; because she was the mother of all living. Unto Adam also and to his wife did the LORD God make coats of skins, and clothed them. And the LORD God said, Behold, the man is become as one of us, to know good and evil: and now, lest he put forth his hand, and take also of the tree of life, and

> eat, and live for ever: Therefore the LORD God sent him forth from the garden of Eden, to till the ground from whence he was taken. So he drove out the man; and he placed at the east of the garden of Eden Cherubims, and a flaming sword which turned every way, to keep the way of the tree of life.
> (Genesis 3:1–24)

In fact, the serpent is not likened to Satan until the very last book of the New Testament, The Book of Revelation:

> And the great dragon was cast out, that old serpent called the Devil, and Satan which deceived the whole world: he was cast out into the earth and his angels where cast out with him.
> (Revelation 12:9)

The explanation in the Qur'án did eventually find its way into the Judeo-Christian stream of thought through the work of the poet John Milton. In his retelling of the story of Adam and Eve, Milton calls on the heavenly muse for inspiration, but proceeds to repeat the story of the first temptation exactly as it is told in the Qur'án.

It is also interesting to note that in the Qur'án, Adam and Eve are jointly and equally responsible for accepting Eiblis's proposition and were beguiled by Satan's deceits, while in the Old Testament story, Eve is the principal responsible party.

Perchance this may enable a few to cease to be perturbed by the clamor and protestations of the divines and the foolish of this age.[28]

28. There is a similarity between the lives, actions, and suffering of the various prophets and Manifestations of God. There is also similarity between the forces of opposition the divines and foolish leaders that arise against them in each age. By relating the stories of some of the Manifestations of God, Bahá'u'lláh shows the uncle of the Báb and other readers that the rejection of the Báb by the religious leaders of His time was of the same nature as the rejection of the prophets and Manifestations of the past by the divines and leaders of their age.

Paragraph No. 7:

Among the Prophets was Noah.[29]

29. Noah was a Prophet mentioned both in the Qur'án and in Genesis, the first book of the Old Testament.

According to Genesis, Noah was thirty generations removed from Adam, and first appears in the Old Testament when He is five hundred years old and when He begets his three children (Genesis 5:32). Then the story in the Old Testament says that the Lord, noticing the evil ways of man, "repented" that he had made man on the earth and vowed to destroy man and the rest of creation:

> And it came to pass, when men began to multiply on the face of the earth, and daughters were born unto them, That the sons of God saw the daughters of men that they were fair; and they took them wives of all which they chose. And the LORD said, My spirit shall not always strive with man, for that he also is flesh: yet his days shall be an hundred and twenty years. There were giants in the earth in those days; and also after that, when the sons of God came in unto the daughters of men, and they bare children to them, the same became mighty men which were of old, men of renown. And God saw that the wickedness of man was great in the earth, and that every imagination of the thoughts of his heart was only evil continually. And it repented the LORD that he had made man on the earth, and it grieved him at his heart. And the LORD said, I will destroy man whom I have created from the face of the earth; both man, and beast, and the creeping thing, and the fowls of the air; for it repenteth me that I have made them.
> (Genesis 6:1–7)

God, however, shows favor to Noah and His family and instructs Noah to build an Ark to His exact specifications and to gather onto the Ark, His own family, a pair of each unclean beast, seven of each clean beast, and provisions to last several months. The Lord then causes rain to fall for forty days and forty nights and everything that is not on the arc is destroyed (Genesis 6:8–7:24). It takes about seven months for the flood waters to clear, and Noah sends a raven and then a dove to scout for dry land. When the dove brings back an olive branch, Noah knows that it had spotted land. The dove does not return from its next flight (Genesis 8). In the Old Testament Noah is presented as a just man, but He has a passive role, and there is no mention of Him being an active prophet or a teacher of people.

In the Qur'án, however, Noah is mentioned several times in different chapters, and is regarded as a major prophet on a par with Abraham, Moses, Christ, and Muḥammad. There is a Súrah named for him in the Qur'án, the Súrah of Noah (Súrah 71), in which it is clearly stated that it is by Noah's request, when no one listens to his repeated behests, rather than by God's own wrath towards man (as in the Old Testament), that God destroys the infidels. In this Súrah, Muḥammad likens the plight of Noah to his own struggles against idol worship:

> In the Name of God, the Compassionate, the Merciful.
> WE sent NOAH to his people, and said to him, "Warn thou thy people ere there come on them an afflictive punishment." He said, "O my people! I come to you a plain-spoken warner: Serve God and fear Him, and obey me: Your sins will He forgive you, and respite you till the fixed Time; for when God's fixed Time hath come, it shall not be put back. Would that ye knew this!" He said, "Lord I have cried to my people night and day; and my cry doth but make them flee from me the more. So oft as I cry to them, that thou mayest forgive them, they thrust their fingers into their ears, and wrap themselves in their garments, and persist in their error, and are disdainfully disdainful. Then I cried aloud to them: Then again spake I with plainness, and in private did I secretly address them. And I said, 'Beg forgiveness of your Lord, for He is ready to forgive. He will send down the very Heaven upon you in plenteous rains; And will increase you in wealth and children; and will give you gardens, and will give you watercourses: What hath come to you that ye hope not for goodness from the hand of God? For He it is who hath formed you by

> successive steps. See ye not how God hath created the seven heavens one over the other? And He hath placed therein the moon as a light, and hath placed there the sun as a torch; And God hath caused you to spring forth from the earth like a plant; Hereafter will He turn you back into it again, and will bring you forth anew. And God hath spread the earth for you like a carpet. That ye may walk therein along spacious paths.'" Said Noah, "O my Lord! they rebel against me, and they follow those whose riches and children do but aggravate their ruin. And they plotted a great plot; And they said, "Forsake not your Gods; forsake not Wadd nor Sowah, Nor Yaghuth and Yahuk and Nesr;"* And they caused many to err;—and thou, too, . . . Shalt be the means of increasing only error in the wicked—Because of their sins they were drowned, and made to go into the Fire; And they found that they had no helper save God. And Noah said, "Lord, leave not one single family of Infidels on the Earth: For if thou leave them they will beguile thy servants and will beget only sinners, infidels. O my Lord, forgive me, and my parents, and every one who being a believer, shall enter my house, and believers men and women: and add to the wicked naught but perdition."
> (The Qur'án 71:1–29)

* These are names of some major Idols.

Noah is also mentioned in the Súrah of Al-A'ráf (Súrah 7), along with Húd and Sálih, in which it is recounted that the people of Noah's time were drowned because of their disobedience to Him:

> Of old sent We Noah to his people, and he said, "O my people! worship God. Ye have no God but Him: indeed I fear for you the chastisement of the great day."
> The chiefs of his people said, "We clearly see that thou art in a palpable error."
> He said, "There is no error in me, O my people! but I am a messenger from the Lord of the Worlds. I bring to you the messages of my Lord, and I give you friendly counsel; for I know from God what ye know not. Marvel ye that a Warning should come to you from your Lord through one of yourselves, that he may Warn you, and that ye may fear

> for yourselves, and that haply ye may find mercy?" But they treated him as a liar: so we delivered him and those who were with him in the ark, and we drowned those who charged our signs with falsehood; for they were a blind people.
> (The Qur'án 7:57–63)

In the Súrah of Húd, Noah is mentioned and the theme of the Súrah of Húd is reiterated in His story:

> We sent Noah of old unto his people:— "Verily I come to you a plain admonisher, That ye worship none but God. Verily I fear for you the punishment of a grievous day." Then said the chiefs of his people who believed not, "We see in thee but a man like ourselves; and we see not who have followed thee except our meanest ones of hasty judgment, nor see we any excellence in you above ourselves: nay, we deem you liars." He said: "O my people! how think you? If I am upon a clear revelation from my Lord, who hath bestowed on me mercy from Himself to which ye are blind, can we force it on you, if ye are averse from it? And, O my people! I ask you not for riches: my reward is of God alone: and I will not drive away those who believe that they shall meet their Lord: - but I see that ye are an ignorant people. And, O my people! were I to drive them away, who shall help me against God? Will ye not therefore consider? And I tell you not that with me are the treasurers of God: nor do I say, 'I know the things unseen;' nor do I say, 'I am an angel;' nor do I say of those whom you eye with scorn, No good thing will God bestow on them:— God best knoweth what is in their minds - for then should I be one of those who act unjustly." They said, "O Noah! already hast thou disputed with us, and multiplied disputes with us: Bring then upon us what thou hast threatened, if thou be of those who speak truth." He said, "God will bring it on you at His sole pleasure, and it is not you who can weaken him; Nor, if God desire to mislead you, shall my counsel profit you, though I fain would counsel you aright. He is your Lord, and unto Him shall ye be brought back. Do they say, "This Koran is of his own devising?" Say: On me be my own guilt, if I have devised

> it, but I am clear of that whereof ye are guilty. And it was revealed unto Noah. Verily, none of thy people shall believed, save they who have believed already; therefore be not thou grieved at their doings. But build the Ark under our eye and after our revelation: and plead not with me for the evil doers, for they are to be drowned.
> (The Qur'án 11:27–50)

As before, it is clear that Noah proved that His Message was from God through the occurrence of the flood. However, before the flood, when he was admonishing the people, they denied him saying that he looked like an ordinary man and was not "excellent" above them.

Although the allegoric nature of this story is very clear, and the fact that the Ark's dimensions as specified in the Old Testament would not contain even a fraction of the number of clean and unclean animals, and the food they require, those people who believe in the literal interpretation of the Bible and the Qur'án insist that the accounts of these events are literal; some Biblical archeologists are even actively searching for Noah's Ark. Recently one of them claimed that he had spotted it on Mount Ararat.

For nine hundred and fifty years[30] He prayerfully exhorted His people and summoned them to the haven of security and peace.

30. While Bahá'u'lláh does not dispute the tradition that Noah lived nine hundred and fifty years —because the length of time was not the main point of argument—a letter from the Guardian explains that these 950 years are not to be taken literally:

> The Guardian advises that the period of nine hundred and fifty years referred to in the Iqan as the time Noah exhorted His people and summoned them to the haven of security and peace, refers to the period of His ministry. The term year does not refer to a period of time such as our year. It was entirely different."
> (The Guardian in a letter dated March 3, 1957 in answer to the question of a believer. Quoted in Hooper C. Dunbar's *A Companion to the Study of The Kitáb-i-Íqán*)

Moreover, 'Abdu'l-Bahá in a Tablet in Persian and Arabic cited in the book *Amr-va-khalq* (Vol. 2, p. 192) explains that such passages quoted in the ancient scriptures that indicate that Noah lived for nine hundred and fifty years do not signify solar years. Some authors, he explains, have counted each month as a year. Otherwise, he explains that the length of their lives was the same in the past as it is now, but because their lifestyle was simpler they were stronger."

But when the hour struck, the divine promise was not fulfilled.[31]

31. The story of Noah and the flood in the Qur'án is a story which clearly demonstrates the consequences of disobedience to God and the fulfillment of the divine promise of punishment of those who disobey the Manifestation of God. Ironically, however, it is also in the story of Noah that the troublesome concept of the non-fulfillment of the divine promise is explored. In the Qur'ánic and Islamic version of Noah's story, people did not believe His preaching and they beat Him. Sometimes he was beaten so badly that his ears would gush with blood and he would lose consciousness. Noah beseeched God to punish them. According to commentaries of the Qur'án God tells Noah to tell His followers to plant a date seed, and that when it grows and brings fruit God would punish the nonbelievers. Noah's followers complied but when the datetree gave fruit God did not punish the nonbelievers. Noah returns to remind God of His promise and God tells Him the same thing. This causes many of Noah's followers to lose faith in Him.

    This story brings forth the concept of *Badá* or the non-fulfillment of a divine promise (See Note No. 34, below).

    In addition, in the days before the flood came, Noah was building His Ark. Each time people saw Him building the Ark they would laugh at him. He told them that while they ridiculed Him now, they would be punished. In Genesis, at this point God opens the window of heaven to rain down upon earth. In the Qur'án at this point an old woman opens her bread oven and the flood waters from it engulf the earth. According to the Old Testament all three sons of Noah entered the ship with Him. According to the Qur'án one of his sons does not come into the Ark, and when Noah calls to Him he tells Noah that he will climb the mountain. Noah warns him that there is no refuge for him. When the flood comes, this son is drowned. Noah complains to God about drowning His son and God tells Him that this was not Noah's true son because he was spiritually estranged from Him (The Qur'án 11:35–50). Thus in this story Muḥammad demonstrates the difference between a spiritual and a physical relation. Another of the commentaries of the Qur'án states that this same son of Noah in the days before the flood associated with bad people and lost the treasure of spirituality that God had given him.

Bahá'u'lláh clarifies the meaning of the story of the Ark and the flood by explaining that the Ark symbolizes the Covenant between God and man. Thus being outside the Ark symbolizes being outside the religion of God and the Covenant of God. In the Writings of the Báb and Bahá'u'lláh, the Cause of God is referred to as the Crimson Ark and the people of Bahá are those who enter this Ark. This concept is very clearly presented in the Tablet of the Holy Mariner. It is interesting to note that this concept of Ark symbolizing the Covenant of God was presented in the Old Testament as well, but due to the literal interpretation of the Biblical events, the true meaning of the Ark was not realized.

> But with thee will I establish my covenant; and thou shalt come into the ark, thou, and thy sons, and thy wife, and thy sons' wives with thee.
> (Genesis 6:18)

and to this testify the records of the best-known books.[32]

32. ". . . the records of the best known books":

This refers to the books of tradition in Islam from Muḥammad and the Imáms and the commentaries on the Qur'án. An example of this is the *Bahár'u'l-Anvár* (Oceans of Light), a twenty-six volume encyclopedia of Shí'ah Islam by the famous Shí'ah scholar 'Alámeh Muḥammad Báqer Ibn Muḥammad Taqí Majlisí Isfahání. The thirteenth volume of this encyclopedia concerns the Twelfth Imám (the Qá'im), the Promised One of Islam, and is extensively quoted by Bahá'u'lláh later in the Kitáb-i-Íqán as proof of the Báb's mission. For additional information see Introduction Notes numbers 28–30: The Twelfth Imám, His occultation, and return.

Paragraph No. 8:

What could have induced them to refuse to put off the garment of denial, and to adorn themselves with the robe of acceptance[33]?

33. The terms garment and robe are also used in sacred writings to signify the revelation and words of God and also the attitudes of denial or acceptance of the Manifestations of God.

> And they came to Jericho: . . . blind Bartimaeus, the son of Timaeus, sat by the highway side begging. And when he heard that it was Jesus of Nazareth, he began to cry out, and say, Jesus, thou son of David, have mercy on me. . . . And Jesus stood still, and commanded him to be called. And they call the blind man, saying unto him, Be of good comfort, rise; he calleth thee. And he, casting away his garment, rose, and came to Jesus. And Jesus answered and said unto him, What wilt thou that I should do unto thee? The blind man said unto him, Lord, that I might receive my sight. And Jesus said unto him, Go thy way; thy faith hath made thee whole. And immediately he received his sight, and followed Jesus in the way.
> (Mark 10:46–52)

> And now concerning thy question regarding the nature of religion. Know thou that they who are truly wise have likened the world unto the human temple. As the body of man needeth a garment to clothe it, so the body of mankind must needs be adorned with the mantle of justice and wisdom. Its robe is the Revelation vouchsafed unto it by God. Whenever this robe hath fulfilled its purpose, the Almighty will assuredly renew it. For every age requireth a fresh measure of the light of God. Every Divine Revelation hath been sent down in a manner that befitted the circumstances of the age in which it hath appeared.
> (Bahá'u'lláh, *Gleanings from the Writings of Bahá'u'lláh*, p. 79)

Nonfulfillment of the divine promise which led the seekers to reject that which they had accepted?[34]

34. The "nonfulfillment of divine promises" is a translation of the word *Badá*. Shí'ah commentators of the Qur'án were puzzled and disturbed by the fact that the divine promise to Noah was not fulfilled. Thy thought that two scenarios were possible. Either Noah, a Prophet of God, was not telling the truth about God's promise, or God Himself made a promise, which He did not intend to keep. If God promised Noah victory, and one of the attributes of God is that He is All-knowing, He must have known that this promise would not be fulfilled. If He did not know that this promise could not be fulfilled, then He is not All-Knowing and therefore could not be God. Because He is All-knowing, He must have known, but if God knew that this promise would not be fulfilled why did He make a false promise to His own prophet?

    Scholars and commentators of the Qur'án have spent a lot of time and effort trying to explain this, but as is often the case with human endavors in these subjects, they constructed their own unusual explanation:

    They postulated that God has two books. One is the book of Divine Decree. All that God has promised in this book will be fulfilled. The other book is a book of Conditional Promises, which may or may not happen, and the promise God made to Noah was inscribe in this latter book.

    However, the literal meaning of Badá is, something that is begun anew, a point of initiation. The word is used in the Bahá'í Writings in reference to the appearance of the Manifestations of God, and to the renewal of the Covenant and establishment of new laws and teachings suitable for a new Dispensation.

    This meaning of the term is used, for example, in the Tablet of Visitation of Bahá'u'lláh:

    > I testify that through thee the sovereignty of God and His dominion, and the majesty of God and His grandeur, were revealed, and the Daystars of ancient splendor have shed their radiance upon the heaven of Thine irrevocable decree,

> and the beauty of the Unseen hath shown from above the horizon of creation.
> (Bahá'u'lláh, *Prayers and Meditations,* p. 310)

Here "irrevocable decree" refers to the declaration of the Manifestation of God, and "horizon of creation" is the English translation of the phrase "Ofouq-i-Badá."

Badá is a concept also mentioned by the Báb in the Persian Bayán (Chapter 3 of Unit 4). He explains the reason for Badá, and states that the most proper way, and highest level of worshiping God is attained by understanding the concept of Badá. Because Badá is the realization and confession to the power and might of God to do what He willet, and if a person worships God to the extent that higher and more intense worship beyond that is not imaginable, when he/she confesses to Badá (God doeth what He willeth), his/her worship will be exalted to a higher level.

It is furthermore explained in the Kitáb-i-Íqán that every Manifestation of God promises His followers spiritual victory. However, this victory is conditional upon their obedience and effort. If the followers keep God's commandments then the divine promise is fulfilled. If the believers fall short of obedience to the Word of God, however, the promise to them is not fulfilled because they did not uphold their part of the Covenant.

Bahá'u'lláh, however, continues in this verse of the Kitáb-i-Íqán to explain that the seeming nonfulfillment, or in reality the non-literal fulfillment of prophecies, has often been a test of spiritual perception and faith.

the sweetness of a spiritual and imperishable fragrance. [35]

35. There are many references in the scriptures of the Bahá'í Faith to inhaling the spiritual fragrances, which will cause the inner eyes to be opened and spiritual knowledge to be gained, truth to be known, faith to be strengthened, and certitude achieved. A few quotations are cited here.

> Whoso hath inhaled the sweet fragrance of the All-Merciful, and recognized the Source of this utterance, will

welcome with his own eyes the shafts of the enemy, that he may establish the truth of the laws of God amongst men.
(Bahá'u'lláh, The Kitáb-i-Aqdas, ¶7)
Blessed be the man that turneth his face towards thee, that perceiveth from thee the fragrance of God's Presence, the Lord of all worlds.
(Bahá'u'lláh, *Gleanings from the Writings of Bahá'u'lláh*, p. 121)

If the learned and worldly-wise men of this age were to allow mankind to inhale the fragrance of fellowship and love, every understanding heart would apprehend the meaning of true liberty, and discover the secret of undisturbed peace and absolute composure.
(Bahá'u'lláh, *Gleanings from the Writings of Bahá'u'lláh*, p. 260)

Happy is the lover that hath inhaled the divine fragrance of his Best-Beloved from these words, laden with the perfume of a grace which no tongue can describe.
(Bahá'u'lláh, The Kitáb-i-Aqdas, ¶4)

This is the Day whereon every sweet smelling thing hath derived its fragrance from the smell of My garment—a garment that hath shed its perfume upon the whole of creation.
(Bahá'u'lláh, *Gleanings from the Writings of Bahá'u'lláh*, p. 30)

These are the ones whom no word except Thy most exalted word can move, whom nothing whatever save the sweet smelling fragrance of the robe of Thy remembrance can enrapture, O Thou Who art the Possessor of all names and the Maker of earth and heaven!
(Bahá'u'lláh, *Prayers and Meditations*, p. 15)

This allegory has its origin in the story of Joseph (see Appendix III).

Even as He hath revealed: "Do men think when they say 'We believe' they shall be let alone and not be put to proof?" (Qur'án 29:2).[36]

36. In addition to the above explanation from the Báb, Bahá'u'lláh reiterates the theme that the servants are continuously tested for purity of heart. Through these prophecies and promises it is

ascertained who among them is able to see the spiritual significance of the divine promise and who is unable to surpass the material meaning.

Paragraph No. 9:

And after Noah the light of the countenance of Húd.[37]

37. Please see the previous references to Húd (Note No. 22, above).

For well-nigh seven hundred years,[38] **according to the sayings of men,**

38. Please see the explanation of the long life spans of Noah and Húd (Note No. 29).

    Also, note that while Bahá'u'lláh does not refute the belief in the long life spans, He does qualify it with the statement: ". . . according to the sayings of men," which naturally is indicative of lack of authority.

and draw nearer unto the Riḍván[39]

39. *Riḍván:* This word is the Arabic word for garden. In Islamic tradition it is both the garden of heaven and the name of the gardener of heaven. Here Bahá'u'lláh with the words "Riḍván of Divine presence". makes clear that heaven in actuality is a condition in which the soul is in the divine presence, which is the recognition of the true station of the Manifestation of God.

Paragraph No. 10:

the holy person of Ṣáliḥ[40]

40. The story of Ṣáliḥ is mentioned in Súrah 11 of the Qur'án (the same chapter which describes Húd). Ṣáliḥ, was a prophet who came to the cousin tribe of the 'Aud, known as Thamud, a tribe of stone masons. Bahá'u'lláh refers to the story of Ṣáliḥ, both with the reference here and also in the Epistle to the Son of the Wolf

(pp.100–102) where He refers specifically to the story of Ṣáliḥ and the she-camel.

According to the Qur'ánic story, when Ṣáliḥ first tried to teach the tribe of Thamud about God they did not listen to Him. He left, and upon His return, God had changed His face and the tribe did not recognize Him. The tribe insisted that in order to believe that He was the same person and was sent by God to guide them, they needed to see a sign. Therefore, God brought out of the rocks of the mountain a she-camel, which in ancient Arabia was considered quite a prized possession, and Ṣáliḥ told the people of the tribe that the she-camel was a present for them to use and to partake of its milk. However, in order to do so they had to share with the camel some of their precious water. In return, the tribe not only did not thank him or give water to the camel, but carried out an act against God's present to them, which in ancient Arabia, one would only perpetrate against one's worst enemy in order to destroy his property. They cut the hamstrings of the camel so that she could no longer walk or serve them. The she-camel then left the tribe and disappeared.

'Abdu'l-Bahá explained the symbolism of the story of the she-camel in the Súrah of Húd, in a Tablet printed in *Ma'idih-i-Ásmáni,* Vol. 2, p. 99. According to His explanation, the She-Camel represents the Manifestation of God Who brought the word of God. The water that the people of Thamud were asked to supply to the she-camel symbolizes the dedication of one's life to the word of God. The milk of the she-camel, then, represents the life-sustaining benefit one can derive from the word of God. Instead of using the she-camel, or God's gifts to them, the people of Thamud chose to kill it rather than give it water. Their refusal resulted in the disappearance of divine guidance.

Paragraph No. 11:

the beauty of the countenance of the Friend of God[41]

41. Abraham was titled *Khalil'u'lláh,* Arabic for the friend of God. the Qur'án in the Súrah of Women states:

> And who hath a better religion than he who resigneth himself to God, who doth what is good, and followeth the faith of Abraham in all sincerity? And God took Abraham for his friend."
> (The Qur'án 4:124)

Though the person of Abraham appears in both Genesis and in the Qur'án, the stories in the two books differ markedly. In Genesis, the story of Abraham Himself is told in Chapters 11–26. The story of His descendants fills the remainder of the book of Genesis. His story in Genesis is briefly summarized as follows:

Abraham was an inhabitant of Chaldees of Ur in the Tigris-Euphrates river valley (present-day Iraq). He was a descendent of Noah and appears on the scene shortly after the incident of the Tower of Babel. When He first appears He is called Abram (the excellent father), not Abraham:

> And the whole earth was of one language, and of one speech. And it came to pass, as they journeyed from the east, that they found a plain in the land of Shinar; and they dwelt there. And they said one to another, Go to, let us make brick, and burn them thoroughly. And they had brick for stone, and slime had they for mortar. And they said, Go to, let us build us a city and a tower, whose top may reach unto heaven; and let us make us a name, lest we be scattered abroad upon the face of the whole earth. And the LORD came down to see the city and the tower, which the children of men builded. And the LORD said, Behold, the people is one, and they have all one language; and this they begin to do: and now nothing will be restrained from them, which they have imagined to do. Go to, let us go down, and there confound their language, that they may not understand one another's speech. So the LORD scattered them abroad from thence upon the face of all the earth: and they left off to build the city. Therefore is the name of it called Babel; because the LORD did there confound the language of all the earth: and from thence did the LORD scatter them abroad upon the face of all the earth.
> (Genesis 11: 1–9)

The generations leading to Abraham are traced from Shem, the son of Noah, to Abraham after this incident.

> These are the generations of Shem (son of Noah): Shem was an hundred years old, and begat Arphaxad two years after the flood: And Shem lived after he begat Arphaxad five hundred years, and begat sons and daughters. And Arphaxad lived five and thirty years, and begat Salah. And Arphaxad lived after he begat Salah four hundred and three years, and begat sons and daughters. And Salah lived thirty years, and begat Eber. And Salah lived after he begat Eber four hundred and three years, and begat sons and daughters. . . . And Nahor lived after he begat Terah an hundred and nineteen years, and begat sons and daughters. And Terah lived seventy years, and begat Abram, Nahor, and Haran. Now these are the generations of Terah: Terah begat Abram, Nahor, and Haran; and Haran begat Lot. And Haran died before his father Terah in the land of his nativity, in Ur of the Chaldees.
> (Genesis 11:10–28)

Some commentators speculate that the Salah named in the generations between Shem and Abraham may be the prophet Ṣáliḥ of the Súrah of Húd in the Qur'án (see above, Note No. 40).

Terah, then sets out with his son, Abram; Abram's wife Sarai; and the son of the deceased Haran, Abrams nephew, Lot. They leave Ur of the Chaldees to settle in the land of Canaan (present-day Israel). Instead, they settle in a land along the way called Haran.

The Lord then commands Abram to leave His father's house and to go to the land of Canaan, and in exchange the Lord will make Him a great nation. Abram takes Sarai and Lot with Him and when He arrives He makes an altar to the Lord. But there is a famine in Canaan and they journey to Egypt where Abram tells Sarai to pretend that they are brother and sister so that no one will kill him to have her. The Pharaoh notices that she is fair and takes her as his wife and recompenses Abram generously with animals. The Lord then plagues Pharaoh for taking Abram's wife. When Pharaoh realizes what he has done, he gives Abram Sarai, asks Him why He lied and sends them out of Egypt under His protection back to Canaan {Genesis Chapter 12}. In Canaan, Lot and Abram's herds grow too large for the land, and so at Abram's bidding, Lot journeys east to Jordan near Sodom and Gomorrah, where the people are wicked. And the Lord tells Abram that all the land that He sees around Him will be His and His seed will multiply to the extent of the sands of the earth. Abram then moves to Hebron and makes an altar to the Lord (see the Old Testament, Genesis, Chapter 13).

In the next chapter, other kings join Chedorlaomer, king of Elam, to attack the kings of Sodom and Gomorrah. As the kings of Sodom and Gomorrah flee, they take all their possessions and on their way capture Lot, the nephew of Abram, and take him with them. When Abram finds out what happened he gathers his servants and defeats the invading kings and retrieves Lot and all the goods that were taken. One of the friendly kings, Mēl-chĭźe-dēk, king of Salem (Jerusalem), a priest of the most high God, blesses Abram, and Abram pays him tithes from all the goods he has captured.

> "And Mēl-chĭźe-dēk king of Salem brought forth bread and wine: and he was the priest of the most high God. And he blessed him, and said, Blessed be Abram of the most high God, possessor of heaven and earth: And blessed be the most high God, which hath delivered thine enemies into thy hand. And he gave him tithes of all.
> (Genesis 14:18–20)

There is another reference in the Bible to Mēl-chĭźe-dēk (also spelled as Mēl-chĭśe-dēc) as the mysterious figure (the priest and king of Salem or Jerusalem) that Abram paid tithes to. In the New Testament, in Hebrews chapters 6 and 7, he is presented as an exalted deity and the head of a priesthood order, the order of Mēl-chĭśe-dēc, and Jesus is presented as a priest of that order:

> Wherein God, willing more abundantly to shew unto the heirs of promise the immutability of his counsel, confirmed it by an oath: That by two immutable things, in which it was impossible for God to lie, we might have a strong consolation, who have fled for refuge to lay hold upon the hope set before us: Which hope we have as an anchor of the soul, both sure and stedfast, and which entereth into that

> within the vail; Whither the forerunner is for us entered, even Jesus, made an high priest for ever after the order of Mēl-chĭśe-dēc.
>
> For this Mēl-chĭśe-dēc, king of Salem, priest of the most high God, who met Abraham returning from the slaughter of the kings, and blessed him; To whom also Abraham gave a tenth part of all; first being by interpretation King of righteousness, and after that also King of Salem, which is, King of peace; Without father, without mother, without descent, having neither beginning of days, nor end of life; but made like unto the Son of God; abideth a priest continually. Now consider how great this man was, unto whom even the patriarch Abraham gave the tenth of the spoils.
> (Hebrews 6:17–7:4)

Going back to the story of Abram:

According to Genesis, chapter 15, Abram complains to the Lord that He has no heir and the Lord tells Him He will have as many of His seed as there are stars in heaven. God then asks Him to sacrifice a goat, a ram, a three-year-old heifer, a turtledove, and a young pigeon. The Lord tells Him that His seed shall be servants on a strange land for four hundred years, that God will afflict that strange land, and that His seed will return to the land of Canaan after four generations. God then gives Abram's seed the land from the river of Egypt (the Nile) to the Euphrates. Next, Sarai, Abram's wife gives Him her Egyptian handmaid, Hagar, and tells Him that since she cannot bear children He should have children through Hagar. Abram obeys her, and when Hagar conceives, Sarai becomes despised in her eyes. Sarai complains to Abram, and Abram tells her that she can do with her handmaid as she pleases. Sarai is harsh to Hagar and Hagar flees with her son Ishmael to the wilderness. The angel of the Lord then appears to her and tells her to return to her mistress. The angel also gives her the following prophecy:

> And the angel of the LORD said unto her, Behold, thou art with child, and shalt bear a son, and shalt call his name Ishmael; because the LORD hath heard thy affliction. And

> he will be a wild man; his hand will be against every man, and every man's hand against him; and he shall dwell in the presence of all his brethren. And she called the name of the LORD that spake unto her, Thou God seest me: for she said, Have I also here looked after him that seeth me?.... And Hagar bare Abram a son: and Abram called his son's name, which Hagar bare, Ishmael. And Abram was fourscore and six years old, when Hagar bare Ishmael to Abram.
> (Genesis 16:11–16)

The importance of this chapter is that it gives the Biblical documentation of the birth of Ishmael, who would become the father of the Arab nations, and contains the Lord's promise that His seed would multiply and that He would dwell among His brethren (the Jews).

In the next chapter, the Lord appears to Abram at the age of ninety-nine and renames Him Abraham, and from that point on he is called Abraham (the father of many people). He says that the Lord's part of the Covenant is to give Abraham's seed the area of Canaan. Abraham's part is to circumcise every male member of His house over eight days old, and His seed thereafter:

> And the uncircumcised man child whose flesh of his foreskin is not circumcised, that soul shall be cut off from his people; he hath broken my covenant.
> (Genesis 17:14)

The Lord also renames Sarai as Sarah and says that she will bear a son:

> And I will bless her, and give thee a son also of her: yea, I will bless her, and she shall be a mother of nations; kings of people shall be of her. Then Abraham fell upon his face, and laughed, and said in his heart, Shall a child be born unto him that is a hundred years old? and shall Sarah, that is ninety years old, bear? And Abraham said unto God, O that Ishmael might live before thee! And God said, Sarah thy wife shall bear thee a son indeed; and thou shalt call his name Isaac: and I will establish my covenant with him for an everlasting covenant, and with his seed after him. And as

> for Ishmael, I have heard thee: Behold, I have blessed him, and will make him fruitful, and will multiply him exceedingly; twelve princes shall he beget, and I will make him a great nation. But my covenant will I establish with Isaac, which Sarah shall bear unto thee at this set time in the next year.
> (Genesis 17:16–21)

Abraham then complies with the Lord's command and circumcises all the males of his household. This chapter is noteworthy in two aspects:

First, the reference to Ishmael becoming the father of a great nation and begetting twelve princes. This is often interpreted to mean that he would begin the Arab nation. The twelve princes are interpreted by some Moslems as Muḥammad and the eleven Imáms of Islam. Another reference to the number twelve is in the Revelation to St. John the Divine:

> And there appeared a great wonder in the Heaven; a woman clothed with the sun, and the moon under her feet, and upon her head a crown of twelve stars. And she being with child cried, travailing in birth, and pained to be delivered. And there appeared another great wonder in the heaven; and behold a red dragon having seven heads and ten horns, and seven crowns upon his head. And his tail drew the third part of the stars of heaven and did cast them to the earth; and the dragon stood before the woman which was ready to be delivered, for they devour her child as soon as it was born. And she brought forth a man child who was to rule all nations with a rod of iron; and her child was caught up unto God and to his throne. And the woman fled into the wilderness where she hath a place prepared by of God, that they should feed her there a thousand and two hundred and three score days.
> (Revelation 12:1–6)

This passage, in which the number twelve is used, mentions the number 1260 days in which the woman flees to the wilderness. This is the exact number of years between the commencement of the Islamic calendar (the establishment of Islam) and the declaration of the Báb. The twelve stars

> on the woman's head, as mentioned above could then be interpreted as Muḥammad and the eleven Imáms and the seven-headed dragon as the Umayyad dynasty, the enemies of true Islam who ruled the Islamic Empire and its seven parts. The woman in Revelation, chapter 12, is interpreted by ‘Abdu'l-Bahá in *Some Answered Questions*, no. 13, as the "religion of God, that descended upon Muḥammad."
> (Thomas Tai-Seale, *Thy Kingdom Come*, p. 94)

The second important point of this chapter is that the Lord says He will make His covenant with Isaac who came to be the father of Israel and thus the Jews. This is the Biblical verse from which the Jews draw their claim to the covenant. It also establishes the tradition of circumcision among the Jews.

In the next chapter the Lord appears to Abraham in the form of three men, and Abraham feeds them with his finest foods. God says that He will visit Sarah and she will have a son (Genesis 18:4–9). Sarah overhears their conversation and cannot believe that she will have a child. The reply she hears is : "Is anything too hard for the Lord?" Abraham finds out that the Lord wants to destroy the evil cities of Sodom and Gomorrah and begs the Lord to spare Lot. The Lord agrees. The next chapter is devoted to Lot.

In Genesis, chapter 20, Abraham and Sarah journey to Gerar and a smilar episode to the one involving the Pharaoh of Egypt occurs with Abimelech, King of Gerar. And in the end the king gives Abraham silver and cattle and sends him on His way as the pharaoh had done.

In Genesis, chapter 21, Sarah finally gives Abraham His son Isaac when she is a hundred years old. She also forces Abraham to send Hagar and her son into the wilderness of Beer-sheba with bread and a bottle of water. When the water runs out, the Lord makes a well appear to Ishmael and repeats His promise to make Him a great nation. Abraham then has a meeting of good faith with the leaders of the Philistines and interestingly complains that their servants took His well away.

This chapter is noteworthy because it establishes the Sonship of Israelites (Jews). As promised (Chapter 18), God visited Sarah (Genesis 21:1–2).

> And the LORD visited Sarah as he had said, and the LORD did unto Sarah as he had spoken. For Sarah conceived,
> (Genesis 21:1–2)

Some Jewish scholars state that by the authority of this verse, Isaac was the son of God. They also state that Jacob was born by divine intervention.

> And Isaac was forty years old when he took Rebekah to wife, the daughter of Bethuel the Syrian of Padanaram, the sister to Laban the Syrian. And Isaac intreated the LORD for his wife, because she was barren: and the LORD was intreated of him, and Rebekah his wife conceived.
> (Genesis 25:20–21)

In Genesis, chapter 22, the Lord asks Abraham to sacrifice Isaac, and Abraham complies, taking Isaac to the place the Lord appoints. Just as Abraham is about to sacrifice His son in obedience to God, the angel of the Lord stops Him and the Lord furnishes a ram to be sacrificed in Isaac's place.

The last chapters of Genesis concerning Abraham deal with the death of Sarah and her burial in Hebron; the marriage of Isaac to his cousin Rebekah, who came from Mesopotami; the marriage of Abraham to his third wife, Keturah; and finally the death of Abraham and His burial next to Sarah, performed by Isaac and Ishmael. Ishmael's death and his fathering of twelve children is also dealt with in Genesis, chapters 23–25.

The Qur'ánic story of Abraham has a different focus than the story in Genesis. It focuses on Abraham's belief in God and His embracing of monotheism and the trials this belief brought upon Him. Essentially, it focuses on the spiritual life of Abraham more than on the details of His travels. All His activities were for the purpose of teaching monotheism. The Qur'ánic story also does not contain any of the stories about the passing off of His wife as His sister.

Abraham's evolutionary process of faith, and the progressive stages of His spiritual development, ending in monotheism and the recognition of the One True God is detailed in the Qur'án in the Súrah of Cattle (Al-An'ám):

> And thus did we shew Abraham the kingdom of the Heavens and of the Earth, that he might be stablished in knowledge. And when the night overshadowed him, he beheld a star. "This," said he, "is my Lord:" but when it set, he said, "I love not gods which set."
>
> And when he beheld the moon uprising, "This," said he, "is my Lord:" but when it set, he said, "Surely, if my Lord guide me not, I shall surely be of those who go astray."
>
> And when he beheld the sun uprise, he said, "This is my Lord; this is greatest." But when it set, he said, "O my people! I share not with you the guilt of joining gods with God;
>
> I turn my face to him who hath created the Heavens and the Earth, following the right religion: I am not one of those who add gods to God."
>
> And his people disputed with him. - He said: "Dispute ye with me about God, when He hath guided me? And I fear not the deities whom ye join with Him, for only by the will of my Lord have they any power: My Lord embraceth all things in His knowledge. Will ye not then consider?
>
> This is our reasoning with which we furnished Abraham against his people: We uplift to grades of wisdom whom we will; Verily thy Lord is Wise, Knowing.
> (The Qur'án 6:75–83)

In one of His Writings, His Holiness the Báb states that Abraham's progression of belief from star to moon to sun and finally to God, is symbolic of humanity's maturation of belief. The stages of star and moon are the symbolic presentation of humanity's understanding under the dispensations of the past, while the progression to sun is equated to His own (the Báb's) dispensation, and finally his further progress and belief in an unseen God Who is

the creator of the Heavens and the Earth is symbolically consonant with the progress of humanity, which comes with the revelation of "He whom God will make manifest" (Bahá'u'lláh).
(Source: Persian Publication, *Khoosh-i-Há'i Az Kharman-I Adab Va Honar*, Vol. 3, p. 77)
In the Qur'án, it is Ishmael who is the one offered to God as a sacrifice. Abraham asked God to give Him a son:

> O Lord give me a son, of the righteous." We announced to him a youth of meekness. And when he became a full-grown youth, His father said to him, "My son, I have seen in a dream that I should sacrifice thee; therefore, consider what thou seest right." He said, "My father, do what thou art bidden; of the patient, if God please, shalt thou find me." And when they had surrendered them to the will of God, he laid him down upon his forehead: We cried unto him, "O Abraham! Now hast thou satisfied the vision,." See how we recompense the righteous. This was indeed a decisive test. And we ransomed his son with a costly victim, And we left this for him among posterity, "Peace be on Abraham!"
> (The Qur'án 37:98–109)

The Báhá'í Writings agree with the Qur'án, naming Ishmael as the sacrifice. In Epistle to the Son of the Wolf, p. 101, Bahá'u'lláh, referring to the martyrdom of the King of the Martyrs and the Beloved of the Martyrs at his hands and the hands of the Wolf (the father of the addressee), warns the addressee, who is still a center of the opposition to the Faith in Iran:

> O heedless one! The tale of the Sacrifice (Ishmael) hath been retold, and he who was to be offered up hath directed his steps towards the place of sacrifice, and returned not, by reason of that which thy hands have wrought, O perverse hater!

And referring to the many pure souls that chose to sacrifice their lives and not recant their faith, and to the sufferings He endured because of His love of each one of them as His own son, Bahá'u'lláh states:

> Do thou ponder on the penetrative influence of the Word of God. Every single one of these souls was first ordered to blaspheme and curse his faith, yet none was found to prefer his own will to the Will of God.
>
> O Shaykh! In former times he that was chosen to be slain was but one person, whereas now this Wronged One hath produced for thee that which causeth every fair-minded man to marvel.
> (Bahá'u'lláh, Epistle to the Son of the Wolf, p. 75)

Furthermore, when speaking of Abraham, Bahá'u'lláh explains:

> That which thou hast heard concerning Abraham, the Friend of the All merciful is the truth, and no doubt is there about it. The voice of God commanded him to offer up Ishmael as a sacrifice so that His steadfastness in the Faith of God and His detachment from all else but Him may be demonstrated unto men.
> (Bahá'u'lláh, *Gleanings from the Writings of Bahá'u'lláh*, p. 75)

In response to Hakim Hezghil Hayem, a Báhá'í from Jewish background, who asked who the real sacrifice was because the Old Testament identifies Isaac and the Qur'án Ishmael, Bahá'u'lláh states that these stations were conferred by the Manifestations of God in the sacred books of the past, and that both Isaac and Ishmael, therefore have this same station (see Amr va Khalq, Vol. 2, page 195)

'Abdu'l-Bahá, when speaking of Abraham in *Some Answered Questions,* compares His exile to that of the Blessed Beauty and affirms the great results that He was able to achieve:

> Among those who possessed this divine power and were assisted by it was Abraham. The proof is this: Abraham was born in Mesopotamia of a family that was ignorant of the oneness of God; He opposed His own people and government, and even His own kin; He rejected all their gods; and, alone and single-handed, He withstood a powerful nation. Such opposition and resistance were not simple or trivial. It is as though one were in this day to deny Christ among Christian nations who firmly cling to

the Bible, or as though one were—God forbid!—to blaspheme Christ in the papal court, oppose all His followers, and to act thus in the most vehement manner.

These people believed not in one God but in many gods, to whom they ascribed miracles, and hence they all rose up against Abraham. No one supported Him except His nephew Lot and one or two other individuals of no consequence. At last the intensity of His enemies' opposition obliged Him, utterly wronged, to forsake His native land. In reality He was banished that He might be reduced to naught and that no trace of Him might remain. Abraham then came to these regions, that is, to the Holy Land.

My point is that His enemies imagined that this exile would lead to His destruction and ruin. And indeed, if a man is banished from his native land, deprived of his rights, and oppressed from every side, he is bound—even if he be a king—to be reduced to naught. But Abraham stood fast and showed forth extraordinary constancy, and God changed His exile into abiding honour, till at last He established the oneness of God, for at that time the generality of mankind were idol worshippers.

This exile became the cause of the progress of Abraham's descendants. This exile resulted in their being given the Holy Land. This exile resulted in the diffusion of Abraham's teachings. This exile resulted in the appearance of a Jacob from the seed of Abraham, and of a Joseph who became ruler in Egypt. This exile resulted in the appearance of a Moses from that same seed. This exile resulted in the appearance of a being such as Christ from that lineage. This exile resulted in a Hagar being found, of whom Ishmael was begotten, and from whom Muḥammad in turn descended. This exile resulted in the appearance of the Báb from the lineage of Abraham. This exile resulted in the appearance of the Prophets of Israel from the progeny of Abraham—and so will it continue forevermore. This exile resulted in the whole of Europe and most of Asia entering under the shadow of the God of Israel. Behold what a

> power it was that enabled an emigrant to establish such a family, to found such a nation, and to promulgate such teachings. Now, can anyone claim that all this was purely fortuitous? We must be fair: Was this Man an Educator or not?
>
> It behoves us to ponder awhile that if the emigration of Abraham from Ur to Aleppo in Syria produced such results, what will be the effect of the exile of Bahá'u'lláh from Ṭihrán to Baghdád, and from thence to Constantinople, to Rumelia, and to the Holy Land!
>
> Behold then what an accomplished Educator Abraham was!
> ('Abdu'l-Bahá, *Some Answered Questions,* no. 4.1–6)

Shoghi Effendi also commented on the similarity of the banishments of Abraham and Bahá'u'lláh from Their native lands:

> [E]nforced and hurried departure of Bahá'u'lláh from His native land, accompanied by some of His relatives, recalls in some of its aspects, . . . above all the banishment of Abraham from Ur of the Chaldees to the Promised Land—a banishment which, in the multitudinous benefits it conferred upon so many divers peoples, faiths and nations, constitutes the nearest historical approach to the incalculable blessings destined to be vouchsafed, in this day, and in future ages, to the whole human race, in direct consequence of the exile suffered by Him Whose Cause is the flower and fruit of all previous Revelations.
> (Shoghi Effendi, *God Passes By*, p. 107)

And after the episode of the fire[42]

42. Among the sufferings and trials that His belief in monotheism brought upon Abraham is an incident that is related in a story contained exclusively in the Qur'ánic Súrah of Al-Anbiya (The Prophets). According to some of the Qur'án commentators, Abraham's father Azar was the master idol sculptor, this is supported or based on the Qur'án Súrah VI:

> And remember when Abraham said to his father Azar, Takest thou images as gods? Verily, I see that thou and thy people are in manifest error.
> (The Qur'án 6:74)

In the story, when the people of Chaldees do not heed Abraham's call to stop idol worship and embrace monotheism, He takes action by destroying all the idols in the Idol House except for the chief idol. When the people come back to the Idol House and see this, they ask Abraham if he has destroyed the idols. He answers that the chief idol destroyed the others, and asks why they don't you ask him. They point out that this idol does not speak or move and is unable to destroy other idols. He then asks why they worship an idol that is not capable of doing anything instead of worshiping God. At this point they decide to burn Him as punishment for His act. So they place him on a mound of wood and ignite a fire to burn him. Then God says "O fire! be thou cold, and to Abraham a safety!" He is saved by divine intervention, but banished from his homeland. This story is mentioned in two places in the Qur'án with slight variation. The following is from the Súrah of Al-Anbiya (The Prophets):

> Of old we gave unto Abraham his direction, for we knew him worthy. When he said to his Father and to his people, "What are these images to which ye are devoted?" They said, "We found our fathers worshipping them." He said, "Truly ye and your fathers have been in a plain mistake." They said, "Hast thou come unto us in earnest? or art thou of those who jest?" He said, "Nay, your Lord is the Lord of the Heavens and of the Earth, who hath created them both; and to this am I one of those who witness:— And, by God, I will certainly lay a plot against your idols, after ye shall have retired and turned your backs." So, he broke them all in pieces, except the chief of them, that to it they might return, inquiring. They said, "Who hath done this to our gods? Verily he is one of the unjust." They said, "We heard a youth make mention of them: they call him Abraham." They said, "Then bring him before the people's eyes, that they may witness against him." They said, "Hast thou done this to our gods, O Abraham?" He said, "Nay, that their chief hath done it: but ask ye them, if they can speak. "So they turned their thoughts upon themselves, and said, "Ye

> truly are the impious persons:" Then became headstrong in their former error and exclaimed, "Thou knowest that these speak not." He said, "What! do ye then worship, instead of God, that which doth not profit you at all, nor injure you? Fie on you and on that ye worship instead of God! What! do ye not then understand?" They said: "Burn him, and come to the succour of your gods: if ye will do anything at all." We said, "O fire! be thou cold, and to Abraham a safety!" And they sought to lay a plot against him, but we made them the sufferers.
> (The Qur'án 21:51–69)

There is a beautiful Tablet from 'Abdu'l-Bahá, addressed to a friend who was in the fire of tribulation, in which He refers to Abraham's story. This author could not find an authorized translation of this Tablet, therefore, a rendering of his understanding (not a translation of the Tablet) is presented here:

It is related that when Abraham, the Friend of God, was placed on a devouring fire, Gabriel called and asked: What is your request and what do you desire? The glorious Abraham (Friend of God) answered and said I do not have any request from you, your asking and God's attention to my situation is sufficient.

'Abdu'l-Bahá then advises the recipient of the Tablet to also turn his heart in supplication to the Divine Kingdom and say: O Thou the knower of the secrets, O Thou the guide of the chosen ones, O Thou the Lord of the righteous ones, . . . may my life be a sacrifice in Thy path. . . . Although You are hidden from the eyes, You always know the needs and desires, . . . may my life be a sacrifice in Thy path. There are several other supplications with the same refrain "may my life be a sacrifice in Thy path.

Paragraph No. 12:

And when His day was ended, there came the turn of Moses. Armed with the rod of celestial dominion, adorned with the white hand of divine knowledge,[43]

43. Moses, a Prophet mentioned in both the Old Testament and the Qur'án, was according to the book of Exodus, chapter 2, a member of one of the twelve tribes of Israel (the tribe or house of Levi).

    Following is a brief history of the tribes of Israel based on the Old Testament's book of Genesis, chapters 26–33:

    The Israelites were descendants of Abraham. Abraham had two sons, Isaac and Ishmael. After Abraham's death, Isaac carried the mantle of spiritual leadership. Isaac had twin sons Esau and Jacob. According to the Old Testament, Isaac favored his firstborn twin, Esau, while Rebekah, his wife, favored the second son, Jacob. The rights of the progenitor (the firstborn son) were very important in ancient times and still are in some societies. According to the Hebrew traditions, the firstborn would inherit all that the father had, both his physical estate and his spiritual leadership. Rebekah, Isaac's wife was concerned for her younger twin and was trying to arrange to deprive Esau of his birthright. Esau and Jacob were quite different in both physique and temperament. Esau was hirsute and liked to go hunting while Jacob enjoyed staying near home.

    One day when Esau came from hunting and was very hungry, Jacob went out with a bowl of soup. Esau sold his birthright to Jacob in exchange for it. Isaac at this time was old, blind, and was ready to transfer the mantle of prophethood to his eldest son, Esau. He asked Esau to hunt venison and prepare Isaac's favorite food and bring it to him so that he could bless Esau and perform the right of transference. Meanwhile, Rebekah asked Jacob to bring a young goat from the flock so that she could prepare Isaac's favorite food. She prepared the goat as Isaac liked it and then she gave Jacob Esau's cloths to wear and placed the skin of the goat on the hands and shoulders of Jacob so that he would feel hirsute to Isaac. Jacob then took the meal to his father. Isaac told him that his voice was that of Jacob, but when he smelled his cloths and touched his arms and neck, it felt like Esau. Being suspicious, "Are you Esau?" he asked him. Jacob replied that he was. Isaac then blessed Jacob and prayed for him, and gave him the mantle of leadership. Then Esau came with venison and Isaac said, "well I have already eaten." Then Esau and Isaac found out that Jacob had cheated them. Esau wanted to kill Jacob, so Rebekah arranged for him to escape and go and live with his uncle. Jacob then married the daughter of his uncle, Leban.

After a number of years God told Jacob to return to the land of his father. Thus, Jacob returned with a large flock and many servants. Fearing his brother, Jacob divided the flock among his servants and sent them ahead to tell Esau that his brother had sent him gifts and wanted forgiveness. He also divided his two wives and children and sent them forward to soften Esau's heart. Then Jacob stayed away by himself at night, waiting to hear from his servants, and giving himself chance to run away in case Esau wanted to kill him. Then, a man appeared and wrestled with him throughout the night until morning but was unable to overcome him. The man hit Jacob in the sinew of his thigh and made him weak. The man then told Jacob to let him go. Jacob told him he would not do so until he blessed him. The man blessed him. The man who had wrestled with him was God, who renamed him and told him that from that point forward his name would not be Jacob, but *Israel,* which means "the one who wrestled with God," and that his children would be known as the "Children of Israel":

> And he rose up that night, and took his two wives, and his two women servants, and his eleven sons, and passed over the ford Jabbok. And he took them, and sent them over the brook, and sent over that he had. And Jacob was left alone; and there wrestled a man with him until the breaking of the day. And when he saw that he prevailed not against him, he touched the hollow of his thigh; and the hollow of Jacob's thigh was out of joint, as he wrestled with him. And he said, Let me go, for the day breaketh. And he said, I will not let thee go, except thou bless me. And he said unto him, What is thy name? And he said, Jacob. And he said, Thy name shall be called no more Jacob, but Israel: for as a prince hast thou power with God and with men, and hast prevailed. And Jacob asked him, and said, Tell me, I pray thee, thy name. And he said, Wherefore is it that thou dost ask after my name? And he blessed him there. And Jacob called the name of the place Penuel: or I have seen God face to face, and my life is preserved. And as he passed over Penuel the sun rose upon him, and he halted upon his thigh. Therefore the children of Israel eat not of the sinew

> which shrank, which is upon the hollow of the thigh, unto this day: because he touched the hollow of Jacob's thigh in the sinew that shrank.
> (Genesis 32:22–32)

The word *sinew* refers to a tendon in the leg that is a major force of stability. (Webster's Third International Dictionary, 1976). It is the tendon that connect the Quadricep muscles to the bones of the leg over the knee.

Jacob had twelve sons, each of whom became the father and originator of a tribe. The story of Moses grows out of the story of the Children of Israel. Jacob's eleventh son Joseph was taken to Egypt, and later Jacob himself and all the Children of Israel migrated there. Reference to Joseph is made in the second part of the Kitáb-i-Íqán. However, due to the importance of the story of Joseph and the many references to this story in the Bible, the Qur'án, and the Writings of the Bahá'í Faith, a brief Biblical and Qur'ánic account of this story is presented in Appendix III (under Note No. 35).

Initially, due to the high status of Joseph in the court of Pharaoh, the Israelites enjoyed a high social status in Egypt. Four Centuries later, however, by the time of the birth of Moses, they were enlisted as manual laborers making brick and were among the lowest class of Egyptian society.

When Moses was born, according to the Encyclopedia of the Holy Book, Pharaoh had a dream that his power and government was to be destroyed and thus he ordered that all the firstborn of the Israelites be killed. The Old Testament indicates that the pharaoh perceived the increasing number of Israelites as a threat and that was the motive behind the genocide (Exodus 1:8–22). Moses' mother, fearful of death of her son, placed Him into a hand-made wooden box and set Him afloat on the River Nile where the currents carried Him to the daughter of Pharaoh who was bathing in the river. The daughter of Pharaoh liked the baby and took it as her own. Moses' sister was watching what happened, approached the daughter of Pharaoh, and asked if she wanted a wet nurse for the baby and then arranged for Moses' mother to nurse Him. Moses then grew up as the son of Pharaoh's daughter. The name Moses means, "one who was pulled out of Water."[44]

Moses' activity begins at the age of forty when He leaves to go and visit His people. On His way He witnesses a fight between an Egyptian and an Israelite. He then intervenes and kills the Egyptian. The next day when He visited His people He witnesses a fight between two Israelis and asks them to stop fighting. They ask him, "Who said you are in charge. Are you going to kill us as you killed the Egyptian?"

From this, Moses knows that the people knew about His crime and He runs into the wilderness. In the wilderness, He comes upon a well where several shepherds are not allowing two women to draw water for their flock. Moses helps the women and when they tell their father of this, their father (who was called Jēth'rō) and is the priest of the Mĭdí-ans (also spelled Mĭdí-an in the Old Testament), takes Him into his house and marries his oldest daughter, Sephora (spelled Zĭp-pórah in the Old Testament), to Moses. Moses is a shepherd for His father-in-law when He is given His mission. The Lord appears to Moses in a Burning Bush on Mount Sinai, and bids Him to go to Pharaoh and arrange to free the Israelites from captivity and slavery.

> Now Moses kept the flock of Jēth'rō * his father in law, the priest of Mĭdí-an: and he led the flock to the backside of the desert, and came to the mountain of God, even to Horeb.
>
> And the angel of the LORD appeared unto him in a flame of fire out of the midst of a bush: and he looked, and, behold, the bush burned with fire, and the bush was not consumed. And Moses said, I will now turn aside, and see this great sight, why the bush is not burnt. And when the LORD saw that he turned aside to see, God called unto him out of the midst of the bush, and said, Moses, Moses. And he said, Here am I. And he said, Draw not nigh hither: put off thy shoes from off thy feet, for the place whereon thou standest is holy ground. Moreover he said, I am the God of thy father, the God of Abraham, the God of Isaac, and the God of Jacob. And Moses hid his face; for he was afraid to

[44] Source: 'Abdu'l-Ḥamíd Is͟hráq-K͟hávari, *Qámus-i-Íqán,* Vol. 4, p. 1542.

look upon God. And the LORD said, I have surely seen the affliction of my people which are in Egypt, and have heard their cry by reason of their taskmasters; for I know their sorrows; And I am come down to deliver them out of the hand of the Egyptians, and to bring them up out of that land unto a good land and a large, unto a land flowing with milk and honey; unto the place of the Canaanites, and the Hittites, and the Amorites, and the Perizzites, and the Hivites, and the Jebusites. Now therefore, behold, the cry of the children of Israel is come unto me: and I have also seen the oppression wherewith the Egyptians oppress them. Come now therefore, and I will send thee unto Pharaoh, that thou mayest bring forth my people the children of Israel out of Egypt. And Moses said unto God, Who am I, that I should go unto Pharaoh, and that I should bring forth the children of Israel out of Egypt? And he said, Certainly I will be with thee; and this shall be a token unto thee, that I have sent thee: When thou hast brought forth the people out of Egypt, ye shall serve God upon this mountain. And Moses said unto God, Behold, when I come unto the children of Israel, and shall say unto them, The God of your fathers hath sent me unto you; and they shall say to me, What is his name? what shall I say unto them? And God said unto Moses, I AM THAT I AM: and he said, Thus shalt thou say unto the children of Israel, I AM hath sent me unto you. And God said moreover unto Moses, Thus shalt thou say unto the children of Israel, the LORD God of your fathers, the God of Abraham, the God of Isaac, and the God of Jacob, hath sent me unto you: this is my name for ever, and this is my memorial unto all generations. Go, and gather the elders of Israel together, and say unto them, The LORD God of your fathers, the God of Abraham, of Isaac, and of Jacob, appeared unto me, saying, I have surely visited you, and seen that which is done to you in Egypt:

And I have said, I will bring you up out of the affliction of Egypt unto the land of the Canaanites, and the Hittites, and the Amorites, and the Perizzites, and the Hivites, and the Jebusites, unto a land flowing with milk and honey. And they shall hearken to thy voice: and thou shalt come, thou and the elders of Israel, unto the king of Egypt, and ye shall

> say unto him, The LORD God of the Hebrews hath met with us: and now let us go, we beseech thee, three days' journey into the wilderness, that we may sacrifice to the LORD our God. And I am sure that the king of Egypt will not let you go, no, not by a mighty hand. And I will stretch out my hand, and smite Egypt with all my wonders which I will do in the midst thereof: and after that he will let you go.
> (Exodus 3:2–20)

* Moses' father-in-law is named differently in three places in the Old Testament as Jēth'rō or Reū'el (in Exodus, chapters 2&3), and Rā-gū'el (in Numbers 10:29). Except for the name of Moses' father-in-law, Shuaibe (designated as a prophet that came to Mĭdíans), this part of the Qur'ánic version of the story is very close to the Biblical version:

> And when Moses had fulfilled the term, and was journeying with his family, he perceived a fire on the mountain side. He said to his family, "Wait ye, for I perceive a fire. Haply I may bring you tidings from it, or a brand from the fire to warm you." And when he came up to it, a Voice cried to him out of the bush from the right side of the valley in the sacred hollow, "O Moses, I truly am God, the Lord of the Worlds: Throw down now thy rod." And when he saw it move as though it were a serpent, he retreated and fled and returned not. "O Moses," cried the Voice, "draw near and fear not, for thou art in safety. Put thy hand into thy bosom; it shall come forth white, but unharmed: and draw back thy hand to thee without fear. These shall be two signs from thy Lord to Pharaoh and his nobles; for they are a perverse people.
> (The Qur'án 28: 29–32)

The Burning Bush has, in religious history, become the symbol of divine presence. The Báb addressing His own relatives regarding His own station states:

> O YE kinsmen of the Most Great Remembrance!* This Tree of Holiness, dyed crimson with the oil of servitude, hath verily sprung forth out of your own soil in the midst of the Burning Bush, yet ye comprehend nothing whatever

> thereof, neither of His true, heavenly attributes, nor of the actual circumstances of His earthly life, nor of the evidences of His powerful and unblemished behavior.
> (The Báb, *Selections from the Writings of the Báb*, p. 51)

* the Most Great Remembrance is a title of the Báb.
The concept of God's communication with Moses through a tree was the subject of extensive discourse in Islamic mystical thought. A very famous ninth century mystic, Mansúr-i-Ḥalláj, who went around saying "I am God," was condemned to death by the Caliph in Ba<u>gh</u>dád. Subsequent to this, a question was posed in the mystical discourse that is best reflected in a poem by the Persian mystic poet, Shabestari:

> It is permitted and acceptable from a tree to say, "I am God,"
> Why is it not permitted and acceptable from a noble man?
> (Gul<u>sh</u>an-i-Ráz, Rose garden of Secrets)

Mullá Hádí Sabzivárí,[45] a well-known mystic contemporary of Bahá'u'lláh made reference to this same Qur'ánic verse in a poem, in which he said, No Moses is there to hear the voice of God proclaiming "Verily, I am God," else there is no tree in which this chant does not exist.

Bahá'u'lláh commented regarding Mullá Hádí Sabzivárí and his poem in a Tablet titled "Láwḥ Basít al-Haqíqa." This Tablet was revealed in honor of one of the believers who asked a question regarding a mystical subject that was alluded to in the writings of Mullá Hádí Sabzivárí. This author could not find an authorized translation of this Tablet, therefore, the relevant passage from a provisional translation of this Tablet by Dr. Moojan Momen titled "Tablet of The Uncompounded Reality,"[46] is presented below:

---

[45] Mullá Hádí Sabzivárí (d. 1878), the most prominent of the Iranian mystic philosophers of the nineteenth century. An English translation of one of his major works was published under the title *The Metaphysics of Sabzavárí* (trans. T. Izutsu and M. Mohaghegh, New York, 1977).

[46] A provisional translation of this tablet by Dr. Moojan Momen is presented as: Bahá'u'lláh's Tablet of Uncompounded Reality (Láwḥ Basít al-Haqíqa), in *Lights of 'Irfán*, Book 11, p. 217.

> Consider the philosopher Sabzivárí. Among his verses, there is a poem, which conveys the following meaning: "No Moses is alive to hear it, otherwise the chant of `I verily am God!' exists in every tree [bush]." Such words as these has he spoken and his meaning is that the true knower of God rises to such a station that his eyes perceive the lights of the effulgences of the luminous Source of manifestation (*mujallí*) and his ears discern His call from all things. There is no objection to these words of the philosopher[47], but, as we have already stated, this is the realm of words. In the realm of deeds, however, it can be seen that although the call of the divine lote-tree has been raised upon the highest spot in creation in clear and unambiguous (*min ghayr ta'wíl*) language and is inviting all beings through the loftiest of summonses, he has paid no heed whatsoever. For had he hearkened, he would have arisen to make mention of it. Either we must say that these were empty words which flowed from his mouth, or that, for fear for his reputation and love of his livelihood (lit. his bread), he remained deprived of this station (of belief) and of testifying to it. Either he understood and concealed [his belief] or he understood and denied [Bahá'u'lláh's claim].

Interestingly in this part of the story when Moses is setting out on His mission, He tarries at an inn instead of moving promptly forward. The Lord meets Him at the inn to slay Him, which is reminiscent of the Lord wrestling with Israel (Jacob). However, when the blood of His son's circumcision hits Him, Moses' life is spared:

> And Moses took his wife and his sons, and set them upon an ass, and he returned to the land of Egypt: and Moses took the rod of God in his hand. And the LORD said unto Moses, When thou goest to return into Egypt, see that thou do all those wonders before Pharaoh, which I have put in thine hand: but I will harden his heart, that he shall not let

---

[47] Indeed Bahá'u'lláh in describing the nature of His Cause, states in one of the prayers for the fast: ". . . this Revelation—a Revelation the potency of which hath caused every tree to cry out what the Burning Bush had aforetime proclaimed unto Moses, Who conversed with Thee" (*Prayers and Meditations*, no. 85, p. 144).

> the people go. And thou shalt say unto Pharaoh, Thus saith the LORD, Israel is my son, even my firstborn: And I say unto thee, Let my son go, that he may serve me: and if thou refuse to let him go, behold, I will slay thy son, even thy firstborn. And it came to pass by the way in the inn, that the LORD met him, and sought to kill him. Then Zĭp-pórah took a sharp stone, and cut off the foreskin of her son, and cast it at his feet, and said, Surely a bloody husband art thou to me. So he let him go: then she said, A bloody husband thou art, because of the circumcision.
> (Exodus 4:24–26)

This section of the story of Moses has confused Bible scholars for centuries. Why did the Lord attempt to kill Moses after charging Him with such a great mission? However, in light of Bahá'u'lláh's explanations in the Kitáb-i-Íqán, the symbolic nature of the events of the life of Moses becomes evident. It is possible to look at this confusing section of the story of Moses in a new light. When originally charged with His mission, Moses tarries and is disobedient to the Lord's wishes to promptly confront Pharaoh. The figure of God coming to kill him in the inn (just as when God wrestled with his ancestor Jacob) can thus be interpreted as the Prophet struggling with His own conscience and feelings of inadequacy with respect to His obedience to God. According to both the Torah and Talmud (the collection of ancient Rabbinic writings consisting of the Mishnah and the Gemara, constituting the basis of religious authority in Orthodox Judaism), circumcision was one way in which the Jews showed their obedience to the commandment of the Lord to Abraham, and their distinction as God's chosen people. Thus by the act of circumcising His son, Moses showed obedience to the Lord. In addition, in Hebrew society, a man ascends to a full station of manhood and responsibility after the circumcision of his firstborn son. One interpretation of this short parable, then, is that Moses, while originally disobedient to the Lord, became aware of His responsibility and His mission, and was spared.

When Moses is charged with His mission to go and talk to Pharaoh and move the Israelites out of Egypt, He is afraid and does not want to do it, but the Lord bids Him to go forward. Moses then asks the Lord how it could be proved to pharaoh that He is indeed the Messenger of God. The Lord supplies Him with several supernatural signs. In Exodus, these are recorded as physical and actual occurrences:

> And Moses answered and said, But, behold, they will not believe me, nor hearken unto my voice: for they will say, The LORD hath not appeared unto thee. And the LORD said unto him, What is that in thine hand? And he said, A rod. And he said, Cast it on the ground. And he cast it on the ground, and it became a serpent; and Moses fled from before it. And the LORD said unto Moses, Put forth thine hand, and take it by the tail. And he put forth his hand, and caught it, and it became a rod in his hand: That they may believe that the LORD God of their fathers, the God of Abraham, the God of Isaac, and the God of Jacob, hath appeared unto thee. And the LORD said furthermore unto him, Put now thine hand into thy bosom. And he put his hand into his bosom: and when he took it out, behold, his hand was leprous as snow. And he said, Put thine hand into thy bosom again. And he put his hand into his bosom again; and plucked it out of his bosom, and, behold, it was turned again as his other flesh. And it shall come to pass, if they will not believe thee, neither hearken to the voice of the first sign, that they will believe the voice of the latter sign. And it shall come to pass, if they will not believe also these two signs, neither hearken unto thy voice, that thou shalt take of the water of the river, and pour it upon the dry land: and the water which thou takest out of the river shall become blood upon the dry land. And Moses said unto the LORD, O my Lord, I am not eloquent, neither heretofore, nor since thou hast spoken unto thy servant: but I am slow of speech, and of a slow tongue. And the LORD said unto him, Who hath made man's mouth? or who maketh the dumb, or deaf, or the seeing, or the blind? have not I the LORD? Now therefore go, and I will be with thy mouth, and teach thee what thou shalt say. And he said, O my Lord, send, I pray thee, by the hand of him whom thou wilt send. And the anger of the LORD was kindled against Moses, and he said, Is not Aaron the Levite thy brother? I know that he can speak well. And also, behold, he cometh forth to meet thee, and when he seeth thee, he will be glad

> in his heart. And thou shalt speak unto him, and put words in his mouth: and I will be with thy mouth, and with his mouth, and will teach you what ye shall do. And he shall be thy spokesman unto the people: and he shall be, even he shall be to thee instead of a mouth, and thou shalt be to him instead of God. And thou shalt take this rod in thine hand, wherewith thou shalt do signs."
> (Exodus 4:1–16)

The following chapters of the Book of Exodus indicate that Moses goes to Pharaoh and delivers the message of the Lord, stating "Israel is my son, even my firstborn: And I say unto thee, Let my son go, that he may serve me," and that Pharaoh refuses to let the Israelites go. Moses then performs the miracles, but the Pharaoh's magicians perform similar acts and produce snakes and shining hands. The actual acts of the signs carried out by Moses, if interpreted literally, are not very extraordinary if one considers the contextual fact that sorcerers and magicians in Egypt during this time are said to have been able to transform rods into serpents and manipulate the appearance and temperature of their hands. The only distinction in this case would be that the serpent Moses conjured could eat other conjured serpents, and that his hands appeared more brilliant. A literal interpretation of these signs, then, would not demonstrate His uniqueness as a Manifestation of God.

This part of the story of Moses is so beautifully clarified by Bahá'u'lláh. He interprets the Rod of Moses as the rod of celestial dominion, or the Cause and law of God, and His white hand as the white hand of divine knowledge—an interpretation in which both of these signs illustrate the divine distinction of Moses, as the distinction of a Manifestation of God is His divine authority and knowledge. Speaking on the same theme, and with regards to His own Revelation, Bahá'u'lláh states:

> Say: Were all the divines, all the wise men, all the kings and rulers on earth to gather together, I, in very truth, would confront them, and would proclaim the verses of God, the Sovereign, the Almighty, the All-Wise. I am He Who feareth no one, though all who are in heaven and all who are on earth rise up against me. . . . This is Mine hand which God hath turned white for all the worlds to behold.

> This is My staff; were We to cast it down, it would, of a truth, swallow up all created things.
> (Bahá'u'lláh quoted in Shoghi Effendi, *God Passes By,* p. 169)

In spite of the literal interpretation by the majority of the followers of the past religions, it seems that the Prophets of Israel understood the symbolic meaning of these signs. In several places in the Old Testament, the Rod is mentioned as a symbol of the Revelation and teachings of the promised one.

> And there shall come forth a rod out of the stem of Jesse, and a Branch shall grow out of his roots: And the spirit of the LORD shall rest upon him, the spirit of wisdom and understanding, the spirit of counsel and might, the spirit of knowledge and of the fear of the LORD; And shall make him of quick understanding in the fear of the LORD: and he shall not judge after the sight of his eyes, neither reprove after the hearing of his ears: But with righteousness shall he judge the poor, and reprove with equity for the meek of the earth: and he shall smite the earth: with the rod of his mouth, and with the breath of his lips shall he slay the wicked.
> (Isaiah 11:1–4)

and proceeding from the Paran[44]

44. Paran is the land where the mountain of God was located, between the present land of Israel and Sinai and where Moses' mission began. The phrase "Paran of the love God" links the origin of Moses's mission with the love of God.

and wielding the serpent of power and everlasting majesty,[45] He shone forth from the Sinai of light upon the world.[46]

45. See the last section of Note No.43 for the discussion of the miracles of the rod and white hand.

46. Sinai is a mountain in the northeast of Egypt that is holy because it is the site where Moses received the revelation of the Ten Commandments, the foundation of Jewish law and society.

And God spake all these words, saying, I am the LORD thy God, which have brought thee out of the land of Egypt, out of the house of bondage. Thou shalt have no other gods before me. Thou shalt not make unto thee any graven image, or any likeness of any thing that is in heaven above, or that is in the earth beneath, or that is in the water under the earth. Thou shalt not bow down thyself to them, nor serve them: for I the LORD thy God am a jealous God, visiting the iniquity of the fathers upon the children unto the third and fourth generation of them that hate me; And shewing mercy unto thousands of them that love me, and keep my commandments. Thou shalt not take the name of the LORD thy God in vain; for the LORD will not hold him guiltless that taketh his name in vain. Remember the sabbath day, to keep it holy. Six days shalt thou labour, and do all thy work: But the seventh day is the sabbath of the LORD thy God: in it thou shalt not do any work, thou, nor thy son, nor thy daughter, thy manservant, nor thy maidservant, nor thy cattle, nor thy stranger that is within thy gates: For in six days the LORD made heaven and earth, the sea, and all that in them is, and rested the seventh day: wherefore the LORD blessed the sabbath day, and hallowed it. Honour thy father and thy mother: that thy days may be long upon the land which the LORD thy God giveth thee. Thou shalt not kill. Thou shalt not commit adultery. Thou shalt not steal. Thou shalt not bear false witness against thy neighbour. Thou shalt not covet thy neighbour's house, thou shalt not covet thy neighbour's wife, nor his manservant, nor his maidservant, nor his ox, nor his ass, nor any thing that is thy neighbour's. And all the people saw the thunderings, and the lightnings, and the noise of the trumpet, and the mountain smoking: and when the people saw it, they removed, and stood afar off. And they said unto Moses, Speak thou with us, and we will hear: but let not God speak with us, lest we die. And Moses said unto the people, Fear not: for God is come to prove you, and that his fear may be before your faces, that ye sin not. And the people stood afar off, and Moses drew near unto the thick darkness where God was. And the LORD said unto Moses, Thus thou shalt say unto the children of

> Israel, Ye have seen that I have talked with you from heaven.
> (Exodus 20: 1–22)

This same story is recounted by the prophet Muḥammad in the Qur'án.

Sinai is also important as the setting of a significant event in the description of the station of Moses and the nature of His relationship with God, specifically when He asks God to show Himself and God says that He can allow Moses to see Him as He passes by.

> And he said, I beseech thee, shew me thy glory. And he said, I will make all my goodness pass before thee, and I will proclaim the name of the LORD before thee; and will be gracious to whom I will be gracious, and will shew mercy on whom I will shew mercy. And he said, Thou canst not see my face: for there shall no man see me, and live. And the LORD said, Behold, there is a place by me, and thou shalt stand upon a rock: And it shall come to pass, while my glory passeth by, that I will put thee in a clift of the rock, and will cover thee with my hand while I pass by: And I will take away mine hand, and thou shalt see my back parts: but my face shall not be seen. And the LORD said unto Moses, Hew thee two tables of stone like unto the first: and I will write upon these tables the words that were in the first tables, which thou brakest. And be ready in the morning, and come up in the morning unto mount Sinai, and present thyself there to me in the top of the mount. And no man shall come up with thee, neither let any man be seen throughout all the mount; neither let the flocks nor herds feed before that mount. And he hewed two tables of stone like unto the first; and Moses rose up early in the morning, and went up unto mount Sinai, as the LORD had commanded him, and took in his hand the two tables of stone. And the LORD descended in the cloud, and stood with him there, and proclaimed the name of the LORD. And the LORD passed by before him, and proclaimed, The LORD, The LORD God, merciful and gracious, longsuffering, and abundant in goodness and truth, Keeping

> mercy for thousands, forgiving iniquity and transgression and sin, and that will by no means clear the guilty; visiting the iniquity of the fathers upon the children, and upon the children's children, unto the third and to the fourth generation. And Moses made haste, and bowed his head toward the earth, and worshipped.
> (Exodus 33:18–34)

Several passages in the Bahá'í Writings recall the episode of Sinai, and elucidate the spiritual significance of it.

> The episode of Sinai hath been re-enacted in this Revelation and He Who conversed upon the Mount is calling aloud: Verily, the Desired One is come, seated upon the throne of certitude, could ye but perceive it. He hath admonished all men to observe that which is conducive to the exaltation of the Cause of God and will guide mankind unto His Straight Path.
> (Bahá'u'lláh, *Tablets of Bahá'u'lláh*, p. 246)

It is noteworthy that the history of the Bahá'í Faith written by Shoghi Effendi is titled "God Passes By," as it makes reference to this defining moment between God and Moses as well as imbuing the phrase with new significance for the current age.

The Qur'ánic version of Moses' request and God's response is as follows:

> And when Moses came at our set time and his Lord spake with him, he said, "O Lord, shew thyself to me, that I may look upon thee." He said, "Thou shalt not see Me; but look towards the mount, and if it abide firm in its place, then shalt thou see Me." And when God manifested Himself to the mountain he turned it to dust! and Moses fell in a swoon. And when he came to himself, he said, "Glory be to thee! To thee do I turn in penitence, and I am the first of them that believe."
> (The Qur'án 7:139–40)

A Persian poet writes "when you reach Mount Sinai don't ask 'O Lord, shew thyself to me' and move over, because it is not worth asking, and hearing the response 'Thou shalt not see me.'" But another poet says "when you reach Mount Sinai do ask "O Lord, shew thyself to me," how sweet is it to hear from Him whether "Behold and see me or Thou shalt not see Me."

Bahá'u'lláh explains the spiritual meaning of Moses only being able to see God as He is passing by as signifying the loftiness and mystery of God even above the comprehension of Moses, and specifically as a shared experience among all the Manifestations of God.

> So perfect and comprehensive is His creation that no mind nor heart, however keen or pure, can ever grasp the nature of the most insignificant of His creatures; much less fathom the mystery of Him Who is the Daystar of Truth, Who is the invisible and unknowable Essence. The conceptions of the devoutest of mystics, the attainments of the most accomplished amongst men, the highest praise which human tongue or pen can render are all the product of man's finite mind and are conditioned by its limitations. Ten thousand Prophets, each a Moses, are thunderstruck upon the Sinai of their search at His forbidding voice, "Thou shalt never behold Me!"; whilst a myriad Messengers, each as great as Jesus, stand dismayed upon their heavenly thrones by the interdiction, "Mine Essence thou shalt never apprehend!" From time immemorial He hath been veiled in the ineffable sanctity of His exalted Self, and will everlastingly continue to be wrapt in the impenetrable mystery of His unknowable Essence. Every attempt to attain to an understanding of His inaccessible Reality hath ended in complete bewilderment, and every effort to approach His exalted Self and envisage His Essence hath resulted in hopelessness and failure.
>
> How bewildering to me, insignificant as I am, is the attempt to fathom the sacred depths of Thy knowledge! How futile my efforts to visualize the magnitude of the power inherent in Thine handiwork—the revelation of Thy creative power! How can mine eye, which hath no faculty to perceive itself, claim to have discerned Thine Essence, and how can mine heart, already powerless to apprehend the significance of its own potentialities, pretend to have comprehended Thy

nature? How can I claim to have known Thee, when the entire creation is bewildered by Thy mystery, and how can I confess not to have known Thee, when, lo, the whole universe proclaimeth Thy Presence and testifieth to Thy truth

(Bahá'u'lláh, *Gleanings from the Writings of Bahá'u'lláh*, p 62)

So much so that Pharaoh and his people[47] finally arose and exerted their utmost endeavor to extinguish with the waters of falsehood and denial the fire of that sacred Tree[48]

47. Pharaoh is the title of the ancient rulers of Egypt. Archeological findings indicate that their dynasties ruled Egypt since 3,000 BC and that the Pharaoh mentioned in the Old Testament as a contemporary of Moses ruled Egypt during the fourteenth century BC. The story of Moses taking the Israelites out of Egypt and Pharaoh chasing them to catch them in the desert by the sea to either kill them all or drive them into the sea to be drowned and perished in the water, is recounted in the Book of Exodus 14:1–7.

48. In the Bahá'í scriptures, the Manifestations of God and the Faith of God are often symbolized by a tree. Another term referring to the Manifestation of God is *Sadratu'l-Muntahá,* literally meaning "the Tree beyond which there is no passing." In ancient times Arabs would plant a tree at the end of a road in the desert to serve as a guide and a sign, indicating that the road terminated and that there was no passage beyond that point. The following two excerpts from the notes to the Kitáb-i-Aqdas explain this term:

> Sadratu'l-Muntahá. Literally "the furthermost Lote-Tree", translated by Shoghi Effendi as "*the Tree beyond which there is no passing.*" This is used as a symbol in Islam, for example in the accounts of Muḥammad's Night Journey, to mark the point in the heavens beyond which neither men nor angels can pass in their approach to God, and thus to delimit the bounds of divine knowledge as revealed to mankind. Hence it is often used in the Bahá'í Writings to designate the Manifestation of God Himself.
>
> (The Kitáb-i-Aqdas, note 128, p. 220)

> The “sacred Lote-Tree” is a reference to the Sadratu’l-Muntahá, the “Tree beyond which there is no passing.” It is used here symbolically to designate Bahá’u’lláh.
> (The Kitáb-i-Aqdas, note 164, p. 236)

The blessed and sacred Tree is in this case Moses. Based on references found in Bahá’í Writings, it seems that the Burning Bush was the metaphor for the condition of Moses contemplating within Himself, His own spiritual essence enkindled and the state in which He was receiving revelation from God.

Nay, rather, such water cannot but intensify the burning of the flame, and such blasts cannot but ensure the preservation of the lamp[49]

49. The history of religion shows that the opposition to the Manifestations of God and the persecution of Their followers has been the cause of the progress and spread of Their religions in every age. The same subject is also beautifully described in another one of Bahá’u’lláh’s Writings:

> I know not, O my God, what the Fire is with which Thou didst light the Lamp of Thy Cause, or what the Glass wherewith Thou didst preserve it from Thine enemies. By Thy might! I marvel at the wonders of Thy Revelation, and at the tokens of Thy glory. I recognize, O Thou Who art my heart's Desire, that were fire to be touched by water it would instantly be extinguished, whereas the Fire which Thou didst kindle can never go out, though all the seas of the earth be poured upon it. Should water at any time touch it, the hands of Thy power would, as decreed in Thy Tablets, transmute that water into a fuel that would feed its flame. I, likewise, recognize, O my God, that every lamp, when exposed to the fury of the winds, must cease from burning. As to Thy Lamp, however, O Beloved of the worlds, I cannot think what power except Thy power could have kept it safe for so many years from the tempests that have continually been directed upon it by the rebellious among Thy creatures.
> (Bahá’u’lláh, *Prayers and Meditations*, p. 150)

In truth God guideth not him who is a transgressor, a liar."' (Qur'án 40:28)[50]

50. The story of this believer is mentioned in the Qur'án:

> And when he came to them from our presence with the truth, they said, "Slay the sons of those who believe as he doth, and save their females alive;" but the stratagem of the unbelievers issued only in failure. And Pharaoh said, "Let me alone, that I may kill Moses; and let him call upon his Lord: I fear lest he change your religion, or cause disorder to shew itself in the land." And Moses said, "I take refuge with my Lord and your Lord from every proud one who believeth not in the day of reckoning." And a man of the family of Pharaoh, who was a believer, but hid his faith, said, "Will ye slay a man because he saith my Lord is god, when he hath already come to you with proofs of his mission from your Lord? and if he be a liar, on him will be his lie: but if he be a man of truth, part at least of what he threateneth will fall upon you. Truly God guideth not him who is a transgressor, a liar. O my people! this day is the kingdom yours, the eminent of the earth! but who shall defend us from the vengeance of God if it come on us?" Pharaoh said, "I would have you see only what I see; and in a right way only will I guide you. "Then said he who believed, "O my people! truly I fear for you the like of the day of the allies, The like of the state of the people of Noah and Ad and Themoud. And of those who came after them; yet God willeth not injustice to his servants. And, O my people! I indeed fear for you the day of mutual outcry— The day when ye shall be turned back from the Judgment into hell. No protector shall ye have then against God. And he whom God shall mislead no guide shall there be for him. (The Qur'án 40:20–40)

Paragraph No. 13:

Why is it that the advent of every true Manifestation of God hath been accompanied by such strife and tumult, by such tyranny and upheaval[51]?

51. The history of religion indicates that every Manifestation of God suffered persecution, imprisonment, and/or martyrdom. Even Muḥammad, Who in the last few years of His life overcame His enemies, suffered greatly for the first fifteen to twenty years of His ministry. It is related that He said no prophet had suffered as much as He did.

This notwithstanding the fact that all the Prophets of God, whenever made manifest unto the peoples of the world, have invariably foretold the coming of yet another Prophet after them, and have established such signs as would herald the advent of the future Dispensation[52]

52. The well-known Bahá'í scholar Mírzá Abu'l-Faḍl, in an article written in response to a British clergyman, Reverend Peter Z. Easton states:

> But the greatest obstacles among the nations are the signs and conditions which shall appear with this praiseworthy Manifestation and promised Day; for all the Manifestations of God and founders of religion who have formerly come have mentioned the signs of this great event in their respective books and emphasized and clearly recorded them in their utterances. But every prophet who appeared recorded the self-same signs mentioned by his predecessor and repeated the same words; yet without undertaking to explain the meaning of those signs and conditions or make his object therein known. For instance, consider how for a thousand years His Holiness Moses and the Israelite prophets spoke and uttered glad tidings to the people of the coming of the Lord of Hosts who would harmonize and unite all the worship of One God. Among the signs of the day of His coming announced by them are:
>
> > First: The rolling up of the heavens.
> > Second: The sun will be darkened.
> > Third: The moon shall not give her light.
> > Fourth: The stars shall fall from heaven.
> > Fifth: The dead shall arise from their tombs.
> > Sixth: Ferocious animals will make peace with grazing animals.

> Seven: They will share the same pasture and food.
> Eight: The children will play with poisonous serpents.
> Ninth: The people of Israel who in that day shall have become scattered and humiliated throughout all the nations of the East and West will be again assembled together by the Lord of Hosts, who will establish them in their promised land and confer upon them eternal glory and everlasting dominion.

> These are, in short, some of the prophecies which all the Israelite prophets announced to their people and recorded in their books. They did not state however that these promises were to be taken in a literal sense without symbolism and interpretation, or that the symbolic texts were not subject to commentary.
> (*The Brilliant Proof,* pp. 31–32)

To this the records of all sacred books bear witness.[53]

53. In Judaism the advent or coming of three personages were prophesied

1. A prophet like Moses:

> And the LORD said unto me, They have well spoken that which they have spoken. I will raise them up a Prophet from among their brethren, like unto thee, and will put my words in his mouth; and he shall speak unto them all that I shall command him. And it shall come to pass, that whosoever will not hearken unto my words which he shall speak in my name, I will require it of him. But the prophet, which shall presume to speak a word in my name, which I have not commanded him to speak, or that shall speak in the name of other gods, even that prophet shall die.
> (Deuteronomy 18:17–20)

2. The return of Elijah or Elias, who was taken to heaven:

> And it came to pass, when the LORD would take up Elijah into heaven by a whirlwind, that Elijah went with Elisha

from Gilgal. And Elijah said unto Elisha, Tarry here, I pray thee; for the LORD hath sent me to Bethel. And Elisha said unto him, As the LORD liveth, and as thy soul liveth, I will not leave thee. So they went down to Bethel. And the sons of the prophets that were at Bethel came forth to Elisha, and said unto him, Knowest thou that the LORD will take away thy master from thy head to day? And he said, Yea, I know it; hold ye your peace. And Elijah said unto him, Elisha, tarry here, I pray thee; for the LORD hath sent me to Jericho. And he said, As the LORD liveth, and as thy soul liveth, I will not leave thee. So they came to Jericho. And the sons of the prophets that were at Jericho came to Elisha, and said unto him, Knowest thou that the LORD will take away thy master from thy head to day? And he answered, Yea, I know it; hold ye your peace. And Elijah said unto him, Tarry, I pray thee, here; for the LORD hath sent me to Jordan. And he said, As the LORD liveth, and as thy soul liveth, I will not leave thee. And they two went on. And fifty men of the sons of the prophets went, and stood to view afar off: and they two stood by Jordan. And Elijah took his mantle, and wrapped it together, and smote the waters, and they were divided hither and thither, so that they two went over on dry ground. And it came to pass, when they were gone over, that Elijah said unto Elisha, Ask what I shall do for thee, before I be taken away from thee. And Elisha said, I pray thee, let a double portion of thy spirit be upon me. And he said, Thou hast asked a hard thing: nevertheless, if thou see me when I am taken from thee, it shall be so unto thee; but if not, it shall not be so. And it came to pass, as they still went on, and talked, that, behold, there appeared a chariot of fire, and horses of fire, and parted them both asunder; and Elijah went up by a whirlwind into heaven. And Elisha saw it, and he cried, My father, my father, the chariot of Israel, and the horsemen thereof. And he saw him no more: and he took hold of his own clothes, and rent them in two pieces. He took up also the mantle of Elijah that fell from him, and went back, and stood by the bank of Jordan; And he took the mantle of Elijah that fell from him, and smote the waters, and said, Where is the LORD God of Elijah? and when he also had smitten the waters, they parted hither and thither: and

Elisha went over. And when the sons of the prophets which were to view at Jericho saw him, they said, The spirit of Elijah doth rest on Elisha. And they came to meet him, and bowed themselves to the ground before him. And they said unto him, Behold now, there be with thy servants fifty strong men; let them go, we pray thee, and seek thy master: lest peradventure the Spirit of the LORD hath taken him up, and cast him upon some mountain, or into some valley. And he said, Ye shall not send. And when they urged him till he was ashamed, he said, Send. They sent therefore fifty men; and they sought three days, but found him not. And when they came again to him, (for he tarried at Jericho,) he said unto them, Did I not say unto you, Go not?
(II Kings 2:1–18)

Behold, I will send my messenger, and he shall prepare the way before me: and the LORD, whom ye seek, shall suddenly come to his temple, even the messenger of the covenant, whom ye delight in: behold, he shall come, saith the LORD of hosts. But who may abide the day of his coming? and who shall stand when he appeareth? for he is like a refiner's fire, and like fullers' soap: And he shall sit as a refiner and purifier of silver: and he shall purify the sons of Levi, and purge them as gold and silver, that they may offer unto the LORD an offering in righteousness. Then shall the offering of Judah and Jerusalem be pleasant unto the LORD, as in the days of old, and as in former years. And I will come near to you to judgment; and I will be a swift witness against the sorcerers, and against the adulterers, and against false swearers, and against those that oppress the hireling in his wages, the widow, and the fatherless, and that turn aside the stranger from his right, and fear not me, saith the LORD of hosts.
(Malachi 3:1–5)

For, behold, the day cometh, that shall burn as an oven; and all the proud, yea, and all that do wickedly, shall be stubble: and the day that cometh shall burn them up, saith the LORD of hosts, that it shall leave them neither root nor branch. But unto you that fear my name shall the Sun of righteousness arise with healing in his wings; and ye shall go forth, and grow up as calves of the stall. And ye shall

> tread down the wicked; for they shall be ashes under the soles of your feet in the day that I shall do this, saith the LORD of hosts. Remember ye the law of Moses my servant, which I commanded unto him in Horeb for all Israel, with the statutes and judgments. Behold, I will send you Elijah the prophet before the coming of the great and dreadful day of the LORD: And he shall turn the heart of the fathers to the children, and the heart of the children to their fathers, lest I come and smite the earth with a curse.
> (Malachi 4:1–5)

3. The Coming of the Messiah or Christ:

> And this is the record of John, when the Jews sent priests and Levites from Jerusalem to ask him, Who art thou? And he confessed, and denied not; but confessed, I am not the Christ. And they asked him, What then? Art thou Elias? And he saith, I am not. Art thou that prophet? And he answered, No. Then said they unto him, Who art thou? that we may give an answer to them that sent us. What sayest thou of thyself? He said, I am the voice of one crying in the wilderness, Make straight the way of the Lord,* as said the prophet Esaias. And they which were sent were of the Pharisees. And they asked him, and said unto him, Why baptizest thou then, if thou be not that Christ, nor Elias, neither that prophet? John answered them, saying, I baptize with water: but there standeth one among you, whom ye know not; He it is, who coming after me is preferred before me, whose shoe's latchet I am not worthy to unloose.
> (John 1:19–27)

* "The voice of him that crieth in the wilderness, Prepare ye the way of the LORD, make straight in the desert a highway for our God."
(Isaiah 40:3)

The Qur'án also foretells of the coming of other Apostles (messengers) who will come with divine Revelation to mankind:

> O children of Adam! there shall come to you Apostles from among yourselves, rehearsing my signs to you; and whoso shall fear God and do good works, no fear shall be upon them, neither shall they be put to grief.

(The Qur'án 7:33)

Even as He hath revealed: "As oft as an Apostle cometh unto you with that which your souls desire not, ye swell with pride, accusing some of being impostors and slaying others."[54]

54. The Qur'án 2:87.

Paragraph No. 14:

Whatever in days gone by hath been the cause of the denial and opposition of those people hath now led to the perversity of the people of this age.[55]

55. Considering the life and suffering of the previous Manifestations of God, it is clear that the cause of opposition and denial of the people of each age is essentially the same. The leaders of religions oppose the Manifestations of God, deny Their claims, and call Them false prophets because they don't see the signs and proofs of Their station as they expected. The Pharisees and Jewish leaders expected Elijah to descend from heaven prior to the coming of their Messiah, and for their Messiah to appear with physical and temporal power, authority and ascendency, and to free the Jews from the rule of Gentiles and to perform miracles for them. However, they did not see what they expected. Jesus identified John the Baptist as Elijah:

> Verily I say unto you, Among them that are born of women there hath not risen a greater than John the Baptist: notwithstanding he that is least in the kingdom of heaven is greater than he. And from the days of John the Baptist until now the kingdom of heaven suffereth violence, and the violent take it by force. For all the prophets and the law prophesied until John. And if ye will receive it, this is Elias, which was for to come. He that hath ears to hear, let him hear.
> (Matthew 11:11–14)

John the Baptist, whom Jesus identified as Elijah did not descend from heaven, but was born to Zacharias and Elizabeth (the cousin of Mary mother of Jesus) and Jesus himself was known as the son of Joseph the carpenter and did not have any temporal or physical power and authority. When they asked Him to perform a miracle, His response was not what they expected:

> They said therefore unto him, What sign shewest thou then, that we may see, and believe thee? what dost thou work? Our fathers did eat manna in the desert; as it is written, He gave them bread from heaven to eat [Jews regarded this as a miracle of Moses (Exodus 16:4)]. Then Jesus said unto them, Verily, verily, I say unto you, Moses gave you not that bread from heaven; but my Father giveth you the true bread from heaven. For the bread of God is he which cometh down from heaven, and giveth life unto the world. Then said they unto him, Lord, evermore give us this bread. And Jesus said unto them, I am the bread of life: he that cometh to me shall never hunger; and he that believeth on me shall never thirst. . . . For I came down from heaven, not to do mine own will, but the will of him that sent me. . . . And this is the will of him that sent me, that every one which seeth the Son, and believeth on him, may have everlasting life: and I will raise him up at the last day. The Jews then murmured at him, because he said, I am the bread which came down from heaven. And they said, Is not this Jesus, the son of Joseph, whose father and mother we know? how is it then that he saith, I came down from heaven? Jesus therefore answered and said unto them, Murmur not among yourselves . . . I am that bread of life. . . . This is the bread which cometh down from heaven, that a man may eat thereof, and not die. I am the living bread which came down from heaven: if any man eat of this bread, he shall live for ever: and the bread that I will give is my flesh, which I will give for the life of the world. The Jews therefore strove among themselves, saying, How can this man give us his flesh to eat? Then Jesus said unto them, Verily, verily, I say unto you, Except ye eat the flesh of the Son of man, and drink his blood, ye have no life in you. . . . Many therefore of his disciples, when they had heard this, said, This is an hard saying; who can hear it?"

(John 6:30–60)

To maintain that the testimony of Providence was incomplete, that it hath therefore been the cause of the denial of the people, is but open blasphemy.[56]

56. The testimony of Providence is the combination of the signs, proofs, and divine power and authority that the Manifestations of God possess. Failure to recognize the Manifestation of God can only have two causes:

I. The flaw is in the divine plan:

   a. The Manifestations of God appear in the human world without adequate signs and proofs to completely satisfy people's expectations.
   b. Their testimony in terms of the alignment of prophecies and their fulfillment is incomplete.

II. The flaw is with the people, due to their lack of understanding and in their following of corrupt religious leaders.

To claim that the flaw is in the plan of God is impossible and blasphemous for any person who claims to be a believer. Therefore, the only possible explanation for the rejection of a Manifestation of God by His contemporaries is:

a. The flaw is in people's understanding of the scriptures and interpretation of the prophecies.
b. Deficient spiritual perception and an inclination to follow ignorant and corrupt religious leaders.

> Never would the Pharisees have been emboldened to calumniate Him [Jesus] and charge Him with that grievous sin, but for their ignorance of the inner core of mysteries and the fact that they paid no heed to His splendors and regarded not His proofs. Else would they have acknowledged His words, and borne witness to the verses He revealed, confessed the truth of His utterances, sought shelter under the protective

> shadow of His banner, learned of His signs and tokens, and rejoiced in His blissful tidings.
> ('Abdu'l-Bahá, *Selections from the Writings of 'Abdu'l-Bahá*, p. 39)

Not for a moment hath His grace been withheld, nor have the showers of His loving-kindness ceased to rain upon mankind.[57]

57. The concept of the continuity of divine grace demonstrated in the Bahá'í principle of progressive revelation is central to Bahá'í theology. Bahá'u'lláh explains this using the metaphor of the sun, which is the source of energy and life that the rest of creation depends upon for existence. The sun burns bright and gives light, representing the grace of God, even during the night when one side of the earth is turned away from it. Though we don't see it, it is still giving light and sustaining our survival. For the followers of previous dispensations to believe that their Manifestation of God was the last one is to hold that divine grace has ceased. This interpretation not only contradicts scriptural references to continued divine guidance through other figures (Deuteronomy 18:15–19, John 14:16, John 16:12–15), but also contradicts the overarching concept that grace would continue to flow from an All-Bountiful God.

Consequently, such behavior can be attributed to naught save the petty-mindedness of such souls as tread the valley of arrogance and pride, are lost in the wilds of remoteness[58]

58. The phrase "wilds of remoteness," is significant because it stands in contrast, to the "city of faith," a very important concept in latter parts of the Íqán associated with aligning oneself with the continuing divine message of God via the holy books of each Manifestation. Those who reject the Manifestation of God for their day and age and do not believe in Him, will not enter the "city of faith" (which requires acceptance and obedience to Him) and are said to be "lost in the wilds of remoteness."

    Bahá'u'lláh when addressing the Christian clergy states:

> "O concourse of priests! The Day of Reckoning hath appeared, the Day whereon He Who was in heaven hath come. He, verily, is the One Whom ye were promised in the Books of God, the Holy, the Almighty, the All-Praised. How long will ye wander in the wilderness of heedlessness and superstition? Turn with your hearts in the direction of your Lord, the Forgiving, the Generous."
> (Quoted in Shoghi Effendi, *The Promised Day is Come*, p. 101)

But having weighed the testimony of God by the standard of their own knowledge, gleaned from the teachings of the leaders of their faith, and found it at variance with their limited understanding, they arose to perpetrate such unseemly acts.[59]

59. Bahá'u'lláh returns to this same theme—that it's not possible to receive the light of the Manifestation unless one cleanse one's heart from manmade constructs which are mostly based on the interpretations of leaders of religions. As He stated in the Seven Valleys:

> The true seeker hunteth naught but the object of his quest, and the lover hath no desire save union with his beloved. Nor shall the seeker reach his goal unless he sacrifice all things. That is, whatever he hath seen, and heard, and understood, all must he set at naught, that he may enter the realm of the spirit, which is the City of God. Labor is needed, if we are to seek Him; ardor is needed, if we are to drink of the honey of reunion with Him; and if we taste of this cup, we shall cast away the world.
> (Bahá'u'lláh, The Seven Valleys and The Four Valleys, p. 7)

He further states that weighing the words and teachings of the Manifestations of God with these constructs will become obstacles for many in recognizing the truth and divine authority in every dispensation. As people fail to cleanse their hearts from the sayings, opinions, or commonly held beliefs of this nature, they repeat the same acts of opposition and denial toward each Manifestation of God. Bahá'u'lláh also makes this point in the Kitáb-i-Aqdas.

> Say: O leaders of religion! Weigh not the Book of God with such standards and sciences as are current amongst you, for the Book itself is the unerring Balance established amongst men. In this most perfect Balance whatsoever the peoples and kindreds of the earth possess must be weighed, while the measure of its weight should be tested according to its own standard, did ye but know it.
> (Kitáb-i-Aqdas, ¶99)

Paragraph No. 15:

Leaders of religion, in every age, have hindered their people from attaining the shores of eternal salvation, inasmuch as they held the reins of authority in their mighty grasp. Some for the lust of leadership, others through want of knowledge and understanding, have been the cause of the deprivation of the people. By their sanction and authority, every Prophet of God hath drunk from the chalice of sacrifice.[60]

60. While their motivations might have differed, whether stemming from ignorance or from malice with full knowledge of Who they were betraying, it has always been religious leaders who have led people astray and prevented them from recognizing the Manifestations of God and who have been instrumental in Their suffering and sacrifice.

> But woe unto you, scribes and Pharisees, hypocrites! for ye shut up the kingdom of heaven against men: for ye neither go in yourselves, neither suffer ye them that are entering to go in.
> (Matthew 23:13)

In the time of Moses, the leaders of religion were the Pharaoh and the Egyptian priests. It was the Jewish leaders of Christ's time, such as Annas and Caiaphas, that condemned Him and caused Him to drink from the chalice of sacrifice and to wing His flight. Muḥammad suffered the oppression of His own relatives especially His uncles, who were the leaders and aristocracy of their region. One of the leaders—Abu'l- Ḥikam (a title meaning the father of all knowledge or wisdom), the most knowledgeable religious leader of their society—slapped the Prophet in the face at the time of His declaration of His mission. Muḥammad gave him the title of

Abu'l-Jahl, meaning the Father of all ignorance, and he and other leaders were the means by which Muḥammad suffered and "drank from the chalice of sacrifice." In like manner the Báb, through His years of imprisonment and his brutal execution at the hands of the ecclesiastics and Shah of Persia, drank from the chalice of sacrifice, stepped in the arena of martyrdom and winged His flight.

For this reason, in all sacred books mention hath been made of the divines of every age. Thus He saith: "O people of the Book![61]

61. In Islam, both Christians and Jews are called People of the Book because Muḥammad asserts the divine origin and validity of their religions and their sacred books (Torah and Gospels). Historically in Islamic societies the People of the Book were accorded a protected status (unlike the pagans or idolaters who did not enjoy any rights and could be taken for slavery) and were protected provided they paid a special tax known as "Dhimmeh." In the Súrah of the Family of Imran (The Qur'án, Súrah 3), the phrase "O People of the Book" appears fourteen times as a refrain, and the verse being cited here (The Qur'án 3:70) is one of these instances. Bahá'u'lláh explains that in these verses where Muḥammad addresses the People of the Book, He is referring to the leaders of these Faiths, not to the generality of the Jews and Christians, and that this becomes apparent if we observe with the eye of God.

    The Báb addressed all the leaders of religions, especially the Muslim clergy, with the same term in the Qayyúmu'l-Asmá, the commentary on the Súrah of Joseph:

    > "O concourse of the people of the Book! Fear ye God and pride not yourselves in your learning. Follow ye the Book which His Remembrance hath revealed in praise of God, the True One. He Who is the Eternal Truth beareth me witness, whoso followeth this Book hath indeed followed all the past Scriptures which have been sent down from heaven by God, the Sovereign Truth. Verily, He is well informed of what ye do."
    > (The Báb, *Selections from the Writings of the Báb*, p. 44)

It is evident that by the "people of the Book," who have repelled their fellow-men from the straight path of God, is meant none other than the divines of that age, whose names and character have been revealed in the sacred books, and alluded to in the verses and traditions recorded therein, were you to observe with the eye of God.[62]

62. Bahá'u'lláh explains that what is meant by the "people of the Book" in this verse of the Qur'án is not the generality of the Jews and Christians but their leaders, and this will be easily realized if we observe this with the eye of God (for more details regarding observing with the eye of God see below, Note No. 63).

Paragraph No. 16:

With fixed and steady gaze, born of the unerring eye of God, scan for a while the horizon of divine knowledge, and contemplate those words of perfection which the Eternal hath revealed, that haply the mysteries of divine wisdom, hidden ere now beneath the veil of glory[63]

63. The concept of gazing, seeing, examining or observing with the eye of God has appeared in a number of passages in the Bahá'í Writings. To gaze or observe with the eye of God is to examine, to understand, and to measure everything with the standard of divine words as presented by the utterances of the Manifestations of God.

> If it be your wish, O people, to know God and to discover the greatness of His might, look, then, upon Me with Mine own eyes, and not with the eyes of any one besides Me. Ye will, otherwise, be never capable of recognizing Me, though ye ponder My Cause as long as My Kingdom endureth, and meditate upon all created things throughout the eternity of God, the Sovereign Lord of all, the Omnipotent, the Ever-Abiding, the All-Wise.
> (Bahá'u'lláh, *Gleanings from the Writings of Bahá'u'lláh*, p. 272)

> . . . [T]he Primal Point[48] saith: "Behold ye Him with His own eyes. Were ye to behold Him with the eyes of another, ye would never recognize and know Him."
> (Bahá'u'lláh, Epistle to the Son of the Wolf, p. 151)

[48] Primal Point is one of the Báb's titles.

> Where is that fair-minded soul, O my God, who will judge equitably Thy Cause, and where is the man of insight to be found who will behold Thee with Thine own eyes? Is there any man of hearing who will hear Thee with Thine ears, or one endued with eloquence who will speak the truth in Thy days?
> (Bahá'u'lláh, *Prayers and Meditations*, p. 285)

> O SON OF MAN!
> Bestow My wealth upon My poor, that in heaven thou mayest draw from stores of unfading splendor and treasures of imperishable glory. But by My life! To offer up thy soul is a more glorious thing couldst thou but see with Mine eye.
> (Bahá'u'lláh, The Hidden Words, Arabic, no. 57)

'Abdu'l-Bahá defines this condition in one of His Tablets:

> As to your question about the meaning of the Arabic Hidden words: 'Couldst thou but see with mine eye', when man reacheth the station of selflessness, and his love of self is entirely wiped out, his existence becomes like non-existence, and a ray from God's presence sheddeth its light upon him. Then he can see with the eye of God, and hear can with His ear. This is like iron in the fire. The qualities of the iron, its coldness, darkness and hardness are concealed, and it manifests heat, luminosity and fluidity, which are qualities of the fire.
> ('Abdu'l-Bahá, cited in Hooper Dunbar, *A Companion to the study of the Kitáb-i-Íqán, pp.* 87–88)

A similar statement is found in the Seven Valleys regarding a person being able to see with the eye of God and hear with His ear:

> Whensoever the light of Manifestation of the King of Oneness settleth upon the throne of the heart and soul, His shining becometh visible in every limb and member. At that time the mystery of the famed tradition gleameth out of the darkness: "A servant is drawn unto Me in prayer until I answer him; and when I have answered him, I become the ear wherewith he heareth . . . " For thus the Master of the

> house hath appeared within His home, and all the pillars of the dwelling are ashine with His light.
> (Bahá'u'lláh, The Seven Valleys and The Four Valleys, p. 21)

The famed tradition referred to here and partially quoted by Bahá'u'lláh, is a holy tradition called *Ḥadíth an-Naváfil*, which has greatly influenced the formation of ideas and schools of thought in Islamic mysticism. A translation of this tradition was offered by Annemarie Schimmel:

> Eternally and always, a servant is drawn nigh unto Me by works of supererogative piety and prayers, until I love him, and when I love him, I am his ear by which he hears, and his eyes by which he sees . . .
> (*As Through a Veil*, pp. 273, 329)

This ḥadíth has also been referenced in other Bahá'í Writings, such as in the following statement from the Báb, which was quoted in its original Arabic in *Safíniy-i 'Irfán*, vol. 2, p. 133. It appears that there is no authorized translation of this statement, but a provisional translation of the statement has been made by this author and reads as follows:

> No servant will achieve perfection in his servitude unless this state appears in him, as mentioned in the Holy Tradition: "Eternally and always, a servant is drawn nigh unto Me by works of supererogative piety and prayers, until I love him, and when I love him, I am his ear by which he hears, and his eyes by which he sees, and his hand that he grabs with. If he prays to Me, I will accept his prayers, and if he asks for something I will provide it to him." . . . And for a person who reaches this station, there are infinite other stations.

The phrase "supererogative piety and prayers" is a translation of the Arabic word *naváfil.* The concept of naváfil (additional prayers in excess of what is required), is also mentioned in the the Qur'án, translated as "excess in service."

> And watch unto it in the night: this shall be an excess in service: it may be that thy Lord will raise thee to a glorious station.

(The Qur'án 17:81)

It seems that Bahá'u'lláh explains here that a person gazing and observing with the eye of God, examines and measures everything with the standard of Divine Words as presented by the utterances of the Manifestations of God, as a result he will apprehend the meanings of the figurative language of the prophecies, which have been until this time hidden beneath the veils of glory (see Note No. 9 above) and which the leaders of religion have prevented their followers from comprehending.

Those words uttered by the Revealers of the beauty of the one true God, setting forth the signs that should herald the advent of the Manifestation to come, they never understood nor fathomed.[64]

64. Please see Note No. 52 above for the signs that should herald the advent of Manifestations to come. The following Old Testament passage indicates the signs that must appear prior to or accompany the coming of Christ:

> And it shall come to pass afterward, that I will pour out my spirit upon all flesh; and your sons and your daughters shall prophesy, your old men shall dream dreams, your young men shall see visions: And also upon the servants and upon the handmaids in those days will I pour out my spirit. And I will shew wonders in the heavens and in the earth, blood, and fire, and pillars of smoke. The sun shall be turned into darkness, and the moon into blood, before the great and terrible day of the LORD come. And it shall come to pass, that whosoever shall call on the name of the LORD shall be delivered: for in mount Zion and in Jerusalem shall be deliverance, as the LORD hath said, and in the remnant whom the LORD shall call.
> (Joel 2:28–32)

Although the present popular Christian belief assigns these signs to the events heralding the second coming of Christ, it is evident that these signs are related to the first coming of Christ, as it is confirmed by Peter in the Book of Acts that Joel's prophesies had been fulfilled.

> But Peter, standing up with the eleven, lifted up his voice, and said unto them, Ye men of Judaea, and all ye that dwell at Jerusalem, be this known unto you, and hearken to my words: For these are not drunken, as ye suppose, seeing it is but the third hour of the day. But this is that which was spoken by the prophet Joel; And it shall come to pass in the last days, saith God, I will pour out of my Spirit upon all flesh: and your sons and your daughters shall prophesy, and your young men shall see visions, and your old men shall dream dreams: And on my servants and on my handmaidens I will pour out in those days of my Spirit; and they shall prophesy: And I will shew wonders in heaven above, and signs in the earth beneath; blood, and fire, and vapour of smoke: The sun shall be turned into darkness, and the moon into blood, before the great and notable day of the Lord come: And it shall come to pass, that whosoever shall call on the name of the Lord shall be saved. Ye men of Israel, hear these words; Jesus of Nazareth, a man approved of God among you by miracles and wonders and signs, which God did by him in the midst of you, as ye yourselves also know: Him, being delivered by the determinate counsel and foreknowledge of God, ye have taken, and by wicked hands have crucified and slain.
> (Acts 2:14–23)

It is obvious and manifest that the true meaning of the utterances of the Birds of Eternity is revealed to none except those that manifest the Eternal Being, and the melodies of the Nightingale of Holiness can reach no ear save that of the denizens of the everlasting realm.[65]

65. The Báb stated that the fruits of each dispensation are the people who will accept and follow the next Manifestation of God (see also the Báb's statement in Note 61). The idea is that religion is a living being. The purpose of the teachings of every Manifestation is realized in the next dispensation, and the meaning of anything a previous Manifestation has revealed which has been recorded in the Holy Scriptures, is only truly understood in light of what is revealed by the Manifestation following Him. (Deut. 18:18 "I will raise them[Israel] up a Prophet from among their brethren, like unto thee, and will put my words in his mouth; and he shall speak

unto them all that I shall command him," as compared with John 5:46 "For had ye believed Moses, ye would have believed me; for he wrote of me.") No other being has this exclusive understanding and authority with respect to the scriptures and mysteries of past dispensations. The reason that the Kitáb-i-Íqán is the key to all previous scriptures is that Bahá'u'lláh, being the Promised One prophesied by these religions, Has provided the divine guidance to explain the mysteries and unlock the scriptures of these religions.

The Copt of tyranny can never partake of the cup touched by the lips of the Sept of justice,[66]

66. *Copt* is the name of the ancient tribe of the original Egyptians before the Christian and Islamic eras. While in current usage this word refers to Egyptian Christians, the original meaning of the word predates Christianity. The word Copt comes from the New Latin word "Coptus," which is derived from the Arabic "qubti," which was an Arabisation of the original name of Egypt in the ancient Egyptian language, "Hut-ka-Ptah." This word literally means the "house" or "estate" of Ptah, who was the oldest known deity of the ancient Egyptians in the first kingdom at Memphis. The name was applied to the kingdom at Memphis and eventually to the country as a whole. The Sept (Septs) is another name for the people of Israel. Here the Copt of tyranny symbolizes the Pharaoh, while the Sept of justice symbolizes Moses. The "Copts" are the allegorical representation of the opposition to the Faith of God, and the same way that Pharaoh and his "Copts" could never understand what Moses represented, people in every dispensation, including those who opposed the Báb, are incapable of understanding the words of God. The Copt of tyranny and Sept of justice recall the reappearing distinction in the Judeo-Christian and Islamic religious traditions between those who recognize the Manifestation of God and receive increased spiritual perception to correctly interpret religious verses, and those who fail to recognize Him and are deprived of this capability.

Pharaoh of unbelief can never hope to recognize the hand of the Moses of truth.[67]

67. The hand of Moses is a reference to the story of Moses when He received His mission to go and bring the Israelites out of Egypt, He told God that no one would believe His claim that He was sent by God for this mission. God provided Him with two signs and evidences to prove the truth of His mission. The first was His rod, which would become a serpent when cast upon the ground, and the second sign was His hand, which would become white and shining when He put it in His bosom and then revealed it (see Note No. 43 above).

    However, when Moses went to Pharaoh, he did not believe in Him and even after seeing the white hand of Moses, he did not recognize His truth.

Even as He saith: "None knoweth the meaning thereof except God and them that are well-grounded in knowledge.[68]

68. This is affirmation of what was discussed above, that the meaning of all the figurative and symbolic statements of the previous Manifestation are only truly understood in light of what is revealed by the following Manifestations. Muḥammad revealed this concept in the Qur'án, where it states that some of the revealed verses are simple and clear while some are figurative. An example is verse 7 of the Súrah of the Family of Imrán (Imrán was the Father of Moses). Three translations of the same verse are presented here:

    > He it is who hath sent down to thee "the Book." Some of its signs are of themselves perspicuous;—these are the basis of the Book—and others are figurative. But they whose hearts are given to err, follow its figures, craving discord, craving an interpretation; yet none knoweth its interpretation but God. And the stable in knowledge say, "We believe in it: it is all from our Lord." But none will bear this in mind, save men endued with understanding.
    > (The Qur'án 7:3)

    > He it is Who hath revealed unto thee (Muḥammad) the Scripture wherein are clear revelations—they are the substance of the Book—and others (which are) allegorical. But those in whose hearts is doubt pursue, forsooth, that

> which is allegorical seeking (to cause) dissension by seeking to explain it. None knoweth its explanation save Allah. And those who are of sound instruction say: We believe therein; the whole is from our Lord; but only men of understanding really heed.
> (The Qur'án, Pickthall tr, 3:7)

> He, the mighty, the wise. He it is who has revealed to thee the Book, of which there are some verses that are decisive, they are the mother of the Book; and others ambiguous; but as for those in whose hearts is perversity, they follow what is ambiguous, and do crave for sedition, craving for (their own) interpretation of it; but none know the interpretation of it except God. But those who are well grounded in knowledge say, 'We believe in it; it is all from our Lord; but none will remember save those who possess minds.
> (The Qur'án, E.H. Palmer tr, 3:7)

These translations place a period after the word "God" or "Allah" in the phrase "yet none knoweth its interpretation but God." However, when Bahá'u'lláh cites this verse, He places the period not after "God" but further on in the sentence to read, "but none know the interpretation of it except God and those who are well grounded in knowledge."

This verse and its implications as to whether only God knows the meaning of the figurative verses (not even the Prophet or Imáms) or whether those who are aided and inspired by God and are grounded in divine knowledge can also distinguish between the literal and figurative verses and understand the intent of the figurative verses of the Qur'án, was the subject of much controversy among Islamic divines.

The corpus of the Qur'án can be divided into two parts: the "Muh'kamát" (Solids or literal) which have precise and literal meaning such as laws for fasting during the month of Ramaḍán and the daily obligatory prayers. There is no interpretation or meaning beyond what is clearly stated in these verses. Then there is the second, the figurative part, known as the "Mutashábihát" (Allegorical), which are verses that have a different meaning from the literal form. Examples are the statement that nonbelievers after passing from this world will say "woe unto us that we missed the opportunity when we were 'at the side' or side by side with God," or the one that states that God "winds up the earth with His right hand." Knowing for example, that God does not literally have "sides" or "hands," one must interpret these verses as figurative, just as with Biblical verses involving messianic advent and its circumstances such as the "sun being darkened" and "stars falling from heaven."

A majority of the Sunni interpreters of the Qur'án believed the period should be placed where it appears in the above cited translations, to maintain that only God could distinguish between the literal and figurative verses and understand the true meaning of the figurative ones. Some Shí'ah authorities such as Imám Ja'fár-i-Ṣádiq, the sixth Imám of the Shí'ah (see Appendix II), have declared that it is far from the justice of God to reveal something in His Book that no one could understand but Himself. They have further asked why such things, if God never intended for humanity to comprehend them, would even be revealed and placed before a human audience that could never hope to understand much less adhere to them. Thus, Imám Ja'fár-i-Ṣádiq interprets that this verse should be read as "no one knoweth the meaning except God and those who are well-grounded in knowledge," placing the period later in the verse to maintain that human beings with spiritual knowledge and perception are also capable of distinguishing between literal and figurative scripture.

In citing this verse, Bahá'u'lláh validates this interpretation of the Shí'ah by placing the period after "those who are well-grounded in knowledge" to support the fact that those who are inspired and are grounded in divine knowledge can have the capability to understand the meaning of figurative verses in the holy books.

This concept is also taught by Christ in explaining the parable of the sower and quoting the prophet Isaiah of the Old Testament when His disciples asked Him why He spoke in parables.

> On the same day Jesus went out of the house and sat by the sea. And great multitudes were gathered together to Him, so that He got into a boat and sat; and the whole multitude stood on the shore. Then He spoke many things to them in parables, saying: "Behold, a sower went out to sow. And as

he sowed, some seed fell by the wayside; and the birds came and devoured them. Some fell on stony places, where they did not have much earth; and they immediately sprang up because they had no depth of earth. But when the sun was up they were scorched, and because they had no root they withered away. And some fell among thorns, and the thorns sprang up and choked them. But others fell on good ground and yielded a crop: some a hundredfold, some sixty, some thirty. He who has ears to hear, let him hear!

And the disciples came and said to Him, "Why do You speak to them in parables?" He answered and said to them, "Because it has been given to you to know the mysteries of the kingdom of heaven, but to them it has not been given. For whoever has, to him more will be given, and he will have abundance; but whoever does not have, even what he has will be taken away from him. Therefore I speak to them in parables, because seeing they do not see, and hearing they do not hear, nor do they understand. And in them the prophecy of Isaiah is fulfilled, which says:

"Hearing you will hear and shall not understand,
And seeing you will see and not perceive;
For the hearts of this people have grown dull.
Their ears are hard of hearing,
And their eyes they have closed,
Lest they should see with their eyes and hear with their ears,
Lest they should understand with their hearts and turn,
So that I should heal them."

But blessed are your eyes for they see, and your ears for they hear; for assuredly, I say to you that many prophets and righteous men desired to see what you see, and did not see it, and to hear what you hear, and did not hear it.

Hear ye therefore the parable of the sower: When anyone hears the word of the kingdom, and does not understand it, then the wicked one comes and snatches away what was sown in his heart. This is he who received seed by the wayside. But he who received the seed on stony places, this

> is he who hears the word and immediately receives it with joy; yet he has no root in himself, but endures only for a while. For when tribulation or persecution arises because of the word, immediately he stumbles. Now he who received seed among the thorns is he who hears the word, and the cares of this world and the deceitfulness of riches choke the word, and he becomes unfruitful. But he who received seed on the good ground is he who hears the word and understands it, who indeed bears fruit and produces: some a hundredfold, some sixty, some thirty.
> (Matthew 13:1–23)

And yet, they have sought the interpretation of the Book from those that are wrapt in veils, and have refused to seek enlightenment from the fountainhead of knowledge.[69]

69. This statement by Bahá'u'lláh is very similar in meaning to what Jesus said about the religious leaders of His time:

> Let them alone: they be blind leaders of the blind. And if the blind lead the blind, both shall fall into the ditch.
> (Matthew 15:14)

Paragraph No. 17:

And when the days of Moses were ended.[70]

70. The "days of Moses" here refers to the Dispensation of Moses, which ended with the appearance of Christ.

the light of Jesus, shining forth from the dayspring of the Spirit.[71]

71. One of the titles of Christ in both the Qur'án and Bahá'í Writings is "Spirit" or "Spirit of God."

They clamoured that He Whose advent the Bible had fortold.[72]

72. By the Bible here is meant the Torah or Old Testament.

whereas this youthful Nazarene[73]

73. Some Biblical scholars believe that Jesus was called Nazarene not only because He was from the town of Nazareth in the Galilee, but because before the commencement of His ministry He belonged to a Jewish ascetic sect called the Nazarite.

who laid claim to the station of the divine Messiah.[74]

74. Messiah means the anointed one. Israelites were in the practice of anointing the chosen ones or the kings and leaders with fragrant holy oil. David was anointed three times. In Hebrew belief, the promised savior of Israel was anointed by Jehovah, and was therefore titled Messiah (Christ).

annulled the law of divorce[75] **and of the Sabbath day—the most weighty of all the laws of Moses.**[76]

75. On the issue of divorce the Mosaic law states:

> When a man hath taken a wife, and married her, and it come to pass that she find no favour in his eyes, because he hath found some uncleanness in her: then let him write her a bill of divorcement, and give it in her hand, and send her out of his house.
> (Deuteronomy 24:1)

The annulment of the law of divorce by Jesus is based on several statements found in the synoptic Gospels. Jesus annulled it in the Sermon on the Mount and in the Gospel of Mark:

> It hath been said, Whosoever shall put away his wife, let him give her a writing of divorcement: But I say unto you, That whosoever shall put away his wife, saving for the cause of fornication, causeth her to commit adultery: and whosoever shall marry her that is divorced committeth adultery.
> (Matthew 5:31–32)

> And the Pharisees came to him, and asked him, Is it lawful for a man to put away his wife? tempting him. And he answered and said unto them, What did Moses command you? And they said, Moses suffered to write a bill of divorcement, and to put her away. And Jesus answered and said unto them, For the hardness of your heart he wrote you this precept. But from the beginning of the creation God made them male and female. For this cause shall a man leave his father and mother, and cleave to his wife; And they twain shall be one flesh: so then they are no more twain, but one flesh. What therefore God hath joined together, let not man put asunder. And in the house his disciples asked him again of the same matter. And he saith unto them, Whosoever shall put away his wife, and marry another, committeth adultery against her. And if a woman shall put away her husband, and be married to another, she committeth adultery.
> (Mark 10:2–11)
>
> A similar statement is made by Him in the Gospel of Luke:
>
> Whosoever putteth away his wife, and marrieth another, committeth adultery: and whosoever marrieth her that is put away from her husband committeth adultery.
> (Luke 16:18)

It seems that the annulment of the law of divorce by Jesus at that time was for the protection of women, because according to the Jewish law, women did not have the right of property ownership, did not inherit from their family members, and could not earn a wage for their work, and if they were divorced and put away by their husbands they had no means of living.

76. The importance of the keeping of the Sabbath is evident when reviewing the law of the Sabbath in Exodus and Deuteronomy. Exodus, Chapter 20, states:

> Remember the sabbath day, to keep it holy. Six days shalt thou labour, and do all thy work: But the seventh day is the sabbath of the LORD thy God: in it thou shalt not do any work, thou, nor thy son, nor thy daughter, thy manservant, nor thy maidservant, nor thy cattle, nor thy stranger that is

> within thy gates: For in six days the LORD made heaven and earth, the sea, and all that in them is, and rested the seventh day: wherefore the LORD blessed the sabbath day, and hallowed it.
> (Exodus 20:8–11)

> Ye shall keep the sabbath therefore; for it is holy unto you: every one that defileth it shall surely be put to death: for whosoever doeth any work therein, that soul shall be cut off from among his people. Six days may work be done; but in the seventh is the Sabbath of rest, holy to the LORD: whosoever doeth any work in the Sabbath day, he shall surely be put to death.
> (Exodus 31:14–15)

The breaking and annulment of the law of Sabbath is mentioned in all four Gospels:

> At that time Jesus went on the sabbath day through the corn; and his disciples were an hungred, and began to pluck the ears of corn and to eat. But when the Pharisees saw it, they said unto him, Behold, thy disciples do that which is not lawful to do upon the sabbath day. But he said unto them, Have ye not read what David did, when he was an hungred, and they that were with him; How he entered into the house of God, and did eat the shewbread, which was not lawful for him to eat, neither for them which were with him, but only for the priests? Or have ye not read in the law, how that on the sabbath days the priests in the temple profane the sabbath, and are blameless? But I say unto you, That in this place is one greater than the temple. But if ye had known what this meaneth, I will have mercy, and not sacrifice**, ye would not have condemned the guiltless. For the Son of man is Lord even of the sabbath day.
> (Matthew 12:1–8)

** This phrase "I will have mercy, and not sacrifice" is also another reference to the scriptures:

> O Ephraim, what shall I do unto thee? O Judah, what shall I do unto thee? for your goodness is as a morning cloud, and as the early dew it goeth away. Therefore have I hewed

> them by the prophets; I have slain them by the words of my mouth: and thy judgments are as the light that goeth forth. For I desired mercy, and not sacrifice; and the knowledge of God more than burnt offerings.
> (Hosea 6:1–6)

The above scriptural reference emphasizes the primacy of spiritual matters, such as knowledge of God, over the mere material traditions and rituals, such as burnt offering, and is indicative of His station which is higher than the temple. But this argument was not acceptable to the Pharisees, because in their eyes He was an ordinary man, He was not David or the high priest of the temple, and there was a precedence for punishing one who broke the Sabbath, as stated in scriptures:

> And while the children of Israel were in the wilderness, they found a man that gathered sticks upon the sabbath day. And they that found him gathering sticks brought him unto Moses and Aaron, and unto all the congregation. And they put him in ward, because it was not declared what should be done to him. And the LORD said unto Moses, The man shall be surely put to death: all the congregation shall stone him with stones without the camp. And all the congregation brought him without the camp, and stoned him with stones, and he died; as the LORD commanded Moses.
> (Numbers 15:33–36)

The Gospels of Mark 2:23–28, and Luke 6:1–5 have similar accounts, but the Gospel of John relates a different story:

> And a certain man was there, which had an infirmity thirty and eight years. When Jesus saw him lie, and knew that he had been now a long time in that case, he saith unto him, Wilt thou be made whole? The impotent man answered him, Sir, I have no man, when the water is troubled, to put me into the pool: but while I am coming, another steppeth down before me. Jesus saith unto him, Rise, take up thy bed, and walk. And immediately the man was made whole, and took up his bed, and walked: and on the same day was the sabbath. The Jews therefore said unto him that was cured, It is the sabbath day: it is not lawful for thee to carry thy bed. He answered them, He that made me whole, the

> same said unto me, Take up thy bed, and walk. Then asked they him, What man is that which said unto thee, Take up thy bed, and walk? And he that was healed wist not who it was: for Jesus had conveyed himself away, a multitude being in that place. Afterward Jesus findeth him in the temple, and said unto him, Behold, thou art made whole: sin no more, lest a worse thing come unto thee. The man departed, and told the Jews that it was Jesus, which had made him whole. And therefore did the Jews persecute Jesus, and sought to slay him, because he had done these things on the sabbath day. But Jesus answered them, My Father worketh hitherto, and I work. Therefore the Jews sought the more to kill him, because he not only had broken the sabbath, but said also that God was his Father, making himself equal with God.
> (John 5:6–18)

Another problem was the law of sacrifice and burnt offering for redemption of sins. The Pentateuch (the first five books of the Old Testament—Genesis, Exodus, Numbers, Leviticus, and Deuteronomy—the authorship of which is attributed to Moses), particularly Leviticus has more than a hundred references to the sacrifice of calves, lambs, turtledoves, and pigeons, and burnt offerings for redemption of sins. But Jesus practically annulled this and replaced it with Baptism and repentance.

Another issue was that the leaders of the Jews claimed that Jesus was leading people away from the path the God of Israel had commanded them to walk, and was teaching them to serve another God. They felt that it was their duty to oppose Him and arrange to kill Him, as stated in Deuteronomy:

> Ye shall walk after the LORD your God, and fear him, and keep his commandments, and obey his voice, and ye shall serve him, and cleave unto him. And that prophet, or that dreamer of dreams, shall be put to death; because he hath spoken to turn you away from the LORD your God, which brought you out of the land of Egypt, and redeemed you out of the house of bondage, to thrust thee out of the way which the LORD thy God commanded thee to walk in. So shalt thou put the evil away from the midst of thee. If thy

> brother, the son of thy mother, or thy son, or thy daughter, or the wife of thy bosom, or thy friend, which is as thine own soul, entice thee secretly, saying, Let us go and serve other gods, which thou hast not known, thou, nor thy fathers; Namely, of the gods of the people which are round about you, nigh unto thee, or far off from thee, from the one end of the earth even unto the other end of the earth; Thou shalt not consent unto him, nor hearken unto him; neither shall thine eye pity him, neither shalt thou spare, neither shalt thou conceal him: But thou shalt surely kill him; thine hand shall be first upon him to put him to death, and afterwards the hand of all the people. And thou shalt stone him with stones, that he die; because he hath sought to thrust thee away from the LORD thy God, which brought thee out of the land of Egypt, from the house of bondage. And all Israel shall hear, and fear, and shall do no more any such wickedness as this is among you.
> (Deuteronomy 13:4–10)

Their claim that Jesus was turning people away from the Lord and teaching them not to observe the Law appeared to have been supported by some of His own statements, such as the following:

> The law and the prophets were until John: since that time the kingdom of God is preached.
> (Luke 16:16)

The other accusation that Jesus was promoting another God, which was not the same as the God of Israel, might not seem to be a very important and significant issue in our time, but it was a very significant issue at the time of Jesus and for the first two Christian Centuries. The ideas presented by Marcion, an early second century philosopher-theologian who had a very large following, is indicative of the importance and impact of this issue. Marcion taught, as many Christians of that time believed, that:

> [t]here were two different gods—one of the Old Testament (a god of wrath) and one of the New Testament (a God of love and mercy). These were not simply two different facets of the same God: they were actually two different gods. . . .

> Marcion was completely absorbed by the life and teachings of the apostle Paul, whom he considered to be the one "true" apostle from the early days of the church. In some of his letters, such as Romans and Galatians, Paul had taught that a right standing before God came only by faith in Christ, not by doing any of the works prescribed by the Jewish law. Marcion took this differentiation between the law of the Jews and faith in Christ to what he saw as its logical conclusion, that there was an absolute distinction between the law on the one hand and the gospel on the other. So distinct were the law and the gospel, in fact, that both could not possibly have come from the same God. Marcion concluded that the God of Jesus (and Paul) was not, therefore, the God of the Old Testament. There were, in fact, two different Gods: the God of the Jews, who created the world, called Israel to be his people, and gave them his harsh law; and the God of Jesus, who sent Christ into the world to save people from the wrathful vengeance of the Jewish creator God.
> (Bart Ehrman, *Misquoting Jesus*, p. 33)

what of the signs of the Manifestation yet to come?[77]

77. As mentioned above in Note No. 64, In Judaism the advent or coming of the Messiah was to follow several important events:

    a) The descent of Elijah with his corporal body from heaven.
    b) The appearance of those signs prophesied by Joel and Malachi (e.g., the day will burn hot like an oven and the powers of earth will be released (such as volcanic activities and earthquakes), and the Sun and Moon will not give light).
    c) The coming of the Messiah with power and authority to restore the rule of Israel and the glory of the time of David and Solomon.

    The expectations of Israel for the literal materialization of the signs of the coming of their Messiah and their objections to Jesus, as well as the true meaning of prophesies are best explained by 'Abdu'l-Bahá:

When Christ appeared, twenty centuries ago, although the Jews were eagerly awaiting His Coming, and prayed every day, with tears, saying:
"O God, hasten the Revelation of the Messiah," yet when the Sun of Truth dawned, they denied Him and rose against Him with the greatest enmity, and eventually crucified that divine Spirit, the Word of God, and named Him Beelzebub, the evil one, as is recorded in the Gospel. The reason for this was that they said: 'The Revelation of Christ, according to the clear text of the Torah, will be attested by certain signs, and so long as these signs have not appeared, whoso layeth claim to be a Messiah is an impostor. Among these signs is this, that the Messiah should come from an unknown place, yet we all know this man's house in Nazareth, and can any good thing come out of Nazareth? The second sign is that He shall rule with a rod of iron, that is, He must act with the sword, but this Messiah has not even a wooden staff. Another of the conditions and signs is this: He must sit upon the throne of David and establish David's sovereignty. Now, far from being enthroned, this man has not even a mat to sit on. Another of the conditions is this: the promulgation of all the laws of the Torah; yet this man has abrogated these laws, and has even broken the sabbath day, although it is the clear text of the Torah that whosoever layeth claim to prophethood and revealeth miracles and breaketh the sabbath day, must be put to death. Another of the signs is this, that in His reign justice will be so advanced that righteousness and well-doing will extend from the human even to the animal world—the snake and the mouse will share one hole, and the eagle and the partridge one nest, the lion and the gazelle shall dwell in one pasture, and the wolf and the kid shall drink from one fountain. Yet now, injustice and tyranny have waxed so great in His time that they have crucified Him! Another of the conditions is this, that in the days of the Messiah the Jews will prosper and triumph over all the peoples of the world, but now they are living in the utmost abasement and servitude in the empire of the Romans. Then how can this be the Messiah promised in the Torah? In this wise did they object to that Sun of Truth, although that Spirit of God was indeed the One promised in the Torah.

('Abdu'l-Bahá, *Selections from the Writings of 'Abdu'l-Bahá,* p. 44)

How many Manifestations of Holiness, how many Revealers of the light everlasting, have appeared since the time of Moses.[78]

78. According to the Bahá'í Writings and considering the concept of progressive revelation, to date at least six Manifestations have appeared since the time of Moses (we do not have the records of any Manifestations that might have appeared in the new world among the American Indians).

Israel, wrapt in the densest veils of satanic fancy and false imaginings, is still expectant that the idol of her own handiwork[79]

79. The belief among the Jews regarding their Messiah and the image they constructed of him was that he would be a descendant of David, who was living in an imaginary City and would come to rule the world, destroy the enemies of Israel, promote the laws of the Torah, and establish a kingdom similar to that of David and Solomon.

hath extinguished in them the spirit of faith[80]

80. The spirit of faith is defined by 'Abdu'l-Bahá, when he describes the five aspects of the spirit:

> As to the fourth degree of spirit, it is the heavenly spirit, which is the spirit of faith and the outpouring grace of the All-Merciful. This spirit proceeds from the breath of the Holy Spirit, and through a power born of God it becomes the cause of everlasting life. It is that power which makes the earthly soul heavenly and the imperfect man perfect. It cleanses the impure, unlooses the tongue of the silent, sanctifies the bondslaves of passion and desire, and confers knowledge upon the ignorant.
> ('Abdu'l-Bahá, *Some Answered Questions*, no. 36.6)

tormented them with the flames of the nethermost fire[81]

81. "The flames of the nethermost fire" is a figurative phrase signifying remoteness from God, burning in the fire of pride and enmity, and not experiencing the joy of recognizing the Manifestation of God. Malachi, chapter 4:1, which is the prophesy of the coming of the Messiah, is applicable to this condition:

> For, behold, the day cometh, that shall burn as an oven; and all the proud, yea, and all that do wickedly, shall be stubble: and the day that cometh shall burn them up, saith the Lord of hosts, that it shall leave them neither root nor branch."
> (Malachi 4:1)

The similitude of the attitude of negation to the fire is also expressed by the Báb:

> Verily it is incumbent upon you to recognize your Lord at the time of His manifestation, that haply ye may not enter into negation, and that, ere a prophet is raised by God, ye may find yourselves securely established upon the sea of affirmation. For if a prophet cometh to you from God and ye fail to walk in His Way, God will, thereupon, transform your light into fire. Take heed then that perchance ye may, through the grace of God and His signs, be enabled to redeem your souls.
> (The Báb, *Selections from the Writings of the Báb*, p. 147)

As she never grasped their true significance, and, to outward seeming, such events never came to pass[82]

82. Commenting on the same subject of how the people of Israel were expecting the literal fulfillment of the signs and prophesies, and therefore did not accept Jesus as their promised Messiah, 'Abdu'l-Bahá stated:

> In this wise did they object to that Sun of Truth, although that Spirit of God was indeed the One promised in the Torah. But as they did not understand the meaning of these signs, they crucified the Word of God. Now the Bahá'ís hold that the recorded signs did come to pass in the Manifestation of Christ, although not in the sense which the

> Jews understood, the description in the Torah being allegorical. For instance, among the signs is that of sovereignty. For Bahá'ís say that the sovereignty of Christ was a heavenly, divine, everlasting sovereignty, not a Napoleonic sovereignty that vanisheth in a short time. For well nigh two thousand years this sovereignty of Christ hath been established, and until now it endureth, and to all eternity that Holy Being will be exalted upon an everlasting throne. In like manner all the other signs have been made manifest, but the Jews did not understand. Although nearly twenty centuries have elapsed since Christ appeared with divine splendour, yet the Jews are still awaiting the coming of the Messiah and regard themselves as true and Christ as false."
>
> (Abdu'l-Baha, *Selections from the Writings of Abdu'l-Baha*, p. 45)

remained deprived of recognizing the beauty of Jesus and of beholding the face of God[83]

83. Please see Note No. 19 above.

From time immemorial even unto this day, all the kindreds and peoples of the earth have clung to such fanciful and unseemly thoughts, and thus have deprived themselves of the clear waters streaming from the springs of purity and holiness.[84]

84. This clear water is the revelation of God as stated by Jesus:

> Now Jacob's well was there. Jesus therefore, being wearied with his journey, sat thus on the well: and it was about the sixth hour. There cometh a woman of Samaria to draw water: Jesus saith unto her, Give me to drink. (For his disciples were gone away unto the city to buy meat.) Then saith the woman of Samaria unto him, How is it that thou, being a Jew, askest drink of me, which am a woman of Samaria? for the Jews have no dealings with the Samaritans. Jesus answered and said unto her, If thou knewest the gift of God, and who it is that saith to thee, Give me to drink; thou wouldest have asked of him, and he

> would have given thee living water. The woman saith unto him, Sir, thou hast nothing to draw with, and the well is deep: from whence then hast thou that living water? Art thou greater than our father Jacob, which gave us the well, and drank thereof himself, and his children, and his cattle? Jesus answered and said unto her, Whosoever drinketh of this water shall thirst again: But whosoever drinketh of the water that I shall give him shall never thirst; but the water that I shall give him shall be in him a well of water springing up into everlasting life.
> (John 4: 6–11)

Bahá'u'lláh also states:

> This is the Day whereon the rushing waters of everlasting life have gushed out of the Will of the All-Merciful. Haste ye, with your hearts and souls, and quaff your fill, O Concourse of the realms above.
> (Bahá'u'lláh, *Gleanings from the Writings of Bahá'u'lláh*, p. 30)

Paragraph No. 18:

In unfolding these mysteries, We have, in Our former Tablets which were addressed to a friend in the melodious language of Ḥijáz [85]

85. The melodious language of Ḥijáz is the Arabic language. Ḥijáz is the western region of present-day Saudi Arabia where the important cities of Mecca and Medina are located. It is the land from where Muḥammad came, and the dialect of the Arabic language spoken there at the time of Muḥammad became the revelatory language of the Qur'án. In the Writings of Bahá'u'lláh, terms like the "melodious language of Hijaz" or "Arabian melodies" are used in referring to the Arabic Writings of Bahá'u'lláh and the Báb.

    The former Tablets referred to here are some Tablets revealed in Arabic—more specifically a treatise titled Javáhiru'l-Asrár (Gems of Divine Mysteries). This same Tablet is referred to in paragraph 24, below, as the "Tablets revealed in the Arabic tongue." This Tablet was translated and published by the Universal House of Justice in

2002 under the title "Gems of Divine Mysteries." Following are a few paragraphs from the introduction to this book:

> Among these early effusions of the Pen of Glory is a lengthy epistle known as Javáhiru'l-Asrár, meaning literally the "gems" or "essences" of mysteries. A number of themes it enunciates are also elaborated in Persian—through different revelatory modes—in the Seven Valleys and the Book of Certitude, those two immortal volumes which Shoghi Effendi has characterized, respectively, as Bahá'u'lláh's greatest mystical composition and His pre-eminent doctrinal work. Undoubtedly the Gems of Divine Mysteries figures among those "Tablets revealed in the Arabic tongue" which were referred to in the latter volume.
>
> One of the central themes of the book, Bahá'u'lláh indicates, is that of "transformation," meaning here the return of the Promised One in a different human guise. Indeed, in a prefatory note written above the opening lines of the original manuscript, Bahá'u'lláh states:
>
> This treatise was written in reply to a seeker who had asked how the promised Mihdí could have become transformed into 'Alí-Muḥammad (the Báb). The opportunity provided by this question was seized to elaborate on a number of subjects, all of which are of use and benefit both to them that seek and to those who have attained, could ye perceive with the eye of divine virtue.
>
> The seeker alluded to the above passage was Siyyid Yúsuf-i-Sidihí Iṣfáháni, who at the time was residing in Karbilá. His questions were presented to Bahá'u'lláh through an intermediary, and this Tablet was revealed in response on the same day.
>
> A number of other important themes are addressed in this work as well: the cause of the rejection of the Prophets of the past; the danger of a literal reading of scripture; the meaning of the signs and portents of the Bible concerning the advent of the new Manifestation; the continuity of divine revelation; intimations of Bahá'u'lláh's own approaching declaration; the significance of such symbolic terms as "the Day of

Judgement," "the Resurrection," "attainment to the Divine Presence," and "life and death;" and the stages of the spiritual quest through "the Garden of Search," "the City of Divine Unity," "the Garden of Wonderment," "the City of Absolute Nothingness," "the City of Immortality," and "the City that hath no name or description."
(*Gems of Divine Mysteries*, Introduction, pp. ii–iv)

uttered this time in the wondrous accents of 'Iráq[86]

86. "The wondrous accents of 'Iráq" is a reference to the Persian or Farsi language. At the time of the revelation of The Book of Certitude, the western part of Iran was referred to as the *'Iráq-i-'Ajam*, or "Persian 'Iráq."

The Báb, Bahá'u'lláh, and 'Abdu'l-Bahá have all written both in the Arabic and Persian languages. The terms, "wondrous accents of 'Iraq" or the "sweet Iranian songs" in the Writings of Bahá'u'lláh are references to the Persian Writings of Bahá'u'lláh and the Báb.

Bahá'u'lláh calls the Arabic "Fus'ha" (eloquent) and Persian "Nura" (illumined) languages.

the sore athirst in the wilds of remoteness[87]

87. Please see Note No. 58.

that haply there may flow from this pen that which shall quicken the souls of men, that they may all arise from their beds of heedlessness[88]

88. Several terms such as "beds of heedlessness," "Couch of heedlessness," and "abode of heedlessness" are interchangeably used in the Bahá'í Writings to describe the mental and spiritual condition of the people who are unaware of their own spiritual condition, are complacent and self-satisfied, and do not feel a need for enhancing their spiritual life. For more details see Note No. 24 above.

and hearken unto the rustling of the leaves of Paradise, from the tree which the hand of divine power hath, by the permission of God, planted in the Riḍván[89] of the All-Glorious[90].

89. Riḍván, which means paradise, is allegorically used in some places in the Bahá'í Writings to signify the presence of God—i, e. the Manifestation of God. See Note No. 39 above .

90. This is the reason for the revelation of the Kitáb-i-Íqán. It seems that the last three sentences of this paragraph are also allusions to the impending revelation and to the exalted station of the person of Bahá'u'lláh.

    What flows from His pen is the divine Revelation which will quicken the souls of men. The tree which the hand of divine power had planted in the Riḍván of the All-Glorious is the person of the Manifestation of God. The leaves of the tree are His teachings or Tablets. The Báb, when describing the importance and exalted nature of Revelation of Bahá'u'lláh, compares the Bayán to a leaf among the leaves of His Paradise:

    > The whole of the Bayán is only a leaf amongst the leaves of His Paradise. Be fair, O people, and be not of such as are accounted as lost in the Book of God, the Lord of the worlds.
    > (The Báb, quoted in Bahá'u'lláh, Epistle to the Son of the Wolf, p. 151)

    Quoting this statement of the Báb, Bahá'u'lláh states:

    > "Ponder ye these blessed words. He saith: 'The whole of the Bayán is only a leaf amongst the leaves of His Paradise.' Be fair, O people, and be not of such as are accounted as lost in the Book of God, the Lord of the worlds."
    >
    > The blessed Lote-Tree standeth, in this day, before thy face, laden with heavenly, with new and wondrous fruits. Gaze on it, detached from all else save it. Thus hath the Tongue of might and power spoken at this Spot which God hath adorned with the footsteps of His Most Great Name and Mighty Announcement"
    > (Bahá'u'lláh, Epistle to the Son of the Wolf, p. 151)

Paragraph No. 19:

To them that are endowed with understanding, it is clear and manifest that when the fire of the love of Jesus consumed the veils of Jewish limitations, and His authority was made apparent and partially enforced[91]

91. Bahá'u'lláh Has in previous paragraphs mentioned some of the veils that prevented the Jews from seeing the exalted station of Jesus and from putting Him on the same level as Moses and following His commandments. He also describes the limitations that barred them from recognizing Him as the Christ they were waiting.

One of the veils that was a result of the misunderstanding of the signs and prophesies was the belief among the Jews that before the coming of their Messiah, and in preparation for His advent, Elijah (Elias) would descend from heaven in His physical/corporal body. Being raised and nurtured in that religious culture, it took some time for the disciples of Jesus to remove those veils and overcome those limitations and recognize Him as the promised Messiah.

According to the text of the Gospels, it was almost half way through the ministry of Jesus that the fire of His love burned those veils. That process is recorded in the synoptic Gospels (Matthew, Mark, and Luke) and in 2 Peter. Due to the differences in the accounts of the same event as recorded in the synoptic Gospels, all three are presented below:

> And after six days Jesus taketh Peter, James, and John his brother, and bringeth them up into an high mountain apart, And was transfigured before them: and his face did shine as the sun, and his raiment was white as the light. And, behold, there appeared unto them Moses and Elias talking with him. Then answered Peter, and said unto Jesus, Lord, it is good for us to be here: if thou wilt, let us make here three tabernacles; one for thee, and one for Moses, and one for Elias. While he yet spake, behold, a bright cloud overshadowed them: and behold a voice out of the cloud, which said, This is my beloved Son, in whom I am well

pleased; hear ye him. And when the disciples heard it, they fell on their face, and were sore afraid. And Jesus came and touched them, and said, Arise, and be not afraid. And when they had lifted up their eyes, they saw no man, save Jesus only. And as they came down from the mountain, Jesus charged them, saying, Tell the vision to no man, until the Son of man be risen again from the dead. And his disciples asked him, saying, Why then say the scribes that Elias must first come? And Jesus answered and said unto them, Elias truly shall first come, and restore all things. But I say unto you, That Elias is come already, and they knew him not, but have done unto him whatsoever they listed. Likewise shall also the Son of man suffer of them. Then the disciples understood that he spake unto them of John the Baptist.
(Matthew 17:1–11)

And after six days Jesus taketh with him Peter, and James, and John, and leadeth them up into an high mountain apart by themselves: and he was transfigured before them. And his raiment became shining, exceeding white as snow; so as no fuller on earth can white them. And there appeared unto them Elias with Moses: and they were talking with Jesus. And Peter answered and said to Jesus, Master, it is good for us to be here: and let us make three tabernacles; one for thee, and one for Moses, and one for Elias. For he wist not what to say; for they were sore afraid. And there was a cloud that overshadowed them: and a voice came out of the cloud, saying, This is my beloved Son: hear him. And suddenly, when they had looked round about, they saw no man any more, save Jesus only with themselves. And as they came down from the mountain, he charged them that they should tell no man what things they had seen, till the Son of man were risen from the dead. And they kept that saying with themselves, questioning one with another what the rising from the dead should mean. And they asked him, saying, Why say the scribes that Elias must first come? And he answered and told them, Elias verily cometh first, and restoreth all things; and how it is written of the Son of man, that he must suffer many things, and be set at nought. But I say unto you, That Elias is indeed come, and they have done unto him whatsoever they listed, as it is written

> of him. And when he came to his disciples, he saw a great multitude about them, and the scribes questioning with them.
> (Mark 9:2–12)
>
> And it came to pass about an eight days after these sayings, he took Peter and John and James, and went up into a mountain to pray. And as he prayed, the fashion of his countenance was altered, and his raiment was white and glistering. And, behold, there talked with him two men, which were Moses and Elias: Who appeared in glory, and spake of his decease which he should accomplish at Jerusalem. But Peter and they that were with him were heavy with sleep: and when they were awake, they saw his glory, and the two men that stood with him. And it came to pass, as they departed from him, Peter said unto Jesus, Master, it is good for us to be here: and let us make three tabernacles; one for thee, and one for Moses, and one for Elias: not knowing what he said. While he thus spake, there came a cloud, and overshadowed them: and they feared as they entered into the cloud. And there came a voice out of the cloud, saying, This is my beloved Son: hear him. And when the voice was past, Jesus was found alone. And they kept it close, and told no man in those days any of those things which they had seen.
> (Luke 9:28–36)

When the veils were removed and the disciples realized that Jesus was in truth the expected Messiah (Christ), they were wondering why they did not see the literal fulfilment of the prophecies and appearance of the signs. “And his disciples asked him, saying, Why then say the scribes that Elias must first come?” And now that His authority was established, “Jesus answered and said unto them, Elias truly shall first come, and restore all things. But I say unto you, That Elias is come already, and they knew him not, but have done unto him whatsoever they listed. . . . Then the disciples understood that he spake unto them of John the Baptist.”

"I go and another will come Who will tell you all that I have not told you, and will fulfil all that I have said."[92]

92. These words of Jesus are recorded in the Gospel of John. There are seven places in the Gospel of John where Jesus speaks about His passing or going and coming back again, or of Him going and another one coming after Him. These passages are presented below:

> Little children, yet a little while I am with you. Ye shall seek me: and as I said unto the Jews, Whither I go, ye cannot come; so now I say to you. . . . In my Father's house are many mansions: if it were not so, I would have told you. I go to prepare a place for you. And if I go and prepare a place for you, I will come again, and receive you unto myself; that where I am, there ye may be also.
> (John 13:33, 14:2–3)

> And I [Jesus] will pray the Father, and he shall give you another Comforter [Paraclete] , that he may abide with you for ever; Even the Spirit of truth; whom the world cannot receive, because it seeth him not, neither knoweth him: but ye know him; for he dwelleth with you, and shall be in you.
> (John 14:16–17)

> But the Comforter [Paraclete], the Holy Ghost, whom the Father will send in my name, he shall teach you all things, and bring all things to your remembrance, whatsoever I have said unto you.
> (John 14:26)

> Ye have heard how I said unto you, I go away, and come again unto you. If ye loved me, ye would rejoice, because I said, I go unto the Father: for my Father is greater than I.
> (John 14:28)

> But when the Comforter [Paraclete] is come, whom I will send unto you from the Father, *even* the Spirit of truth, which proceedeth from the Father, he shall testify of me:
> (John 15:26)

> Nevertheless I tell you the truth; It is expedient for you that I go away: for if I go not away, the Comforter will not come unto you; but if I depart, I will send him unto you.

> And when he is come, he will reprove the world of sin, and of righteousness, and of judgment.
> (John 16:7–8)

> A little while, and ye shall not see me: and again, a little while, and ye shall see me, because I go to the Father. Then said some of his disciples among themselves, What is this that he saith unto us, A little while, and ye shall not see me: and again, a little while, and ye shall see me: and, Because I go to the Father? They said therefore, What is this that he saith, A little while? we cannot tell what he saith.
> (John 16:16–18)

> And ye now therefore have sorrow: but I will see you again, and your heart shall rejoice, and your joy no man taketh from you.
> (John 16:22)

Both these sayings have but one meaning, were you to ponder upon the Manifestations of the Unity of God with divine insight.[93]

93. Bahá'u'lláh introduces the concept of the unity of the essence, reality, and spiritual identity of the Manifestations of God. This is a very important theological concept that is fully elucidated in the Kitáb-i-Íqán.

    Although the statements of Jesus in the Gospel of John—that He would go and would come back, and that He would go and another would be sent after Him—seem contradictory in a literal sense[49], by introducing this concept, Bahá'u'lláh removes the contradiction and demonstrates that the two visions and two personalities are the same. If we consider the fact that the divine reality of Jesus and that of Muḥammad, the Manifestation that followed Him, are the same, there is no contradiction.

[49] Chapters 14–17 of the Gospel of John in general and more specifically the above statements are known as "Jesus' Farewell Discourse." Some biblical scholars hold that these statements provide two contradictory visions of the future with two distinct personalities. One in which Jesus will go away and will return Himself, and another in which Jesus will go away and the Comforter will come. Biblical scholars have not been able to resolve this contradiction. For a detailed discussion of this subject see (Christopher Buck, *Symbol & Secret,* pp. 114–120).

This is also a reference to the fact that these words of Jesus are prophesies of the coming of another Manifestation (Muslims claim that this is a reference to the coming of Muḥammad). The Qur'án states that Jesus gave the glad tiding of the coming of Muḥammad and mentioned Him by His name "Aḥmad."

The Qur'án in the Súrah of (al-Saff) "The Ranks" states:

> And when Jesus the son of Mary said, 'Children of Israel, I am indeed the Messenger of God to you, confirming the Torah that is before me, and giving good tidings of a Messenger who shall come after me, whose name shall be Aḥmad. Yet when He came to them with clear signs, they said: 'This is a Plain sorcery"
> (The Qur'án, Arberry tr, 61:6)

The Rodwell translation reads:

> And remember when Jesus the son of Mary said, "O Children of Israel! Of a truth I am God's Apostle to you to confirming the law which was given before me, and to announce an apostle that shall come after me, whose name shall be Aḥmad!"[50] But when he (Aḥmad) presented himself with clear proofs of his mission, they said: "This is manifest sorcery."
> (The Qur'án 61:6)

Some Christians contend that the name "Aḥmad" is never mentioned in the Gospels, to which Muslims have responded that the promises made by Jesus in the Gospel of John for the coming of the Paraclete are references to Aḥmad, as to them Paraclete is synonymous with Aḥmad. The names "Aḥmad" and "Muḥammad," are both derived from the Arabic verb "Ḥamda" (to

---

[50] The footnote in the Rodwell translation on the word "Aḥmad" in this verse states:

> Muḥmmad had no doubt heard that Jesus had promised a *Paracletos*, John xvi. 7. This title, understood by him, probably from the similarity of sound, as equivalent to *Periclytos*, he applied to himself with reference to his own name Muḥammad (i.e. *praised, glorified*) from the same root and of the same meaning as Aḥmad, also one of the Prophet's names. It may be here remarked that the name Muḥammad, if pronounced Muḥamm*e*d, "might be understood by an Arab in an active instead of a passive sense." (Lane, Kor p. 52.)

praise). "Aḥmad" means "highly-esteemed, or worthy of praise" and "Muḥammad" means "often praised." To Muslims, these statements of Jesus are the clearest prophecies for the coming of Muḥammad.

The English word "Paraclete" is a transliteration of the Latin word "Paracletus" and Greek "Parakletos," which means helper or comforter. Some Muslim apologists state that in Arabic and Syriac and other Semitic languages there are no vowels in the written form of "Parakletos" (PRKLTS) and it is written exactly as the word " Periklutos" (PRKLTS) meaning "celebrated," "illustrious," "highly-esteemed, or praised," which is equivalent to Aḥmad.
(Source: 'Abdu'l-Ḥamíd Ishráq-Khávari, *Qámous-i-Íqán, Vol. 2*, p. 749. Stephen Lambden, "Prophecy in Johannine Farewell Discourse," in *Scripture & Revelation,* Bahá'í Studies, Vol. III, edited by Moojan Momen, pp. 69–124)

Some scholars maintain that during the almost fourteen centuries before Bibles were printed, many words, especially those that were similar in spelling or sound, were replaced in the process of transcription. In the book *Misquoting Jesus,* Bart Ehrman cites several examples of words in the New Testament that have been changed or substituted by other similar words by scribes who were either not familiar with the original words or thought that the substituted words made better sense.

> An interesting illustration of the intentional change of a text is found in one of the finest old manuscripts, Codex Vaticanus (so named because it was found in the Vatican library), made in the fourth century. In the opening of the book of Hebrews there is a passage in which, according to most manuscripts, we are told that "Christ bears [Greek: PHERÓN] all things by the word of his power" (Heb. 1:3). In Codex Vaticanus, however, the original scribe produced a slightly different text, with a verb that sounded similar in Greek; here the text instead reads: "Christ manifests [Greek: PHANERÓN] all things by the word of his power." Some centuries later, a second scribe read this passage in the manuscript and decided to change the unusual word *manifests* to the more common reading *bears*—erasing the one word and writing in the other. Then, again some centuries later, a third scribe read the manuscript and noticed the alteration his predecessor had made; he, in turn,

> erased the word *bears* and rewrote the word *manifests*. He then added a scribal note in the margin to indicate what he thought of the earlier, second scribe. The note says: "Fool and knave! Leave the old reading, don't change it!"
> (Bart Ehrman, *Misquoting Jesus*, p. 56)

> Sometimes accidental mistakes were made not because words *looked* alike, but because they *sounded* alike. This could happen, for example, when a scribe was copying a text by dictation—when one scribe would be reading from a manuscript and one or more other scribes would be copying the words into new manuscripts, as sometimes happened in scriptoria after the fourth century. If two words were pronounced the same, then the scribe doing the copying might inadvertently use the wrong one in his copy, especially if it made perfectly good (but wrong) sense. This appears to be what happened, for example, in REV. 1:5, where the author prays to "the one who released us from our sins." The word for "released" (LUSANTI) sounds exactly like the word for "washed" (LOUSANTI), and so it is no surprise that in a number of medieval manuscripts the author prays to the one "who washed us from our sins."
> (Bart Ehrman, *Misquoting Jesus*, p. 92)

Whether due to conversion from Middle-Eastern languages to Greek, or due to the scribal substitution, The Muslim apologists argue that the word "Parakletos" has somehow substituted the original and correct word "Periklutos" in the above verses, and in truth Muḥammad is the promised figure of the Johannine Gospel. There are several traditions (Aḥadith) ascribed to Muḥammad and the Imáms that seem to affirm this concept.

Paragraph No. 20:

Dispensation of the Qur'án[94]

94. The Dispensation of the Qur'án and the religion of Islam began with the ministry of its Prophet-Founder Muḥammad and the revelation of the Qur'án, circa 610 AD, and ended with the Declaration of the Báb in 1844. Please see Notes 5 and 6 above and Appendix I.

Book and the Cause of Jesus were confirmed[95]

95. The Qur'án confirms the divine origin of Christ and the Gospels in many places:

> In truth hath He sent down to thee "the Book," which confirmeth those which precede it: For He had sent down the Law, and the Evangel aforetime, as man's Guidance; and now hath He sent down the "Illumination." (Furkan)[51]
> (The Qur'án 3:3)

> Moreover, to Moses gave we "the Book," and we raised up apostles after him; and to Jesus, son of Mary, gave we clear proofs of his mission, and strengthened him by the Holy Spirit.
> (The Qur'án 2:81)

> Say ye: "We believe in God, and that which hath been sent down to us, and that which hath been sent down to Abraham and Ismael and Isaac and Jacob and the tribes: and that which hath been given to Moses and to Jesus, and that which was given to the prophets from their Lord. No difference do we make between any of them: and to God are we resigned (Muslims).
> (The Qur'án 2:130)

> Some of the apostles we have endowed more highly than others: Those to whom God hath spoken, He hath raised to the loftiest grade, and to Jesus the Son of Mary we gave manifest signs, and we strengthened him with the Holy Spirit.
> (The Qur'án 2:255)

> Remember when the angel said, "O Mary! Verily God announceth to thee the Word from Him: His name shall be, Messiah Jesus the son of Mary, illustrious in this world,

[51] In the Qur'ánic terminology "the Law" is the Old Testament, "the Evangel" is the New Testament, and "Furkan" is another name for the Qur'án.

> and in the next, and one of those who have near access to God;
> (The Qur'án 3:40)
>
> And in the footsteps of the prophets caused we Jesus, the son of Mary, to follow, confirming the law which was before him: and we gave him the Evangel with its guidance and light, confirmatory of the preceding Law; a guidance and warning to those who fear God;
> (The Qur'án 5:50)

As to the matter of names, Muḥammad[96] Himself, declared: "I am Jesus."[97]

96. Muḥammad was born in Mecca. Jesus was born 570 years earlier in Bethlehem. For details about the life and person of Muḥammad, see Appendix I.

97. There are several traditions (Aḥadith), in which Muḥammad identifies Himself with the Prophets before Him. This statement is a part of one of those traditions. He stated: "I am the first Adam, the Noah, the Moses and Jesus."

    There is another tradition in which Muḥammad says: "I am the Prophets." The story behind this tradition—as related in several of the Qur'án commentaries—is that one of the believers asked Muḥammad to interpret the following verse of the Qur'án for him:

    > And whoever shall obey God and the Apostle, these shall be with those of the Prophets, and of the Sincere, and of the Martyrs, and of the Just, to whom God hath been gracious. These are a goodly band!
    > (The Qur'án 4: 71)

    Muḥammad stated that "I am the Prophets, the Sincere is 'Alí, the Martyr is Ḥamzeh (one of Muḥammad's uncles who became a believer, followed Muḥammad to Medina and was killed in one of the wars with the idolators). . ."
    (Source: 'Abdu'l-Ḥamíd Ishráq-Khávari, *Qámus-i-Íqán, Vol. 1*, pp. 137)

He recognized the truth of the signs, prophecies, and words of Jesus, and testified that they were all of God[98]

98. As mentioned in Note No. 95 above, in many places in the Qur'án and traditions from Muḥammad the divine origin of the words and works of Jesus are confirmed. the Qur'án also confirms the signs and miracles of Jesus:

> When He shall say: O Jesus! Son of Mary! call to mind my favour upon thee and upon thy mother, when I strengthened thee with the Holy Spirit, that thou shouldest speak to men alike in the cradle,* and when grown up; And when I taught thee the Scripture, and Wisdom, and the Law, and the Evangel: and thou didst create of clay, as it were, the figure of a bird, by my leave, and didst breathe into it, and by my leave it became a bird,** and thou didst heal the blind and the leper, by my leave; and when, by my leave, thou didst bring forth the dead; and when I withheld the children of Israel from thee, when thou hadst come to them with clear tokens: and such of them as believed not said, "This is nought but plain sorcery;"
> (The Qur'án 5:108–111)

* This is a reference to the miracle of Jesus speaking like a grown up man a few days after His birth while in the cradle.

** This is a reference to the miracle of Jesus forming figurines of birds out of clay and making them fly.

These two miracles of Jesus—speaking like a grown man a few days after His birth, and creating birds from clay and causing them to fly in His childhood—are not recorded in the canonical Gospels (Matthew, Mark, Luke, and John). For several centuries Christians accused Muḥammad of inventing stories that had no basis in the scriptures. But the discovery and translation of a collection of thirteen ancient codices in Nag Ḥammadi in Egypt in 1945 and several Infancy Gospels that were extant in the early Christian era proved that Muḥammad did not invent these stories. The Infancy Gospels, i.e., *The Infancy Gospel of James*, *The Infancy Gospel of Pseudo-Matthew,* and *The Infancy Gospel of Thomas*, which were available to Christians from the middle of the second century AD, contain accounts of these miracles.

These Gospels are part of Christian Apocrypha (quasi-scriptural, non-canonical books, or books that, although accepted for a period of time by certain churches as scripture, were not eventually included in the Canon or present Bible). Willis Barnstone the author of the "*The Other Bible*" in his introduction to these gospels writes:

> *The Infancy Gospel of James (The Birth of Mary)*: Although the New Testament gospels say little of Jesus' childhood—Mark and John say nothing at all—and the earliest theological interest was in Christ the teacher, the crucified, and the resurrected, by the second century infancy gospels were very popular. The sources were outside the synoptic gospels, for between the nativity scene and the story of Jesus at the age of twelve in the temple, there is only one reference to the young Jesus: "the child grew and became strong" (Luke 2:40). As for the formal observance of Christmas, this did not take place until the fourth century.
>
> There was great human interest in Jesus' childhood and, in several infancy gospels, tales of children of gods are introduced. Jesus becomes a divine prankster. There were also theological and political reasons for the infancy gospels. A common "slander" of the time was that Jesus was the illegitimate son of a soldier called Panthera, and indeed the story (including the discovery of a gravestone in Germany with the name "Panthera") has never failed to interest historians and pseudohistorians. The problem of legitimacy was caused by the assertion on the one hand that Jesus was born of a virgin birth, and the genealogies in Mathew and Luke on the other hand demonstrate Jesus' Davidic descent through Joseph. A solution was found in the infancy *Gospel of James* by making Mary descend from David. . . . *The Gospel of James*, also called the *Protevangelism Jacobi*. . . . The *Gospel of James* was attributed to Jesus' brother James. James (Jacob) was thought to be Jesus' younger brother by Mary, or, by those

> who maintained Mary's perpetual virginity, Joseph's son by a previous marriage. In any case, the *Gospel* could not have been written before A.D. 150, which eliminates James as the author. It was probably written, scholars agree, not by a Jewish Christian but a Gentile. . . . Early manuscripts of the *Gospel* exist in Greek, Syriac, Armenian, and later in many languages, including Ethiopic, Georgian, and Slavonic. No Latin manuscript survived the early condemnation of the book in the west.
> (Willis Barnstone, *The Other Bible,* p. 383)

> *The Infancy Gospel of Pseudo-Matthew* is a strangely poetic version of the *Infancy Gospel of James*. Joseph is accused of defiling Mary, but he exonerates himself. Then Mary is accused of deceiving Joseph, but she "drank the water of testing" to prove her innocence. Mary calls on her God, "Adonai of hosts," to declare that she has never known a man. Since infancy she has vowed to live without stain. Then Jesus is born in the cave and placed in the manger where he is worshiped by a donkey and an ox. So the prophecy of Habbakuk is fulfilled: "You will be known by these two animals."

> Thereafter Jesus, who asks not to be considered a child but "a perfect man," charms dangerous dragons, lions, and leopards, and causes them to worship him. . . . The infant Jesus, still at his mother's breast in the third day of his life, hears that his mother is hungry and thirsty. He orders a palm tree to bend down which it does, so his mother can gather fruit from it.
> (Willis Barnstone, *The Other Bible,* p. 393)

This miracle of Jesus as recorded in *The Infancy Gospel of Pseudo-Matthew* is as follows:

> When they came to a certain cave and wanted to rest in it, Mary got down from the pack mule, and, sitting down, held Jesus in her lap. There were three boys traveling with Joseph and a girl with Mary. And behold, suddenly, many dragons came out of the cave. When the boys saw them in front of them they shouted with great fear. Then Jesus got down from his mother's lap, and stood on his feet before

> the dragons. They, however, worshiped him, and while they worshiped, they backed away. Then what was said through the prophet David was fulfilled: "You dragons of the earth, praise the Lord, you dragons and all creatures of the abyss." Then the infant Jesus walked before them and ordered them not to harm any man. But Mary and Joseph were very afraid lest the child should be harmed by the dragons. Jesus said to them, "Do not be afraid, nor consider me a child; I always have been a perfect man and am so now; it is necessary that all the wild beasts of the forest be tame before me."
> (Willis Barnstone, *The Other Bible,* p. 396)
>
> The *Infancy Gospel of Thomas* is one of the earliest infancy gospels, written about A.D. 150, and was extremely popular in the first centuries. It appears in translation in many languages. The *Gospel* deals with the period between Jesus' birth and the incident of Jesus in the Temple, which is recounted in Luke 2:40. For modern apologists, the work is an ethical embarrassment, for the little Jesus is not only a child prodigy but a child terror, performing nasty miracles. The author was probably Gentile, since the work betrays no knowledge of Judaism. In keeping with other apocryphal scriptures, Jesus and his family are depicted as surrounded by unfriendly Jews but they themselves, somehow, are not Jews. Cartlidge and Dungan, the translators of this text from the Greek, speak of the gospel as "a classic example of the influence of the Hellenistic "divine man" concept on a Christian description of Jesus Christ.
> (Willis Barnstone, *The Other Bible,* p. 398)

This miracle of Jesus as recorded in *The Infancy Gospel of Thomas* is as follows:

> I, Thomas the Israelite, announce and make known to all you brethren from the Gentiles the childhood and great deeds of our Lord Jesus Christ, which he did when he was born in our country. This is the beginning.
>
> When this child Jesus was five years old, he was playing *at the ford of a stream. He* made pools of the rushing water and made it immediately pure; he ordered and this by word

alone. He made soft clay and molded twelve sparrows from it. It was the Sabbath when he did this. There were many other children playing with him. A certain Jew saw what Jesus did while playing on the Sabbath; he immediately went and announced to his father Joseph, "See, you child is at the stream, and has taken and molded twelve birds; he has profaned the Sabbath." Joseph came to the place, and seeing what Jesus did he cried out, "Why do you do on the Sabbath what it is not lawful to do?" Jesus clapped his hands and cried to the sparrows, "Be gone." And the sparrows flew off chirping. The Jews saw this and were amazed. They went away and described to their leaders what they had seen Jesus do.
(*The Infancy Gospel of Thomas,* p. 399)

Thus it is that Jesus, Himself, declared: "I go away and come again unto you." Consider the sun. Were it to say now, "I am the sun of yesterday,"[99]

99. The same concept is also stated in the Writings of the Báb:

Thou beholdest how vast is the number of people who go to Mecca each year on pilgrimage and engage in circumambulation, while He, through the potency of Whose Word the Ka'bah [the sanctuary in Mecca] hath become the object of adoration, is forsaken in this mountain. He is none other but the Apostle of God Himself, inasmuch as the Revelation of God may be likened to the sun. No matter how innumerable its risings, there is but one sun, and upon it depends the life of all things. It is clear and evident that the object of all preceding Dispensations hath been to pave the way for the advent of Muḥammad, the Apostle of God. These, including the Muḥammadan Dispensation, have had, in their turn, as their objective the Revelation proclaimed by the Qá'im. The purpose underlying this Revelation, as well as those that preceded it, has, in like manner, been to announce the advent of the Faith of Him Whom God will make manifest. And this Faith—the Faith of Him Whom God will make manifest—in its turn, together with all the Revelations gone before it,

> have as their object the Manifestation destined to succeed it. And the latter, no less than all the Revelations preceding it, prepare the way for the Revelation which is yet to follow. The process of the rise and setting of the Sun of Truth will thus indefinitely continue—a process that hath had no beginning and will have no end.
> (The Báb, *Selections from the Writings of the Báb,* p. 105)

Conceive accordingly the distinction, variation, and unity characteristic of the various Manifestations of holiness, that thou mayest comprehend the allusions made by the creator of all names and attributes to the mysteries of distinction and unity[100]

100. The elements of distinctions are the physical attributes, the location and time of the appearance of the Manifestations God. Each came from a different country and at different times. But the basis of Their unity is that They are all emanations of one spirit, reflect the light of one divine reality, and manifest the attributes of one God. This concept is discussed and developed more extensively further on in the Kitáb-i-Íqán.

and discover the answer to thy question as to why that everlasting Beauty should have, at sundry times, called Himself by different names and titles[101]

101. One of the questions posed by the uncle of the Báb was why the Báb had appeared with a different name than the one associated with promised one of Islam. According to the Shi'ah traditions the Twelfth Imám, the promised Qá'im was named "Abu'l-Qásim Muḥammad" and the Báb's given name was "'Alí Muḥammad."

Bahá'u'lláh here explains why the same divine reality appears under different names. On the same theme 'Abdu'l-Bahá states:

> The sun is one, but the dawning points of the sun are numerous and changing. The ocean is one body of water, but different parts of it have particular designations—Atlantic, Pacific, Mediterranean, Antarctic, etc. If we consider the names, there is differentiation; but the water,

> the ocean itself, is one reality. Likewise, the divine religions of the holy Manifestations of God are in reality one, though in name and nomenclature they differ.
> ('Abdu'l-Bahá, *The Promulgation of Universal Peace*, p. 151)

> Bahá'u'lláh spread the Cause of Christ and opened the book of the Christians and Jews. He removed the barriers of names. He proved that all the divine Prophets taught the same reality and that to deny One is to deny the Others, for all are in perfect oneness with God.
> ('Abdu'l-Bahá, *The Promulgation of Universal Peace*, p. 212)

Jesus promised that He would come with a new name:

> He who overcomes, I will make him a pillar in the temple of My God, and he shall go out no more. And I will write on him the name of My God and the name of the city of My God, the New Jerusalem, which comes down out of heaven from My God. And I will write on him My new name. He who has an ear, let him hear what the Spirit says to the churches.
> (Revelation 3:12–13)

The above is an answer to the question that if Bahá'u'lláh is the return of Christ, why did He appear with a different name? The question is based on the following quote from St. Peter:

> Nor is there salvation in any other, for there is no other name under heaven given among men by which we must be saved.
> (Acts 4:12)

The fulfillment of the above mentioned promise of Jesus, a great divine hint, appears in the same Book:

> And he carried me away in the Spirit to a great and high mountain, and showed me the great city, the holy Jerusalem, descending out of heaven from God, having the glory of God.
> (Revelation 21:10–11)

Paragraph No. 21:

To this testify the records of the four Gospels.[102]

102. The signs that according to the scriptures will generally accompany the advent of each Manifestation of God were presented in Note Nos. 51, 52, and 72 above. In the Gospels the same signs are cited for the second advent of Christ.

These are mainly found in the synoptic Gospels, more specifically in Chapter 24 of the Gospel of Matthew, Chapter 13 of the Gospel of Mark, and Chapter 21 of the Gospel of Luke.

Although the Gospel of John has references to the return of Christ, as cited above in a few verses of Chapters 14, 15, and 16, there are no specific signs provided to accompany His return. In the synoptic Gospels, the discourse starts when Jesus and some of His disciples are passing by the Temple, and continues when they go to the garden on Mount Olive. The details of this discourse are discussed in Note No. 121 below.

Paragraph No. 22:

This wronged One[103]

103. "This Wronged One," is a title that Bahá'u'lláh chose for Himself and often used to refer to Himself in His writing. Some examples are provided below:

> Give ear, O distinguished divine, unto the voice of this Wronged One. He verily, counselleth thee for the sake of God, and exhorteth thee unto that which will cause thee to draw nigh unto Him under all conditions.
>
> These words have streamed from the pen of this Wronged One in one of His Tablets: The purpose of the one true God, exalted be His glory, hath been to bring forth the Mystic Gems out of the mine of man.

> This Wronged One hath frequented no school, neither hath He attended the controversies of the learned.
> (Bahá'u'lláh, Epistle to the Son of the Wolf, pp. 2, 11, 132)

Bahá'u'lláh refers to Himself and other Manifestations of God as those whom the world wronged, because They are the most exalted beings, the "Revealers of the Divine revelation," "the Treasury of God's wisdom and the Dawning-Place of His majesty and power," whom, at the time of Their life in this world, instead of being treated with respect, honor, love, and obedience to their teachings, are wronged and subjected to the most cruel and inhumane persecutions. 'Abdu'l-Bahá briefly explains this, when He refers to Bahá'u'lláh as "He Whom the world hath wronged."

> The sacred breast of His Holiness, the Exalted One,[52] (may my life be a sacrifice unto Him) was made a target to many a dart of woe, and in Mázindarán, the Blessed feet of the Abhá Beauty (may my life be offered up for His loved ones) were so grievously scourged as to bleed and be sore wounded. His neck also was put into captive chains and His feet made fast in the stocks. In every hour, for a period of fifty years, a new trial and calamity befell Him and fresh afflictions and cares beset Him. One of them: after having suffered intense vicissitudes, He was made homeless and a wanderer and fell a victim to still new vexations and troubles. In 'Iráq, the Day-Star of the world was so exposed to the wiles of the people of malice as to be eclipsed in splendor. Later on He was sent an exile to the Great City (Constantinople) and thence to the Land of Mystery (Adrianople), whence, grievously wronged, He was eventually transferred to the Most Great Prison ('Akká). He Whom the world hath wronged (may my life be offered up for His loved ones) was four times banished from city to city, till at last condemned to perpetual confinement, He was incarcerated in this Prison, the prison of highway robbers, of brigands and of manslayers. All this is but one of the trials that have afflicted the Blessed Beauty, the rest being even as grievous as this.
> ('Abdu'l-Bahá, quoted in Shoghi Effendi, *Bahá'í Administration*, p. 4)

[52] "His Holiness, the Exalted One," is a title of the Báb.

'Abdu'l-Bahá also refers to Himself as "this wronged one" and "this wronged servant":

> This wronged one hath in no wise borne nor doth he bear a grudge against any one; towards none doth he entertain any ill-feeling and uttereth no word save for the good of the world.
> (*Bahá'í Administration*, p. 11)

> Thou seest this wronged servant of Thine, held fast in the talons of ferocious lions, of ravening wolves, of bloodthirsty beasts.
> ('Abdu'l-Bahá, *Will and Testament of 'Abdu'l-Bahá*, p. 9)

> When the hour cometh that this wronged and broken winged bird will have taken its flight unto the celestial concourse, when it will have hastened to the Realm of the Unseen and its mortal frame will have been either lost or hidden neath the dust,
> ('Abdu'l-Bahá, *Will and Testament of 'Abdu'l-Bahá*, p. 9)

Adib Taherzadeh, in a section titled "The Wronged One of the World," provides an explanation for the submission of Bahá'u'lláh to trials and sufferings:

> In the Fire Tablet we observe two different features of Bahá'u'lláh. The first is the station of sovereignty and lordship, a station exalted above the world of man. In this station He is not affected by the tumult and conflicts of this life, because He is animated by the Most Great Spirit which makes Him independent of all things except God. The other station is that of meekness and submission to God. This is a station in which Bahá'u'lláh is referred to in many of His Tablets as the "Wronged One of the World." In this station He submits Himself to His enemies, welcomes sufferings and accepts bondage and imprisonment so that mankind in this Dispensation may become freed from the fetters of tyranny and oppression and attain the light of unity.
> (Adib Taherzadeh, *The Revelation of Bahá'u'lláh,* vol. 3, p. 231)

> Thou didst manifest Him Who is the Revealer of Thyself and the Treasury of Thy wisdom and the Dawning-Place of

Thy majesty and power. Thou didst establish His covenant with every one who hath been created in the kingdoms of earth and heaven and in the realms of revelation and of creation. Thou didst raise Him up to such heights that the wrongs inflicted by the oppressors have been powerless to deter Him from revealing Thy sovereignty, and the ascendancy of the wayward hath failed to prevent Him from demonstrating Thy power and from exalting Thy Cause.
(Bahá'u'lláh, *Prayers and Meditations,* p. 35)

Glorified art Thou, O Lord my God! I beseech Thee by Thy Name, the Restrainer, to withhold from us the maleficence of Thine adversaries who have disbelieved in Thy testimony, and caviled at Thy beauty. Overpower by Thy Name, the All-Subduing, such as have wronged Thy Previous Manifestation Who hath now appeared invested with Thy title, the All-Glorious.
(Bahá'u'lláh, *Prayers and Meditations,* p. 119)

thus conferring upon mankind, for the sake of God, such bounties as are yet concealed[104]

104. As mentioned above, the signs of the advent of the Manifestations of God as stated in all the sacred scriptures of the past are very similar. The signs of the advent of the Messiah in the Old Testament, and the return of Christ in the New testament, and those of the appearance of the Promised One of Islam in the Islamic traditions are very similar, yet no Manifestations of God in the past explained the meanings of these signs and the symbolic events that would accompany the advent of these Manifestations. Bahá'u'lláh, in the Kitáb-i-Íqán, opened the seals of the treasuries of their true meanings as foretold by the Prophet Daniel, and vouchsafed to mankind those gems that were until that time concealed.

treasury of the hidden and sacred Tree[105]

105. The sacred Tree is the Person of the Manifestation of God as was presented in Note Nos. 24, 42, and 47. The fruit of this tree is the

Revelation that is brought to humanity by the Manifestation of God. It seems that the hidden sacred Tree is the person of Bahá'u'lláh before His public declaration.

> Say: O people! The Tree of Life hath verily been planted in the heart of the heavenly paradise and bestoweth life in every direction. How can ye fail to perceive and recognize it?
> (Bahá'u'lláh, *Gems of Divine Mysteries,* p. 50)

> Verily He is the Tree of Life that bringeth forth the fruits of God, the Exalted, the Powerful, the Great.
> ("Tablet of Ahmad," in *Bahá'í Prayers,* p. 209)

and attain to a dewdrop of the waters of everlasting life[106]

106. Waters of everlasting life are the words of God, which are revealed by the Manifestations of God.

> Verily, verily, I say unto you, He that heareth my word, and believeth on him that sent me, hath everlasting life,
> (John 5:24)

> But whosoever drinketh of the water that I shall give him shall never thirst; but the water that I shall give him shall be in him a well of water springing up into everlasting life.
> (John 4: 14)

from Baghdád, the "Abode of Peace[107]

107. Baghdád, also known as Dár-al-salám in Arabic, meaning "the abode of peace," is located on the banks of the Tigris River. The city dates back to at least the eighth century, and probably to pre-Islamic times. Once the center of the Muslim world, it was the site of the largest university in the world. The name Baghdád might have a Persian origin. Several alternatives have been proposed regarding its specific etymology. The most accepted among these is that the name Baghdád is a Middle Persian compound of two words Bhaga (God) and dád (given), translating to "God-given" or "God's gift."

Dár-al-salám (the abode of peace) is mentioned in two places in the Qur'án:

> And God calleth to the abode of peace; and He guideth whom He will into
> the right way.
> (The Qur'án 10:26)

And also in the Súrah of Cattle:

> This is the path of thy Lord, a straight path. We have detailed Our revelations for a people who take heed. For them is the abode of peace with their Lord. He will be their Protecting Friend because of what they used to do.
> (The Qur'án 6:126–127)

Some Bahá'í scholars hold that these verses of the Qur'án are prophecies for the Declaration of Bahá'u'lláh in Baghdád (the abode of peace), where God calls people to the abode of peace in the presence of the Manifestation of God, Who brings God's Revelation and guides whom He will into His Faith, the right path, and serves as their protecting friend. The above statement by Bahá'u'lláh seems to be an allusion to this Qur'ánic verse and His own upcoming Declaration. The Kitáb-i-Íqán was revealed approximately one year before His public Declaration, and the waters of everlasting life which were flowing from Baghdád refer to the Writings, Tablets, and Books He revealed in Baghdád.

Shoghi Effendi, in describing the flow of divine Revelation in Baghdád, states:

> In that city, described in Islamic traditions as "Ẓahru'l-Kúfih," designated for centuries as the "Abode of Peace," and immortalized by Bahá'u'lláh as the "City of God," . . . From it radiated, wave after wave, a power, a radiance and a glory which insensibly reanimated a languishing Faith, sorely-stricken, sinking into obscurity, threatened with oblivion. From it were diffused, day and night, and with ever-increasing energy, the first emanations of a Revelation which, in its scope, its copiousness, its driving force and

> the volume and variety of its literature, was destined to excel that of the Báb Himself.
> (Shoghi Effendi, *God Passes By*, p. 109)

For more information regarding Baghdád, see the Appendix II.

"We nourish your souls for the sake of God; we seek from you neither recompense nor thanks.[108]

108. Súrah of Man, the Qur'án, 76:9.

This is the bread of which it is said: "Lord, send down upon us Thy bread from heaven."[109]

109. This verse is a part of the Súrah of Table:

> Remember when the Apostles said—"O Jesus, son of Mary! is thy Lord able to send down a furnished table to us out of Heaven?" He said—"Fear God if ye be believers." They said—"We desire to eat therefrom, and to have our hearts assured; and to know that thou hast indeed spoken truth to us, and to be witnesses thereof." Jesus, Son of Mary, said—"O God, our Lord! send down a table to us out of Heaven, that it may become a recurring festival to us, to the first of us and to the last of us, and a sign from thee; and do thou nourish us, for thou art the best of nourishers." And God said—Verily, I will cause it to descend unto you; but whoever among you after that shall disbelieve, I will surely chastise him with a chastisement, wherewith I will not chastise any other creature.
> (The Qur'án 5:115–117)

The above is from the Rodwell translation. Rodwell translated the Arabic word "Maedeh," which means an assortment of delicious foods, as "table," but a better translation is "food" as found in the following translation:

> When the disciples said: O Jesus, son of Mary! Is thy Lord able to send down for us a table spread with food from heaven ? He said: Observe your duty to Allah, if ye are true

> believers. (They said:) We wish to eat thereof, that we may satisfy our hearts and know that thou hast spoken truth to us, and that thereof we may be witnesses. Jesus, son of Mary, said: O Allah, Lord of us! Send down for us a table spread with food from heaven, that it may be a feast for us, for the first of us and for the last of us, and a sign from Thee. Give us sustenance, for Thou art the Best of Sustainers. Allah said: Lo! I send it down for you. And whoso disbelieveth of you afterward, him surely will I punish with a punishment wherewith I have not punished any of (My) creatures.
> (The Qur'án, Pickthall tr, Súrah 5, The Food)

In Biblical terminology the word bread is also used for food in general. As discussed in Note No. 25 above, the bread or food or "manna" that comes down from heaven is the divine Revelation, as related in the Gospel of John, Chapter 6, when the Jews tell Jesus that their fathers eat from the manna that came down from heaven, and ask Him to bring down bread or manna so that they will believe in Him. Jesus states that the Manifestation of God and His Revelation are the real food that comes from Heaven:

> They said therefore unto him, What sign showest thou then, that we may see, and believe thee? what dost thou work? Our fathers did eat manna in the desert; as it is written, He gave them bread from heaven to eat. Then Jesus said unto them, Verily, verily, I say unto you, Moses gave you not that bread from heaven; but my Father giveth you the true bread from heaven. For the bread of God is he which cometh down from heaven, and giveth life unto the world. Then said they unto him, Lord, evermore give us this bread. And Jesus said unto them, I am the bread of life: he that cometh to me shall never hunger; and he that believeth on me shall never thirst.
> (John 6:30–35)

Despite this explanation, the Jews were still confused:

> The Jews then murmured at him, because he said, I am the bread which came down from heaven. And they said, Is not this Jesus, the son of Joseph, whose father and mother we know? how is it then that he saith, I came down from heaven?
> (John 6:41–42)

He added to their confusion with the following:

> I am that bread of life. Your fathers did eat manna in the wilderness, and are dead. This is the bread which cometh down from heaven, that a man may eat thereof, and not die. I am the living bread which came down from heaven: if any man eat of this bread, he shall live for ever: and the bread that I will give is my flesh, which I will give for the life of the world. The Jews therefore strove among themselves, saying, How can this man give us his flesh to eat? Then Jesus said unto them, Verily, verily, I say unto you, Except ye eat the flesh of the Son of man, and drink his blood, ye have no life in you. Whoso eateth my flesh, and drinketh my blood, hath eternal life; and I will raise him up at the last day. For my flesh is meat indeed, and my blood is drink indeed. He that eateth my flesh, and drinketh my blood, dwelleth in me, and I in him. As the living Father hath sent me, and I live by the Father: so he that eateth me, even he shall live by me. This is that bread which came down from heaven: not as your fathers did eat manna, and are dead: he that eateth of this bread shall live for ever. These things said he in the synagogue, as he taught in Capernaum. Many therefore of his disciples, when they had heard this, said, This is an hard saying; who can hear it? When Jesus knew in himself that his disciples' murmured at it, he said unto them, Doth this offend you? What and if ye shall see the Son of man ascend up where he was before? It is the spirit that quickeneth; the flesh profiteth nothing: the words that I speak unto you, they are spirit, and they are life. . . . From that time many of his disciples went back, and walked no more with him.
> (John 6:48–66)

'Abdu'l-Bahá also explains and clarifies the meanings of the words of Christ that are as confusing to the present-day Christians as it was to the Jews at the time of Christ.

> It is evident that the loaves of which the disciples ate, and with which they were filled, were the heavenly grace, for in verse 33 of the same chapter it is said: "For the bread of God is He which cometh down from heaven, and giveth life

unto the world." It is evident that the body of Christ did not descend from heaven but came from the womb of Mary: What descended from the heaven of God was the spirit of Christ. The Jews, presuming that Christ was speaking of His body, objected, as is recorded in verse 42 of the same chapter: "And they said, Is not this Jesus, the son of Joseph, whose father and mother we know? how is it then that he saith, I came down from heaven?"

Consider how evident it is that what Christ intended by the heavenly bread was His spirit, His manifold grace, His perfections, and His teachings; for in verse 63 of the aforementioned chapter it is said: "It is the spirit that quickeneth; the flesh profiteth nothing."

It has therefore been made evident that the spirit of Christ was a celestial bounty which descended from heaven, and that whosoever receives the outpourings of this spirit—that is, embraces its heavenly teachings—will attain everlasting life. Thus it is said in verse 35: "And Jesus said unto them, I am the bread of life: he that cometh to Me shall never hunger; and he that believeth on Me shall never thirst."

Observe that He expresses "coming to Him" as eating, and "believing in Him" as drinking. It is therefore clearly established that the heavenly sustenance consists in the divine bounties, spiritual splendours, heavenly teachings, and all-embracing truths of Christ, and that to eat means to draw nigh unto Him and to drink means to believe in Him. For Christ had both an elemental and a heavenly body. The elemental body was crucified, but the heavenly one is alive, eternal, and the source of everlasting life. The elemental body was His human nature and the heavenly body His divine nature. Gracious God! Some imagine that the bread of the Eucharist is the reality of Christ, and that the Divinity and the Holy Spirit have descended into it and are present therein, whereas when once the Eucharist is taken, in a few minutes it is wholly disintegrated and entirely transformed. How then can such an error be conceived? I beg the forgiveness of God for such a grave delusion!
('Abdu'l-Bahá, *Some Answered Questions*, no. 21.3–6)

Bahá'u'lláh clarifies the true meaning of the bread that comes down from heaven:

> Know thou that, according to what thy Lord, the Lord of all men, hath decreed in His Book, these favors vouchsafed by Him unto mankind have been, and will ever remain, limitless in their range. First and foremost among these gifts that the Almighty hath conferred upon man is the gift of understanding. . . . Next in rank is the power of vision, the chief instrument whereby his understanding can function. . . .
>
> These gifts are inherent in man himself. That which is preeminent above all other gifts, is incorruptible in nature, and pertaineth to God Himself, is the gift of Divine Revelation. Every bounty conferred by the creator, be it material or spiritual, is subservient unto this. It is, in its essence, and will ever so remain, the Bread that cometh down from Heaven. It is God's supreme testimony, the clearest evidence of His truth, the sign of His consummate bounty, the token of His all-encompassing mercy, the proof of His most loving providence, the symbol of His most perfect grace. He hath, indeed, partaken of this highest gift of God who hath recognized His Manifestation in this Day.
> (*Gleanings from the Writings of Bahá'u'lláh,* p. 195)

Even as He saith: "Seest thou not to what God likeneth a good word? To a good tree; its root firmly fixed, and its branches reaching unto heaven: yielding its fruit in all seasons."[110]

110. This verse is from the Qur'án, Súrah 14:

> But they who shall have believed and done the things that be right, shall be brought into gardens beneath which the rivers flow: therein shall they abide for ever by the permission of their Lord: their greeting therein shall be, "Peace." Seest thou not to what God likeneth a good word? To a good tree: its root firmly fixed, and its branches in the Heaven: Yielding its fruit in all seasons by the will of its

> Lord. God setteth forth these similitudes to men that haply they may reflect."
> (The Qur'án 14:24–30)

Paragraph No. 23:

It behooveth him to prize this food that cometh from heaven, that perchance, through the wondrous favours of the Sun of Truth, the dead may be brought to life, and the withered souls be quickened by the infinite Spirit[111]

111. The dead might be brought to life by receiving the Revelation of God, and the withered souls be quickened and revived. As Jesus and Bahá'u'lláh both stated:

> Jesus said unto her, I am the resurrection, and the life: he that believeth in me, though he were dead, yet shall he live: And whosoever liveth and believeth in me shall never die.
> (John 11:25–26)

> My God, my Adored One, my King, my Desire! What tongue can voice my thanks to Thee? I was heedless, Thou didst awaken me. I had turned back from Thee, Thou didst graciously aid me to turn towards Thee. I was as one dead, Thou didst quicken me with the water of life. I was withered, Thou didst revive me with the heavenly stream of Thine utterance which hath flowed forth from the Pen of the All-Merciful.

> O Divine Providence! All existence is begotten by Thy bounty; deprive it not of the waters of Thy generosity, neither do Thou withhold it from the ocean of Thy mercy. I beseech Thee to aid and assist me at all times and under all conditions, and seek from the heaven of Thy grace Thine ancient favor. Thou art, in truth, the Lord of bounty, and the Sovereign of the kingdom of eternity.
> (Bahá'u'lláh, *Prayers and Meditations*, p. 264)

Make haste, O my brother, that while there is yet time our lips may taste of the immortal draught[112]

112.Immortal draught" is also a reference to divine revelation. The very beautiful "Ode of the Divine Cupbearer" by Bahá'u'lláh speaks of the immortal/eternal wine in the first couplet:

> O Cupbearer, from the unseen immortal realm, cast aside the veil from your countenance
> That I may drink the eternal wine from the beauty of the Devine Providence
>
> That which you have in the wine Cellar will not break the bile of love
> From that wine of inner meaning, Cupbearer, bring forth an ocean
> (Bahá'u'lláh, "Ode of the Divine Cupbearer," "Sáqí az ghayb-i-baghá")

For full text of a provisional translation of this Ode, See Appendix II, Note No. 11.

for the breeze of life, now blowing from the city of the Well-Beloved[113]

113. The breeze of life blowing from the city of the Well-Beloved,[53] is an allusion to the story of Joseph in the Qur'án. See Appendix III, the story of Joseph.

and the portals of the Riḍván cannot for ever remain open[114]

114. Riḍván, in the sacred Writings, is a reference to the garden of Heaven or paradise. In many places in the Bahá'í Writings, Riḍván is used as a reference to the presence of the Manifestations of God and/or Their sacred Writings (see also above, Note Nos. 89 and 90).

The day will surely come when the Nightingale of Paradise[115]

115. In the Writings of Bahá'u'lláh, the Nightingale or Dove is used to symbolize the Manifestation of God, especially Himself.

---

[53] The City of the Well-Beloved is a translation of (مصر جانان, literally "the Egypt of the Well-Beloved").

He is the King, the All-Knowing, the Wise! Lo, the Nightingale of Paradise singeth upon the twigs of the Tree of Eternity, with holy and sweet melodies, proclaiming to the sincere ones the glad tidings of the nearness of God, calling the believers in the Divine Unity to the court of the Presence of the Generous One, informing the severed ones of the message which hath been revealed by God, the King, the Glorious, the Peerless, guiding the lovers to the seat of sanctity and to this resplendent Beauty.
(*Bahá'í Prayers*, p. 208)

O Shaykh! We have enabled thee to hear the melodies of the Nightingale of Paradise, and unveiled to thine eyes the signs which God, by His all-compelling behest, hath sent down in the Most Great Prison, that thine eye might be cheered, and thy soul be well-assured. He, verily, is the All-Bounteous, the Generous.
(Bahá'u'lláh, Epistle to the Son of the Wolf, p. 103)

O SON OF SPIRIT! The time cometh, when the nightingale of holiness will no longer unfold the inner mysteries and ye will all be bereft of the celestial melody and of the voice from on high.
(Bahá'u'lláh, The Hidden Words, Persian, no. 15)

Alas, alas, for that which befell Him Who was the Manifestation of the Self of God, and for that which He and His loved ones were made to suffer! The people inflicted upon them what no soul hath ever inflicted upon another, and what no infidel hath wrought against a believer or suffered at his hand. Alas, alas! That immortal Being sat upon the darksome dust, the Holy Spirit lamented in the retreats of glory, the pillars of the Throne crumbled in the exalted dominion, the joy of the world was changed into sorrow in the crimson land, and the voice of the Nightingale was silenced in the golden realm. Woe betide them for what their hands have wrought and for what they have committed!
(Bahá'u'lláh, *Gems of Divine Mysteries*, p. 20)

But for Him, how could the Celestial Dove have uttered its songs or the Heavenly Nightingale, according to the decree of God, have warbled its melody?
(Bahá'u'lláh, *Prayers and Meditations*, p. 295)

I bear witness that thou hast hearkened unto the melody of God and His sweet accents, inclined thine ear to the cooing of the Dove of divine Revelation and hast heard the Nightingale of fidelity pouring forth its notes upon the Branch of Glory: Verily there is none other God but Me, the Incomparable, the All-Informed.
(Bahá'u'lláh, *Tablets of Bahá'u'lláh*, p. 240)

Say, by the righteousness of God! The All-Merciful is come invested with power and sovereignty. Through His power the foundations of religions have quaked and the Nightingale of Utterance hath warbled its melody upon the highest branch of true understanding. Verily, He Who was hidden in the knowledge of God and is mentioned in the Holy Scriptures hath appeared. Say, this is the Day when the Speaker on Sinai hath mounted the throne of Revelation and the people have stood before the Lord of the worlds.
(Bahá'u'lláh, *Tablets of Bahá'u'lláh*, p. 107)

Hearken ye, O Rulers of America and the Presidents of the Republics therein, unto that which the Dove is warbling on the Branch of Eternity.
(Bahá'u'lláh, The Kitáb-i-Aqdas, ¶88)

Then will its melody be heard no more, and the beauty of the rose cease to shine[116]

116. References to the bounty of the presence of the Manifestation of God ,which is the essence of beauty, are repeated in other places in the Writings:

Hear Me, ye mortal birds! In the Rose Garden of changeless splendor a Flower hath begun to bloom, compared to which every other flower is but a thorn, and before the brightness of Whose glory the very essence of beauty must pale and wither. Arise, therefore, and, with the

> whole enthusiasm of your hearts, with all the eagerness of your souls, the full fervor of your will, and the concentrated efforts of your entire being, strive to attain the paradise of His presence, and endeavor to inhale the fragrance of the incorruptible Flower, to breathe the sweet savors of holiness, and to obtain a portion of this perfume of celestial glory. Whoso followeth this counsel will break his chains asunder, will taste the abandonment of enraptured love, will attain unto his heart's desire, and will surrender his soul into the hands of his Beloved. Bursting through his cage, he will, even as the bird of the spirit, wing his flight to his holy and everlasting nest.
> (Bahá'u'lláh, *Gleanings from the Writings of Bahá'u'lláh,* p. 320)

> The everlasting Candle shineth in its naked glory. Behold how it hath consumed every mortal veil. O ye moth-like lovers of His light! Brave every danger, and consecrate your souls to its consuming flame. O ye that thirst after Him! Strip yourselves of every earthly affection, and hasten to embrace your Beloved. With a zest that none can equal make haste to attain unto Him. The Flower, thus far hidden from the sight of men, is unveiled to your eyes. In the open radiance of His glory He standeth before you. His voice summoneth all the holy and sanctified beings to come and be united with Him. Happy is he that turneth thereunto; well is it with him that hath attained, and gazed on the light of so wondrous a countenance.
> (Bahá'u'lláh, *Gleanings from the Writings of Bahá'u'lláh,* p. 321)

Seize the time, therefore, ere the glory of the divine springtime hath spent itself[117]

117. The divine springtime is the time of the appearance of the Manifestations of God, and the theme of the importance and preciousness of the divine springtime is mentioned in many places in the Writings. Bahá'u'lláh, referring to His Declaration in the Garden of Riḍván, revealed a Tablet with this opening:

> The Divine Springtime is come, O Most Exalted Pen, for the Festival of the All-Merciful is fast approaching. Bestir thyself, and magnify, before the entire creation, the name of

> God, and celebrate His praise, in such wise that all created things may be regenerated and made new. Speak, and hold not thy peace.
> (Bahá'u'lláh, *Gleanings from the Writings of Bahá'u'lláh*, p. 27)

> O friends! It behooveth you to refresh and revive your souls through the gracious favors which in this Divine, this soul-stirring Springtime are being showered upon you. The Daystar of His great glory hath shed its radiance upon you, and the clouds of His limitless grace have overshadowed you. How high the reward of him that hath not deprived himself of so great a bounty, nor failed to recognize the beauty of his Best-Beloved in this, His new attire.
> (Bahá'u'lláh, *Gleanings from the Writings of Bahá'u'lláh*, p. 94)

> The hearts of Thy dear ones, however, will rejoice only at the Divine Springtime of Thy tender mercies, whereby the hearts are quickened, and the souls are renewed, and the trees of human existence bear their fruits. The plants that have sprung forth, O my Lord, in the hearts of Thy loved ones have withered away. Send down upon them, from the clouds of Thy spirit, that which will cause the tender herbs of Thy knowledge and wisdom to grow within their breasts.
> (Bahá'u'lláh, *Prayers and Meditations*, p. 199)

Whosoever wisheth, let him turn thereunto: whosoever wisheth, let him turn away[118]

118. This is the most important case of the freedom of choice that man is endowed with, the recognition of the Manifestation of God for his age, and acceptance or rejection of His call and His Cause.

> Thus doth the Nightingale utter His call unto you from this prison. He hath but to deliver this clear message. Whosoever desireth, let him turn aside from this counsel and whosoever desireth let him choose the path to his Lord.
> (*Bahá'í Prayers*, p. 209)

Those who miss this privilege and turn away do this to their own peril, because God is independent of their acceptance or rejection.

Paragraph No. 24:

These are the melodies, sung by Jesus, Son of Mary[119]

119. In the Qur'án, as well as in some Islamic traditions and some of the Writings of the Báb and Bahá'u'lláh, Jesus is referred to as "Jesus, Son of Mary." This is an allusion to the Immaculate Conception of Jesus. Although among the Jews and other Middle-Eastern people, a young man was usually referred to as the son of "name of his father" (such as Isaac, son of Jacob), in the Qur'án Jesus is called "Son of Mary," because no man was His father. Jesus is also referred to by other titles in those sacred Writings such as the "Spirit of God," the "Messiah," and the "Word of God." There is only one place in the Gospels where Jesus is called "Son of Mary."

> Is not this the carpenter, the son of Mary, the brother of James, and Joses, and of Juda, and Simon? and are not his sisters here with us?
> (Mark 6:3)

in accents of majestic power in the Riḍván of the Gospel[120]

120. Please see Note No. 114 above.

revealing those signs that must needs herald the advent of the Manifestation after Him[121]

121. As mentioned in Note No. 102, above, the signs of the next advent of Christ are mainly found in the synoptic Gospels, more specifically in Chapter 24 of the Gospel of Matthew, Chapter 13 of the Gospel of Mark, and Chapter 21 of the Gospel of Luke. Although the Gospel of John has references to the return of Christ in a few verses of Chapters 14, 15, and 16, there are no specific signs provided to accompany His return. Those chapters of the synoptic Gospels are known as the "Olivet Discourse." The Olivet Discourse begins when Jesus prophesies regarding the destruction of the Temple, and His words are very similar in all three Gospels:

> And Jesus went out, and departed from the temple: and his disciples came to him for to shew him the buildings of the temple. And Jesus said unto them, See ye not all these things? verily I say unto you, There shall not be left here one stone upon another, that shall not be thrown down.
> (Matthew 24:1–3)

> And as he went out of the temple, one of his disciples saith unto him, Master, see what manner of stones and what buildings are here! And Jesus answering said unto him, Seest thou these great buildings? there shall not be left one stone upon another, that shall not be thrown down.
> (Mark 13:1–2)

> And as some spake of the temple, how it was adorned with goodly stones and gifts, he said, As for these things which ye behold, the days will come, in the which there shall not be left one stone upon another, that shall not be thrown down.
> (Luke 21:5–6)

Then the Disciples asked Him to elaborate more about His statement:

> And as he sat upon the mount of Olives, the disciples came unto him privately, saying, Tell us, when shall these things be? and what shall be the sign of thy coming, and of the end of the world?.
> (Matthew 24:4)

> And as he sat upon the mount of Olives over against the temple, Peter and James and John and Andrew asked him privately, Tell us, when shall these things be? and what shall be the sign when all these things shall be fulfilled?
> (Mark 13:3–4)

> And they asked him, saying, Master, but when shall these things be? and what sign will there be when these things shall come to pass?
> (Luke 21:7)

According to the Gospel of Matthew, upon Mount Olive the disciples asked Him three questions:

a) Tell us, when shall these things be?
b) and what shall be the sign of thy coming,
c) and of the end of the world?

According to the Gospel of Mark, upon Mount Olive, Peter, James, John, and Andrew asked Him two questions:

a) Tell us, when shall these things be?
b) and what shall be the sign when all these things shall be fulfilled?

According to the Gospel of Luke, upon Mount Olive, they [the disciples] asked Him two questions:

a) but when shall these things be?
b) and what sign will there be when these things shall come to pass?

The prophecy of Jesus was regarding the destruction of the Temple. As stated in Mark and Luke, the disciples' questions were only related to this prophecy. They were asking: when shall these things be, and what shall be the sign when all these things shall be fulfilled? However, according to the Gospel of Matthew, the Disciples asked three questions. Only the first one is related to the destruction of the Temple: "when shall these things be?" The second is regarding the signs of His coming, and the third is regarding the end of the world. Although the present popular evangelical Christian belief is that His coming and the end of the world are synonymous events, some Biblical scholars hold that these are two chronologically different events, and that in reality three questions were asked.

In the first Gospel according to Matthew[122]

122. The Gospel of Matthew is the first book or first Gospel among the four Gospels that are included in the New Testament. However, historically and chronologically, as Bart Ehrman stated:

> Scholars have long recognized that Mark was the first Gospel to be written, and that both Matthew and Luke used Mark's account as a source for their own stories about Jesus.
> (Bart Ehrman, *Misquoting Jesus*, p. 135)

It is noteworthy that although as indicated above, the Gospel of Mark was the source material for both Matthew and Luke, the record of this discourse in the Gospels of Mark (the source) and Luke, does not indicate that the disciples asked a question regarding the second advent of Christ. However, His response, (the contents of the relevant chapters in the three Gospels) is very similar in all three, with each containing statements regarding His next advent. This discourse as recorded in the Gospel of Matthew is more detailed (see the full text and the Table of comparison of the Olivet Discourse in the Synoptic Gospels in Appendix IV), and because Bahá'u'lláh made direct reference to the Gospel of Matthew, the contents of chapter 24 of this Gospel are examined here in detail.

when they asked Jesus concerning the signs of His coming[123]

123. Matthew, Chapter 24, states:

> And Jesus went out, and departed from the temple: and his disciples came to him for to shew him the buildings of the temple. And Jesus said unto them, See ye not all these things? verily I say unto you, There shall not be left here one stone upon another, that shall not be thrown down. And as he sat upon the mount of Olives, the disciples came unto him privately, saying, Tell us, when shall these things be? and what shall be the sign of thy coming, and of the end of the world? And Jesus answered and said unto them, Take heed that no man deceive you. For many shall come in my name, saying, I am Christ; and shall deceive many. And ye shall hear of wars and rumors of wars: see that ye be not troubled: for all these things must come to pass, but the end is not yet. For nation shall rise against nation, and kingdom against kingdom: and there shall be famines, and pestilences, and earthquakes, in divers places. All these are

the beginning of sorrows. Then shall they deliver you up to be afflicted, and shall kill you: and ye shall be hated of all nations for my name's sake. And then shall many be offended, and shall betray one another, and shall hate one another. And many false prophets shall rise, and shall deceive many. And because iniquity shall abound, the love of many shall wax cold. But he that shall endure unto the end, the same shall be saved. And this gospel of the kingdom shall be preached in all the world for a witness unto all nations; and then shall the end come. When ye therefore shall see the abomination of desolation, spoken of by Daniel the prophet, stand in the holy place, (whoso readeth, let him understand:) Then let them which be in Judaea flee into the mountains: Let him which is on the housetop not come down to take any thing out of his house: Neither let him which is in the field return back to take his clothes. And woe unto them that are with child, and to them that give suck in those days! But pray ye that your flight be not in the winter, neither on the sabbath day: For then shall be great tribulation, such as was not since the beginning of the world to this time, no, nor ever shall be. And except those days should be shortened, there should no flesh be saved: but for the elect's sake those days shall be shortened. Then if any man shall say unto you, Lo, here is Christ, or there; believe it not. For there shall arise false Christs, and false prophets, and shall shew great signs and wonders; insomuch that, if it were possible, they shall deceive the very elect. Behold, I have told you before. Wherefore if they shall say unto you, Behold, he is in the desert; go not forth: behold, he is in the secret chambers; believe it not. For as the lightning cometh out of the east, and shineth even unto the west; so shall also the coming of the Son of man be. For wheresoever the carcase is, there will the eagles be gathered together. Immediately after the tribulation of those days shall the sun be darkened, and the moon shall not give her light, and the stars shall fall from heaven, and the powers of the heavens shall be shaken: And then shall appear the sign of the Son of man in heaven: and then shall all the tribes of the earth mourn, and they shall see the Son of man coming in the clouds of heaven with power and great glory. And he shall send his angels

> with a great sound of a trumpet, and they shall gather together his elect from the four winds, from one end of heaven to the other. Now learn a parable of the fig tree; When his branch is yet tender, and putteth forth leaves, ye know that summer is nigh: So likewise ye, when ye shall see all these things, know that it is near, even at the doors. Verily I say unto you, This generation shall not pass, till all these things be fulfilled. Heaven and earth shall pass away, but my words shall not pass away. But of that day and hour knoweth no man, no, not the angels of heaven, but my Father only. But as the days of Noe were, so shall also the coming of the Son of man be. For as in the days that were before the flood they were eating and drinking, marrying and giving in marriage, until the day that Noe entered into the ark, And knew not until the flood came, and took them all away; so shall also the coming of the Son of man be. Then shall two be in the field; the one shall be taken, and the other left. Two women shall be grinding at the mill; the one shall be taken, and the other left. Watch therefore: for ye know not what hour your Lord doth come. But know this, that if the goodman of the house had known in what watch the thief would come, he would have watched, and would not have suffered his house to be broken up. Therefore be ye also ready: for in such an hour as ye think not the Son of man cometh. Who then is a faithful and wise servant, whom his lord hath made ruler over his household, to give them meat in due season? Blessed is that servant, whom his lord when he cometh shall find so doing. Verily I say unto you, That he shall make him ruler over all his goods. But and if that evil servant shall say in his heart, My lord delayeth his coming; And shall begin to smite his fellow servants, and to eat and drink with the drunken; The lord of that servant shall come in a day when he looketh not for him, and in an hour that he is not aware of, And shall cut him asunder, and appoint him his portion with the hypocrites: there shall be weeping and gnashing of teeth.
> (Matthew 24:1–51)

The Chapter 24 of the Gospel of Matthew, known as "Olivet Discourse," also called the Synoptic Gospels' Apocalypse (the Greek word meaning revelation), as a parallel to the St. John's

Apocalypse or the "Book of Revelation" (the last book of the New Testament), has close connections to the Book of Revelation and the Book of Daniel in the Old Testament, as all these documents deal with eschatological issues (issues related to the end of the age or the end of time).

Many scholars maintain that the Olivet Discourse and Christ's Resurrection are the two most important, theologically complex, and widely discussed subjects presented in the Gospels. While the Resurrection, whether literal and physical or spiritual and allegorical, has already taken place, Christian perception of the nature, the unfoldment of the process, and the chronological schedule of the Olivet Discourse as a complex combination of future historical and theological processes has been evolving over the past twenty centuries.

There has historically been opposing views regarding the nature of the statements made by Christ regarding the destruction of the Temple and His next advent:

1. The first view is that the prophecies of the Olivet Discourse are all literal, and as the prophecies regarding the destruction of the Temple were fulfilled literally, the other prophecies regarding His next advent will also be fulfilled literally, and the same Jesus of Nazareth with the same corporal body will descend from heaven riding the physical clouds for all eyes to see.
2. The second view holds that the destruction of the Temple and the return of Christ as presented in the Olivet Discourse were not intended as physical events to take place in physical form, but as events that have or will occur spiritually.
3. The third view maintains that the questions the Disciples asked Jesus are three parts of the same question, and that Jesus' response (the totality of the Olivet Discourse) only refers to the destruction of the Temple and Jewish state, and that nothing is spoken concerning the end of time or age.
4. The fourth view asserts that the text of the Olivet Discourse, like other parts of the Gospels, is a mixture of

> literal and figurative or allegorical statements, and can be understood if put in the proper context.

There have also been opposing views regarding the Unfoldment process and the timeline of the events. The Unfoldment process is generally believed to have four important parts and components:

- The destruction of the Temple
- The tribulation and persecution of the elect (believers)
- The establishment of the Kingdom of God and commencement of a millennium of peace
- The second advent of Christ

Although there has been general agreement throughout Christian history regarding the sequence of events concerning the destruction of the Temple and tribulation and persecution of the elect before the establishment of the Kingdom, the time and nature of the Second Advent has been the subject of disagreement among Biblical scholars. The two opposing views are represented by "post-millennialism" and "pre-millennialism." The group that holds the first view believes that the Second Advent will take place after the Christians overcome evil and establish the Kingdom of God on earth, while the other group believes that when Christ returns, He will destroy the evil and Himself establish the kingdom of God and start the millennium.

The chronological aspects of the eschatological statements in the Olivet Discourse have also been the subject of much controversy among Biblical scholars. There are four types of eschatology presented in the Gospels, namely: the realized, the near, the far, and the indefinite (see Daniel Gorlin, *Jesus and Early Christians in the Gospels,* pp. 205–8).

The first, the "realized eschatology," is that the Kingdom of God or the Kingdom of Heaven, the imminent advent of which was proclaimed by John the Baptist, was established in the hearts of the people who received the Word of God:

> And when he was demanded of the Pharisees, when the kingdom of God should come, he answered them and said, The kingdom of God cometh not with observation: Neither

> shall they say, Lo here! or, lo there! for, behold, the kingdom of God is within you.
> (Luke 17:20–21)

The second or the "near eschatology" is the proclamation of the eminent coming of the end of the world or time and the Second Advent. This intends to invoke a sense of urgency as when John the Baptist preached that the Kingdom of God was at hand, or when Jesus said that all this will happen within the span of one generation.

> Verily I say unto you, This generation shall not pass, till all these things be fulfilled.
> (Matthew 24:34)

Also the statement made by Jesus in answer to Caiaphas the Jewish high priest at His trial, when He was asked if He was the Christ, the son of the Blessed:

> Again the high priest asked him, and said unto him, Art thou the Christ, the Son of the Blessed? And Jesus said, I am: and ye shall see the Son of man sitting on the right hand of power, and coming in the clouds of heaven.
> (Mark 14:61–62)

In this statement Jesus is predicting that the high priest will himself see Jesus coming in the clouds of heaven.

The third or "far away eschatology" holds that the time of the end is some time in the distant future. The scriptural basis for this is found in the following statement of Christ:

> And this gospel of the kingdom shall be preached in all the world for a witness unto all nations; and then shall the end come. When ye therefore shall see the abomination of desolation, spoken of by Daniel the prophet, stand in the holy place, (whoso readeth, let him understand).
> (Matthew 24:14–15)

The fact that Jesus makes reference to the Book of Daniel focuses the attention and evokes the enquiry regarding the prophecies and dates given in the last five chapters of this book. The

eschatological vision is punctuated by time periods related to "the abomination of desolation." According to Daniel's vision the desolation which will come upon the Temple will end after a period of "two thousand three hundred days" (or 2300 years), and as mentioned by Daniel, this vision refers to the time of the end. By referring to the Book of Daniel, Christ is connecting His response to the Disciples' question regarding the time of the end and His coming, to the time of the end specified by Daniel. As additional prophecies provided in chapter 9 of the Book of Daniel (seventy weeks), are related to the coming of the Messiah, and they clearly correspond to the first advent, the starting and ending dates of these prophecies are ascertained and the scriptural basis of the "far eschatology" is established.
(For additional materials on this subject, see the section related to Notes No. 121 and 122 in Appendix IV)

The fourth or "indefinite eschatology" indicates that the time of the end will definitely come, but we do not know when. Would it be within the life of one generation, within one or two centuries, or millenniums? This keeps the believers in a state of constant alertness to be ready for the Second Advent at any time. The scriptural basis for the indefinite eschatology are found in several of Jesus' statements in the Olivet Discourse:

> 36: But of that day and hour knoweth no man, no, not the angels of heaven, but my Father only . . . 43: Watch therefore: for ye know not what hour your Lord doth come. But know this, that if the goodman of the house had known in what watch the thief would come, he would have watched, and would not have suffered his house to be broken up. 44: Therefore be ye also ready: for in such an hour as ye think not the Son of man cometh."
> (Matthew 24:36–44)

It is interesting to note that in the Gospel of Mark (which as mentioned above, was the source for the Gospels of Matthew and Luke), this lack of knowledge regarding the time of the end and second advent is mentioned in the following verse:

> But of that day and that hour knoweth no man, no, not the angels which are in heaven, neither the Son, but the Father.
> (Mark 13:32)

Some Biblical scholars cite this as an example of changes made in the text by scribes either to correct what they perceived to be an error, or for theological reasons:

> Scribes found this passage difficult: the Son of God, Jesus himself, does not know when the end will come? How could that be? Isn't he all-knowing? To resolve the problem, some scribes simply modified the text by taking out the words" nor even the Son." Now the angels may be ignorant, but the Son of God isn't.
> (Bart Ehrman, *Misquoting Jesus,* p. 95)

The majority view of the Christians has in different historical eras been close to some combination of the above alternatives in accordance to the situation and the prevailing conditions of the Christian communities at different times.

The first View

The Temple was the permanent structure that was built as the replacement for the Tabernacle that was constructed during the Exodus when the Israelites established their rule in the Holy land. As stated in Note No. 4 above, the Tabernacle and, later on, the Temple was the place and sign of the presence of God amidst His chosen people, where the sacrifices were offered for atonement of the sins. It was the heart, the focal center, and the sign of the unity of their tribes and their independence as a nation.

Although at the time of Christ, the Holy Land and the nation of Israel were under the rule of the Roman Empire for almost a century, the Temple was in operation by the Jewish religious establishment. However, within a few decades of the Olivet Discourse, the Jews could not tolerate the rule of the Romans much longer and in AD 66 revolted against the Roman rule, and subsequently Titus the Roman Emperor issued an order for the destruction of Jerusalem. Adam Clarke, in his commentary on Matthew 24:2 ("There shall not be left here one stone upon another"), states:

> These seem to have been the last words he spoke as he left the temple, into which he never afterwards entered; and,

> when he got to the mount of Olives, he renewed the discourse. From this mount, on which our Lord and his disciples now sat, the whole of the city, and particularly the temple, were clearly seen. This part of our Lord's prediction was fulfilled in the most literal manner. Josephus says, War, book vii. c. 1: "Caesar gave orders that they should now demolish the whole city and temple, . . . except the three towers, Phaselus, Hippicus, and Mariamne, and a part of the western wall, and these were spared; but, for all the rest of the wall, it was laid so completely even with the ground, by those who dug it up to the foundation, that there was left nothing to make those that came thither believe it had ever been inhabited." Maimonides, a Jewish rabbin, in Tract. Taanith, c. 4, says, "That the very foundations of the temple were digged up, according to the Roman custom." His words are these: "On that ninth day of the month Ab, fatal for vengeance, the wicked Turnus Rufus, of the children of Edom, ploughed up the temple, and the places round about it, that the saying might be fulfilled, Zion shall be ploughed as a field." This Turnus, or rather Terentius Rufus, was left general of the army by Titus, with commission, as the Jews suppose, to destroy the city and the temple, as Josephus (an early Christian historian) observes. The temple was destroyed, 1st. Justly; because of the sins of the Jews. 2dly. Mercifully; to take away from them the occasion of continuing in Judaism: and 3dly. Mysteriously; to show that the ancient sacrifices were abolished, and that the whole Jewish economy was brought to an end, and the Christian dispensation introduced."

Regarding the next verse "For many shall come in my name" Adam Clarke states:

> "1. Josephus says, (War, b. ii. c. 13), that there were many who, pretending to Divine inspiration, deceived the people, leading out numbers of them to the desert, pretending that God would there show them the signs of liberty, meaning redemption from the Roman power: and that an Egyptian false prophet led 30,000 men into the desert, who were almost all cut off by Felix. See Acts 21:38. It was a just judgment for God to deliver up

that people into the hands of false Christs who had rejected the true one. Soon after our Lord's crucifixion, Simon Magus appeared, and persuaded the people of Samaria that he was the great power of God, Acts 8:9, 10; and boasted among the Jews that he was the son of God.

2. Of the same stamp and character was also Dositheus, the Samaritan, who pretended that he was the Christ foretold by Moses.
3. About twelve years after the death of our Lord, when Cuspius Fadus was procurator of Judea, arose an impostor of the name of Theudas, who said he was a prophet, and persuaded a great multitude to follow him with their best effects to the river Jordan, which he promised to divide for their passage; and saying these things, says Josephus, he deceived many: almost the very words of our Lord.
4. A few years afterwards, under the reign of Nero, while Felix was procurator of Judea, impostors of this stamp were so frequent that some were taken and killed almost every day. Josephus. Ant. b. xx. c. 4. and 7."

(Adam Clarke Commentary at: http://www.studylight.org/commentaries/acc/matthew-24.html)

Other people were also mentioned in the historical accounts or in New Testament that claimed or were regarded to be the promised Christ. One such person was Bar-Jesus as mentioned in Acts 13:16: "And when they had gone through the isle unto Paphos, they found a certain sorcerer, a false prophet, a Jew, whose name was Barjesus" Another very influential person who appeared in the early second Century AD/CE, was Simon bar Kokhba or Cochba who was the most important leader of the Jewish revolts and wars against the Roman Empire. He established an independent Jewish state in 132 AD/CE and ruled for three years as Nasi (meaning the Prince). He was originally named Simon ben Kosba (Simon son of Kosba), but was given the surname Bar Kokhba (Aramaic for "Son of a Star") by his contemporary Jewish sage Rabbi Akiva referring to the Star prophecy in Book of Numbers 24:17:

> there shall come a Star out of Jacob, and a Sceptre shall rise out of Israel, and shall smite the corners of Moab, and destroy all the children of Sheth.

In the religious and political environment of the time of Christ in the first and second centuries AD, when the Jews were longing for their Messiah and savior to come and release them from the rule of the Gentiles and restore the glory of the time of David and Solomon, Bar Cochba's personality and image was more closely aligned to the image of the warrior Messiah that the Jews had in mind, than the poor homeless and peace-loving carpenter of Nazareth Who could not even save Himself from their persecution and abuse.

Bar Cochba found a lot of followers, who considered him the Christ, but was eventually defeated by the Romans in 135 AD/CE.

In the same manner, those Biblical commentators who subscribe to the literal interpretation of the Olivet Discourse, present specific examples of the fulfillment of the rest of the prophecies, such as the hearing about wars and rumors of wars; the rising of nations against other nations and kingdoms against kingdoms; the occurrences of famines, pestilences, and earthquakes; the tribulations and afflictions; the persecution and betrayals of the believers; and the rise of false prophets within the first two centuries.

Regarding the rise of the false prophets mentioned in verse 11, Adam Clarke states:

> False prophets also were to be raised up; such as Simon Magus and his followers; and the false apostles complained of by St. Paul in 2 Corinthians 11:13, "For such are false apostles, deceitful workers, transforming themselves into the apostles of Christ. Such also were Hymeneus and Philetus, 2 Timothy 2:17, 18." And their word will eat as doth a canker: of whom is Hymenaeus and Philetus; Who concerning the truth have erred, saying that the resurrection is past already; and overthrow the faith of some. Eusebius (Eusebius of Caesarea referred to as the father of the Church history) records the activities and claims of Simon and his successor Menander who claimed to be the savior and Montanus who claimed to be the Paraclete, with his

female followers Maximilla and Priscilla were all prophets who brought revelations from God.[54]

The Second View

Those who held the second view, that the destruction of the Temple and return of Christ did not take place physically, but had already taken place spiritually, maintained that the Temple was the person of Christ as stated in the Gospel of John 2:19–22:

> Then answered the Jews and said unto him, What sign shewest thou unto us, seeing that thou doest these things? Jesus answered and said unto them, Destroy this temple, and in three days I will raise it up. Then said the Jews, Forty and six years was this temple in building, and wilt thou rear it up in three days? But he spake of the temple of his body. When therefore he was risen from the dead, his disciples remembered that he had said this unto them; and they believed the scripture, and the word which Jesus had said.
> (John 2:19–22)

The annual ritual of the high priest offering sacrifice at the Temple for atonement of the sins of the Jews stopped due to the destruction of the Temple shortly after the crucifixion of Jesus. Some Christians believe that this was the outward manifestation of the fact that Christ, acting as high priest (see Note No. 40 above and Heb. Chapters 6 and 7), offered Himself as sacrifice for the redemption of the sins of people, and therefore, the Temple sacrifices were abrogated and replaced by repentance. Following His crucifixion, Christ as the Temple or the sign of the presence of God, is present in the Church and His risen body is the new Temple, the focal point of the unity of the believers:

> Now therefore ye are no more strangers and foreigners, but fellow citizens with the saints, and of the household of God; And are built upon the foundation of the apostles and prophets, Jesus Christ himself being the chief corner stone; In whom all the building fitly framed together groweth unto

[54] For more information see: https://en.wikipedia.org/wiki/Simon_bar_Kokhba.

> an holy temple in the Lord: In whom ye also are builded together for an habitation of God through the Spirit.
> (Ephesians 2:19–22)

The Third View

As stated above, those who maintain this view, assert that the questions the disciples asked Jesus are essentially three parts of the same question, and that Jesus' response (the totality of the Olivet Discourse) refers only to the destruction of the Temple and Jewish state, and that nothing is spoken concerning the end of time or age. They maintain that these prophecies were all fulfilled between the crucifixion of Christ and the end of the first Century AD/CE. All elements of the tribulations mentioned here are very specific to Jerusalem and Judaea and the first and second century era. The abomination of desolation was the presence of the Roman Army in Jerusalem and in the Temple, where they hoisted their ensign and images. More over the text of verse 34 where Jesus states that "This generation shall not pass, till all these things be fulfilled" indicates that these things would occur within one generation. The span (the number of years) of one generation as indicated in the Old Testament is thirty-eight years:

> Surely there shall not one of these men of this evil generation see that good land, which I sware to give unto your fathers.
> (Deuteronomy 1:35)

> And the space in which we came from Kadeshbarnea, until we were come over the brook Zered, was thirty and eight years; until all the generation of the men of war were wasted out from among the host, as the LORD sware unto them.
> (Deuteronomy 2:14)

The Olivet Discourse took place shortly before the Christ's crucifixion in AD 32, and the destruction of the Temple happened thirty-eight years later in AD 70. All other verses are also interpreted in this manner. Even verse 30, "And then shall appear the sign of the Son of man," which is accepted by the majority of Biblical commentators and scholars as the prophecy of the coming of Christ, is interpreted to be related to the destruction of the Temple and the Jewish State. Adam Clarke states:

> The plain meaning of this is, that the destruction of Jerusalem will be such a remarkable instance of Divine vengeance, such a signal manifestation of Christ's power and glory, that all the Jewish tribes shall mourn, and many will, in consequence of this manifestation of God, be led to acknowledge Christ and his religion. . . . the land, in the text, is evidently meant here, as in several other places, the land of Judea and its tribes, either its then inhabitants, or the Jewish people wherever found.
> (Adam Clarke, in commentary to Bible)

The Historical Evolution of the Interpretation of Prophecies

As mentioned above, the Christians' views regarding the nature and the process of the fulfillment of prophecies have been evolving during the past twenty centuries.

The persecution of the Christians, and the tribulations that accompanied the Jewish revolt and the destruction of Jerusalem and the Temple took place within a short span of time after the event of the Olivet Discourse and crucifixion of Christ. This raised the expectations for the immanent return of Christ among Christians. As the persecutions and tribulations worsened under the rule of Nero (AD 37–68), Decius (AD 201–251), and Diocletian (AD 236–316), Christians remembered those words of Christ that "there shall be great tribulation such as was not since the beginning of the world to this time" (see Notes No. 121 and 122 in Appendix IV). The Church Fathers were expecting the immanent return of Christ and the beginning of the millennium. However, when Constantine (AD 280–337) embraced Christianity by issuance of the Edict of Milan with his co-emperor Licinius in AD 313, the persecution of the Christians ended. Within the span of a few decades, the tribulation largely ended and Christianity became the official religion of the Roman Empire. The common and dominant view in this era was that the apocalyptic visions of the New Testaments (both the Olivet Discourse and the Book of Revelation) were fulfilled, and the building of the Kingdom of God on earth had commenced. However, since Christ had not appeared after the passage of almost a century from the establishment of Christianity as the official and dominant religion of the Empire, the original apocalyptic model based on the pre-millennial view, the near eschatology, and on literal interpretation of prophecies, had to be modified and replaced with a new model. The great Christian theologian, philosopher, and writer, St. Augustine of Hippo (CE 354–430), was the person who offered the new model in his writings and especially his famous book "The City of God."

Although Augustine originally believed that Christ would appear first and would literally establish a one-thousand-year Kingdom prior to the end of time and the general resurrection (pre-millennialism view), he changed his view and offered the doctrine of amillennialism, which was related to his ideas regarding the church as a heavenly city or kingdom. He stated more specifically that the Christian Church, which was developing and gathering strength, was the "City of God" or the "New Jerusalem" prophesied in the Book of Revelation. Based on the amillennial model of eschatology, it is not necessary for the Christ to physically return to earth to rule, because "he rules the earth spiritually through His triumphant church."

The medieval Catholic Church adopted Augustine's amillennial eschatological model as the basis and foundation of the supreme rule of the Catholic Church over all earthly empires. The acceptance of the amillennial model by the Church, removed the millennial expectations from the arena of public interest for several centuries.

However, as the year AD 1000 approached, expectations for the return of Christ re-emerged. This was due to various factors—interpretation of the prophecies in the Book of Revelation, the division of the Church into the eastern and western churches, general discontent with the Church due to corruption and the heavy involvement of the Popes and the hierarchy of the Church in politics, and concerns over the rule of Muslims over the Christian holy places that resulted in Crusades toward the end of the first century of the new Millennium.

During the Reformation period, the concerns and protests against the corruption of the Roman Catholic Church, which resulted in the emergence of Protestant Christianity, found some ideological basis in the prophecies. Some regarded the Church as the Antichrist and saw the signs of the approach of the pre-millennial advent.

From the middle of eighteenth century some Biblical scholars, through the interpretation of the Olivet Discourse and specially the chronological prophecies of chapters 7, 8, and 12 of the Book of Daniel and chapter 11 of the Book of Revelation, determined that the time of the end was approaching. Based on their calculations, the Second Advent would take place between 1836 and 1848. Those who publicized their findings and found a following were referred to as Adventists (expecting the second advent of Christ). One of the pioneers in this field was the German Biblical scholar Johan Albrecht Bengal, who in 1736 predicted that the Second Advent would take place in 1836. The most famous Adventist was William Miller, a Baptist preacher, who in 1833 predicted that the Second Advent would take place in 1843 or 1844. He presented a very strong argument, backed up by a timeline that calculated the dates of the First and Second Advents, and as the calculated date for the First Advent corresponded exactly with the ministry of Jesus, it created a lot of excitement, and in spite of strong opposition by some clerics, attracted a great number of people to the Adventist movement. However, when on the predicted dates, the Second Advent did not appear to take place literally—the Sun was not darkened and the Moon continued to give light, the stars were still in the heaven and did not all fall, and Christ did not descend in clouds from heaven—there was great disappointment, and Miller became the subject of ridicule and condemnation for misleading the believers. In spite of the disappointment, the Adventist movement continues to the present time and has large number of followers. The pre-millennial view is presently the dominant view among Christians.

As mentioned above, the majority of Christians believe that verses 29 and 30 of chapter 24 of Matthew are the signs of the Second Coming of Christ.

> 24:29 Immediately after the tribulation of those days shall the sun be darkened, and the moon shall not give her light, and the stars shall fall from heaven, and the powers of the

> heavens shall be shaken: 24:30 And then shall appear the sign of the Son of man in heaven: and then shall all the tribes of the earth mourn, and they shall see the Son of man coming in the clouds of heaven with power and great glory.

As mentioned above in Note No. 64, these signs are exactly the same signs that are given for the first coming, the advent of the Messiah, in the Old Testament prophecies:

> And I will shew wonders in the heavens and in the earth, blood, and fire, and pillars of smoke. The sun shall be turned into darkness, and the moon into blood, before the great and terrible day of the LORD come. And it shall come to pass, that whosoever shall call on the name of the LORD shall be delivered: for in mount Zion and in Jerusalem shall be deliverance, as the LORD hath said, and in the remnant whom the LORD shall call.
> (Joel 2:28–32)

It is interesting to note that in Islamic prophecies the same signs are given for the advent of the Promised One and the Day of Resurrection.

He said unto them: "Immediately after the oppression[124] of those days shall the sun be darkened, and the moon shall not give her light, and the stars shall fall from heaven, and the powers of the earth shall be shaken[125]

124. Shoghi Effendi in footnote 19 of the Book of Certitude states: “The Greek word used (Thlipsis) has two meanings: pressure and oppression.”

125. As presented above (see Note Nos. 52, 64, 77, and 123), the prophecies in the Old Testament regarding the advent of the Messiah (i.e., the first advent of Christ) contain very similar signs, which were to appear before the coming of the Messiah, and Jews were expecting to see those signs heralding the advent of their promised savior.

Rendered into the Persian tongue[126]

126. Shoghi Effendi states: "The passage is quoted by Bahá'u'lláh in Arabic and interpreted in Persian." Bahá'u'lláh first quoted Matthew 24:29–31 in Arabic and then rendered it in Persian.

As We have referred at length to these in Our Tablets revealed in the Arabic tongue, We have made no mention of them in these pages, and have confined Ourselves to but one reference.[127]

127. The Tablets mentioned here are some Tablets revealed in Arabic, more specifically the treatise titled Javáhiru'l-Asrár (Gems of Divine Mysteries). Please see note No. 85 above.

Paragraph No. 25:

they therefore became deprived of the streaming grace of the Muḥammadan Revelation and its showering bounties.[128]

128. The same attachment to the form and the literal interpretation of the prophecies and signs that caused the Jews to be veiled and not accept Jesus as the promised Messiah, has caused the Christians to be veiled and deprived of the divine grace vouchsafed by the Manifestations that appeared after Christ. Shoghi Effendi states:

> It seems both strange and pitiful that the Church and clergy should always, in every age, be the most bitter opponents of the very Truth they are continually admonishing their followers to be prepared to receive! They have become so violently attached to the form that the substance itself eludes them!"
> (*The Compilation of Compilations, vol. I*, p. 149)

The ignorant among the Christian community, following the example of the leaders of their faith[129]

129. The Báb states:

> It is recorded in a tradition that of the entire concourse of the Christians no more than seventy people embraced the Faith of the Apostle of God. The blame falleth upon their doctors, for if these had believed, they would have been followed by the mass of their countrymen. Behold, then, that which hath come to pass! The learned men of Christendom are held to be learned by virtue of their safeguarding the teaching of Christ, and yet consider how they themselves have been the cause of men's failure to accept the Faith and attain unto salvation! Is it still thy wish to follow in their footsteps? The followers of Jesus submitted to their clerics to be saved on the Day of Resurrection,[55] and as a result of this obedience they eventually entered into the fire, and on the Day when the Apostle of God[56] appeared they shut themselves out from the recognition of His exalted Person. Dost thou desire to follow such divines?
> (The Báb, *Selections from the Writings of the Báb,* p. 122)

In another passage from His Writings, the Báb states:

> If ye entertain any doubts in this matter consider the people unto whom the Gospel was given. Having no access to the apostles of Jesus, they sought the pleasure of the Lord in their churches, hoping to learn that which would be acceptable unto God, but they found therein no path unto Him. Then when God manifested Muḥammad as His Messenger and as the Repository of His good-pleasure, they neglected to quicken their souls from the Fountain of living waters which streamed forth from the presence of their Lord and continued to rove distraught upon the earth seeking a mere droplet of water and believing that they were doing righteous deeds. They behaved as the people unto whom the Qur'án was given are now behaving.
> (The Báb, *Selections from the Writings of the Báb,* p. 136)

---

[55] In the Writings of the Báb and Bahá'u'lláh, the advent of each Manifestation of God is the Day of Resurrection of the followers of all the previous religions.

[56] The Apostle of God is one of the titles of Muḥammad.

inasmuch as those signs which were to accompany the dawn of the sun of the Muḥammadan Dispensation did not actually come to pass.[130]

130. As mentioned in Note No. 52 above, the followers of all religions were expecting the advent of the promised one of their religion to be accompanied by certain extraordinary signs and events. Some of those signs that are listed by Jews, Christian, and Muslims alike are as follows:

First: The rolling up of the heavens.
Second: The sun will be darkened.
Third: The moon shall not give her light.
Fourth: The stars shall fall from heaven.
Fifth: The dead shall arise from their tombs.
Sixth: Ferocious animals will make peace with grazing animals.
Seven: They will share the same pasture and food.
Eight: The children will play with poisonous serpents.

Once more hath the eternal Spirit breathed into the mystic trumpet[131]

131. In the Judeo-Christo-Islamic eschatology, it is perceived that at the end of time a general resurrection will take place and the dead will be raised to face the judgment, and according to the outcome of the judgment, will either enter Paradise or be sent to Hell. In Islamic eschatology the imagery is more expanded and the sequence of events are related with more detail. According to Islamic traditions, at the time of the end, Isráfíl, one of the four exalted archangels that are close to the throne of God, sounds the trumpet on the Day of Judgment, and in so doing he resurrects the dead so that they may be judged. The Judeo-Christian counterpart of Isráfíl is Raphael.

In the Writings of the Bahá'í Faith, the time of the end for the followers of each religion is the appearance of the next Manifestation of God, the resurrection and the sound of trumpet is His call to all humanity to rise and accept His cause, and the judgment is their reaction to this call. If they accept to enter into His Cause they enter the Paradise of the faith and if they reject it they will be in the fire of remoteness and deprivation.

Bahá'u'lláh called His Pen the trumpet that will resurrect all mankind:

> We have heard the voice of thy pleading, O Pen, and excuse thy silence. What is it that hath so sorely bewildered thee? The inebriation of Thy presence, O Well-Beloved of all worlds, hath seized and possessed me. Arise, and proclaim unto the entire creation the tidings that He Who is the All-Merciful hath directed His steps towards the Riḍván and entered it. Guide, then, the people unto the garden of delight which God hath made the Throne of His Paradise. We have chosen thee to be our most mighty Trumpet, whose blast is to signalize the resurrection of all mankind.
> (Bahá'u'lláh, *Gleanings from the Writings of Bahá'u'lláh,* p. 30)

and caused the dead[132] to speed out of their sepulchers of heedlessness and error[133] unto the realm of guidance and grace[134]

132. The dead mentioned in the holy scriptures are those who are deprived of the spirit of faith.

> And another of his disciples said unto him, Lord, suffer me first to go and bury my father. But Jesus said unto him, Follow me; and let the dead bury their dead.
> (Matthew 8:21–22)

They are revived and raised from the sepulchers and graves of unbelief when they receive the spirit of faith.

> Verily, verily, I say unto you, He that heareth my word, and believeth on him that sent me, hath everlasting life, and shall not come into condemnation; but is passed from death unto life.
> (John 5:24)

> Verily, verily, I say unto you, He that believeth on me hath everlasting life.
> (John 6:47)

'Abdu'l-Bahá defines the dead mentioned in the Book of Revelation as: "those who are deprived of the spirit of the love of God and bereft of that life which is holy and everlasting."

> Thus if the Sacred Scriptures speak of raising the dead, the meaning is that they attained everlasting life . . .
> ('Abdu'l-Bahá, *Some Answered Questions,* nos. 11.39, 22.7)

133. The state of heedlessness and ignorance and opposition to the light of God is like the darkness of the grave. Christ likens the divines of His time to sepulchers:

> Woe unto you, scribes and Pharisees, hypocrites! for ye are like unto whited sepulchres, which indeed appear beautiful outward, but are within full of dead men's bones, and of all uncleanness.
> (Matthew 23:27)

The same theme is recorded in the Old Testament:

> And ye shall know that I am the LORD, when I have opened your graves, O my people, and brought you up out of your graves, And shall put my spirit in you, and ye shall live, and I shall place you in your own land: then shall ye know that I the LORD have spoken it, and performed it, saith the LORD.
> (Ezekiel 37:13–14)

134. "Once more the eternal Spirit breathed into the mystic trumpet that caused the dead to speed out of their sepulchres of heedlessness and error unto the realm of guidance and grace." The "once more" after the advent of Muḥammad is the advent of the Revelation of the Báb.

And yet, that expectant community still crieth out: When shall these things be? When shall the promised One, the object of our expectation, be made manifest, . . . that we may offer up our lives in His path?[135]

135. The Jewish communities all over the world pray every Sabbath day for the advent of the Messiah. They do not accept Jesus as their promised Messiah because their expected signs did not appear

before or accompany His advent. Many Christians, followers of different denominations, pray for the return of Christ, but believe that His second advent will be accompanied by the literal or physical appearance of the above mentioned signs. When in the middle of the twentieth century, the state of Israel was formed (1948), and subsequently during the 1967 Arab-Israeli war, the City of Jerusalem was taken by the Israeli army and came under Jewish rule, there was great excitement because some Christians argued that these events are the precursors of the Second Advent, as Jesus stated in the Parable of the fig tree in Matt. 24:32:

> Now learn a parable of the fig tree; When his branch is yet tender, and putteth forth leaves, ye know that summer is nigh.

In the book "The Late Great planet Earth," Hal Lindsey, argues that these events were milestones in the unfolding process leading to the coming of Christ. In the closing years of the twentieth century, the authors of a series of books under the title of "Left Behind" took advantage of public sentiments regarding this subject, and enjoyed strong sales as a result. The expectations were raised to a level that a group of people who were more passionate regarding the coming of Christ moved to the Holy Land prior to the turn of the Millennium, expecting to see the Second Advent. When the end of the millennium came and passed and Jesus did not appear riding on the clouds, the subject dropped out of public attention and interest.

to stray from the Kaw<u>th</u>ar of the infinite mercy of Providence, and to be busied with their own idle thoughts.[136]

136. The word Kaw<u>th</u>ar in Arabic means abundance, and a generous person, but in Islamic terminology it is the name of a fountain in Paradise from which all the rivers in Paradise initiate. The Islamic traditions relate that the water from this fountain is cooler than ice, whiter than milk, sweeter than honey, and those that drink from it shall never thirst. It is also the name of Súrah No. 108 of the Qur'án, in which God addresses Muḥammad: "Truly we have given thee an Abundance." In the Bahá'í sacred Writings it is

translated as "fountain," but more frequently as "the living waters":

> Thou beholdest, O Lord, the ignorant seeking the ocean of Thy knowledge, the sore athirst the living waters of Thine utterance, the abased the tabernacle of Thy glory, the poor the treasury of Thy riches, the suppliant the dawning-place of Thy wisdom, the weak the source of Thy strength, the wretched the heaven of Thy bounty, the dumb the kingdom of Thy mention.
> (Bahá'u'lláh, Epistle to the Son of the Wolf, p. 3)

Or:

> Seize ye the living waters of immortality in the name of your Lord, the Lord of all names, and drink ye in the remembrance of Him, Who is the Mighty, the Peerless.
> (Bahá'u'lláh, Epistle to the Son of the Wolf, p. 38)

Paragraph No. 26:

"Heaven and earth shall pass away: but My words shall not pass away.[137]

137. Matthew 24:35. Some Christians use this statement to support their view that there will never be another divine Revelation, and that the words of Christ will never pass away. The Jews used similar statements regarding the words, laws, and Revelation of Moses, considering those statements as the proof that the laws and religion of Moses are the eternal truth and the only true religion, which will never be superseded.

> Now therefore hearken, O Israel, unto the statutes and unto the judgments, which I teach you, for to do them, that ye may live, and go in and possess the land which the LORD God of your fathers giveth you. Ye shall not add unto the word which I command you, neither shall ye diminish ought from it, that ye may keep the commandments of the LORD your God which I command you. . . . Behold, I have taught you statutes and judgments, even as the LORD my God commanded me, that ye should do so in the land

whither ye go to possess it. Keep therefore and do them; for this is your wisdom and your understanding in the sight of the nations, which shall hear all these statutes, and say, Surely this great nation is a wise and understanding people. For what nation is there so great, who hath God so nigh unto them, as the LORD our God is in all things that we call upon him for? And what nation is there so great, that hath statutes and judgments so righteous as all this law, which I set before you this day? Only take heed to thyself, and keep thy soul diligently, lest thou forget the things which thine eyes have seen, and lest they depart from thy heart all the days of thy life: but teach them thy sons, and thy sons' sons
(Deuteronomy 4:1–9)

All flesh is grass, and all the goodliness thereof is as the flower of the field: The grass withereth, the flower fadeth: because the spirit of the LORD bloweth upon it: surely the people is grass. The grass withereth, the flower fadeth: but the word of our God shall stand for ever.
(Isaiah 40:6–8)

Jesus maintained that the law of the Gospel shall never be annulled, and that whensoever the promised Beauty is made manifest and all the signs are revealed, He must needs re-affirm and establish the law proclaimed in the Gospel, so that there may remain in the world no faith but His faith[138]

138. This expectation is very similar to the expectations of the Jews that their Messiah would not change their religion, but would promote it and establish the rule of Jewish law in the world. This is the reason for their objections to Christ breaking the law of the Sabbath (please see Notes No. 75 and 76 above). This is also the reason for the following statement of Christ:

Think not that I am come to destroy the law, or the prophets[57]: I am not come to destroy, but to fulfil. For

[57] The "law" is a reference to the first five Books of the Old Testament, i.e., the five books attributed to Moses (Pentateuch), which contain the Judaic laws. The "prophets" is

> verily I say unto you, Till heaven and earth pass, one jot or one tittle shall in no wise pass from the law, till all be fulfilled. Whosoever therefore shall break one of these least commandments, and shall teach men so, he shall be called the least in the kingdom of heaven: but whosoever shall do and teach them, the same shall be called great in the kingdom of heaven.
> (Matthew 5: 17–19)

Christ's admonition to His followers to observe and follow the Law, and His statement in Matthew 15:4, where He says "I am not sent but unto the lost sheep of the house of Israel," was the cause of a very serious dispute among His Disciples in the early years following His crucifixion. The most important issues were:

- Whether Christ came solely for the Jews, who would not have any difficulties with observance and compliance with the laws of the Torah, or if He also came for the Gentiles.
- Whether the Gentiles would be required to live in compliance with the Judaic laws from the moment they accepted Christ, or if they would be exempt from observing the Judaic laws.

Some Christian historians indicate that the two most important Christian leaders of the time, namely Peter and Paul, were on the opposing sides of these issues. Among the major issues were compliance with the law of circumcision, the laws governing food preparation and consumption (the Kosher), and the laws governing association with non-Jews.

Peter and some of the Disciples held that Christ was the promised Messiah of the Jews, and that He came not to change or break any laws but to fulfill and promote the laws of the Torah, and that a Christian had to live in total and strict obedience of the laws. Paul and other leaders believed that Christ came for all men, and when they started to teach the Gentiles, these issues came into focus and had to be addressed.

---

a reference to the books of the prophets of Israel. Together, these books form the foundation of the Jewish religion.

These issues were brought to the council of disciples in Jerusalem and eventually all agreed to exempt the Gentiles from observing these important laws. The book of Acts, describes how Peter changed his position

> On the morrow, as they went on their journey, and drew nigh unto the city, Peter went up upon the housetop to pray about the sixth hour: And he became very hungry, and would have eaten: but while they made ready, he fell into a trance, And saw heaven opened, and a certain vessel descending upon him, as it had been a great sheet knit at the four corners, and let down to the earth: Wherein were all manner of fourfooted beasts of the earth, and wild beasts, and creeping things, and fowls of the air. And there came a voice to him, Rise, Peter; kill, and eat. But Peter said, Not so, Lord; for I have never eaten any thing that is common or unclean. And the voice spake unto him again the second time, What God hath cleansed, that call not thou common. This was done thrice: and the vessel was received up again into heaven. Now while Peter doubted in himself what this vision which he had seen should mean, behold, the men which were sent from Cornelius had made enquiry for Simon's house, and stood before the gate, And called, and asked whether Simon, which was surnamed Peter, were lodged there. While Peter thought on the vision, the Spirit said unto him, Behold, three men seek thee. Arise therefore, and get thee down, and go with them, doubting nothing: for I have sent them. Then Peter went down to the men which were sent unto him from Cornelius; and said, Behold, I am he whom ye seek: what is the cause wherefore ye are come? And they said, Cornelius the centurion, a just man, and one that feareth God, and of good report among all the nation of the Jews, was warned from God by an holy angel to send for thee into his house, and to hear words of thee.
>
> Then called he them in, and lodged them. And on the morrow Peter went away with them, and certain brethren from Joppa accompanied him. And the morrow after they entered into Caesarea. And Cornelius waited for them, and he had called together his kinsmen and near friends. And as

> Peter was coming in, Cornelius met him, and fell down at his feet, and worshipped him. But Peter took him up, saying, Stand up; I myself also am a man. And as he talked with him, he went in, and found many that were come together. And he said unto them, Ye know how that it is an unlawful thing for a man that is a Jew to keep company, or come unto one of another nation; but God hath shewed me that I should not call any man common or unclean. Therefore came I unto you without gainsaying, as soon as I was sent for: I ask therefore for what intent ye have sent for me? And Cornelius said, Four days ago I was fasting until this hour; and at the ninth hour I prayed in my house, and, behold, a man stood before me in bright clothing, And said, Cornelius, thy prayer is heard, and thine alms are had in remembrance in the sight of God. Send therefore to Joppa, and call hither Simon, whose surname is Peter; he is lodged in the house of one Simon a tanner by the sea side: who, when he cometh, shall speak unto thee. Immediately therefore I sent to thee; and thou hast well done that thou art come. Now therefore are we all here present before God, to hear all things that are commanded thee of God. Then Peter opened his mouth, and said, Of a truth I perceive that God is no respecter of persons: But in every nation he that feareth him, and worketh righteousness, is accepted with him. The word which God sent unto the children of Israel, preaching peace by Jesus Christ: (he is Lord of all:). . . . Then prayed they him to tarry certain days. And the apostles and brethren that were in Judaea heard that the Gentiles had also received the word of God. And when Peter was come up to Jerusalem, they that were of the circumcision contended with him, Saying, Thou wentest in to men uncircumcised, and didst eat with them. But Peter rehearsed the matter from the beginning, and expounded it by order unto them. . . .
> (Acts 10:9–11:4)

As mentioned before, the law of circumcision was one of the most important laws of Judaism. This is the law that was established among Israelites from the time of Abraham (see notes No. 41 and 43 above). The Gentile converts were all grown men, mostly middle-aged and older, who were troubled when they learned that they had to be circumcised. As stated in the book of Acts, the disciples had to find a compromise, otherwise all those new believers would be lost to the Church:

> And certain men which came down from Judaea taught the brethren, and said, Except ye be circumcised after the manner of Moses, ye cannot be saved. When therefore Paul and Barnabas had no small dissension and disputation with them, they determined that Paul and Barnabas, and certain other of them, should go up to Jerusalem unto the apostles and elders about this question. And being brought on their way by the church, they passed through Phenice and Samaria, declaring the conversion of the Gentiles: and they caused great joy unto all the brethren. And when they were come to Jerusalem, they were received of the church, and of the apostles and elders, and they declared all things that God had done with them. But there rose up certain of the sect of the Pharisees which believed, saying, That it was needful to circumcise them, and to command them to keep the law of Moses. And the apostles and elders came together for to consider of this matter. And when there had been much disputing, Peter rose up, and said unto them, Men and brethren, ye know how that a good while ago God made choice among us, that the Gentiles by my mouth should hear the word of the gospel, and believe. And God, which knoweth the hearts, bare them witness, giving them the Holy Ghost, even as he did unto us; And put no difference between us and them, purifying their hearts by faith. Now therefore why tempt ye God, to put a yoke upon the neck of the disciples, which neither our fathers nor we were able to bear? But we believe that through the grace of the LORD Jesus Christ we shall be saved, even as they. Then all the multitude kept silence, and gave audience to Barnabas and Paul, declaring what miracles and wonders God had wrought among the Gentiles by them. And after they had held their peace, James answered, saying, Men and brethren, hearken unto me: Simeon hath declared how God at the first did visit the Gentiles, to take out of them a people for his name. . . . Wherefore my sentence is, that we trouble not them, which from among the Gentiles are turned to God: But that we write unto them, that they

> abstain from pollutions of idols, and from fornication, and from things strangled, and from blood. For Moses of old time hath in every city them that preach him, being read in the synagogues every sabbath day. Then pleased it the apostles and elders with the whole church, to send chosen men of their own company to Antioch with Paul and Barnabas; namely, Judas surnamed Barsabas and Silas, chief men among the brethren: And they wrote letters by them after this manner; The apostles and elders and brethren send greeting unto the brethren which are of the Gentiles in Antioch and Syria and Cilicia. Forasmuch as we have heard, that certain which went out from us have troubled you with words, subverting your souls, saying, Ye must be circumcised, and keep the law: to whom we gave no such commandment: It seemed good unto us, being assembled with one accord, to send chosen men unto you with our beloved Barnabas and Paul, Men that have hazarded their lives for the name of our Lord Jesus Christ. We have sent therefore Judas and Silas, who shall also tell you the same things by mouth. For it seemed good to the Holy Ghost, and to us, to lay upon you no greater burden than these necessary things; That ye abstain from meats offered to idols, and from blood, and from things strangled, and from fornication: from which if ye keep yourselves, ye shall do well. . . ."
> (Acts 15:1–28)

Although the Gentiles became exempt from following the laws, the Jewish converts were required to follow them:

> Then came he to Derbe and Lystra: and, behold, a certain disciple was there, named Timotheus, the son of a certain woman, which was a Jewess, and believed; but his father was a Greek: Which was well reported of by the brethren that were at Lystra and Iconium. Him would Paul have to go forth with him; and took and circumcised him because of the Jews which were in those quarters: for they knew all that his father was a Greek.
> (Acts 16:1–3)

Compliance with the letter of the law was so important for the Jews, even those who became Christians, that the elders and Disciples made Paul publicly demonstrate it.

> And the day following Paul went in with us unto James; and all the elders were present. And when he had saluted them, he declared particularly what things God had wrought among the Gentiles by his ministry. And when they heard it, they glorified the Lord, and said unto him, Thou seest, brother, how many thousands of Jews there are which believe; and they are all zealous of the law: And they are informed of thee, that thou teachest all the Jews which are among the Gentiles to forsake Moses, saying that they ought not to circumcise their children, neither to walk after the customs. What is it therefore? the multitude must needs come together: for they will hear that thou art come. Do therefore this that we say to thee: We have four men which have a vow on them; Them take, and purify thyself with them, and be at charges with them, that they may shave their heads: and all may know that those things, whereof they were informed concerning thee, are nothing; but that thou thyself also walkest orderly, and keepest the law. As touching the Gentiles which believe, we have written and concluded that they observe no such thing, save only that they keep themselves from things offered to idols, and from blood, and from strangled, and from fornication. Then Paul took the men, and the next day purifying himself with them entered into the temple, to signify the accomplishment of the days of purification, until that an offering should be offered for every one of them.
> (Acts 21:18–26)

From the early days of Christianity to the present time, the Jews contend that the true Messiah has to promote the laws of the Torah, and that because the Judaic laws were annulled and abrogated in Christianity, Jesus has violated the Covenant of God and is therefore not the true Messiah.

Similarly the Christians, quoting the statement of Christ in Matthew 24:35: "Heaven and earth shall pass away, but my words shall not pass away," contend that Christ's Revelation is the final one. It is interesting to note that Muslims also forward a similar claim regarding the finality of the Revelation of Muḥammad, while contending that Jews and Christians are wrong to claim finality for their respective religions.

This is proved by that which came to pass when the sun of the Muḥammadan Revelation was revealed.[139]

139. The history of Islam shows that from the early years of the ministry of Muḥammad, not withstanding Muḥammad's affirmation of the divine origin of their Faith, the large Jewish community of Arabia opposed Him and did not accept His claims. Not only did the signs they expected fail to appear, but rather than promote Judaic laws, Muḥammad abrogated them and promulgated a new set of religious laws and ordinances. The Jewish tribes entered into alliance with Muḥammad's enemies and fought in several battles against Muslims. Although the Christians of Arabia did not have a similar contentious relation with Muslims, they never the less did not accept Muḥammad's claim, and their leaders opposed and ridiculed Him. This is indicated in the Báb's statement (see Note No. 129), that of "the entire concourse of the Christians no more than seventy people embraced" the Faith of Muḥammad.

Had they sought with a humble mind from the Manifestations of God in every Dispensation[140]

140. Dispensation is defined as:

> The period of time during which the authority of a Manifestation of God's social or temporal teachings endure.
>
> A prophet's dispensation begins with the declaration of His prophetic mission and ends with the declaration of the next Manifestation of God, whose teachings supersede those of the former prophet.
> (*A Basic Baha'i Dictionary*, p. 72)

words the misapprehension of which hath caused men to be deprived of the recognition of the Sadratu'l-Muntahá[141]

141. Please see Note No. 48 above. Bahá'u'lláh defines "Sadratu'l-Muntahá as He states:

> The Holy Tree [Sadrah] is, in a sense, the Manifestation of the One True God, exalted be He.
> (Bahá'u'lláh, *Tablets of Bahá'u'lláh,* p. 137)

the ultimate Purpose[142]

142. The Bahá'í Writings indicate that the recognition of the Manifestation of God in every age, and steadfastness and service in His Cause, is the greatest achievement of every human being, and that deprivation from this recognition and allegiance is the greatest loss that a person can suffer:

> The second Tajalli is to remain steadfast in the Cause of God—exalted be His glory—and to be unswerving in His love. And this can in no wise be attained except through full recognition of Him; and full recognition cannot be obtained save by faith in the blessed words: "He doeth whatsoever He willeth." Whoso tenaciously cleaveth unto this sublime word and drinketh deep from the living waters of utterance which are inherent therein, will be imbued with such a constancy that all the books of the world will be powerless to deter him from the Mother Book. O how glorious is this sublime station, this exalted rank, this ultimate purpose!
> (Bahá'u'lláh, *Tablets of Bahá'u'lláh*, p. 50)

> Let us pray to God that He will exhilarate our spirits so we may behold the descent of His bounties, illumine our eyes to witness His great guidance and attune our ears to enjoy the celestial melodies of the heavenly Word. This is our greatest hope. This is our ultimate purpose.
> ('Abdu'l-Bahá, *The Promulgation of Universal Peace*, p. 171)

> The friends of God must arise with such steadfastness that if, at any moment, a hundred souls like 'Abdu'l-Bahá

become the target for the arrows of affliction, they will not shift or waver in their resolve, their determination, their enkindlement, their devotion and service in the Cause of God. 'Abdu'l-Bahá is himself a servant at the Threshold of the Blessed Beauty and a manifestation of pure and utter servitude at the Threshold of the Almighty. He hath no other station or title, no other rank or power. This is my ultimate Purpose, my eternal Paradise, my holiest Temple and my Sadratu'l-Muntahá.
(‘Abdu’l-Bahá, *Selections from the Writings of ‘Abdu’l-Bahá*, p. 294)

and would have discovered the mysteries of divine knowledge and wisdom[143]

143. As discussed above, the religious leaders’ misinterpretations of the signs given in their sacred books regarding the advent of the promised one of their religion has always been the cause of their denial and the people’s failure to recognize and accept the Manifestations of God. It is very unfortunate that in every age and in past Dispensations they failed to ask the divine Manifestations to explain the true meaning of those signs. This is the purpose of the revelation of the Book of Certitude. In this Dispensation every one owes a debt of gratitude to the uncle of the Báb, who by humbly asking those questions as the representative of the whole of humanity, became the recipient of this great gift that Bahá’u’lláh in His love and mercy brought forward from the fathomless ocean of His knowledge to assist every sincere seeker of truth to comprehend the true meaning of those signs and not be deprived of the recognition of the Manifestation of God, which is the ultimate purpose of every man’s creation.

Paragraph No. 27:

This servant[144]

144. As mentioned before, in many of His Writings, Bahá’u’lláh refers to Himself as “this servant.” This is to signify that in all His majesty and exalted station, He is the servant of God and lives, moves, and speaks as bidden by God.

share with thee a dewdrop out of the fathomless ocean[145]

145. To illustrate the vastness of the subject matter, Bahá'u'lláh uses the analogy of the ocean and a dewdrop:

> O Thou Who art the All-Knowing! Wayward though we be, we still cling to Thy bounty; and though ignorant, we still set our faces toward the ocean of Thy wisdom. Thou art that All-Bountiful Who art not deterred by a multitude of sins from vouchsafing Thy bounty, and the flow of Whose gifts is not arrested by the withdrawal of the peoples of the world. From eternity the door of Thy grace hath remained wide open. A dewdrop out of the ocean of Thy mercy is able to adorn all things with the ornament of sanctity, and a sprinkling of the waters of Thy bounty can cause the entire creation to attain unto true wealth.
> (Bahá'u'lláh, *Prayers and Meditations*, p. 245)

that haply discerning hearts may comprehend all the allusions and the implications of the utterances of the Manifestations of Holiness[146]

146. In the Kitáb-i-Íqán, Bahá'u'lláh clarifies the allusions, parables and implications of the sacred books of the past religions.

> Another asked why the teachings of all religions are expressed largely by parables and metaphors and not in the plain language of the people.
>
> 'Abdu'l-Bahá replied: "Divine things are too deep to be expressed by common words. The heavenly teachings are expressed in parable in order to be understood and preserved for ages to come. When the spiritually minded dive deeply into the ocean of their meaning they bring to the surface the pearls of their inner significance. There is no greater pleasure than to study God's Word with a spiritual mind."
> ('Abdu'l-Bahá, *'Abdu'l-Bahá in London,* p. 79)
>
> The divine Words are not to be taken according to their outer sense. They are symbolical and contain realities of spiritual meaning. . . . All the texts and teachings of the holy

Testaments have intrinsic spiritual meanings. They are not to be taken literally. I, therefore, pray in your behalf that you may be given the power of understanding these inner real meanings of the Holy Scriptures and may become informed of the mysteries deposited in the words of the Bible so that you may attain eternal life and that your hearts may be attracted to the Kingdom of God.
('Abdu'l-Bahá, *The Promulgation of Universal Peace*, p. 459)

so that the overpowering majesty of the Word of God[147]

147. It seems there are certain words that if interpreted literally, and their meanings not explained and clarified by the Manifestations of God, may confuse the people. The outward overpowering majesty of these words and statements might prevent people from recognizing the Manifestations of God and deprive them from attaining to the station of faith. Some of these are:

- Words pertaining to the signs, events, or conditions that according to public belief must appear prior or simultaneously with the advent of their promised one.
- Words pertaining to the claims of the new Manifestations to their own special station, which does not correspond with their physical and social condition and status.
- Words in regard to the abrogation of the established laws and ordinances of the previous Dispensation, and the promulgation of new laws and teachings.

A review of the available history of the life of all Manifestations of God indicates that in every case, all or the majority of the above mentioned conditions not only prevented the peoples of their time from recognizing the station of the Manifestations, but prompted the ignorant to repudiate Their claims, oppose, and persecute Them. The most clear examples are Jesus, the Báb, and Bahá'u'lláh, and to some degree Moses and Muḥammad.

In the case of Jesus, the Jews were expecting Elijah to descend from heaven in his physical corporal body before the day of the coming of the Messiah. That day was going to be hot like an oven, in which the Sun was not going to give light and the Moon was going to be like blood, and the powers of earth would be released. The Messiah was expected to come descending from heaven. None of these expected signs appeared to occur before or during the advent of Jesus (please see Notes No. 52 and 64).

The public were expecting the Messiah to come with worldly power and dominion, and rescue Jews from the rule of Gentiles. Jesus did not fulfill these expectations.

Jesus, Who was known to people as the Son of Joseph the carpenter and Who's brothers and sisters they knew and were living among them (see Mark 6:3 and Note No. 8), not only claimed that God was His Father, but claimed that God and Him were one:

> But Jesus answered them, My Father worketh hitherto, and I work. Therefore the Jews sought the more to kill him, because he not only had broken the sabbath, but said also that God was his Father, making himself equal with God.
> (John 5:17–18)

> My Father, which gave them me, is greater than all; and no man is able to pluck them out of my Father's hand. I and my Father are one. Then the Jews took up stones again to stone him.
> (John 10:29–31)

Jesus also broke the law of the Sabbath and abrogated the law of divorce (see Note No. 76).

deprive them of recognizing the Lamp of God which is the seat of the revelation of His glorified Essence[148]

148. "The Lamp of God" and the "seat of the revelation of His glorified Essence" are references to the Manifestation of God as other titles given in the Kitáb-i-Aqdas:

> The first duty prescribed by God for His servants is the recognition of Him Who is the Dayspring of His Revelation and the Fountain of His laws, Who representeth the

Godhead in both the Kingdom of His Cause and the world of creation.
(Bahá'u'lláh, The Kitáb-i-Aqdas, ¶1)

Paragraph No. 28:

the fruit of the Tree of knowledge and wisdom[149]

149. The Tree of knowledge and wisdom is the religion of God, 'Abdu'l-Bahá states:

> From the days of Adam until today, the religions of God have been made manifest, one following the other, and each one of them fulfilled its due function, revived mankind, and provided education and enlightenment. They freed the people from the darkness of the world of nature and ushered them into the brightness of the Kingdom. As each succeeding Faith and Law became revealed it remained for some centuries a richly fruitful tree and to it was committed the happiness of humankind. However, as the centuries rolled by, it aged, it flourished no more and put forth no fruit, wherefore was it then made young again.
> ('Abdu'l-Bahá, *Selections from the Writings of 'Abdu'l-Bahá*, p. 51)

the portals of divine unity[150]

150. The portals of divine unity are the Manifestations of God. Divine unity is defined by Bahá'u'lláh in the following terms:

> The essence of belief in Divine unity consisteth in regarding Him Who is the Manifestation of God and Him Who is the invisible, the inaccessible, the unknowable Essence as one and the same. By this is meant that whatever pertaineth to the former, all His acts and doings, whatever He ordaineth or forbiddeth, should be considered, in all their aspects, and under all circumstances, and without any reservation, as identical with the Will of God Himself. This is the loftiest station to which a true believer in the unity of God can ever hope to attain. Blessed is the

> man that reacheth this station, and is of them that are steadfast in their belief.
> (Bahá'u'lláh, *Gleanings from the Writings of Bahá'u'lláh*, p. 166)

We find the same theme in the words of Christ, as He explained this concept:

> Then answered Jesus and said unto them, Verily, verily, I say unto you, The Son can do nothing of himself, but what he seeth the Father do: for what things soever he doeth, these also doeth the Son likewise. . . . I can of mine own self do nothing: as I hear, I judge: and my judgment is just; because I seek not mine own will, but the will of the Father which hath sent me.
> (John 5:19)

> 8:16 for I am not alone, but I and the Father that sent me . . 8:19 if ye had known me, ye should have known my Father also . . . 10:30 I and my Father are one. . . . 10:38 and believe, that the Father is in me, and I in him.
> (John)

> whatsoever I speak therefore, even as the Father said unto me, so I speak.
> (John 12:50)

> Jesus saith unto him, Have I been so long time with you, and yet hast thou not known me, Philip? he that hath seen me hath seen the Father; and how sayest thou then, Shew us the Father? Believest thou not that I am in the Father, and the Father in me? the words that I speak unto you I speak not of myself: but the Father that dwelleth in me, he doeth the works.
> (John 14:9–10)

the essential and highest purpose in creation—will have been closed[151]

151. Bahá'u'lláh states that the purpose of the creation of man is for man to know and worship God:

> I bear witness, O my God, that Thou hast created me to know Thee and to worship Thee.
> (Bahá'u'lláh, *Prayers and Meditations by Bahá'u'lláh*, p. 313)

The Bahá'í Writings clearly state that the knowledge of God is in essence the knowledge of the Manifestation of God:

> The knowledge of the reality of the Divinity is in no wise possible, but the knowledge of the Manifestations of God is the knowledge of God, for the bounties, splendours, and attributes of God are manifest in Them. Thus, whoso attains to the knowledge of the Manifestations of God attains to the knowledge of God, and whoso remains heedless of Them remains bereft of that knowledge. It is therefore clearly established that the Holy Manifestations are the focal centres of the heavenly bounties, signs, and perfections. Blessed are those who receive the light of divine bounties from those luminous Daysprings!
> ('Abdu'l-Bahá, *Some Answered Questions*, no. 59.9)

> The source of all learning is the knowledge of God, exalted be His Glory, and this cannot be attained save through the knowledge of His Divine Manifestation.
> (Bahá'u'lláh, *Tablets of Bahá'u'lláh*, p. 156)

> And when the sanctified souls rend asunder the veils of all earthly attachments and worldly conditions, and hasten to the stage of gazing on the beauty of the Divine Presence and are honoured by recognizing the Manifestation and are able to witness the splendour of God's Most Great Sign in their hearts, then will the purpose of creation, which is the knowledge of Him Who is the Eternal Truth, become manifest.
> (Bahá'u'lláh, The Kitáb-i-Aqdas, Notes, p. 175)

as this is witnessed in this day when the reins of every community have fallen into the grasp of foolish leaders, who lead after their own whims and desire. On their tongue the mention of God hath become an empty name; in their midst His holy Word a dead letter[152]

152. We are witnessing this situation so clearly in the world—that so many communities, especially certain religious communities, are controlled by the kinds of leaders described by Bahá'u'lláh. Both the Christian and Muslim scriptures contain many references to these foolish and self-centered religious leaders who grasp the rein of religious communities and prevent them from recognizing and accepting the new Manifestation of God:

> Jesus said, "The Pharisees and the scribes have taken the keys of Knowledge and hidden them. They themselves have not entered, nor have they allowed to enter those who wish to. You, however, be as wise as serpents and as innocent as doves."
> (The Gospel of Thomas 39, *The Other Bible*, p. 303)

A tradition from Muḥammad describes the characteristics of the religious doctors of the time of the coming of the promised one of Islam:

> A day shall be witnessed by My people, whereon there will have remained of Islam naught but a name, and of the Qur'án naught but a mere appearance. The doctors of that age shall be the most evil the world hath ever seen. Mischief hath proceeded from them, and on them it will recoil." And again: "Most of His enemies will be the divines. His bidding they will not obey, but will protest saying: 'This is contrary to that which hath been handed down unto us by the Imáms of the Faith.'" And still again: "At that hour His malediction shall descend upon you, and your curse shall afflict you, and your religion shall remain an empty word on your tongues. And when these signs appear amongst you, anticipate the day when the red-hot wind will have swept over you, or the day when ye will have been disfigured, or when stones will have rained upon you."
> (Shoghi Effendi, *The Promised Day is Come,* p. 98)

portals of the knowledge of God[153]

153. The Jews believe that by the end of the Jewish prophetic era (approximately the fifth century BCE), the portals of divine

knowledge and revelation were closed. Almost all Christian denominations also believe that by the end of the first century AD the doors of divine knowledge were closed. The Majority of Muslims (Sunnis) also believe that after the passing of the prophet Muḥammad, and for the Shi'is, after the occultation and hiding of the last Imám (see Note No. 31 above), the doors to the divine knowledge were closed. Therefore, in each case they sought guidance from the leaders of their religion who ruled and guided them based on their own personal and deficient human understanding and conjecture, which would naturally be contrary to the ideas, guidance, and conjectures of the other religious leaders. This caused a myriad sectarian divisions and problems among the followers of each religion. In all these religions the clerics arrogated themselves to interpret the scriptures based on conjecture and idle fancy. Moreover, at the time of the advent of each Manifestation of God, the same leaders claimed that the doors of knowledge were still closed and did not acknowledge or recognize the new source of divine knowledge.

Clinging unto idle fancy, they have strayed far from the 'Urvatu'l-Vuthqá of divine knowledge[154]

154. 'Urvatu'l-Vuthqá, meaning "the sure handle" or "the strongest handle," signifies a reliable support that preserves a person from slipping and falling. This term first appeared in the Qur'án:

> Let there be no compulsion in Religion. Now is the right way made distinct from error. Whoever therefore shall deny Thagout (the Idol) and believe in God—he will have taken hold on a strong handle that shall not be broken: and God is He who Heareth, Knoweth."
> (The Qur'án 2:257)
>
> But whoso setteth his face toward God with self-surrender, and is a doer of that which is good, hath laid hold on a sure handle; for unto God is the issue of all things.
> (The Qur'án 31:21)

This term also appears in many places in the Bahá'í Writings where it generally signifies the faith and recognition of the Manifestation of God:

> From this exalted station We send Our greetings unto such believers as have taken fast hold on the Sure Handle and quaffed the choice wine of constancy from the hand of favour of their Lord, the Almighty, the All-Praised.
> (Bahá'u'lláh, *Tablets of Bahá'u'lláh*, p. 239)

> Certain people seem to be entirely bereft of understanding. By clinging to the cord of idle fancy they have debarred themselves from the Sure Handle. I swear by My life! Were they to reflect a while with fairness on that which the All-Merciful hath sent down, they would, one and all, spontaneously give utterance to these words, "Verily Thou art the Truth, the manifest Truth."
> (Bahá'u'lláh, *Tablets of Bahá'u'lláh*, p. 242)

This is the same concept expressed in the Gospels in Christ's parable of building a house on a sure and strong foundation:

> Therefore whosoever heareth these sayings of mine, and doeth them, I will liken him unto a wise man, which built his house upon a rock: And the rain descended, and the floods came, and the winds blew, and beat upon that house; and it fell not: for it was founded upon a rock. And every one that heareth these sayings of mine, and doeth them not, shall be likened unto a foolish man, which built his house upon the sand: And the rain descended, and the floods came, and the winds blew, and beat upon that house; and it fell: and great was the fall of it.
> (Matthew 7:24–27)

'Abdu'l-Bahá states that this is the covenant of God that protects those who hold fast unto it:

> The glory of God rest upon thee and upon them that hold fast unto the sure handle of His Will and holy Covenant.
> ('Abdu'l-Bahá, *Selections from the Writings of 'Abdu'l-Bahá,* p. 205)

> "Know thou," He has written, "that the 'Sure Handle' mentioned from the foundation of the world in the Books, the Tablets and the Scriptures of old is naught else but the Covenant and the Testament."
> (Shoghi Effendi, *God Passes By*, p. 238)

Their hearts seem not to be inclined to knowledge and the door thereof, neither think they of its manifestations, inasmuch as in idle fancy they have found the door that leadeth unto earthly riches, whereas in the manifestation of the Revealer of knowledge they find naught but the call to self-sacrifice[155]

155. The history of the Bahá'í Faith is replete with examples of these contrasting situations. There were many famous, highly stationed, and widely recognized religious leaders, who upon embracing the new Manifestation of God and His Faith, lost their position and everything they had, and in many cases sacrificed their lives, while their colleagues, some of whom even privately acknowledged the truth of the Báb and Bahá'u'lláh, did not have the courage to embrace the Manifestations of God and denounced them or rose against them to protect their own position and earthly riches. An example of the former is Vaḥíd Dárábí who was the greatest divine of his time. He was sent by Muḥammad Shah to investigate the Cause of the Báb. When he accepted the station of the Báb and announced the truth of the Báb's claims, he lost his position, power, and worldly riches, and was eventually martyred and sacrificed his life (see *God Passes By*, pp. 11–12). An example of the latter is Mírzá Muḥiṭ (please see Note No. 11, above for his story).

Were the eye to be anointed and illumined with the collyrium[156] **of the knowledge of God it would surely discover that a number of voracious beasts have gathered and preyed upon the carrion of the souls of men.**[157]

156. The word "collyrium" comes from the Greek word *κολλύρον,* meaning eye-salve. It is a liquid wash that is used in eyecare. A diseased eye will have viscous secretion that will disturb, and in many cases, prevent clear vision. The collyrium will wash and clean away the secretion, and restore the health and vision to the eye. The knowledge of God is that collyrium which will heal the inner eye and will clean and wash away all those materials that cloud the vision and will restore sight to the inner eye.

157. The "carrion of the souls of men" is an allusion to the spiritually dead people. The corrupt religious leaders are those voracious beasts who are preying upon these dead bodies.

Paragraph No. 29:

What "oppression" is more grievous than that a soul seeking the truth, and wishing to attain unto the knowledge of God, should know not where to go for it and from whom to seek it?[158]

158. This is one of the most important keys for unlocking the mysteries of the prophecies in the sacred books of the past religions. The oppression that, according to the prophecies must precede the appearance of the promised ones, is the absence of truth and the knowledge of God. Although, this concept was presented in the Old Testament, the religious leaders either did not understand it themselves or interpreted it literally to mean famine or other natural disasters, and in doing so prevented the people from comprehending.

> And it shall come to pass in that day, saith the Lord GOD, that I will cause the sun to go down at noon, and I will darken the earth in the clear day: And I will turn your feasts into mourning, and all your songs into lamentation; and I will bring up sackcloth upon all loins, and baldness upon every head; and I will make it as the mourning of an only son, and the end thereof as a bitter day. Behold, the days come, saith the Lord GOD, that I will send a famine in the land, not a famine of bread, nor a thirst for water, but of hearing the words of the LORD: And they shall wander from sea to sea, and from the north even to the east, they shall run to and fro to seek the word of the LORD, and shall not find it.
> (Amos 8:9–12)

For the break of the morn of divine guidance must needs follow the darkness of the night of error.[159]

159. In some of the Bahá'í Writings, "night" is meant to symbolize the period between two divine Revelations when the Sun of Truth is not manifest among men.

As the traditions referred to are well known, and as the purpose of this servant is to be brief, He will refrain from quoting the text of these traditions.[160]

160. There are a number of Islamic traditions and prophecies from Muḥammad and 'Alí and other Imáms regarding the conditions of the world and human society at the time of the end, when the promised one of Islam would appear. Several famous traditions of this kind appear in the well-known, multi-volume traditions books, the *Bahár'u'l-Anvár* (Oceans of Light, see Note No. 31 above), more specifically in volume 13. In one of those long traditions quoted in Qámus-i-Íqán, Imám 'Alí describes the conditions of that time. He states that at that time people will not care about religion much, bribery and lying will be prevalent, people who lack knowledge or experience will occupy high positions, killing people will be easy, the rulers will be unjust, and religious leaders will be decadent and barter their religion and their soul for worldly gains. They will make ornate Qur'áns and build large mosques with very tall minarets and large numbers of people will go to the Mosques for prayer, but their hearts will be full of worldly desires and satanic fancies. The most unworthy and spiritually deprived people will become leaders of the religious communities. Also women will be consulted and will participate in politics and commerce. At that time, when these conditions are observed, according to the Imám, haste should be made to go to the Holy Land, as everyone will wish to reside there.
(Source: 'Abdu'l-Ḥamíd Ishráq-Khávari, *Qámus-i-Íqán, Vol. 2*, p. 708)

There is another tradition from Muḥammad that states:

> A day shall be witnessed by My people, whereon there will have remained of Islam naught but a name, and of the Qur'án naught but a mere appearance.
> (Quoted by Shoghi Effendi, The Promised Day is Come, p. 98)

Similar statements are also found in the Old and New Testaments:

> And because iniquity shall abound, the love of many shall wax cold.
> (Matthew 24:12)

Paragraph No. 30:

Were this "oppression" (which literally meaneth pressure) to be interpreted that the earth is to become contracted, or were men's idle fancy to conceive similar calamities to befall mankind, it is clear and manifest that no such happenings can ever come to pass.[161]

161. Bahá'u'lláh is referring to Mathew 24:29 "Immediately after the tribulation of those days shall the sun be darkened, and the moon shall not give her light . . ." The word "tribulation" in this verse is the translation of the Greek word "thlipsis." Strong's Hebrew and Greek Dictionaries of the Bible defines this word as: "*pressure* (literally or figuratively):—afflicted, (-tion), anguish, burdened, persecution, tribulation, trouble."

The same word "thlipsis" used by Christ in John 16:21, is translated as anguish: "A woman when she is in travail hath sorrow, because her hour is come: but as soon as she is delivered of the child, she remembereth no more the anguish, for joy that a man is born into the world."

This indicates that both Christ and Bahá'u'lláh consider this a spiritual condition, and confirms the fact that the correct meaning of the word and the true description of the condition referred to in Mathew 24:29 is what Bahá'u'lláh described and not what the generality of Christians understand and describe as tribulation, i.e. physical calamities.

Whereas, by "oppression" is meant the want of capacity to acquire spiritual knowledge and apprehend the Word of God.[162]

162. This lack of capacity to comprehend the words of God and instead follow the dictates of the religious leaders, is the condition that the majority of the people have been afflicted with at the time of the appearance of every Manifestation of God. A very clear example of this is found in Mathew chapter 13, where Christ relates the parable of the sower and the disciples ask why He speaks in parables:

> And the disciples came, and said unto him, Why speakest thou unto them in parables? He answered and said unto them. Because it is given unto you to know the mysteries of the kingdom of heaven, but to them it is not given. For whosoever hath, to him shall be given, and he shall have more abundance: but whosoever hath not, from him shall be taken away even that he hath. Therefore speak I to them in parables: because they seeing see not; and hearing they hear not, neither do they understand. And in them is fulfilled the prophecy of Esaias, which saith, By hearing ye shall hear, and shall not understand; and seeing ye shall see, and shall not perceive: For this people's heart is waxed gross, and their ears are dull of hearing, and their eyes they have closed; lest at any time they should see with their eyes and hear with their ears, and should understand with their heart, and should be converted, and I should heal them. But blessed are your eyes, for they see: and your ears, for they hear.
> (Matthew 13:10–16)

By it is meant that when the Day-star of Truth hath set, and the mirrors that reflect His light have departed[163]

163. In the Bahá'í Writings the Manifestations of God are often referred to as the Daystars of Truth.

mankind will become afflicted with "oppression" and hardship, knowing not whither to turn for guidance.[164]

164. Again Christ and Bahá'u'lláh speak of the same concept—that if people, instead of receiving spiritual knowledge from the Manifestations of God, seek guidance from religious leaders, they will be afflicted with oppression and hardship.

> Let them alone: they be blind leaders of the blind. And if the blind lead the blind, both shall fall into the ditch.
> (Matthew 15:14)

Thus We[165] instruct thee in the interpretation of the traditions, and reveal unto thee the mysteries of divine wisdom

165. In this sentence Bahá'u'lláh provides the readers with an intimation of His station by using the pronoun "We," and also indicates that One that occupies a divine station can reveal the mysteries of divine wisdom:

> When Bahá'u'lláh uses the plural—"We," "Our" etc.—He is merely using a form which is regal and has greater power than the singular "I." We have this same usage in English, when the King says "we." The Pope does the same thing.
> (From a letter written on behalf of Shoghi Effendi to an individual believer, February 18, 1951)

Paragraph No. 31:

These Suns of Truth are the universal Manifestations of God in the worlds of His attributes and names[166]

166. As mentioned in Note No. 14 above, the term "Manifestation of God"—referring to Moses, Jesus, Muḥammad, Zoroaster, Buddha, etc.—was used for the first time in sacred scriptures by the Báb and Bahá'u'lláh. The concept of the "Universal Manifestations of God" is also a very important theological concept that is presented for the first time in the sacred Bahá'í Writings. The universality of these Manifestations is based on two factors:

a) Although their life or surroundings might have remained confined to one region or culture, their Cause has a universal nature and is revealed for the whole and generality of the human race.
b) All these Manifestations have been endowed with divine power and excellence by the same divine universal spirit.

> True knowledge, therefore, is the knowledge of God, and this is none other than the recognition of His Manifestation in each Dispensation.
> (The Báb, *Selections from the Writings of the Báb*, p. 89)

> The knowledge of the reality of the Divinity is in no wise possible, but the knowledge of the Manifestations of God is the knowledge of God, for the bounties, splendours, and attributes of God are manifest in Them. Thus, whoso attains to the knowledge of the Manifestations of God attains to the knowledge of God, and whoso remains heedless of Them remains bereft of that knowledge. It is therefore clearly established that the Holy Manifestations are the focal centres of the heavenly bounties, signs, and perfections. Blessed are those who receive the light of divine bounties from those luminous Daysprings!
> ('Abdu'l-Bahá, *Some Answered Questions*, no. 59.9)

so do the divine Luminaries,[167] by their loving care and educative influence, cause the trees of divine unity, the fruits of His oneness, the leaves of detachment, the blossoms of knowledge and certitude, and the myrtles of wisdom and utterance, to exist and be made manifest.[168]

167. Although direct reference to Manifestations as divine Luminaries appears in the Bahá'í Writings, the concept has also appeared in the scriptures of the past:

> Then spake Jesus again unto them, saying, I am the light of the world: he that followeth me shall not walk in darkness, but shall have the light of life. . . .As long as I am in the world, I am the light of the world. . . .I am come a light into the world, that whosoever believeth on me should not abide in darkness.
> (John 8:12, 9:5, and 12:46)

168. Christ also explained the same concept when He stated:

> I am the true vine, and my Father is the husbandman. Every branch in me that beareth not fruit he taketh away: and every branch that beareth fruit, he purgeth it, that it may bring forth more fruit. Now ye are clean through the word which I have spoken unto you. Abide in me, and I in you. As the branch cannot bear fruit of itself, except it abide in the vine; no more can ye, except ye abide in me. I am the vine, ye are the branches: He that abideth in me, and I in

> him, the same bringeth forth much fruit: for without me ye can do nothing.
> (John 15:1–5)

Thus it is that through the rise of these Luminaries of God the world is made new, the waters of everlasting life stream forth,[169] the billows of loving-kindness surge, the clouds of grace are gathered, and the breeze of bounty bloweth upon all created things.

169. The same concept that the Revelation and teachings of the Manifestations of God bestow everlasting life is also expressed by Christ:

> Jesus answered and said unto her, If thou knewest the gift of God, and who it is that saith to thee, Give me to drink; thou wouldest have asked of him, and he would have given thee living water. The woman saith unto him, Sir, thou hast nothing to draw with, and the well is deep: from whence then hast thou that living water? . . . Jesus answered and said unto her, Whosoever drinketh of this water shall thirst again: But whosoever drinketh of the water that I shall give him shall never thirst; but the water that I shall give him shall be in him a well of water springing up into everlasting life.
> (John 4:10–14)

Paragraph No. 32:

The quintessence of every name can hope for no access unto their court of holiness, and the highest and purest of all attributes can never approach their kingdom of glory.[170]

170. This subject is explained by the Báb and 'Abdu'l-Bahá:

> For instance, were ye to place unnumbered mirrors before the sun, they would all reflect the sun and produce impressions thereof, whereas the sun is in itself wholly independent of the existence of the mirrors and of the suns which they reproduce. Such are the bounds of the

contingent beings in their relation to the manifestation of the Eternal Being. . . .
(The Báb, *Selections from the Writings of the Báb*, p. 93)

. . . the reality of the Divinity lies hidden from all understanding and is concealed from the minds of all men, and to ascend to that station is in no wise possible.

We observe that every lower thing is incapable of comprehending the reality of that which is higher. Thus, no matter how far they may evolve, the stone, the earth, and the tree can never comprehend the reality of man or imagine the powers of sight, hearing, or the other senses, even though the former and the latter alike are created things. How then can man, a mere creature, comprehend the reality of the sanctified Essence of the Creator? No human understanding can approach this station, no utterance can unfold its truth, and no allusion can intimate its mystery. What has the speck of dust to do with the world of sanctity, and what relationship can ever hold between the limited mind and the expanse of the limitless realm? Minds are powerless to comprehend Him, and souls are bewildered as they attempt to describe His reality. . . .

Thus, in this connection, every statement and explanation is deficient, every description and characterization is unworthy, every conception is unfounded, and every attempt to contemplate its depths is futile. Yet for that Essence of essences, that Truth of truths, that Mystery of mysteries, there are splendours, effulgences, manifestations, and appearances in the world of existence. The Daysprings of those effulgences, the Dawning-places of those revelations, and the Sources of those manifestations are those Exponents of holiness, those universal Realities and divine Beings Who are the true mirrors of the sanctified Essence of the Divinity. All the perfections, bounties, and splendours of the one true God are plainly visible in the realities of His Holy Manifestations, even as the light of the sun is fully reflected with all its perfections and bounties in a clear and spotless mirror. And if it be said that the mirrors are the

> manifestations of the sun and the dawning-places of the daystar of the world, this is not meant to imply that the sun has descended from the heights of its sanctity or has become embodied in the mirror, or that that limitless Reality has been confined to this visible plane. God forbid! This is the belief of the anthropomorphists. No, all these descriptions, all these expressions of praise and glory, refer to these holy Manifestations; that is, every description, praise, name, or attribute of God that we mention applies to Them. But no soul has ever fathomed the reality of the Essence of the Divinity so as to be able to intimate, describe, praise, or glorify it. Thus all that the human reality knows, discovers, and understands of the names, attributes, and perfections of God refers to these holy Manifestations and leads nowhere else: "The way is cut off, and all seeking rejected."
> ('Abdu'l-Bahá, *Some Answered Questions*, no. 37.3–5)

Glorified are they above the praise of men; exalted are they above human understanding![171]

171. Bahá'u'lláh states in many places in His writing that the Manifestation of God can only be known by His own self:

> It behooveth us, therefore, to make the utmost endeavor, that, by God's invisible assistance, these dark veils, these clouds of Heaven-sent trials, may not hinder us from beholding the beauty of His shining Countenance, and that we may recognize Him only by His own Self.
> (Bahá'u'lláh, *Gleanings from the Writings of Bahá'u'lláh*, p. 27)

> The first and foremost testimony establishing His truth is His own Self. Next to this testimony is His Revelation. For whoso faileth to recognize either the one or the other He hath established the words He hath revealed as proof of His reality and truth. This is, verily, an evidence of His tender mercy unto men.
> (Bahá'u'lláh, *Gleanings from the Writings of Bahá'u'lláh*, p. 105)

> He hath manifested unto men the Daystars of His divine guidance, the Symbols of His divine unity, and hath

ordained the knowledge of these sanctified Beings to be identical with the knowledge of His own Self. Whoso recognizeth them hath recognized God. Whoso hearkeneth to their call, hath hearkened to the Voice of God, and whoso testifieth to the truth of their Revelation, hath testified to the truth of God Himself.
(Bahá'u'lláh, *Gleanings from the Writings of Bahá'u'lláh,* p. 50)

O My servant that believest in God! . . . Meditate diligently upon the Cause of thy Lord. Strive to know Him through His own Self and not through others. For no one else besides Him can ever profit thee. To this all created things will testify, couldst thou but perceive it.
(Bahá'u'lláh, *Gleanings from the Writings of Bahá'u'lláh,* p. 148)

Say, God is my witness! The Promised One Himself hath come down from heaven, seated upon the crimson cloud with the hosts of revelation on His right, and the angels of inspiration on His left, and the Decree hath been fulfilled at the behest of God, the Omnipotent, the Almighty. Thereupon the footsteps of everyone have slipped except such as God hath protected through His tender mercy and numbered with those who have recognized Him through His Own Self and detached themselves from all that pertaineth to the world.
(Bahá'u'lláh, *Tablets of Bahá'u'lláh,* p. 182)

Paragraph No. 33:

The term "suns" hath many a time been applied in the writings of the "immaculate Souls"[172]

172. The "immaculate Souls" is a reference to the Imáms of Shí'ah Islam. These are the descendants of Muḥammad through His daughter Fátima and His cousin and son-in-law 'Alí. The Shí'ah sect of Islam believe that 'Alí was the rightful temporal and spiritual successor to Muḥammad, and after him, his sons and their descendants were the rightful leaders. They believe that Muḥammad appointed 'Alí as His successor during His last trip to Mecca. However, from the very day of the passing of Muḥammad, disagreement and division started in Islam as prominent people

and tribal leaders selected Abu-Bakr as the temporal and spiritual leader (Caliph), and after him other people usurped the power and leadership position, and 'Alí and his descendants, who were the legitimate temporal and spiritual leaders of the Islamic Empire were set aside. Shí'ah Muslims also believe that these Imáms were infallible (they were free from error, and the infallibility was conferred upon them by virtue of their lineage). The Bahá'í Writings confirm the station of 'Alí and his descendants as rightful successors to Muḥammad. In response to a question Shoghi Effendi stated:

> 'Ali's appointment was clear to the Khalifs, who actually disregarded the Prophet's oral statements. The usurpation occurred immediately after the Prophet's death. Ali did not feel unqualified, but wished to avoid schism, which, unfortunately, could not be prevented. The schisms that have afflicted the religions preceding the Faith of Bahá'u'lláh establish its distinction from all previous Revelations, and single it out among all other Dispensations, as stated by 'Abdu'l-Bahá. The guidance vouchsafed to the Imáms regarding the laws and institutions of Islam was absolute and unqualified. Their infallibility was derived directly from the Manifestation. The Báb's descent from the Imám Ḥusayn is no doubt a proof of the validity of the Imámate.
> (*Lights of Guidance*, p. 496)

Among those writings are the following words recorded in the "Prayer of Nudbih"[173]:

173. The word "Nudbih" means lamentations or wailing (the Wailing Wall in Jerusalem is also called the Wall of Nudbih). This is a famous prayer among the Shí'ah Muslims, and is said on four special days of the year. The prayer starts with the praise of Muḥammad and His descendants (the Imáms), and then continues with lamentation for their absence, "Whither are gone the resplendent Suns? Whereunto have departed those shining Moons and sparkling Stars?" By referring to this prayer, Bahá'u'lláh reminds the readers that the application of the terms sun, moon, and star to Manifestations and spiritual luminaries has precedence in the

scriptures and when these terms are mentioned in prophecies, they do not refer to the physical sun, moon, or stars, as Christ also stated:

> Then shall the righteous shine forth as the sun in the kingdom of their Father. Who hath ears to hear, let him hear."
> (Matthew 13:43)

Paragraph No. 34:

If these divines be illumined by the light of the latter Revelation they will be acceptable unto God, and will shine with a light everlasting.[174]

174. The same theme is also developed in some other Writings of Bahá'u'lláh:

> "O CONCOURSE of divines! Can any one of you race with the Divine Youth in the arena of wisdom and utterance, or soar with Him into the heaven of inner meaning and explanation? Nay, by My Lord, the God of mercy! All have swooned away in this Day from the Word of thy Lord. They are even as dead and lifeless, except him whom thy Lord, the Almighty, the Unconstrained, hath willed to exempt. Such a one is indeed of those endued with knowledge in the sight of Him Who is the All-Knowing. The inmates of Paradise, and the dwellers of the sacred Folds, bless him at eventide and at dawn. Can the one possessed of wooden legs resist him whose feet God hath made of steel? Nay, by Him Who illumineth the whole of creation!
>
> When We observed carefully, We discovered that Our enemies are, for the most part, the divines. . . . Among the people are those who said: He hath repudiated the divines. Say: Yea, by My Lord! I, in very truth, was the One Who abolished the idols! We, verily, have sounded the Trumpet, which is Our Most Sublime Pen, and lo, the divines and the learned, and the doctors and the rulers, swooned away except such as God preserved, as a token of His grace, and He, verily, is the All-Bounteous, the Ancient of Days. . . .

> O concourse of divines! Fling away idle fancies and imaginings, and turn, then, towards the Horizon of Certitude. I swear by God! All that ye possess will profit you not, neither all the treasures of the earth, nor the leadership ye have usurped. Fear God, and be not of the lost ones. . . . Say: O concourse of divines! Lay aside all your veils and coverings. Give ear unto that whereunto calleth you the Most Sublime Pen, in this wondrous Day. . . . The world is laden with dust, by reason of your vain imaginings, and the hearts of such as enjoy near access to God are troubled because of your cruelty. Fear God, and be of them that judge equitably."
> (Bahá'u'lláh, *The Proclamation of Bahá'u'lláh*, p. 75)

Otherwise, they will be declared as darkened, even though to outward seeming they be leaders of men, inasmuch as belief and unbelief, guidance and error, felicity and misery, light and darkness, are all dependent upon the sanction of Him Who is the Daystar of Truth.[175]

175. The same concept is also presented in the Kitáb-i-Aqdas:

> By the righteousness of the one true God! Were anyone to wash the feet of all mankind, and were he to worship God in the forests, valleys, and mountains, upon high hills and lofty peaks, to leave no rock or tree, no clod of earth, but was a witness to his worship—yet, should the fragrance of My good pleasure not be inhaled from him, his works would never be acceptable unto God. Thus hath it been decreed by Him Who is the Lord of all. . . . Say: The very life of all deeds is My good pleasure, and all things depend upon Mine acceptance.
> (Bahá'u'lláh, The Kitáb-i-Aqdas, ¶36)

Whosoever among the divines of every age receiveth, in the Day of Reckoning, the testimony of faith from the Source of true knowledge, he verily becometh the recipient of learning, of divine favour, and of the light of true understanding. Otherwise, he is branded as guilty of folly, denial, blasphemy, and oppression.[176]

176. As stated above, in the Bahá'í Writings, the Day of Reckoning or the Day of Resurrection is defined as the day of the appearance or declaration of a Manifestation of God. Therefore, the day of the advent of each Manifestation of God is the Day of Resurrection of the followers of all the previous religions. Bahá'u'lláh in the Tablet to Christians states:

> O concourse of bishops! Ye are the stars of the heaven of My knowledge. My mercy desireth not that ye should fall upon the earth. My justice, however, declareth: "This is that which the Son hath decreed." And whatsoever hath proceeded out of His blameless, His truth-speaking, trustworthy mouth, can never be altered.* The bells, verily, peal out My Name, and lament over Me, but My spirit rejoiceth with evident gladness. The body of the Loved One yearneth for the cross, and His head is eager for the spear, in the path of the All-Merciful. The ascendancy of the oppressor can in no wise deter Him from His purpose. We have summoned all created things to attain the presence of thy Lord, the King of all names. Blessed is the man that hath set his face towards God, the Lord of the Day of Reckoning.
> (Bahá'u'lláh, *Tablets of Bahá'u'lláh*, p. 13)

* The religious leaders at the time of Christ, Pharisees and scribes, were like the bishops in present-day Christianity. Jesus spoke of them in many places in the Gospels such as the following:

> But woe unto you, scribes and Pharisees, hypocrites! for ye shut up the kingdom of heaven against men: for ye neither go in yourselves, neither suffer ye them that are entering to go in. . . . Even so ye also outwardly appear righteous unto men, but within ye are full of hypocrisy and iniquity. . . . Woe unto you, scribes and Pharisees, hypocrites! because ye build the tombs of the prophets, and garnish the sepulchres of the righteous, And say, If we had been in the days of our fathers, we would not have been partakers with them in the blood of the prophets. Wherefore ye be witnesses unto yourselves, that ye are the children of them which killed the prophets. Fill ye up then the measure of

> your fathers. Ye serpents, ye generation of vipers, how can ye escape the damnation of hell?
> (Matthew 23:13–31)

Paragraph No. 35:

It is evident and manifest unto every discerning observer that even as the light of the star fadeth before the effulgent splendour of the sun, so doth the luminary of earthly knowledge, of wisdom, and understanding vanish into nothingness when brought face to face with the resplendent glories of the Sun of Truth, the Day-star of divine enlightenment.[177]

177. The same theme is discussed by Bahá'u'lláh in the Epistle to the Son of the Wolf:

> O Shaykh! Reflect upon these words addressed by Him Who is the Desire of the world to Amos[58]. He saith: "Prepare to meet thy God, O Israel, for, lo, He that formeth the mountains[59] and createth the wind, and declareth unto man what is his thought, that maketh the morning darkness, and treadeth upon the high places of the earth, the Lord, the God of Hosts, is His name." He saith that He maketh the morning darkness. By this is meant that if, at the time of the Manifestation of Him Who conversed on Sinai anyone were to regard himself as the true morn, he will, through the might and power of God, be turned into darkness. He truly is the false dawn, though believing himself to be the true one. Woe unto him, and woe unto such as follow him without a clear token from God, the Lord of the worlds.
> (Bahá'u'lláh, Epistle to the Son of the Wolf, p. 145)

---

[58] (Amos 4:13)

[59] The Eternal Sovereignty descends from heaven, the body is of the earth. The mountains are men of high renown, whose famous names sink into insignificance when the dawn of the Manifestation fills the world with light. The pomp of Annas and Caiaphas* is outshone by the simple glory of the Christ. The earthquake is the wave of spiritual life that moves through all living things and makes creation quiver.
(H.M. Balyuzi, *'Abdu'l-Bahá - The Centre of the Covenant*, p. 499)

* Annas and Caiaphas were the high priests of Israel, who following their interrogation of Jesus, as described in Mathew, Chapter 26 and John, Chapter 18, issued their decree to crucify Christ.

Paragraph No. 36:

If they be in the likeness of the Sun of Truth, they will surely be accounted as the most exalted of all luminaries.[178]

178. Bahá'u'lláh, in extolling the station of the divines and learned people of the past religions, who were earnestly searching for truth, and who accepted and followed the Manifestations of God when They appeared, states:

> The divine who hath seized and quaffed the most holy Wine, in the name of the sovereign Ordainer, is as an eye unto the world. Well is it with them who obey him, and call him to remembrance.
>
> Great is the blessedness of that divine that hath not allowed knowledge to become a veil between him and the One Who is the Object of all knowledge, and who, when the Self-Subsisting appeared, hath turned with a beaming face towards Him. He, in truth, is numbered with the learned. The inmates of Paradise seek the blessing of his breath, and his lamp sheddeth its radiance over all who are in heaven and on earth. He, verily, is numbered with the inheritors of the Prophets. He that beholdeth him hath, verily, beheld the True One, and he that turneth towards him hath, verily, turned towards God, the Almighty, the All-Wise."
> (Bahá'u'lláh, *The Proclamation of Bahá'u'lláh*, p. 78)

Even as He saith: "Verily, the sun and the moon are both condemned to the torment of infernal fire.[179]

179. This verse (Súrah 55, The Merciful, verse 5) has been interpreted differently by the Sunni and Shí'ah commentators of the Qur'án. The Shí'ah sources present this verse as:

> "Verily, the sun and the moon are both condemned to the torment of infernal fire."

Sunnis, and English translations by non-Shí'ah translators, present this verse as:

> "The Sun and the Moon have each their times," (The Qur'án, Rodwell tr)
>
> "The sun and the moon are made punctual." (The Qur'án, Pickthall tr)
>
> "The sun and the moon follow courses (exactly) computed;" (The Qur'án, Yusuf Ali tr)

The operating word is the Arabic word "Husbán," which means Hell, and comes from the root of "Hesáb," which means calculation. Those that considered the sun and moon mentioned in this verse as the physical sun and moon, interpreted it to mean that the sun and moon are in a regulated or calculated course. However, some of the commentators have, based on the Shí'ah traditions, considered the "Husbán" as Hell and Sun and Moon as certain people who had high stations among the people of their time, but were condemned to the torment of Hell.

You are no doubt familiar with the interpretation of the term "sun" and "moon" mentioned in this verse; no need therefore to refer unto it.[180]

180. The interpretation referred to here by Bahá'u'lláh is based on a tradition related to one of the Shí'ah Imáms (Imám Riḍá) who interpreted "Husbán" as the divine torment, and Sun and Moon as some of the important figures and leaders in early Islamic history, who, as a result of their opposition to Islam, would be condemned to the torment of Hell.
(Source: 'Abdu'l-Ḥamíd Ishráq-Khávari, *Qámus-i-Íqán,* Vol. 4, p. 1480)

Paragraph No. 37:

O seeker, it behooveth us firmly to cling unto the Urvatu'l-Vuthqá[181]

181. Please see Note No. 154 above.

Shall we not free ourselves from the horror of satanic gloom, and hasten towards the rising light of the heavenly Beauty?[182]

182. Bahá'u'lláh here expounds on the theme of dawning of a new Day and rising of the divine sun in contrast to the forces of denial that intend to keep people in the gloom of darkness (the spiritual night season). He Has also written on this theme in His other Writings:

> O CHILDREN OF FANCY!
> Know, verily, that while the radiant dawn breaketh above the horizon of eternal holiness, the satanic secrets and deeds done in the gloom of night shall be laid bare and manifest before the peoples of the world.
> (Bahá'u'lláh, The Hidden Words, Persian, no. 67)
>
> O thou who art mentioned in this outspread roll and who, amidst the gloomy darkness that now prevaileth, hast been illumined by the splendours of the sacred Mount in the Sinai of divine Revelation! Cleanse thy heart from every blasphemous whispering and evil allusion thou hast heard in the past, that thou mayest inhale the sweet savours of eternity from the Joseph of faithfulness , gain admittance into the celestial Egypt, and perceive the fragrances of enlightenment from this resplendent and luminous Tablet. . . .
> (Bahá'u'lláh, *Gems of Divine Mysteries,* p. 23)

In such wise, we bestow upon you the fruit of the Tree of divine knowledge that ye may gladly and joyously abide in the Riḍván of divine wisdom[183]

183. Although the Book of Certitude was revealed more than a year before Bahá'u'lláh's public declaration, this is an allusion to His divine station, through which He bestows upon the uncle of the Báb and all the seekers who read this Book, the fruits of the Tree of divine knowledge (Manifestation of God), and assists them to turn away from the gloom and darkness of denial and move towards the light of faith.

Paragraph No. 38:

In another sense, by the terms "sun," "moon," and "stars" are meant such laws and teachings as have been established and proclaimed in every Dispensation, such as the laws of prayer and fasting[184]

184. The prayer, as mentioned here, is the translation of the Arabic word "ṣalát." In some religions such as Zoroastrianism, Islam, and the Bahá'í Faith, prayers are in two forms: obligatory and supererogatory. Ṣalát is a form of prayer that is known as the obligatory prayer. This is a prayer that has a special format, both with regard to the content and the method of its performance.

> In Arabic, there are several words for prayer. The word "ṣalát," which appears here in the original, refers to a particular category of prayers, the recitation of which at specific times of the day is enjoined on the believers. To differentiate this category of prayers from other kinds, the word has been translated as "*obligatory prayer.*"
> Bahá'u'lláh states that "*obligatory prayer and fasting occupy an exalted station in the sight of God*".
> (The Kitáb-i-Aqdas, Notes, p. 166)

Nay rather, in every Dispensation the law concerning prayer hath been emphasized and universally enforced[185]

185. The laws of prayer and fasting, although existing in general form in all religions, have evolved and taken different forms in different religious practices.

In Judaism, supplication and prayer has been regarded as a very important act that the Jews were required to perform. Although no specific form of prayer has been prescribed in the Old Testament, over the centuries Jews have, based on the scriptures and traditions, developed many structured prayers, which were recorded and passed on to later generations, for different occasions. In Judaism, prayers and sacrifice rituals are closely related, but since the destruction of the Temple in Jerusalem, the sacrifice and burnt offerings have stopped. Jewish prayer is related to, and is specified for, times and seasons. There are special prayers for specific times of day, days of the week (both for regular days and the sacred days), as well as ordinary seasons and festival seasons. There are prayers for special events such as a birth, naming a child, and circumcision. The prayers are compiled in prayer books called *Siddurim*. The Hebrew word for prayer book is *Siddur*, which is a book that contains certain Hebrew prayers in a very specific, time-based order. Observant Jews pray three times a day following the tradition of David as he stated:

> As for me, I will call upon God; and the LORD shall save me. Evening, and morning, and at noon, will I pray, and cry aloud: and he shall hear my voice.
> (Psalms 55:16–17)

Formal prayer services are held in Synagogues three times a day, every day, commemorating the historical sacrifice rituals offered at the Temple in Jerusalem. The daily prayers consist of morning prayers, afternoon prayers, and evening prayers. The Sabbath prayers have their own special routine. Historically, the prayers were recited facing the Temple, which contained the Ark of the Covenant, as stated in the Old Testament:

> If thy people go out to war against their enemies by the way that thou shalt send them, and they pray unto thee toward this city which thou hast chosen, and the house which I have built for thy name; Then hear thou from the heavens their prayer and their supplication, and maintain their cause.
> (2 Chronicles 6:34–35)

However, in contemporary times the prayers are recited while facing the Aron Kodesh (the ark that houses the Torah scrolls in the Synagogues). Different Jewish sects use different *Siddurim*. The major Jewish sects such as the Orthodox, Conservative, Reformed, Messianic, and Reconstructionist Jews, have their own *Siddurim*.

Fasting is also observed by Jews. Fasting for Jews means completely abstaining from food and drink, including water. Observant Jews fast on up to six days of the year. With the exception of Yom Kippur (the day of atonement and redemption of sins), fasting is never permitted on Shabbat for the commandment of keeping Shabbat is biblically ordained and overrides the later rabbinically-instituted fast days. Yom Kippur is the only fast day that is explicitly stated in the Torah.

Yom Kippur is considered to be the most important day of the Jewish year, and fasting as a means of repentance is expected of every Jewish man and boy above the age of bar mitzvah (thirteen years old). This is the age at which a Jewish boy is considered to be mature enough to observe religious precepts and is eligible to take part in public worship). For Jewish woman and girls, the age of maturity is twelve years old (known as bat mitzvah). It is considered so important to fast on this day that only those who would be put in danger by fasting are exempt, such as the ill, elderly, or pregnant or nursing women, as endangering one's life is against a core principle of Judaism. Those that do eat on this day are encouraged to eat as little as possible at a time and to avoid a full meal. For some, fasting on Yom Kippur is considered more important than the prayers of this holy day. If one fasts, even if one is at home in bed, one is considered as having participated in the full religious service. In addition to fasting and prayer, Yom Kippur—as the "Sabbath of Sabbaths"—has the same restrictions regarding work as the Sabbath, such as striking a fire, carrying objects outside the home, using tools, and so on. Traditionally, leather shoes are not worn on this day. Men may wear a white gown over their clothes, symbolic of a burial shroud on this Day of Judgment.

The second major day of fasting is Tisha B'Av, the day nearly 2,000 years ago on which the Romans destroyed the Holy Temple in Jerusalem and the Jews were banished from their homeland. Both of these holy days are considered major fasting days and are observed from sunset to sunset on the following day by both men and women. The remaining four fasts are considered minor, and fasting is only observed from sunrise to sunset.
(Based on information from Wikipedia).

Zoroastrians have to pray five times in every twenty-four hours. First from dawn to mid-day, second from noon to three hours after noon, third from three hours after noon to sunset, fourth from sunset to midnight, and fifth from midnight to dawn. Prior to

performing the payer, the arms from the tip of the fingers to the elbow, the face, behind the ears, and under the chin, must be washed (ablution). Fasting is also observed by the Zoroastrians. They fast five days a year in the beginning of the first month of the year (five days after the Naw-Ruz or the first day of the year) from sunrise to sunset.
In Christianity, although prayer and fasting are prescribed by Christ, there is only one prayer that is recorded in the Gospels, the Lord's Prayer:

> Our Father which art in heaven, Hallowed be thy name. Thy kingdom come, Thy will be done in earth, as it is in heaven. Give us this day our daily bread. And forgive us our debts, as we forgive our debtors. And lead us not into temptation, but deliver us from evil: For thine is the kingdom, and the power, and the glory, for ever. Amen.
> (Matthew 6:9–13)

Although following and practicing the requirements of the law such as prayers and fasting was sanctioned by Jesus, as stated in the Gospel of Matthew:

> Think not that I am come to destroy the law, or the prophets[60]: I am not come to destroy, but to fulfil. For verily I say unto you, Till heaven and earth pass, one jot or one tittle shall in no wise pass from the law, till all be fulfilled. Whosoever therefore shall break one of these least commandments, and shall teach men so, he shall be called the least in the kingdom of heaven: but whosoever shall do and teach them, the same shall be called great in the kingdom of heaven.
> (Matthew 5:17–19)

His very strong admonitions against the hypocritical practices of some Jews, especially some of the clergy, caused most of the Christians to abandon the strict observance of the law such as the

[60] As mentioned above in Note No. 19, Judaism is based on two pillars of Law and Prophets. The law is what is revealed in the Pentateuch (the five books of Moses) and is represented by Moses the law giver. The Prophets is the teachings of the prophets of Israel as recorded in their books and symbolically represented by Elijah.

Jewish fasting and the daily practice of prayers, and to pray as they were instructed in the following verses:

> And when thou prayest, thou shalt not be as the hypocrites are: for they love to pray standing in the synagogues and in the corners of the streets, that they may be seen of men. Verily I say unto you, They have their reward. But thou, when thou prayest, enter into thy closet, and when thou hast shut thy door, pray to thy Father which is in secret; and thy Father which seeth in secret shall reward thee openly. But when ye pray, use not vain repetitions, as the heathen do: for they think that they shall be heard for their much speaking. Be not ye therefore like unto them: for your Father knoweth what things ye have need of, before ye ask him. After this manner therefore pray ye: Our Father which art in heaven, Hallowed be thy name. Thy kingdom come, Thy will be done in earth, as it is in heaven. Give us this day our daily bread. And forgive us our debts, as we forgive our debtors. And lead us not into temptation, but deliver us from evil: For thine is the kingdom, and the power, and the glory, for ever. Amen. For if ye forgive men their trespasses, your heavenly Father will also forgive you: But if ye forgive not men their trespasses, neither will your Father forgive your trespasses. Moreover when ye fast, be not, as the hypocrites, of a sad countenance: for they disfigure their faces, that they may appear unto men to fast. Verily I say unto you, They have their reward. But thou, when thou fastest, anoint thine head, and wash thy face; That thou appear not unto men to fast, but unto thy Father which is in secret: and thy Father, which seeth in secret, shall reward thee openly.
> (Matthew 6:5–15)

In Islam, fasting and daily prayers (obligatory prayers) are the two most important laws. For Sunni Muslims, these are two of the five pillars of Islam (the primary principles of religion), and for Shi'ah Muslims, they also are among the most important articles of the faith.

Muslims fast one Lunar month per year, called the month of Ramaḍán, from dawn to twilight. The Islamic calendar is a lunar calendar, therefore the months move through the seasons, the fasting period might fall in summer, fall, winter, or spring and the number of days might differ from year to year ranging from twenty-six to thirty days. The obligatory prayers are performed five times in twenty-four hours at dawn, noon, mid-afternoon, sunset, and night fall. The prayer is performed facing toward the Ka‘bih[61] in Mecca and with ablution (similar to Zoroastrian ablution) prior to performing the prayers. In Islam it is preferred that the obligatory prayers be performed in congregation and in the Mosque. Some Muslim theologians maintain (based on some traditions related to the Prophet Muḥammad) that the obligatory prayers not performed in a congregational setup (as in a Mosque in company of other people) are not acceptable.

To this testify the recorded traditions ascribed to the lights that have emanated from the Daystar of Truth, the essence of the Prophet Muḥammad[186]

186. "the lights that have emanated from the Daystar of Truth, the essence of the Prophet Muḥammad" is a reference to Shí‘ah Imáms. Please see Note No. 173.

Paragraph No. 39:

The traditions established the fact that in all Dispensations the law of prayer hath constituted a fundamental element of the Revelation of all the Prophets of God[187]

187. In the Bahá'í Faith also, fasting and obligatory prayers are important as demonstrated in the following words of ‘Abdu'l-Bahá and Shoghi Effendi:

> The obligatory prayers are binding inasmuch as they are conducive to humility and submissiveness, to setting one's face towards God and expressing devotion to Him.

[61] The Arabic word ka‘bih literally means cube, and it refers to the holy sanctuary (a cubical building containing a black meteorite rock) located at the heart of the structure in Mecca called the House of Ka‘bih, which is the Qiblih, or point of adoration of Muslims, toward which they face when saying their daily obligatory prayers.

Through such prayer man holdeth communion with God, seeketh to draw near unto Him, converseth with the true Beloved of one's heart, and attaineth spiritual stations.
('Abdu'l-Bahá, in *The Compilation of Compilations*, Vol. II, p. 232)

As regards fasting, it constitutes, together with the obligatory prayers, the two pillars that sustain the revealed Law of God. They act as stimulants to the soul, strengthen, revive and purify it, and thus insure its steady development.

The ordinance of fasting is, as is the case with these three prayers (obligatory) a spiritual and vital obligation enjoined by Bahá'u'lláh upon every believer who has attained the age of fifteen. In the Aqdas He thus writes: "We have commanded you to pray and fast from the beginning of maturity; this is ordained by God, your Lord and the Lord of your forefathers. He has exempted from this those who are weak from illness or age, as a bounty from His Presence, and He is the Forgiving, the Generous."
(Shoghi Effendi, *Directives from the Guardian*, p. 27)

"That He might prove you, which of you excel in deeds."[188]

188. The Qur'án, Súrah 67: Verse 2

Paragraph No. 40:

"Fasting is illumination, prayer is light."[189]

189. This is a tradition attributed to the Prophet Muḥammad through the Sunni sources.
('Abdu'l-Ḥamíd Ishráq-Khávari, *Qámus-i-Íqán, Vol. 2*, p. 706)

One day, a well-known divine came to visit Us. . . . Thereupon We realized that that poor man had not been favoured with a single drop of the ocean of true understanding, and had strayed far from the burning Bush of divine wisdom.[190]

190. Although Bahá'u'lláh had no religious education, His knowledge of scriptures and command of all theological matters astonished the learned religious leaders and scholars who came in contact with Him and knew about His family and His life story. He explains the source of His knowledge in the Tablet of Wisdom:

> Thou knowest full well that We perused not the books which men possess and We acquired not the learning current amongst them, and yet whenever We desire to quote the sayings of the learned and of the wise, presently there will appear before the face of thy Lord in the form of a tablet all that which hath appeared in the world and is revealed in the Holy Books and Scriptures. Thus do We set down in writing that which the eye perceiveth. Verily His knowledge encompasseth the earth and the heavens.
> (Bahá'u'lláh, *Tablets of Bahá'u'lláh,* p. 148)

The interpretation your honor hath given to this tradition is the one current amongst the people[191]

191. Bahá'u'lláh in many places in His writings demonstrates how the interpretations of the scriptures current amongst the people are not correct:

> This is the Day when the loved ones of God should keep their eyes directed towards His Manifestation, and fasten them upon whatsoever that Manifestation may be pleased to reveal. Certain traditions of bygone ages rest on no foundations whatever, while the notions entertained by past generations, and which they have recorded in their books, have, for the most part, been influenced by the desires of a corrupt inclination. Thou dost witness how most of the commentaries and interpretations of the words of God, now current amongst men, are devoid of truth. Their falsity hath, in some cases, been exposed when the intervening veils were rent asunder. They themselves have acknowledged their failure in apprehending the meaning of any of the words of God.
> (Bahá'u'lláh, *Gleanings from the Writings of Bahá'u'lláh,* p. 171)

Muḥammad, the Seal of the Prophets[192]

192. The Seal of Prophets is a title of Muḥammad, which is based on the station and designation conferred upon Him in the Qur'án:

> Muḥammad is not the father of any man among you, but he is the messenger[62] of Allah and the Seal[63] of the Prophets; and Allah is ever Aware of all things.
> (The Qur'án, Pickthall tr, 33:40)

Although the above verse indicates that Muḥammad is both the Messenger of God and the Seal of Prophets, Muslims believe that the "Seal of Prophets" means that He is both the last Prophet and the last Messenger of God, after whom no other Prophet or Messenger will come, and therefore Islam is the final Revelation of God for humanity.

It is interesting to note that the Qur'án names and describes two classes of revealers and promoters of the words of God, namely the Messengers and the Prophets. The Qur'án, in many verses, indicates that Messengers and Prophets are not the same and that the Messengers have a higher station. They are those who receive Revelation, are endowed with a Book, and inaugurate a Dispensation (in Bahá'í terminology They are designated as Manifestations of God. See Note No. 15 above). The Prophets on the other hand, are the promoters of the Faith of God and help the Messengers (see Appendix V). Therefore, the above mentioned verse, by stating that Muḥammad is the Messenger of God and the Seal of Prophets, does not proclaim the termination of Messengers and divine Revelations. On the contrary, the Qur'án, in several verses such as the following, states that Messengers (or Apostles) will come and will bring divine Revelation to mankind:

---

[62] The word "Messenger" is the literal translation of the Arabic word "Rasool" o also transliterated as "Rasoul" (Muḥammad is designated as Rasool-al-Allah, the Messenger of God throughout the Qur'án), but some translators of the Qur'án have translated the word Rasool as "apostle."

[63] The word "Seal" is translation of the Arabic word "خاتَم". Webster's Dictionary lists several meanings for the word "Seal," among those are, the end and closure, and an indication of status, especially of approved superior or desirable status.

> O sons of Adam! verily, there will come to you apostles from amongst you, narrating unto you my signs; then whoso fears God and does what is right, there is no fear for them, nor shall they grieve.
> (The Qur'án, E.H. Palmer tr, 7:33)

> O children of Adam! there shall come to Apostles from among yourselves, rehearsing my signs[64] to you; and whoso shall fear God and do good works, no fear shall be upon them, neither shall they be put to grief.
> (The Qur'án 7:33)

The Bahá'í Writings indicate that the most distinguished characteristic of all of the previous Dispensations that were established during the Adamic Cycle, is that they provided prophecy for, and prepared humanity for, the advent of the Day of God and the inauguration of a new universal cycle in human spiritual evolution. They were all Prophetic Dispensations. The Dispensation of Muḥammad was therefore the last of the Prophetic Dispensations. The following explains this concept:

> Through Bahá'u'lláh, the glory of God's Revelation to mankind is unveiled, a glory which the Manifestations of the past foretold. Indeed, Their purpose throughout all ages was to herald the coming of Bahá'u'lláh and prepare mankind for His advent. Muḥammad was the last to do so, referring to Himself as the "Seal of the Prophets," for His was the last Dispensation of the prophetic cycle of religion. With the appearance of the Báb, this cycle closed, and He announced Bahá'u'lláh, Whose Mission was not to foretell the Day of God, but to inaugurate it, as God's supreme Manifestation.
> (Adib Taherzadeh, *The Revelation of Bahá'u'lláh*, Vol. 1, p. 66)

The Báb stated:

> When God sent forth His Prophet Muḥammad, on that day the termination of the prophetic cycle was foreordained in

[64] The word "signs" is the translation of the Arabic word "Áyát, آيات", the plural of "Áyeh, آيه", which means a verse, a sign or a miracle. The Qur'án declares that its verses are the direct divine Revelation, God's signs and miracles given to Prophet Muḥammad.

> the knowledge of God. Yea, that promise hath indeed come true and the decree of God hath been accomplished as He hath ordained. Assuredly we are today living in the Days of God. These are the glorious days on the like of which the sun hath never risen in the past. These are the days which the people in bygone times eagerly expected.
> (The Báb, *Selections from the Writings of the Báb*, p. 161)

Bahá'u'lláh stated:

> It is evident that every age in which a Manifestation of God hath lived is divinely ordained, and may, in a sense, be characterized as God's appointed Day. This Day, however, is unique, and is to be distinguished from those that have preceded it. The designation "Seal of the Prophets" fully revealeth its high station. The Prophetic Cycle hath, verily, ended. The Eternal Truth is now come. He hath lifted up the Ensign of Power, and is now shedding upon the world the unclouded splendor of His Revelation.
> (*Gleanings from the Writings of Bahá'u'lláh*, p. 60)

This concept is also explained in the writings of Shoghi Effendi, who states that the advent of the Báb "at once signalized the termination of the "Prophetic Cycle" and the inception of the "Cycle of Fulfillment" (Shoghi Effendi, *God Passes By*, p. 57). Regarding the Revelation of Bahá'u'lláh, he states:

> The Revelation of Bahá'u'lláh, whose supreme mission is none other but the achievement of this organic and spiritual unity of the whole body of nations, should, if we be faithful to its implications, be regarded as signalizing through its advent the (coming of age of the entire human race. It should be viewed not merely as yet another spiritual revival in the ever-changing fortunes of mankind, not only as a further stage in a chain of progressive Revelations, nor even as the culmination of one of a series of recurrent prophetic cycles, but rather as marking the last and highest stage in the stupendous evolution of man's collective life on this planet.
> (Shoghi Effendi, in *The Compilation of Compilations*, vol. II, p. 182)

> The weight of the potentialities with which this Faith, possessing no peer or equal in the world's spiritual history, and marking the culmination of a universal prophetic cycle, has been endowed, staggers our imagination.
> (Shoghi Effendi, *God Passes By*, p. xi)

> Nor does the Bahá'í Revelation, claiming as it does to be the culmination of a prophetic cycle and the fulfillment of the promise of all ages, attempt, under any circumstances, to invalidate those first and everlasting principles that animate and underlie the religions that have preceded it.
> (Shoghi Effendi, *The World Order of Bahá'u'lláh*, p. 114)

Dispensation of the Qur'án[193]

193. Please see Note No. 94.

and the fact that it comprehendeth all religions[194]

194. This concept that every religion includes or comprehends all religions before it and is the fruit, the perfection, or maturation of these religions has been presented in the Writings of the Báb and Bahá'u'lláh, and is closely connected to the concept of progressive revelation.

"Islam is heaven; fasting is its sun, prayer, its moon."[195]

195. In addition to explaining the true meaning of the Sun and Moon in prophetic scriptures, Bahá'u'lláh clarifies the meaning of yet another very important symbol, "heaven," by concluding His discourse with the phrase "Islam is heaven; fasting is its sun, prayer, its moon." This indicates that the heaven mentioned in the previous scriptures and prophecies symbolizes the religion. The significance of fasting and obligatory prayers in the Bahá'í Faith is demonstrated in the following statements:

> In truth, I say that obligatory prayer and fasting occupy an exalted station in the sight of God.
> (Bahá'u'lláh, The Kitáb-i-Aqdas, p. 134)

> Fasting and obligatory prayer constitute the two pillars that sustain the revealed Law of God. Bahá'u'lláh in one of His Tablets affirms that He has revealed the laws of obligatory prayer and fasting so that through them the believers may draw nigh unto God.
> (The Kitáb-i-Aqdas, Notes, p. 176)

Paragraph No. 41:

This is the purpose underlying the symbolic words of the Manifestations of God[196]

196. There are many symbolic statements in the scriptures of the past religions. Many of the books of the Old Testament, especially Geneses, Exodus, Isaiah, and Daniel contain many symbolic terms. As mentioned in Note Nos. 64, 65, and 68 above, Christ often spoke in symbolic language and parables, and the Qur'án also contains a significant amount of symbolic or figurative language.

"The righteous shall drink of a cup tempered at the camphor fountain."[197]

197. This is a verse from the Qur'án, Súrah "Man."

> For the unbelievers We have prepared chains and fetters, and a blazing Fire. But the righteous shall drink of a cup tempered at the Camphor Fountain.
> (The Qur'án, N. J. Dawood tr, 76:4–5)

> We have created man from the union of the sexes that we might prove him; and hearing, seeing, have we made him. In a right way have we guided him, be he thankful or ungrateful. For the Infidels we have got ready chains and collars and flaming fire. But a wine cup tempered at the camphor fountain the just shall quaff. Fount whence the servants of God shall drink, and guide by channels from place to place; They who fulfilled their vows, and feared the day whose woes will spread far and wide; Who though

> longing for it themselves, bestowed their food on the poor and the orphan and the captive"
> (The Qur'án 76:2–7)

Camphor, derived from Arabic word "káfur," is a spice that is a preservative and is sweet, fragrant, and cooling.

In Middle Eastern pharmacopoeia, camphor was used for its medicinal properties as an anti-allergic, anti-infection, analgesic, and metabolic equalizer, and was used to reduce the heat of natural and animalistic passion and desires and induce calm and cool temper.

In Islamic traditions, it is held that there is a fountain in Paradise (based on the above verses of Súrah 76) that has camphor properties, from which the believers will drink.

Therefore, the people who understand the meaning of the symbolic language of the scriptures realize that the above verse means that the righteous will recognize the Manifestation of God, enter into the Paradise of His Faith, and will drink from the spiritual wine that has camphor characteristics.

This metaphor of drinking from a "wine cup tempered at the camphor fountain" has been used frequently in the Writings of Bahá'u'lláh and 'Abdu'l-Bahá, to signify the spiritual joy and felicity resulting from recognition of the Manifestation of God.

> He who hath attained this station is sanctified from all that pertaineth to the world. Wherefore, if those who have come to the sea of His presence are found to possess none of the limited things of this perishable world, whether it be outer wealth or personal opinions, it mattereth not. For whatever the creatures have is limited by their own limits, and whatever the True One hath is sanctified therefrom; this utterance must be deeply pondered that its purport may be clear. "Verily the righteous shall drink of a wine cup tempered at the camphor fountain." If the interpretation of "camphor" become known, the true intention will be evident.
> (Bahá'u'lláh, The Seven Valleys, p. 36)

Paragraph No. 42:

and would not have become afflicted and oppressed by the darkness of their selfish desires. Yea, but since they have failed to acquire true knowledge from its very Source, they have perished in the perilous vale of waywardness and misbelief.[198]

198. As stated in Note No. 138 above, people have a history of following and believing the words of the religious leaders. If the people in every Dispensation were like the uncle of the Báb, seeking enlightenment from the source of knowledge, they would receive the guidance and would be able to comprehend the meanings of these symbolic words. Christ has a similar statement:

> Verily, verily, I say unto you, He that heareth my word, and believeth on him that sent me, hath everlasting life, and shall not come into condemnation. . . . And ye have not his word abiding in you: for whom he hath sent, him ye believe not.
>
> Search the scriptures; for in them ye think ye have eternal life: and they are they which testify of me. And ye will not come to me, that ye might have life. . . . For had ye believed Moses, ye would have believed me; for he wrote of me. But if ye believe not his writings, how shall ye believe my words?
> (John 5:24, 39–47)

They still have not awakened to perceive that all the signs foretold have been made manifest, that the promised Sun hath risen above the horizon of divine Revelation[199]

199. The concepts of wakefulness and sleep and life and death as mentioned in the scriptures, are the symbolic language signifying the spiritual awareness and ignorance and the state of faith and unbelief. This concept is fully explained in paragraphs 110–130 below. Bahá'u'lláh states that each Manifestation of God is the spiritual Sun in the heaven of divine Revelation and those who do not recognize Them are like people who are asleep when the physical sun rises. If people become spiritually awake they will

realize that all the signs have appeared and all prophecies and promises have been fulfilled, as Bahá'u'lláh states in the Epistle to the Son of the Wolf:

> Vague fancies have encompassed the dwellers of the earth and debarred them from turning towards the Horizon of Certitude, and its brightness, and its manifestations and its lights. Vain imaginings have withheld them from Him Who is the Self-Subsisting. They speak as prompted by their own caprices, and understand not.
>
> Among them are those who have said: "Have the verses been sent down?" Say: "Yea, by Him Who is the Lord of the heavens!" "Hath the Hour come?" "Nay, more; it hath passed, by Him Who is the Revealer of clear tokens! Verily, the Inevitable is come, and He, the True One, hath appeared with proof and testimony. The Plain is disclosed, and mankind is sore vexed and fearful. Earthquakes have broken loose, and the tribes have lamented, for fear of God, the Lord of Strength, the All-Compelling." Say: "The stunning trumpet blast hath been loudly raised, and the Day is God's, the One, the Unconstrained." "Hath the Catastrophe come to pass?" Say: "Yea, by the Lord of Lords!" "Is the Resurrection come?" "Nay, more; He Who is the Self-Subsisting hath appeared with the Kingdom of His signs." "Seest thou men laid low?" "Yea, by my Lord, the Exalted, the Most High!" "Have the tree-stumps been uprooted?" "Yea, more; the mountains have been scattered in dust; by Him the Lord of attributes!" They say: "Where is Paradise, and where is Hell?" Say: "The one is reunion with Me; the other thine own self, O thou who dost associate a partner with God and doubtest." They say: "We see not the Balance." Say: "Surely, by my Lord, the God of Mercy! None can see it except such as are endued with insight." "Have the stars fallen?" Say: "Yea, when He Who is the Self-Subsisting dwelt in the Land of Mystery (Adrianople).
>
> Take heed, ye who are endued with discernment!" All the signs appeared when We drew forth the Hand of Power from the bosom of majesty and might. Verily, the Crier

hath cried out, when the promised time came, and they that have recognized the splendors of Sinai have swooned away in the wilderness of hesitation, before the awful majesty of thy Lord, the Lord of creation. The trumpet asketh: 'Hath the Bugle been sounded?' Say: "Yea, by the King of Revelation!, when He mounted the throne of His Name, the All-Merciful." Darkness hath been chased away by the dawning-light of the mercy of thy Lord, the Source of all light. The breeze of the All-Merciful hath wafted, and the souls have been quickened in the tombs of their bodies. Thus hath the decree been fulfilled by God, the Mighty, the Beneficent. They that have gone astray have said: "When were the heavens cleft asunder?" Say: "While ye lay in the graves of waywardness and error." Among the heedless is he who rubbeth his eyes, and looketh to the right and to the left. Say: "Blinded art thou. No refuge hast thou to flee to." And among them is he who saith: "Have men been gathered together?" Say: "Yea, by my Lord!, whilst thou didst lie in the cradle of idle fancies." And among them is he who saith: "Hath the Book been sent down through the power of the true Faith?" Say: "The true Faith itself is astounded. Fear ye, O ye men of understanding heart!" And among them is he who saith: "Have I been assembled with others, blind?" Say: "Yea, by Him that rideth upon the clouds!" Paradise is decked with mystic roses, and hell hath been made to blaze with the fire of the impious. Say: "The light hath shone forth from the horizon of Revelation, and the whole earth hath been illumined at the coming of Him Who is the Lord of the Day of the Covenant!" The doubters have perished, whilst he that turned, guided by the light of assurance, unto the Dayspring of Certitude hath prospered.
(Bahá'u'lláh, Epistle to the Son of the Wolf, p. 131)

A fire from the Kingdom hath been kindled in the heart of the world,—in the Blessed Tree, whose flame shall ere long set aglow the pillars of the world and its rays illumine the horizons of nations. All the signs have appeared, all the prophetic references become clear, all that was revealed in Books and Scriptures hath become fully manifest. There is no ground for any one to hesitate in regard thereto. Some people of former times and sects avoided certain others as

strangers. But now the glorious Beloved One hath ridden upon His swift coursing steed, circling about in the arena of truth, and all that was hidden hath become manifest. Let there be no more silence or reticence, taciturnity or negligence.
('Abdu'l-Bahá, *Tablets of 'Abdu'l-Bahá*, Vol. 2, p. 405)

Paragraph No. 43:

And now, with fixed gaze and steady wings enter thou the way of certitude and truth[200]

200. In this phrase Bahá'u'lláh summarizes the three progressive stages of attaining to certitude. In this statement, "fixed" is a translation of the term 'Ilm al-yaqín, "steady" is 'Ayn al-Yaqín, and "certitude" is Ḥaq al Yaqín. In eastern epistemology these three hierarchical stages of knowledge that lead to certitude have been defined:

a. 'Ilm al-yaqín: this is acquiring the knowledge regarding something, the subject of the knowing, by inference or hearing or reading about it.

b. 'Ayn al-Yaqín: to be personally or directly observing the subject of the knowing.

c. Ḥaq al Yaqín: the true knowledge of the subject of knowing by personally experiencing it or coming in close contact with the reality of the subject of knowing.

Some Bahá'í scholars have cited different allegorical examples to facilitate understanding of this subject. For example, if we read or hear from a trustworthy source that there is a fire in a fireplace in the next room and we believe it, we gain certitude by knowledge; if we go to the next room and see the fire, we gain certitude by seeing and observing the subject of knowing; and if we experience the heat and light of the fire, we have gained true knowledge or certitude that this in reality is a fire.
(For more details regarding the above subject see 'Abdu'l-Ḥamíd Ishráq-Khávari, *Qámus-i-Íqán, Vol 2*, p. 1146)

"Say: It is God; then leave them to entertain themselves with their cavilings."[201]

201. By quoting this verse of the Qur'án 6:91, which was revealed in reference to Jewish and Christian clergy who maintained that Muḥammad was not a true prophet because he looked like an ordinary man, and the signs as they expected did not appear at His advent, Bahá'u'lláh draws a comparison to the objections of Muslim clergy who maintained that the promised one of Islam who they believed was living in hiding for a thousand years, would look like a superman and not a normal human like the Báb and the signs as they expected did not appear with the advent of the Báb. The Qur'án states:

> This is God's guidance: He guideth by it such of his servants as he will: But if they join other gods with Him, vain assuredly shall be all their works. These are they to whom we gave the Scripture and Wisdom and Prophecy: but if these their posterity believe not therein, we will entrust these gifts to a people who will not disbelieve therein. These are they whom God hath guided: follow therefore their guidance. Say: No pay do I ask of you for this: Verily it is no other than the teaching for all creatures. No just estimate do they form of God when they say, "Nothing hath God sent down to man." Say: Who sent down the Book which Moses brought, a light and guidance to man, which ye set down on paper, publishing part, but concealing most; though ye have now been taught that which neither ye nor your fathers knew? Say: It is God: then leave them in their pastime of cavillings.
> (The Qur'án 6:88–91)

"They that say 'Our Lord is God,' and continue steadfast in His way, upon them, verily, shall the angels descend."[202]

202. This is from the Qur'án 41:30. Súrah 41 of the Qur'án is mostly about how the unbelievers rejected the Prophets that God sent for their guidance, as it states:

> [W]e had vouchsafed them guidance; but to guidance did they prefer blindness; wherefore the tempest of a shameful punishment overtook them for their doings:
> (The Qur'án 41:17)

> Yet the unbelievers say, "Hearken not to this Koran, but keep up a talking, that ye may overpower the voice of the reader." Surely therefore will we cause the unbelievers to taste a terrible punishment; And recompense them according to the worst of their actions. This the reward of the enemies of God, - the Fire! it shall be their eternal abode, in requital for their gainsaying our signs.
> (The Qur'án 41:25–28)

In contrast to those who rejected the message, the believers will be rewarded, as it states:

> But as for those who say, "Our Lord is God;" and who go straight to Him, the angels shall descend to them and say, "Fear ye not, neither be ye grieved, but rejoice ye in the paradise which ye have been promised.
> (The Qur'án 41:30)

The meaning of the angels, which will descend upon the believers, is explained in the Bahá'í Writings. 'Abdu'l-Bahá offers two definitions for the angels:

> Look ye not upon the fewness of thy numbers, rather, seek ye out hearts that are pure. One consecrated soul is preferable to a thousand other souls. If a small number of people gather lovingly together, with absolute purity and sanctity, with their hearts free of the world, experiencing the emotions of the Kingdom and the powerful magnetic forces of the Divine, and being at one in their happy fellowship, that gathering will exert its influence over all the earth. The nature of that band of people, the words they speak, the deeds they do, will unleash the bestowals of Heaven, and provide a foretaste of eternal bliss. The hosts of the Company on high will defend them, and the angels of the Abhá Paradise, in continuous succession, will come down to their aid.

> The meaning of "angels" is the confirmations of God and His celestial powers. Likewise angels are blessed beings who have severed all ties with this nether world, have been released from the chains of self and the desires of the flesh, and anchored their hearts to the heavenly realms of the Lord. These are of the Kingdom, heavenly; these are of God, spiritual; these are revealers of God's abounding grace; these are dawning-points of His spiritual bestowals.
> ('Abdu'l-Bahá, *Selections from the Writings of 'Abdu'l-Bahá*, p. 80)

Paragraph No. 44:

O my brother! Take thou the step of the spirit,[203] so that, swift as the twinkling of an eye, thou mayest flash through the wilds of remoteness and bereavement, attain the Riḍván of everlasting reunion[204]

203. The same concept is also found in other Bahá'í Writings:

> O SON OF LOVE! Thou art but one step away from the glorious heights above and from the celestial tree of love. Take thou one pace and with the next advance into the immortal realm and enter the pavilion of eternity. Give ear then to that which hath been revealed by the pen of glory.
> (Bahá'u'lláh, The Hidden Words, Persian, no. 7)

204. As mentioned in Note No. 58, the metaphor "wilds of remoteness," takes its significance from serving in contrast to, and as the opposite of, the "City of Faith," which is equivalent to the "Riḍván (paradise) of the everlasting reunion." This indicates that the person who uses his spiritual insight can leave the wilds of remoteness and bereavement and enter into the paradise of reunion (state of faith and certitude). Those who reject the Manifestation of God for their day and age and do not believe in Him, will not be able to enter the "paradise of reunion with the beloved," which requires acceptance and obedience to Him, and they are said to be "lost in the wilds of remoteness."

Bahá'u'lláh, when addressing the Christian clergy, states:

> O concourse of priests! The Day of Reckoning hath appeared, the Day whereon He Who was in heaven hath

> come. He, verily, is the One Whom ye were promised in the Books of God, the Holy, the Almighty, the All-Praised. How long will ye wander in the wilderness of heedlessness and superstition? Turn with your hearts in the direction of your Lord, the Forgiving, the Generous.
> (Bahá'u'lláh, *The Proclamation of Bahá'u'lláh*, p. 94)

The same concept is also presented with a different analogy elsewhere:

> The one true God is My witness! This most great, this fathomless and surging Ocean is near, astonishingly near, unto you. Behold it is closer to you than your life-vein! Swift as the twinkling of an eye ye can, if ye but wish it, reach and partake of this imperishable favor, this God-given grace, this incorruptible gift, this most potent and unspeakably glorious bounty.
> (Bahá'u'lláh, *Gleanings from the Writings of Bahá'u'lláh*, p. 325)

Peace be upon him whom the light of truth guideth unto all truth[205]

205. Guidance and assistance of the Holy Spirit must supplement the human endeavor to attain the state of faith and certitude, as was promised by Christ to the believers:

> I have yet many things to say unto you, but ye cannot bear them now. Howbeit when he, the Spirit of truth, is come, he will guide you into all truth: for he shall not speak of himself; but whatsoever he shall hear, that shall he speak: and he will shew you things to come.
> (John 16:12–13)

A promise that finds fulfilment with the following announcement of Bahá'u'lláh:

> Announce thou unto the priests: Lo! He Who is the Ruler is come. Step out from behind the veil in the name of thy Lord, He Who layeth low the necks of all men. Proclaim then unto all mankind the glad-tidings of this mighty, this glorious Revelation. Verily, He Who is the Spirit of Truth is come to guide you unto all truth. He speaketh not as

> prompted by His own self, but as bidden by Him Who is the All-Knowing, the All-Wise.
> (Bahá'u'lláh, *Tablets of Bahá'u'lláh*, p. 12)

and who, in the name of God, standeth in the path of His Cause, upon the shore of true understanding.[206]

206. This guidance and assistance is necessary for the believer to remain in the path of the Cause of God:

> Send down, therefore, O my God, upon all that seek Thee that which will entirely strip them of all that pertaineth not unto Thee, and will draw them nigh unto Thy Self. Assist them, by Thy grace, to love Thee and to conform unto that which shall please Thee. Grant, then, that they may go straight on in the path of Thy Cause, the path wherein have slipped the footsteps of the doubters among Thy people and the froward among Thy servants. Thou art, verily, the All-Powerful, the Almighty, the Most Great."
> (Bahá'u'lláh, *Prayers and Meditations*, p. 254)

Please see Note No. 2 above, regarding the term "true understanding."

Paragraph No. 45:

This is the meaning of the sacred verse: "But nay! I swear by the Lord of the Easts and the Wests,[207]

207. The Qur'án, in Súrah 70:40, states: "But nay! I swear by the Lord of the Easts and the Wests." This is an exact and correct translation of the Arabic text of this verse. However, because the English translators of the Qur'án, much like many commentators, did not understand the true meaning of the verse they translated it inaccurately and changed and distorted the English text. A few examples are presented below:

> "But nay! I swear by the Lord of the rising-places and the setting-places of the planets"
> (The Qur'án, Pickthall tr, 70:40)

> It needs not that I swear by the Lord of the East and of the West.
> (The Qur'án, Rodwell tr, 70:40)

> Now I do call to witness the Lord of all points in the East and the West.
> (The Qur'án, Yusuf Ali tr, 70:40)

> I swear by the Lord of the East and the West.
> (The Qur'án, N. J. Dawood. tr, 70:40)

There is a similar verse in the Qur'án, Súrah 55, in which the words East and West are pluralized—i.e, "the Easts and the Wests," but the translators have modified it:

> He is the Lord of the East, He is the Lord of the West.
> (The Qur'án 55:17)

The commentators made similar erroneous arguments when commenting on this verse, because they did not understand the proper meaning of sun and moon in these prophesies.

Paragraph No. 46:

In like manner, strive thou to comprehend from these lucid, these powerful, conclusive, and unequivocal statements the meaning of the "cleaving of the heaven"—one of the signs that must needs herald the coming of the last Hour, the Day of Resurrection. As He hath said: "When the heaven shall be cloven asunder"[208]

208. This is from the Súrah of Cataclysm or Cleaving:

> When the Heaven shall Cleave asunder, And when the stars shall disperse, And when the seas shall be commingled.
> (The Qur'án 82:1)

Muslims considered the cleaving of Heaven as one of the signs of the Day of Resurrection, mostly based on this and a few other versus of the Qur'án such as those in the Súrahs "Merciful" and "Folded Up":

> When the Heaven shall be cleft asunder, and become rose red, like stained leather.
> (The Qur'án 55:37)

> When the sun shall be folded up, And when the stars shall fall, And when the mountains shall be set in motion.
> (The Qur'án 81:1–3)

Similar statements are found in the Old and New Testaments in verses concerning the second coming of the Messiah and the signs of the Day of Resurrection:

> Therefore I will shake the heavens, and the earth shall remove out of her place, in the wrath of the LORD of hosts, and in the day of his fierce anger.
> (Isaiah 13:13)

> Oh that thou wouldest rend the heavens, . . . that the mountains might flow down at thy presence, As when the melting fire burneth, the fire causeth the waters to boil!
> (Isaiah 64:1)

> Blow ye the trumpet in Zion, and sound an alarm in my holy mountain: let all the inhabitants of the land tremble: for the day of the LORD cometh, . . . heavens shall tremble: the sun and the moon shall be dark, and the stars shall withdraw their shining. . . . And the LORD shall utter his voice before his army: for his camp is very great: for he is strong that executeth his word: for the day of the LORD is great and very terrible; . . . And I will shew wonders in the heavens and in the earth, blood, and fire, and pillars of smoke. . . . The sun shall be turned into darkness, and the moon into blood, before the great and terrible day of the LORD come.
> (Joel 2:1, 10, 29)

> For, behold, the day cometh, that shall burn as an oven.
> (Malachi 4:1)

> But the day of the Lord will come as a thief in the night; in the which the heavens shall pass away with a great noise, and the elements shall melt with fervent heat, the earth also

> and the works that are therein shall be burned up. . . . Looking for and hasting unto the coming of the day of God, wherein the heavens being on fire shall be dissolved, and the elements shall melt with fervent heat?
> (2 Peter 3:10–12)

By "heaven" is meant the heaven of divine Revelation[209]

209. As mentioned in Note No. 5, and other places, Bahá'u'lláh's interpretation of the "Heaven" mentioned in the Bible and the Qur'án as "religion" opens up the mysteries of the prophecies related to the time of the end and solves the problem of the literal nonfulfillment of those prophecies.

By "cloven asunder" is meant that the former Dispensation is superseded and annulled. I swear by God! That this heaven being cloven asunder is, to the discerning, an act mightier than the cleaving of the skies! Ponder a while. That a divine Revelation which for years hath been securely established; beneath whose shadow all who have embraced it have been reared and nurtured; by the light of whose law generations of men have been disciplined; the excellency of whose word men have heard recounted by their fathers; in such wise that human eye hath beheld naught but the pervading influence of its grace, and mortal ear hath heard naught but the resounding majesty of its command[210]

210. The excellency of the words are mentioned in the text of the Old Testament with the admonition to the followers to recount it to their sons for future generations:

> For what nation is there so great, who hath God so nigh unto them, as the LORD our God is in all things that we call upon him for? And what nation is there so great, that hath statutes and judgments so righteous as all this law, which I set before you this day? Only take heed to thyself, and keep thy soul diligently, lest thou forget the things which thine eyes have seen, and lest they depart from thy heart all the days of thy life: but teach them thy sons, and thy sons' sons
> (Deuteronomy 4:7–9)

Therefore thou shalt love the LORD thy God, and keep his charge, and his statutes, and his judgments, and his commandments, always.
(Deuteronomy 11:10)

Therefore shall ye lay up these my words in your heart and in your soul, and bind them for a sign upon your hand, that they may be as frontlets between your eyes.[65]

And ye shall teach them your children, speaking of them when thou sittest in thine house, and when thou walkest by the way, when thou liest down, and when thou risest up.
(Deuteronomy 11:18–19)

And know ye this day: for I speak not with your children which have not known, and which have not seen the chastisement of the LORD your God, his greatness, his mighty hand, and his stretched out arm, And his miracles, and his acts, which he did in the midst of Egypt unto Pharaoh the king of Egypt, and unto all his land; And what he did unto the army of Egypt, unto their horses, and to their chariots; how he made the water of the Red sea to overflow them as they pursued after you, and how the LORD hath destroyed them unto this day; And what he did unto you in the wilderness, until ye came into this place; And what he did unto Dathan and Abiram, the sons of Eliab, the son of Reuben: how the earth opened her mouth, and swallowed them up, and their households, and their tents, and all the substance that was in their possession, in the midst of all Israel: But your eyes have seen all the great acts of the LORD which he did.
(Deuteronomy 11:2–7)

We have heard with our ears, O God, our fathers have told us, what work thou didst in their days, in the times of old. How thou didst drive out the heathen with thy hand, and plantedst them; how thou didst afflict the people, and cast them out. For they got not the land in possession by their

[65] The small leather boxes (phylacteries) that the orthodox Jews place on their foreheads between their eyes, is in compliance with this commandment.

> own sword, neither did their own arm save them: but thy right hand, and thine arm, and the light of thy countenance, because thou hadst a favour unto them.
> (Psalms 44:1–3)

> [S]hewing to the generation to come the praises of the LORD, and his strength, and his wonderful works that he hath done. For he established a testimony in Jacob, and appointed a law in Israel, which he commanded our fathers, that they should make them known to their children: That the generation to come might know them, even the children which should be born; who should arise and declare them to their children:
> (Psalms 78:4–6)

So for centuries Jews heard from their fathers and religious leaders regarding the majesty and excellency of their religion, and the power and might of their expected Messiah, Who was to come with worldly power, establish the ascendency of Jews over gentiles, and promote the laws of the Torah. However, Jesus was known to Jews as the son of a carpenter as attested to in the Bible:

> Is not this the carpenter's son? is not his mother called Mary? and his brethren, James, and Joses, and Simon, and Judas? And his sisters, are they not all with us? Whence then hath this man all these things? And they were offended in him. But Jesus said unto them, A prophet is not without honour, save in his own country, and in his own house.
> (Matthew 13:55–57)

Therefore, when the son of the local carpenter, who had no power or might, declared His mission, claimed the exalted and mighty station of Messiah, and broke the most important Judaic law, the law of Sabbath, the Jews as stated above, were shocked and offended. This was, in the eyes of the people of the time, an act more shocking and disturbing than the cleaving of the Heavens.

Similar statements are found in the New Testament regarding the excellency, majesty, and importance of the words and works of Jesus Christ:

> Heaven and earth shall pass away, but my words shall not pass away.
> (Matthew 24:35)

> This beginning of miracles did Jesus in Cana of Galilee, and manifested forth his glory; and his disciples believed on him.
> (John 2:11)

> The Father loveth the Son, and hath given all things into his hand. He that believeth on the Son hath everlasting life: and he that believeth not the Son shall not see life; but the wrath of God abideth on him.
> (John 3:35–36)

> If ye had known me, ye should have known my Father also: and from henceforth ye know him, and have seen him. Philip saith unto him, Lord, shew us the Father, and it sufficeth us. Jesus saith unto him, Have I been so long time with you, and yet hast thou not known me, Philip? he that hath seen me hath seen the Father; and how sayest thou then, Shew us the Father? Believest thou not that I am in the Father, and the Father in me? the words that I speak unto you I speak not of myself: but the Father that dwelleth in me, he doeth the works. Believe me that I am in the Father, and the Father in me: or else believe me for the very works' sake.
> (John 14:7–11)

> For unto us a child is born, unto us a son is given: and the government shall be upon his shoulder: and his name shall be called Wonderful, Counsellor, The mighty God, The everlasting Father, The Prince of Peace.
> (Isaiah 9:6)

Throughout the centuries, based on these and similar statements, the words and the person of Jesus were considered the words and the person of God, and Christianity was the religion of the most mighty empire of the world. Then an Arab man, who was born an orphan in a small village in backward Arabia (and surely did not descend from the Heavens accompanied by a flock of Angels), stood up and claimed that He was not only equal to Jesus, but that

He brought a new religion that superseded and annulled Christianity and abolished the mighty institution of the Christian Church. This also was, in the eyes of the people of the time, an act that was mightier than the cleaving of the Heavens.

Similarly, after the passage of thirteen centuries from that time, when the excellency and ascendency of the Qur'án (the words of Muḥammad) over all the sacred books of other religions was established in the hearts and minds of all Muslims, and the exalted station of Muḥammad as the foremost Being to ever have appeared in the world was established, and Who's religion was perceived as the highest and final stage of divine Revelation by almost half of the human world, a young simple man stood up against the mighty Islamic orthodoxy and claimed that He was entrusted with a Revelation from God that not only placed Him at an equal station with Muḥammad, but that His Revelation superseded that of Muḥammad. This young man went on to annul the religion of Islam and abolish the mighty ecclesiastical institutions of both the Shí'ah and Sunni orthodoxy. This was in the eyes of the generality of Muslims an act that was mightier than the cleaving of the Heavens.

Reflect, is this a mightier act than that which these abject and foolish men[211] have imagined the "cleaving of the heaven" to mean?

211. "Abject and foolish men," is the translation of the term "hemaj-i-reá'a," which also means the pack of gnats that fly around the cattle and, devoid of a direction or a goal for their motion, are driven in different directions and locations by the wind.

Paragraph No. 47:

Moreover, consider the hardships and the bitterness of the lives of those Revealers of the divine Beauty[212]

212. In another place in His Writings, Bahá'u'lláh comments on the same theme and recounts the sufferings of the Manifestations of God:

Consider the former generations. Witness how every time the Daystar of Divine bounty hath shed the light of His Revelation upon the world, the people of His Day have arisen against Him, and repudiated His truth. They who were regarded as the leaders of men have invariably striven to hinder their followers from turning unto Him Who is the Ocean of God's limitless bounty.

Behold how the people, as a result of the verdict pronounced by the divines of His age, have cast Abraham, the Friend of God, into fire; how Moses, He Who held converse with the Almighty, was denounced as liar and slanderer. Reflect how Jesus, the Spirit of God, was, notwithstanding His extreme meekness and perfect tender-heartedness, treated by His enemies. So fierce was the opposition which He, the Essence of Being and Lord of the visible and invisible, had to face, that He had nowhere to lay His head. He wandered continually from place to place, deprived of a permanent abode. Ponder that which befell Muḥammad, the Seal of the Prophets, may the life of all else be a sacrifice unto Him. How severe the afflictions which the leaders of the Jewish people and of the idol-worshipers caused to rain upon Him, Who is the sovereign Lord of all. . . .

Thou hast known how grievously the Prophets of God, His Messengers and Chosen Ones, have been afflicted. Meditate a while on the motive and reason which have been responsible for such a persecution. At no time, in no Dispensation, have the Prophets of God escaped the blasphemy of their enemies, the cruelty of their oppressors, the denunciation of the learned of their age, who appeared in the guise of uprightness and piety. Day and night they passed through such agonies as none can ever measure, except the knowledge of the one true God, exalted be His glory.

Consider this wronged One. Though the clearest proofs attest the truth of His Cause; though the prophecies He, in an unmistakable language, hath made have been fulfilled; though, in spite of His not being accounted among the learned, His being unschooled and inexperienced in the disputations current among the divines, He hath rained upon men the showers of His manifold and Divinely-inspired knowledge; yet, behold how this generation hath rejected His authority, and rebelled against Him! He hath, during the greater part of His life, been sore-tried in the clutches of His enemies. His sufferings have now reached their culmination in this afflictive Prison, into which His oppressors have so unjustly thrown Him. God grant that, with a penetrating vision and radiant heart, thou mayest observe the things that have come to pass and are now happening, and, pondering them in thine heart, mayest recognize that which most men have, in this Day, failed to perceive.

(Bahá'u'lláh, *Gleanings from the Writings of Bahá'u'lláh*, p. 56)

Reflect, how single-handed and alone they faced the world and all its peoples[213]

213. Jesus refers to the fact that in spite of the suffering and tribulations He would face alone, He would overcome the world:

> His disciples said unto him, Lo, now speakest thou plainly, and speakest no proverb. Now are we sure that thou knowest all things, and needest not that any man should ask thee: by this we believe that thou camest forth from God. Jesus answered them, Do ye now believe? Behold, the hour cometh, yea, is now come, that ye shall be scattered, every man to his own, and shall leave me alone: and yet I am not alone, because the Father is with me. These things I have spoken unto you, that in me ye might have peace. In the world ye shall have tribulation: but be of good cheer; I have overcome the world.
>
> (John 16:28–33)

'Abdu'l-Bahá explains how Bahá'u'lláh, single-handed and alone, faced the world and all its people:

> One prisoner, single and solitary, without assistant or defender, a foreigner and stranger imprisoned in the fortress of 'Akká writing such letters to the emperor of France and

sultan of Turkey. Reflect upon this how Bahá'u'lláh upraised the standard of His Cause in prison. Refer to history. It is without parallel. No such thing has happened before that time nor since; a prisoner and an exile advancing His Cause and spreading His teachings broadcast so that eventually He became powerful enough to conquer the very king who banished Him. His Cause spread more and more. The Blessed Perfection was a prisoner twenty-five years. During all this time He was subjected to the indignities and revilement of the people. He was persecuted, mocked and put in chains.
('Abdu'l-Bahá, *The Promulgation of Universal Peace*, p. 28)

It is clear, however, that mere human power is incapable of fulfilling this great office, and that the results of human thought alone cannot secure such bounties. How can a single person, with no aid or assistance, lay the foundations of such a lofty edifice? A divine and spiritual power is therefore needed to enable him to carry out this mission. Behold! One sanctified Soul revives the world of humanity, transforms the face of the globe, develops the minds, quickens the souls, inaugurates a new life, establishes new foundations, orders the world, gathers the nations and religions under the shadow of one banner, delivers man from the realm of baseness and deficiency, and exhorts and encourages him to develop his innate and acquired perfections. Certainly nothing short of a divine power could accomplish this feat! One must examine this matter fairly, as this indeed is an occasion for fairness.

A Cause which all the governments and peoples of the earth, notwithstanding all their powers and their armies, are unable to promote and promulgate, one holy Soul promulgates without aid or assistance! Can this be accomplished through the agency of mere human power? No, by God! For example, Christ, alone and single-handed, raised the banner of peace and amity—a feat that the combined forces of all the mighty governments of the world are unable to accomplish.
('Abdu'l-Bahá, *Some Answered Questions*, no. 3.12–13)

those holy, those precious, and tender Souls[214]

214. The holy and precious Manifestations of God:

> The Báb in His Tablet to Muḥammad Sháh stated: "The substance wherewith God hath created Me is not the clay out of which others have been formed. He hath conferred upon Me that which the worldly-wise can never comprehend, nor the faithful discover . . ."
> (*Selections from the Writings of the Báb*, p. 11)

> Bahá'u'lláh also stated: "Barter not away this Youth,[66] O people, for the vanities of this world or the delights of heaven. By the righteousness of the one true God! One hair of Him excelleth all that is in the heavens and all that is on the earth."
> (Bahá'u'lláh, *Gleanings from the Writings of Bahá'u'lláh*, p. 38)

they still remained, in the plenitude of their power, patient, and, despite their ascendancy, they suffered and endured[215]

215. The power and ascendancy of the Manifestations of God has been manifested on most crucial occasions:

> Now the chief priests, and elders, and all the council, sought false witness against Jesus, to put him to death; But found none: yea, though many false witnesses came, yet found they none. At the last came two false witnesses, And said, This fellow said, I am able to destroy the temple of God, and to build it in three days. And the high priest arose, and said unto him, Answerest thou nothing? what is it which these witness against thee? But Jesus held his peace, And the high priest answered and said unto him, I adjure thee by the living God, that thou tell us whether thou be the Christ, the Son of God. Jesus saith unto him, Thou hast said: nevertheless I say unto you, Hereafter shall ye see the Son of man sitting on the right hand of power, and coming in the clouds of heaven. Then the high priest rent his clothes, saying, He hath spoken blasphemy; what further need have we of witnesses? behold, now ye have heard his blasphemy. What think ye? They answered and said, He is guilty of death. Then did they spit

[66] Youth is a title that Bahá'u'lláh chose for Himself.

in his face, and buffeted him; and others smote him with the palms of their hands, Saying, Prophesy unto us, thou Christ, Who is he that smote thee?
(Matthew 26:60–67)

When three years had passed, Muḥammad was commanded to preach in public, and withdraw from the idolaters; the Qur'án reads: "Profess publicly then what Thou hast been bidden, and withdraw from those who join gods to God." (15:94). He invited His kinsmen, the leaders of Mecca, . . . He freely told them what had happened, ending, "Never before has an Arab bestowed on his people what I now bring you. . . . Who will act as my brother and helper?" There was icy silence. Abu Lahab, one of the uncles [uncles of Muḥammad were the leaders of Mecca at that time], shrugged his shoulders. . . . And they all laughed, and the meeting broke up. . . . The Meccans did not know what to make of Him. For a time they mocked Him, they pursued Him, they covered Him and His disciples with filth when they were praying, they incited children and the rabble to follow and mock them, a woman strewed thorns where He would walk.
(Marzieh Gail, *Six Lessons on Islam*, pp. 6–7)

The circumstances attending the examination of the Báb, as a result of so precipitate an act, may well rank as one of the chief landmarks of His dramatic career. The avowed purpose of that convocation was to arraign the Prisoner, and deliberate on the steps to be taken for the extirpation of His so-called heresy. It instead afforded Him the supreme opportunity of His mission to assert in public, formally and without any reservation, the claims inherent in His Revelation. In the official residence, and in the presence, of the governor of Ádhirbáyján, Náṣiri'd-Dín Mírzá, the heir to the throne; under the presidency of Ḥájí Mullá Maḥmúd, the Niẓámu'l-'Ulamá, the Prince's tutor; before the assembled ecclesiastical dignitaries of Tabríz, the leaders of the Shaykhí community, the Shaykhu'l-Islám, and the Imám-Jum'ih, the Báb, having seated Himself in the chief place which had been reserved for the Valí-'Ahd (the heir to the throne), gave, in ringing tones, His celebrated answer to the question put to Him by the President of that assembly. *"I am,"* He exclaimed,

"I am, I am the Promised One! I am the One Whose name you have for a thousand years invoked, at Whose mention you have risen, Whose advent you have longed to witness, and the hour of Whose Revelation you have prayed God to hasten. Verily, I say, it is incumbent upon the peoples of both the East and the West to obey My word, and to pledge allegiance to My person."

Awe-struck, those present momentarily dropped their heads in silent confusion. Then Mullá Muḥammad-i-Mamáqání, that one-eyed white-bearded renegade, summoning sufficient courage, with characteristic insolence, reprimanded Him as a perverse and contemptible follower of Satan; to which the undaunted Youth retorted that He maintained what He had already asserted. To the query subsequently addressed to Him by the Niẓámu'l-'Ulamá, the Báb affirmed that His words constituted the most incontrovertible evidence of His mission, adduced verses from the Qur'án to establish the truth of His assertion, and claimed to be able to reveal, within the space of two days and two nights, verses equal to the whole of that Book. In answer to a criticism calling His attention to an infraction by Him of the rules of grammar, He cited certain passages from the Qur'án as corroborative evidence, and, turning aside, with firmness and dignity, a frivolous and irrelevant remark thrown at Him by one of those who were present, summarily disbanded that gathering by Himself rising and quitting the room. The convocation thereupon dispersed, its members confused, divided among themselves, bitterly resentful and humiliated through their failure to achieve their purpose. Far from daunting the spirit of their Captive, far from inducing Him to recant or abandon His mission, that gathering was productive of no other result than the decision, arrived at after considerable argument and discussion, to inflict the bastinado on Him, at the hands, and in the prayer-house of the heartless and avaricious Mírzá 'Alí-Aṣghar, the Shaykhu'l-Islám of that city.
(Shoghi Effendi, *God Passes By*, p. 21)

His arrival at the penal colony of 'Akká, far from proving the end of His afflictions, was but the beginning of a major crisis, . . . Explicit orders had been issued by the Sulṭán and his ministers to subject the exiles, who were accused of having grievously erred and led others far astray, to the strictest confinement. Hopes were confidently expressed that the sentence of life-long imprisonment pronounced against them would lead to their eventual extermination. The farmán [edict] of Sulṭán, . . . not only condemned them to perpetual banishment, but stipulated their strict incarceration, and forbade them to associate either with each other or with the local inhabitants.

Bahá'u'lláh Himself, as attested by Nabíl in his narrative, had, as far back as the first years of His banishment to Adrianople, alluded to that same city in His Lawḥ-i-Sayyáḥ, designating it as the "Vale of Nabíl," the word Nabíl being equal in numerical value to that of Akká. *"Upon Our arrival," . . . "We were welcomed with banners of light, whereupon the Voice of the Spirit cried out saying: 'Soon will all that dwell on earth be enlisted under these banners.'"*
(Shoghi Effendi, *God Passes By*, pp. 184–86)

Bahá'u'lláh was peremptorily summoned to the Governorate, interrogated, kept in custody the first night, with one of His sons, in a chamber in the K͟hán-i-S͟hávirdí, . . . When interrogated, He was asked to state His name and that of the country from which He came. *"It is more manifest than the sun,"* He answered. The same question was put to Him again, to which He gave the following reply: *"I deem it not proper to mention it. Refer to the farmán of the government which is in your possession."* Once again they, with marked deference, reiterated their request, whereupon Bahá'u'lláh spoke with majesty and power these words: *"My name is Bahá'u'lláh* (Light of God), *and My country is Núr* (Light). *Be ye apprized of it."* Turning then, to the Muftí, He addressed him words of veiled rebuke, after which He spoke to the entire gathering, in such vehement and exalted language that none made bold to answer Him. Having quoted verses from the Súriy-i-Múlúk, He, afterwards, arose and left the gathering.
(Shoghi Effendi, *God Passes By*, p. 190)

Paragraph No. 48:

Know thou, that upon whatever hearts the bountiful showers of mercy, raining from the "heaven" of divine Revelation, have fallen, the earth of those hearts hath verily been changed into the earth of divine knowledge and wisdom.[216]

216. In the prophecies related to the Day of resurrection, both the Bible and Qur'án, speak of the establishment of a new Earth and a new Heaven:

> Looking for and hasting unto the coming of the day of God, wherein the heavens being on fire shall be dissolved, and the elements shall melt with fervent heat? Nevertheless we, according to his promise, look for new heavens and a new earth, wherein dwelleth righteousness.
> (2 Peter 3:12–13)

> On the day when the Earth shall be changed into another Earth, and the Heavens also, men shall come forth unto God, the Only, the Victorious.
> (The Qur'án 14:49)

The meaning of "Heaven," as explained by Bahá'u'lláh, is the Heaven of divine Revelation (the new religion) that is established by the new Manifestation of God, and the meaning of "the Earth" is the heart of the people of the world. This concept is also supported by the statement of Christ in the parable of the sower who spreads the seeds, in Matthew, Chapter 13:

> Then He spoke many things to them in parables, saying: "Behold, a sower went out to sow. And as he sowed, some seed fell by the wayside; and the birds came and devoured them. Some fell on stony places, where they did not have much earth; and they immediately sprang up because they had no depth of earth. But when the sun was up they were scorched, and because they had no root they withered away. And some fell among thorns, and the thorns sprang up and choked them. But others fell on good ground and yielded a crop: some a hundredfold, some sixty, some thirty. He who has ears to hear, let him hear!

And the disciples came and said to Him, "Why do You speak to them in parables?" He answered and said to them, "Because it has been given to you to know the mysteries of the kingdom of heaven, but to them it has not been given. For whoever has, to him more will be given, and he will have abundance; but whoever does not have, even what he has will be taken away from him. Therefore I speak to them in parables, because seeing they do not see, and hearing they do not hear, nor do they understand. And in them the prophecy of Isaiah is fulfilled, which says:

'Hearing you will hear and shall not understand,
And seeing you will see and not perceive;
For the hearts of this people have grown dull.
Their ears are hard of hearing,
And their eyes they have closed,
Lest they should see with their eyes and hear with their ears, Lest they should understand with their hearts and turn,
So that I should heal them.'

But blessed are your eyes for they see, and your ears for they hear; for assuredly, I say to you that many prophets and righteous men desired to see what you see, and did not see it, and to hear what you hear, and did not hear it.

Hear ye therefore the parable of the sower: When anyone hears the word of the kingdom, and does not understand it, then the wicked one comes and snatches away what was sown in his heart. This is he who received seed by the wayside. But he who received the seed on stony places, this is he who hears the word and immediately receives it with joy; yet he has no root in himself, but endures only for a while. For when tribulation or persecution arises because of the word, immediately he stumbles. Now he who received seed among the thorns is he who hears the word, and the cares of this world and the deceitfulness of riches choke the word, and he becomes unfruitful. But he who received seed on the good ground is he who hears the word and understands it, who indeed bears fruit and produces: some a hundredfold, some sixty, some thirty."
(Matthew 13:3–23)

With this explanation, the meaning of "the Earth" in many versus of scripture becomes clear.

Were the earth of their hearts to remain unchanged, how could such souls who have not been taught one letter, have seen no teacher, and entered no school, utter such words and display such knowledge as none can apprehend[217]

217. The transforming effects of the divine Revelation has been demonstrated through the life, works, and accomplishments of the simple and unlettered disciples of each and every one of the Manifestations of God. 'Abdu'l-Bahá stated:

> Peter, the chief of the apostles, used to divide the proceeds of his fishing into seven parts, and when, having taken one part for each day's use, he arrived at the seventh portion, he knew it was the Sabbath day. Consider this! and then think of his future position; to what glory he attained because the Holy Spirit wrought great works through him.
> ('Abdu'l-Bahá, *Paris Talks*, p. 164)

> Why were these disciples able to do what philosophers and scientists failed to accomplish? You have the example in Peter who was assisted by the Holy Spirit, as have been all those who have enlightened humanity—for universal education can be accomplished only through the Holy Spirit.
> ('Abdu'l-Bahá, *Divine Philosophy,* p. 89)

> The two great apostles, St Peter and St John the Evangelist, were once simple, humble workmen, toiling for their daily bread. By the Power of the Holy Spirit their souls were illumined, and they received the eternal blessings of the Lord Christ.
> ('Abdu'l-Bahá, *Paris Talks*, p. 59)

> The apostles, who were the disciples of Jesus Christ, were just as other men are; they, like their fellows, were attracted by the things of the world, and each thought only of his own advantage. They knew little of justice, nor were the Divine perfections found in their midst. But when they

followed Christ and believed in Him, their ignorance gave place to understanding, cruelty was changed to justice, falsehood to truth, darkness into light. They had been worldly, they became spiritual and divine. They had been children of darkness, they became sons of God, they became saints! Strive therefore to follow in their steps, leaving all worldly things behind, and striving to attain to the Spiritual Kingdom.
('Abdu'l-Bahá, *Paris Talks*, p. 60)

This is the stone which was set at nought of you builders, which is become the head of the corner. . . . Now when they saw the boldness of Peter and John, and perceived that they were unlearned and ignorant men, they marvelled; and they took knowledge of them, that they had been with Jesus.
(Acts 4:7–13)

And We desired to show favour unto those who were oppressed in the earth, and to make them examples and to make them the inheritors,
(The Qur'án, Pickthall tr, 28:4)

And we were minded to shew favour to those who were brought lo in the land, and to make them spiritual chiefs, and to make them Pharaoh's heirs,
(The Qur'án 28:4)

How often—and the early history of the Faith in the land of its birth offers many a striking testimony—have the lowliest adherents of the Faith, unschooled and utterly inexperienced, and with no standing whatever, and in some cases devoid of intelligence, been capable of winning victories for their Cause, before which the most brilliant achievements of the learned, the wise, and the experienced have paled.
(Shoghi Effendi, *The Advent of Divine Justice*, p. 45)

Therefore, hath it been said: "Knowledge is a light which God casteth into the heart of whomsoever He willeth.[218]

218. This is a tradition (Ḥadi_th_) from Muḥammad. Bahá'u'lláh defines the meaning of the knowledge that is displayed by those unschooled people, the earth of whose hearts have been changed through the outpourings of the divine revelation. As was stated in Note No. 2 above, this knowledge is different from what is acquired in the religious schools and seminaries. One contemporary Bahá'í scholar, the late Adib Taherzadeh, has provided the following explanation on this subject:

> This is a stage in which the light of knowledge will shine within the heart of the believer and he will be "apprised" of the things he could not comprehend earlier. The knowledge of God and a true understanding of His teachings can come about when the believer approaches Him in a spirit of utter humility and submissiveness, and opens his heart fully to the outpourings of His Revelation. Then and only then will the vernal showers of His unfailing grace cause the tree of knowledge and wisdom to grow within the heart, and enable him to bring forth, in the fullness of time, the fruit of understanding. When this stage is reached, the individual will be aided to comprehend the truth of the Word and discover the manifold mysteries that are enshrined within God's Revelation. Knowledge of spiritual truth comes through the heart of man. The intellect will then grasp the subject and reason will emerge. There is a tradition in Islam which Bahá'u'lláh confirms in the Kitáb-i-Íqán, stating that "knowledge is a light which God sheddeth into the heart of whomsoever He willeth." This is a knowledge which wells out of the heart of the believer and is Independent of academic learning.
> (Adib Taherzadeh, *The Revelation of Bahá'u'lláh,* vol. 4, p. 213)

It is this kind of knowledge which is and hath ever been praiseworthy, and not the limited knowledge that hath sprung forth from veiled and obscured minds.[219]

219. Historically, in most societies the religious leaders were recognized and regarded as the most knowledgeable people. The term "knowledge" generally referred to what those religious scholars knew and the subjects that were taught in religious

schools, seminaries, and madrasehs (Islamic traditional schools). This knowledge, which in most cases was the result of the study of obscure, impractical, and useless subjects was the source of their pride and arrogance and became a veil that prevented them from recognizing the Manifestations of God.

> We have decreed, O people, that the highest and last end of all learning be the recognition of Him Who is the Object of all knowledge; and yet, behold how ye have allowed your learning to shut you out, as by a veil, from Him Who is the Dayspring of this Light, through Whom every hidden thing hath been revealed. Could ye but discover the source whence the splendor of this utterance is diffused, ye would cast away the peoples of the world and all that they possess, and would draw nigh unto this most blessed Seat of glory
> (Bahá'u'lláh, *Gleanings from the Writings of Bahá'u'lláh*, p. 198)

Paragraph No. 49:

Consider now, were the parched and barren soil of these hearts to remain unchanged, how could they ever become the Recipients of the revelation of the mysteries of God, and the Revealers of the divine Essence?[220]

220. This concept is very similar to what Christ explained in the parable of the sower in Chapter 13 of Matthew (see Note No. 208 above), in which the words of God are exemplified as seeds and the hearts of men as the earth. He said that those seeds that fall on stony places or the parched earth do not develop root and whither.

Thus hath He said: "On the day when the earth shall be changed into another earth."[221]

221. This is from the Qur'án, Súrah 14, Abrahim:

> On the day when the Earth shall be changed into another Earth, and the Heavens also, men shall come forth unto God, the Only, the Victorious.
> (The Qur'án 14:49)

Paragraph No. 50:

The breeze of the bounty of the King of creation hath caused even the physical earth to be changed.[222]

222. After explaining the meanings of the symbolic words and statements of the sacred books of previous dispensations, Bahá'u'lláh states that the forces released by this new Revelation are not only changing the symbolic earth (the hearts of the people), but have also caused the physical earth to be changed. He states:

> Were ye to be fair in your judgment, ye would readily recognize how the realities of all created things are inebriated with the joy of this new and wondrous Revelation, how all the atoms of the earth have been illuminated through the brightness of its glory.
> (Bahá'u'lláh, *Gleanings from the Writings of Bahá'u'lláh*, p. 324)

> Through the mere revelation of the word "Fashioner," issuing forth from His lips and proclaiming His attribute to mankind, such power is released as can generate, through successive ages, all the manifold arts which the hands of man can produce. This, verily, is a certain truth. No sooner is this resplendent word uttered, than its animating energies, stirring within all created things, give birth to the means and instruments whereby such arts can be produced and perfected. All the wondrous achievements ye now witness are the direct consequences of the Revelation of this Name. In the days to come, ye will, verily, behold things of which ye have never heard before. Thus hath it been decreed in the Tablets of God, and none can comprehend it except them whose sight is sharp. In like manner, the moment the word expressing My attribute "The Omniscient" issueth forth from My mouth, every created thing will, according to its capacity and limitations, be invested with the power to unfold the knowledge of the most marvelous sciences, and will be empowered to manifest them in the course of time at the bidding of Him Who is the Almighty, the All-Knowing.
> (Bahá'u'lláh, *Gleanings from the Writings of Bahá'u'lláh*, p. 141)

Paragraph No. 51:

And now, comprehend the meaning of this verse: "The whole earth shall on the Resurrection Day be but His handful, and in His right hand shall the heavens be folded together.[223]

223. This is a verse from the Qur'án, Súrah Al-Zumar (the Hordes):

> But they have not deemed of God as is He due; for on the resurrection day the whole Earth shall be but his handful, and in his right hand shall the Heavens be folded together. Praise be to Him! and high be He uplifted above the partners they join with Him!
> (The Qur'án 39:67)

Some Qur'ánic commentators maintained that on the Day of Resurrection, God would by His own hands roll up the heavens like a scroll around the earth and would throw this to a corner of the Plain of Resurrection. Similar imagery is presented in the Old and New Testaments:

> . . . the heavens shall be rolled together as a scroll: and all their host shall fall down, as the leaf falleth off from the vine, and as a falling fig from the fig tree.
> (Isaiah 34:4)

> And I beheld when he had opened the sixth seal, and, lo, there was a great earthquake; and the sun became black as sackcloth of hair, and the moon became as blood; And the stars of heaven fell unto the earth, even as a fig tree casteth her untimely figs, when she is shaken of a mighty wind. And the heaven departed as a scroll when it is rolled together; and every mountain and island were moved out of their places.
> (Revelation 6:12–14)

thus causing the freshest and loveliest blossoms, and the mightiest and loftiest trees to spring forth from the illumined bosom of man.[224]

224. The flowers and trees that spring forth from the earth of the hearts of men are the flowers and trees of faith, which bring forth the fruits of spiritual character.

> The fruits of the human tree are exquisite, highly desired and dearly cherished. Among them are upright character, virtuous deeds and a goodly utterance. The springtime for earthly trees occurreth once every year, while the one for human trees appeareth in the Days of God—exalted be His glory. Were the trees of men's lives to be adorned in this divine Springtime with the fruits that have been mentioned, the effulgence of the light of Justice would, of a certainty, illumine all the dwellers of the earth and everyone would abide in tranquillity and contentment beneath the sheltering shadow of Him Who is the Object of all mankind. The Water for these trees is the living water of the sacred Words uttered by the Beloved of the world. In one instant are such trees planted and in the next their branches shall, through the outpourings of the showers of divine mercy, have reached the skies.
> (Bahá'u'lláh, *Tablets of Bahá'u'lláh*, p. 257)

Similar statements are found in the Bible:

> The righteous shall flourish like the palm tree: he shall grow like a cedar in Lebanon. Those that be planted in the house of the LORD shall flourish in the courts of our God. They shall still bring forth fruit in old age; they shall be fat and flourishing;
> (Psalms 92:12–14)

Paragraph No. 52:

In like manner, reflect how the elevated heavens of the Dispensations of the past have, in the right hand of power, been folded together, how the heavens of divine Revelation have been raised by the command of God, and been adorned by the sun, the moon, and stars of His wondrous commandments[225]

225. This folding of the previous dispensation and unfolding of the new one takes place in fulfillment of the prophecies every time

that a new Manifestation appears. The earth of Judaic knowledge and the heaven of Judaic laws were folded up by Christ and a new earth of knowledge and a new heaven of understanding were unfolded in Christianity. The same process was repeated when Muḥammad appeared and a new earth of knowledge was unfolded under the heaven of Islamic laws. Even in the case of the Revelation of the Bayán, the main purpose of which was to prepare the way for revelation of Bahá'u'lláh, the earth of understanding and the heaven of the laws of the Bayán were folded up and a new earth and a new heaven were unfolded:

> Our Exalted Herald—may the life of all else besides Him be offered up for His sake—hath revealed certain laws. However, in the realm of His Revelation these laws were made subject to Our sanction, hence this Wronged One hath put some of them into effect by embodying them in the Kitáb-i-Aqdas in different words. Others We set aside. He holdeth in His hand the authority. He doeth what He willeth and He ordaineth whatsoever He pleaseth. He is the Almighty, the All-Praised. There are also ordinances newly revealed. Blessed are they that attain. Blessed are they that observe His precepts.
> (Bahá'u'lláh, *Tablets of Bahá'u'lláh*, p. 131)

Such are the mysteries of the Word of God, which have been unveiled and made manifest.[226]

226. The mysteries of the sacred books of the past are revealed by Bahá'u'lláh:

> Great is the Cause, and great the Announcement! Patiently and calmly ponder thou upon the resplendent signs and the sublime words, and all that hath been revealed in these days, that haply thou mayest fathom the mysteries that are hid in the Books, and mayest strive to guide His servants.
> (Bahá'u'lláh, Epistle to the Son of the Wolf, p. 143)

> For otherwise, unto them that have recognized the Repositories of divine Revelation and beheld through His inspiration the mysteries of divine authority, all the verses of God are perspicuous and all His allusions are clear. Such

men discern the inner mysteries that have been clothed in the garment of words as clearly as ye perceive the heat of the sun or the wetness of water, nay even more distinctly. Immeasurably exalted is God above our praise of His loved ones, and beyond their praise of Him!
(Bahá'u'lláh, *Gems of Divine Mysteries*, p. 22)

that haply thou mayest apprehend the morning light of divine guidance, mayest quench, by the power of reliance and renunciation, the lamp of idle fancy, of vain imaginings, of hesitation, and doubt, and mayest kindle, in the inmost chamber of thine heart, the new-born light of divine knowledge and certitude.[227]

227. This concept is also explained by 'Abdu'l-Bahá:

> When the darkness of ignorance and heedlessness concerning the realm of eternity and bereavement from the True One had encircled the universe, then the resplendent Luminary dawned and the brilliant Light illumined the horizon of the East. Hence, the Sun of Reality shone forth, scattering the sparkling lights of the Kingdom to the East and to the West. Those who had seeing eyes found the Most Great Glad-Tidings, began to cry the call, "O blessed are we! O blessed are we!"—and have beheld the reality of things in themselves, have discovered the mysteries of the Kingdom, were released from superstition and doubts, perceived the lights of Truth and became so intoxicated with the cup of the love of God, that, wholly forgetting themselves and the world while dancing, they ran with utmost joy and ecstasy to the city of Martyrdom, sacrificing their minds and their lives upon the altar of Love.
> ('Abdu'l-Bahá, *Tablets of Abdu'l-Bahá*, vol. 3, p. 502)

> Shouldst thou come with the whole of thy being to God and be attracted to the lights of the Kingdom of God and be enkindled by the fire of the love of God, then wilt thou see that which thou canst not see today, wilt comprehend the inner significance of the Word of God and thoroughly understand the mysteries contained in the holy Books.
> ('Abdu'l-Bahá, *Tablets of Abdu'l-Bahá*, vol. 3, p. 622)

All the texts and teachings of the holy Testaments have intrinsic spiritual meanings. They are not to be taken literally. I, therefore, pray in your behalf that you may be given the power of understanding these inner real meanings of the Holy Scriptures and may become informed of the mysteries deposited in the words of the Bible so that you may attain eternal life and that your hearts may be attracted to the Kingdom of God. May your souls be illumined by the light of the Words of God, and may you become repositories of the mysteries of God, for no comfort is greater and no happiness is sweeter than spiritual comprehension of the divine teachings. If a man understands the real meaning of a poet's verses such as those of Shakespeare, he is pleased and rejoiced. How much greater his joy and pleasure when he perceives the reality of the Holy Scriptures and becomes informed of the mysteries of the Kingdom!

I pray that the divine blessings may descend upon you day by day, that your hearts may be opened to perceive the inner significances of the Word of God. There is no fruit in knowing the mere letters of the Book. Most of the Jews had memorized the texts of the Old Testament and repeated them night and day, but inasmuch as they were ignorant of the meanings, they were deprived of the bounties of Christ. I pray that you may be quickened by the breaths of the Holy Spirit and illumined by the rays of the Sun of Truth. May you be favored with heavenly blessings in the threshold of God and attain to eternal life. This is my prayer. May God bless and enlighten you.
('Abdu'l-Bahá, *The Promulgation of Universal Peace*, p. 459)

Paragraph No. 53:

* There are no Notes for Paragraph No. 53.

Paragraph No. 54:

And likewise, reflect upon the revealed verse concerning the "Qiblih."[228]

228. Qiblih or Qiblah (also transliterated as Kiblah) is an Arabic word which literarily means the direction toward which one faces, but actually means the "Point of Adoration." It is the point or the location toward which Muslim worshippers must face when offering their obligatory prayers. The concept of Qiblih existed in previous religions including Judaism.

Historically, as recorded in the Mishnah, Jews were to face the Temple in Jerusalem while praying. This practice was recorded in the Book of Kings:

> When thy people Israel be smitten down before the enemy, because they have sinned against thee, and shall turn again to thee, and confess thy name, and pray, and make supplication unto thee in this house: Then hear thou in heaven, and forgive the sin of thy people Israel. . . . When heaven is shut up, and there is no rain, because they have sinned against thee; if they pray toward this place, and confess thy name, and turn from their sin, when thou afflictest them: Then hear thou in heaven, and forgive the sin of thy servants, . . . If there be in the land famine, if there be pestilence, blasting, mildew, locust, or if there be caterpiller; if their enemy besiege them in the land of their cities; whatsoever plague, whatsoever sickness there be; What prayer and supplication soever be made by any man, or by all thy people Israel, which shall know every man the plague of his own heart, and spread forth his hands toward this house: Then hear thou in heaven thy dwelling place, and forgive, and do, and give to every man according to his ways, whose heart thou knowest.
> (3 Kings 8:33–38)

After the destruction of the Temple in 70 AD, Jews prayed toward or at the Temple grounds and the remaining Wailing Wall, but throughout the ages this was changed and in contemporary times Jews in other parts of the world recite prayers while facing the Aron Kodesh (the ark that houses the Torah scrolls in each Synagogue).

In Christianity, partly because soon after the crucifixion of Christ the gentile believers became the majority, and partly because of the teachings of Paul, who considered the body of Christ as replacing the Holy Temple and His crucifixion as replacing the ritual of sacrifice offering, the concept of Qiblih was not introduced.

In Islam there were two Qiblih. In the first few years, the Qiblih was the same Temple grounds in Jerusalem, which was called Bayt-al-Muqadas (the Sacred House) or sometimes Masjid-al-Aqsá (the faraway Mosque), and Muḥammad and His followers faced Jerusalem during the obligatory prayers. Later on (approximately one and a half years after the arrival of Muḥammad and his followers in Medina) it was changed to the House of Ka'bih in Mecca. The Arabic word "Ka'bih" literally means cube, and it refers to the holy sanctuary (a cubical building containing a black meteorite rock) located at the heart of the structure in Mecca (called the House of Ka'bih). In the above paragraph Bahá'u'lláh relates the story and the effects and the wisdom of this change of Qiblih.

The concept of Qiblih in the Bahá'í Faith is explained in the Kitáb-i-Aqdas:

> The "Point of Adoration," that is, the point to which the worshipper should turn when offering obligatory prayer, is called the Qiblih. The concept of Qiblih has existed in previous religions. Jerusalem in the past had been fixed for this purpose. Muḥammad changed the Qiblih to Mecca. The Báb's instructions in the Arabic Bayán were:
>
> The Qiblih is indeed He Whom God will make manifest; whenever He moveth, it moveth, until He shall come to rest.
>
> This passage is quoted by Bahá'u'lláh in the Kitáb-i-Aqdas (¶137) and confirmed by Him in the above-noted verse. He has also indicated that facing in the direction of the Qiblih is a "fixed requirement for the recitation of obligatory prayer"
> (Kitáb-i-Aqdas, Q and A, 14 and 67, p. 168)

When Muḥammad, the Sun of Prophethood, had fled from the dayspring of Baṭḥá[229]

229. Baṭḥá and Yat͟hrib (Mecca and Medina) are the two most sacred cities of Islam, located in the land of Ḥijáz (present-day Saudi Arabia). Baṭḥá is sometimes used in reference to Mecca. Baṭḥá was the central part of the City of Mecca where the House of Ka'bih, the most sacred shrine of Islam, is located. At the time of Muḥammad, the ten main clans of the tribe of Quraysh, Muḥammad's family (His grandfather and his ten sons), the aristocracy of Mecca, who were the custodians of the House of Kaaba, which was the main Idol House of the Arabian peninsula, were living in Baṭḥá. Bahá'u'lláh called it the dayspring of Baṭḥá because Muḥammad declared His mission in Baṭḥá—i.e., the Sun of His Prophethood rose from there. Yat͟hrib is the original name of Medina. It is a city approximately 200 miles north of Mecca. After Islam was established, Yat͟hrib was named Medinat-ul-Nabí (the City of the Prophet). In English it is abbreviated to Medinah or Medina. Muḥammad took refuge in Medina, and ten years later passed away there. His burial place in Medina is the second holiest shrine of Islam.

When Muḥammad, the Sun of Prophethood, had fled from the dayspring of Baṭḥá unto Yat͟hrib[230]

230. This is a reference to the Ḥijrah (Emigration) of Muḥammad from Mecca to Medina. In reference to the migration of Muḥammad and a group of His followers from Mecca to Medina in 622 AD, Marzieh Gail writes:

> The Meccans said, "Know this, O Muḥammad, we shall never cease to stop thee from preaching till either thou or we perish" (Ameer Ali, op. cit., 107).
>
> For three years (617–619) they blockaded Him and His kinsmen in a remote quarter of the town and forbade the other towns-people to have any dealings with them whatever [We should remember that, as R. L. Gulick points out in his Muḥammad The Educator (ms. p. 21), "Tribal opinion was of supreme importance as a regulator of

behavior. The worst punishment was expulsion from the tribe . . ."]. Then Khadíjih [Muḥammad's first wife] died (December 619) and five weeks later, Muḥammad's uncle and protector. Since His own people refused Him, He then went to another city—Ta'if, a beautiful place about seventy miles distant, where fruit trees grew—but the people stoned Him away. . . . He and a tiny group, shut away in the sand, alone on the planet, encircled by men so wild they buried children alive as a point of honor, who killed casually, and who— because His teachings meant the destruction of the national religion and the loss of their own wealth and power—had for thirteen long years been waiting to shed His blood. An enemy of His has written: "We search in vain through the pages of profane history for a parallel to the struggle in which for thirteen years the Prophet of Arabia, in face of discouragement and threats, rejection and persecution, retained thus his faith unwavering, preached repentance . . . he met insults, menace, and danger with a lofty and patient trust in the future." (Muir, op. cit., 518).

It was now that the tide of history turned . . . What happened in Islam was this: Muḥammad had often preached to other tribes, people who would come to the Ka'bih or the great fairs. On such occasions, His uncle, the squint-eyed Abu Lahab (he and Zayd, Muḥammad's adopted son, are the only two contemporaries named in the Qur'án) would follow and cry: "He is an impostor who seeks to lead you away from the faith of your fathers!" And the visitors would laugh, saying, "Thine own kindred know thee best. Wherefore do they not believe?" But there were some men of Medina (Yathrib) who listened to Him. They were weary of the fighting between rival clans in their own city, and they asked Him to come and be their Chief. Muḥammad sent His disciples on to Medina. It was the fateful year 622—the year of the Ḥijra (Emigration) from which the Muslim calendar was afterward reckoned.

At this juncture the Meccans united to murder Muḥammad. They arranged for members of all the clans to attack Him at once, so that the blood-guilt would not rest on any one of them. They waited outside His house, watching as He lay in

His cloak on the bed, but when the dawn came, they saw it was not Muḥammad there but 'Ali[67]. Muḥammad had escaped to Medina, which from this time on was called the City of the Prophet.

Muḥammad entered Medina in triumph; a shaykh put his turban on the end of a lance for a banner, and a parasol of palm branches was held over the Prophet's head, while the Helpers (Ansar), the Medina believers, surrounded Him, brandishing swords and spears. He dismounted on the outskirts, and turned toward the Point of Adoration, Jerusalem . . . ; He prayed, with all the multitude; then, the accounts say, He let His camel go free into the town, and where it knelt, a mosque was later erected. As He entered, He greeted all the people, even the children.
(Marzieh Gail, *Six Lessons on Islam*, p. 8)

He continued to turn His face, while praying, unto Jerusalem, the holy city[231]

231. While in Mecca, Muḥammad and His followers were facing Jerusalem when performing their obligatory prayers. This practice of facing Jerusalem during the prayers continued for almost one and a half years after the arrival of Muḥammad in Medina.

words which if mentioned would ill befit these pages and would weary the reader[232]

232. The Islamic historians have recorded the Jews' objections and unseemly words in detail, and Bahá'u'lláh stated that it was not necessary to repeat them in the Kitáb-Íqán. Briefly, the essence of

[67] There are a lot of stories in Islamic literature regarding the way Muḥammad escaped the enemies who were surrounding His house, and accompanied by two of His followers, made His way to Medina. It is related that they left Mecca before midnight and hid in a cave a few miles from Mecca. When the enemies who were searching for Him reached the cave the next day, they saw that the entrance to the cave was covered by spiderwebs. They thought that no one had entered the cave for a long time, otherwise the spiderwebs would have been disturbed. Therefore they left without entering. Muḥammad and His companion left the cave after three days and eventually arrived at Medina.

what they were saying (in proper language) was: If Muḥammad does not follow our religion and is claiming to be God’s Messenger, why is He praying toward our Qiblih (Jerusalem) and why does His God not give him a Qibilih of His own?

He heard the kindly Voice of Gabriel[233]

233. In Islamic tradition, there are four exalted archangels who dwell near the throne of God: ‘Izrá’íl, Isráfíl, Michael (pronounced Míká’íl in Arabic), and Gabriel (pronounced Jibra’íl in Arabic). Three of these archangels—Gabriel, Michael, and Isráfíl, who is also called Raphael—are also mentioned in the Bible. Gabriel is the one that according to Islamic belief brought the Revelation from God to Muḥammad, i.e., he is the symbol or equivalent of the Holy Spirit in the Islamic Dispensation. The Qur’án states:

> Say: Whoso is the enemy of Gabriel—For he it is who by God's leave hath caused the Koran to descend on thy heart, the confirmation of previous revelations, and guidance, and good tidings to the faithful—Whoso is an enemy to God or his angels, or to Gabriel, or to Michael, shall have God as his enemy: for verily God is an enemy to the Infidels.
> (The Qur’án 2:96–97)

> Thus have we sent the Spirit (Gabriel) to thee with a revelation, by our command. Thou knowest not, ere this, what "the Book" was, or what the faith.
> (The Qur’án 42:52)

We will have Thee turn to a Qiblih which shall please Thee.[234]

234. This verse is from the Súrah of the Cow, 2:144. In some Qur’ánic translations, such as Rodwell’s, this is verse 139, and in some, such as Pickthall’s, the wording is slightly different.

> We have seen thee turning thy face towards every part of Heaven; but we will have thee turn to a kebla which shall please thee. Turn then thy face towards the sacred Mosque, and wherever ye be, turn your faces towards that part.
> (The Qur’án 2:139)

> We have seen the turning of thy face to heaven (for guidance, O Muhammad). And now verily We shall make thee turn (in prayer) toward a qiblah which is dear to thee.
> (The Qur'án, Pickthall tr, 2:144)

performed two of the prescribed Rik'ats[235]

235. Rik'ats or rak'ahs are defined in the Kitáb-i-Aqdas in the following terms:

> A rak'ah is the recitation of specifically revealed verses accompanied by a prescribed set of genuflections and other movements.
> (The Kitáb-i-Aqdas, p. 167)

The Rik'at, which is the unit of obligatory prayers in Islam, consists of recitation of special verses accompanied by movements such as standing, standing with the raising of the hands, bowing with hands placed on the knees, prostrating with forehead on a piece of clay or a rock, sitting in specified position and form (legs folded under the thighs). The noon obligatory prayers in Islam consist of performing five Rik'ats—i.e., repeating each Rik'at five times. Muslims have to perform a total of seventeen Rik'at of prayers within every twenty-four hours (see Note No. 184 above).

"Turn Thou Thy face towards the sacred Mosque"[236]

236. "Sacred Mosque" is the House of Ka'bih. Ka'bih is the holiest place in Islam. Ka'bih (Arabic word meaning the Cube), is a large masonry cubical structure, more than a few thousand years old, which, according to Islamic traditions, dates back to the time of Abraham. The Ka'bih is located inside the al-Masjid al-Harám (meaning the most sacred mosque) located in Mecca in Saudi Arabia. The mosque was built around the original Ka'bih. The House of Ka'bih is the Qiblih, the point of adoration, toward which Muslims face during their daily obligatory prayers from any location on Earth, and which they circumambulate during the pilgrimage season.

So great was their alarm, that many of them, discontinuing their prayer, apostatized their faith[237]

237. According to the accounts of the companions of Muḥammad, who were present at that event, the change of Qiblih took place suddenly and without prior warning. Muḥammad was leading the noon obligatory prayers in a mosque in Medina, which later became known as the Masjid-al-Qiblatain (the Mosque of two Qiblihs) in the direction of Jerusalem when He received the Revelation from God through Gabriel instructing Him to turn from the direction of Jerusalem toward the House of Ka'bih in Mecca. According to these accounts, this act of changing direction in the middle of prayers caused great confusion and consternation among the people who were standing behind Him performing their prayers. At that point many of His followers left Him and turned back to their previous faiths. Some of them said they were told that He was a mad poet, but had to see this to believe it. The Qur'án provides the account of the change of Qiblih in the Súrah of the Cow 2:130–147:

> Say ye: "We believe in God, and that which hath been sent down to us, and that which hath been sent down to Abraham and Ismael and Isaac and Jacob and the tribes: and that which hath been given to Moses and to Jesus, and that which was given to the prophets from their Lord. No difference do we make between any of them: and to God are we resigned (Muslims)." If therefore they believe even as ye believe, then have they true guidance; but if they turn back, then do they cut themselves off from you: and God will suffice to protect thee against them, for He is the Hearer, the Knower. Islam is the Baptism of God, and who is better to baptise than God? And Him do we serve.[68]

---

[68] Verse 137–139, especially verse 138, of the second Súrah (Súrah of the Cow) is translated very differently by different translators of the Qur'án. Below is Pickthall's translation:

137 And if they believe in the like of that which ye believe, then are they rightly guided. But if they turn away, then are they in schism, and Allah will suffice thee (for defense) against them. He is the Hearer, the Knower. 138 (We take our) colour from Allah, and who is better than Allah at colouring. We are His worshippers. 139 Say (unto the People of the Scripture): Dispute ye with us concerning Allah when He is our Lord and your Lord ? Ours are our works and yours your works. We look to Him alone.

Say: Will ye dispute with us about God? when He is our Lord and your Lord! We have our works and ye have your works; and we are sincerely His. Will ye say, "Verily Abraham, and Ismael, and Isaac, and Jacob, and the tribes, were Jews or Christians?" Say: Who knoweth best, ye, or God? And who is more in fault than he who concealeth the witness which he hath from God? But God is not regardless of what ye do. That people have now passed away: they have the reward of their deeds, and for you is the meed of yours; but of their doings ye shall not be questioned. The foolish ones will say, "What hath turned them from the kebla which they used?" Say: The East and the West are God's He guided whom he will into the right path. Thus have we made you a central people, that ye may be witnesses in regard to mankind, and that the apostle may be a witness in regard to you. We appointed the kebla which thou formerly hadst, only that we might know him who followeth the apostle, from him who turneth on his heels: The change is a difficulty, but not to those whom God hath guided. But God will not let your faith be fruitless; for unto man is God Merciful, Gracious. We have seen thee turning thy face towards every part of Heaven; but we will have thee turn to a kebla which shall please thee. Turn then thy face towards the sacred Mosque, and wherever ye be, turn your faces towards that part. They, verily, to whom "the Book" hath been given, know this to be the truth from their Lord: and God is not regardless of what ye do. Even thou thou shouldst bring every kind of sign to those who have received the Scriptures, yet thy kebla they will not adopt; nor shalt thou adopt their kebla; nor will one part of them adopt the kebla of the other. And if, after the knowledge which hath come to thee, thou follow their wishes, verily then will thou become of the unrighteous. They to whom we have given the Scriptures know him—the apostle—even as they know their own children: but truly a part of them do conceal the truth, though acquainted with it. The truth is from thy Lord. Be not then of those who doubt. All have a quarter of the Heavens to which they turn them; but wherever ye be, hasten emulously after good: God will one

---

(The Qur'án, Pickthall tr, Súrah 2, The Cow)

> day bring you all together; verily, God is all-powerful. And from whatever place thou comest forth, turn thy face toward the sacred Mosque; for this is the truth from thy Lord; and God is not inattentive to your doings. And from whatever place thou comest forth, turn thy face toward the sacred Mosque; and wherever ye be, to that part turn your faces, lest men have cause of dispute against you: but as for the impious among them, fear them not; but fear me, that I may perfect my favours on you, and that ye may be guided aright. And we sent to you an apostle from among yourselves to rehearse our signs unto you, and to purify you, and to instruct you in "the Book," and in the wisdom, and to teach you that which ye knew not: Therefore remember me: I will remember you; and give me thanks and be not ungrateful.
> (The Qur'án 2:130–147)

Verily, God caused not this turmoil but to test and prove His servants.[238]

238. A similar test was presented to the followers of Jesus as recorded in the Gospel of John, Chapter 6, according to which some of the followers of Jesus were tested by His words and left Him:

> Verily, verily, I say unto you, He that believeth on me hath everlasting life. I am that bread of life. Your fathers did eat manna in the wilderness, and are dead. This is the bread which cometh down from heaven, that a man may eat thereof, and not die. I am the living bread which came down from heaven: if any man eat of this bread, he shall live forever: and the bread that I will give is my flesh, which I will give for the life of the world. The Jews therefore strove among themselves, saying, How can this man give us his flesh to eat? Then Jesus said unto them, Verily, verily, I say unto you, Except ye eat the flesh of the Son of man, and drink his blood, ye have no life in you. Whoso eateth my flesh, and drinketh my blood, hath eternal life; and I will raise him up at the last day. For my flesh is meat indeed, and my blood is drink indeed.

> He that eateth my flesh, and drinketh my blood, dwelleth in me, and I in him. As the living Father hath sent me, and I live by the Father: so he that eateth me, even he shall live by me. This is that bread which came down from heaven: not as your fathers did eat manna, and are dead: he that eateth of this bread shall live forever. These things said he in the synagogue, as he taught in Capernaum. Many therefore of his disciples, when they had heard this, said, This is an hard saying; who can hear it? When Jesus knew in himself that his disciples murmured at it, he said unto them, Doth this offend you? What and if ye shall see the Son of man ascend up where he was before? . . From that time many of his disciples went back, and walked no more with him.
> (John 6:47–60)

Paragraph No. 55:

Messengers of the Word of God, such as David[239]

239. David, son of Jesse of Bethlehem, whose name in Hebrew means "beloved," is presented in the Old Testament mainly based on the books of Samuel, as a prophet, a divinely inspired poet, the author of Psalms, a musician, and the second king of the united Kingdom of Israel. According to biblical chronology, his reign was between the time of Moses and Jesus, around 1000 BC. Accounts of his life are found in the Old Testament, 1 Samuel 16 to 1 Kings 2. David, who was born in Bethlehem, is portrayed as the chosen one (the anointed or Messiah), as God sends the prophet Samuel to Anoint him, and he is guided and supported to overcome his enemies such as the champion giant Goliath and Ish-Bosheth the son of Saul, and becomes the king of the united Israel (some recent biblical scholars doubt the accuracy of these stories and the size and nature of David's kingdom). The Old Testament accounts indicate that he committed a sin by taking the wife of Uriah (one of his army commanders) and arranging for Uriah to be killed. In contrast to the Old Testament accounts, in accordance with some Rabbinic traditions, David was so pious that he could bring heavenly miracles, and his committing adultery was to demonstrate the power of repentance and the

vastness of God's forgiveness. Some Talmudic traditions hold that David did not commit a sin. As based on the Jewish practice of prevention of Agunah (chaining of women in marriage, as a result of a women not having a bill of divorcement (*Get*) if the husband was killed in war or disappeared), Uriah had already divorced his wife when he left for battle.

During his forty-year reign, David formed the Jewish Kingdom and the institution of an eternal royal prophetic dynasty. He brought the Ark of the Covenant to Jerusalem, which was later placed in the Temple built by Solomon. Some historians hold that the failure of this eternal Davidic dynasty (due to the defeat of David's kingdom of the united Israel by its enemies) was the basis for the development of the concept of the Messiah being an apocalyptic figure, a descendant of David, who would restore his kingdom and sit on his throne.

In Christianity the accounts of the birth and life of Jesus in the Gospels name Bethlehem as His birth place, trace His lineage to David, call Him the Good Shepherd, and liken the five wounds that were inflicted on Him on the Cross to the five stones that David used to slay Goliath—the means by which Jesus defeated death. All these are considered as fulfillment of those Jewish prophecies.

In the Qur'án David (in Arabic, Dáwood) is named as one of the Major Prophets, to whom God revealed the Psalms (Zabur). He is presented as an epitome of wisdom, piety, justice, and fair judgment, and as having a heavenly voice and magical musical abilities that captivated all living things. As mentioned above, the accounts of the life and personal characteristics of Noah, Abraham, David, and Solomon in the Qur'án are different from what is recorded in the Old Testament. In Islamic theology, especially in Shí'ah Islam, the prophets of God are considered infallible. Consequently, the negative portrayal of these holy prophets in the Old Testament—i.e. of Noah as a drunken man who curses his son, of Abraham as a coward who gives away his wife for fear of his life, and of David as an adulterer and murderer—are categorically rejected.

There are many references to David and his Psalms in the Bahá'í Writings, such as:

> Lend an ear unto the song of David. He saith: "Who will bring me into the Strong City?" The Strong City is 'Akká, which hath been named the Most Great Prison, and which possesseth a fortress and mighty ramparts.
> (Bahá'u'lláh, Epistle to the Son of the Wolf, p. 144)

In referring to the prophecies of the sacred books of the past Dispensations regarding Bahá'u'lláh and His station, Shoghi Effendi States:

> Of Him David had sung in his Psalms, acclaiming Him as the "Lord of Hosts" and the "King of Glory."
> (Shoghi Effendi, *God Passes By*, p. 94)

> David, in his Psalms, had predicted: "Lift up your heads, O ye gates; even lift them up, ye everlasting doors; and the King of Glory shall come in. Who is this King of Glory? The Lord of Hosts, He is the King of Glory." "Out of Zion, the perfection of beauty, God hath shined. Our God shall come, and shall not keep silence.
> (Shoghi Effendi, *God Passes By*, p. 183)

Jesus, and others among the more exalted Manifestations[240]

240. "More exalted Manifestations" is a reference to the major prophets who received Revelation from God and in their Dispensations established laws and ordinances, in contrast to the minor prophets such as those of Israel. In this sentence, the term "More exalted Manifestations" refers to Jesus, although in accordance to Islamic belief, David was also a Messenger of the Word of God. This concept is clarified by the following statement from 'Abdu'l-Bahá:

> The universal Prophets Who have appeared independently include Abraham, Moses, Christ, Muḥammad, the Báb, and Bahá'u'lláh. The second kind, which consists of followers and promulgators, includes Solomon, David, Isaiah, Jeremiah, and Ezekiel. For the independent Prophets are

founders; that is, They establish a new religion, recreate the souls, regenerate the morals of society, and promulgate a new way of life and a new standard of conduct. Through Them a new Dispensation appears and a new religion is inaugurated. Their advent is even as the springtime, when all earthly things don a new garment and find a new life.

As to the second kind of Prophets, who are followers, they promulgate the religion of God, spread His Faith, and proclaim His Word. They have no power or authority of their own, but derive theirs from the independent Prophets.
('Abdu'l-Bahá, *Some Answered Questions,* no. 43.5–6)

the law of the Qiblih[241]

241. The Temple in Jerusalem was built by Solomon, son of David, where David built an altar on the Temple Mount on the spot designated by God, as stated in the Old Testament:

> And Gad came that day to David, and said unto him, Go up, rear an altar unto the LORD in the threshing floor of Araunah the Jebusite. And David, according to the saying of Gad, went up as the LORD commanded. . . . And Araunah said, Wherefore is my lord the king come to his servant? And David said, To buy the threshing floor of thee, to build an altar unto the LORD, that the plague may be stayed from the people. . . . And David built there an altar unto the LORD, and offered burnt offerings and peace offerings. So the LORD was intreated for the land, and the plague was stayed from Israel."
> (2 Kings 24:18–25)

According to 2 Chronicles, David brought the Ark of the Covenant to the place of the altar, and Solomon brought the Tabernacle of Congregation and built the Temple:

> Then Solomon began to build the house of the LORD at Jerusalem in mount Moriah, where the Lord appeared unto David his father, in the place that David had prepared in the threshing floor of Ornan the Jebusite.
> (2 Chronicles 3:1)

Historically, as recorded in the Mishnah (a major work of Rabbinic Judaism, and the first major redaction into written form of Jewish oral traditions, called the Oral Torah), Jews faced the Temple in Jerusalem while praying. This practice was recorded in the Book of Kings. Muslims also faced Jerusalem while praying until this was changed by Muḥammad (see Note No. 231 above).

excepting that place which, in the days of His Manifestations, He doth appoint for a particular purpose[242]

242. Although as stated above, all locations on earth are the same in the sight of God, those places that are appointed for a particular purpose by the Manifestations of God—such as the resting places of the Báb and Bahá'u'lláh—have special distinction. Regarding this, Shoghi Effendi states:

> The reflection of the qualities of holy souls can take place at any time; it is not confined to the period when the Manifestation is on this Earth.
>
> The atoms of the prophets are just atoms, like all others, but the association of the great spiritual power with them lives, in the place they are laid to rest, a spiritual atmosphere, if one can use this expression. They are, no doubt, endowed with a tremendous spiritual influence and far-reaching power. But the physical character of Their atoms are not different from other peoples, any more than Their bodies and physical functions are different."
>
> (From a letter written on behalf of Shoghi Effendi to an individual believer, October 28, 1949, in *Lights of Guidance*, p. 507)

"The East and West are God's: therefore whichever way ye turn, there is the face of God.[243]

243. This verse is from the Qur'án 2:115. Bahá'u'lláh makes reference to the same verse in the Kitáb-i-Aqdas:

> QUESTION: The believers have been enjoined to face in the direction of the Qiblih when reciting their Obligatory

Prayers; in what direction should they turn when offering other prayers and devotions?

ANSWER: Facing in the direction of the Qiblih is a fixed requirement for the recitation of obligatory prayer, but for other prayers and devotions one
may follow what the merciful Lord hath revealed in the Qur'án: "Whichever way ye turn, there is the face of God."
(The Kitáb-i-Aqdas, p. 111)

that the true may be known and distinguished from the false.[244]

244. Bahá'u'lláh indicates that these events are just tests that are presented to the followers of the Manifestations to differentiate between those who are really faithful and those that lack deep faith. For a discussion of the same theme, please see Notes Nos. 36 and 238 above.

"We did not appoint that which Thou wouldst have to be the Qiblih, but that We might know him who followeth the Apostle from him who turneth on his heels.[245]

245. The Qur'án 2:143. Also see Note No. 237 above.

"Affrighted asses fleeing from a lion."[246]

246. The Qur'án Súrah 74 (The Enwrapped), verse 50. The preceding verse puts this in context:

> Then what hath come to them that they turn aside from the Warning. As if they affrighted asses fleeing from a lion?
> (The Qur'án 74:50)

Paragraph No. 56:

Were you to ponder, but for a while, these utterances in your heart, you would surely find the portals of understanding unlocked before your

face, and would behold all knowledge and the mysteries thereof unveiled before your eyes[247]

247. In several places in the Kitáb-i-Íqán and in His other Writings, Bahá'u'lláh explains a concept, then advises the reader to ponder His utterances in order to absorb and understand the subject matter, to gain the knowledge and understanding of complex subjects and to see the mysteries of the sacred books being revealed:

> O concourse of the fair-minded! Observe and reflect upon the billows of the ocean of the utterance and knowledge of God, so that ye may testify with your inner and outer tongues that with Him is the knowledge of all that is in the Book. Nothing escapeth His knowledge. He, verily, hath manifested that which was hidden, when He, upon His return, mounted the throne of the Bayán. All that hath been sent down hath and will come to pass, word for word, upon earth. No possibility is left for anyone either to turn aside or protest. As fairness, however, is disgraced and concealed, most men speak as prompted by their own idle fancies.
> (Bahá'u'lláh, Epistle to the Son of the Wolf, p. 150)

> In such manner hath the Kitáb-i-Aqdas been revealed that it attracteth and embraceth all the divinely appointed Dispensations. Blessed those who peruse it. Blessed those who apprehend it. Blessed those who meditate upon it. Blessed those who ponder its meaning. So vast is its range that it hath encompassed all men ere their recognition of it.
> (Bahá'u'lláh, *Tablets of Bahá'u'lláh,* p. 200)

> If you read the utterances of Bahá'u'lláh and 'Abdu'l-Bahá with selflessness and care and concentrate upon them, you will discover truths unknown to you before and will obtain an insight into the problems that have baffled the great thinkers of the world.
> (From a letter dated 30 January 1925 written on behalf of Shoghi Effendi to an individual believer, in *The Compilation of Compilations,* vol. II, p. 2)

> Praise be to God that the spirit of the Holy Writings and Tablets which have been revealed in this wondrous

Dispensation concerning matters of major or minor importance, whether essential or otherwise, related to the sciences and the arts, to natural philosophy, literature, politics or economics, have so permeated the world that since the inception of the world in the course of past Dispensations and bygone ages nothing like it has ever been seen or heard. Indeed if an avowed follower of Bahá'u'lláh were to immerse himself in, and fathom the depths of, the ocean of these heavenly teachings, and with utmost care and attention deduce from each of them the subtle mysteries and consummate wisdom that lie enshrined therein, such a person's life, materially, intellectually and spiritually, will be safe from toil and trouble, and unaffected by setbacks and perils, or any sadness or despondency.
(13 January 1923 to the Bahá'ís of Ádhirbáyján, in *The Compilation of Compilations,* vol. I, p. 204)

Such things take place only that the souls of men may develop and be delivered from the prison-cage of self and desire[248]

248. There are several references in the Hidden Words of Bahá'u'lláh to the prison cage of self and desire. A few from the Persian Hidden Words are quoted here:

O SON OF DESIRE!
The learned and the wise have for long years striven and failed to attain the presence of the All-Glorious; they have spent their lives in search of Him, yet did not behold the beauty of His countenance. Thou without the least effort didst attain thy goal, and without search hast obtained the object of thy quest. Yet, notwithstanding, thou didst remain so wrapt in the veil of self, that thine eyes beheld not the beauty of the Beloved, nor did thy hand touch the hem of His robe. Ye that have eyes, behold and wonder.
(Bahá'u'lláh, The Hidden Words, Persian, no. 22)

O BEFRIENDED STRANGER!
The candle of thine heart is lighted by the hand of My power, quench it not with the contrary winds of self and passion. The healer of all thine ills is remembrance of Me,

forget it not. Make My love thy treasure and cherish it even as thy very sight and life.
(Bahá'u'lláh, The Hidden Words, Persian, no. 32)

O MY SERVANT!
Free thyself from the fetters of this world, and loose thy soul from the prison of self. Seize thy chance, for it will come to thee no more.
(Bahá'u'lláh, The Hidden Words, Persian, no. 40)

O MY SERVANT!
Thou art even as a finely tempered sword concealed in the darkness of its sheath and its value hidden from the artificer's knowledge. Wherefore come forth from the sheath of self and desire that thy worth may be made resplendent and manifest unto all the world.
(Bahá'u'lláh, The Hidden Words, Persian, no. 72)

Every man of insight will, in this day, readily admit that the counsels which the Pen of this Wronged One hath revealed constitute the supreme animating power for the advancement of the world and the exaltation of its peoples. Arise, O people, and, by the power of God's might, resolve to gain the victory over your own selves, that haply the whole earth may be freed and sanctified from its servitude to the gods of its idle fancies—gods that have inflicted such loss upon, and are responsible for the misery of their wretched worshippers. These idols form the obstacle that impedeth man in his efforts to advance in the path of perfection. We cherish the hope that the Hand of divine power may lend its assistance to mankind and deliver it from its state of grievous abasement.
(Bahá'u'lláh, *Tablets of Bahá'u'lláh*, p. 85)

His own Being to be exalted above the adoration of every soul[249]

249. Please refer to Note No. 6 above for Bahá'u'lláh's statement on this subject.

Regard thou the one true God as One Who is apart from, and immeasurably exalted above, all created things. The

whole universe reflecteth His glory, while He is Himself independent of, and transcendeth His creatures. This is the true meaning of Divine unity.
(Bahá'u'lláh, *Gleanings from the Writings of Bahá'u'lláh*, p. 165)

GOD hath, at all times and under all conditions, been wholly independent of His creatures.
(The Báb, *Selections from the Writings of the Báb*, p. 86)

Moreover, just as people are in need of God in this world, so too are they in need of Him in the next. The creatures are ever in need, and God is ever completely independent of them, whether in this world or in the world to come.
('Abdu'l-Bahá, *Some Answered Questions*, no. 62.3)

Question.— What is the nature of the connection between God and His creation, between the Absolute and Inaccessible One and all other beings?

Answer.— The connection between God and His creation is that of the originator and the originated, of the sun and the dark bodies of the universe, of the craftsman and his handiwork. Not only is the sun sanctified in its very essence above all the bodies that receive its illumination, but its light is also, in its essence, sanctified from and independent of the earth. So, though the earth is nurtured by the sun and is the recipient of its light, the sun and its rays are nonetheless sanctified above it. But were it not for the sun, the earth and all terrestrial life could not exist.
('Abdu'l-Bahá, *Some Answered Questions*, no. 53.1–2)

He hath, therefore, in every season sent down upon mankind the showers of tests from His realm of glory[250]

250. On the same theme, 'Abdu'l-Bahá states:

To the sincere ones, tests are as a gift from God, the Exalted, for a heroic person hasteneth, with the utmost joy and gladness, to the tests of a violent battlefield, but the coward is afraid and trembles and utters moaning and lamentation. Likewise, an expert student prepareth and

memorizeth his lessons and exercises with the utmost effort, and in the day of examination he appeareth with infinite joy before the master. Likewise, the pure gold shineth radiantly in the fire of test.
('Abdu'l-Bahá, *Tablets of 'Abdu'l-Bahá*, vol. 3, p. 722)

The necessity and the particularity of the assured and believing ones is to be firm in the Cause of God and withstand the hidden and evident tests.
('Abdu'l-Bahá, *Tablets of 'Abdu'l-Bahá*, vol. 2, p. 263)

As ye have heard of the former times, when (for example) Christ—glory be to Him!—appeared, a storm of trials arose, afflictions appeared, the winds of tests blew, the thunder of temptation descended and hosts of people (Pharisees) surrounded the houses of the friends; then the weak ones were shaken and were misled after once being guided; but the disciples withstood the hardships and endured the storms of ordeals, remaining firm in the Religion of God. Then observe that which occurred after the storm and what appeared subsequent to that severity, whereby the members (followers) trembled.
('Abdu'l-Bahá, *Tablets of 'Abdu'l-Bahá*, vol. 1, p. 13)

Caiaphas lived a comfortable and happy life while Peter's life was full of sorrow and trial; which of these two is the more enviable? Assuredly we should choose the present state of Peter, for he possesses immortal life whilst Caiaphas has won eternal shame. The trials of Peter tested his fidelity. Tests are benefits from God, for which we should thank Him.
('Abdu'l-Bahá, *Paris Talks*, p. 50)

Paragraph No. 57:

Were men to meditate upon the lives of the Prophets of old, so easily would they come to know and understand the ways of these Prophets that they would cease to be veiled by such deeds and words as are contrary to their own worldly desires, and thus consume every intervening veil with the fire burning in the Bush of divine knowledge, and abide secure upon the throne of peace and certitude[251]

251. As attested by the sacred books of the past Dispensations, the Manifestations of God, during Their lifetime and in Their physical characteristics looked like ordinary people. However, with the passage of time, as They are glorified by Their followers, Their normal human appearance is forgotten, supernatural characteristics and actions are attributed to Them, and They are placed behind several veils of glory.

Therefore, as Bahá'u'lláh states here, if people think and meditate upon the lives of the prophets of old, the man-made veils that prevent them from seeing the reality of their lives will be removed, they will gain insight, and will understand that the human appearance of the new Manifestation of God does not disqualify Him from assuming the station of divine authority (Please see Note No. 9 above).

consider Moses[252]

252. The story of Moses (partially presented above in Note No. 43) is related in both the Old Testament (in Exodus, Chapters 2 and 3) and in many places in the Qur'án, particularly in the Súrah of the "Story" (Al-Qasas). There is essentially a harmony between the Old Testament and the Qur'án regarding the major events of the life and ministry of Moses. The differences are in some details such as, why His mother was chosen to nurse Him, the name of His father-in-law (Reuel or Jethro in the Old Testament, and Shoeb or Shoaib in The Qur'án), and the number of Jethro's or Shoaib's daughters (seven daughters in Exodus 2:16–17, versus two in the Qur'án 28:22–28).

son of Imran[253]

253. Imran (in the Islamic literature) and Amram (in the Old Testament, Exodus 6:18–20) is the name of the father of Moses, His brother Aaron, and His sister Miriam (Mary). As stated in the Old Testament, Moses' father was from the house of Levi, and took as his wife a daughter of Levi. Moses' mother's name was Jochebed, and was either Amram's cousin or aunt. Because both of them were from the priestly house of Levi, their male

descendants, especially Aaron and his descendants, were the hereditary priests. Due to the importance of Amram in Jewish priesthood, Moses is sometimes identified as the son of Amram.

Amram was born, as a grandson of Levi when Levi was sixty-four years old. Commentaries on Exodus state that when the Pharaoh ordered the Israelite midwives to throw the male children of the Israelites into the Nile river in order to decrease their number and force, Amram divorced Jochebed, who was three months pregnant with Moses at the time, arguing that there was no justification for the Israelite men to father children if they were just to be killed; however, the text goes on to state that Miriam, his daughter, chided him for his lack of care for his wife's feelings, persuading him to recant and marry Jochebed again. According to the Talmud, Amram promulgated the laws of marriage and divorce amongst the Jews in Egypt. The Talmud also states that Amram had extreme longevity, which he used to ensure that doctrines were preserved through several generations. Despite the legend of his divorce and remarriage, Amram was also said to have been entirely sinless throughout his life, and was rewarded for this by his corpse remaining without any signs of decay.

(based on materials from Wikipedia, the free encyclopedia)

one of the exalted Prophets and Author of a divinely-revealed Book[254]

254. In spite of the ramifications of the story of transfiguration, in which Moses, Jesus, and Elijah are considered equals, in Christian theological discourse the divine station of Moses is not generally affirmed and He is regarded as a man and prophet who was not sinless. However, in Jewish theology, the divine station of Moses as reflected in the Rabbinic literature and ancient traditions is unique, and has been the source of much of the theological constructs regarding the divine station of Jesus in Christian theology. These Rabbinic sources state that:

Moses' influence and activity reach back to the days of Creation. Heaven and earth were created only for his sake. The account of the creation of the water on the second day, therefore, does not close with the usual formula, "And God saw that it was good,"

because God foresaw that Moses would suffer through water. Although Noah was not worthy to be saved from the Flood, he was saved because Moses was destined to descend from him. The angels, which Jacob in his nocturnal vision saw ascending to and descending from heaven were really Moses and Aaron.
The birth of Moses as the liberator of the people of Israel was foretold to Pharaoh by his soothsayers, in consequence of which he issued the cruel command to cast all the male children into the river. Later on, Miriam (Moses' older sister) also foretold to her father, Amram, that a son would be born to him who would liberate Israel from the yoke of Egypt.

According to Rabbinic sources, Moses was born in the year 2377 after the creation of the world. He was born circumcised, and was able to walk immediately after His birth; but according to another story He was circumcised on the eighth day after birth. A peculiar and glorious light filled the entire house at His birth, indicating that he was worthy of the gift of prophecy. He spoke with His father and mother on the day of his birth, and prophesied at the age of three. His mother kept His birth secret for three months, when Pharaoh was informed that she had borne a son. The mother put the child into a casket, which she hid among the reeds of the sea before the king's officers came to her. For seven days His mother went to him at night to nurse Him, His sister Miriam protecting Him from the birds by day.
(based on Moses in Rabbinic Literature from Wikipedia, the free encyclopedia)

He saw two men engaged in fighting. One of them asked the help of Moses against his opponent[255]

255. Regarding this incident 'Abdu'l-Bahá states:

> Moses struck down an Egyptian to prevent an act of oppression, became known among men as a murderer—especially since the victim belonged to the ruling nation—and was obliged to flee, and it was after all this that He was raised up as a Prophet.
> ('Abdu'l-Bahá, *Some Answered Questions,* no. 5.6)

To this testifieth the record of the sacred Book[256]

256. The sacred Book is a reference to the Qur'án, Súrah 28, "Story," and also the book of Exodus, Chapters 2 and 3.

"O Moses! of a truth, the chiefs take counsel to slay Thee"[257]

257. This is a part of verse 20 of Súrah 28:

> And there came a man, running, from the furthest end of the City. He said: "O Moses! the Chiefs are taking counsel together about thee, to slay thee: so get thee away, for I do give thee sincere advice."
> (The Qur'án, Yusuf Ali tr, 28:20)

> But a man came running up from the city's end. He said, "O Moses, of a truth, the nobles consult to slay thee—Begone then—I counsel thee as a friend."
> (The Qur'án 28:20)

He went forth from the city, and sojourned in Midian[258]

258. Midian is an area south of present-day Israel, and is part of the Sinai Peninsula, on the eastern side of the Red Sea and Gulf of Aqaba. On the north it extends to the area southeast of the Dead Sea. Historically, it was the area where the descendants of Midian, one of the sons of Abraham from his third wife Keturah, were residing. Genesis, Chapter 25:1–2, names all the sons of Abraham from Ketura.

in the service of Shoeb[259]

259. According to the Qur'án, Shoeb or Shoaib was a descendent of Abraham. He was a prophet who was sent to the people of Midian:

> And we sent to Madian their brother Shoaib. He said, "O my people! worship God; ye have no other God than Him: now hath a clear sign come to you from your Lord: give

therefore the full in measures and weights; take from no man his chattels, and commit no disorder on the earth after it has been made so good. This will be better for you, if you will believe it. And lay not in ambush by every road in menacing sorts; nor mislead him who believeth in God, from His way, nor seek to make it crooked; and remember when ye were few and that he multiplied you, and behold what hath been the end of the authors of disorder! And if a part of you believe in that with which I am sent, and a part of you believe not, then wait steadfastly until God shall judge between us, for He is the best of judges." Said the chiefs of his people puffed up with pride, "We will surely banish thee, O Shoaib, and thy fellow-believers from our cities, unless indeed ye shall back to our religion." "What!" said he, "though we abhor it? Now shall we have devised a lie concerning God, if after he hath delivered us from your religion we shall return to it; nor can we return to it, unless by the will of God our Lord: our Lord embraceth all things in his ken. In God have we put our trust: O our Lord! decide between us and between our people, with truth; for the best to decide art Thou." And the chiefs of his people who believed not, said, "If ye follow Shoaib, ye shall then surely perish." An earthquake therefore surprised them, and they were found in the morning dead on their faces, in their dwellings."
(The Qur'án 7: 83–89)

He became Moses' father-in-law. In the Old Testament he is named as Jethro, the priest of Midian (Exodus 3:1), and is also named Reuel in another place (Exodus 2:18).

Moses entered the holy vale, situate in the wilderness of Sinai[260]

260. "Holy Vale" is a valley by Mount Sinai, in the Sinai Peninsula, which is the location where Moses received both the Revelation and the laws and commandments. Although in Deuteronomy the place is called Mount Horeb, in other places in the Old Testament, Mount Horeb and Mount Sinai are used to refer to the same place. In the Qur'án it is called the holy valley of Towa.

> When he saw a fire, and said to his family, "Tarry ye here, for I perceive a fire: Haply I may bring you a brand from it, or find at the fire a guide." And when he came to it, he was called to, "O Moses! Verily, I am thy Lord: therefore pull off they shoes: for thou art in the holy valley of Towa. And I have chosen thee: hearken then to what shall be revealed.
> (The Qur'án 20:9–12)

Mount Sinai is also called Tur in the Qur'án:

> Now when Moses had fulfilled the term, and was travelling with his family, he perceived a fire in the direction of Mount Tur. He said to his family: "Tarry ye; I perceive a fire; I hope to bring you from there some information, or a burning firebrand, that ye may warm yourselves."
> (The Qur'án, Yusuf Ali tr, 28:29)

"Tree that belongeth neither to the East nor to the West."[261]

261. This is a part of the Súrah of Light.

> God is the light of the Heavens and of the Earth. His Light is like a niche in which is a lamp—the lamp encased in glass—the glass, as it were, a glistening star. From a blessed tree it is lighted, the olive neither of the East nor of the West, whose oil would well nigh shine out, even though fire touched it not! It is light upon light. God guideth whom He will to His light, and God setteth forth parables to men, for God knoweth all things.
> (The Qur'án 24:35)

> Allah is the Light of the heavens and the earth. The parable of His Light is as if there were a Niche and within it a lamp: the Lamp enclosed in Glass: the glass as it were a brilliant star: lit from a blessed Tree, an Olive, neither of the East nor of the West, whose Oil is well-nigh luminous, though fire scarce touched it: Light upon Light! Allah doth guide whom He will to His Light. Allah doth set forth Parables for men: and Allah doth know all things.
> (The Qur'án, Yusuf Ali tr, 24:35)

In the Writings of the Bahá'í Faith, the Holy or Blessed Tree, which is neither of the East or the West, is a reference to the universal Manifestation of God.

> Through the power of God and His might, I shall now relate certain passages revealed in the Books of old, and mention some of the signs heralding the appearance of the Manifestations of God in the sanctified persons of His chosen Ones, that thou mayest recognize the Dayspring of this everlasting morn and behold this Fire that blazeth in the Tree which is neither of the East nor of the West.
> (Bahá'u'lláh, *Gems of Divine Mysteries*, p. 7)
>
> O God, my God! Praise be unto Thee for kindling the fire of divine love in the Holy Tree on the summit of the loftiest mount: that Tree which is neither of the east nor of the west, that fire which blazed out till the flame of it soared upward to the Concourse on high, and from it those realities caught the light of guidance, and cried out: "Verily have we perceived a fire on the slope of Mount Sinai."
>
> O God, my God! Increase Thou this fire, as day followeth day, till the blast of it setteth in motion all the earth. O Thou, my Lord! Kindle the light of Thy love in every heart, breathe into men's souls the spirit of Thy knowledge, gladden their breasts with the verses of Thy oneness. Call Thou to life those who dwell in their tombs, warn Thou the prideful, make happiness world-wide, send down Thy crystal waters, and in the assemblage of manifest splendours, pass round that cup which is tempered at the camphor fountain.
> ('Abdu'l-Bahá, *Selections from the Writings of 'Abdu'l-Bahá*, p. 253)
>
> . . . until suddenly Moses, the All-Beauteous, beheld the Divine Light streaming out of the blessed Vale, the place that was holy ground, and heard the quickening voice of God as it spoke from the flame of that Tree "neither of the East nor of the West," and He stood up in the full panoply of His universal prophethood.
> ('Abdu'l-Bahá, *The Secret of Divine Civilization*, p. 75)

There He heard the soul-stirring Voice of the Spirit speaking from out of the kindled Fire, bidding Him to shed upon Pharaonic souls[262]

262. Pharaoh is the title of the ancient kings of Egypt. The mission of Moses, as mentioned in the Old Testament and the Qur'án, was to go to the Pharaoh and ask him to release the Israelites that were living in slavery in Egypt. But Bahá'u'lláh comments on the universal nature of Moses' divine Revelation by stating that He was charged with the mission of guiding the "Pharaonic souls," that is all the souls that had pharaonic attitudes and characteristics (such as pride, vainglory, tyranny, and attachment to worldly power and riches), not only His contemporaries, but those of future generations as well.

He might enable them to attain the meads of heavenly delight, and delivering them, through the Salsabil[263]

263. "Salsabil" (pronounced sal-sa-beel), as described in the Qur'án (76:17–18), is the name of a softly flowing river or fountain in Paradise, where the faithful will drink ginger-flavored water.

In the Bahá'í Writings, Salsabil (i.e., the life-giving water) is the symbol of the words of God and divine Revelation, which spiritually revives and gives spiritual life.

> Consider the grace of thy Master; how He hath directed thee to the fountain of salvation, until thou hast drunk from the salsabil (i. e., clear water of life) of the guidance of God, in this holy and rich garden.
> ('Abdu'l-Bahá, *Tablets of 'Abdu'l-Bahá*, Vol. 2, p. 255)

> [D]irect these bewildered souls unto the fountain of Thy guidance, and cause these wanderers to abide in the shelter of Thy might. Suffer the thirst ones to drink from the Salsabil of Thy gifts, and quicken the dead by eternal life. Endow the blind with light, the deaf with hearing, the dumb with speech, the lukewarm with energy, the heedless with mindfulness, the sleepers with wakefulness, and the proud with humility. Verily, Thou art the Powerful, Thou art the Forgiver! Thou

art the Loving! Verily, Thou art the Generous, the Most High! [1 Salsabil, i. e., Sweet Water of Life.]
('Abdu'l-Bahá, *Tablets of 'Abdu'l-Bahá*, Vol. 2, p. 369)

Blessed the sore athirst who hasteneth to the soft-flowing waters* of My loving-kindness.
(Bahá'u'lláh, *Tablets of Bahá'u'lláh*, p. 16)

Blessed is the man who hath detached himself from all else but Me, hath soared in the atmosphere of My love, hath gained admittance into My Kingdom, gazed upon My realms of glory, quaffed the living waters[69] of My bounty, hath drunk his fill from the heavenly river of My loving providence, acquainted himself with My Cause, apprehended that which I concealed within the treasury of My Words, and hath shone forth from the horizon of divine knowledge engaged in My praise and glorification. Verily, he is of Me. Upon him rest My mercy, My loving-kindness, My bounty and My glory.
(Bahá'u'lláh, *Tablets of Bahá'u'lláh*, p. 16)

from the bewilderment of remoteness, cause them to enter the peaceful city of the divine presence[264]

264. Please see Note No. 58 above.

"What a deed is that which Thou hast done! Thou art one of the ungrateful. He said: 'I did it indeed, and I was one of those who erred. And I fled from you when I feared you, but My Lord hath given Me wisdom, and hath made Me one of His Apostles."[265]

265. The Qur'án, Súrah of Poets, 26:19.

Paragraph No. 58:

[69] *The "soft-flowing waters" and "the living waters" are translations of the Arabic word Salsabil. Please see Note No. 136 above.

There are no notes for this paragraph.

Paragraph No. 59:

Likewise, reflect upon the state and condition of Mary[266]

266. Mary is the mother of Jesus.

"O would that I had died ere this, and been a thing forgotten, forgotten quite!"[267]

267. This is a verse of the Súrah of Mary in the Qur'án, 19:22.

Two Gospels of Matthew and Luke contain an account of the birth of Jesus. The story in the Gospel of Matthew begins with the marriage of Joseph and Mary, when he found that Mary was pregnant, but offers no details regarding the conception process or why Jesus was born in Bethlehem, although His family resided in Nazareth:

> Now the birth of Jesus Christ was on this wise: When as his mother Mary was espoused to Joseph, before they came together, she was found with child of the Holy Ghost. Then Joseph her husband, being a just man, and not willing to make her a publick example, was minded to put her away privily. But while he thought on these things, behold, the angel of the LORD appeared unto him in a dream, saying, Joseph, thou son of David, fear not to take unto thee Mary thy wife: for that which is conceived in her is of the Holy Ghost. And she shall bring forth a son, and thou shalt call his name JESUS: for he shall save his people from their sins. Now all this was done, that it might be fulfilled which was spoken of the Lord by the prophet, saying, Behold, a virgin shall be with child, and shall bring forth a son, and they shall call his name Emmanuel, which being interpreted is, God with us[70] Then Joseph being raised from sleep did

70 "The Gospel of Matthew presents the virgin birth of Jesus as fulfilling a prophecy in Isaiah 7:14, which Matthew adapts to his purpose. Hebrew language has a specific word,

> as the angel of the Lord had bidden him, and took unto him his wife: And knew her not till she had brought forth her firstborn son: and he called his name JESUS."
> (Matthew 1:17–26)

The Gospel of Luke presents a detailed account of the process of holy conception, which is closely linked to the conception and birth of John the Baptist, and provides the reason for the birth of Jesus in Bethlehem, but is totally silent regarding the reaction of Joseph to Mary being pregnant before their wedding:

> And in the sixth month [after the day of the conception of the John the Baptist] the angel Gabriel was sent from God unto a city of Galilee, named Nazareth, To a virgin espoused to a man whose name was Joseph, of the house of David; and the virgin's name was Mary. And the angel came in unto her, and said, Hail, thou that art highly favoured, the Lord is with thee: blessed art thou among women. And when she saw him, she was troubled at his saying, and cast in her mind what manner of salutation this should be. And the angel said unto her, Fear not, Mary: for thou hast found favour with God. And, behold, thou shalt conceive in thy womb, and bring forth a son, and shalt call his name JESUS. He shall be great, and shall be called the Son of the Highest: and the Lord God shall give unto him the throne of his father David: And he shall reign over the house of Jacob for ever; and of his kingdom there shall be no end. Then said Mary unto the angel, How shall this be, seeing I know not a man? And the angel answered and said unto her, The Holy Ghost shall come upon thee, and the power of the Highest shall overshadow thee: therefore also

---

betulah, for a virgin, and a more general word, *`almah*, for a young woman. Since *`almah* is the word used in the Hebrew text of Isaiah, some commentators, whether Christian or not, have believed it at least possible that Isaiah had in mind only a normal conception by a young mother and that Matthew applied this text of Scripture to the birth of the one he believed to be Messiah, as John seems to have applied to his death another text of Scripture that in its original context referred to the Passover lamb. Others believe that Isaiah was indeed directly prophesying the future virgin birth of the Messiah. The author of Matthew may have recounted the virgin birth story to answer contemporary Jewish slanders about Jesus' origin."
(Based on entry in Wikipedia, the free Encyclopedia)

> that holy thing which shall be born of thee shall be called the Son of God. And, behold, thy cousin Elisabeth, she hath also conceived a son in her old age: and this is the sixth month with her, who was called barren. For with God nothing shall be impossible. And Mary said, Behold the handmaid of the Lord; be it unto me according to thy word. And the angel departed from her. . . .
> And it came to pass in those days, that there went out a decree from Caesar Augustus that all the world should be taxed. (And this taxing was first made when Cyrenius was governor of Syria.) And all went to be taxed, every one into his own city. And Joseph also went up from Galilee, out of the city of Nazareth, into Judaea, unto the city of David, which is called Bethlehem; (because he was of the house and lineage of David:) To be taxed with Mary his espoused wife, being great with child. And so it was, that, while they were there, the days were accomplished that she should be delivered. And she brought forth her firstborn son, and wrapped him in swaddling clothes, and laid him in a manger; because there was no room for them in the inn.
> (Luke 1:26–37, 2:1–7)

As mentioned above, some biblical scholars contend that the virgin birth stories were recounted to answer the contemporary Jewish slanders, i.e., Mary's purity and chastity and the legitimacy of Jesus. The Christians of the first and second centuries, especially those who were living among the Jews, were facing these issues. In fact these charges were brought against Mary and Jesus by the Jews as well as by non-Jewish opponents of Christianity when Christianity was growing and emerging from obscurity:

A charge of illegitimacy against Jesus can be traced back at least to about 177–180 AD, when Celsus[71] drawing on Jewish sources,

[71] A polemical writer against Christianity, Celsus flourished towards the end of the second century. Very little is known about his personal history except that he lived during the reign of Marcus Aurelius, that his literary activity falls between the years 175 and 180 AD, and that he wrote his *The True Word* against the Christian religion. . . . Celsus divided the work into two sections, the one in which objections are put in the mouth of a Jewish interlocutor and the other in which Celsus speaks as the pagan philosopher that he is. Celsus ridiculed Christians for what he perceived to be an advocacy of blind faith instead of reason. About 60 years after it was first published, the book written by Celsus inspired a massive refutation by Origen in *Contra Celsum.*

wrote: "It was Jesus himself who fabricated the story that he had been born of a virgin. In fact, however, his mother was a poor country woman who earned her money by spinning. She had been driven out by her carpenter husband when she was convicted of adultery with a soldier named Panthera. She then wandered about and secretly gave birth to Jesus. Later, because he was poor, Jesus hired himself out in Egypt where he became adept in magical powers. Puffed up by these, he claimed for himself the title of God." According to this view, the accounts in Matthew and Luke were intended as a response to this charge.

The story of the birth of Jesus in the Qur'án is related in the Súrah of Maryam (Mary):

> And make mention in the Book, of Mary, when she went apart from her family, eastward, And took a veil to shroud herself from them: and we sent our spirit to her, and he took before her the form of a perfect man. She said: "I fly for refuge from thee to the God of Mercy! If thou fearest Him, begone from me." He said: "I am only a messenger of thy Lord, that I may bestow on thee a holy son." She said: "How shall I have a son, when man hath never touched me? And I am not unchaste." He said: "So shall it be. Thy Lord hath said: 'Easy is this with me:' and we will make him a sign to mankind, and mercy from us. For it is a thing decreed." And she conceived him, and retired with him to a far-off place. And the throes came upon her by the trunk of a palm. She said: "Oh, would that I had died ere this, and been a thing forgotten, forgotten quite!" And one cried to her from below her: "Grieve not thou, thy Lord hath provided a streamlet at thy feet:—And shake the trunk of the palm-tree toward thee: it will drop fresh ripe dates upon thee. Eat then and drink, and be of cheerful eye: and shouldst thou see a man, Say—Verily, I have vowed abstinence to the God of mercy. To no one will I speak this day." Then came she with the babe to her people, bearing him. They said, "O Mary! now hast thou done a strange thing! O sister of Aaron! Thy father was not a man of wickedness, nor unchaste thy mother." And she made a

(Based on entry in Wikipedia, the free Encyclopedia)

> sign to them, pointing towards the babe. They said, "How shall we speak with him who is in the cradle, an infant?" It said, "Verily, I am the servant of God; He hath given me the Book, and He hath made me a prophet; And he hath made me blessed wherever I may be, and hath enjoined me prayer and almsgiving so long as I shall live; And to be duteous to her that bare me: and he hath not made me proud, depraved. And the peace of God was on me the day I was born, and will be the day I shall die, and the day I shall be raised to life." This is Jesus, the son of Mary; this is a statement of the truth concerning which they doubt. It beseemeth not God to beget a son. Glory be to Him! when he decreeth a thing. He only saith to it, Be, and it Is. And verily, God is my Lord and your Lord; adore Him then. This is the right way. But the Sects have fallen to variance among themselves about Jesus: but woe, because of the assembly of a great day, to those who believe not! Make them hear, make them behold the day when they shall come before us! But the offenders this day are in a manifest error.
> (The Qur'án 19:16–39)

No sooner had the eyes of the people fallen upon her than they raised their voice saying: "O sister of Aaron! Thy father was not a man of wickedness, nor unchaste thy mother."[268]

268. This verse is from the Qur'án, Súrah of Mary 19:28, presented above in Note No. 267. A comparison of the accounts of the birth of Jesus in the Gospels and the Qur'án indicates that a harmony exists between the texts on the most important issues, i.e., the immaculate conception and the purity of Mary, but the texts of the Gospels do not mention anything regarding the reaction of family members, neighbors, or other people to Mary's pregnancy before the wedding and the charges of wrongdoing and of the illegitimacy of her child, while the Qur'án recounts the following:

> Then came she with the babe to her people, bearing him. They said, "O Mary! now hast thou done a strange thing! O sister of Aaron! Thy father was not a man of wickedness, nor unchaste thy mother."
> (The Qur'án 19:28–29)

As mentioned above, these charges were brought against Mary by the Jews and were repeated and recorded in the books of the Jewish and Roman writers and philosophers, such as in Celsus' book *The True Word.*

However, the Qur'án defends Mary and affirms her purity and the immaculate conception of Jesus.

It is interesting to note that the above Qur'ánic verse: "O Mary! now hast thou done a strange thing! O sister of Aaron!" has been the subject of a historical controversy between Muslims and Jews and Christians. It has been used by the opponents of Muḥammad as a proof of His lack of knowledge of the sacred scriptures and of the non-divine or non-revelatory nature of the Qur'án.

They claim that Muḥammad mistakenly assumed that Mary (called Miriam in both Hebrew and Arabic), the mother of Jesus, and Miriam, the sister of Moses and Aaron and daughter of Imran, are the same person. J. M. Rodwell in his translation of the Qur'án in the footnotes to two Qur'ánic verses (19:29 and 3:1) related to Mary, Aaron and Imran, states:

> The anachronism is probably only apparent. Muḥammad may have supposed that this Aaron (or Harun) was son of Imran and Anna. Or, if Aaron the brother of Moses be meant, Mary may be called his sister, either because she was of the Levitical race, or by way of comparison. . . . Muḥammad supposed Imarn or Amran to be the father of the Virgin Mary. . . . It is difficult to avoid the conclusion that Muḥammad is guilty of anachronism of confounding Miriam with the Virgin Mary.

The Muslim apologists hold that according to some non-canonical Christian Gospels or apocryphal[72] writings such as the Proto-

[72] Apocrypha: Fourteen books of the Septuagint that are rejected in Judaism and regarded by Protestants as not canonical . . . or various other writings falsely attributed to Biblical characters or kept out of the New Testament because not accepted as resulting from revelation.

Gospel of James, Anna the mother of Mary dedicated her from the time of her birth to a life of service to God and at the age of 3 she was taken to live in the Temple in Jerusalem. There she grew up under the Aaronic priests in absolute purity until the age of 12, and that is the reason why she was given the title of the sister of Aaron. The term is used to denote her attachment to the Temple and to Aaronic Priests.

As stated here in the Book of Certitude, and in other Writings of Bahá'u'lláh and 'Abdu'l-Bahá, the Bahá'í teachings uphold the purity and innocence of the Virgin Mary.

> It would be sacrilege for a Bahá'í to believe that the parents of Jesus were illegally married and that the latter was consequently of an illegal union. Such a possibility cannot be even conceived by a believer who recognizes the high station of Mary and the Divine Prophethood of Jesus Christ. It is this same false accusation which the people of His Day attributed to Mary that Bahá'u'lláh indirectly repudiated in the Íqán. The only alternative therefore is to admit that the birth of Jesus has been miraculous. The operation of miracles is not necessarily irrational or illogical. It does by no means constitute a limitation of the Omnipotence of God. The belief in the possibilities of miracles, on the contrary, implies that God's power is beyond any limitation whatsoever. For it is only logical to believe that the Creator, Who is the sole Author of all the laws operating in the universe, is above them and can, therefore, if He deems it necessary, alter them at His Own Will. We, as humans, cannot possibly attempt to read His Mind, and to fully grasp His Wisdom. Mystery is therefore an inseparable part of true religion, and as such, should be recognized by the believers."
>
> (From a letter of Shoghi Effendi to an individual believer, October 1, 1935, in *Lights of Guidance*, p. 490)
>
> First regarding the birth of Jesus Christ. In the light of what Bahá'u'lláh and 'Abdu'l-Bahá have stated concerning this subject it is evident that Jesus came into this world through the direct intervention of the Holy Spirit, and that consequently His birth was quite miraculous. This is an established fact, and the friends need not feel at all

surprised, as the belief in the possibility of miracles has never been rejected in the Teachings. Their importance, however, has been minimized.
(From a letter dated December 31, 1937 written on behalf of the Guardian to an individual believer)

Miracles are Always Possible

Again with regard to your question relative to the birth of Jesus; he wishes me to inform you that there is nothing further he can add to the explanation he have you in his previous communication regarding this point. One thing, however, he wishes again to bring to your attention, namely that miracles are always possible, even though they do not constitute a regular channel whereby God reveals His power to mankind. To reject miracles on the ground that they imply a breach of the laws of nature is a very shallow, well-nigh a stupid argument, inasmuch as God Who is the Author of the universe can, in His Wisdom and Omnipotence, bring any change, no matter how temporary, in the operation of the laws which He Himself has created.

The Teachings do not tell us of any miraculous birth besides that of Jesus.
(From a letter dated February 27, 1938 written on behalf of the Guardian to an individual believer, in *Lights of Guidance*, p. 489)

The Bahá'í Faith recognizes the divine origin of Christianity and the Immaculacy of the Virgin Mary:

As to the position of Christianity, let it be stated without any hesitation or equivocation that its Divine origin is unconditionally acknowledged, that the Sonship and Divinity of Jesus Christ are fearlessly asserted, that the Divine inspiration of the Gospel is fully recognized, that the reality of the mystery of the Immaculacy of the Virgin Mary is confessed, and the primacy of Peter, the Prince of the Apostles, is upheld and defended. The Founder of the Christian Faith is designated by Bahá'u'lláh as the "Spirit of God," is proclaimed as the One Who "appeared out of the breath of the Holy Ghost', and is even extolled as the 'Essence of the Spirit." His mother is described as "that

veiled and immortal, that most beauteous countenance," and the station of her Son eulogized as a "station which hath been exalted above the imaginings of all that dwell on earth," whilst Peter is recognized as one whom God has caused "the mysteries of wisdom and of utterance to flow out of his mouth."
(Shoghi Effendi, *The Promised Day is Come*, pp. 113–14)

With regard to your question concerning the Virgin Birth of Jesus; on this point, as on several others, the Bahá'í Teachings are in full agreement with the doctrines of the Catholic Church. In the 'Kitáb-i-Íqán' (Book of Certitude) p. 56, and in a few other Tablets still unpublished, Bahá'u'lláh confirms, however, indirectly, the Catholic conception of the Virgin Birth. Also 'Abdu'l-Bahá in the 'Some Answered Questions', Chap. XII, p. 73, explicitly states that 'Christ found existence through the Spirit of God' which statement necessarily implies, when viewed in the light of the text, that Jesus was not the son of Joseph."
(From a letter dated October 14, 1945 written on behalf of the Guardian to an individual believer, in *Lights of Guidance,* p. 489)

Paragraph No. 60:

Notwithstanding all these things, God conferred upon that essence of the Spirit[269], Who was known amongst the people as fatherless, the glory of Prophethood, and made Him His testimony unto all that are in heaven and on earth.

269. "Essence of the Spirit" is a reference to Jesus Christ. Bahá'u'lláh, in many places in the Kitáb-i-Íqán and His other Writings, referred to Jesus Christ with titles such as "the Spirit of God," "the Lord of all being," "The Essence of Being," "the Lord of visible and invisible," "the Divine Spirit," "the Word of God," "the Daystar of the heaven of divine Revelation," and other similar titles.

Paragraph No. 61:

As thou comest to comprehend the essence of these divine mysteries, thou wilt grasp the purpose of God, the divine Charmer, the Best-Beloved.[270]

270. As mentioned in the previous pages, the physical and human appearance, station, and life of the Manifestations of God have never been in harmony with the expectations and fanciful imagination of the people of Their time. The texts of the Bible and the Qur'án attest to this fact. 'Abdu'l-Bahá explains the expectation of the Jews regarding the characteristics of their Messiah:

> When Christ appeared, twenty centuries ago, although the Jews were eagerly awaiting His Coming, and prayed every day, with tears, saying: "O God, hasten the Revelation of the Messiah," yet when the Sun of Truth dawned, they denied Him and rose against Him with the greatest enmity, and eventually crucified that divine Spirit, the Word of God, and named Him Beelzebub, the evil one, as is recorded in the Gospel. The reason for this was that they said: "The Revelation of Christ, according to the clear text of the Torah, will be attested by certain signs, and so long as these signs have not appeared, whoso layeth claim to be a Messiah is an impostor. Among these signs is this, that the Messiah should come from an unknown place, yet we all know this man's house in Nazareth, and can any good thing come out of Nazareth? The second sign is that He shall rule with a rod of iron, that is, He must act with the sword, but this Messiah has not even a wooden staff. Another of the conditions and signs is this: He must sit upon the throne of David and establish David's sovereignty. Now, far from being enthroned, this man has not even a mat to sit on."
>
> ('Abdu'l-Bahá, *Selections from the Writings of 'Abdu'l-Bahá*, p. 44)

The Qur'án also contains statements regarding the fact that Muḥammad's appearance as a normal man was contrary to the expectations of people, who expected the Prophet to be a superman:

> And they say, "What sort of apostle is this? He eateth food and he walketh the streets! [we will not believe in Him] Unless an angel be sent down and take part in his warnings, Or a treasure be thrown down to him, or he have a garden that supplieth him with food" and those unjust persons say, "Ye follow but a man enchanted." See what likenesses they strike out for thee! But they err, and cannot find their way.
> (The Qur'án 25:6–10)

Thus it is that outwardly such deeds and words are the fire of vengeance unto the wicked, and inwardly the waters of mercy unto the righteous. Were the eye of the heart to open, it would surely perceive that the words revealed from the heaven of the will of God are at one with, and the same as, the deeds that have emanated from the Kingdom of divine power.[271]

271. This concept is also explained in other places in the Writings:

> These verses, clear and conclusive, are a token of the mercy of thy Lord and a source of guidance for all mankind. They are a light unto those who believe in them and a fire of afflictive torment for those who turn away and reject them.
> (The Báb, *Selections from the Writings of the Báb*, p. 162)

> All things of the world arise through man and are manifest in him, through whom they find life and development; and man is dependent for his (spiritual) existence upon the Sun of the Word of God. All the good names and lofty qualities are of the Word. The Word is the fire of God which, glowing in the hearts of people, burns away all things that are not of God. The minds of the lovers are ever aflame with this fire. Outwardly it is burning fire, while inwardly it is calm light. This is the Water which giveth life to all things.
> (*Bahá'i Scriptures*, p. 156)

Paragraph No. 62:

And now, take heed, O brother! If such things be revealed in this Dispensation, and such incidents come to pass, at the present time, what would the people do? I swear by Him Who is the true Educator of mankind[272] and the Revealer of the Word of God that the people would instantly and unquestionably pronounce Him an infidel and would sentence Him to death.

272. The "true Educators" are Manifestations of God as declared in the Writings:

> Then it is clear and evident that this glorious Being was a true Educator of the world of humanity and that He was aided and assisted by a divine power.
> ('Abdu'l-Bahá, *Some Answered Questions*, no. 6.5)

> The sending of Prophets has ever been for the training of humanity. They are the first Educators and Trainers. If Moses has developed the body politic, there is no doubt that He was a true Teacher and Educator.
> ('Abdu'l-Bahá, *The Promulgation of Universal Peace*, p. 345)

> Observe the influence on material situations of that training which is inculcated by the true Educator.
> ('Abdu'l-Bahá, *The Secret of Divine Civilization*, p. 88)

> He, verily, is the True Educator, and the Spiritual Teacher.
> (Bahá'u'lláh, Epistle to the Son of the Wolf, p. 143)

> And likewise are the daily prayer, fasting, and the laws which shone forth above the horizon of the Book of God, the Lord of the World and the true Educator of the peoples and kindreds of the earth.
> (Bahá'u'lláh, *Tablets of Bahá'u'lláh*, p. 108)

> That is why man is said to be the greatest sign of God—that is, he is the Book of Creation—for all the mysteries of the universe are found in him. Should he come under the shadow of the true Educator and be rightly trained, he becomes the gem of gems, the light of lights, and the spirit of spirits; he becomes the focal centre of divine blessings,

the wellspring of spiritual attributes, the dawning-place of heavenly lights, and the recipient of divine inspirations. Should he, however, be deprived of this education, he becomes the embodiment of satanic attributes, the epitome of animal vices, and the source of all that is oppressive and dark.
(Abdu'l-Bahá, *Some Answered Questions*, no. 64.4)

O Company of God! To each created thing, the Ancient Sovereignty hath portioned out its own perfection, its particular virtue and special excellence, so that each in its degree may become a symbol denoting the sublimity of the true Educator of humankind, and that each, even as a crystalline mirror, may tell of the grace and splendour of the Sun of Truth.
(*The Compilation of Compilations,* vol. I, p. 25)

Paragraph No. 63:

If the eye of justice be opened, it will readily recognize, in the light of that which hath been mentioned, that He, Who is the Cause and ultimate Purpose of all these things, is made manifest in this day[273].

273. The Bahá'í Writings state that the appearance of each Manifestation of God is the ultimate purpose of the preceding Revelations.

In as much as the Revelation of God may be likened to the sun. No matter how innumerable its risings, there is but one sun, and upon it depends the life of all things. It is clear and evident that the object of all preceding Dispensations hath been to pave the way for the advent of Muḥammad, the Apostle of God. These, including the Muḥammadan Dispensation, have had, in their turn, as their objective the Revelation proclaimed by the Qá'im. The purpose underlying this Revelation, as well as those that preceded it, has, in like manner, been to announce the advent of the Faith of Him Whom God will make manifest. And this Faith—the Faith of Him Whom God will make manifest—in its turn, together with all the Revelations gone before it, have as their object the Manifestation destined to succeed

it. And the latter, no less than all the Revelations preceding it, prepare the way for the Revelation which is yet to follow. The process of the rise and setting of the Sun of Truth will thus indefinitely continue—a process that hath had no beginning and will have no end.
(The Báb, *Selections from the Writings of the Báb*, p. 105)

And when Thou didst purpose to make Thyself known unto men, Thou didst successively reveal the Manifestations of Thy Cause, and ordained each to be a sign of Thy Revelation among Thy people, and the Dayspring of Thine invisible Self amidst Thy creatures, until the time when, as decreed by Thee, all Thy previous Revelations culminated in Him Whom Thou hast appointed as the Lord of all who are in the heaven of revelation and the kingdom of creation, Him Whom Thou hast established as the Sovereign Lord of all who are in the heavens and all who are on the earth.
(Bahá'u'lláh, *Prayers and Meditations*, p. 128)

This enforced and hurried departure of Bahá'u'lláh from His native land, accompanied by some of His relatives, recalls in some of its aspects, the precipitate flight of the Holy Family into Egypt; the sudden migration of Muḥammad, soon after His assumption of the prophetic office, from Mecca to Medina; the exodus of Moses, His brother and His followers from the land of their birth, in response to the Divine summons, and above all the banishment of Abraham from Ur of the Chaldees to the Promised Land—a banishment which, in the multitudinous benefits it conferred upon so many divers peoples, faiths and nations, constitutes the nearest historical approach to the incalculable blessings destined to be vouchsafed, in this day, and in future ages, to the whole human race, in direct consequence of the exile suffered by Him Whose Cause is the flower and fruit of all previous Revelations.
(Shoghi Effendi, *God Passes By*, p. 107)

Though similar events have not occurred in this Dispensation, yet the people still cling to such vain imaginings as are cherished by the reprobate. How grievous the charges brought against Him![274]

274. In another place in His Writings, Bahá'u'lláh explains the charges that were brought against the Báb by the religious and governmental authorities:

> Ages rolled away, until they attained their consummation in this, the Lord of days, the Day whereon the Daystar of the Bayán manifested itself above the horizon of mercy, the Day in which the Beauty of the All-Glorious shone forth in the exalted person of 'Alí-Muḥammad, the Báb. No sooner did He reveal Himself, than all the people rose up against Him. By some He was denounced as one that hath uttered slanders against God, the Almighty, the Ancient of Days. Others regarded Him as a man smitten with madness, an allegation which I, Myself, have heard from the lips of one of the divines. Still others disputed His claim to be the Mouthpiece of God, and stigmatized Him as one who had stolen and used as his the words of the Almighty, who had perverted their meaning, and mingled them with his own. The Eye of Grandeur weepeth sore for the things which their mouths have uttered, while they continue to rejoice upon their seats. . . .
>
> The more He exhorted them, the fiercer grew their enmity, till, at the last, they put Him to death with shameful cruelty.
> (Bahá'u'lláh, *Gleanings from the Writings of Bahá'u'lláh*, p. 145)

How severe the persecutions inflicted upon Him -- charges and persecutions the like of which men have neither seen nor heard![275]

275. The Báb Himself described some of His sufferings:

> In this mountain I have remained alone, and have come to such a pass that none of those gone before Me have suffered what I have suffered, nor any transgressor endured what I have endured!
>
> Verily, behold My habitation—a lofty mountain wherein no one dwelleth. Woe betide them that wrongfully do injustice to people, and unjustly and deceitfully usurp the property of the believers in violation of His lucid Book; whereas I,

> Who, in very truth, am the rightful Sovereign of all men, designated by the true, the undeniable Leader, would never infringe on the integrity of the substance of the people, were it to the extent of a grain of mustard, nor would I treat them unjustly. Rather would I consort with them even as one of themselves, and I would be their witness.
> (The Báb, *Selections from the Writings of the Báb*, pp.15, 26)

A brief summary of the persecutions inflicted upon the Báb is given by Shoghi Effendi:

> The Báb—"the Point [of the Bayán]," . . . —was the One first swept into the maelstrom which engulfed His supporters. Sudden arrest and confinement in the very first year of His short and spectacular career; public affront deliberately inflicted in the presence of the ecclesiastical dignitaries of Shíráz; strict and prolonged incarceration in the bleak fastnesses of the mountains of Ádhirbáyján; a contemptuous disregard and a cowardly jealousy evinced respectively by the Chief Magistrate of the realm and the foremost minister of his government; the carefully staged and farcical interrogatory sustained in the presence of the heir to the Throne and the distinguished divines of Tabríz; the shameful infliction of the bastinado in the prayer house, and at the hands of the Shaykhu'l-Islám of that city; and finally suspension in the barrack-square of Tabríz and the discharge of a volley of above seven hundred bullets at His youthful breast under the eyes of a callous multitude of about ten thousand people, culminating in the ignominious exposure of His mangled remains on the edge of the moat without the city gate—these were the progressive stages in the tumultuous and tragic ministry of One Whose age inaugurated the consummation of all ages, and Whose Revelation fulfilled the promise of all Revelations.
> (Shoghi Effendi, *The Promised Day is Come*, p. 8)

Paragraph No. 64:

Great God! When the stream of utterance reached this stage, We beheld, and lo! the sweet savours of God were being wafted from the dayspring of Revelation[276].

276. In this and the next paragraph, which were both revealed in 1862 approximately one year before Bahá'u'lláh's public declaration in the Garden of Riḍván, He provides intimation of His impending declaration:

"Dayspring of Revelation" is a reference to the Manifestation of God, as stated in the first verse of the Kitáb-i-Aqdas:

> The first duty prescribed by God for His servants is the recognition of Him Who is the Dayspring of His Revelation and the Fountain of His laws, Who representeth the Godhead in both the Kingdom of His Cause and the world of creation.
> (Bahá'u'lláh, The Kitáb-i-Aqdas, Paragraph 1)

> This is the day whereon He Who is the Dayspring of Revelation hath come with clear tokens which none can number.
> (Bahá'u'lláh, Epistle to the Son of the Wolf, p. 101)

and the morning breeze[277] was blowing out of the Sheba of the Eternal[278]

277. The word "breeze" here is a translation of the word *ṣabá*. The Persian and Arabic word typically connotes a breeze or a wind that is blowing from the east and south, i.e., from the direction of sabá ("Sheba"). Sheba is an area in the south of the Arabian Peninsula; at the end of winter a breeze or a wind often blows north from Sheba into the rest of the Middle East, signaling the changing of the seasons. In Persian literature, the *naseem-i-sabá* or *bád-i-sabá*, the breeze or wind of Sheba—often just shortened to ṣabá—is well-known as a fragrant and refreshing breeze that is the harbinger of spring and in this case the spiritual springtime. (Note that the term *sabá*, which refers to the area of Sheba, is spelled with the letter "sín" in Persian (س), which is transliterated as "s," while the term *ṣabá*, which refers to the wind that comes from Sheba, is spelled with the letter "sát" in Persian (ص), which is transliterated as "ṣ.")

278. The term "Sheba of the Eternal" is a translation of the term سبای لایزالی. Most likely the term is an allegorical reference to connote

the spiritual breeze blowing from the spiritual realm or the Kingdom of God.

In mystical Persian literature and poetry, the wind or breeze (ṣabá) that comes from Sheba carries fragrances, or messages and glad tidings, and Sheba is the allegorical spiritual realm that is not known to mankind. This bares a reference to the story of Solomon and the Queen of Sheba as it is related in the Qur'án. Solomon is portrayed in the Qur'án as a prophet who was wise and knew everything, who could command the wind, speak the language of animals, birds, and insects, and could order them to do his bidding:

> And unto Solomon did we subject the wind, which travelled in the morning a month's journey, and a month's journey in the evening. And we made a fountain of molten brass to flow for him. And of the Djinn were some who worked in his presence, by the will of his Lord; and such of them as swerved from our bidding will we cause to taste the torment of the flame. They made for him whatever he pleased, of lofty halls, and images, and dishes large as tanks for watering camels, and cooking pots that stood firmly. "Work," said we, "O' family of David with thanksgiving:" But few of my servants are the thankful!
> (Qur'án 34:12, Súrah of Sheba)

In another place (Súrah of Ant) it states:

> And of old we gave knowledge to David and Solomon: and they said, "Praise be to God, who hath made us to excel many of his believing servants!"
>
> And in knowledge Solomon was David's heir. And he said, "O men, we have been taught the speech of birds, and are endued with everything. This is indeed a clear boon from God." And to Solomon were gathered his hosts of Djinn[73] and men and birds, and they were marched on in bands, Till they reached the Valley of Ants. Said an ant, "O ye ants, enter your dwellings, lest Solomon and his army crush you and know it not." Then smiled Solomon, laughing at her

[73] For details regarding the Djinns, see Appendix II.

> words, and he said, "Stir me up, O Lord, to be thankful for thy favour which thou hast shewed upon me and upon my parents, and to do righteousness that shall be well pleasing to thee, and bring me in, by thy mercy, among thy servants the righteous."
> And he reviewed the birds, and said, "How is it that I see not the lapwing? Is it one of the absent? Surely, with a severe chastisement will I chastise it, or I will certainly slaughter it, unless it bring me a clear excuse." Nor tarried it long ere it [the lapwing] came and said, "I have gained the knowledge that thou knowest not, and with sure tidings have I come to thee from Saba [Sheba].
> (The Qur'án 27:15–22)

The significance of this story is that for Solomon, who knew everything, the Lapwing, or hoopoe (*hudhud* in Arabic and Persian), brought knowledge from a place of which Solomon knew nothing. Sheba is the allegorical spiritual realm that is not known to mankind, even to Solomon, who had extraordinary knowledge. Of course the rest of the story is an ordinary tale, as the lapwing says that "I found a woman reigning over them [in Sheba], gifted with everything, and she hath a splendid throne; And I found her and her people worshipping the sun instead of God." Solomon sends the Lapwing back with a message to invite the Queen of Sheba to come to the Solomon's Court.

Therefore, the breeze (ṣabá) that comes from the eternal Sheba (the divine realm) carries spiritual glad tidings from the source of Revelation and is the harbinger of the spiritual springtime.

In the Writings of the Bahá'í Faith there are many references to Sheba, such as the following from the Hidden Words:

> O YE PEOPLE THAT HAVE MINDS TO KNOW AND EARS TO HEAR!
> The first call of the Beloved is this: O mystic nightingale! Abide not but in the rose-garden of the spirit. O messenger of the Solomon of love! Seek thou no shelter except in the Sheba of the well-beloved, and O immortal phoenix! dwell not save on the mount of faithfulness. Therein is thy

> habitation, if on the wings of thy soul thou soarest to the realm of the infinite and seekest to attain thy goal.
> (The Hidden Words, Persian, no. 1)

Another reference to the glad tidings that are brought from Sheba has great historical significance in the Bahá'í Faith. Shoghi Effendi states:

> Áqá Buzurg of Khurásán, the illustrious Badí' (Wonderful); converted to the Faith by Nabíl; surnamed the "Pride of Martyrs"; the seventeen-year old bearer of the Tablet addressed to Násiri'd-Dín Sháh; in whom, as affirmed by Bahá'u'lláh, "the spirit of might and power was breathed" . . . After visiting Bahá'u'lláh in the barracks, during the second year of His confinement, he had arisen with amazing alacrity to carry that Tablet, alone and on foot, to Ṭihrán and deliver it into the hands of the sovereign. A four months' journey had taken him to that city, and, after passing three days in fasting and vigilance, he had met the Sháh proceeding on a hunting expedition to Shimírán. He had calmly and respectfully approached His Majesty, calling out, "O King! I have come to thee from Sheba with a weighty message . . ."
> (Shoghi Effendi, *God Passes By,* p. 199)

It made all things new, and brought unnumbered and inestimable gifts from the unknowable Friend[279]

279. The unknowable Friend: is the translation of the Persian term "Yár-e-bee-neshán," which is also translated as "the traceless Friend," (see The Seven Valleys, paragraph number 15).

    It seems that the unknowable or traceless friend is an allusion to the Manifestation of God during the period of concealment. There is a beautiful Tablet by 'Abdu'l Bahá that starts with "O the lover of the traceless friend," for which, this author could not find an authorized English translation. In this Tablet 'Abdu'l Bahá addresses one of the friends and mentions that thousands of mystics have been in search of the "Traceless Friend" (Bahá'u'lláh), but they were deprived, because they did not recognize Him, but that this friend found Him and recognized

Him. He says that it is a strange story that they could not find Him, but that this friend did. Then He states that the reason was that their search was not a whole-hearted and selfless search, it was not like the search of a really thirsty person who is in search of water and their quest was a cautious and calculated quest and not the quest of a real lover.

At this hour, so liberal is the outpouring of Its grace that the holy Spirit itself is envious![280]

280. This is to signify that in this Dispensation a greater measure of divine Revelation has been bestowed on humanity. In the past Dispensations, the Holy Spirit was the medium of Revelation and the source of inspiration. Bahá'u'lláh describes His relationship to the Most Great Spirit in the following passage:

> I have no will but Thy will, O my Lord, and cherish no desire except Thy desire. From my pen floweth only the summons which Thine own exalted pen hath voiced, and my tongue uttereth naught save what the Most Great Spirit hath itself proclaimed in the kingdom of Thine eternity. I am stirred by nothing else except the winds of Thy will, and breathe no word except the words which, by Thy leave and Thine inspiration, I am led to pronounce.
> (Bahá'u'lláh, *Prayers and Meditations*, p. 108)

So great are the overflowings of Its bounty that the foulest beetle[281] hath sought the perfume of the musk[282]

281. The word "beetle" is the translation of "Jou'al," which is a special beetle that grows and lives in horse droppings, and is used to living in an environment full of foul odor.

282. Musk has been known as a most fragrant substance since ancient times, and was used as the base of the most exquisite perfumes. It was historically prepared by collecting the glandular secretions from a special species of gazelles, and later on from some special plants.

It hath quickened the dead with the breath of life, and caused them to speed out of the sepulchres of their mortal bodies[283]

283. The "breath of life" is the spirit of faith that confers spiritual life and causes those who are spiritually dead to be vivified:

> Blessed the soul that hath been raised to life through My quickening breath and hath gained admittance into My heavenly Kingdom
> (Bahá'u'lláh, *Tablets of Bahá'u'lláh*, p. 16)
>
> The beloved of God in this mortal world are each a spiritual trumpet. They breathe the breath of life and thus confer upon them that are dead in negligence and ignorance, the life eternal.
> ('Abdu'l-Bahá, *Tablets of 'Abdu'l-Bahá,* vol. 3, p. 632)
>
> We must understand the interpretation of Christ's words concerning the dead. A certain disciple came to Christ and asked permission to go and bury his father. He answered, "Let the dead bury their dead." Therefore, Christ designated as dead some who were still living—that is, let the living dead, the spiritually dead, bury your father. They were dead because they were not believers in Christ. Although physically alive, they were dead spiritually.
> ('Abdu'l-Bahá, *The Promulgation of Universal Peace*, p. 245)

established the ignorant upon the seats of learning, and elevated the oppressor to the throne of justice.[284]

284. There are many examples of this spiritual transformation in the histories of all religions, especially in both Christianity and the Bahá'í Faith. The story of Peter, who before becoming a disciple of Christ was a simple unlettered person, but after receiving the spirit of faith and the bounties of the Holy Spirit, was debating and defeating the most learned Jewish and Roman scholars, is one example. Saul, who was an oppressor before receiving the bounty of the faith and the outpouring of the grace of God, became Paul, the symbol of kindness and justice for the whole world. There are many examples of this kind of transformation in the Bahá'í Faith. Mulla Jafar, the sifter of wheat, Mírzá Haydar

'Alí of Iṣfahán, and many other unlettered and simple men, when they received the spirit of faith, were debating and defeating the most learned Islamic scholars and were established upon the seat of learning.

Paragraph No. 65:

The universe is pregnant with these manifold bounties[285]

285. This whole paragraph is a clear intimation of the fast-approaching and climatic hour of Bahá'u'lláh's public declaration. At the time of the Revelation of the Kitáb-i-Íqán, which was less than two years before His public declaration, the universe was pregnant with all the bounties that the new revelation was bringing to the world.

awaiting the hour when the effects of Its unseen gifts will be made manifest in this world[286]

286. This indicates that the declaration of the Manifestation of God and appearance of the divine bounties will take place at the divinely ordained hour. The last section of 'Abdu'l-Bahá's commentary on the Islamic holy tradition of the "Hidden Treasure" illuminates the subject. The tradition states:

> I was a Hidden Treasure. I wished to be made known, and thus I called creation into being in order that I might be known.
> (See The Kitáb-i-Aqdas, note 23, pp. 174–76)

'Abdu'l-Bahá, in His commentary on the above-cited tradition, states:

> O wayfarer in the path of the Beloved! Know thou that the main purpose of this holy tradition is to make mention of the stages of God's concealment and manifestation within the Embodiments of Truth, They who are the Dawning-places of His All-Glorious Being. For example, before the flame of the undying Fire is lit and manifest, it existeth by

> itself within itself in the hidden identity of the universal Manifestations, and this is the stage of the "Hidden Treasure." And when the blessed Tree is kindled by itself within itself, and that Divine Fire burneth by its essence within its essence, this is the stage of "I wished to be made known." And when it shineth forth from the Horizon of the universe with infinite Divine Names and Attributes upon the contingent and placeless worlds, this constituteth the emergence of a new and wondrous creation which correspondeth to the stage of "Thus I called creation into being." And when the sanctified souls rend asunder the veils of all earthly attachments and worldly conditions, and hasten to the stage of gazing on the beauty of the Divine Presence and are honoured by recognizing the Manifestation and are able to witness the splendour of God's Most Great Sign in their hearts, then will the purpose of creation, which is the knowledge of Him Who is the Eternal Truth, become manifest.
>
> (A part of 'Abdu'l-Bahá's commentary on the Islamic Holy Tradition of the "Hidden Treasure," quoted in the Kitáb-i-Aqdas, pp. 175–76)

Regarding the energies that will be released and the bounties and unseen gifts that will be vouchsafed by His Revelation, Bahá'u'lláh states:

> Every word that proceedeth out of the mouth of God is endowed with such potency as can instill new life into every human frame, if ye be of them that comprehend this truth. All the wondrous works ye behold in this world have been manifested through the operation of His supreme and most exalted Will, His wondrous and inflexible Purpose. Through the mere revelation of the word "Fashioner," issuing forth from His lips and proclaiming His attribute to mankind, such power is released as can generate, through successive ages, all the manifold arts which the hands of man can produce. This, verily, is a certain truth. No sooner is this resplendent word uttered, than its animating energies, stirring within all created things, give birth to the means and instruments whereby such arts can be produced and perfected. All the wondrous achievements ye now witness are the direct consequences of the Revelation of this Name. In the days to come, ye will, verily, behold

> things of which ye have never heard before. Thus hath it been decreed in the Tablets of God, and none can comprehend it except them whose sight is sharp. In like manner, the moment the word expressing My attribute "The Omniscient" issueth forth from My mouth, every created thing will, according to its capacity and limitations, be invested with the power to unfold the knowledge of the most marvelous sciences, and will be empowered to manifest them in the course of time at the bidding of Him Who is the Almighty, the All-Knowing.
> (Bahá'u'lláh, *Gleanings from the Writings of Bahá'u'lláh*, p. 141)

It is evident that since the time of Bahá'u'lláh, new sciences and arts have come into existence and will continue to develop at an ever-increasing rate to provide mankind with manifold bounties for years and centuries to come.

athirst will attain the living Kawthar[287] of their Well-Beloved, and the erring wanderer, lost in the wilds of remoteness[288] and nothingness, will enter the tabernacle[289] of life, and attain reunion with his heart's desire.

287. Please see Note No. 136 above.

288. Please see Note Nos. 58 and 204 above.

289. Please see Note No. 4 above.

In the soil of whose heart will these holy seeds germinate[290]?

290. A similar allegory is made by Christ in Mathew, Chapter 13, symbolizing the words of God as seeds that grow in the hearts of the believers (see Note No. 68 above).

    Regarding the germination and growth of the holy seeds in the heart of the people, Shoghi Effendi states:

    > When a person becomes a Bahá'í, actually what takes place is that the seed of the spirit starts to grow in the human soul. This seed must be watered by the outpourings of the

Holy Spirit. These gifts of the spirit are received through prayer, meditation, study of the Holy Utterances and service to the Cause of God. The fact of the matter is that service in the Cause is like the plough which ploughs the physical soil when seeds are sown. It is necessary that the soil be ploughed up, so that it can be enriched, and thus cause a stronger growth of the seed. In exactly the same way the evolution of the spirit takes place through ploughing up the soil of the heart so that it is a constant reflection of the Holy Spirit. In this way the human spirit grows and develops by leaps and bounds.
(Shoghi Effendi, in *The Compilation of Compilations,* vol. II, p. 24)

Verily, I say, so fierce is the blaze of the Bush of love, burning in the Sinai of the heart[291]

291. This is another allusion to the station of Bahá'u'lláh, Whose heart is the Sinai in which the Revelation of the holy utterance takes place. As 'Abdu'l-Bahá states (see Note No. 286 above), this is the second stage of the four stages identified in the process of divine revelation:

> And when the blessed Tree is kindled by itself within itself, and that Divine Fire burneth by its essence within its essence, this is the stage of "I wished to be made known."

Oceans can never allay this Leviathan's[292]

292. "Leviathan" is a mythical, huge, marine animal such as a whale or anything of immense size and power. There are several references to the Leviathan in the Old Testament, i.e in the Book of Job, Chapter 41, where it is referenced as a symbol of strength and power.

and this Phoenix[293]

293. The "Phoenix" is a mythical bird of great beauty that has been mentioned in ancient myths as a bird of magnificent size, shape,

and color, which possessed superhuman intellect and wisdom. The Islamic and Ṣúfí traditions maintain that the Phoenix lived in a mountain called Qá'f which is located at the end of the world. According to these traditions it lived a very long life, e.g., a thousand years, and at the end of its life would burn itself on a funeral pyre which it made by igniting its own feathers. From its ashes a new Phoenix would rise in the freshness of youth and live through another cycle of years. Often used as an emblem of immortality or of reborn idealism or hope, a person or thing of peerless beauty or excellence. In mystical literature the Phoenix is the symbol of divinity.

The Phoenix of the undying fire might be a reference to the Manifestation of God and the eternal religion of God, which, when it gets old, is reborn with vigor and power by the coming of the new Manifestation. Bahá'u'lláh in other places in His Writings also refers to Himself as a Phoenix:

> The Pen of Revelation exclaimeth: "On this Day the Kingdom is God's!" The Tongue of Power is calling: "On this Day all sovereignty is, in very deed, with God!" The Phoenix of the realms above crieth out from the immortal Branch: "The glory of all greatness belongeth to God, the Incomparable, the All-Compelling!"
> (Bahá'u'lláh, *Gleanings from the Writings of Bahá'u'lláh*, p. 35)

O brother! kindle with the oil of wisdom the lamp of the spirit within the innermost chamber of thy heart, and guard it with the globe of understanding, that the breath of the infidel may extinguish not its flame nor dim its brightness.[294]

294. This is similar to Christ's statement that the seed of faith which is sown in the heart of a believer can be snatched away by the wicked one (see Note No. 216 above). There is another statement by Bahá'u'lláh in which He advises the believers to protect the light of faith and the flame of the love of God in their hearts from being extinguished by the ungodly:

> O My servants! Deprive not yourselves of the unfading and resplendent Light that shineth within the Lamp of Divine

> glory. Let the flame of the love of God burn brightly within your radiant hearts. Feed it with the oil of Divine guidance, and protect it within the shelter of your constancy. Guard it within the globe of trust and detachment from all else but God, so that the evil whisperings of the ungodly may not extinguish its light.
> (Bahá'u'lláh, *Gleanings from the Writings of Bahá'u'lláh*, p. 325)

Thus have We illuminated the heavens of utterance with the splendours of the Sun of divine wisdom and understanding,[295]

295. This is another allusion to the divine station of Bahá'u'lláh in which, He, as the Manifestation of God presently in the second stage of the four stages identified in the process of divine Revelation (see Note No. 291 above), is illuminating "the heavens of utterance with the splendours of the Sun of divine wisdom and understanding."

Paragraph No. 66:

And now, concerning His words: "And then shall appear the sign of the Son of man[296] in heaven."

296. The term "Son of man" first appeared in the Old Testament denoting mankind in general, as in Psalms:

> What is man, that thou art mindful of him? and the son of man, that thou visitest him? For thou hast made him a little lower than the angels, and hast crowned him with glory and honour. Thou madest him to have dominion over the works of thy hands; thou hast put all things under his feet:
> (Psalms 8:4–6)

This term is mentioned in other parts of the Old Testament, with special reference to man's weakness and frailty, as in Job 25:6, Psalms 144:3, 146:3, and Isaiah 51:12. This title was also given to the prophet Ezekiel as the representative of mankind who fails to achieve its rightful station and falls short of God's expectation.

In the book of Ezekiel at the end of the first chapter and the beginning of the second chapter, God calls Ezekiel "Son of man":

> As the appearance of the bow that is in the cloud in the day of rain, so was the appearance of the brightness round about. This was the appearance of the likeness of the glory of the LORD. And when I saw it, I fell upon my face, and I heard a voice of one that spake.
>
> And he said unto me, Son of man, stand upon thy feet, and I will speak unto thee. And the spirit entered into me when he spake unto me, and set me upon my feet, that I heard him that spake unto me. And he said unto me, Son of man, I send thee to the children of Israel, to a rebellious nation that hath rebelled against me: they and their fathers have transgressed against me, even unto this very day. For they are impudent children and stiffhearted. I do send thee unto them; and thou shalt say unto them, Thus saith the Lord GOD.
> (Ezekiel 1:28–2:4)

It was also used to denote the person who is chosen to represent God among man and to receive God's power and authority, as stated in Psalms:

> Let thy hand be upon the man of thy right hand, upon the son of man whom thou madest strong for thyself.
> (Psalms 80:17)

And in the Book of Daniel Chapter 7:

> I saw in the night visions, and, behold, one like the Son of man came with the clouds of heaven and came to the Ancient of days, and they brought him near before him. And there was given him dominion, and glory, and a kingdom, that all people, nations, and languages, should serve him: his dominion is an everlasting dominion, which shall not pass away, and his kingdom that which shall not be destroyed.
> (Daniel 7:13–14)

"Son of man," is the title that Jesus distinctively chose for Himself as evidenced in the Gospels, where it is used forty-three times. Jesus used this self-designation particularly in passages relating to "Parousia" (a Greek word adopted as the technical term for the coming of Christ at the end of time or history; the second coming. The English word is "coming"). A description of Parousia is given in Matt. 24:4–36, 25:31–46, 26:1–64, Mark 13:5–37, LK 21:8–36 (see Appendix IV, The Olivet Discourse).

The term "Son of man" has a parallel in the term "Son of God," which appears first in Genesis and further in the Book of Hosea and other places in the Old Testament:

> And it came to pass, when men began to multiply on the face of the earth, and daughters were born unto them, That the sons of God saw the daughters of men that they were fair; and they took them wives of all which they chose.
> (Genesis 6:1–2)

> Yet the number of the children of Israel shall be as the sand of the sea, which cannot be measured nor numbered; and it shall come to pass, that in the place where it was said unto them, Ye are not my people, there it shall be said unto them, Ye are the sons of the living God.
> (Hosea 1:10)

In the New Testament, it is used for Christ and refers also to whomever is obedient to God, receives guidance, lives a righteous life, and believes in Christ:

> Behold, what manner of love the Father hath bestowed upon us, that we should be called the sons of God: therefore the world knoweth us not, because it knew him not. Beloved, now are we the sons of God, and it doth not yet appear what we shall be: but we know that, when he shall appear, we shall be like him; for we shall see him as he is.
> (1 John 3:1–2)

> He came unto his own, and his own received him not. But as many as received him, to them gave he power to become the sons of God, even to them that believe on his name:

> Which were born, not of blood, nor of the will of the flesh, nor of the will of man, but of God.
> (John 1:11–13)

> Do all things without murmurings and disputings: That ye may be blameless and harmless, the sons of God, without rebuke, in the midst of a crooked and perverse nation, among whom ye shine as lights in the world; Holding forth the word of life; that I may rejoice in the day of Christ, that I have not run in vain, neither laboured in vain.
> (Philippians 2:14–16)

> For as many as are led by the Spirit of God, they are the sons of God.
> (Romans 8:14)

It is interesting to note that Jesus referred to Himself as "Son of man," and to God as "my Father," "the Father," or "our Father" when describing His or the believers relationship with God.

> Then came the Jews round about him, and said unto him, How long dost thou make us to doubt? If thou be the Christ, tell us plainly. Jesus answered them, I told you, and ye believed not: the works that I do in my Father's name, they bear witness of me. But ye believe not, because ye are not of my sheep, as I said unto you. My sheep hear my voice, and I know them, and they follow me: And I give unto them eternal life; and they shall never perish, neither shall any man pluck them out of my hand. My Father, which gave them me, is greater than all; and no man is able to pluck them out of my Father's hand. I and my Father are one. Then the Jews took up stones again to stone him.
> (John 10:24–31)

There are several statements denoting the believers as sons of God, such as:

> For as many as are led by the Spirit of God, they are the sons of God.
> (Romans 8:14)

In general, in the Gospels, Jesus refers to Himself as "Son of man" and is addressed or referred to as "Son of God" by others.

By these words it is meant that when the sun of the heavenly teachings hath been eclipsed, the stars of the divinely-established laws have fallen, and the moon of true knowledge—the educator of mankind—hath been obscured[297]

297. Bahá'u'lláh here explains the true meanings of the sun, the moon, and the stars that were referred to in the Olivet discourse (see Note Nos. 121–23 above and Appendix IV).

> Immediately after the tribulation of those days shall the sun be darkened, and the moon shall not give her light, and the stars shall fall from heaven, and the powers of the heavens shall be shaken: And then shall appear the sign of the Son of man in heaven:
> (Matthew 24:29–30)

By "heaven" is meant the visible heaven, inasmuch as when the hour draweth nigh on which the Daystar of the heaven of justice[298] shall be made manifest, and the Ark of divine guidance shall sail upon the sea of glory,[299] a star will appear in the heaven, heralding unto its people the advent of that most great light.

298. Bahá'u'lláh, in other places in the Kitáb-i-Íqán (The Book of Certitude) refers to Manifestations of God as the "Daystar of truth" and the "Daystar of divine enlightenment."

299. It seems that the Ark of divine guidance, or the Ark of salvation or safety, are allusions to the Revelation and Faith of God. Whoever believes in the divine Revelation and enters the Faith of God, enters the Ark of Guidance, safety, and salvation.

> For in this station, the City of Divine Unity, are to be found those who have entered within the ark of divine guidance and journeyed through the heights of divine unity.
> (Bahá'u'lláh, *Gems of Divine Mysteries*, p. 64)

Ere long will God sail His Ark upon thee, and will manifest the people of Bahá who have been mentioned in the Book of Names.
(Bahá'u'lláh, *Tablets of Bahá'u'lláh*, p. 5)

O Holy Mariner! Bid thine ark of eternity appear before the Celestial Concourse,
Glorified be my Lord, the All-Glorious! Launch it upon the ancient sea, in His Name, the Most Wondrous, Glorified be my Lord, the All-Glorious! And let the angelic spirits enter, in the Name of God, the Most High. Glorified be my Lord, the All-Glorious! Unmoor it, then, that it may sail upon the ocean of glory,
(Bahá'u'lláh, in *Bahá'í Prayers,* p. 220)

He will come to your aid with invisible hosts, and support you with armies of inspiration from the Concourse above; He will send unto you sweet perfumes from the highest Paradise, and waft over you the pure breathings that blow from the rose gardens of the Company on high. He will breathe into your hearts the spirit of life, cause you to enter the Ark of salvation, and reveal unto you His clear tokens and signs.
('Abdu'l-Bahá, *Selections from the Writings of ('Abdu'l-Bahá*, p. 186)

Verily, I pray God to make thee firm in this Path; to cause thee to enter the Ark of Safety.
('Abdu'l-Bahá, *Tablets of 'Abdu'l-Bahá,* vol. 1, p. 129)

O thou messenger in the command of God! Blessed art thou for guiding . . . unto the Fountain of the Water of Life, caused him to enter the Ark of Safety, demonstrated unto him the manifest signs, and proved to him the elegant proofs.
('Abdu'l-Bahá, *Tablets of 'Abdu'l-Bahá,* vol. 1, p. 189)

Through him a considerable number found their way into the Ark of Salvation.
('Abdu'l-Bahá, *Memorials of the Faithful*, p. 135)

In like manner, in the invisible heaven[300] a star shall be made manifest who, unto the peoples of the earth,

300. As mentioned above, Bahá'u'lláh in many of His Writings, and specifically in the Kitáb-i-Íqán, explains that the heaven described in the Scriptures symbolizes a religion or dispensation (see Note No. 6 above)

These twofold signs, in the visible and the invisible heaven, have announced the Revelation of each of the Prophets of God, as is commonly believed.[301]

301. By this statement, "as is commonly believed," Bahá'u'lláh in the next paragraph utilizes the stories and references to the life and times of the prophets of the past such as Abraham, Moses, Jesus, and Muḥammad, as related in the major commentaries of the Qur'án or other Islamic sources, without confirming their accuracies.

Paragraph No. 67:

Among the Prophets was Abraham, the Friend of God,[302]

302. As mentioned above, the title of "the Friend of God" for Abraham comes from the Qur'án, Súrah of Women:

> And who hath a better religion than he who resigneth himself to God, who doth what is good, and followeth the faith of Abraham in all sincerity? And God took Abraham for his friend.
> (The Qur'án 4:124)

For further details regarding Abraham see Notes No. 41–43 above.

Nimrod[303]

303. There are three mentions of Nimrod in the Old Testament, in Genesis and Chronicles when the generation of the children of Noah is listed:

> And Cush begat Nimrod: he began to be a mighty one in the earth. He was a mighty hunter before the LORD: wherefore it is said, Even as Nimrod the mighty hunter before the LORD. And the beginning of his kingdom was Babel, and Erech, and Accad, and Calneh, in the land of Shinar.
> (Genesis 10:8–10)

> And the sons of Cush; Seba, and Havilah, and Sabta, and Raamah, and Sabtecha. And the sons of Raamah; Sheba, and Dedan. And Cush begat Nimrod: he began to be mighty upon the earth.
> (1 Chronicles 1: 9–10)

As mentioned above, Nimrod was the son of Cush, the great-grandson of Nova, the king of Shinar, and based on this some extra-biblical sources associate him with the Tower of Bable, because the Tower of Bable was located in the land of Shinar:

> And the whole earth was of one language, and of one speech. And it came to pass, as they journeyed from the east, that they found a plain in the land of Shinar; and they dwelt there. And they said one to another, Go to, let us make brick, and burn them thoroughly. And they had brick for stone, and slime had they for morter. And they said, Go to, let us build us a city and a tower, whose top may reach unto heaven; and let us make us a name, lest we be scattered abroad upon the face of the whole earth. And the LORD came down to see the city and the tower, which the children of men builded. And the LORD said, Behold, the people is one, and they have all one language; and this they begin to do: and now nothing will be restrained from them, which they have imagined to do. Go to, let us go down, and there confound their language, that they may not understand one another's speech. So the LORD scattered them abroad from thence upon the face of all the earth: and they left off to build the city. Therefore is the name of it called Babel; because the LORD did there confound the language of all the earth.
> (Genesis 11:1–9)

According to the Old Testament, Nimrod was not Abraham's contemporary and had no encounter with him. But in Midrash and other Rabbinical sources Nimrod was identified with Amraphel, who was a contemporary of Abraham and was known as the king who built the Tower of Babel. However, commentators on the Qur'án and some other Islamic sources state that a king called Namrood was Abraham's contemporary and his antagonist in the stories of his life. He was the ruler of the land who ordered Abraham to be burned (see Note Nos. 41–43). They wrote many stories regarding him in relation to Abraham. One recounted that before Abraham was born, Namrood saw a dream that when it was interpreted, warned him of the birth of a child that would eventually destroy his kingdom, and at his order for three years every male newborn child was killed. But Abraham's father who was the astrologer and vizier of the Namrood was able to hide and protect his son.

Paragraph No. 68:

After Him came Moses, He Who held converse with God.[304]

304. One of the titles of Moses in the Qur'án is "Kalím'u'lláh," meaning "He Who held converse with God." This is based on the many statements in the Old Testament, more specifically in Exodus, indicating that Moses was conversing with God, such as the following:

> And it came to pass, when Moses came down from mount Sinai with the two tables of testimony in Moses' hand, . . . And Moses called unto them; and Aaron and all the rulers of the congregation returned unto him: and Moses talked with them. And afterward all the children of Israel came nigh: and he gave them in commandment all that the LORD had spoken with him in mount Sinai. And till Moses had done speaking with them, he put a vail on his face. But when Moses went in before the LORD to speak with him, he took the vail off, until he came out.
> (Exodus 34:29–33)

"A star hath risen in the heaven, and lo! it foreshadoweth the conception of a Child Who holdeth your fate and the fate of your people in His hand.[305]

305. See Note No. 43 above.

Were the details to be mentioned, this epistle would swell into a book. Moreover, it is not Our wish to relate the stories of the days that are past. God is Our witness that what We even now mention is due solely to Our tender affection for thee, that haply the poor of the earth may attain the shores of the sea of wealth, the ignorant be led unto the ocean of divine knowledge, and they that thirst for understanding partake of the Salsabil[74] of divine wisdom. Otherwise, this servant regardeth the consideration of such records a grave mistake and a grievous transgression.[306]

306. Bahá'u'lláh makes a similar statement in the Seven Valleys:

> I mislike the copious citation from sayings of the past; for quotation from the words of others proveth acquired learning, not the divine bestowal. Even so much as We have quoted here is out of deference to the wont of men and after the manner of the friends. . . . Our unwillingness to recount their sayings is not from pride, rather is it a manifestation of wisdom and a demonstration of grace.
> (Bahá'u'lláh, The Seven Valleys and The Four Valleys, p. 26)

Elsewhere in the Kitáb-i-Íqán, He states:

> Although We did not intend to make mention of the traditions of a bygone age, yet, because of Our love for thee, We will cite a few which are applicable to Our argument. We do not feel their necessity, however, inasmuch as the things We have already mentioned suffice the world and all that is therein. In fact, all the Scriptures and the mysteries thereof are condensed into this brief account. So much so, that were a person to ponder it a while in his heart, he would discover from all that hath

[74] Please see Note No. 263 above.

> been said the mysteries of the Words of God, and would apprehend the meaning of whatever hath been manifested by that ideal King. As the people differ in their understanding and station, We will accordingly make mention of a few traditions, that these may impart constancy to the wavering soul, and tranquility to the troubled mind. Thereby, will the testimony of God unto the people, both high and low, be complete and perfect.
> (Bahá'u'lláh, The Kitáb-i-Íqán, ¶266)

Paragraph No. 69:

In like manner, when the hour of the Revelation of Jesus drew nigh, a few of the Magi[307] aware that the star of Jesus had appeared in heaven, sought and followed it.

307. "Magi," is the Latin plural of "Magus." This word is used in the original Greek Gospel of Matthew, but in English translations such as the King James Version, it is translated as "wise men." The word Magus comes from the Persian word "Majus," meaning Zoroastrian priest.

> Magus: one of the Magi, a member of priestly caste of ancient Media and Persia.
> (Webster's New World College Dictionary, Third Edition, © 1997)

The Gospel of Matthew is the only Gospel that mentioned the visit by the Magi or the wise men who came from the east to find and worship the infant Jesus:

> Now when Jesus was born in Bethlehem of Judaea in the days of Herod the king, behold, there came wise men from the east to Jerusalem, Saying, Where is he that is born King of the Jews? for we have seen his star in the east, and are come to worship him.
> (Matthew 2:1–2)

Although the number of the wise men is not specified in the Bible, Christian traditions assume that there were three men (possibly because they brought three gifts of gold, frankincense, and myrrh) for the infant Jesus. Traditions differ about their status (clergy, rulers, or kings), origins, names, and nationalities. Most agree, however, that they were Persians, and some indicate that they came from one of the ancient Persian cities, the City of Cassan (present-day Káshán):

> According to Odoric of Pordenone (1320), this was the city from which came the Three Wise Men; and from here these Kings got to Jerusalem, with God's help, in thirteen days.
> (Marzieh Gail, *Dawn Over Mount Hira and other essays*, p. 72)

The appearance of the "Star of Jesus," which is also known as the "Star of Bethlehem," is only mentioned as part of the nativity story in the Gospel of Matthew (Matt. 2:2). The Gospels of Mark and John do not contain any reference to the birth of Jesus and there is no mention of a star in the nativity story in the Gospel of Luke.

Although the Star of Bethlehem was considered a miraculous symbol of the birth of Jesus, for many centuries some Christian astronomers were trying to identify an astronomical event such as a nova, comet, or conjunction that occurred at the time of the birth of Jesus that could explain the phenomena of the star of Bethlehem. Some thought that the conjunction of the stars or planets (a conjunction is when two astronomical bodies, although in different orbits appear, as seen from the earth, to merge together for a period of time) might produce this effect. Conjunctions of Jupiter and Venus, the two brightest planets visible from Earth, are frequent astronomical events which cause the two planets to appear as a very bright star. However, some conjunctions might be more spectacular than others.

According to some Biblical scholars Jesus was born between 6 and 1 BC. The "handbook of Biblical Chronology" indicates that the majority of the ancient Biblical scholars place the date between 3 and 2 BC. The records of a few relevant astronomical events in that time period were found. A bright comet appearing in the constellation of Capricorn in 5 BC was recorded by Chinese astronomers. Jupiter and Venus might have had an exceptionally bright conjunction around the years 3 to 2 BC. One of these events might have been what was referred to as the Star of Bethlehem.

the city which was the seat of the Kingdom of Herod[308]

308. "Herod," which means "son of a hero," was the name of several rulers of the Herodian kingdom who ruled in Judea. There are two Herods mentioned in the Bible who were contemporaries of Jesus. The first one was Herod I or Herod the Great and the second was Herod Antipater.

Herod I was the son of Antipas of Idumaea, who was the ruler of Judea and was assassinated in 43 BC. Supported by the Roman Empire, Herod I became the king of Judea and established the Herodian Kingdom in 37 BC. The seat of his kingdom was Jerusalem. According to the Gospel of Matthew, the wise men first went to Jerusalem to enquire about the birth of the King of Jews.

Herod ruled Judea until 4 BC. He has been regarded as a mad man who murdered three of his sons, some other family members, and many Jewish leaders. According to the Gospel of Matthew, he ordered the massacre of infants and children under the age of two in order to prevent the fulfilment of a prophecy regarding the loss of his kingdom. This act, known as the Massacre of Innocents in Christian history, is only mentioned in the Gospel of Matthew:

> Now when Jesus was born in Bethlehem of Judaea in the days of Herod the king, behold, there came wise men from the east to Jerusalem, Saying, Where is he that is born King of the Jews? for we have seen his star in the east, and are come to worship him. When Herod the king had heard these things, he was troubled, and all Jerusalem with him. And when he had gathered all the chief priests and scribes of the people together, he demanded of them where Christ should be born. And they said unto him, In Bethlehem of Judaea: for thus it is written by the prophet, And thou Bethlehem, in the land of Juda, art not the least among the princes of Juda: for out of thee shall come a Governor, that shall rule my people Israel. Then Herod, when he had privily called the wise men, enquired of them diligently what time the star appeared. And he sent them to Bethlehem, and said, Go and search diligently for the

> young child; and when ye have found him, bring me word again, that I may come and worship him also. When they had heard the king, they departed; and, lo, the star, which they saw in the east, went before them, till it came and stood over where the young child was. When they saw the star, they rejoiced with exceeding great joy. And when they were come into the house, they saw the young child with Mary his mother, and fell down, and worshipped him: and when they had opened their treasures, they presented unto him gifts; gold, and frankincense and myrrh. And being warned of God in a dream that they should not return to Herod, they departed into their own country another way. And when they were departed, behold, the angel of the Lord appeareth to Joseph in a dream, saying, Arise, and take the young child and his mother, and flee into Egypt, and be thou there until I bring thee word: for Herod will seek the young child to destroy him. When he arose, he took the young child and his mother by night, and departed into Egypt: And was there until the death of Herod: that it might be fulfilled which was spoken of the Lord by the prophet, saying, Out of Egypt have I called my son. Then Herod, when he saw that he was mocked of the wise men, was exceeding wroth, and sent forth, and slew all the children that were in Bethlehem, and in all the coasts thereof, from two years old and under, according to the time which he had diligently enquired of the wise men.
> (Matthew 2:1–16)

The accounts of the massacre of infants and children as mentioned in the Gospel of Matthew (above) have not been corroborated by any ancient historians, including Josephus (the first century Jewish historian) who recorded the details of the life and political career of Herod I. If Matthew's story is correct, Jesus' birth must have taken place between 6 and 4 BC, as Herod died in 4 BC. After his death, Herod's kingdom was divided into four parts, with one part going to each of his three sons and daughter.

Herod Antipater (*Antipatros*; born before 20 BCE – died after 39 CE), known by the nickname Antipas, was a first-century CE ruler of Galilee and Petra, and bore the title of Tetrarch ("ruler of a quarter"). He is best known for the accounts in the New Testament of his role in the execution (beheading) of John the Baptist and crucifixion of Jesus. After inheriting his territories when the kingdom of his father Herod the Great was divided upon his death in 4 BCE, Antipas ruled them as a client state of the Roman Empire. Antipas divorced his first wife Phasaelis, the daughter of King Aretas IV of Nabatea, in favor of Herodias, who had formerly been married to his brother Herod Phillip I. According to the New Testament, it was John the Baptist's condemnation of this arrangement that led Antipas to have him arrested; John was subsequently put to death.

> For Herod had laid hold on John, and bound him, and put him in prison for Herodias' sake, his brother Philip's wife. For John said unto him, It is not lawful for thee to have her. And when he would have put him to death, he feared the multitude, because they counted him as a prophet. But when Herod's birthday was kept, the daughter of Herodias danced before them, and pleased Herod. Whereupon he promised with an oath to give her whatsoever she would ask. And she, being before instructed of her mother, said, Give me here John Baptist's head in a charger. And the king was sorry: nevertheless for the oath's sake, and them which sat with him at meat, he commanded it to be given her. And he sent, and beheaded John in the prison. And his head was brought in a charger, and given to the damsel: and she brought it to her mother.
> (Matthew 14:3–10)

Besides provoking his conflict with the Baptizer, the tetrarch's divorce added a personal grievance to previous disputes with Aretas over territory on the border of Perea and Nabatea. The result was a war that proved disastrous for Antipas; a Roman counter-offensive was ordered by Tiberius, but abandoned upon that emperor's death in 37 CE. In 39 CE Antipas was accused by his nephew Agrippa of conspiracy against the new Roman emperor Caligula, who sent him into exile in Gaul. Accompanied there by Herodias, he died at an unknown date[75]. The Gospel of Luke states that when Jesus was brought before Pontius Pilate for trial, Pilate

[75] (Based on Dictionary of the Bible: http://www.biblestudytools.com/dictionary/herod/#)

handed him over to Antipas, in whose territory Jesus had been active. However, Antipas sent him back to Pilate.

> When Pilate heard of Galilee, he asked whether the man were a Galilaean. And as soon as he knew that he belonged unto Herod's jurisdiction, he sent him to Herod, who himself also was at Jerusalem at that time. And when Herod saw Jesus, he was exceeding glad: for he was desirous to see him of a long season, because he had heard many things of him; and he hoped to have seen some miracle done by him. Then he questioned with him in many words; but he answered him nothing. And the chief priests and scribes stood and vehemently accused him. And Herod with his men of war set him at nought, and mocked him, and arrayed him in a gorgeous robe, and sent him again to Pilate. And the same day Pilate and Herod were made friends together: for before they were at enmity between themselves. And Pilate, when he had called together the chief priests and the rulers and the people, Said unto them, Ye have brought this man unto me, as one that perverteth the people: and, behold, I, having examined him before you, have found no fault in this man touching those things whereof ye accuse him: No, nor yet Herod: for I sent you to him; and, lo, nothing worthy of death is done unto him. I will therefore chastise him, and release him. (For of necessity he must release one unto them at the feast.) And they cried out all at once, saying, Away with this man, and release unto us Barabbas: (Who for a certain sedition made in the city, and for murder, was cast into prison.) Pilate therefore, willing to release Jesus, spake again to them.
>
> But they cried, saying, Crucify him, crucify him. And he said unto them the third time, Why, what evil hath he done? I have found no cause of death in him: I will therefore chastise him, and let him go. And they were instant with loud voices, requiring that he might be crucified. And the voices of them and of the chief priests prevailed. And Pilate gave sentence that it should be as they required.
> (Luke 23:6–24)

Paragraph No. 70:

These Magi said: "Where is He that is born King of the Jews? for we have seen His star in the east and are come to worship Him!"[309]

309. This verse is from the Gospel of Mathew, Matt 2:2.

When they had searched, they found out that in Bethlehem[310], in the land of Judea, the Child had been born.

310. Bethlehem or *Bēt Laḥm*, literally meaning "House of Flesh"; is a city located in the central part of the present West Bank and approximately 8 kilometers (5.0 mi) south of Jerusalem. The Hebrew Bible identifies Bethlehem as the city that David was from and the location where he was crowned as the King of Israel.

The New Testament identifies Bethlehem as the birthplace of Jesus of Nazareth. The town is inhabited by one of the oldest Christian communities in the world, although the size of the community has shrunk due to emigration. Bethlehem was destroyed by the Emperor Hadrian during the second-century Bar Kokhba revolt; its rebuilding was promoted by Empress Helena, mother of Emperor Constantine, who commissioned the building of its great Church of the Nativity in 327 CE. The church was badly damaged by the Samaritans, who sacked it during a revolt in 529, but was rebuilt a century later by Emperor Justinian I.

Bethlehem was conquered by the Arabs during the Caliphate of the 'Umar ibn al Khaṭṭáb in 637, who guaranteed safety for the city's religious shrines. In 1099, Crusaders captured and fortified Bethlehem and replaced its Greek Orthodox clergy with a Latin one. The Latin clergy were expelled after the city was captured by Saladin, the Sultan of Egypt and Syria. Muslim rule continued in Bethlehem. In the mid-thirteenth century, the Mamluks (the rulers that followed Saladin) demolished the city's walls, which were subsequently rebuilt in the early sixteenth century, after Bethlehem became part of the Ottoman Empire. Control of Bethlehem passed from the Ottomans to the British at the end of World War I. Bethlehem came under Jordanian rule during the 1948 Arab-Israeli War and was later captured by Israel in the 1967

Six-Day War. Since the 1995 Oslo Accord, Bethlehem has been administered by the Palestinian Authority.
(Based on Wikipedia and Dictionary of the Bible)

As to the sign in the invisible heaven—the heaven of divine knowledge and understanding—it was Yaḥyá,[311] son of Zachariah

311. In the Qur'án and Bahá'í Writings, John the Baptist is called "Yaḥyá" or the son of Zachariah. John the Baptist was a prophet from a priestly family, who preached a message of repentance, announced the coming of the Messiah, baptized Jesus, and was beheaded by Herod Antipas (see above, Note No. 308).

Luke 1:5–80 records the birth of John the Baptist in terms similar to the birth of Isaac, which was the result of divine intervention. Zachariah, John's father, was a priest from the division of Abijah. Elizabeth, his mother, was a descendant of Aaron (Moses' brother) and a cousin of Mary the mother of Jesus. Both John's parents were at very advanced age when he was born. The angel Gabriel announced John's birth, while Zachariah was burning incense in the Temple.

John lived the life an ascetic and would not drink wine or strong drinks. He was the same age as Jesus and started his mission around age thirty, baptizing people in the River Jordan. He would be filled with the Holy Spirit, preach a message of repentance, warning people that the time of the end was approaching. He had a considerable number of followers who believed that he was a prophet that had the spirit and power of Elijah.

The Gospel of Mark 1:2–4 records that John was in the wilderness from the beginning of his public ministry:

> As it is written in the prophets, Behold, I send my messenger before thy face, which shall prepare thy way before thee. The voice of one crying in the wilderness, Prepare ye the way of the Lord, make his paths straight. John did baptize in the wilderness, and preach the baptism of repentance for the remission of sins.
> (Mark 1:2–4)

There he ate locusts and wild honey and wore the dress made of camel's hair and a leather girdle:

> In those days came John the Baptist, preaching in the wilderness of Judaea, And saying, Repent ye: for the kingdom of heaven is at hand. For this is he that was spoken of by the prophet Esaias, saying, The voice of one crying in the wilderness, Prepare ye the way of the Lord, make his paths straight. And the same John had his raiment of camel's hair, and a leathern girdle about his loins; and his meat was locusts and wild honey.
> (Matthew 3:1–4)

Because of his life in the wilderness, his priestly background, his preaching of repentance to Israel, and his practice of baptism, it is often suggested that John grew up among the Essenes at Qumran.[76] The origin of John's practice of baptizing cannot be traced with certainty. However, washings had long been part of Jewish piety, and by the time of John, Gentile converts to Judaism washed themselves as a form of ceremonial cleansing. The Essenes at Qumran practiced ritual washings and had an elaborate procedure for admission to the community. John was using the practice and ritual of baptism (washing or cleaning of the physical body by dipping or emersion of the body in the water) as a symbol of repentance and outer expression of spiritual cleaning in preparation for entering the kingdom of God, which was going to be established with the imminent appearance of the Messiah

According to the Gospel of Luke, John began his ministry on the banks of the River Jordan in the fifteenth year of the reign of Caesar Tiberius (Luke 3:1–3), which must have been 26 or 27 AD. John's preaching emphasized the approaching time of judgment, the need for repentance, and the coming of the Messiah. Luke also emphasizes the ethical teachings of John: he called the multitudes a "generation of vipers" (Luke 3:7); one who had two coats should give one to a person who had none; tax collectors were warned to

---

[76] Essenes were a group of Jewish ascetics that flourished between the second century BCE and the first century CE. Qumeran was a settlement that was established around the second century BCE in the area approximately one mile northeast of the Dead Sea and was destroyed by Romans in 68 CE. The famous Dead Sea Scrolls were found in the caves near Qumran.

collect no more than their due; and soldiers were instructed to rob no one and be content with their wages (Luke 3:10–14).

Jesus was baptized by John, a fact that all the evangelists except Mark attempted to explain. Matthew explains that it was "to fulfill all righteousness."

> Then cometh Jesus from Galilee to Jordan unto John, to be baptized of him. But John forbad him, saying, I have need to be baptized of thee, and comest thou to me? And Jesus answering said unto him, Suffer it to be so now: for thus it becometh us to fulfil all righteousness. Then he suffered him.
> (Matthew 3:13–15)

Luke recorded that John baptized Jesus before he was thrown in prison by Herod:

> And as the people were in expectation, and all men mused in their hearts of John, whether he were the Christ, or not; John answered, saying unto them all, I indeed baptize you with water; but one mightier than I cometh, the latchet of whose shoes I am not worthy to unloose: he shall baptize you with the Holy Ghost and with fire. . . . But Herod the tetrarch, being reproved by him for Herodias his brother Philip's wife, and for all the evils which Herod had done, Added yet this above all, that he shut up John in prison. Now when all the people were baptized, it came to pass, that Jesus also being baptized,
> (Luke 3:15–21)

The Gospel of John mentions the baptism of Jesus but only through the testimony of John the Baptist himself:

> John bare witness of him, and cried, saying, This was he of whom I spake, He that cometh after me is preferred before me: for he was before me.
> (John 1:15)

Various sayings give some glimpses of John's ministry. His disciples practiced fasting (Mark 2:18), and he taught them to pray (Luke 11:1). John was vigorous in his attacks on Herod and strongly criticized Herod for marrying his sister-in-law Herodias (see Note Nos. 308 and 311 above). According to Josephus, Herod arrested and imprisoned John because "he feared that John's so extensive influence over the people might lead to an uprising." John's popularity with the people is reflected in Matthew 21:31–32, Mark 11:27–32, Luke 7:29–30, and John 10:41. In contrast to Herod's household, John lived an austere existence (Matthew 11:7–9). Some criticized John for his ascetic lifestyle (Matthew, 11:16–19), but Jesus praised John as the greatest of the prophets (Matthew 11:9–11)

While John was in prison, one night in a party for Herod's birthday celebration, Herod asked Salome, Herodias' daughter, to dance for him and promised that he would give her whatever she asked for. Herodias told Salome to ask for John's head. She asked Herod to kill John and bring his head to her. Herod did not like this but to fulfill his promise, he ordered John to be killed and his head brought to Salome.

Many Christians believed that the defeat of Herod's armies by the Nabateans was God's judgment on Herod for the death of John the Baptist. While John was in prison, he sent two of his disciples to inquire whether Jesus was "he that should come" (Matt. 11:2–3; Luke 7:18–23). This is when Jesus stated that John was the return of Elijah "And if ye will receive it, this is Elias, which was for to come" (Matt. 11:14). John's death is recorded in detail in the Gospel of Mark 6:14–29.

According to the Gospel of John, the ministry of Jesus overlapped with that of John (3:22–24; contrast Mark 1:14), and some of Jesus' first disciples had also been disciples of John the Baptist (John 1:35–37). Jesus even identified John with the person and the eschatological role of Elijah:

> And as they departed, Jesus began to say unto the multitudes concerning John, What went ye out into the wilderness to see? A reed shaken with the wind? But what went ye out for to see? A man clothed in soft raiment? behold, they that wear soft clothing are in kings' houses. But what went ye out for to see? A prophet? yea, I say unto you, and more than a prophet. For this is he, of whom it is

> written, Behold, I send my messenger before thy face, which shall prepare thy way before thee. Verily I say unto you, Among them that are born of women there hath not risen a greater than John the Baptist: notwithstanding he that is least in the kingdom of heaven is greater than he. And from the days of John the Baptist until now the kingdom of heaven suffereth violence, and the violent take it by force. For all the prophets and the law prophesied until John. And if ye will receive it, this is Elias, which was for to come.
> (Matthew 11:7–14)

> And his disciples asked him, saying, Why then say the scribes that Elias must first come? And Jesus answered and said unto them, Elias truly shall first come, and restore all things. But I say unto you, That Elias is come already, and they knew him not, but have done unto him whatsoever they listed. Likewise shall also the Son of man suffer of them. Then the disciples understood that he spake unto them of John the Baptist.
> (Matthew 17:11–13)

John's movement did not stop with his death. Indeed, some believed that Jesus was John, raised from the dead (Mark 6:14–16; 8:28). Years later, a group of John's followers were found around Ephesus, among them the eloquent Apollos (Acts 18:24–19:7); and for centuries John's influence survived among the Mandeans, who claimed to perpetuate his teachings.
(Excerpts from the entries under "John the Baptist" presented in the International Standard Bible Encyclopedia and the Holman Bible Dictionary)

At the present time, a group of the followers of John the Baptist who are called Sobies (Sabians) live in the southern regions of Iran and Iraq.

In one of His Tablets, Bahá'u'lláh states that the relationship of His Revelation with the Revelation of the Point of the Bayán (the Báb) is like that of the relationship between the Revelations of Christ and John the Baptist. Bahá'u'lláh also states that the son of Zachariah (John the Baptist) with the exalted station of prophethood was giving people the glad tidings of the Revelation of the Spirit (Christ), but people did not understand some of his

teachings. Therefore, after his martyrdom, some of his followers did not accept the Manifestation of God (Jesus). If they properly understood John's teachings, they would not turn away from his beloved (Christ).
(This Tablet in Persian is quoted in the book "The Religion of Sábiun" by Rúhu'lláh Mihrábkháni, p 1. This author could not find an authorized translation of this Tablet)

John was baptizing people with water in anticipation and preparation for the Manifestation of Christ and baptism with the Holy Spirit by Jesus. 'Abdu'l-Bahá states:

> John would first admonish the people, lead them to repent of sin, and exhort them to anticipate the advent of Christ. Then, whoever received the purification of baptism would repent of his sins with utmost meekness and humility, cleanse and purify his body likewise from outward defilements, and with perfect yearning await, night and day and from moment to moment, the advent of Christ and admittance into His Kingdom.
> ('Abdu'l-Bahá, *Some Answered Questions*, no. 20.5)

Even as He hath revealed: "God announceth Yaḥyá to thee, who shall bear witness unto the Word from God, and a great one and chaste.[312] By the term "Word" is meant Jesus.[313]

312. This verse is from the Qur'án 3:39.

313. "Word" or "Word of God" is among the titles of Jesus in the Qur'án. As with other titles such as "Spirit" or "Spirit of God," these titles are based on a statement in the Gospel of John:

> In the beginning was the Word, and the Word was with God, and the Word was God. The same was in the beginning with God. . . .
>
> And the Word was made flesh, and dwelt among us, (and we beheld his glory, the glory as of the only begotten of the Father,) full of grace and truth.
> (John 1:1, 1:14)

"John the Baptist was preaching in the wilderness of Judea, and saying, Repent ye: for the Kingdom of heaven is at hand."[314]

314. This verse is from Matthew 3:1–2: "In those days came John the Baptist, preaching in the wilderness of Judaea, And saying, Repent ye: for the kingdom of heaven is at hand."

Paragraph No. 71:

Likewise, ere the beauty of Muḥammad was unveiled, the signs of the visible heaven were made manifest.[315]

315. An account is related in some famous early Islamic books regarding this. They stated that a Jewish astronomer in Mecca at the time of the birth of Muḥammad declared that the star that is the sign of the birth of a Prophet had appeared in heaven.
(Source: 'Abdu'l-Ḥamíd Ishráq-Khávari, *Qámus-i-Íqán, Vol, 3*, pp. 12–17)

Rúz-bih, later named Salmán.[316]

316. "Rúz-bih," who in Islamic history is referred to as Salmán or Salmán-i-Fársí (Salmán the Persian), was named "Salmán" by Prophet Muḥammad. He was a Persian man who was born either in the city of Kazeroon in the Fárs (Pars) province, or in a suburb of Iṣfahán, a major city in central Persia. The Muslim scholars who wrote regarding Salmán relate that he was born in a rich Zoroastrian farming family from the descendants of Manuchehr, one of the Persian kings. One day during his teenage years, he passed by a Christian church and heard the sound of singing and music. He went inside and was attracted to Christianity. A few years later he decided to study Christianity more deeply and traveled to Syria, which was one of the learning centers of Christianity. He studied with a learned priest and stayed with him until the end of his master's life. Based on the recommendation of his master, he traveled to Mousel, a City in Iraq, to study and serve under a certain priest there. He then served and studied under this second master, and based on his recommendation, after the death of this second master he traveled to the city of Nasibain and served and studied under a monk there. At the time of death of

this third person, he was sent to a fourth person in the city of Amourah near Rome. Salmán served and studied with that priest, who, close to the time of his death, told Salmán to travel to Arabia, where a new prophet of God would shortly appear. Salmán traveled to Arabia, but when traveling with a caravan in Arabia, he was captured and sold as a slave and was brought to the city of Yat͟hreb which was later called "Medina," where he was living and working as a slave. When Prophet Muḥammad migrated from Mecca to Medina, and Salmán heard that a man who claimed to be the prophet of God had arrived, he went and met Prophet Muḥammad, accepted His faith, and became a Muslim.

Salmán was released from slavery by Prophet Muḥammad, Who paid his master the price he asked for to free Salmán and He named him Salmán, which means wise or protector. Salmán became one of the close companions of Prophet Muḥammad and assisted Him in struggles and wars with non-Muslim Arabs. When a 10,000-man army of Meccan Arabs were coming to fight Muslims and take Medina, Salmán planned for the digging of a big trench around the city, which was completed before the opposing army arrived. That trench saved the Muslims and the city of Medina from defeat. This battle is known as the Battle of Trench in the history of Islam.

Salmán was among the ten close companions of Muḥammad who were assured of their place in Heaven. He was liked by all Muslims, it was reported that the Muhájerun (the immigrant Muslims who migrated from Mecca to Medina) said that Salmán was from them and the Ansár (the Muslim natives of Medina) claimed that Salmán was from them, and when they asked Prophet Muḥammad to determine which group Salmán belonged to, He said that Salmán was from His own family. He was a very knowledgeable and wise person, and was given the title of Abu-Al Kitábyn (the father of two books, i.e., the Bible and the Qur'án) and some enemies of Muḥammad claimed that the Qur'án was dictated to Prophet Muḥammad by Salmán. Salmán was the first person to translate the Qur'án into a foreign language, he translated a major part of the Qur'án to Persian. After the passing of Prophet Muḥammad, Salmán supported the choice of 'Alí as the successor to the Prophet.

After Muslims defeated the Persian army and established their rule over the Persian Empire. Salmán was installed as the governor of Al-Madá'in (Ctesiphon, the pre-Islamic capital of the Persian Empire). His time of death is not precisely recorded, but it is assumed that he passed away about twenty or thirty years after the passing of Prophet Muḥammad.
(Excerpts from 'Abdu'l-Ḥamíd Ishráq-Khávari, *Qámus-i-Íqán, Vol, 1,* pp. 522 and *Vol, 2*, pp. 787, and Wikipedia the free encyclopedia)

Paragraph No. 72:

And now concerning this wondrous and most exalted Cause. Know thou verily that many an astronomer hath announced the appearance of its star in the visible heaven.[317]

317. Bahá'u'lláh stated that prior to the birth of the Báb, astronomers had also announced the appearance of its star in the visible heaven. Taymour-i-Kh͟áwrazmi, who was a famous Persian astronomer residing in Iṣfahán predicted that based on his astronomical observations, between the years 1230 and 1250 AH (1814–1834 AD), a great event would occur that would revolutionize the affairs of the world. Mírzá Áqá Kh͟án, of the Iṣfáhán who was the astronomer of the Manúch͟ihr Kh͟án, the Mu 'Tamidu'd-Dawlih, the governor of Iṣfáhán, also predicted that a person will appear in the world who will renovate and reform the laws of the religion, because his star has appeared in the heavens.
(Excerpts from 'Abdu'l-Ḥamíd Ishráq-Khávari, *Qámus-i-Íqán, Vol, 4*, pp. 1532, quoted from the book "Kitábu'l-Fará'id by Mírzá Abu'l Faḍl, the renowned Bahá'í scholar and teacher)

Western astronomers sighted a great non-retuning comet, which was later designated as the Great Comet of 1819.

> GREAT COMET; O.S. 1819 II. Period of naked-eye visibility spanned the month of July. Also known as "Comet Tralles". Spotted on July first in the evening sky, a little to the north of the sun, the head being of about zeroth magnitude. Comet crossed eastern Auriga and was visible at both dusk and dawn for several weeks. At the end of the first week of July, at first magnitude with a 7- to 8-degree tail. Comet faded rapidly as it moved toward the northeast,

almost pacing the sun. At mid-month, situated in Lynx, an object of third magnitude with a short tail. In the last few days of July, the comet's brightness rapidly approached the naked-eye threshold.
(THE BRIGHT-COMET CHRONICLES, by John E. Bortle (W. R. Brooks Observatory), http://www.icq.eps.harvard.edu/bortle.html)

The Great Comet of 1819: It ascended above the northwest horizon as a conspicuous naked-eye object and was generally detected in Europe in the first days of July. The earliest observation was made by Professor Tralles at Berlin in the beginning of the month and the latest observations were made by Struve and Dorpat and by Olbers in Bremen at the middle of October.
(Monthly Notices of the Royal Astronomical Society, 1876 - Astronomy, https://books.google.com/books?id=GC9DAQAAMAAJ)

Likewise, there appeared on earth Aḥmad and Káẓim.[318]

318. Aḥmad and Káẓim is a reference to Shaykh Aḥmad-i-Aḥsá'i and Siyyid Káẓim-i-Rashtí, who Bahá'u'lláh referred to as the "twin luminous lights".

Shaykh Aḥmad (1753–1831), the first of the "twin luminous lights" who was the founder of the Shaykhí School of Shí'ah Islam, was born in 1753 in the town of Aḥsá in the district of Aḥsá which is part of the historical area called Baḥrain. Located in the eastern part of Arabia, the area historically stretched from the south of Iraq along the Persian Gulf coast and included present day Kuwait, Qatar, the Emirates and the Awal Islands, presently known as Baḥrain.

As a result of decades of study and research of the sacred scriptures of Islam such as the Qur'án and Islamic traditions, Shaykh Aḥmad felt that the time of the appearance of the Qá'im or Mahdi, the Promised One of Islam was near. At the age of forty, he left Aḥsá and resided in Najaf and Karbilá[77], two centers of

[77] Karbilá is about 55 miles S.W. of Baghdad on the banks of the Euphrates. . . . The tomb of Husayn is in the centre of the city, and of his brother 'Abbás in the S.E. quarter are the chief buildings. Najaf is revered by the shi'ahs, as it enshrines the tomb of Imám 'Alí.

learning and scholarship of Shi'ah Islam, where he soon became famous for his knowledge as a mujtahid (Doctor of Islamic law) and for his teachings regarding messianic expectations. Regarding this period of S͟haykh Aḥmad's life, Nabil-i-A'zam, the author of *The Dawn-Breakers* states:

> . . . in a few years he acquired familiarity with the prevailing thoughts and standards current among the learned men of Islám. There he came to be recognized as one of the authorized expounders of the Islamic Holy Writ, was declared a mujtahid, and soon obtained an ascendancy over the rest of his colleagues, who either visited or were residing in those holy cities. These came to regard him as one initiated into the mysteries of Divine Revelation, and qualified to unravel the abstruse utterances of Muḥammad and of the imáms of the Faith. As his influence increased, and the scope of his authority widened, he found himself besieged on every side by an ever-increasing number of devoted enquirers who asked to be enlightened regarding the intricacies of the Faith, all of which he ably and fully expounded.
> (*The Dawn-Breakers*, p. 2)

After a decade long stay in Iraq, he traveled to Persia and resided for several years in some major cities there, everywhere as the guest of the king and other members of the royal family or governors of different provinces of Persia. Regarding his trip to Shiraz, which took place at the beginning of his sojourn in Persia, Nabil-i-A'zam, states:

> "Having achieved his purpose in those cities [Najaf and Karbilá], and inhaling the fragrance which wafted upon him from Persia, he felt in his heart an irrepressible yearning to hasten to that country. He concealed from his friends, however, the real motive that impelled him to direct his steps towards that land. By way of the Persian Gulf, he hastened unto the land of his heart's desire, ostensibly for the purpose of visiting the shrine of the Imám

---

(Shoghi Effendi, *The Dawn-Breakers*, p. 2)

Riḍá in Mashhad[78]. He was filled with eagerness to unburden his soul, and searched zealously for those to whom he could deliver the secret which to no one he had as yet divulged.

Upon his arrival at Shíráz, the city which enshrined that concealed Treasure of God, and from which the voice of the Herald of a new Manifestation was destined to be proclaimed, he repaired to the Masjid-i-Jum'ih, a mosque which in its style and shape bore a striking resemblance to the holy shrine of Mecca. Many a time did he, whilst gazing upon that edifice, observe: "Verily, this house of God betokens such signs as only those who are endowed with understanding can perceive. Methinks he who conceived and built it was inspired of God."[79] How often and how passionately he extolled that city! Such was the praise he lavished upon it that his hearers, who were only too familiar with its mediocrity, were astonished at the tone of his language. "Wonder not," he said to those who were surprised, "for ere long the secret of my words will be made manifest to you. Among you there shall be a number who will live to behold the glory of a Day which the prophets of old have yearned to witness." So great was his authority in the eyes of the ulamás who met and conversed with him, that they professed themselves incapable of comprehending the meaning of his mysterious allusions and ascribed their failure to their own deficient understanding."
(*The Dawn-Breakers*, pp. 4–5)

---

[78] In the ninth century the remains of the Imám Riḍá, son of the Imám Músá and eighth of the twelve Imáms, were interred in Mashhad.
(Shoghi Effendi, *The Dawn-Breakers*, p. 4)

[79] "In the country of Fars, there is a Mosque in the center of which rises a structure similar to the Ka'bih, (Masjid-i-Jum'ih). It was built only as a sign indicating the Manifestation of the Will of God through the erection of the house in that land. [Allusion to the new Mecca, i.e., the house of the Báb in Shíráz.] Blessed be he who worships God in that land; truly we, too, worshipped God there, and prayed for him who had erected that building." ("Le Bayán Persan," vol. 2, p. 151.)
(Shoghi Effendi, *The Dawn-Breakers*, pp. 4–5). The above English translation is quoted from the book, Translation of French Foot-Notes of the Dawn-Breakers, By Emily McBride Pėrigord, Bahá'í Publishing Trust, Wilmette, Illinois.

Shaykh Aḥmad then traveled to Yazd, a city in the central region of Iran. He resided in Yazd for several years, where he was engaged in teaching and writing. Many of his major books were written while he was residing in Yazd. His foremost disciple and successor, Siyyid Káẓim-i-Rashtí joined Shaykh Aḥmad in Yazd. After few weeks, Shaykh Aḥmad trusted his followers and disciples to the care of Siyyid Káẓim and resumed his travels. Nabil-i-A'zam states:

> Shaykh Aḥmad, having thus committed his disciples to the care of Siyyid Káẓim, left for Khurásán. There he tarried awhile, in the close vicinity of the holy shrine of the Imám Riḍá in Mashhad. Within its precincts he pursued with undiminished zest the course of his labours. By resolving the intricacies that agitated the minds of the seekers, he continued to prepare the way for the advent of the coming Manifestation. In that city he became increasingly conscious that the Day which was to witness the birth of the promised One could not be far distant. The promised hour, he felt, was fast approaching.
> (*The Dawn-Breakers*, pp. 11–12)

Shaykh Aḥmad then traveled accompanied by Siyyid Káẓim to Núr and Tehran, where he was the guest of Fath-'Ali Sháh, king of Persia. He then traveled to the province of Kirmánsháh (in the western part of Iran) and stayed there for several years as the guest of the governor of Kirmánsháh, Prince Muḥammad-'Alí Mírzá, the Shah's eldest son. After the death of Prince Muḥammad-'Alí Mírzá he returned to Iraq and after several years traveled to and resided in Medina, where he passed away in 1831.

In addition to his general teachings regarding the nearness of the appearance of the Promised One of Islam, Shaykh Aḥmad made some specific prophecies for the time of the advent and even the person of promised one, although in coded language that only his disciples particularly Siyyid Káẓim could decipher. Nabil-i-A'zam records some of these details:

> In the very year the Báb was born, Shaykh Aḥmad suffered the loss of his son, whose name was Shaykh 'Alí. To his disciples who mourned his loss he spoke these words of

comfort: "Grieve not, O my friends, for I have offered up my son, my own 'Alí, as a sacrifice for the 'Alí whose advent we all await. To this end have I reared and prepared him."
(*The Dawn-Breakers*, p. 13)

Ere he departed from Karbilá, he confided to Siyyid Káẓim, his chosen successor, the secret of his mission and instructed him to strive to kindle in every receptive heart the fire that had burned so brightly within him. However much Siyyid Káẓim insisted on accompanying him as far as Najaf, Shaykh Aḥmad refused to comply with his request. "You have no time to lose," were the last words which he addressed to him. . . . "For verily I say, the Hour is drawing nigh, the Hour I have besought God to spare me from witnessing, for the earthquake of the Last Hour will be tremendous. You should pray to God to be spared the overpowering trials of that Day, for neither of us is capable of withstanding its sweeping force. Others, of greater endurance and power, have been destined to bear this stupendous weight, men whose hearts are sanctified from all earthly things, and whose strength is reinforced by the potency of His power."

Having spoken these words, Shaykh Aḥmad bade him farewell, urged him to face valiantly the trials that must needs afflict him, and committed him to the care of God. In Karbilá, Siyyid Káẓim devoted himself to the work initiated by his master, expounded his teachings, defended his Cause, and answered whatever questions perplexed the minds of his disciples. The vigour with which he prosecuted his task inflamed the animosity of the ignorant and envious. . . . The louder their clamour and protestations, the firmer grew the determination of Siyyid Káẓim to prosecute his mission and fulfil his trust. He addressed an epistle to Shaykh Aḥmad, wherein he set forth at length the calumnies that had been uttered against him, and acquainted him with the character and extent of their opposition. In it he ventured to enquire as to how long he was destined to submit to the unrelenting fanaticism of a stubborn and ignorant people, and prayed to be enlightened regarding the time when the promised One was to be made manifest. To this Shaykh Aḥmad replied: "Be assured of the grace of your God. Be not grieved at their doings. The mystery of this Cause must needs be made manifest, and the secret of this Message must needs be divulged.* I can say no more, I can appoint no time. His Cause will be made known after Hin.** 'Ask me not of things which, if revealed unto you, might only pain you.'"

* The Báb, Himself, refers to this passage and confirms it in the "Dalá'il-i-Sab'ih": "The words of the revered Shaykh Aḥmad-i-Aḥsá'i are well known. They contain numerous allusions to the subject of the Manifestation. For example, he has written with his own hand to Siyyid Káẓim-i-Rashtí: 'Just as it is necessary in order to build a house to have suitable ground, so also for this Manifestation must the moment be propitious. But here one cannot give an answer clearly foretelling the moment. Soon we shall know it with certainty.' That which you have heard so often yourself from Siyyid Káẓim, is not that an explanation? Did he not reiterate every minute—'You do not wish then that I should go away so that God may appear?'" ("The Book of the Seven Proofs," translated by A. L. M. Nicolas, p. 58.)

"There is also the anecdote referring to Shaykh Aḥmad-i-Aḥsá'i on his way to Mecca. It has been proven that this anecdote is authentic and hence there is something which is certain. The disciples of the deceased have related the sayings which they have heard and also certain personages were mentioned such as Mullá 'Abdu'l-Kháliq and Murtaḍá-Qulí. Mullá 'Abdu'l-Kháliq relates that the Shaykh said to them one day: 'Pray that you may not be present at the beginning of the Manifestation and of the Return, as there will be many civil wars.' He added: 'If any one of you should still be living at that time, he shall see strange things between the years sixty and sixty-seven. And what strange thing can be more strange than the very Being of the Manifestation? You will be there and you will witness another extraordinary event; that is to say, God, in order to bring about the victory of the Manifestation, will

> raise up a Being who will speak his own thoughts without ever having been instructed by anyone.'"
> (Shoghi Effendi, *The Dawn-Breakers*, p. 17, Footnote 2. The above English translation is quoted from the book, Translation of French Foot-Notes of the Dawn-Breakers, By Emily McBride Pèrigord, Bahá'í Publishing Trust, Wilmette, Illinois, p. 3)
>
> ** According to the Abjad notation, the numerical value of the word "Ḥín" is 68. It was in the year 1268 A.H. that Bahá'u'lláh, while confined in the Síyáh-Chál of Ṭihrán received the first intimations of His Divine Mission. Of this He hinted in the odes which He revealed in that year.
> (Shoghi Effendi, *The Dawn-Breakers*, p. 18)

Bahá'u'lláh in one of His books (Kitáb-i-Badi'[80]) mentions that Shaykh Aḥmad-i-Aḥsá'i said to a merchant, who was one of his admirers, "give my regards to Siyyid-i-Báb." The merchant wondered what the Shaykh meant by Siyyid-i-Báb, until after the Báb's declaration (some fifteen to twenty years later) when His fame under the name "Siyyid-i-Báb" was spread all over Iran and Iraq. The merchant hearing the name and learning of the station and claims of the Báb, attained the presence of the Báb and conveyed Shaykh Aḥmad's regards and greetings to the Báb.
(Source: 'Abdu'l-Ḥamíd Ishráq-Khávari, *Qámus-i-Íqán, Vol 4*, p. 1646)

Bahá'u'lláh also confirmed that:

> The followers of Shaykh-i-Aḥsá'i (Shaykh Aḥmad) have, by the aid of God, apprehended that which was veiled from

[80] [t]he Kitáb-i-Badi', His [Bahá'u'lláh's] apologia, written to refute the accusations levelled against Him by Mírzá Mihdiy-i-Rashtí, corresponding to the Kitáb-i-Íqán, revealed in defense of the Bábí Revelation;
(Shoghi Effendi, God Passes By, p. 171)

The Kitáb-i-Badi' is Bahá'u'lláh's apologia written in defence of His Faith and to demonstrate the validity and the truth of His Own Mission. It is mainly in Persian, but also contains many passages in Arabic.
(Adib Taherzadeh, The Revelation of Baha'u'llah v 2, p. 369)

The Kitab-i-Badi' was revealed in Adrianople in response to accusations and objections made by Mírzá Mihdiy-i-Rashtí who was a follower of Mírzá Yaḥyá (Azal). The objections were centerd upon the notion that the dispensation of Bayán (the Bábí Faith) should have lasted 2000 years instead of nine years.

> the comprehension of others, and of which they remained deprived.
> (Epistle to the Son of the Wolf, p. 120)

Siyyid Káẓim-i-Rashtí, the second of the "twin luminous lights" came from a family of merchants from north of Iran who resided in the area around Caspian Sea. Regarding his life before joining Shaykh Aḥmad -i-Aḥsá'i, Nabil-i-A'zam states:

> This Siyyid Káẓim had already, from his early boyhood, shown signs of remarkable intellectual power and spiritual insight. He was unique among those of his own rank and age. At the age of eleven, he had committed to memory the whole of the Qur'án. At the age of fourteen, he had learned by heart a prodigious number of prayers and recognized traditions of Muḥammad. At the age of eighteen, he had composed a commentary on a verse of the Qur'án known as the Áyatu'l-Kursi, which had excited the wonder and the admiration of the most learned of his day. His piety, the gentleness of his character, and his humility were such that all who knew him, whether young or old, were profoundly impressed.
> (*The Dawn-Breakers*, p. 10)

In the year 1231 A.H. (1815–1816) Shaykh Aḥmad was preparing to leave Yazd and travel to Mashhad in the province of Khurásán. Siyyid Káẓim who was twenty-two years old left his home and traveled to Yazd to join him. Nabil-i-A'zam states:

> During those days when Shaykh Aḥmad was preparing to depart from Yazd, Siyyid Káẓim-i-Rashtí,[81] that other luminary of Divine guidance, set out from his native

[81] "His [Siyyid Kázim's] family were merchants of repute. His father was named Áqá Siyyid Qásim. When twelve years old, he was living at Ardibíl near the tomb of Shaykh Safi'u'd-Din Ishaq, the descendant of the seventh Imám Músá Kázim and the ancestor of the Safaví kings. One night in a dream it was signified to him by one of the illustrious progenitors of the buried saint that he should put himself under the spiritual guidance of Shaykh Aḥmad-i-Ahsá'í, who was at this time residing at Yazd. He accordingly proceeded thither and enrolled himself amongst the disciples of Shaykh Aḥmad, in whose doctrine he attained such eminence that on the Shaykh's death he was unanimously recognised as the leader of the Shaykhí school." ("A Traveller's Narrative," Note E, p. 238)

> province of Gílán with the object of visiting Shaykh Aḥmad, ere the latter undertook his pilgrimage to Khurásán. In the course of his first interview with him, Shaykh Aḥmad spoke these words: "I welcome you, O my friend! How long and how eagerly have I waited for you to come and deliver me from the arrogance of this perverse people! . . ."
>
> He had been in the company of Shaykh Aḥmad for only a few weeks, when the latter, turning to him one day, addressed him in these words: "Remain in your house and cease attending my lectures. Such of my disciples as may feel perplexed will turn henceforth to you, and will seek to obtain from you directly whatsoever assistance they may require. You will, through the knowledge which the Lord your God has bestowed upon you, resolve their problems and tranquillise their hearts. By the power of your utterance you will help to revive the sorely neglected Faith of Muḥammad, your illustrious ancestor." These words addressed to Siyyid Káẓim excited the resentment and kindled the envy of the prominent disciples of Shaykh Aḥmad, among whom figured Mullá Muḥammad-i-Mámáqání and Mullá 'Abdu'l-Kháliq-i-Yazdí. So compelling was the dignity of Siyyid Káẓim, however, and so remarkable were the evidences of his knowledge and wisdom, that these disciples were awed and felt compelled to submit.
> (*The Dawn-Breakers*, pp. 8–11)

As mentioned above, Siyyid Káẓim accompanied Shaykh Aḥmad in his travels and after Shaykh Aḥmad left Karbilá and resided in Medina, he took charge of Shaykh Aḥmad's disciples and continued to lead the Shaykhi movement until the end of his own life. Nabil-i-A'zam in describing the work of Siyyid Káẓim in preparing his followers for the advent of the Promised One states:

> In Karbilá, Siyyid Káẓim devoted himself to the work initiated by his master, expounded his teachings, defended his Cause, and answered whatever questions perplexed the minds of his disciples.
> (*The Dawn-Breakers*, p. 17)

In those days Siyyid Káẓim became increasingly aware of the approach of the Hour at which the promised One was to be revealed. He realised how dense were those veils that hindered the seekers from apprehending the glory of the concealed Manifestation. He accordingly exerted his utmost endeavour to remove gradually, with caution and wisdom, whatever barriers might stand in the way of the full recognition of that Hidden Treasure of God. He repeatedly urged his disciples to bear in mind the fact that He whose advent they were expecting would appear neither from Jábulqá nor from Jábulsá.'[82] He even hinted at His presence in their very midst. "You behold Him with your own eyes," he often observed, "and yet recognise Him not!" To his disciples who questioned him regarding the signs of the Manifestation, he would say: "He is of noble lineage. He is a descendant of the Prophet of God, of the family of Há<u>sh</u>im. He is young in age, and is possessed of innate knowledge. His learning is derived, not from the teachings of <u>Sh</u>ay<u>kh</u> Aḥmad, but from God. My knowledge is but a drop compared with the immensity of His knowledge; my attainments a speck of dust in the face of the wonders of His grace and power. Nay, immeasurable is the difference. He is of medium height, abstains from smoking, and is of extreme devoutness and piety."[83] Certain of the Siyyid's disciples, despite the testimonies of their master, believed him to be the promised One, for in him they recognised the signs to which he was alluding. Among them was a certain Mullá Mihdíy-i-<u>Kh</u>ú'í, who went so far as to make public this belief. Whereupon the Siyyid was sore displeased, and would have cast him out from the company of his chosen followers had he not begged forgiveness and expressed his repentance for his action.
(*The Dawn-Breakers*, pp. 24–25)

---

[82]See the Introduction.

[83]"There seems to be conclusive evidence that Siyyid Kázim adverted often near the close of life to the divine Manifestation which he believed to be at hand. He was fond of saying, 'I see him as the rising sun.'" (Dr. T. K. Cheyne's the Reconciliation of Races and Religions," p. 19.)
(Shoghi Effendi, *The Dawn-Breakers*, p. 25)

Toward the end of his life, Siyyid Káẓim advised his disciples to go in search of the Promised One Who's advent was at hand. Nabil-i-A'zam states:

> And as the days of Siyyid Káẓim drew to a close, he, whenever he met his disciples, whether in private converse or public discourse, exhorted them, saying: "O my beloved companions! Beware, beware, lest after me the world's fleeting vanities beguile you. Beware lest you wax haughty and forgetful of God. It is incumbent upon you to renounce all comfort, all earthly possessions and kindred, in your quest of Him who is the Desire of your hearts and of mine. Scatter far and wide, detach yourselves from all earthly things, and humbly and prayerfully beseech your Lord to sustain and guide you. Never relax in your determination to seek and find Him who is concealed behind the veils of glory. Persevere till the time when He, who is your true Guide and Master, will graciously aid you and enable you to recognise Him.
> (*The Dawn-Breakers*, pp. 24–25)

Siyyid Káẓim passed away on December 31, 1843, after which a significant number of his faithful disciples who were prepared by him for the immanent approach of the time of the advent, left Karbilá in search of the Promised One.

Shaykh Aḥmad-i-Aḥsá'i and Siyyid Káẓim-i-Rashtí were the two luminaries in the Middle East, who, based on the proper interpretation of the prophecies of the Qur'an and Islamic traditions, not only predicted the time of the advent, but also provided their followers with clues regarding the person of the new Manifestation and the non-literal interpretations of the signs of the advent. The majority of the Báb's first group of disciples known as "The Letters of Living," were Siyyid Káẓim's followers.

There were others in other parts of the world especially in the West, who, based on Biblical prophecies, particularly those of the Old Testament Book of Daniel and the New Testament Book of Revelation, thought that the second advent of Christ was near and predicted the time of the advent. Among them, Isaac Newton the greatest scientist of the eighteenth century who presented the concept of gravitational field, Johann Bengel, Edward Irving, Joseph Wolf, Heinrich Kelber, William Davis, Alexander Campbell and William Miller, were prominent and achieved international fame. These biblical scholars who were concerned with and made predictions regarding the time of the Second Advent are called Adventists.

Among the Adventists William Miller[84] who in 1836 made very specific prediction and indicated that the Second Advent will take place some times in spring 1843 to spring 1844, became the most prominent preacher of the Second Coming and found a great following. Miller's lectures and writings such as those that appeared in the publication "Evidence From Scripture and History of the Second Coming of Christ About the Year 1843[85]," created great sense of expectation among the masses. Millions of people in America, Europe and other areas of the world prepared to see and receive Christ as He descended from heaven.

When the spring of 1844 arrived and past and the signs of the coming of Christ did not appear, the date was revised to be the fall of 1844. However, as the year 1844 ended without Christ riding on the clouds and descending from heaven followed by the multitude of angels and saints, the literal nonfulfillment of the Second Advent prophecies was called "the Great Disappointment." However, in spite of disappointment, several groups of Adventists continued to believe that their interpretation of the prophecies and their determination of the date of the second coming were correct. They did not know why Christ did not appear in 1844, but believed that He might decide to appear any day. Among the groups that continued their Adventist belief and expectations to present time,

---

[84] William Miller (February 15, 1782–December 20, 1849) was an American Baptist preacher who is credited with beginning the mid-19th century North American religious movement known as the Millerites. After his prophecies of the Second Coming did not occur as expected in the 1840s, new heirs of his message emerged, including the Advent Christians (186 0) and the Seventh-day Adventists (1863). Later movements found inspiration in Miller's emphasis on Bible prophecy and the Bahá'í faith believes his predictions of 1844 events to be accurate.
(Based on entry for William Miller in Wikipedia, the free encyclopedia)

[85] Evidence From Scripture and History of the Second Coming of Christ About the Year 1843, In a Course of Lectures, By William Miller, Boston, Published By Moses A. Dow, 107 Hanover Street. 1841.

"The Seventh-Day Adventists" and "Jehovah's Witnesses" are well known.

Approximately two decades after the Great Disappointment, a group of German Adventists called "German Templars" who based on their interpretation of the prophecies were expecting the return of Christ to take place in Holy Land at Mount Carmel, the "Vineyard of God" which is overlooking the plain of Sharon, moved to that area and established a community at the foot of Mount Carmel.

The first half of the 1800s was also witnessing the birth of other Adventist churches in America, the most important one of those was the Church of Jesus Christ of the Latter-Day Saints (LDS Church also known as the Mormon Church). Joseph Smith the prophet founder of the LDS Church believed that they were living in the latter-days, the days just before the end of times and second coming of Jesus. That is the reason why he named his church "the Church of Jesus Christ of the Latter-Day Saints." In his book the "*Doctrines and Covenants*" Joseph Smith wrote:

> I was once praying very earnestly to know the time of the coming of the Son of Man, when I heard a voice repeat the following: Joseph, my son, if thou livest until thou art eighty-five years old, thou shalt see the face of the Son of Man; therefore let this suffice, and trouble me no more on this matter.
> (Joseph Smith, *Doctrines and Covenants, Section 130, No. 14–15 & 17, https://www.lds.org/scriptures/dc-testament/dc/130.18?lang=eng*)

Joseph Smith was born in Vermont in 1805 and was killed during a gun fight while he was jailed in Carthage, Illinois in June 1844 and did not live to the age of eighty five[86]. This statement in the *Doctrines and Covenants* places the time of the Second Advent in the year 1890. It is interesting to note that Bahá'u'lláh who was living in exile in Holy Land since 1868, visited the Mont Carmel and Templar colony in 1890.

For more details regarding the Adventist movement see Appendix II, Note No. 318.

[86] Fawn M. Brodie, "*No Man Knows My History, the life of Joseph Smith,*" pp. 390–95.

As mentioned above, both the middle-eastern and western Adventists predicted the time of the advent correctly, and in the case of William Miller with great precision. However, the difference between the disciples of Siyyid Káẓim who recognized the Báb and realized the fulfilment of the prophecies and the western Adventists especially William Miller and his followers who experienced the great Disappointment, was that the latter group were expecting the literal fulfilment of the prophecies.

Paragraph No. 73:

From all that We have stated it hath become clear and manifest that before the revelation of each of the Mirrors reflecting the divine Essence, the signs heralding their advent must needs be revealed in the visible heaven as well as in the invisible, wherein is the seat of the sun of knowledge, of the moon of wisdom, and of the stars of understanding and utterance.[319]

319. As mentioned above (see Note Nos. 5 and 199), Bahá'u'lláh teaches that religion and Revelation of God are the spiritual counterpart of the physical heaven, i.e, religion is the spiritual or invisible heaven. The Manifestation of God is like the sun in this spiritual invisible heaven.

The sign of the invisible heaven must needs be revealed in the person of that perfect man[320] **who, before each Manifestation appeareth, educateth, and prepareth the souls of men for the advent of the divine Luminary, the Light of the unity of God amongst men.**

320. The term "perfect man" here seems to be referring to those pure and illumined people who through their spiritual insight and deep understanding of the prophecies of the sacred books, develop the ability to not only sense the approaching of the time of the advent, but also prepare people of their time to recognize the Manifestation of God. Elsewhere in the Bahá'i Writings the term perfect man has also been used as a reference to the Manifestation of God. 'Abdu'l-Bahá states:

> In the human kingdom we find all the attributes of the lower worlds, with much more added thereto. Man is the sum of every previous creation, for he contains them all. To man is given the special gift of the intellect by which he is able to receive a larger share of the light Divine. The Perfect Man is as a polished mirror reflecting the Sun of Truth, manifesting the attributes of God.
> (*Paris Talks*, p. 25)

> . . . the full splendour of the perfections, bounties, and attributes of the Divinity shines forth from the reality of the Perfect Man, that is, that unique Individual Who is the universal Manifestation of God. For the other beings have each received only a portion of that light, but the universal Manifestation of God is the mirror held before this Sun, and the latter manifests itself therein with all its perfections, attributes, signs, and effects.
> (*Some Answered Questions*, no. 59.8)

Paragraph No. 74:

And now, with reference to His words: "And then shall all the tribes of the earth mourn, and they shall see the Son of man coming in the clouds of heaven with power and great glory[321]

321. This is from the Gospel of Matthew :

> Immediately after the tribulation of those days shall the sun be darkened, and the moon shall not give her light, and the stars shall fall from heaven, and the powers of the heavens shall be shaken: And then shall appear the sign of the Son of man in heaven: and then shall all the tribes of the earth mourn, and they shall see the Son of man coming in the clouds of heaven with power and great glory.
> (Matthew 24:29–30)

In the sentences that follow in this paragraph, Bahá'u'lláh describes the meanings of the allegorical terms such as the "sun," "the moon," and "the stars" and explains the significance of the metaphors concerning the darkening of the sun and falling of the stars. Many Christians believe, however, that these are the signs that predicate the second coming of Christ and should be interpreted literally and not metaphorically.

It is interesting to note that a very similar set of prophecies and signs were given to predicate the coming of the promised Messiah for the Jews. The Jews in addition to the physical and corporal descent of Elijah (see above, Note Nos. 19, 53) were expecting the same occurrences of the darkening of the sun and moon and falling of the stars to take place indicating and heralding the appearance of their Messiah (for details see Note No. 64 above).

Thereupon, they will behold the countenance of the promised One, the adored Beauty, descending from heaven and riding upon the clouds.[322]

322. ‘Abdú’l-Bahá explains what the metaphor of the cloud means:

> Christ said, “They shall see the Son of Man coming in the clouds of Heaven.”[87] Bahá'u'lláh said, “When Christ came for the first time He came upon the clouds.” Christ said that He had come from the sky, from Heaven[88]—that He came forth from God—while He was born of Mary, His Mother. But when He declared that He had come from Heaven, it is clear that He did not mean the blue firmament but that He spoke of the Heaven of the Kingdom of God, and that from this Heaven He descended upon the clouds. As clouds are obstacles to the shining of the sun, so the clouds of the world of humanity hid from the eyes of men the radiance of the Divinity of Christ. Men said, “He is of Nazareth, born of Mary, we know Him and we know his brethren.[89] What

[87] (Matthew 24:30 and 16:27)

[88] And no man hath ascended up to heaven, but he that came down from heaven, even the Son of man which is in heaven.
(John 3:13)

[89] And they said, Is not this Jesus, the son of Joseph, whose father and mother we know? how is it then that he saith, I came down from heaven?
(John 6: 42)

can He mean? What is He saying? That He came forth from God?"

The Body of Christ was born of Mary of Nazareth, but the Spirit was of God. The capacities of His human body were limited but the strength of His spirit was vast, infinite, immeasurable. Men asked, "Why does He say He is of God?" If they had understood the reality of Christ, they would have known that the body of His humanity was a cloud that hid His Divinity. The world only saw His human form, and therefore wondered how He could have "come down from Heaven."

Bahá'u'lláh said, "Even as the clouds hide the sun and the sky from our gaze, even so did the humanity of Christ hide from men His real Divine character." I hope that you will turn with unclouded eyes towards the Sun of Truth, beholding not the things of earth, lest your hearts be attracted to the worthless and passing pleasures of the world; let that Sun give you of His strength, then will not the clouds of prejudice veil His illumination from your eyes! Then will the Sun be without clouds for you.

Breathe the air of purity. May you each and all share in the Divine Bounties of the Kingdom of Heaven. May the world be for you no obstacle hiding the truth from your sight, as the human body of Christ hid His Divinity from the people of His day. May you receive the clear vision of the Holy Spirit, so that your hearts may be illumined and able to recognize the Sun of Truth shining through all material clouds, His splendor flooding the universe. Let not the things of the body obscure the celestial light of the spirit, so

---

Is not this the carpenter, the son of Mary, the brother of James, and Joses, and of Juda, and Simon? and are not his sisters here with us?
(Mark 6:3)

Is not this the carpenter's son? is not his mother called Mary? and his brethren, James, and Joses, and Simon, and Judas?
(Matthew 13:55)

that, by the Divine Bounty, you may enter with the children of God into His Eternal Kingdom.
This is my prayer for you all.
('Abdu'l-Bahá, *Paris Talks*, p. 43)

These ancient Beings, though delivered from the womb of their mother, have in reality descended from the heaven[323] of the will of God.

323. The allegorical concept of ascending to and descending from heaven found in the sacred books of the past religions has largely been interpreted literally by the followers of those religions. The expectation for the Promised One to physically and with his corporal body descend from the heaven is common among Jews, Christians and Muslims. Jews have been expecting Elijah to descend from heaven before the appearance of their Messiah. Likewise there are Christians expecting Jesus to physically descend from heaven in his second coming, and Muslims who are expecting their Promised One (Mahdi) to appear and for Christ to descend from heaven before the Day of Resurrection at the end of time.

As mentioned above in Note No. 19, according to the Old Testament, Elijah (Elias) was taken to heaven in his corporeal body:

> And it came to pass, when they were gone over, that Elijah said unto Elisha, Ask what I shall do for thee, before I be taken away from thee. And Elisha said, I pray thee, let a double portion of thy spirit be upon me. And he said, Thou hast asked a hard thing: nevertheless, if thou see me when I am taken from thee, it shall be so unto thee; but if not, it shall not be so. And it came to pass, as they still went on, and talked, that, behold, there appeared a chariot of fire, and horses of fire, and parted them both asunder; and Elijah went up by a whirlwind into heaven. And Elisha saw it, and he cried, My father, my father, the chariot of Israel, and the horsemen thereof. And he saw him no more: and he took hold of his own clothes, and rent them in two pieces.
> (4 Kings 2:9–12)

Jews were expecting Elijah to return to Earth at the time of the coming of the Messiah:

> Behold, I will send you Elijah the prophet before the coming of the great and dreadful day of the LORD:
> (Malachi 4:5)

This is the reason that after the episode of the Transfiguration, when Christ's disciples realized that He was the promised Messiah, they asked Him about the coming of Elijah, which was supposed to take place prior to His appearance and Jesus said that John the Baptist was Elijah:

> And his disciples asked him, saying, Why then say the scribes that Elias must first come? And Jesus answered and said unto them, Elias truly shall first come, and restore all things. But I say unto you, That Elias is come already, and they knew him not, but have done unto him whatsoever they listed. Likewise shall also the Son of man suffer of them. Then the disciples understood that he spake unto them of John the Baptist.
> (Matthew 17:13)

When speaking about John the Baptist, Jesus stated:

> And as they departed, Jesus began to say unto the multitudes concerning John, What went ye out into the wilderness to see? A reed shaken with the wind? But what went ye out for to see? A man clothed in soft raiment? behold, they that wear soft clothing are in kings' houses. But what went ye out for to see? A prophet? yea, I say unto you, and more than a prophet. For this is he, of whom it is written, Behold, I send my messenger before thy face, which shall prepare thy way before thee.
>
> Verily I say unto you, Among them that are born of women there hath not risen a greater than John the Baptist: notwithstanding he that is least in the kingdom of heaven is greater than he. And from the days of John the Baptist until now the kingdom of heaven suffereth violence, and the violent take it by force. For all the prophets and the law prophesied until John. And if ye will receive it, this is Elias,

> which was for to come. He that hath ears to hear, let him hear.
> (Matthew 11:7–15)

In these statements, Jesus interprets and explains the meaning of the allegorical prophecy of the descent of Elijah from heaven before His (the Messiah's) coming. The Jews were expecting that Elijah who was taken in his physical corporal body to heaven, would return/descend to earth in his physical corporal body to prepare people for the coming of Messiah. By this logic, a person who was a contemporary of Jesus and was born of a mother (a woman) and grew among them in their society, could not be Elijah. Nevertheless, Jesus stated that John the Baptist who was born of a woman was "Elias, which was for to come." He therefore, demonstrated that the fulfilment of the prophecy of coming of Elias was conditioned upon people's understanding of the meaning of "heaven," and how a person who was born of a woman could have come from heaven. He further stated:

> And if ye will receive it, this is Elias, which was for to come. He that hath ears to hear, let him hear.
> (Matthew 11:14)

It seems that in this passage Jesus is describing the spiritual hearing, which results in acceptance and readiness for understanding (willingness to receive) the real meaning of descending from heaven.

In this paragraph Bahá'u'lláh provides the real meanings of the allegorical terms such as: "the Sun," "the Moon," and "heaven."

'Abdú'l-Bahá states:

> Now, I would like in turn to say a further word on this subject, which is the following. The first coming of Christ was also from heaven, as has been explicitly stated in the Gospel. Even Christ Himself says that the Son of man came down from heaven, and the Son of man is in heaven; and no man hath ascended up to heaven but He that came down from heaven. Thus it is admitted by all that Christ came down from heaven, whereas to outward seeming He came from the womb of Mary. Thus it is admitted by all that

> Christ came down from heaven, whereas to outward seeming He came from the womb of Mary.
> ('Abdu'l-Bahá, *Some Answered Questions*, no. 26.2)

and at every moment traverse the kingdoms of the visible and the invisible.[324]

324. The word "kingdom" in Bahá'i scriptures is used interchangeably with the world and sometimes with realm, station or degree. These kingdoms are called by different names. Four of these kingdoms or worlds are listed in the Seven Valleys:

> Thus, some have said that the world of perpetuity hath neither beginning nor end, and have named the world of eternity as the invisible, impregnable Empyrean. Others have called these the worlds of the Heavenly Court (Láhút), of the Empyrean Heaven (Jabarút), of the Kingdom of the Angels (Malakút), and of the mortal world (Násút).
> (Bahá'u'lláh, The Seven Valleys and The Four Valleys, p. 24)

These four worlds are also mentioned in one of the famous Tablets of Bahá'u'lláh, the *Láwḥ-i-Kullu't-Ṭa'ám* (The Tablet of All Food), which was revealed during the Baghdád period. Adib Taherzadeh provides the following description of the circumstances of its revelation:

> Shortly before Bahá'u'lláh's departure for Kurdistán, the *Láwḥ-i-Kullu'ṭ- Ṭa'ám* (Tablet of All Food) was revealed by Him. This was addressed to Ḥájí Mírzá Kamálu'd-Dín of the town of Naráq. . . . Ḥájí Mírzá Kamálu'd-Dín was a man of culture and knowledge, and had been converted to the Bábí Faith by a certain Mullá Ja'far, who had attained the presence of the Báb in Káshán. He travelled to Baghdád in order to meet and receive enlightenment from Mírzá Yaḥyá, the nominee of the Báb. Unable to trace him, he wrote a letter to Bahá'u'lláh requesting Him to ask Mírzá Yaḥyá for a commentary on the following verse of the *Qur'án* by which he had been puzzled: 'All food was allowed to the children of Israel except what Israel made unlawful for itself.' Bahá'u'lláh passed on this letter to Mírzá Yaḥyá whose inadequate and superficial answer caused Ḥájí Mírzá Kamálu'd-Dín to become completely

> disillusioned and to lose all faith in him. Ḥájí Mírzá Kamálu'd-Dín then turned to Bahá'u'lláh and requested Him to enlighten him on the subject. The *Tablet of Kullu'ṭ-Ṭa'ám* was revealed in Arabic in answer to his question.
>
> Upon receiving and perusing the Tablet, Ḥájí Mírzá Kamálu'd-Dín was inspired and uplifted; his heart was filled with a new spirit and his soul became illumined by the light of the New Day. Through this Tablet he found the Source of all knowledge and recognized the station of Bahá'u'lláh as 'Him Whom God shall make manifest'. On attaining this state of recognition, he declared his belief and pledged his loyalty to Bahá'u'lláh, Who cautioned him not to divulge to anyone the truth he had found. He was directed to return to his native town of Naráq, and to share his Tablet with the friends there. This he did, serving the Cause of Bahá'u'lláh with devotion and self-sacrifice until his death in Naráq about the year A.D. 1881.
> (Adib Taherzadeh, *The Revelation of Bahá'u'lláh*, Vol. 1, pp. 55–56)

Regarding the four worlds mentioned in this Tablet, Taherzadeh provides the following brief explanations:

> Because the *Tablet of Kullu'ṭ- Ṭa'ám* is not translated into English in its entirety, it is not possible adequately to convey its significance. The verse of the *Qur'án* concerning food and the children of Israel was apparently revealed in answer to the Jews' assertion that the laws of Islam on the prohibition of certain foods, contrary to the claims of the Muslims, did not conform to Jewish laws. Bahá'u'lláh explained that this verse in the spiritual worlds of God has infinite meanings, most of which are beyond the comprehension of man, and that He could, through His All-encompassing knowledge, continue to reveal them for many years. But He elucidated some of these, including the spiritual meaning of 'food', and in so doing unveiled in an infinitesimal measure the glory, the mystery and the vastness of the spiritual worlds of God which are without limit and far beyond the understanding of men.

Of these worlds He mentioned four in this Tablet. To gain some appreciation of their mysteries, let us turn our thoughts to God's creation on this earth, where different kingdoms exist together, each one fulfilling its particular purpose. And let us consider the human being who, in this life, functions on three different levels simultaneously. In relation to the lower kingdoms, such as the vegetable and animal, man is superior and dominant. Within his own kingdom, however, man is created to live in unity with his fellow men; whereas, in relation to the Manifestations of God, he is vastly inferior. In this example it can be seen that although man remains the same being, he manifests three degrees of qualities and attributes: those of unity, of inferiority and superiority.

Likewise, the spiritual worlds of God mentioned in this Tablet are of different degrees. The world of Háhút is described by Bahá'u'lláh as the Heaven of Oneness, the realm of the Divine Being, the imperishable Essence, a realm so exalted that even the Manifestations of God are unable to understand it. Bahá'u'lláh has written in one of His Tablets:

> From time immemorial, He, the Divine Being, hath been veiled in the ineffable sanctity of His exalted Self, and will everlastingly continue to be wrapt in the impenetrable mystery of His unknowable Essence. . . Ten thousand Prophets, each a Moses, are thunderstruck upon the Sinai of their search at God's forbidding voice, 'Thou shalt never behold Me!'; whilst a myriad Messengers, each as great as Jesus, stand dismayed upon their heavenly thrones by the interdiction 'Mine Essence thou shalt never apprehend!'

The next is the world of Láhút which is the plane of Divinity, the Heavenly Court. In the Writings of Bahá'u'lláh it appears that the realm of Láhút is perhaps the world of God in relation to His Manifestations and Chosen Ones. Immersed in the ocean of His Presence, They claim no station for Themselves on this plane and are as utter nothingness in relation to Him. In this realm no one is identified with God and the designation "He alone, and no one else beside Him, is God" becomes manifest here.

Yet another spiritual world which Bahá'u'lláh describes in this Tablet is that of Jabarút, the All-Highest Dominion. The station of those who abide therein is closely identified with God, insofar as they manifest all the attributes of God, speak with His voice and are united with Him. This world appears to be the realm in which God's Chosen Ones, in relation to created things, are invested with His authority.

In the Writings of Bahá'u'lláh there are many statements concerning the dual station of the Manifestations of God and His Chosen Ones. In relation to God, these Holy Souls appear as utter nothingness, but in relation to the world of creation They are endowed with all the attributes of God and are closely identified with Him. As Bahá'u'lláh has stated in one of His prayers:

> When I contemplate, O my God, the relationship that bindeth me to Thee, I am moved to proclaim to all created things 'verily I am God!'; and when I consider my own self, lo, I find it coarser than clay![90]

Similar statements have also been made in Islam. The following tradition attributed to Muḥammad, the Prophet of Islam, clearly indicates the dual nature of the Messengers of God. 'Manifold are Our relationships with God. At one time, We are He Himself, and He is We Ourself. At another He is that He is, and We are that We are.'[91]

Another plane in the spiritual worlds of God is that of Malakút, the Kingdom of God, often referred to by the Prophets of the past. In the Tablet of *Kullu'ṭ- Ṭa'ám*, Bahá'u'lláh has described it as the Heaven of Justice.

---

[90] See The Kitáb-i-Aqdas, note 160, p. 234.

[91] This tradition is quoted by Bahá'u'lláh in Epistle to the Son of the Wolf, p. 43, and *Gleanings from the Writings of Bahá'u'lláh*, pp. 66–67.

> Apart from these four spiritual worlds, Bahá'u'lláh also refers in this Tablet to the realm of Násút—this mortal world—which He describes as the Heaven of Bounty. In many of His Tablets He has confirmed that both the human world and Divine Revelation have come into being through the bounty of God alone, and that if His bounty were to be replaced for one moment by the operation of His justice, the whole of creation would cease to exist. (Adib Taherzadeh, *The Revelation of Bahá'u'lláh*, Vol. 1, pp. 57–59)

Based on the above explanations, it seems that the invisible kingdoms are the spiritual kingdoms and the visible kingdom is the physical world, and the Manifestations of God are simultaneously present in and traverse all these kingdoms. Bahá'u'lláh's explanations clarify Jesus' statement in the Gospel of John 3:13:

> And no man hath ascended up to heaven, but he that came down from heaven, even the Son of man which is in heaven.

The verses of this kind serve to demonstrate how Jesus could have come from heaven while also being born from a mother and how He could be in heaven while He was standing on earth.

Paragraph No. 75:

In the utterances of the divine Luminaries the term "heaven" hath been applied to many and divers things; such as the "heaven of Command," the "heaven of Will," the "heaven of the divine Purpose," the "heaven of divine Knowledge," the "heaven of Certitude," the "heaven of Utterance," the "heaven of Revelation," the "heaven of Concealment," and the like.[325]

325. Bahá'u'lláh here lists several examples of the symbolic use of the term "heaven." This term has also been used as the symbol of divine Revelation in the Gospels.

> In those days came John the Baptist, preaching in the wilderness of Judaea, And saying, Repent ye: for the kingdom of heaven is at hand.
> (Matthew 3:1–2)

The kingdom of heaven that was at hand was the appearance of Jesus and the Revelation and ministry of Christ.

> From that time Jesus began to preach, and to say, Repent: for the kingdom of heaven is at hand.
> (Matthew 4:17)

> These twelve [His disciples] Jesus sent forth, and commanded them, saying, Go not into the way of the Gentiles, and into any city of the Samaritans enter ye not: But go rather to the lost sheep of the house of Israel. And as ye go, preach, saying, The kingdom of heaven is at hand.
> (Matthew 10:5–7)

Jesus uses the term heaven in conjunction with other symbolic terms such as bread, water, blood, and flesh:

> For the bread of God is he which cometh down from heaven, and giveth life unto the world. Then said they unto him, Lord, evermore give us this bread. And Jesus said unto them, I am the bread of life: he that cometh to me shall never hunger; and he that believeth on me shall never thirst. …For I came down from heaven, not to do mine own will, but the will of him that sent me. And this is the Father's will which hath sent me, that of all which he hath given me I should lose nothing, but should raise it up again at the last day. And this is the will of him that sent me, that every one which seeth the Son, and believeth on him, may have everlasting life: and I will raise him up at the last day. The Jews then murmured at him, because he said, I am the bread which came down from heaven.
> (John 6:33–41)

He also said:

> Your fathers did eat manna in the wilderness, and are dead. This is the bread which cometh down from heaven, that a man may eat thereof, and not die. I am the living bread which came down from heaven: if any man eat of this bread, he shall live for ever: and the bread that I will give is my flesh, which I will give for the life of the world. The Jews therefore strove among themselves, saying, How can

> this man give us his flesh to eat? Then Jesus said unto them, Verily, verily, I say unto you, Except ye eat the flesh of the Son of man, and drink his blood, ye have no life in you. Whoso eateth my flesh, and drinketh my blood, hath eternal life; and I will raise him up at the last day. For my flesh is meat indeed, and my blood is drink indeed. He that eateth my flesh, and drinketh my blood, dwelleth in me, and I in him. As the living Father hath sent me, and I live by the Father: so he that eateth me, even he shall live by me. This is that bread which came down from heaven: not as your fathers did eat manna, and are dead: he that eateth of this bread shall live for ever.
> (John 6:49–58)

It is interesting to note that although the symbolic nature of words such as "bread," "flesh," "blood" and phrases such as "dwelling in Jesus" that are used in association with "heaven" in these statements are well understood by all Christians, many ignore this close and clear association and do not consider the symbolic nature of the word "heaven" as used in the Gospels. Muslims have the same type of misunderstanding and Bahá'u'lláh clarifies this by citing the verse from the Qur'án.

The term "heaven" with different meanings as listed above has also appeared in many places in the Writings of Bahá'u'lláh. Examples of several uses of the term are listed below:

The "heaven of Command":

> The second glad tidings: it is sanctioned that all the nations of the world consort with each other with joy and fragrance. Consort ye, O people, with all religions with joy and fragrance! Thus hath the orb of permission and desire shone forth from the horizon of the heaven of the command of God, the lord of the creatures.
> (*Tablets of Bahá'u'lláh,* p. 22)

The "heaven of Will":

> If any man were to meditate on that which the Scriptures, sent down from the heaven of God's holy Will, have revealed, he would readily recognize that their purpose is

> that all men shall be regarded as one soul, so that the seal bearing the words 'The Kingdom shall be God's' may be stamped on every heart, and the light of Divine bounty, of grace, and mercy may envelop all mankind.
> (Bahá'u'lláh, *Tablets of Bahá'u'lláh*, p. 161)

The "heaven of immutable purpose":

> Magnified, O Lord my God, be Thy Name, whereby the trees of the garden of Thy Revelation have been clad with verdure, and been made to yield the fruits of holiness during this Springtime when the sweet savors of Thy favors and blessings have been wafted over all things, and caused them to bring forth whatsoever had been preordained for them in the Kingdom of Thine irrevocable decree and the Heaven of Thine immutable purpose. I beseech Thee by this very Name not to suffer me to be far from the court of Thy holiness, nor debarred from the exalted sanctuary of Thy unity and oneness.
> (Bahá'u'lláh, *Prayers and Meditations*, p. 160)

The "heaven of divine Knowledge":

> Wherefore, O My servants, defile not your wings with the clay of waywardness and vain desires, and suffer them not to be stained with the dust of envy and hate, that ye may not be hindered from soaring in the heavens of My divine knowledge.
> (Bahá'u'lláh, *Gleanings from the Writings of Bahá'u'lláh*, p. 327)

The "heaven of Certitude":

> He it is Who hath unveiled to your eyes the treasures of His knowledge, and caused you to ascend unto the heaven of certitude—the certitude of His resistless, His irrefutable, and most exalted Faith.
> (Bahá'u'lláh, *Gleanings from the Writings of Baha'u'llah*, p. 104)

The "heaven of Utterance":

> That which is conducive to the regeneration of the world and the salvation of the peoples and kindreds of the earth

> hath been sent down from the heaven of the utterance of Him Who is the Desire of the world. Give ye a hearing ear to the counsels of the Pen of Glory. Better is this for you than all that is on the earth. Unto this beareth witness My glorious and wondrous Book.
> (Bahá'u'lláh, *Tablets of Bahá'u'lláh*, p. 222)

The "heaven of Revelation":

> Glory be unto Thee, O Lord of the world and Desire of the nations, O Thou Who hast become manifest in the Greatest Name whereby the pearls of wisdom and utterance have appeared from the shells of the great sea of Thy knowledge, and the heavens of divine revelation have been adorned with the light of the appearance of the Sun of Thy countenance.
> (Bahá'u'lláh, *Tablets of Baha'u'llah*, p. 33)

Wert thou to cleanse the mirror of thy heart from the dust of malice, thou wouldst apprehend the meaning of the symbolic terms revealed by the all-embracing Word of God made manifest in every Dispensation, and wouldst discover the mysteries of divine knowledge. Not, however, until thou consumest with the flame of utter detachment those veils of idle learning, that are current amongst men, canst thou behold the resplendent morn of true knowledge.[326]

326. The veils of idle learning include those opinions and beliefs that the clerics and religious leaders consider religious knowledge and use to create veils that prevent people from embracing the new Manifestations of God. The veils created for Jews by their religious leaders were the literal interpretation of the symbolic prophecies such as expecting the descent of Elijah from the physical heaven and the darkening of the Sun and Moon prior to the appearance of their Messiah who they believed would come with temporal worldly power and authority (See Note Nos. 19, 55, 77 147 and 323). Christian religious leaders also created the same type of veils by misinterpreting symbolic terms such as "heaven," and asserting the corporal ascension of Jesus, as well as creating expectations regarding His second coming prior to which, the stars would fall on earth, the Sun and Moon would be darkened, and He would descend from physical heaven in His corporal body over

the clouds. The same is true of Muslims, who expect their Promised One to appear descending from the physical heaven.

Paragraph No. 76:

Know verily that Knowledge is of two kinds: Divine and Satanic. The one welleth out from the fountain of divine inspiration; the other is but a reflection of vain and obscure thoughts. The source of the former is God Himself; the motive-force of the latter the whisperings of selfish desire.[327]

327. The word knowledge here is the translation of the Arabic and Persian word ‘Ilm علم. A knowledgeable person is called ‘Álem عالم (the one who has ‘Ilm علم). Divine knowledge is the source of the positive knowledge that is the cause of advancement in both the physical and intellectual realms in the human world.

There are many references in the Bahá’í Writings that acknowledge the fact that the source of all positive knowledge is the divine Revelation.

> Through Him the ocean of knowledge hath surged amidst mankind and the river of divine wisdom hath gushed out at the behest of God, the Lord of Days.
> (Bahá'u'lláh, *Tablets of Bahá'u'lláh*, p. 47)

> From the Source of His knowledge countless Luminaries of learning and wisdom have risen, and out of the Paradise of His Pen the breath of the All-Merciful hath continually been wafted to the hearts and souls of men.
> (Bahá'u'lláh, *Gleanings from the Writings of Bahá'u'lláh*, p. 144)

Acquisition of positive knowledge is highly commended in the Bahá’í Faith.

> Knowledge is one of the wondrous gifts of God. It is incumbent upon everyone to acquire it. Such arts and material means as are now manifest have been achieved by virtue of His knowledge and wisdom which have been revealed in Epistles and Tablets through His Most Exalted Pen—a Pen out of whose treasury pearls of wisdom and

> utterance and the arts and crafts of the world are brought to light.
> (Bahá'u'lláh, *Tablets of Bahá'u'lláh*, p. 39)

Bahá'u'lláh defines satanic knowledge as being "a reflection of vain and obscure thoughts," and this is what some leaders of the religions called knowledge. Throughout the Dark Ages in Europe, the priests and fathers of the Church were pursuing useless subjects, superstitions and obscure concepts and were calling it knowledge. An example was the arguments they had about the ascension of Jesus to heaven after He appeared to His disciples. The focus of their discussions centered on whether He ascended with His clothes or if His clothing fell off, and if it did fall off, where did it go? They considered these obscure and useless subjects true science and were torturing and killing the true men of science and knowledge.

> . . . the papal government entirely forgot Christ and occupied itself with earthly dominion and grandeur, with material comforts and luxuries. It put people to death, opposed the diffusion of learning, persecuted men of science, obstructed the light of knowledge, and gave the order to slay and to pillage. Thousands of people, men of science and learning and innocent souls, perished in the prisons of Rome.
> ('Abdu'l-Bahá, *Some Answered Questions*, no. 34.8)

In the Islamic societies in later centuries, the divines were also pursuing vain and obscure thoughts and were calling it knowledge. They were spending hours and days arguing about the number of wings of some angels, or the length of the legs of the horse or donkey that Muḥammad was riding when, according to traditions (Aḥadith), He ascended to heaven. According to those traditions, in the heavens, He met Jesus in the second heaven and Aaron in the fifth heaven and Moses in the sixth heaven. They were wondering whether Aaron was more important than Jesus, Who was called the spirit of God in the Qur'án?

In the Shí'ah communities the clergy and religious leaders are called 'Ulama علما (plural of 'Álem عالم, those who have 'Ilm, علم, meaning knowledge). In majority of cases what these clerics and religious leaders consider knowledge (‘Ilm علم), are obscure and useless matters that begin with words and end in words.

When the Báb arrived at Iṣfáhán and His popularity increased day by day, the important divines (the ‘Ulama) rose in opposition to Him. Nabil states:

> The growing popularity of the Báb aroused the resentment of the ecclesiastical authorities of Iṣfáhán, who viewed with concern and envy the ascendancy which an unlearned Youth was slowly acquiring over the thoughts and consciences of their followers. They firmly believed that unless they rose to stem the tide of popular enthusiasm, the very foundations of their existence would be undermined. (*The Dawn-Breakers*, p. 204)

Some of the divines “began to calumniate the Báb from the pulpit in the most unseemly language.” They said that this unlearned man had no religious knowledge and demanded an encounter to expose his ignorance. Upon hearing this demand, Manú<u>ch</u>ihr <u>Kh</u>án, the Mu‘tamidu’d-Dawlih, the governor of Iṣfáhán invited the important ‘Ulama to come and meet with the Báb. The divines who attended that meeting asked questions to test the Báb’s knowledge (‘Ilm علم) and expose His ignorance. The famous orientalist A. L. M. Nicolas wrote about that meeting and the questions the divines asked. He mentioned that one of them “requested the Báb to elucidate certain abstruse philosophical doctrines” and that another one,

> [Q]uestioned the Báb in order to induce him to explain three miracles which it would suffice to relate in order to enlighten the reader. The first one was the Tiyyu'l-Arḍ, or the immediate transfer of a human being from one part of the world to another very distant point. The Shiites are convinced that the third Imám, Javád, had adopted this easy and economical way of traveling. For example, he betook himself, in the twinkling of an eye, from Medina in Arabia to Tús in <u>Kh</u>urásán.
>
> “The second miracle was the multiple and simultaneous presence of the same person in many different places. ‘Alí

was, at the same moment, host to sixty different people.

"The third miracle was a problem of cosmography which I submit to our astronomers who will certainly relish it. It is said that, during the reign of a tyrant, the heavens revolve rapidly, while during that of an Imám they revolve slowly. First, how could the heavens have two movements and then, what were they doing during the reign of the 'Umayyads and the 'Abbássids? It was the solution of these insanities that they proposed to the Báb!

"I shall not dwell on them any longer but I believe I must here make clear the mentality of the learned Moslems of Persia. And if one should consider that, for nearly one thousand years, the science of Irán rests upon such trash, that men exhaust themselves in continuous research upon such matters, one will easily understand the emptiness and arrogance of all these minds.
"Be that as it may, the reunion was interrupted by the announcement of dinner of which each one partook, after which they returned to their respective homes."
(A. L. M. Nicolas' "Siyyid 'Alí-Muḥammad dit le Báb," pp. 239–240.)
(Shoghi Effendi, *The Dawn-Breakers*, Footnote No. 2 p. 207, in French. The above English translation is quoted from the book, Translation of French Foot-Notes of the Dawn-Breakers, By Emily McBride Pèrigord, Bahá'í Publishing Trust, Wilmette, Illinois)

Not only was A. L. M. Nicolas astonished that those celebrated divines, who were claiming to be the most learned and knowledgeable people of their nation, were asking the Báb to provide "the solution of these insanities" and stated that "I must here make clear the mentality of the learned Moslems of Persia. And if one should consider that, for nearly one thousand years, the science of Irán rests upon such trash, that men exhaust themselves in continuous research upon such matters, one will easily understand the emptiness and arrogance of all these minds." But also I'tiżád-al-Salṭanah ('Ali-Qulí Mírzá) one of the most staunch enemies of the Báb and Bahá'u'lláh who had written a book against the Faith called "Fitna-yi Báb"[92] (Calamity and disturbance

[92] Mutanabbi'ín. Ed. and annotated. 'A. Navá'í as "Fitna-yi Báb", 2d ed. Tehran, 1350 Shamsi, 1971.

caused by the Báb), wrote in his book about the above mentioned meeting, and stated that those divines were small-minded to ask such ridiculous questions of one who claimed to be the Promised One of Islam. Their most important kernel of knowledge was the subject of Tiyyu'l-Arḍ, on which they asked the Báb whether the Imám's legs were so long as to cover that great distance in one or two steps, or the earth was moving so fast under his legs?[93] I'tiżád-al-Salṭanah stated that Manúchihr Khán found these questions so ridiculous that He told the divines that He considers these discussions a waste of time.

These and similar subjects that the divines were and still are calling the knowledge, are prime examples of what Bahá'u'lláh defines "the satanic knowledge" as being "a reflection of vain and obscure thoughts."

Bahá'u'lláh advises everyone to acquire the positive knowledge:

> Arts, crafts and sciences uplift the world of being, and are conducive to its exaltation. Knowledge is as wings to man's life, and a ladder for his ascent. Its acquisition is incumbent upon everyone. The knowledge of such sciences, however, should be acquired as can profit the peoples of the earth, and not those which begin with words and end with words. Great indeed is the claim of scientists and craftsmen on the peoples of the world.
> (Bahá'u'lláh, Epistle to the Son of the Wolf, p. 26)

"Fear ye God; God will teach you;"[328]

328. This verse of the Qur'án appears in other places in the Bahá'í Writings:

---

[93] Nicolas wrote that the "Shiites are convinced that the third Imám, Javád" performed the "Tiyyu'l-Arḍ". However, the third Shi'ah Imám is "Husayn Ibn 'Alí", titled Sayyid ash-Shúhadá (*Master of the Martyrs*) and Imám Javád (Muḥammad Ibn 'Alí al-Taqi, al-Jawad) was the ninth Shi'ah Imám. The Shi'ah attribute this miracle to Imám Javád's father the eight Shi'ah Imám 'Alí Ibn Músa ar-Riḍa also referred to as "Imám Reza", who was summoned by the 'Abbássid Caliph Al-Ma'mun to go from Medina in Arabia to Tús in Khurásán (the northeast region of Iran) to become his Crown Prince and the Tiyyu'l-Arḍ was performed during that trip.

> Fear God and God will give you knowledge, for God hath knowledge of all things.
> (The Qur'án 2:282)

Similar statements are also found in the Bible:

> The fear of the LORD is the beginning of knowledge
> (Proverbs 1:7)

> The fear of the LORD is to hate evil: pride, and arrogancy, and the evil way
> (Proverbs 8:13)

> The fear of the LORD is the beginning of wisdom: and the knowledge of the holy is understanding.
> (Proverbs 9:10)

In the Bahá'í Writings where the favorable motivation for compliance with the commandments is the love for and not the fear of God, the concept of the fear of God may refer to the fear that a believer has of doing something that is not pleasing to God. This fear may imply being mindful of displeasing Him. It is listed among the favorable characteristics:

> Adorn ye the temple of dominion with the ornament of justice and of the fear of God, and its head with the crown of the remembrance of your Lord, the Creator of the heavens.
> (Bahá'u'lláh, The Kitáb-i-Aqdas, ¶88)

> Adorn your heads with the garlands of trustworthiness and fidelity, your hearts with the attire of the fear of God, your tongues with absolute truthfulness, your bodies with the vesture of courtesy.
> (Bahá'u'lláh, The Kitáb-i-Aqdas, ¶120)

It seems that those people who reach the stage that the meaning of fear of God becomes clear in their heart, who feel that God is present in their consciousness, God will enable them to remove the veils of selfish desire, love of position and leadership and material gain that prevent them from gaining true knowledge, and will lead them to recognize the Manifestation of God Who is:

> the Root of Knowledge, and to Him Who is the Fountain thereof,
> (Bahá'u'lláh, *Gleanings from the Writings of Baha'u'llah*, p. 176)

As the Báb stated:

> True knowledge, therefore, is the knowledge of God, and this is none other than the recognition of His Manifestation in each Dispensation.
> (The Báb, *Selections from the Writings of the Báb*, p. 89)

"Knowledge is the most grievous veil between man and his Creator."[329]

329. This statement is very famous among the mystics. It refers to the same kind of knowledge that is based on vain and obscure thoughts which causes arrogance, vainglory and conceit. These characteristics and this kind of knowledge have become the greatest veils between the people and God and prevent them from recognition and submission to the Manifestation of God for their age.

"Cling unto the robe of the Desire of thy heart, and put thou away all shame; bid the worldly wise be gone, however great their name."[330]

330. This poem is by Ibn-i-Fáriḍ an Arabic-language poet. Abú Ḥafaṣ 'Umar Ibn al-S'adí, known as Ibn-i-Fáriḍ, is considered by many scholars the most famous mystic poet in the Arabic language. Born in 1182 AD, he was a contemporary of Shaykh Muḥyi'd-Dín-i-'Arabí. His masterpiece is a long poem of 761 lines, originally named "Naẓm al-Sulúk" (the order or procedure for treading the mystical path), but it is better known as "Qaṣídiy-i-Tá'íyyih" (the Ode of Tá), because each line ends with the letter Tá. This poem was considered unique in its application of complex poetic and literary art in its composition, structure, meter, and rhyme, and is revered for its exploration of profound mystical concepts and ideas. During Bahá'u'lláh's sojourn in Sulaymáníyyih, the divines of Sulaymáníyyih requested Him to

undertake a task, which no one had previously accomplished, of writing a poem in the same rhyme as Qaṣídiy-i-Tá'íyyih.

> This request was complied with, and no less than two thousand verses, in exactly the manner they had specified, were dictated by Him, out of which He selected one hundred and twenty-seven, which He permitted them to keep, deeming the subject matter of the rest premature and unsuitable to the needs of the times. It is these same one hundred and twenty-seven verses that constitute the Qaṣídiy-i-Varqá'íyyih, so familiar to, and widely circulated amongst, His Arabic speaking followers.
> (Shoghi Effendi, *God Passes By*, p. 123)

In this poem Ibn-i-Fáriḍ states that being in true love is not easy and requires sacrifice. If you are a true lover, cling to the robe of your beloved and abandon the doubt, indecisiveness and shame of being in love. Avoid the way of superficial people or people of pretense who are worldly wise, although they appear acceptable and very fine.

Paragraph No. 77:

The heart must needs therefore be cleansed from the idle sayings of men, and sanctified from every earthly affection, so that it may discover the hidden meaning of divine inspiration, and become the treasury of the mysteries of divine knowledge.[331]

331. The importance of cleansing the heart in preparation for receiving spiritual and divine knowledge is a theme that has been repeated in the Kitáb-i-Íqán and many other places in the Bahá'í Writings (see Notes Nos. 10 and 24 above).

> It is incumbent on these servants that they cleanse the heart—which is the wellspring of divine treasures—from every marking, and that they turn away from imitation, which is following the traces of their forefathers and sires,
> (Bahá'u'lláh, The Seven Valleys, p. 5)

A pure heart is as a mirror; cleanse it with the burnish of love and severance from all save God, that the true sun may shine within it and the eternal morning dawn.
(Bahá'u'lláh, The Seven Valleys, p. 21)

Thus hath it been said: "He that treadeth the snow-white Path, and followeth in the footsteps of the Crimson Pillar, shall never attain unto his abode unless his hands are empty of those worldly things cherished by men."[332]

332. Here Bahá'u'lláh quotes a passage from the writings of Shaykh Muḥyi'd-Dín 'Abdú'l Qádir Gilaní (471–561 AH, 1077–1166 AD). He had many titles such as Shaykh-i-Kul (the leader of all) and Ghawth-i-A'ẓam (the most great helper). He is the founder of the Qádiríyyih sect of Ṣúfísm, which has a great number of followers in the Islamic countries. Bahá'u'lláh has also quoted another passage from the writings of the Ghawth-i-A'ẓam in "The Seven Valleys."[94]

In mystic terminology the "snow-white Path," is the path of "Sulúk" or the path of progression toward God and the "Crimson Pillar" is the station of sacrifice in the path of the true beloved (to die from self and live in God). This statement might imply that whoever wants to acquire true knowledge and is moving in the path of progression to reach the point of sacrifice of his self for the true beloved must empty his hands (and his heart) from earthly (worldly) things (to become detached), otherwise he can never achieve his goal.

Paragraph No. 78:

How many the ḥúrís of inner meaning that are as yet concealed within the chambers of divine wisdom! . . . When will a faithful seeker be found who will don the garb of pilgrimage, attain the Ka'bih of the heart's desire, and, without ear or tongue, discover the mysteries of divine utterance? [333]

333. "Ḥúrís" is plural of "ḥúrí" which is also spelled as houri:

[94] The Seven Valleys Paragraph 4.

The Persian word ḥúrí, Arabic ḥúríah, gazelle-eyed (woman), literally black-eyed like a gazelle. One of the beautiful virgins provided in Paradise for all faithful Muslims.
(Random House *College Dictionary*, 1973 Edition)

Ḥúrís as presented in the Qur'án are fair and beautiful black-eyed women that God promised the believers in Paradise:

> As for righteous, they shall be lodged in peace together amidst gardens and fountains, arrayed in rich silk and fine brocade. Yes, and We shall wed them to dark-eyed houris.
> (The Qur'án, N.J Dawood tr. 44:51–54)

> But the pious shall be in a secure place, amidst gardens and fountains, Clothed in silk and richest robes, facing one another: Thus shall it be: and we will wed them to the virgins with large dark eyes :
> (The Qur'án 44:51–54)

> But for those who dread the majesty of their Lord shall be two gardens, . . .Therein shall be the damsels with retiring glances, whom nor man nor djinn hath touched before them, . . . Like jacynths and pearls.
> (The Qur'án 55:46–58)

In Súrah 56, the Inevitable, more details are provided about the ḥúrís:

> And they who were foremost on earth—the foremost still. These are they who shall be brought nigh to God, In gardens of delight; A crown of the former. And few of the latter generations; On inwrought couches. Reclining on them face to face: Aye-blooming youths go round about to them. With goblets and ewers and a cup of flowing wine; Their brows ache not from it, nor fails the sense: And with such fruits as shall please them best, And with flesh of such birds, as they shall long for: And theirs shall be the Houris, with large dark eyes, like pearls hidden in their shells, . . . Of a rare creation have we created the Houris, And we have made them ever virgins, Dear to their spouses, of equal age with them, For the people of the right hand,
> (The Qur'án 56:10–38)

The great majority of Muslims take Paradise and ḥúrís literally. During the ensuing years and centuries after completion of the Qur'án and passing of Muḥammad, based on some traditions which were attributed to Muḥammad and related by some of His companions, Muslim scholars constructed the image and characteristics of the ḥúrís such as their size and shape, e.g., being very tall with transparent body and luminous bone marrow and not having human needs and limitations.

Some said that the recompense of whoever is killed for Islam (the martyrs) is that upon their death they will immediately enter Paradise in which they will have seventy-two ḥúrís. These are further examples of the same useless matters that have been considered religious knowledge.

Bahá'u'lláh here defines the meaning of ḥúrís, as the spiritual ideas, revelation and inner meanings. He states that these ḥúrís whom no one has touched before, are the new spiritual ideas and inner meanings that "are as yet concealed within the chambers of divine wisdom" and have not been divulged.

Although the Kitáb-i-Íqán is by itself a treasury of spiritual ideas and inner meaning, because its revelation preceded the declaration of Bahá'u'lláh, many pearls of spiritual ideas and ḥúrís of inner meaning remained concealed until after His declaration and the ensuing years to be manifested and vouchsafed to humanity.

As stated in Note No. 185 above, Ka'bih is the *Qiblih*, or point of adoration of Muslims, toward which they face when saying their daily obligatory prayers. Every faithful Muslim if able is obligated to go on pilgrimage to Mecca.

The goal of all pilgrims to Mecca is to reach the House of Ka'bih and circumambulate the Ka'bih. The pilgrims take off all their clothing, jewelry, and leave aside their belongings and don a very simple cotton garb as a sign of their detachment from the world and then go to circumambulate the Ka'bih.

The word Ka'bih has throughout the ages found some allegorical meanings such as "goal," and the "ultimate end."

Paragraph No. 79:

And now regarding His words, that the Son of man shall "come in the clouds of heaven."[334]

334. This phrase is a part of Matthew 24:30, which is believed to be the prophecy for the signs which will accompany the second advent of Christ:

> Immediately after the tribulation of those days shall the sun be darkened, and the moon shall not give her light, and the stars shall fall from heaven, and the powers of the heavens shall be shaken. And then shall appear the sign of the Son of man in heaven: and then shall all the tribes of the earth mourn, and they shall see the Son of man coming in the clouds of heaven with power and great glory.
> (Matthew 24:29–30)

It is interesting to note that similar signs were prophesied to accompany the coming of the Jewish Messiah (the first advent of Christ). As mentioned above, Note No. 64, the prophecies of the Old Testament's Book of Joel indicate that "The sun shall be turned into darkness, and the moon into blood, before the great and terrible day of the LORD come" and that day will be gloomy and covered by clouds and darkness:

> Blow ye the trumpet in Zion, and sound an alarm in my holy mountain: let all the inhabitants of the land tremble: for the day of the LORD cometh, for it is nigh at hand; A day of darkness and of gloominess, a day of clouds and of thick darkness, as the morning spread upon the mountains:
> (Joel 2:1–2)

> And it shall come to pass afterward, that I will pour out my spirit upon all flesh; and your sons and your daughters shall prophesy, your old men shall dream dreams, your young men shall see visions: And also upon the servants and upon the handmaids in those days will I pour out my spirit. And I will shew wonders in the heavens and in the earth, blood, and fire, and pillars of smoke. The sun shall be turned into darkness, and the moon into blood, before the great and terrible day of the LORD come. And it shall come to pass,

> that whosoever shall call on the name of the LORD shall be delivered: for in mount Zion and in Jerusalem shall be deliverance, as the LORD hath said, and in the remnant whom the LORD shall call.
> (Joel 2:28–32)

Because these prophecies were not fulfilled literarily at the first advent of Christ, i.e., the sun did not turn into darkness and the moon into blood and no fires and pillars of smoke were observed, the popular Christian belief assigns the literal fulfilment of these signs to the events heralding the second coming of Christ. But it is evident that these signs are related to the first coming of Christ, as it is confirmed by Peter in the Book of Acts that Joel's prophecies have been fulfilled in Jesus during the first advent (see Note No. 64, above).

"As oft as an Apostle cometh unto you with that which your souls desire not, ye swell with pride, accusing some of being impostors and slaying others."[335]

335. This is a verse from the Qur'án, Súrah 2:87 (2:82 in Rodwell tr.). It was addressing the Jews who were rejecting Muḥammad's claims.

> Moreover, to Moses gave we "the Book," and we raised up apostles after him; and to Jesus, son of Mary, gave we clear proofs of his mission, and strengthened him by the Holy Spirit. So oft then as an apostle cometh to you with that which your souls desire not, swell ye with pride, and treat some as impostors, and slay others?
> (The Qur'án 2:87)

These "clouds" signify, in one sense, the annulment of laws, the abrogation of former Dispensations, the repeal of rituals and customs current amongst men, the exalting of the illiterate faithful above the learned opposers of the Faith. In another sense, they mean the appearance of that immortal Beauty in the image of mortal man, with such human limitations as eating and drinking, poverty and riches, glory and abasement, sleeping and waking, and such other things as

cast doubt in the minds of men, and cause them to turn away. All such veils are symbolically referred to as "clouds."[336]

336. Here Bahá'u'lláh provides the true interpretation of the term "cloud" mentioned in the past sacred books. He states "By the term "clouds" is meant those things that are contrary to the ways and desires of men." He also identifies two groups of "clouds" or issues that are contrary to the ways and desires of men.

The first group consists of those issues that are concerned with and related to the religion or teachings of the former and the new dispensations. A few examples of this group are:

- The annulment of the laws of the previous dispensations and revealing new laws,
- The abrogation of former Dispensations,
- The repeal of rituals and customs current amongst men,
- The exalting of the illiterate faithful above the learned opponents of the Faith.

As demonstrated throughout recorded history, the followers of the religions expected their promised one to follow and uphold the laws, the rituals and customs current among them and to promote their religion. The Manifestations of God when They appeared, acted contrary to these expectations. They annulled the laws, customs and rituals and abrogated the old religion and established new laws and new religions. In the case of Christ, as mentioned above in Notes No. 75 and 76, Christ annulled the two most important and weightiest Judaic laws, namely, the law of Sabbath and the law of divorce. Their objections are most clearly described by 'Abdu'l-Bahá:

> Among other objections they said, "We are promised through the tongue of the prophets that Christ at the time of His coming would proclaim the law of the Torah, whereas now we see this person abrogating the commands of the Pentateuch, disturbing our blessed Sabbath and abolishing the law of divorce. He has left nothing of the ancient law of Moses; therefore, he is the enemy of Moses."
> ('Abdu'l-Bahá, *The Promulgation of Universal Peace*, p. 292)

> At that time Jesus went on the sabbath day through the corn; and his disciples were an hungred, and began to pluck the ears of corn and to eat. But when the Pharisees saw it, they said unto him, Behold, thy disciples do that which is not lawful to do upon the sabbath day. But he said unto them, Have ye not read what David did, when he was an hungred, and they that were with him; How he entered into the house of God, and did eat the shewbread, which was not lawful for him to eat, neither for them which were with him, but only for the priests? Or have ye not read in the law, how that on the sabbath days the priests in the temple profane the sabbath, and are blameless? But I say unto you, That in this place is one greater than the temple. But if ye had known what this meaneth, I will have mercy, and not sacrifice,* ye would not have condemned the guiltless. For the Son of man is Lord even of the sabbath day.
> (Matthew 12:1–8)
>
> * This phrase "I will have mercy, and not sacrifice" is also another reference to the scriptures:
>
> O Ephraim, what shall I do unto thee? O Judah, what shall I do unto thee? for your goodness is as a morning cloud, and as the early dew it goeth away. Therefore have I hewed them by the prophets; I have slain them by the words of my mouth: and thy judgments are as the light that goeth forth. For I desired mercy, and not sacrifice; and the knowledge of God more than burnt offerings.
> (Hosea 6:1–6)

The above scriptural reference emphasizes the primacy of spiritual matters such as knowledge of God over the mere material traditions and rituals such as burnt offering and is indicative of His station which is higher than the temple. But this argument was not acceptable to the Pharisees, because in their eyes He was an ordinary man. He was not David or the high priest of the temple, and there was a precedence for punishing a man who broke the Sabbath, as stated in scripture:

> And while the children of Israel were in the wilderness, they found a man that gathered sticks upon the sabbath day. And they that found him gathering sticks brought him unto

> Moses and Aaron, and unto all the congregation. And they put him in ward, because it was not declared what should be done to him. And the LORD said unto Moses, The man shall be surely put to death: all the congregation shall stone him with stones without the camp. And all the congregation brought him without the camp, and stoned him with stones, and he died; as the LORD commanded Moses.
> (Numbers 15:33–36)

Among the rituals and customs that were repealed as a result of the Revelation of Christ were the important laws and rituals of burned offering for atonement of sins and practice of circumcision which were current and seriously observed amongst the Jews.

Furthermore Christ condemned and discredited the leaders of the religion and exalted the station of a group of illiterate, poor and ordinary people (His disciples) above the most learned Rabbis and the High Priests. 'Abdu'l-Bahá states:

> Peter, the chief of the apostles, used to divide the proceeds of his fishing into seven parts, and when, having taken one part for each day's use, he arrived at the seventh portion, he knew it was the Sabbath day. Consider this! and then think of his future position; to what glory he attained because the Holy Spirit wrought great works through him.
> ('Abdu'l-Bahá, *Paris Talks*, p. 164)

> The two great apostles, St. Peter and St. John the Evangelist, were once simple, humble workmen, toiling for their daily bread. By the Power of the Holy Spirit their souls were illumined, and they received the eternal blessings of the Lord Christ.
> ('Abdu'l-Bahá, *Paris Talks*, p. 59)

> Peter was a fisherman and Mary Magdalene a peasant, but as they were specially favoured with the blessings of Christ, the horizon of their faith became illumined, and down to the present day they are shining from the horizon of everlasting glory.
> ('Abdu'l-Bahá, *Selections from the Writings of 'Abdu'l-Bahá*, p. 105)

> "Caiaphas and Annas were the colossal pillars of the Mosaic Dispensation in the day of His Highness the Spirit; but as they did not acknowledge the Word of God, they fell from the apex of glory to the bottom of the pit of the greatest abasement. But Peter was a catcher of fish; as he turned his face toward the Word of God, the fame of his imperishable, deathless and immortal glory encircled East and West; and he found in the sovereignty of the Kingdom, eternal and everlasting majesty.
> ('Abdu'l-Bahá, *Tablets of 'Abdu'l-Bahá*, vol. 1, p. 223)

> They were not rich and important people. Some of them were catchers of fish. Most of them were ignorant men, not trained in the knowledge of this world. One of the greatest of them, Peter, could not remember the days of the week. All of them were men of the least consequence in the eyes of the world.
> ('Abdu'l-Bahá, *The Promulgation of Universal Peace*, p. 5)

The second group consists of those clouds or issues that are the result of the appearance of the Manifestations of God in the image of mortal man, with such human limitations as:

- Eating and drinking,
- Poverty and riches,
- Glory and abasement,
- Sleeping and waking,

As well as such other things as cast doubt in the minds of men, and cause them to turn away.

In the case of Christ, the Jews were waiting for their Messiah to come with power and authority, sit upon the throne of David and free them from the rule of the Gentiles. However, Jesus was a poor man who was devoid of any power and authority, Who did not have a place to lay down and rest, as He said:

> The foxes have holes, and the birds of the air have nests; but the Son of man hath not where to lay his head.
> (Matthew 8:20)

This situation is best described by 'Abdu'l-Bahá:

> Jews rejected His Holiness Jesus Christ. They were expecting his coming; by day and night they mourned and lamented, saying, "O God! hasten thou the day of the advent of Christ," expressing most intense longing for the Messiah but when His Holiness Christ appeared they denied and rejected him, treated him with arrogant contempt, sentenced him to death and finally crucified him. Why did this happen? Because they were blindly following imitations . . . , they said, "We have heard from our fathers and have read in the old testament that His Holiness Christ must come from an unknown place; now we find that this one has come from Nazareth." Steeped in the literal interpretation and imitating the beliefs of fathers and ancestors they failed to understand the fact that although the body of Jesus came from Nazareth, the reality of the Christ came from the unknown place of the divine Kingdom. They also said that the sceptre of His Holiness Christ would be of iron, that is to say he should wield a sword. When His Holiness Christ appeared, he did possess a sword but it was the sword of his tongue with which he separated the false from the true; but the Jews were blind to the spiritual significance and symbolism of the prophetic words. They also expected that the Messiah would sit upon the throne of David whereas His Holiness the Christ had neither throne nor semblance of sovereignty; nay, rather, he was a poor man, apparently abject and vanquished; therefore how could he be the veritable Christ? This was one of their most insistent objections based upon ancestral interpretation and teaching.
> ('Abdu'l-Bahá, *Foundations of World Unity*, p. 74)

On the subject of human limitations such as eating and drinking, sleeping and waking, the *Gospels* recorded the evidences of those human limitations, which in the eyes of Jews disqualified Jesus from being their expected Messiah. The Gospel of Matthew states:

> Now in the morning as he returned into the city, he hungered. And when he saw a fig tree in the way, he came to it, and found nothing thereon, but leaves only, and said

> unto it, Let no fruit grow on thee henceforward for ever. And presently the fig tree withered away.
> (Matthew 21:18–19)

Jesus Himself described the Jews objections regarding his eating and drinking:

> The Son of man came eating and drinking, and they say, Behold a man gluttonous, and a winebibber, a friend of publicans and sinners.
> (Matthew 11:19)

He was sleeping in houses of poor and ordinary people and was eating with people who did not have good reputations such as the "publicans," and this in their estimation was another sign of Him being disqualified from being their Messiah.

> And it came to pass, as Jesus sat at meat in the house, behold, many publicans and sinners came and sat down with him and his disciples. And when the Pharisees saw it, they said unto his disciples, Why eateth your Master with publicans and sinners?
> (Matthew 9:10–11)

Similar conditions existed at the time of Muḥammad as well. The Arab aristocracy and ruling class of Mecca (the uncles and cousins of Muḥammad) who were the custodians of the Idol House, the House of Ka'bih, were threatened by the Revelation and teachings of Muḥammad. The laws revealed in the Qur'án annulled their laws, the monotheistic religion of Islam abrogated their polytheistic religion and the rituals and customs current in their society. The early followers of Muḥammad, many of whom were poor and ordinary people such as shepherds and camel drivers, were exalted above the aristocrats and learned religious leaders such as Abu'l-Hakam and the custodians of the House of Ka'bih such as Abu'Lahab (see Appendix I).

In the fourth year of His ministry Muḥammad invited Bani Háshem (His clan in the tribe of Quraysh), to publically declare His mission. But one of His uncles, Abu'Lahab scattered them and before He could speak and announce His mission, he threw Muḥammad on the ground and put his foot on Muḥammad's neck.

Paragraph No. 80:

Even as the clouds prevent the eyes of men from beholding the sun, so do these things hinder the souls of men from recognizing the light of the divine Luminary.[337]

337. The appearance of the Manifestations of God, Who are like the sun in the heaven of religions, as normal people with all human limitations, hindered the people of Their time from recognizing their station and seeing the divine light in the same way that clouds can cover the sun. Some of the doubts and objections of the Jews to Christ due to His appearance as an ordinary person were mentioned above. In the case of Muḥammad, although He became the ruler of Arabia in the latter years of His life, He was not immune to severe persecution and ridicule throughout most of His ministry, some of those are recorded in the Qur'án.

People thought that if He was a prophet or Messenger of God He would not be like other normal and ordinary human beings. They expected Him to perform extraordinary feats:

> And they say, "What sort of apostle is this? He eateth food and he walketh the streets! Unless an angel be sent down and take part in his warnings, Or a treasure be thrown down to him, or he have a garden that supplieth him with food..." and those unjust persons say, "Ye follow but a man enchanted."
> (The Qur'án 25:8–9)
>
> They asked Him to perform miracles: turn the hills to gold, make a book fall from heaven, show them Gabriel, bring a well of pure water, prophesy the approaching price of goods: "Cannot your God disclose which articles will rise in price?" Muḥammad would answer,
>
> I am only a man like you. It is revealed to me that your God is one God: go straight then to Him, and implore his pardon. And woe to those who join gods with God.
> (The Qur'án 41:6)
> (Marzieh Gail, *Six Lessons on Islam*, p. 6)

The leaders in Mecca were telling the people that Muḥammad admitted Himself to be a man like them and that they should not follow him because He is crazy, a mad poet.

> And those unjust persons say, "Ye follow but a man enchanted."
> (The Qur'án 25:9)

> For when it was said unto them, There is no God save Allah, they were scornful. And said: Shall we forsake our gods for a mad poet ?
> (The Qur'án, Pickthall tr., 37:35–36)

Other Prophets, similarly, have been subject to poverty and afflictions, to hunger, and to the ills and chances of this world.[338]

338. Examples of ill treatment of other prophets by people of their time are also found in the Qur'án. In the Súrah of Húd the stories of the objections of the people and the sufferings of several prophets are related:

> Then said the chiefs of his people who believed not, "We see in thee but a man like ourselves; and we see not who have followed thee except our meanest ones of hasty judgment, nor see we any excellence in you above ourselves: nay, we deem you liars."
> (The Qur'án 11:29)

> And we sent among them an apostle from out themselves, with, "Worship ye God! ye have no other God than He: will ye not therefore fear Him?" And the chiefs of His people who believed not, and who deemed the meeting with us in the life to come to be a lie, and whom we had richly supplied in this present life, said, "This is but a man like yourselves; he eateth of what ye eat, And he drinketh of what ye drink: And if ye obey a man like yourselves, then ye will surely be undone.
> (The Qur'án 23:33–36)

How, they wondered, could such a person be sent down from God, assert His ascendancy over all the peoples and kindreds of the earth, and claim Himself to be the goal of all creation,[339]

339. Due to misinterpretation of the prophecies of the sacred books, i.e., the expectation for literal and physical fulfilment of those prophecies and the fanciful images that the leaders of religions portrayed of the Promised Ones of their religions, the contemporaries of every Manifestation of God when comparing Their ordinary appearance and natural human limitation with the expected supernatural characteristics of their Promised One, would wonder how such a person could be sent down from God. Accounts of some of these tests that the people of the time of the Manifestations of God were subjected to, are recorded in the Gospels and the Qur'án.

When Jesus and His disciples who looked like a bunch of poor and homeless people, as described in Matthew, Chapter 12, went through the cornfield "and his disciples were an hungred, and began to pluck the ears of corn and to eat." In response to the Pharisees' objection, Jesus compared Himself to David and told them that He was the one Who was "greater than the temple." The Pharisees wondered how a person like this Who could not provide food for Himself and His disciples, and had to go to a cornfield on Sabbath day to pluck corn, could be the promised Messiah Who was sent down by God. Or when the people saw the event described in Matthew Chapter 21, "in the morning as he returned into the city, he hungered. And when he saw a fig tree in the way, he came to it, and found nothing thereon, but leaves only, and said unto it, Let no fruit grow on thee henceforward for ever," they wondered how the expected Messiah, Who was supposed to possess power and authority, could be this man Who did not have anything to eat and came to the fig tree by the wayside to eat some figs to satisfy His hunger. And if He was sent down by God, why did He not command the tree to produce figs for Him to eat instead of cursing the tree?

How, they wondered, could such a person be sent down from God, assert His ascendancy over all the peoples and kindreds of the earth, and claim Himself to be the goal of all creation, —even as He hath

said: "But for Thee, I would not have created all that are in heaven and on earth,"[340]

340. The phrase "But for Thee" is a translation of the Arabic word "Lawlák." There is an Islamic tradition (ḥadíth) which holds that God said to Muḥammad, "O Muḥammad you are the lover and I am the beloved. But for Thee, We would not have created the heavens [or the worlds]" (See Annemarie Schimmel, *As Through a Veil*, p. 178). Based on this tradition, Muslims believe that Muḥammad was the one who was the reason for the creation of the worlds and He was called by titles such as Siyyid-i-Lawlák, which means "the Lord of the Worlds"

Bahá'u'lláh in the Seven Valleys referred to Muḥammad by this title "Siyyid-i-Lawlák."

As stated by the Báb all Prophets are the manifestations of the Primal Will; therefore, this statement applies to all Manifestations of God.[95]

---

[95] If, however, thou art sailing upon the sea of creation, know thou that the First Remembrance, which is the Primal Will of God, may be likened unto the sun. God hath created Him through the potency of His might, and He hath, from the beginning that hath no beginning, caused Him to be manifested in every Dispensation through the compelling power of His behest, and God will, to the end that knoweth no end, continue to manifest Him according to the good-pleasure of His invincible Purpose.

And know thou that He indeed resembleth the sun. Were the risings of the sun to continue till the end that hath no end, yet there hath not been nor ever will be more than one sun; and were its settings to endure for evermore, still there hath not been nor ever will be more than one sun. It is this Primal Will which appeareth resplendent in every Prophet and speaketh forth in every revealed Book. It knoweth no beginning, inasmuch as the First deriveth its firstness from It; and knoweth no end, for the Last oweth its lastness unto It.

In the time of the First Manifestation the Primal Will appeared in Adam; in the day of Noah It became known in Noah; in the day of Abraham in Him; and so in the day of Moses; the day of Jesus; the day of Muḥammad, the Apostle of God; the day of the "Point of the Bayán"; the day of Him Whom God shall make manifest; and the day of the One Who will appear after Him Whom God shall make manifest. Hence the inner meaning of the words uttered by the Apostle of God, "I am all the Prophets," inasmuch as what shineth resplendent in each one of Them hath been and will ever remain the one and the same sun.
(*Selections from the Writings of the Báb*, p. 126)

The statement "But for Thee, We would not have created all that are in heaven and on earth [or the worlds]," and some other statements and stations claimed by Muḥammad—such as "he is the Apostle of God, and the seal of the prophets"[96]; or the tradition from Muḥammad: "Manifold are Our relationships with God. At one time, We are He Himself, and He is We Ourself. At another He is that He is, and We are that We are"[97]—caused misunderstanding. The subsequent interpretations which were based on vain imagination, such as assuming supernatural physical characteristics for Muḥammad, in time became dark veils that prevent people from recognizing the new Manifestation of God.

Similar statements regarding the exalted station of Jesus are found in the Gospels:

> Verily, verily, I say unto you, If a man keep my saying, he shall never see death. Then said the Jews unto him, Now we know that thou hast a devil. Abraham is dead, and the prophets; and thou sayest, If a man keep my saying, he shall never taste of death . . . Jesus answered . . . Your father Abraham rejoiced to see my day: and he saw it, and was glad. Then said the Jews unto him, Thou art not yet fifty years old, and hast thou seen Abraham? Jesus said unto them, Verily, verily, I say unto you, Before Abraham was, I am.
> (John 8:51–58)

> I and my Father are one.
> (John 10:30)

> Thou blasphemest; because I said, I am the Son of God? If I do not the works of my Father, believe me not. But if I do, though ye believe not me, believe the works: that ye may know, and believe, that the Father is in me, and I in him.
> (John 10:36–38)

> Then said Jesus unto them, When ye have lifted up the Son of man, then shall ye know that I am he, and that I do

[96] (The Qur'án 33:40).

[97] Quoted in the Epistle to the Son of the Wolf, p. 43.

> nothing of myself; but as my Father hath taught me, . . . And he that sent me is with me: the Father hath not left me alone;
> (John 8:28–29)

How, they wondered, could such a person be sent down from God, assert His ascendancy over all the peoples and kindreds of the earth, and claim Himself to be the goal of all creation, —even as He hath said: "But for Thee, I would not have created all that are in heaven and on earth," —and yet be subject to such trivial things?[341]

341. As mentioned above, Jews heard Jesus claiming to be the Son of God and stating that "I and my Father are one," which by their literal interpretation meant that He was God and He physically existed before Abraham. In their eyes these claims were not supported by Jesus' appearance and conditions. He was poor and homeless and this did not match their preconceived notions of the characteristics of their expected Messiah. He did not possess worldly power or a kingdom and did not save Jews from the rule of Gentiles. They did not accept Him and applied several tests to prove that He was false:

1 – The test of hanging on a tree.

> And if a man have committed a sin worthy of death, and he be to be put to death, and thou hang him on a tree: His body shall not remain all night upon the tree, but thou shalt in any wise bury him that day; (for he that is hanged is accursed of God;) that thy land be not defiled, which the LORD thy God giveth thee for an inheritance.
> (Deuteronomy 21:22–23)

Their reason was that if Jesus was Christ and Son of God, He would not be accursed of God, and they would not be able to hang Him on a tree. Therefore they applied this test by hanging him on a Cross that was made of a tree to test whether He was accursed of God or not. The Book of Acts states that he was hanged on a tree:

> The God of our fathers raised up Jesus, whom ye slew and hanged on a tree.
> (Acts 5:30)

> Christ hath redeemed us from the curse of the law, being made a curse for us: for it is written, Cursed is every one that hangeth on a tree:
> (Galatians 3:13)

2 – The second test was the test of His alleged Sonship—whether or not He was the Son of God. A father would not give his son vinegar if he asked for water. Why then did God or Jesus not perform a miracle by turning the vinegar to water or wine, when it was claimed that He had done so before.

> If a son shall ask bread of any of you that is a father, will he give him a stone? or if he ask a fish, will he for a fish give him a serpent? Or if he shall ask an egg, will he offer him a scorpion? If ye then, being evil, know how to give good gifts unto your children: how much more shall your heavenly Father give the Holy Spirit to them that ask him?
> (Luke 11:11–13)

> And when they had platted a crown of thorns, they put it upon his head, and a reed in his right hand: and they bowed the knee before him, and mocked him, saying, Hail, King of the Jews! And they spit upon him, and took the reed, and smote him on the head. And after that they had mocked him, they took the robe off from him, and put his own raiment on him, and led him away to crucify him. And as they came out, they found a man of Cyrene, Simon by name: him they compelled to bear his cross. And when they were come unto a place called Golgotha, that is to say, a place of a skull, They gave him vinegar to drink mingled with gall: and when he had tasted thereof, he would not drink.
> (Matthew 27:29–34)

> After this, Jesus knowing that all things were now accomplished, that the scripture might be fulfilled, saith, I thirst. Now there was set a vessel full of vinegar: and they filled a spunge with vinegar, and put it upon hyssop, and put it to his mouth. When Jesus therefore had received the vinegar, he said, It is finished: and he bowed his head, and gave up the ghost.
> (John 19:28–30)

> And the people stood beholding. And the rulers also with them derided him, saying, He saved others; let him save himself, if he be Christ, the chosen of God. And the soldiers also mocked him, coming to him, and offering him vinegar, And saying, If thou be the king of the Jews, save thyself. And a superscription also was written over him in letters of Greek, and Latin, and Hebrew, THIS IS THE KING OF THE JEWS. And one of the malefactors which were hanged railed on him, saying, If thou be Christ, save thyself and us.
> (Luke 23:35–39)

Jesus foretold His crucifixion and said that when He was crucified people would know that He and His Father were one and they would know that the Father had not left Him alone:

> Then said Jesus unto them, When ye have lifted up the Son of man, then shall ye know that I am he, and that I do nothing of myself; but as my Father hath taught me, I speak these things. And he that sent me is with me: the Father hath not left me alone;
> (John 8:28–29)

But when they crucified Him the contrary occurred:

> And at the ninth hour Jesus cried with a loud voice, saying, Eloi, Eloi, lama sabachthani? which is, being interpreted, My God, my God, why hast thou forsaken me? And some of them that stood by, when they heard it, said, Behold, he calleth Elias. And one ran and filled a spunge full of vinegar, and put it on a reed, and gave him to drink, saying, Let alone; let us see whether Elias will come to take him down. And Jesus cried with a loud voice, and gave up the ghost.
> (Mark 15:34–37)

3 – The third test was that they believed that the Messiah would not die. Therefore if He was Messiah He would live forever and could not be killed. As stated in the Gospel of John, when Jesus was speaking of His imminent death, those Jews who were attracted to Him were puzzled. If He was the Messiah, why was He speaking of His death.

> And I, if I be lifted up from the earth, will draw all men unto me. This he said, signifying what death he should die. The people answered him, We have heard out of the law that Christ abideth for ever: and how sayest thou, The Son of man must be lifted up? who is this Son of man?
> (John 12:31–34)

Furthermore, if He was the Messiah (Christ) or Son of God, and they put Him on the Cross, He would come down and save Himself as stated in the Gospels:

> And sitting down they watched him there; And set up over his head his accusation written, THIS IS JESUS THE KING OF THE JEWS. Then were there two thieves crucified with him, one on the right hand, and another on the left. And they that passed by reviled him, wagging their heads, And saying, Thou that destroyest the temple, and buildest it in three days, save thyself. If thou be the Son of God, come down from the cross. Likewise also the chief priests mocking him, with the scribes and elders, said, He saved others; himself he cannot save. If he be the King of Israel, let him now come down from the cross, and we will believe him. He trusted in God; let him deliver him now, if he will have him: for he said, I am the Son of God.
> (Matthew 27:36–43)

> And the soldiers also mocked him, coming to him, and offering him vinegar, And saying, If thou be the king of the Jews, save thyself. And a superscription also was written over him in letters of Greek, and Latin, and Hebrew, THIS IS THE KING OF THE JEWS. And one of the malefactors which were hanged railed on him, saying, If thou be Christ, save thyself and us.
> (Luke 23:36–39)

4 – The fourth test was that if He was God or the Son of God, He would not bleed.

> Then came the soldiers, and brake the legs of the first, and of the other which was crucified with him. But when they came to Jesus, and saw that he was dead already, they brake not his legs: But one of the soldiers with a spear

> pierced his side, and forthwith came there out blood and water.
> (John 19:32–33)

In the case of Muḥammad, as mentioned above, the statement "But for Thee, We would not have created all that are in heaven and on earth," and the station it indicates, when combined with some other statements and stations claimed by Muḥammad—caused confusion for people of His time. Because, if these claims were true and He was the great prophet Who had such a special relationship with God, why could He not perform any miracles or protect Himself from their abuse?

From the inception of His ministry and for thirteen years Muḥammad was despised and an outcast. The people of Mecca and their religious leaders called Him a crazed poet, a madman, a liar, Who was claiming to be the prophet sent by God, but could not perform any extraordinary act:

> They asked Him to perform miracles: turn the hills to gold, make a book fall from heaven, show them Gabriel, bring a well of pure water, prophesy the approaching price of goods: "Cannot your God disclose which articles will rise in price?" Muḥammad would answer, "I am only a man like you." (Qur'án 18:110)
> (Marzieh Gail, *Six Lessons on Islam*, p. 6)

He could not even stop people from hurting or ridiculing Him. They threw a rock at His face and broke one of His teeth.

> They pursued Him, they covered Him and His disciples with filth when they were praying, they incited children and the rabble to follow and mock them, a woman strewed thorns where He would walk.
> (Marzieh Gail, *Six Lessons on Islam*, p. 7)

In order to qualify and provide literal justification for the special relationship of the prophet Muḥammad with God—and in spite of Muḥammad's declaration that His only miracle was the Revelation of the Qur'án and His assertion that "I am only a man like you"—Muslims in subsequent years attributed many miracles and supernatural physical characteristics to Him. These attributions which were based on vain imagination, in time became dark veils that prevented people from recognizing the new Manifestations of God.

You must undoubtedly have been informed of the tribulations, the poverty, the ills, and the degradation that have befallen every Prophet of God and His companions. You must have heard how the heads of their followers were sent as presents unto different cities, how grievously they were hindered from that whereunto they were commanded. Each and every one of them fell a prey to the hands of the enemies of His Cause, and had to suffer whatsoever they decreed.[342]

342. The history of Christianity reflects what happened to the followers and disciples of Jesus. Peter was crucified upside-down and Paul was imprisoned and beheaded. The book of Acts describes the events leading to the arrest and killing of Stephen the first Christian martyr.

> Then there arose certain of the synagogue, which is called the synagogue of the Libertines, and Cyrenians, and Alexandrians, and of them of Cilicia and of Asia, disputing with Stephen. And they were not able to resist the wisdom and the spirit by which he spake. Then they suborned men, which said, We have heard him speak blasphemous words against Moses, and against God. And they stirred up the people, and the elders, and the scribes, and came upon him, and caught him, and brought him to the council, And set up false witnesses, which said, This man ceaseth not to speak blasphemous words against this holy place, and the law: For we have heard him say, that this Jesus of Nazareth shall destroy this place, and shall change the customs which Moses delivered us.
> (Acts 6:9–14)

The high priest asked Stephen if what they said about him was true, and as part of his explanation he said:

> Which of the prophets have not your fathers persecuted? and they have slain them which shewed before of the

> coming of the Just One; of whom ye have been now the betrayers and murderers: Who have received the law by the disposition of angels, and have not kept it. When they heard these things, they were cut to the heart, and they gnashed on him with their teeth. ......Then they cried out with a loud voice, and stopped their ears, and ran upon him with one accord, And cast him out of the city, and stoned him.
> (Acts 7:52–57)

Paragraph No. 81:

Were these men, therefore, to discover suddenly that a Man, Who hath been living in their midst, Who, with respect to every human limitation, hath been their equal, had risen to abolish every established principle imposed by their Faith—principles by which for centuries they have been disciplined, and every opposer and denier of which they have come to regard as infidel, profligate and wicked,—they would of a certainty be veiled and hindered from acknowledging His truth.[343]

343. This obstacle and veil preventing the recognition of Jesus as the expected Messiah is recorded in the Gospels:

> Is not this the carpenter's son? is not his mother called Mary? and his brethren, James, and Joseph, and Simon, and Judas? And his sisters, are they not all with us? Whence then hath this man all these things? And they were offended in him. But Jesus said unto them, A prophet is not without honour, save in his own country, and in his own house. And he did not many mighty works there because of their unbelief.
> (Matthew 13:54–58)

Muḥammad also faced the same situation. The people of Mecca saw Him as an ordinary human that was living in their town and was their equal with the same human limitations, but now was trying to abolish the established principle of their idol worship and teach His monotheistic religion. This became a veil and hindrance for them:

> Muḥammad preached, and the Meccans scoffed. They asked Him to perform miracles: turn the hills to gold, make a book fall from heaven, show them Gabriel, bring a well of pure water, prophesy the approaching price of goods: "Cannot your God disclose which articles will rise in price?" Muḥammad would answer, "I am only a man like you." (Qur'án 18:110). "It is revealed to me that your God is one God: go straight then to Him, and implore His pardon. And woe to those who join gods with God." (Qur'án 41:5). The Qur'án tells us: "But most of them withdraw and hearken not: And they say, 'Our hearts are under shelter from Thy teachings, and in our ears is a deafness, and between us and Thee there is a veil." (The Qur'án 41:3–4)
> (Marzieh Gail, *Six Lessons on Islam*, p. 6)

Therefore the ordinary human appearance of these divine beings "are as 'clouds' that veil the eyes . . ."

those whose inner being hath not tasted the Salsabíl[344] of detachment, nor drunk from the Kawthar[345] of the knowledge of God.

344. See Note No. 263 above.

345. See Note No. 136 above.

Paragraph No. 82:

and that we may recognize Him only by His own Self.[346]

346. In many places in His Writings, Bahá'u'lláh states that the Manifestation of God should be known by His own Self (*nafs*):

> The first and foremost testimony establishing His truth is His own Self. Next to this testimony is His Revelation. For whoso faileth to recognize either the one or the other He hath established the words He hath revealed as proof of His reality and truth. This is, verily, an evidence of His tender mercy unto men.
> (*Gleanings from the Writings of Bahá'u'lláh*, p. 105)

> He hath manifested unto men the Daystars of His divine guidance, the Symbols of His divine unity, and hath ordained the knowledge of these sanctified Beings to be identical with the knowledge of His own Self. Whoso recognizeth them hath recognized God. Whoso hearkeneth to their call, hath hearkened to the Voice of God, and whoso testifieth to the truth of their Revelation, hath testified to the truth of God Himself.
> (*Gleanings from the Writings of Bahá'u'lláh*, p. 50)

And should we ask for a testimony of His truth, we should content ourselves with one, and only one.[347]

347. In the above statement, Bahá'u'lláh has established a hierarchy of testimony and proof for ascertaining the truth of the divine Manifestations of God. The first and foremost is the Manifestation's own Self, and the next is His Revelation and the third is the words He has revealed. Although the previous Manifestations did not accept to provide a testimony for their truth based on the people's request, as stated both in the Bible and the Qur'án:

> Then certain of the scribes and of the Pharisees answered, saying, Master, we would see a sign from thee. But he answered and said unto them, An evil and adulterous generation seeketh after a sign; and there shall no sign be given to it.
> (Matthew 12:38–39)

> And they say, 'We will by no means believe in thee, until there gush forth for thee a fountain from the earth; or there be made for thee a garden of palms and grapes, and rivers come gushing out amidst them; or thou make the sky to fall down upon us in pieces; or thou bring us God and the angels before us; or there be made for thee a house of gold; or thou climb up into the heaven; and even then we will not believe in thy climbing there, until thou send down on us a book that we may read!'
> Say, 'Celebrated be the praises of my Lord! was I aught but a mortal apostle?'
> (The Qur'án, E.H. Palmer tr, Súrah 17:93)

Bahá'u'lláh teaches that this refusal of complying with the wishes of people is not because these Manifestations were not able to perform those extraordinary things:

> Bahá'u'lláh also speaks in this Tablet [Book of the River] about miracles which are attributed to the Prophets. He states that one should not deny the performance of miracles by these Holy Souls, but emphasizes that miracles are not a conclusive proof of the authenticity of Their Messages. The greatest and the most evident sign of Prophethood has always been the Revelation of the Word of God.
> (Adib Taherzadeh, *The Revelation of Bahá'u'lláh,* Vol. *1,* p. 105)

Bahá'u'lláh however, has graciously allowed those people who are not able to discern the truth of the Manifestation of God based on the three criteria mentioned above, to ask for a testimony of His truth, provided that they should all agree on the testimony they want, and be content with one. The Manifestation of God is not the plaything of people so that every one comes and asks for a sign or testimony. This is exactly what He did while living in exile in Baghdád, when one of His enemies, Shaykh 'Abdu'l-Ḥusayn, gathered the influential clerics and religious leaders and made them ask Bahá'u'lláh to perform miracles and provide testimonies for the truth of His Cause. Describing this situation, Shoghi Effendi states:

> Balked in his repeated attempts to achieve his malevolent purpose, Shaykh 'Abdu'l-Ḥusayn now diverted his energies into a new channel. He promised his accomplice [Mírzá Buzurg Khán, a newly-appointed Persian consul-general] he would raise him to the rank of a minister of the crown, if he succeeded in inducing the government to recall Bahá'u'lláh to Ṭihrán, and cast Him again into prison. He despatched lengthy and almost daily reports to the immediate entourage of the Sháh. He painted extravagant pictures of the ascendancy enjoyed by Bahá'u'lláh by representing Him as having won the allegiance of the nomadic tribes of 'Iráq. He claimed that He was in a position to muster, in a day, fully one hundred thousand men ready to take up arms at His bidding. He accused Him of meditating, in conjunction with various leaders in Persia,

an insurrection against the sovereign. By such means as these he succeeded in bringing sufficient pressure on the authorities in Ṭihrán to induce the S͟háh to grant him a mandate, bestowing on him full powers, and enjoining the Persian 'ulamás and functionaries to render him every assistance. This mandate the S͟hayk͟h instantly forwarded to the ecclesiastics of Najaf and Karbilá, asking them to convene a gathering in Káẓimayn, the place of his residence. A concourse of s͟hayk͟hs, mullás and mujtahids, eager to curry favor with the sovereign, promptly responded. Upon being informed of the purpose for which they had been summoned, they determined to declare a holy war against the colony of exiles, and by launching a sudden and general assault on it to destroy the Faith at its heart. To their amazement and disappointment, however, they found that the leading mujtahid amongst them, the celebrated S͟hayk͟h Murtaḍáy-i-Anṣárí, a man renowned for his tolerance, his wisdom, his undeviating justice, his piety and nobility of character, refused, when apprized of their designs, to pronounce the necessary sentence against the Bábís. He it was whom Bahá'u'lláh later extolled in the "Lawḥ-i-Sulṭán," and numbered among "those doctors who have indeed drunk of the cup of renunciation," and "never interfered with Him," and to whom 'Abdu'l-Bahá referred as "the illustrious and erudite doctor, the noble and celebrated scholar, the seal of seekers after truth." Pleading insufficient knowledge of the tenets of this community, and claiming to have witnessed no act on the part of its members at variance with the Qur'án, he, disregarding the remonstrances of his colleagues, abruptly left the gathering, and returned to Najaf, after having expressed, through a messenger, his regret to Bahá'u'lláh for what had happened, and his devout wish for His protection.

Frustrated in their designs, but unrelenting in their hostility, the assembled divines delegated the learned and devout Ḥájí Mullá Ḥasan-i-'Ammú, recognized for his integrity and wisdom, to submit various questions to Bahá'u'lláh for elucidation. When these were submitted, and answers completely satisfactory to the messenger were given, Ḥájí Mullá Ḥasan, affirming the recognition by the 'ulamás of

> the vastness of the knowledge of Bahá'u'lláh, asked, as an evidence of the truth of His mission, for a miracle that would satisfy completely all concerned. "Although you have no right to ask this," Bahá'u'lláh replied, "for God should test His creatures, and they should not test God, still I allow and accept this request. . . . The 'ulamás must assemble, and, with one accord, choose one miracle, and write that, after the performance of this miracle they will no longer entertain doubts about Me, and that all will acknowledge and confess the truth of My Cause. Let them seal this paper, and bring it to Me. This must be the accepted criterion: if the miracle is performed, no doubt will remain for them; and if not, We shall be convicted of imposture." This clear, challenging and courageous reply, unexampled in the annals of any religion, and addressed to the most illustrious Shí'ah divines, assembled in their time-honored stronghold, was so satisfactory to their envoy that he instantly arose, kissed the knee of Bahá'u'lláh, and departed to deliver His message. Three days later he sent word that that august assemblage had failed to arrive at a decision, and had chosen to drop the matter, a decision to which he himself later gave wide publicity, in the course of his visit to Persia, and even communicated it in person to the then Minister of Foreign Affairs, Mírzá Sa'íd Khán. "We have," Bahá'u'lláh is reported to have commented, when informed of their reaction to this challenge, "through this all-satisfying, all-embracing message which We sent, revealed and vindicated the miracles of all the Prophets, inasmuch as We left the choice to the 'ulamás themselves, undertaking to reveal whatever they would decide upon."
> (*God Passes By*, p. 143–144)

However, Shaykh 'Abdu'l-Ḥusayn did not give up his intrigues and machinations and managed to extend Bahá'u'lláh's exile and transfer Him and His companions from Baghdád to far away places in the most western part of the Ottoman Empire.

> In the end, the intrigues and machinations of the Shaykh and the efforts of the Consul-General so influenced the Sháh that he instructed Mírzá Sa'íd Khán, the Persian Foreign Minister, to send a request to the Ottoman

government for the transfer Bahá'u'lláh from Ba<u>gh</u>dád. In the meantime, the enemy was becoming increasingly hostile towards Bahá'u'lláh. Siyyid Mírzá Ḥusayn-i-Mutavallí, a notorious Bábí, suggested in a letter to Him that He remain at home for the sake of His own safety. In reply to this, Bahá'u'lláh revealed a Tablet in Persian known as *<u>Sh</u>ikkar-<u>Sh</u>ikan-<u>Sh</u>avand.*
(Adib Taherzadeh, *The Revelation of Bahá'u'lláh*, Vol. 1, p. 147)

This Tablet (Láwḥ-i-<u>Sh</u>ikkar-<u>Sh</u>ikan-<u>Sh</u>avand) is one of the most beautiful Tablets of Bahá'u'lláh. Translation of a part of this Tablet is presented in Appendix II.

Paragraph No. 83:

Gracious God! Notwithstanding the warning which, in marvelously symbolic language and subtle allusions, hath been uttered in days past, and which was intended to awaken the peoples of the world and to prevent them from being deprived of their share of the billowing ocean of God's grace, yet such things as have already been witnessed have come to pass![348]

348. As mentioned above and more specifically in Note Nos. 64, 123, 131 and 135, in the Judeo-Christo-Islamic chain of religions, the holy books of each religion contain the signs and prophecies related to the coming of the next Manifestation of God in symbolic and allegorical language. The Old Testament contains the signs and prophecies related to the manifestation of Jesus as the promised Messiah, similarly the New Testament and the Qur'án contain the signs and prophecies related to the coming of Muḥammad and the Báb and Bahá'u'lláh. However, the followers of each of these religions ignored those warnings and by literal and eschatological interpretation of these signs and prophecies, missed the advent of their Promised One, and were deprived of their share of the billowing ocean of God's grace."

An example of the warning intended to help people not be deprived of recognizing the future Manifestations was provided by Christ when He was speaking about His second coming, as recorded in the Olivet Discourse (Matthew, Chapter 24):

> Therefore be ye also ready: for in such an hour as ye think not the Son of man cometh. Watch therefore: for ye know not what hour your Lord doth come. But know this, that if the goodman of the house had known in what watch the thief would come, he would have watched, and would not have suffered his house to be broken up. Therefore be ye also ready: for in such an hour as ye think not the Son of man cometh.
> (Matthew 24:43–44)

The same warning with additional explanation is provided in the Gospel of Luke:

> And this know, that if the goodman of the house had known what hour the thief would come, he would have watched, and not have suffered his house to be broken through. Be ye therefore ready also: for the Son of man cometh at an hour when ye think not. Then Peter said unto him, Lord, speakest thou this parable unto us, or even to all? And the Lord said, Who then is that faithful and wise steward, whom his lord shall make ruler over his household, to give them their portion of meat in due season? Blessed is that servant, whom his lord when he cometh shall find so doing. Of a truth I say unto you, that he will make him ruler over all that he hath. But and if that servant say in his heart, My lord delayeth his coming; and shall begin to beat the menservants and maidens, and to eat and drink, and to be drunken; The lord of that servant will come in a day when he looketh not for him, and at an hour when he is not aware, and will cut him in sunder, and will appoint him his portion with the unbelievers.
> (Luke 12:39–45)

Although Christ warned them that He would come like a thief in the night without fanfare or notice and when they were not expecting it, the Christian religious leaders were and are still waiting for the sun to be dark and for the moon to become like blood, the powers of earth to be released, for the sound of trumpets to be heard announcing the Second Coming, and to see Christ descending from heaven riding over the clouds. Therefore, when their Lord came in a way and at an hour that they were not expecting, they did not receive Him and were accounted among the unbelievers.

Reference to these things hath also been made in the Qur'án, as witnessed by this verse: "What can such expect but that God should come down to them overshadowed with clouds?"[349]

349. This verse is a part of a series of Qur'ánic verses that were intended to warn and awaken the people and help them not to be deprived of recognizing the future Manifestations of God.

> O believers! Enter completely into the true religion, and follow not the steps of Satan, for he is your declared enemy. But if ye lapse after that our clear signs have come to you, know that God is Mighty, Wise. What can such expect but that God should come down to them overshadowed with clouds.
> (The Qur'án 2:204–6)

Following in the steps of Satan is essentially following the steps of those who are opposing God. God that comes down to the human level is the Manifestation of God who is the manifestation of divine in the form of the human temple with ordinary physical appearance and characteristics. Their ordinary human appearance like clouds, veil the eyes of people from seeing the reality of a being Who stands as Godhead in the human world. Jesus explains this:

> If ye had known me, ye should have known my Father also: and from henceforth ye know him, and have seen him. Phillip saith unto him, Lord, shew us the Father, and it sufficeth us. Jesus saith unto him. Have I been so long time with you, and yet hast thou not known me, Phillip? He that hath seen me hath seen the Father, and how sayest thou then, Shew us the Father? Believest thou not that I am in the Father and Father in me? The words that I speak unto you I speak not of myself: but the Father that dweleth in me, he doeth the works. Believe me that I am in the Father, and the Father in me . . .
> (John 14:5–20)

The evidence of Muḥammad's station of Godhead is found in verse 10 of the Súrah of Victory in the Qur'án. Commentaries on the Qur'án relate the circumstance of the revelation of this verse. When after several years of wars and hostilities with the tribe of Qurays<u>h</u> (Idolater Arabs of His own tribe), Prophet Muḥammad made a treaty and truce for the cessation of war and hostility at a place near Mecca called Al-Ḥudaybíyyah, and a group of Arabs plighted fealty to Him. As was customary among the Arabs when they were establishing fealty, they put all their hands together and Prophet Muḥammad's hand was placed on the top of all hands. The following verse was revealed in the Qur'án:

> In truth, they who plighted fealty to thee, really plighted that fealty to God: the hand of God was over their hands! Whoever, therefore, shall break his oath shall only break it to his own hurt; but whoever shall be true to his engagement with God, He will give him a great reward.
> (The Qur'án 48:10)

A number of the divines, who hold firmly to the letter of the Word of God, have come to regard this verse as one of the signs of that expected resurrection which is born of their idle fancy. This, notwithstanding the fact that similar references have been made in most of the heavenly Books, and have been recorded in all the passages connected with the signs of the coming Manifestation.[350]

350. Certain verses in the Old Testament such as those in the Book of Joel (see Note No. 64, above) and Book of Isiah (see Note No. 208, above) and the verses in the New Testament such as those in Matthew Chapter 24 (see Appendix IV) that have a symbolic and allegorical nature, were interpreted literally by the Christian religious leaders. When they did not see the literal fulfilment of the signs that were to accompany the appearance of Jesus (such as the darkening of the sun and moon and falling of the stars of heaven over the earth), they maintained that these are eschatological events that will take place at eschaton (end of the time) and on the day of resurrection. They combined their imagination of these events with their assumptions and imaginations about life after death and produced fascinating

scenarios for the Day of Resurrection (see Notes Nos. 123–31, above).

Similarly there are certain verses of the Qur'án that mention the occurrence of extraordinary events, or pertain to the Day of Resurrection or life after death. A few examples are presented below:

> O believers! Enter completely into the true religion, and follow not the steps of Satan, for he is your declared enemy. But if ye lapse after that our clear signs have come to you, know that God is Mighty, Wise. What can such expect but that God should come down to them overshadowed with clouds, and the angels also, and their doom be sealed? And to God shall all things return.
> (The Qur'án 2:204–6)

> When the heaven shall cleave asunder, And when the stars shall disperse, And when the seas shall be comingled.
> (The Qur'án 82:1)

> When the Heaven shall be cleft asunder, and become rose red, like stained leather.
> (The Qur'án 55:37)

> When the sun shall be folded up, And when the stars shall fall, And when the mountains shall be set in motion.
> (The Qur'án 81:1–3)

> And the heaven shall cleave asunder, for on that day it shall be fragile;
> (The Qur'án 69:16–17)

> When the earth shall be shaken with a shock, And the mountains shall be crumbled with a crumbling, And shall become scattered dust,
> (The Qur'án 56:4–6)

> But they have not deemed of God as is He due; for on the resurrection day the whole Earth shall be but his handful, and in his right hand shall the Heavens be folded together.

Praise be to Him! and high be He uplifted above the partners they join with Him!
(The Qur'án 39:67)

He will surely assemble you on the Resurrection day; there is no doubt of it.
(The Qur'án 6:12)

Now thy Lord! He will decide between them on the day of resurrection as to the subject of their disputes.
(The Qur'án 32:25)

And truly thy Lord will gather them together again, for He is Wise, Knowing.
(The Qur'án 15:26)

Unto Him shall ye return, all together: the promise of God is sure: He produceth a creature, then causeth it to return again—that he may reward those who believe and do the things that are right, with equity: but as for the infidels! —for them the draught that boileth and an afflictive torment—because they have not believed.
(The Qur'án 10:5)

And if thou say, "After death ye shall surely be raised again," the infidels will certainly explain, "This is nothing but pure sorcery."
(The Qur'án 11:10)

No soul knoweth what joy of the eye is reserved for the good in recompense of their works. Shall he then who is a believer be as he who sinneth grossly? they shall not be held alike. As to those who believe and do that which is right, they shall have gardens of eternal abode as the meed of their works: But as for those who grossly sin, their abode shall be the fire: so oft as they shall desire to escape out of it, back shall they be turned into it. And it shall be said to them, Taste ye the torment of the fire, which he treated as a lie.
(The Qur'án 32:17–20)

All the above verses are of a symbolic or allegorical nature, but were interpreted literally by the Muslim divines, who failing to comprehend them, combined them into a fanciful scenario for the end of time and the Day of Resurrection.

As mentioned above, the Islamic concept of the Day of Resurrection is very similar to the same concept in Judaism and Christianity and has borrowed some elements from Zoroastrianism. In general the Muslims believe that after their death people will remain in a state of suspended existence until the Day of Resurrection. On that day, heaven shall cleave asunder, the sun shall be folded up, the stars shall fall, the mountains shall be set in motion, and the earth shall be shaken with a shock. That day which will be marked by the appearance of the Promised One of Islam (Mahdí for the Sunnis, or Qá'im for the Shi'ahs) might last as long as one thousand years. In that day all the dead will rise from their graves in their physical bodies and will be present in the plane of resurrection. God will preside over the process of judgment. People will all be judged by the weight of their good deeds in comparison to their bad deeds. All have to pass over a bridge (called Ṣeráṭ) that spans the expanse of Hell and connects the plane of judgment to Heaven (Paradise).

This bridge is narrower than a hair, sharper than a blade and longer than any conceivable measure. The people of the right (those whose good deeds outweigh their bad deeds), will have no trouble passing over the bridge. The more righteous a person the faster he/she passes over the bridge. Those whose bad deeds are heavier will fall from the bridge into Hell. The majority of Muslims believe in corporeal resurrection and a physical Heaven and Hell. Those who go to paradise will sit over brocade couches in a garden in which rivers of milk and honey are flowing. The men will have ever-virgin ḥúrís and women will have young men serving them (see Note No. 333). The pictures and descriptions of the events of the Day of Resurrection and Heaven and Hell developed by the Muslim divines during the past millennium are far more fantastic and colorful than Dante's description in the Divine Comedy.

As stated above, in the Bahá'í Writings the Day of Resurrection is defined as the day of the appearance or declaration of a Manifestation of God. Therefore, the day of the advent of each

Manifestation of God is the Day of Resurrection of the followers of all the previous religions (see Note Nos. 208–10 and 223 above).

Paragraph No. 84:

Likewise, He saith: "On the day when the heaven shall give out a palpable smoke, which shall enshroud mankind: this will be an afflictive torment."[351]

351. This verse is from the Qur'án Súrah 44:

> By virtue of our behest. Lo! we have ever sent forth Apostles, A mercy from thy Lord: he truly heareth and knoweth all things—Lord of the Heavens and of the Earth and of all that is between them,—if ye be firm in faith—There is no God but He!—He maketh alive and killeth!—Your Lord and the Lord of your sires of old!~Yet with doubts do they disport them. But mark them on the day when the Heaven shall give out a palpable smoke, Which shall enshroud mankind: this will be an afflictive torment.
> (The Qur'án 44:4–10)

In these verses the coming of the Manifestations of God (Apostles) is associated with the palpable smoke that enshrouds mankind. God has forever sent the Manifestations of God Who are the evidence of the mercy of God for mankind. But man has always dismissed them in doubt. Bahá'u'lláh, explained that smoke in this verse denotes grave dissensions, the abrogation and demolition of recognized standards, and the utter destruction of their narrow-minded exponents.

The more they are told that this wondrous Cause of God, this Revelation from the Most High, hath been made manifest to all mankind,[352] and is waxing greater and stronger every day, the fiercer groweth the blaze of the fire in their hearts.

352. The universal nature of the Bahá'í Faith is emphasized here. The Báb has also mentioned that His Revelation is for all mankind:

> ALL praise be to God Who hath, through the power of Truth, sent down this Book unto His servant, that it may serve as a shining light for all mankind.
> (The Báb, *Selections from the Writings of the Báb,* p. 39)

However, there are some statements in the sacred scriptures of the past that could be interpreted to mean that they have not been revealed for all mankind, but were aimed to help certain groups of people or certain geographical regions.

Moses' primary mission and objective was to bring the children of Israel out of Egypt and take them to the Holy Land.

> Now therefore, behold, the cry of the children of Israel is come unto me: and I have also seen the oppression wherewith the Egyptians oppress them. Come now therefore, and I will send thee unto Pharaoh, that thou mayest bring forth my people the children of Israel out of Egypt.
> (Exodus 3:9–10)

There was an argument in early Christianity that Jesus Christ came primarily for the Jews.

> And, behold, a woman of Canaan came out of the same coasts, and cried unto him, saying, Have mercy on me, O Lord, thou son of David; my daughter is grievously vexed with a devil. But he answered her not a word. And his disciples came and besought him, saying, Send her away; for she crieth after us. But he answered and said, I am not sent but unto the lost sheep of the house of Israel. Then came she and worshipped him, saying, Lord, help me. But he answered and said, It is not meet to take the children's bread, and to cast it to dogs.
> (Matthew 15:22–26)

There was an argument in the early Islamic era, before the Islamic army's expansionary wars, that Islam had come primarily for Arabs and for Mecca and its surroundings.

> It is thus moreover that we have revealed to thee an Arabic Koran, that thou mayest warn the mother city[98] and all around it, and that thou mayest warn them of that day of the Gathering, of which there is no doubt—when part shall be in Paradise and part in the flame.
> (The Qur'án 42:5)

Paragraph No. 85:

Erelong, thine eyes will behold the standards of divine power unfurled throughout all regions, and the signs of His triumphant might and sovereignty manifest in every land.[353]

353. The Manifestations of God are not bound by time and place and see the future and the victory and exaltation of Their Cause even when They outwardly are powerless, captive, and under the rule of Their enemies.

When Jesus was brought beaten and in a miserable conditions as a captive, to the presence of the high priests and other powerful religious leaders, He announced the future ascendency of His station, a fact that those religious leaders could not see and were not able to comprehend.

> And as soon as it was day, the elders of the people and the chief priests and the scribes came together, and led him into their council, saying, Art thou the Christ? tell us. And he said unto them, If I tell you, ye will not believe: And if I also ask you, ye will not answer me, nor let me go. Hereafter shall the Son of man sit on the right hand of the power of God.
> (Luke 22:66–69)

When Bahá'u'lláh and His companions arrived at the Most Great Prison in the city of ‘Akká, in the eyes of the people who were watching them they were a group of captive exiles in seemingly miserable conditions, but Bahá'u'lláh’s statement regarding that instance indicates His vision of the victory and ascendency of His Cause:

---

[98] The mother city is Mecca.

> Upon Our arrival, . . .We were welcomed with banners of light, whereupon the Voice of the Spirit cried out saying: “Soon will all that dwell on earth be enlisted under these banners.”
> (Bahá'u'lláh, quoted in Shoghi Effendi, *God Passes By*, p. 184)

This contrast is beautifully described by Adib Taherzadeh:

> How incomparable is the difference between the vision of those assembled at the sea gate of 'Akká to jeer at the company of exiles and their leader, and the vision of Bahá'u'lláh. A few years before, in the Tablet of Sayyah foreshadowing His arrival in the city of 'Akká He had disclosed to those endowed with spiritual insight a vastly different spectacle:
>
>> Upon Our arrival We were welcomed with banners of light, whereupon the Voice of the Spirit cried out saying: “Soon will all that dwell on earth be enlisted under these banners.”
>> (Bahá'u'lláh, quoted in Shoghi Effendi, *God Passes By,* p. 184)
>
> The reaction of these onlookers, blind to the world of the spirit and the all-encompassing vision of Bahá'u'lláh, is characteristic of man's attitude to the Revelation of God in every age. Over one hundred years have passed since Bahá'u'lláh uttered these words. The majority of mankind, its rulers and wise men, have so far failed to recognize their truth, either remaining unaware of the coming of the Lord or turning a deaf ear to His voice. But those who have embraced His Cause believe in the vision of their Lord that 'soon will all that dwell on earth be enlisted under these banners'.
> (Adib Taherzadeh, *The Child of the Covenant,* p. 85)

As most of the divines have failed to apprehend the meaning of these verses, and have not grasped the significance of the Day of Resurrection, they therefore have foolishly interpreted these verses according to their idle and faulty conception.[354]

354. As mentioned above the leaders of religion often either do not understand the symbolism of these kinds of verses and interpret them literally, or if they do understand they ignore them and for the purpose of preserving their own position and authority oppose the Manifestations of God and prevent people from receiving and embracing the new Revelation. The Báb explained how the leaders of His time failed to understand the meaning of these verses:

> As to those who have debarred themselves from the Revelation of God, they have indeed failed to understand the significance of a single letter of the Qur'án, nor have they obtained the slightest notion of the Faith of Islam, otherwise they would not have turned away from God, Who hath brought them into being, Who hath nurtured them, hath caused them to die and hath proffered life unto them, by clinging to parts of their religion, thinking that they are doing righteous work for the sake of God.
> (The Báb, *Selections from the Writings of the Báb*, p. 139)

> [w]hat is intended by the Day of Resurrection is the Day of the appearance of the Tree of divine Reality, but it is not seen that any one of the followers of Shí‘ih Islám hath understood the meaning of the Day of Resurrection; rather have they fancifully imagined a thing which with God hath no reality. In the estimation of God and according to the usage of such as are initiated into divine mysteries, what is meant by the Day of Resurrection is this, that from the time of the appearance of Him Who is the Tree of divine Reality, at whatever period and under whatever name, until the moment of His disappearance, is the Day of Resurrection.
> (The Báb, *Selections from the Writings of the Báb*, p. 106)

Such are the strains of celestial melody which the immortal Bird of Heaven, warbling upon the Sadrih of Bahá, poureth out upon thee, that, by the permission of God, thou mayest tread the path of divine knowledge and wisdom.[355]

355. The Arabic word "Sadrih" means "Tree." As mentioned in Note No. 48 above, in Bahá'í scripture, the Manifestations of God and the Faith of God are often symbolized by a "Tree."

> Hearken unto My call, ringing forth from the precincts of this sacred Tree—a Tree set ablaze by the preexistent Fire: There is no God but Him; He is the Exalted, the All-Wise.
> (The Báb, *Selections from the Writings of the Báb*, p. 56)

The "Sadrih of Bahá" is a symbolic allusion to the person of Bahá'u'lláh as the Manifestation of God. This is another instance of Bahá'u'lláh's intimation of His divine station during the ten-year period between receiving Revelation in the dungeon of Tehran and His declaration in the Garden of Riḍván, which is a time period referred to in the Bahá'í Writings as the "Days of Concealment" or the period of "Delay." Shoghi Effendi, describing the declaration of Bahá'u'lláh in the Garden of Riḍván, states:

> Through that solemn act the "delay," of no less than a decade, divinely interposed between the birth of Bahá'u'lláh's Revelation in the Síyáh-Chál and its announcement to the Báb's disciples, was at long last terminated. The "set time of concealment," during which as He Himself has borne witness, the "signs and tokens of a divinely-appointed Revelation" were being showered upon Him, was fulfilled.
> (Shoghi Effendi, *God Passes By*, p. 151)

During this period Bahá'u'lláh, in some of His oral statements and several places in His Writings, provides intimation of His divine station and authority. An example of the former is when He accepted to perform a miracle (see Note No. 347 above) and some examples of the latter in the other passages from the Writings of Bahá'u'lláh are presented here:

> And since I noted thy mention of thy death in God, and thy life through Him, and thy love for the beloved of God and the Manifestations of His Names and the Dawning-Points of His Attributes—I therefore reveal unto thee sacred and resplendent tokens from the planes of glory, to attract thee into the court of holiness and nearness and beauty, and

draw thee to a station wherein thou shalt see nothing in creation save the Face of thy Beloved One, the Honored, and behold all created things only as in the day wherein none hath a mention.
(Bahá'u'lláh, The Seven Valleys and The Four Valleys, p. 2)

There is many an utterance of the mystic seers and doctors of former times which I have not mentioned here, since I mislike the copious citation from sayings of the past; for quotation from the words of others proveth acquired learning, not the divine bestowal. Even so much as We have quoted here is out of deference to the wont of men and after the manner of the friends. Further, such matters are beyond the scope of this epistle. Our unwillingness to recount their sayings is not from pride, rather is it a manifestation of wisdom and a demonstration of grace.
(Bahá'u'lláh, The Seven Valleys, p. 25)

Were I to reveal the full measure of that which He hath ordained for this station, the souls of men would depart from their bodies, the inner realities of all things would be shaken in their foundations, they that dwell within the realms of creation would be dumbfounded, and those who move in the lands of allusion would fade into utter nothingness.
(Bahá'u'lláh, *Gems of Divine Mysteries,* p. 31)

Encompassed as I am at this time by the dogs of the earth and the beasts of every land, concealed as I remain in the hidden habitation of Mine inner Being, forbidden as I may be from divulging that which God hath bestowed upon Me of the wonders of His knowledge, the gems of His wisdom, and the tokens of His power, yet am I loath to frustrate the hopes of one who hath approached the sanctuary of grandeur, sought to enter within the precincts of eternity, and aspired to soar in the immensity of this creation at the dawning of the divine decree. I shall therefore relate unto thee certain truths from among those which God hath vouchsafed unto Me, this only to the extent that souls can bear and minds endure, lest the malicious raise a clamour or the dissemblers hoist their banners. I implore God to graciously aid Me in this, for unto such as beseech Him, He

is the All-Bounteous, and of those who show mercy, He is the Most Merciful.
(Bahá'u'lláh, *Gems of Divine Mysteries*, p. 9)

Paragraph No. 86:

And now, concerning His words: "And He shall send His angels . . ." By "angels"[356] is meant those who, reinforced by the power of the spirit, have consumed, with the fire of the love of God, all human traits and limitations, and have clothed themselves with the attributes of the most exalted Beings and of the Cherubim.[357]

356. Angels in Judeo-Christo-Islamic traditions are defined as supernatural / spiritual beings that act on behalf of God and do His biddings in the human world. They are described in the Bible as having wings and moving in the air. Some of them have more than one face. Angels are made from light (*núr*), and, based on Islamic traditions they are servants of God who have no free will. They do not commit any sin or disobey God, and they always worship Him. They are God's envoys, and are always circling around the Throne of God singing His praise.

> And thou shalt see the Angels circling around the Throne with praises of their Lord: and judgment shall be pronounced between them with equity: and it shall be said, "Glory be to God the Lord of the Worlds."
> (The Qur'án 39:75)

Based on some verses of the Qur'án like the following,

> Praise be to God, Maker of the Heavens and of the Earth! Who employeth the angels as envoys, with pairs of wings, two, three and four: He addeth to his creature what He will! Truly God hath power for all things.
> (The Qur'án 35:1)

And based on some traditions from Muḥammad and Shí'ah Imáms, the Muslims made and wrote stories and books full of incredible, fantastic and utterly ridiculous description of the size, shape, function and peculiar life of angels.

Bahá'u'lláh here provides a new definition of the angels, "By 'angels' is meant those who, reinforced by the power of the spirit, have consumed, with the fire of the love of God, all human traits and limitations, and have clothed themselves with the attributes of the most exalted Beings." And also in this paragraph (below), Bahá'u'lláh provides additional details "in as much as these holy beings have sanctified themselves from every human limitation, have become endowed with the attributes of the spiritual, and have been adorned with the noble traits of the blessed, they therefore have been designated as "angels."

'Abdu'l-Bahá Has also provided a few definitions for angels:

> By angels is meant the divine confirmations and heavenly powers. Angels are also those holy souls who have severed attachment to the earthly world, who are free from the fetters of self and passion and who have attached their hearts to the Divine Realm and the Merciful Kingdom. They are of the Kingdom, heavenly; they are of the Merciful One, divine. They are the manifestations of the divine grace and the dawns of spiritual bounty.
> ('Abdu'l-Bahá, *Tablets of 'Abdu'l-Bahá,* vol. 3, p. 508)

> THE BLESSED Person of the Promised One is interpreted in the Holy Book as the Lord of Hosts—the heavenly armies. By heavenly armies those souls are intended who are entirely freed from the human world, transformed into celestial spirits and have become divine angels. Such souls are the rays of the Sun of Reality who will illumine all the continents. Each one is holding in his hand a trumpet, blowing the breath of life over all the regions. They are delivered from human qualities and the defects of the world of nature, are characterized with the characteristics of God, and are attracted with the fragrances of the Merciful.
> ('Abdu'l-Bahá, *Tablets of the Divine Plan*, p. 49)

357. In the Judeo-Christo-Islamic traditions, cherubims (in Arabic Karubin) are defined as a higher class of angels who are closer than other angels to the Throne of God and they are the angels who hold and support the Throne of God.

> In traditional Christian angelology they are regarded as an angel of the second highest order of the nine fold celestial hierarchy.
>
> The word *cherub* (*cherubim* is the Hebrew masculine plural) is a word borrowed from the Assyrian *kirubu*, from *karâbu*, "to be near," hence it means near ones, familiars, personal servants, bodyguards, courtiers. It was commonly used of those heavenly spirits, who closely surrounded the Majesty of God and paid Him intimate service. Hence it came to mean as much as "Angelic Spirit."
> (Catholic Encyclopedia,http://www.newadvent.org/cathen/03646c.htm)

Cherubim are presented in religious arts (both painting and sculpture) as beautiful winged children or winged lions or eagles with human faces.

That holy man, Ṣádiq,[358] in his eulogy of the Cherubim, saith: "There stand a company of our fellow-Shí'ihs behind the Throne."

358. Imám Ja'far al-Ṣádiq, the sixth Shí'ah Imám. For more details see Appendix II, the article related to Note No. 62.

"A true believer is likened unto the philosopher's stone."[359]

359. The philosopher's stone, or stone of the philosophers, is a legendary alchemical substance capable of turning base metals such as mercury, silver, coper or lead into gold. It is also able to extend one's life and is sometimes referred to as the elixir of life, useful for rejuvenation and for achieving immortality; for many centuries, it was the most sought-after goal in alchemy. The philosopher's stone was the central symbol of the mystical terminology of alchemy, symbolizing perfection at its finest, enlightenment, and heavenly bliss. Efforts to discover the philosopher's stone were known as the Magnum Opus ("Great Work"). . . . Alchemy refers to an ancient philosophical and spiritual discipline that combined chemistry with metal work, medicine, astronomy, and physics. The Magnum Opus (translated from Latin as "Great Work") of alchemy was successfully piecing together the concept of the philosopher's stone, which during the

Middle Ages through to the seventeenth century was believed to not only have the power to impart great riches from base metals, but could also grant eternal life. For centuries, the Philosopher's Stone was the most sought-after object in alchemy, until scientists figured out that everything it promised was entirely impossible and not even worth pursuing.
(Based on entry for the Philosopher's Stone in Wikipedia, the free encyclopedia)

And now consider, how unfair and numerous are those who, although they themselves have failed to inhale the fragrance of belief, have condemned as infidels those by whose word belief itself is recognized and established.[360]

360. This is a reference to the failure of the leaders of religions to recognize the new Manifestations of God or even consider Them as believers. This applies in general to all religious leaders including Jews and Christians and particularly to Muslim and especially to the Shí'ah divines who condemned the Báb and His followers as nonbelievers and infidels. The Báb when referring to the importance of the Day (period) of the appearance of the new Manifestation of God, also mentions that those who fail to recognize Him will also refuse to regard Him as a believer:

> That Day is indeed an infinitely mighty Day, for in it the Divine Tree proclaimeth from eternity unto eternity, "Verily, I am God. No God is there but Me." Yet those who are veiled believe that He is one like unto them, and they refuse even to call Him a believer, although such a title in the realm of His heavenly Kingdom is conferred everlastingly upon the most insignificant follower of His previous Dispensation.
> (The Báb, *Selections from the Writings of the Báb,* p. 78)

> Likewise in this Dispensation of the Point of the Bayán, if the people had not refused to concede the name believer unto Him, how could they have incarcerated Him on this mountain, without realizing that the quintessence of belief oweth its existence to a word from Him? Their hearts are deprived of the power of true insight, and thus they cannot see, while those endowed with the eyes of the spirit circle like moths round the Light of Truth until they are

consumed. It is for this reason that the Day of Resurrection is said to be the greatest of all days, yet it is like unto any other day.
(The Báb, *Selections from the Writings of the Báb*, p. 78)

Paragraph No. 87:

Such is the meaning of these verses,[361] every word of which hath been expounded by the aid of the most lucid texts, the most convincing arguments, and the best established evidences.

361. These are the verses in the Gospel of Matthew to which Bahá'u'lláh refers in Paragraph 24 of the Book of Certitude as "those signs that must needs herald the advent of the Manifestation after Him" (see Paragraph number 24 and Notes Nos. 122 and 123).

These are verses 29–31 in chapter 24 of the Gospel of Matthew:

> Immediately after the tribulation of those days shall the sun be darkened, and the moon shall not give her light, and the stars shall fall from heaven, and the powers of the heavens shall be shaken. And then shall appear the sign of the Son of man in heaven: and then shall all the tribes of the earth mourn, and they shall see the Son of man coming in the clouds of heaven with power and great glory. And he shall send his angels with a great sound of a trumpet, and they shall gather together his elect from the four winds, from one end of heaven to the other.

The imagery presented in the above verses that describe the signs that are associated with the second advent of Christ for Christians are very similar to the signs that herald the coming of the Messiah for the Jews and the coming of the Promised One of Islam for the Muslims. Bahá'u'lláh, within the span of fifty two paragraphs and almost the same number of pages, by the aid of the most lucid texts, and through the most convincing arguments, and the best established evidences, expounds and explains the meaning of each and every one of those signs such as:

- Tribulation
- Darkening of the sun
- Moon not giving light
- Falling of stars from heaven (meaning of the stars and heaven)
- Appearance of the signs of the Son of man in heaven
- The Son of man coming in the clouds of heaven (meaning of the clouds)
- Coming of the Angels (meaning of the Angels)

Paragraph No. 88:

As the adherents of Jesus have never understood the hidden meaning of these words, and as the signs which they and the leaders of their Faith have expected have failed to appear, they therefore refused to acknowledge, even until now, the truth of those Manifestations of Holiness that have since the days of Jesus been made manifest.[362].

362. Although the major cause of rejection of Christ by the Jews was that their expected signs for the appearance of their Messiah did not literally appear, Christians are also expecting the signs mentioned in the Olivet Discourse to literally appear (see Note No. 123 above). The two Manifestations of God that appeared between the time of Jesus and the time of revelation of the Kitáb-i-Íqán (circa 1862) were Muḥammad and the Báb.

in this, the Day of Resurrection![363]

363. The concept of the Day of Resurrection was discussed at length above in Notes Nos. 123, 129, 176, 208, 350 and 354. From a Bahá'í perspective the appearance of the new Manifestation of God (the Báb) represents the Day of Resurrection for the followers of Islam and all other previous religions.

Even as the All-Glorious hath recorded their statement: "Why hath not an angel been sent down to him, so that he should have been a warner with Him?"[364]

364. The objections of the Jewish and Christian divines are recorded in the Qur'án:

> And they say, "What sort of apostle is this? He eateth food and he walketh the streets! Unless an angel be sent down and take part in his warnings, Or a treasure be thrown down to him, or he have a garden that supplieth him with food . . ." and those unjust persons say, "Ye follow but a man enchanted."
> (The Qur'án 25:7)

Paragraph No. 89:

Such objections and differences have persisted in every age and century. The people have always busied themselves with such specious discourses, vainly protesting: "Wherefore hath not this or that sign appeared?"[365]

365. As discussed above in detail, at the time of the appearance of every Manifestation of God, people at the instigation of their religious leaders, question the authenticity of their claim. People protest to and reject the Manifestations of God due to nonfulfillment of the prophecies that according to their vain imagination had to be literally fulfilled preceding or synchronous to Their appearance. The Old Testament, the New Testament, and the Qur'án have documented these expectations and the subsequent protestation and rejection that both Jesus and Muḥammad encountered.

In the case of Jesus, the Jews were expecting Elijah to descend from heaven in his physical corporeal body prior to the appearance of their Messiah[99] and for supernatural events such as the darkening of the sun and moon and the falling of the stars, earthquakes and storms to accompany the appearance of their Messiah who would come with his army and rescue the Jews from the rule of the Gentiles.[100] But Jesus looked like an ordinary man with no army and power. They did not see Elijah descending from

---

[99] Old Testament, Book of Malachi, Chapters 3 and 4.

[100] Old Testament, Book of Joel, Chapter 2.

heaven before He started His ministry, and none of those expected supernatural events took place at that time.

As for Muḥammad, they objected to Him because he also appeared to be an ordinary man, who ate, drank, and walked in the market place. There were no angels by His sides, no halo around His head, and they could assault Him and even break His tooth and pour trash on His head with impunity.[101]

The Báb also suffered at the hands of divines of His time and was subjected to cruelty, imprisonment and martyrdom because the ridiculous scenario imagined by the divines of His age for the coming of their promised Qá'im (such as the emergence of the one-eyed Dajjál and the Sufyání, and other signs mentioned in the "Introduction Note No. 35" above and Appendix I below) did not appear.

And yet they bear witness to this well-known tradition: "Verily Our Word is abstruse, bewilderingly abstruse." In another instance, it is said: "Our Cause is sorely trying, highly perplexing; none can bear it except a favorite of heaven, or an inspired Prophet, or he whose faith God hath tested."[366]

366. These two traditions are attributed to Muḥammad. Bahá'u'lláh quotes these two traditions in confirmation of His statement that the leaders of religion are unable to understand the true meaning of the signs and prophecies and that by literal interpretation of the Word of God they deprived themselves and all their people from the bounties of the new Revelation. The second tradition states that there are only three groups that have the ability to properly interpret and comprehend the true meanings of the abstruse words of the sacred scripture:

- The first group consists of those that are the favorite of heaven (like the angles that are close to the Throne of God). The second group consists of those who are the inspired Prophets. The Qur'án uses two different terms when referring to intermediaries between God and man. One is Messenger (Rasool, also transliterated as Rasoul) and the other is prophet (Nabi). The majority of Muslims

[101] The Qur'án, Súrah 25, also see Appendix I.

do not distinguish between these two. However, these two classes are different and distinct. The Messengers are those Who receive Revelation from God and establish an independent religion, such as Abraham, Moses, Jesus and Muḥammad. These are sometimes referred to as Major Prophets. Prophets are on the other hand those who receive inspiration, promote a religion and guide and assist people in understanding and following the precepts of one of the religions. Examples of prophets are Daniel, Isaiah, Joel and other prophets of Israel. These are the inspired prophets. The third group consists of those whose Faith is tested by God and who pass the test.

Bahá'u'lláh very simply demonstrates that none of these conditions is applicable to the leaders of religion.

When the divine Touchstone[367] appeared, they have shown themselves to be naught but dross.

367. Touchstone is defined as:

> A black siliceous stone used to test the purity of gold and silver by the color of the streak produced on it by rubbing it with either metal. A test or criterion for the quality of a thing.
> (*The Random House Dictionary of English Language.* The unabridged edition)

A touchstone is used to distinguish precious metals from cheap and worthless metals (dross). The above statement indicates that the divine Touchstone is the new Manifestation of God. The leaders of religions have always failed the test of faith by opposing the Manifestation of God and by preventing their followers from receiving the bounty of the new Revelation. Christ, addressing the leaders of religion of His time, stated:

> But woe unto you, scribes and Pharisees, hypocrites! for ye shut up the kingdom of heaven against men: for ye neither go in yourselves, neither suffer ye them that are entering to go in.
> (Matthew 23:13)

Similar vituperative statements regarding the leaders of religions are found in other Writings of Bahá'u'lláh. He—when addressing these leaders of religions who in reality are ignorant and foolish but outwardly are considered learned and wise, who pretend to be the shepherds of the multitude of their followers but in reality are ferocious wolves who outwardly pretend to be just and pious but inwardly are corrupt—states:

> O YE THAT ARE FOOLISH, YET HAVE A NAME TO BE WISE!
> Wherefore do ye wear the guise of shepherds, when inwardly ye have become wolves, intent upon My flock? Ye are even as the star, which riseth ere the dawn[102], and which, though it seem radiant and luminous, leadeth the wayfarers of My city astray into the paths of perdition.
> (Bahá'u'lláh, The Hidden Words, Persian, no. 24)

> O YE SEEMING FAIR YET INWARDLY FOUL!
> Ye are like clear but bitter water, which to outward seeming is crystal pure but of which, when tested by the divine Assayer, not a drop is accepted. Yea, the sun beam falls alike upon the dust and the mirror, yet differ they in reflection even as doth the star from the earth: nay, immeasurable is the difference!
> (Bahá'u'lláh, The Hidden Words, Persian, no. 25)

These religious leaders present the appearance of good shepherds and guiding morning stars, they pretend to be fair ethical and spiritual people, but in reality they are wolves, misguiding stars, and corrupt and the cause of spiritual perdition.

---

[102] From ancient times until almost the middle of the ninteenth century, in most parts of the world caravans and horse drawn carriages were the most prevalent means of travel and the roads were not safe. The caravans and groups who were traveling were often attacked by thieves and highway robbers in the darkness. The travelers that were staying overnight at the inns or other resting places used to get up at dawn, get ready, and move out just before sunrise. As they did not have any watches or clocks, they would rise and move out when they would see the planet Venus (also called the Morning Star) which is very bright and appears at dawn. However, another bright star, Sirius which usually appears a couple of hours before Venus, was sometimes mistakenly assumed to be the morning star and when it appeared, the travelers would move out of their city or safe overnight residence into the wilderness. They had to travel in darkness and would be attacked by the thieves and robbers and would lose their belongings and their lives.

Paragraph No. 90:

[t]hese divines who are still doubtful of, and dispute about, the theological obscurities of their faith, yet claim to be the exponents of the subtleties of the law of God, and the expounders of the essential mysteries of His holy Word.[368]

368. Christian theologians and divines have for more than nineteen hundred years been engaged in arguments and fights and have divided the religion of Christ into hundreds of sects based on disputes regarding a wide array of obscure theological issues in Christology. A few of those are listed below:

- ✓ The nature of Christ, the single or dual substantiation,
- ✓ The Doctrine of the Trinity,
- ✓ The perpetual virginity of Mary,
- ✓ Whether Jesus was resurrected with his cloths or naked
- ✓ On sacramental and procedural issues such as baptism, whether it should be performed by immersion of the individual in water or by pouring or sprinkling water on the individual.

Similarly, Muslim theologians and divines have for more than thirteen hundred years been engaged in arguments and fights and divided the religion of Islam into hundreds of sects based on disputes regarding a wide array of obscure theological issues such as:

- ➢ The nature of the unity of God,
- ➢ The five Pillars of Islam,
- ➢ The station and divinity of Imám ‘Alí,
- ➢ Whether Muḥammad went to His night Journey to heaven with His physical body. Whether while there, He had dinner with God.

- On the nature and the number of the wings of the angels,

- On jurisprudence and procedural issues such as performing daily prayers, fasting or compliance with other religious laws.

The main occupation of these divines has been to make rules for the way to perform the religious obligations, but in many cases these rules are contradictory and the cause of arguments and dispute between the divines and their followers. There has been a long term historical dispute among the Muslim divines as to whether, during the daily obligatory prayers, one should hold his hands and arms on his sides or fold them and keep them on his chest. The same kind of doubts, disagreements and disputes exist for the proper procedure in performing every religious act. For example, there have always been disputes and quarrels about what can nullify prayers and fasting. Even within the same sect, the divines have been and still are, engaged in ongoing disputes regarding minute procedural issues.

How can these divines be capable of understanding the subtleties, and decipher the mysteries of their holy book and the symbolic allusions presented in their traditions?

and are still oblivious of the fact that all the signs foretold have come to pass, that the way of God's holy Cause hath been revealed,[369] and the concourse of the faithful, swift as lightning, are, even now, passing upon that way.

369. The "way of God's holy Cause" is a translation of the Arabic term (Ṣeráṭ-i-Amr). The word "Ṣeráṭ" literally means the way, the path or the road, but in Islamic vernacular refers to a way or a bridge that extends between the plane of resurrection and Paradise (see Footnote No. 29 and Note No. 350 above). In Islamic literature the Ṣeráṭ is said to be narrower than a hair, sharper than a blade and infinitely long. After completion of the judgment, people have to pass through the Ṣeráṭ. Those that are pure and faithful believers will easily and speedily cross it and enter Paradise, but unbelievers and sinners will not be able to pass and will fall into Hell.

In light of the exegesis provided by Bahá'u'lláh here and in other passages from the Bahá'í Writings, it is possible to understand the real meaning of these symbolic terms. It seems that the Day of Resurrection is the time of the appearance of the Manifestation of God and Ṣeráṭ is the symbol of the claim of the new Manifestation of God and His Revelation. The Báb explains the meanings of these symbolic terms in the Kitáb-i-Bayán. In chapter seven of the second Váhid, He states:

> In the estimation of God and according to the usage of such as are initiated into divine mysteries, what is meant by the Day of Resurrection is this, that from the time of the appearance of Him Who is the Tree of divine Reality, at whatever period and under whatever name, until the moment of His disappearance, is the Day of Resurrection.
>
> For example, from the inception of the mission of Jesus—may peace be upon Him—till the day of His ascension was the Resurrection of Moses. For during that period the Revelation of God shone forth through the appearance of that divine Reality, Who rewarded by His Word everyone who believed in Moses, and punished by His Word everyone who did not believe; inasmuch as God's Testimony for that Day was that which He had solemnly affirmed in the Gospel. And from the inception of the Revelation of the Apostle of God—may the blessings of God be upon Him—till the day of His ascension was the Resurrection of Jesus—peace be upon Him—wherein the Tree of divine Reality appeared in the person of Muḥammad, rewarding by His Word everyone who was a believer in Jesus, and punishing by His Word everyone who was not a believer in Him. And from the moment when the Tree of the Bayán appeared until it disappeareth is the Resurrection of the Apostle of God, as is divinely foretold in the Qur'án; the beginning of which was when two hours and eleven minutes had passed on the eve of the fifth of Jamádíyu'l-Avval, 1260 A.H.,[*] which is the year 1270 of the Declaration of the Mission of Muḥammad. This was the beginning of the Day of Resurrection of the Qur'án, and until the disappearance of the Tree of divine Reality is

the Resurrection of the Qur'án. The stage of perfection of everything is reached when its resurrection occurreth. The perfection of the religion of Islám was consummated at the beginning of this Revelation; and from the rise of this Revelation until its setting, the fruits of the Tree of Islám, whatever they are, will become apparent. The Resurrection of the Bayán will occur at the time of the appearance of Him Whom God shall make manifest. For today the Bayán is in the stage of seed; at the beginning of the manifestation of Him Whom God shall make manifest its ultimate perfection will become apparent. He is made manifest in order to gather the fruits of the trees He hath planted; even as the Revelation of the Qá'im [He Who ariseth], a descendant of Muḥammad—may the blessings of God rest upon Him—is exactly like unto the Revelation of the Apostle of God Himself [Muḥammad]. He appeareth not, save for the purpose of gathering the fruits of Islam from the Qur'ánic verses which He [Muḥammad] hath sown in the hearts of men. The fruits of Islám cannot be gathered except through allegiance unto Him [the Qá'im] and by believing in Him. At the present time, however, only adverse effects have resulted; for although He hath appeared in the midmost heart of Islám, and all people profess it by reason of their relationship to Him [the Qá'im], yet unjustly have they consigned Him to the Mountain of Mákú, and this notwithstanding that in the Qur'án the advent of the Day of Resurrection hath been promised unto all by God. For on that Day all men will be brought before God and will attain His Presence; which meaneth appearance before Him Who is the Tree of divine Reality and attainment unto His presence; inasmuch as it is not possible to appear before the Most Holy Essence of God, nor is it conceivable to seek reunion with Him. That which is feasible in the matter of appearance before Him and of meeting Him is attainment unto the Primal Tree.
[* 22 May 1844]
(The Báb, *Selections from the Writings of the Báb*, pp. 106–8)

THE Day of Resurrection is a day on which the sun riseth and setteth like unto any other day. How oft hath the Day

of Resurrection dawned, and the people of the land where it occurred did not learn of the event.
(The Báb, *Selections from the Writings of the Báb*, p. 78)

In chapter twelve of the second Váhid of the Kitáb-i-Bayán, He explains that Ṣeráṭ is the claim and Revelation of each Manifestation of God and that Ṣeráṭ for people who believe is wider than the heavens and the earth. Therefore, when the Manifestation of God appears it is the Day of Resurrection. On that Day those who are faithful to the eternal covenant of God and believe and accept His claim, easily and swift as lightning cross the Ṣeráṭ and enter the paradise of nearness and spiritual delight, and those who do not believe, fall into the hell of remoteness and unbelief.

Paragraph No. 91:

Were they to be questioned concerning those signs that must needs herald the revelation and rise of the sun of the Muḥammadan Dispensation, to which We have already referred, none of which have been literally fulfilled, and were it to be said to them: "Wherefore have ye rejected the claims advanced by Christians and the peoples of other faiths and regard them as infidels," knowing not what answer to give, they will reply: "These Books have been corrupted and are not, and never have been, of God." [370]

370. As mentioned above, the advent of Christ was not accompanied by the literal fulfilment of the Jewish prophecies and the ordinary appearance of Jesus did not satisfy the expectations of the Jews and caused them to reject Him. Christians in their turn were also expecting the literal fulfilment of the prophecies and material appearance of the signs and occurrences mentioned in the Gospels, and therefore rejected Muḥammad as a false Prophet because He appeared as an ordinary man and none of the expected signs and occurrences preceded or accompanied His advent. Another significant issue in this context is that the Qur'án states that not only was the advent of Muḥammad prophesied and described in the Old Testament (the Law) and in the New Testament (Evangel), but He was also clearly named in the Gospels. In the Súrah of (Al-A'ráf) "The Heights" it states:

> Who shall follow the Apostle, the unlettered Prophet—whom they shall find described with them in the Law and Evangel. What is right will he enjoin them, and forbid them what is wrong, and will allow them healthful viands and prohibit the impure, and will ease them of their burden, and of the yokes which were upon them; and those who shall believe in him, and strengthen him, and help him, and follow the light which hath been sent down with him,—these are they with whom it shall be well."
> (The Qur'án 7:156)

In the Súrah of (al-Ṣaff) "The Ranks" it states:

> And when Jesus the son of Mary said, 'Children of Israel, I am indeed the Messenger of God to you, confirming the Torah that is before me, and giving good tidings of a Messenger who shall come after me, whose name shall be Aḥmad.' Yet when He came to them with clear signs, they said: 'This is a Plain sorcery'
> (The Qur'án, Arberry tr, 61:6)

The Rodwell translation reads:

> And remember when Jesus the son of Mary said, "O Children of Israel! Of a truth I am God's Apostle to you to confirming the law which was given before me, and to announce an apostle that shall come after me, whose name shall be Aḥmad!" But when he (Aḥmad) presented himself with clear proofs of his mission, they said: "This is manifest sorcery."
> (The Qur'án 61:6)

Throughout Islamic history, Muslims condemned the Jews and Christians and called them infidels for not believing in Muḥammad and His Revelation. Jews and Christians say that they cannot believe in Muḥammad because no description of Muḥammad or His advent is found in the Old or New Testament, none of the expected signs appeared and the name "Aḥmad" is not found in any of the Gospels (see Note No. 93, above).

Muslim divines not being able to prove the literal fulfilment of the expected signs and occurrences and unable to show the description and the name of Muḥammad or Aḥmad in the Old or the New Testament, devised the concept of the corruption of the Bible (both the Old and New Testament). They claim that "These Books have been corrupted and are not, and never have been, of God." Corruption is translation of the Arabic word “Taḥríf.”

The concept of the corruption of the Books holds that the prophecies related to the advent of Muḥammad, the descriptions of His person and the name Aḥmad were all removed from the texts of the Old and New Testament by Jews and Christians. Some divines take an extreme stance and state that the true Torah and Evangel were taken to heaven and the present Bible is not the divine Book.

In the following paragraphs Bahá'u'lláh clearly demonstrates that these accusations are false.

Reflect: the words of the verses themselves eloquently testify to the truth that they are of God. A similar verse hath been also revealed in the Qur'án, were ye of them that comprehend. Verily I say, throughout all this period they have utterly failed to comprehend what is meant by corrupting the text.[371]

371. Bahá'u'lláh explains that:

- The words of the verses of the Bible “themselves eloquently testify to the truth that they are of God.”
- Verses with similar content and meaning to the verses of the Bible have also been revealed and exist in the Qur'án.

It is noteworthy to mention that the Qur'án itself confirms divine origin of the Torah and Gospels and their similarity with the Qur'án:

> He hath revealed unto thee (Muḥammad) the Scripture with truth, confirming that which was (revealed) before it, even as He revealed the Torah and the Gospel. Aforetime, for a guidance to mankind;
> (The Qur'án, Pickthall tr, 3:3–4)

> He has sent down to thee the Book, in truth, confirming what was before it, and has revealed the law, and the gospel before for the guidance of men, and has revealed the Discrimination.
> (The Qur'án, E.H. Palmer tr, 3:3)

> In truth hath He sent down to thee "the Book," which confirmeth those which precede it: For He had sent down the Law, and the Evangel aforetime, as man's Guidance; and now hath He sent down the "Illumination" (Furkan).[103]
> (The Qur'án 3:3)

Bahá'u'lláh states that "throughout all this period," almost thirteen centuries, the Muslim divines "have utterly failed to comprehend what is meant by corrupting the text," and He in the following seven paragraphs explains the true meaning of the corruption of the Books.

Paragraph No. 92:

Yea, in the writings and utterances of the Mirrors reflecting the sun of the Muḥammadan Dispensation mention hath been made of "Modification by the exalted beings" and "alteration by the disdainful." Such passages, however, refer only to particular cases.[372]

372. The Arabic word "Taḥríf" has been translated in English as alteration, corruption, displacement, distortion and changing of the context. This term has been historically used by the Muslim jurists, Qur'ánic commentators and apologists in their arguments against the criticism of Muḥammad and Islam by Christians and Jews. They claim that the Jews and Christians have altered the texts of the Old Testament (Torah) and the New Testament (Evangel).

    Islamic jurists and apologists identify six kinds of Taḥríf:

---

[103] Ar. *Furkan*—a word derived by Muhammad from the Jews, constantly used in the Talmud, and meaning as in Syr . . . deliverance, liberation . . . and hence, illumination, revelation, generally. . . . The title is applied to the Koran and Pentateuch alike.
(The Qur'an, Rodwell tr, note No. 2, p. 154)

1. To deliberately add or delete a word, phrase or sentence to or from a text that alters or distorts the meaning or intent of the sentence, the story or discourse in that text.
2. To interpret the text or statement in a manner that is clearly opposite to the meaning intended by the author of that text.
3. In translating a word that has more than one meaning, choosing the meaning that makes the translated text contrary to the original.
4. To distort the pronunciations of some words in a manner that alters their meaning.
5. To write something and present it to people as taken from the sacred scripture.
6. To ignore some statements of the holy books that are contrary to their personal position.

The word Taḥríf and its derivatives appeared all together only in four verses in the Qur'án. In none of those verses where the word Taḥríf or its derivatives are used, does the Qur'án claim that any words or phrases were added to or deleted from the Torah or Evangel. In all those places the word is used in terms of misinterpretation of the text, distortion of the pronunciation of the words in a manner that alters their meaning, ignoring some of the laws or teachings that are clearly stated in their scriptures or falsely representing something as sacred scripture. As Bahá'u'lláh states, each one of those verses refers to a particular case.

Among them is the story of Ibn-i-Ṣúríyá.[373] When the people of Khaybar[374] asked the focal center of the Muḥammadan Revelation[375] concerning the penalty of adultery committed between a married man and a married woman,[376]

373. According to the Qur'ánic commentaries, Ibn-i-Ṣúríyá was the most learned Jewish Rabbi contemporary to the Prophet Muḥammad. Ibn-i-Ṣúríyá was living in Fadak (see below).

374. Khaybar is the name of a fortress containing oasis areas that had many dams and water reservoirs. It was located approximately thirty miles to the north of Medina. For several centuries before the rise of Islam, it was inhabited by Jewish tribes. It consisted of

several fortress communities and was a center of commerce and the production of dates.

Khaybar area was mostly owned by the rich Jewish people of Medina. It fell to Muslim forces in 629 AD. Fadak was a garden oasis in the Khaybar area.
(Based partly on information provided in Wikipedia)

375. The focal center of the Muḥammadan Revelation is the Prophet Muḥammad.

376. The story of Ibn-i-Ṣúríyá as related in the most famous Qur'ánic commentaries when cleared of the irrelevant details are in close conformity with the brief story related here.

I adjure thee by God Who clove the sea for you,[377] caused manna to descend upon you,[378] and the cloud to overshadow you,[379] Who delivered you from Pharaoh and his people,[380] and exalted you above all human beings,[381]

377. This is a reference to the parting of the Red Sea during the Jewish exodus from Egypt. The Old Testament recorded this event in the Book of Exodus:

> And the angel of God, which went before the camp of Israel, removed and went behind them; and the pillar of the cloud went from before their face, and stood behind them: And it came between the camp of the Egyptians and the camp of Israel; and it was a cloud and darkness to them, but it gave light by night to these: so that the one came not near the other all the night. And Moses stretched out his hand over the sea; and the LORD caused the sea to go back by a strong east wind all that night, and made the sea dry land, and the waters were divided. And the children of Israel went into the midst of the sea upon the dry ground: and the waters were a wall unto them on their right hand, and on their left.
> (Exodus 14:19–22)

378. This is a reference to the Jews eating manna (food from heaven) in the desert:

> And the LORD spake unto Moses, saying, I have heard the murmurings of the children of Israel: speak unto them, saying, At even ye shall eat flesh, and in the morning ye shall be filled with bread; and ye shall know that I am the LORD your God. And it came to pass, that at even the quails came up, and covered the camp: and in the morning the dew lay round about the host. And when the dew that lay was gone up, behold, upon the face of the wilderness there lay a small round thing, as small as the hoar frost on the ground. And when the children of Israel saw it, they said one to another, It is manna: for they wist not what it was. And Moses said unto them, This is the bread which the LORD hath given you to eat.
> (Exodus 14:11–15)

379. Clouds that overshadowed Jews and protected them from the Egyptian army:

> And the angel of God, which went before the camp of Israel, removed and went behind them; and the pillar of the cloud went from before their face, and stood behind them: And it came between the camp of the Egyptians and the camp of Israel; and it was a cloud and darkness to them, but it gave light by night to these: so that the one came not near the other all the night.
> (Exodus 14:19–20)

380. God delivered Israel from Pharaoh and his people:

> Wherefore say unto the children of Israel, I am the LORD, and I will bring you out from under the burdens of the Egyptians, and I will rid you out of their bondage, and I will redeem you with a stretched out arm, and with great judgments: And I will take you to me for a people, and I will be to you a God: and ye shall know that I am the LORD your God, which bringeth you out from under the burdens of the Egyptians.
> (Exodus 6:6–7)

381. The Pentateuch states that God exalted Israelites above all human beings:

> And thou shalt say unto Pharaoh, Thus saith the LORD, Israel is my son, even my firstborn: And I say unto thee, Let my son go, that he may serve me.
> (Exodus 4:22–23)

> For thou art an holy people unto the LORD thy God: the LORD thy God hath chosen thee to be a special people unto himself, above all people that are upon the face of the earth. The LORD did not set his love upon you, nor choose you, because ye were more in number than any people; for ye were the fewest of all people: But because the LORD loved you, and because he would keep the oath which he had sworn unto your fathers, hath the LORD brought you out with a mighty hand, and redeemed you out of the house of bondmen, from the hand of Pharaoh king of Egypt.
> (Deuteronomy 7:7–8)

tell us what Moses hath decreed concerning adultery between a married man and a married woman." He made reply: "O Muhammad! death by stoning is the law."[382]

382. The punishment of adultery in the Pentateuch is death:

> And the man that committeth adultery with another man's wife, even he that committeth adultery with his neighbour's wife, the adulterer and the adulteress shall surely be put to death.
> (Leviticus 20:10)

When Nebuchadnezzar[383] delivered Jerusalem to the flames, and put the Jews to death, only a few survived. The divines of that age, considering the extremely limited number of the Jews, and the multitude of the Amalekites,[384] took counsel together, and came to the conclusion that were they to enforce the law of the Pentateuch, every survivor who hath been delivered from the hand of Nebuchadnezzar would have to be put to death according to the verdict of the Book.

383. Nebuchadnezzar, (c. 634–562 BC) was the Chaldean King of Neo-Babylonian Empire who reigned between 605 BC and 562 BC. He expanded his dominion by invading Egypt, Syria and

Judea. He invaded Jerusalem in 597 BC and deposed King Jehoiakim. Subsequent to the Jewish rebellion he destroyed and burned the city of Jerusalem and demolished the Temple, killed a great many of the inhabitants, and took a very large group of Jews in captivity to Babylon (some accounts estimate the number of the captives at close to 70,000).
(Based partly on information provided in Wikipedia)

384. Amalekites were descendants of Amalek, grandson of Esau (Jacob's brother). Biblical scholars assume that the word Amalek may mean "dweller in the valley," or possibly "war-like" person. Amalekites were dwelling in the south country of Canaan. They warred with Israel over the centuries. Saul and David went to war and defeated them but did not succeed in exterminating them. After the defeat of Israel and the destruction of Jerusalem by Nebuchadnezzar, Amalekites became stronger and challenged the Israelites more frequently.
(Based partly on information provided in the Dictionary of Bible, King James Version)

They pervert the text of the Word of God."[385]

385. The story of Ibn-i-Ṣúríyá has been cited by Qur'ánic commentators to explain the reason for the revelation of this phrase in verse 45 in the Súrah of Women (verse numbers in the English translations differ):

> Of the Jews there are those who displace words from their (right) places, and say: "We hear and we disobey;" and "Hear what is not heard": and "Ra'ina;" with a twist of their tongues and a slander to faith. If only they had said: "We hear and we obey;" and "Do hear;" and "Do look at us": it would have been better for them, and more proper; but Allah hath cursed them, for their unbelief; and but few of them will believe.
> (The Qur'án, Yusuf Ali tr, 4:46)
>
> Some of those who are Jews change words from their context and say: "We hear and disobey; hear thou as one who heareth not" and "Listen to us!" distorting with their tongues and slandering religion. If they had said: "We hear

and we obey: hear thou, and look at us" it had been better for them, and more upright. But Allah hath cursed them for their disbelief, so they believe not, save a few.
(The Qur'án, Pickthall tr, Súrah 4:46)

Among the Jews are those who displace the words of their Scriptures, and say, "We have heard, and we have not obeyed. Hear thou, but as one that heareth not; and look at us;" perplexing with their tongues, and wounding the Faith by their revilings. But if they would say, "We have heard, and we obey; hear thou, and regard us;" it were better for them, and more right. But God hath cursed them for their unbelief. Few only of them are believers!
(The Qur'an 4:48–49)

But for their breaking their covenant we have cursed them, and have hardened their hearts. They shift the words of Scripture from their places, and have forgotten part of what they were taught. Thou wilt not cease to discover deceit on their part, except in a few of them. But forgive them, and pass it over: verily, God loveth those who act generously!
(The Qur'an 5:15)

Paragraph No. 93:

Verily by "perverting" the text is not meant that which these foolish and abject souls have fancied, even as some maintain that Jewish and Christian divines have effaced from the Book such verses as extol and magnify the countenance of Muhammad, and instead thereof have inserted the contrary.[386]

386. The claims of removal or addition of text from and to the Old and New Testaments are baseless claims and are not supported by any of the four verses of the Qur'án where the word Taḥríf and its derivatives appear. In all those places the word is used in the context of shifting the meaning or misinterpretation of the word and not adding or removing any words, phrases, or sentences.

Of the Jews there are those who displace words from their (right) places…
(The Qur'án, Yusuf Ali tr, 4:46)

> Some of those who are Jews change words from their context...
> (The Qur'án, Pickthall tr, Súrah 4, Women)

> Among the Jews are those who displace the words of their Scriptures,
> (The Qur'án 4:48–49)

> They shift the words of Scripture from their places, and have forgotten part of what they were taught.
> (The Qur'án 5:15)

Moreover, the Pentateuch had been spread over the surface of the earth, and was not confined to Mecca and Medina, so that they could privily corrupt and pervert its text.[387]

387. Biblical scholars maintain that by the end of the second century BC, canonization of the Old Testament containing the Pentateuch was complete and subsequently no addition or deletion to the text took place. The two oldest existing manuscripts of the Bible, the Codex Vaticanous and the Codex Sinaticus, date back to the third and fourth centuries AD some three hundred years before the advent of Prophet Muḥammad. By the first half of the seventh century at the birth of Islam thousands of copies of the Bible were spread all over the world. The existence of the Bible was not confined to Mecca and Medina, where the local Jews could delete, add to or alter its text.

Detailed and accurate lists of the discrepancies between the texts of the above mentioned old manuscripts and the present Bible have been prepared by Biblical scholars. These lists highlight the differences between the contents of those manuscripts and the presently extant Bible.
(Based partly on information provided in Wikipedia, The free Encyclopedia with some modifications)

None of those discrepancies were additions or deletions of the texts related to the signs or prophecies for the advent of the next Prophet, and none of them named the Prophet Muḥammad, described His person or His religion. Those Muslims that claim that verses prophesying the coming of Prophet Muḥammad had been removed and that verses against Him had been added to the Torah or Evangel, have not been able to show any instance of this type of addition or removal.

And as the Jews, in the time of Muḥammad, interpreted those verses of the Pentateuch, that referred to His Manifestation, after their own fancy, and refused to be satisfied with His holy utterance, the charge of "perverting" the text was therefore pronounced against them. Likewise, it is clear, how in this day, the people of the Qur'án have perverted the text of God's holy Book, concerning the signs of the expected Manifestation, and interpreted it according to their inclination and desires.[388]

388. There are several passages in the Pentateuch that Muslims consider prophecies referring to the manifestation of Muḥammad, but Jews do not interpret them as such. A few examples are:

- Deuteronomy 18:18:

  > I will raise them up a Prophet from among their brethren, like unto thee, and will put my words in his mouth; and he shall speak unto them all that I shall command him.

  Muslims consider this verse as the prophecy for the coming of Muḥammad (who was a law giver like Moses) among the Arabs. They indicate that the brethren of Israelites who are descendants of Isaac are Arabs who are descendants of Ishmáel who was Isaac's brother.

- Deuteronomy 33:2:

  > And he said, The LORD came from Sinai, and rose up from Seir unto them; he shined forth from mount Paran, and he came with ten thousands of saints: from his right hand went a fiery law for them.

This verse is also considered by Muslims to be a prophecy for the coming of Muḥammad. Coming of the LORD "from Sinai" is a reference to the Revelation of Moses, "from Seir" is a reference to the Revelation of Jesus, and "from mount Paran" is a reference to the Revelation of Muḥammad, because in the Old Testament terminology Mecca and its surrounding area is referred to as Paran.

There are other verses in both the Old and New Testaments such as Isaiah 31:7, Matthew 20:1–16, John 4:21, and 1 John 4:2–3, that contain allusions that Muslims consider to be references to Muḥammad or His religion.

The people of the Qur'án (Muslims) have also perverted the text of their holy Book (The Qur'án) by misinterpreting the text of the Book. An example of the Corruption of the text (Taḥríf) by misinterpretation concerns the following verse:

> Muḥammad is not the father of any man among you, but he is the Apostle of God, and the seal of the prophets: and God knoweth all things.
> (The Qur'án 33:40)

The word "Apostle" is a translation of the Arabic word "Rasoul," which means messenger. Muḥammad is often called (Rasoul-al'lah) Messenger of God in the Qur'án. Prophet is the translation of the Arabic word "Nabi." As mentioned in Note No. 366 above, in Qur'ánic terminology, Messengers are those Who receive Revelation from God and establish an independent religion, such as Abraham, Moses, Jesus and Muḥammad. These Beings are sometimes referred to as Major Prophets. Prophets are those who receive inspiration, promote a religion and guide and assist people in understanding and following the precepts of one of the religions. Examples of prophets include Daniel, Isaiah, Joel and other prophets of Israel.

Muslims interpret the above mentioned verse of the Qur'án to mean that Muḥammad is the last Messenger of God and Islam the last religion. There will not be another Messenger (Manifestation of God) until the end of the world (the Day of Resurrection), when the Qá'im or Mahdi will come, and the heavens will clive asunder and the sun and moon will not give light (see Note No. 350 above).

Although the above Qur'ánic verse does not say that Muḥammad is the last Messenger and does not mention the end of time, Muslim divines distort the purport of the verse and claim that Muḥammad is the last Messenger of God. They also ignore or misinterpret the following verse of the Qur'án:

> Every nation hath its set time. And when their time is come, they shall not retard it an hour; and they shall not advance it.
>
> O children of Adam! there shall come to you Apostles from among yourselves, rehearsing my signs to you; and whoso shall fear God and do good works, no fear shall be upon them, neither shall they be put to grief.
>
> But they who charge our signs with falsehood, and turn away from them in their pride, shall be inmates of the fire: forever shall they abide therein.
> (The Qur'án 7:32–34)

The word "nation" in the above verse is a translation of the Arabic word "Umat" that is also transliterated as "Umah." In Islamic vernacular every religion and its followers is called an umat.

The Christians are called umat-i-Isa(Jesus) and Jews umat-i-Musa (Moses). The "set time" is a translation of the Arabic word "'Ajal," which also means the end time or time of the death. The word "signs" is a translation of the Arabic word "Áyát" which also means verses and Revelation.

This clearly indicates that every religion has a set time to come to an end and God will send His Messengers to bring His Revelation to humanity (the children of Adam).

These verses do not provide any exception for any religion. The important and functional phrases—"Every nation hath its set time," and "there shall come to you Apostles"—do not indicate that there will be a religion without a set end time or there will be a time that no Apostles shall come.

The Muslim divines, however, misinterpret these verses and say that these verses were only applicable to the religions and messengers before Muḥammad. Therefore, as Bahá'u'lláh states, through misinterpretation they "perverted the text of God's holy Book."

Paragraph No. 94:

In yet another instance, He saith:[389]

389. This is another instance of corruption and perversion of the text (Taḥríf) mentioned in the Qur'án:

> Desire ye then that for your sakes the Jews should believe? Yet a part of them heard the word of God, and then, after they had understood it; perverted, and knew that they did so.
> (The Qur'án 2:70)

This verse, too, doth indicate that the meaning of the Word of God hath been perverted, not that the actual words have been effaced.[390]

390. Some Qur'ánic commentators have provided the following explanation as the reason for the revelation of this verse. They state that some Jews were coming to Prophet Muḥammad and asking questions and that He would answer their questions, but they would go to their fellow Jews and change, pervert, and misrepresent His words and tell them that these were Prophet Muḥammad's responses to those questions. Therefore, this verse refers to their verbal alterations of His words as Taḥríf (perversion or corruption of the words of God).

Some other commentators believe that this verse refers to an incident in which a select group of Jews went to Mount Sinai where God spoke to them and gave them commandments. When they came back they said that God had given them a few commandments but that God had indicated that they were free to follow or not to follow these commandments. It is obvious that God did not give them the option to not follow the commandments and by saying this they perverted the words of God.

The text of the above verse and the commentators explanations clearly indicate that the change or perversion of the words was in verbal communication and there is no indication that Jews changed or perverted the written words or the text of their sacred scriptures.

Paragraph No. 95:

Again in another instance, He saith: "Woe unto those who, with their own hands, transcribe the Book corruptly, and then say: 'This is from God,' that they may sell it for some mean price."[391]

391. Another form of corruption was that because most of the Jews were illiterate and could not read and understand the Book (the Old Testament), some Jewish leaders were writing articles, treatises and tracts against Prophet Muḥammad and would present them as materials that were derived from scripture:

> But there are illiterates among them who are unacquainted with the Book, but with lies only, and have but vague fancies. Woe to those who with their own hands transcribe the Book corruptly, and then say, "This is from God," that they may sell it for some mean price! Woe then to them for that which their hands have written! and, Woe to them for the gains which they have made!
> (The Qur'án 2:74; The Arabic Qur'án 2:79)

Paragraph No. 96:

The same may be witnessed today. Consider how abundant are the denunciations written by the foolish divines of this age against this most wondrous Cause! How vain their imaginings that these calumnies are in conformity with the verses of God's sacred Book, and in consonance with the utterances of men of discernment![392]

392. Even within the short span of eighteen years, from the declaration of the Báb to the time of the Revelation of the Kitáb-i-Íqán, many articles and treatises were written by the Muslim clergy denouncing the Báb and His Revelation. The above quoted Qur'ánic verse 2:74, truly describes the situation that Bahá'u'lláh referred to. The majority of people were illiterate and unacquainted with the Qur'án and traditions, and divines claimed that their books and treatise were derived from and based on the Qur'án (God's Book) and traditions from Prophet Muḥammad and the Imáms (the utterances of men of discernment).

Paragraph No. 97:

Yea "corruption" of the text, in the sense We have referred to, hath been actually effected in particular instances. A few of these We have mentioned, that it may become manifest to every discerning observer that unto a few untutored holy Men hath been given the mastery of human learning, so that the malevolent opposer may cease to contend that a certain verse doth indicate "corruption" of the text, and insinuate that We, through lack of knowledge, have made mention of such things.[393]

393. The few untutored holy Men might be a reference to the Manifestations of God. The Qur'án referred to the Prophet Muḥammad as the unlettered prophet:

> Who shall follow the Apostle, the unlettered Prophet—whom they shall find described with them in the Law and Evangel.
> (The Qur'án 7:156)

The Old and New Testaments and the Qur'án indicate that Moses, Jesus and Muḥammad were untutored. Bahá'u'lláh as well, as mentioned by Himself, was untutored.

> This Wronged One hath frequented no school, neither hath He attended the controversies of the learned. By My life! Not of Mine own volition have I revealed Myself, but God, of His own choosing, hath manifested Me.
> (Bahá'u'lláh, Epistle to the Son of the Wolf, p. 11)

> We have not entered any school, nor read any of your dissertations. Incline your ears to the words of this unlettered One, wherewith He summoneth you unto God, the Ever-Abiding.
> (Bahá'u'lláh, Epistle to the Son of the Wolf, p. 129)

The concept of Taḥríf (corruption and perversion of the text of the Torah and Evangel) is a very complex subject that has been developed and argued by the Islamic clergy and apologists and was taught in the Islamic seminaries during the past thousand years. Within the above seven paragraphs Bahá'u'lláh so eloquently explains and simplifies this complex subject so that a layman like the uncle of the Báb could easily comprehend it. Through the above explanation He demonstrated that the objection of the Muslim clerics to the Báb for the nonliteral fulfilment of the signs and prophecies is equally applicable to Muḥammad, and that Muslims could not justify that by resorting to the excuse of Taḥríf.

Moreover, most of the verses that indicate "corruption" of the text have been revealed with reference to the Jewish people,[394]

394. There are several verses in the Qur'án in which opposition to Prophet Muḥammad and the corruption of the text is mentioned. However, as mentioned above the majority of the verses in which the word Taḥríf or its derivatives are used are in reference to Jews:

> Of old did God accept the covenant of the children of Israel, and out of them we raised up twelve leaders, and God said, "Verily, I will be with you. If ye observe prayer and pay the obligatory alms, and believe in my Apostles and help them, and lend God a liberal loan, I will surely put away from you your evil deeds, and I will bring you into gardens 'neath which the rivers flow! But whoso of you after this believeth not, hath gone astray from the even path." But for their breaking their covenant we have cursed them, and have hardened their hearts. They shift the words of Scripture from their places, and have forgotten part of what they were taught. Thou wilt not cease to discover deceit on their part, except in a few of them. But forgive them, and pass it over: verily, God loveth those who act generously!
> (The Qur'án 5:15)
>
> O Apostle! let not those who vie with one another in speeding to infidelity vex this;—of those who say with their mouths, "We believe," but whose hearts believe not;—of of the Jews—listeners to a lie—listeners to others—but who come not to thee. They shift the words of the law from their places, and say, "If this be brought to you, receive it; but if this be not brought to you, then beware of it." For him whom God would mislead, thou canst in no wise prevail with God! They whose hearts God

> shall not please to cleanse, shall suffer disgrace in this world, and in the next a grievous punishment;
> (The Qur'án 5:45)
>
> Desire ye then that for your sakes the Jews should believe? Yet a part of them heard the word of God, and then, after they had understood it; perverted, and knew that they did so.
> (The Qur'án 2:70)
>
> Of the Jews there are those who displace words from their (right) places . . .
> (The Qur'án, Yusuf Ali tr, 4:46)
>
> Some of those who are Jews change words from their context…
> (The Qur'án, Pickthall tr, Súrah 4, Women)
>
> Among the Jews are those who displace the words of their Scriptures,
> (The Qur'án 4:48–49)

The accusation of Taḥríf (the corruption or perversion of the text) as mentioned in the Qur'án was not made against the Christians who also were expecting the literal fulfilment of the signs and prophecies.

Paragraph No. 98:

We have also heard a number of the foolish of the earth assert that the genuine text of the heavenly Gospel doth not exist amongst the Christians, that it hath ascended unto heaven.[395]

395. As mentioned above in Note No. 270, some Muslim apologists state that the true Torah and Evangel (the Old Testament and the New Testament) were taken to heaven and that the present Bible is not the original divine Book. They base their argument on misinterpretation of the following verse from the Qur'án that states that Jesus was not killed on the Cross and after crucifixion God took Jesus up to heaven:

> And for their saying, "Verily we have slain the Messiah, Jesus the son of Mary, an Apostle of God." Yet they slew him not, and they crucified him not, but they had only his likeness. And they who differed about him were in doubt concerning him: No sure knowledge had they about him, but followed only an opinion, and they did not really slay him, but God took him up to Himself. And God is Mighty, Wise!
> (The Qur'án 41:56)

These Muslim apologists state that the true Evangel (Gospels) were taken to heaven at the same time that Jesus was taken to heaven, but they do not determine when the Torah (the Old testament) was taken to heaven. It is clear that these statements are a result of their lack of knowledge and ignorance.

How could God, when once the Daystar of the beauty of Jesus had disappeared from the sight of His people, and ascended unto the fourth heaven,[396]

396. Muslim theologians and commentators on the Qur'án, when commenting on the last part of the above mentioned verse: "they did not really slay him, but God took him up to Himself," encountered a serious and difficult issue, to determine where Jesus would be residing after God took Him up to Himself. Because according to the Islamic theology, God is alone and no being, not even the Prophets, will reside with Him. They therefore placed Jesus in the fourth heaven. Based on the Ptolemaic geocentric cosmology[104] the fourth sphere or heaven is the sphere of the Sun. Placing Jesus in the fourth heaven was based on the analogy that

---

[104] Ptolemy was the Alexandrian mathematician and Astronomer who presented his geocentric cosmology in 150 AD. His geocentric model was later adopted and subsequently modified by the Islamic astronomers. The Ptolemaic geocentric system assumes that the seven heavenly bodies that are observable by the naked eye (Moon, Mercury, Venus, Sun, Mars, Jupiter and Saturn) are each fixed to a rigid invisible sphere and all the stars are also fixed to one rigid invisible sphere. These seven concentric spheres or heavens revolve around the earth which is located on the center. This model was the dominantly accepted cosmological concept until the 16th and 17th centuries when it was replaced by the Heliocentric model which was proposed by Nicholas Copernicus,and subsequently confirmed by development of the laws of the planetary motion by Johannes Kepler and discoveries of Galileo through the observational astronomy.

in the same way that the Sun is the source of light and life in the material world, the Prophets are the source of divine and spiritual light and life. Therefore, after His crucifixion, Jesus ascended to the fourth heaven which is the heaven of Sun. This was the prevalent belief among all Muslims including the uncle of the Báb, and here Bahá'u'lláh was using this familiar subject to explain an important concept: In the absence of Jesus, it is contrary to both the mercy and justice of God to leave the people without a source of guidance (the holy Book) in the period between the appearance of the two Prophets (Jesus and Muḥammad).
(Source: 'Abdu'l-Ḥamíd Ishráq-Khávari, *Qámus-i-Íqán, Vol 1*, p. 350)

How could such people be made the victims of the avenging wrath of God, the omnipotent Avenger?[397]

397. The following statements help to clarify the nature, the form and the reason for the wrath of God and His retribution:

> As regards the passages in the sacred writings indicating the wrath of God; Shoghi Effendi says that the Divinity has many attributes: He is loving and merciful but also just. Just as reward and punishment, according to Bahá'u'lláh, are the pillars upon which society rests, so mercy and justice may be considered as their counterpart in the world to come. Should we disobey God and work against His commands He will view our acts in the light of justice and punish us for it. That punishment may not be in the form of fire, as some believe, but in the form of spiritual deprivation and degradation. This is why we read so often in the prayers statements such as "God do not deal with us with justice, but rather through thy infinite mercy." The wrath of God is in the administration of His justice, both in this world and in the world to come. A God that is only loving or only just is not a perfect God. The divinity has to possess both of these aspects as every father ought to express both in his attitude towards his children. If we ponder a while, we will see that our welfare can be insured only when both of these divine attributes are equally emphasised and practiced.
> (Shoghi Effendi, *Arohanui - Letters to New Zealand,* p. 32)

> How vast the number of the loved and chosen ones of God who have lamented and moaned by day and by night that haply a sweet and fragrant breeze might blow from the court of His good-pleasure and dispel altogether the loathsome and foul-smelling odors from the world. However, this ultimate goal could not be attained, and men were deprived thereof by virtue of their evil deeds, which brought upon them the retribution of God, in accordance with the basic principles of His divine rule.
> (Bahá'u'lláh, *Tablets of Bahá'u'lláh,* p. 176)

Paragraph No. 99:

Dear friend! Now when the light of God's everlasting Morn[398] is breaking; when the radiance of His holy words: "God is the light of the heavens and of the earth"[399] is shedding illumination upon all mankind.

398. In the Writings of the Bahá'í Faith, The advent of each Manifestation of God is the Day of God. The Kitáb-i-Íqán was revealed at the dawn of the new Revelation when the morning light of the everlasting Day of God was breaking.

399. This is the first sentence of verse 35 of the Súrah of Light:

> God is the light of the Heavens and of the Earth. His Light is like a niche in which is a lamp - the lamp encased in glass - the glass, as it were, a glistening star. From a blessed tree it is lighted, the olive neither of the East nor of the West, whose oil would well nigh shine out, even though fire touched it not! It is light upon light. God guideth whom He will to His light,
> (The Qur'án 24:35)

The rest of the verse with allusion to the blessed tree that is neither of the East nor of the West is indicative of the presence of the divine Manifestation.

The inviolability of His tabernacle is being proclaimed.[400] by His sacred utterance: "God hath willed to perfect His light;"[401] and the

Hand of omnipotence, bearing His testimony: "In His grasp He holdeth the kingdom of all things,"[402]

400. As stated above in Note No. 4, the tabernacle signifies the faith of God and a place where God is present.

401. This is a part of the following verse of the Qur'án:

> Fain would they put out God's light with their mouths: but God only desireth to perfect His light, albeit the Infidels abhor it.
> (The Qur'án 9:33)

The citing of this verse might be an allusion to the efforts of the enemies of the Báb who assumed that by the martyrdom of the Báb, the killing of His followers and the exile of Bahá'u'lláh out of His native land, they could put out God's light, but they were ignorant to the fact that God perfected His Light by the Revelation of Bahá'u'lláh. He states:

> Give heed to My warning, ye people of Persia! If I be slain at your hands, God will assuredly raise up one who will fill the seat made vacant through My death, for such is God's method carried into effect of old, and no change can ye find in God's method of dealing. Seek ye to put out God's light that shineth upon His earth? Averse is God from what ye desire. He shall perfect His light, albeit ye abhor it in the secret of your hearts.
> (Bahá'u'lláh, *Gleanings from the Writings of Bahá'u'lláh,* p. 224)

402. This is a part of the following verse of the Qur'án:

> In whose hand is the empire of all things, who protecteth but is not protected? if ye know:
> (The Qur'án 23:88)

This is an allusion to the power and ascendency of the Manifestation of God Who is the Godhead in the world of Cause and the world of existence.

it behooveth us to gird up the loins of endeavour, that haply, by the grace and bounty of God, we may enter the celestial City: "Verily, we are God's," and abide within the exalted habitation: "And unto Him we do return."[403]

403. This verse is an excerpt from a verse from the Qur'án. The entire verse, found in the Súrah of the Cow, is as follows:

> With somewhat of fear and hunger, and loss of wealth, and lives, and fruits, will we surely prove you: but bear good tidings to the patient, Who when a mischance chanceth them, say, "Verily we are God's, and to Him shall we return:" On them shall be blessings from their Lord, and mercy: and these!—they are rightly guided.
> (The Qur'án 2:150–152)

This verse of the Qur'án: "Verily we are God's, and to Him shall we return." is the restatement of a common teaching among all divine religions that the human soul originates from God, and the purpose of its life in this world is to prepare itself to return to Him.

The Qur'ánic phrase "verily we are God's" is here a translation of the Arabic phrase "*i'nná lellah.*" The phrase "And unto Him do we return" is here a translation of the Arabic phrase "*va i'nná allíhi ráji'ún*". These terms— i'nná and ráji'ún in the Qur'ánic verse "Verily we are God's, and unto Him do we return"—have a significant position in mystical doctrines. In mystical tradition, *i'nná* ("verily we") is the station of individuality and human limitations (the self), the beginning of the path on which the wayfarer journeys. However, if the wayfarer moves away from the station of limitation and self and becomes aware that the human soul belongs to and originates from God, he attains to the spiritually conscious condition that is allegorically defined as entering the celestial City "Verily we are God's." The phrase *allihi ráji'ún* ("unto Him do we return") is the end of this path, the advanced station where the wayfarer has discarded the self (human limitations) and all the veils, the vain imaginations and other barriers in preparation for the return to God and by entering the station of faith abides in the exalted habitation "unto Him do we return."

It is incumbent upon thee, by the permission of God, to cleanse the eye of thine heart from the things of the world, that thou mayest realize the infinitude of divine knowledge,[404]

404. In many places in the Bahá'í Writings, possessing a pure heart, cleaning the heart or cleaning the inner eye are the necessary conditions for receiving spiritual light and the ability to perceive and comprehend divine knowledge. Drawing a parallel between the faculty of vision of the physical or outer eye and perception of the spiritual realities by the inner eye, 'Abdú'l-Bahá states:

> He has given us material gifts and spiritual graces, outer sight to view the lights of the sun and inner vision by which we may perceive the glory of God. He has designed the outer ear to enjoy the melodies of sound and the inner hearing wherewith we may hear the voice of our Creator.
> ('Abdu'l-Bahá, *The Promulgation of Universal Peace,* p. 90)

> When man is not endowed with inner perception, he is not informed of these important mysteries. The retina of outer vision, though sensitive and delicate, may, nevertheless, be a hindrance to the inner eye which alone can perceive. The bestowals of God which are manifest in all phenomenal life are sometimes hidden by intervening veils of mental and mortal vision which render man spiritually blind and incapable, but when those scales are removed and the veils rent asunder, then the great signs of God will become visible, and he will witness the eternal light filling the world.
> ('Abdu'l-Bahá, The Promulgation of Universal Peace, p. 91)

> O SON OF GLORY!
> Be swift in the path of holiness, and enter the heaven of communion with Me. Cleanse thy heart with the burnish of the spirit, and hasten to the court of the Most High.
> (Bahá'u'lláh, The Hidden Words, Persian, no. 8)

> O SON OF MAN!
> The light hath shone on thee from the horizon of the sacred Mount and the spirit of enlightenment hath breathed in the

> Sinai of thy heart. Wherefore, free thyself from the veils of idle fancies and enter into My court, that thou mayest be fit for everlasting life and worthy to meet Me.
> (Bahá'u'lláh, The Hidden Words, Persian, no. 63)

and mayest behold Truth so clearly that thou wilt need no proof to demonstrate His reality, nor any evidence to bear witness unto His testimony.[405]

405. The word "Truth" here is a translation of the Arabic and Persian word "Ḥaq." This is a polysemic word (a word with a diversity and multiplicity of meanings). Some of its most commonly used meanings are: right (such as the right of free speech), truth (conformity with the fact or reality, opposite of falsehood). It is also used symbolically for referring to God (as the absolute truth) and to the Manifestation of God (as the vicegerent of God, the absolute truth). An example is the following statement of Jesus:

> Jesus saith unto him, I am the way, the truth, and the life: no man cometh unto the Father, but by me.
> (John 14:6)

Because the concept of capital letters as understood in English—the use of capitals at the beginning of proper nouns to distinguish them from common nouns—does not exist in Arabic and Persian, the intended meaning of the word in each text is understood by the context of its use. However, in English translations, the word "Ḥaq" in its latter usage (when referring to God or the Manifestation of God) is usually translated as "Truth" (with a capital T). In the Bahá'í Writings the Manifestation of God is sometimes referred to as the "Daystar of Truth," the "Sun of Truth," the "Essence of Truth," or simply as the "Truth."

When the mirror of the heart is clean and the inner eye is open and not barred by the veils of prejudice and vain imagining it will be able to perceive the spiritual realities and will recognize the "Truth." Just as the sun in the sky needs no proof for its presence "the eye will . . . will recognize the Sun through the Sun itself."[105] Explaining this process, 'Abdú'l-Bahá states:

---

[105] 'Abdu'l-Bahá, *Bahá'í World Faith,* p. 383.

> Verily, I say unto thee, that if for the appearance of that Divine Essence thou desirest to have a definite proof, an indisputable testimony and a strong, convincing evidence, thou must prepare thyself to make thy heart empty and thine eye ready to look only toward the Kingdom of God. Then, at that time, the radiance of that widespread effulgence will descend upon thee successively, and that motion rendered thee by the Holy Spirit will make thee dispense with any other strong evidence that leadeth to the appearance of this Light
> (‘Abdu'l-Bahá, *Tablets of ‘Abdu'l-Bahá*, vol. 3, pp. 705–6)

> Judge ye fairly the Cause of God, your Creator, and behold that which hath been sent down from the Throne on high, and meditate thereon with innocent and sanctified hearts. Then will the truth of this Cause appear unto you as manifest as the sun in its noon-tide glory. Then will ye be of them that have believed in Him.
> (Bahá'u'lláh, *Gleanings from the Writings of Bahá'u'lláh,* p. 104)

Paragraph No. 100:

Shouldst thou soar in the holy realm of the spirit, thou wouldst recognize God manifest and exalted above all things, in such wise that thine eyes would behold none else but Him. "God was alone; there was none else besides Him."[406]

406. To further explain the exalted station of the Manifestations of God, the station in which They are alone and no other being shares this position with Them or has any existence in comparison with Them, Bahá’u’lláh quotes a part of an Islamic ḥadí<u>th</u>, "God was alone; there was none else besides Him." This part of ḥadí<u>th</u> has been referenced in many places in the Bahá’í Writings.

> Know then that all thou hast heard and witnessed that Daystar of Truth, the Primal Point, ascribe to Himself from the designations of former times is only on account of the weakness of men and the scheme of the world of creation. Otherwise, all names and attributes revolve round His Essence and circle about the threshold of His sanctuary. For He it is Who traineth all names, revealeth all attributes,

> conferreth life upon all beings, proclaimeth the divine verses, and arrayeth the heavenly signs. Nay, shouldst thou gaze with thine inner eye, thou wouldst find that all save Him fade into utter nothingness and are as a thing forgotten in His holy presence. "God was alone; there was none else besides Him. He remaineth now what He hath ever been." Since it hath been established that God—hallowed and glorified be He!—was alone and there was none besides Him, how can the law of change and transformation apply here? Shouldst thou reflect upon that which We have disclosed unto thee, the daystar of guidance would shine resplendent before thee in this everlasting morn, and thou wouldst be numbered therein with the pious.
> (Bahá'u'lláh, *Gems of Divine Mysteries*, pp. 65–66)

In another place in His Writings, Bahá'u'lláh has explained this tradition as follows:

> As to those sayings, attributed to the Prophets of old, such as, "In the beginning was God; there was no creature to know Him," and "The Lord was alone; with no one to adore Him," the meaning of these and similar sayings is clear and evident, and should at no time be misapprehended. To this same truth bear witness these words which He hath revealed: "God was alone; there was none else besides Him. He will always remain what He hath ever been." Every discerning eye will readily perceive that the Lord is now manifest, yet there is none to recognize His glory. By this is meant that the habitation wherein the Divine Being dwelleth is far above the reach and ken of any one besides Him. Whatsoever in the contingent world can either be expressed or apprehended, can never transgress the limits which, by its inherent nature, have been imposed upon it. God, alone, transcendeth such limitations. He, verily, is from everlasting. No peer or partner has been, or can ever be, joined with Him. No name can be compared with His Name. No pen can portray His nature, neither can any tongue depict His glory. He will, for ever, remain immeasurably exalted above any one except Himself.
> (*Gleanings from the Writings of Bahá'u'lláh*, p. 150)

In another tablet, excerpts of which appear in their original Persian in the article "From the Abode of Dust,"[106] Bahá'u'lláh explains that, in the divine station, the divine being (the Manifestation of God) is alone and nothing else has existence beside Him. Because it appears that there is no authorized translation of this Tablet at present, a provisional translation of a part of it was made by this author and is presented below:

> Say, O Ye who are lost in the desert of ignorance! Your tongues are confessing to these words: "There was God and there was naught beside Him, and He presently exists exactly as He was before." Although you observe that all things are existing now, you still witness that God has been and will continue to be, and besides Him nothing exists. Therefore, witness to the same truth in this Manifestation and testify that all things are, in comparison to Him and at His station, non-existent.

He hath ever been, and will continue for ever to be, known through Himself.[407]

407. As mentioned above in Note No. 171, Bahá'u'lláh states in many places in His Writings that the Manifestation of God can only be known by His own self:

> It behoveth us, therefore, to make the utmost endeavor, that, by God's invisible assistance, these dark veils, these clouds of Heaven-sent trials, may not hinder us from beholding the beauty of His shining Countenance, and that we may recognize Him only by His own Self.
> (*Gleanings from the Writings of Bahá'u'lláh*, XIII, p. 27)

> He hath manifested unto men the Daystars of His divine guidance, the Symbols of His divine unity, and hath ordained the knowledge of these sanctified Beings to be identical with the knowledge of His own Self. Whoso recognizeth them hath recognized God. Whoso hearkeneth to their call, hath hearkened to the Voice of God, and

[106] From the Abode of Dust, by Dr. Vahid Rafati, *Safíniy-i 'Irfán*, Vol. 2, p. 144.

> whoso testifieth to the truth of their Revelation, hath testified to the truth of God Himself.
> (Bahá'u'lláh, *Gleanings from the Writings of Bahá'u'lláh*, p. 50)

We find the same concept spoken by Jesus:

> If ye had known me, ye should have known my Father also: and from henceforth ye know him, and have seen him. Philip saith unto him, Lord, shew us the Father, and it sufficeth us. Jesus saith unto him, Have I been so long time with you, and yet hast thou not known me, Philip? he that hath seen me hath seen the Father; and how sayest thou then, Shew us the Father? Believest thou not that I am in the Father, and the Father in me?
> (John 14: 7–10)

content thyself with that which He, Himself, hath revealed: "Is it not enough for them that We have sent down unto Thee the Book?" This is the testimony which He, Himself, hath ordained; greater proof than this there is none, nor ever will be: "This proof is His Word; His own Self, the testimony of His truth." [408]

408. Here Bahá'u'lláh quotes a part of the following verse from the Qur'án, Súrah of the Spider:

> And they say, "Unless a sign be sent down to him from his Lord...." Say: Signs are in the power of God alone. I am only a plain spoken warner. Is it not enough for them that we have sent down to thee the Book to be recited to them? In this verily is a mercy and a warning to those who believe.
> (The Qur'án 29:49–50)

As stated above in Note No, 388, the word "signs" is a translation of the Arabic word "Áyát" which also means verses and Revelation. The phrase—"This proof is His Word; His own Self, the testimony of His truth"—is a part of a tradition from Imám 'Alí. Both the Qur'án verse and the tradition from Imám 'Alí, indicate that the proof for establishing the truth of the Manifestation of God is His own self and His Revelation (the Book to be recited to people). This concept is most clearly explained by Bahá'u'lláh:

> The first and foremost testimony establishing His truth is His own Self. Next to this testimony is His Revelation. For whoso faileth to recognize either the one or the other He hath established the words He hath revealed as proof of His reality and truth. This is, verily, an evidence of His tender mercy unto men. He hath endowed every soul with the capacity to recognize the signs of God. How could He, otherwise, have fulfilled His testimony unto men, if ye be of them that ponder His Cause in their hearts. He will never deal unjustly with any one, neither will He task a soul beyond its power. He, verily, is the Compassionate, the All-Merciful.
>
> (Bahá'u'lláh, *Gleanings from the Writings of Bahá'u'lláh*, P. 105–106)

Paragraph No. 101:

And now,[409] We beseech the people of the Bayán,[410] all the learned, the sages, the divines, and witnesses amongst them,[411] not to forget the wishes and admonitions revealed in their Book.[412] Let them, at all times, fix their gaze upon the essentials of His Cause,

409. This paragraph is the conclusion of the first part of the Book of Certitude, The first one hundred paragraphs are devoted to describing the plight and sufferings of the previous Manifestations of God, demonstrating that one of the most important factors causing these sufferings and the deprivation of the followers of the previous religions from embracing the new Revelations was the misunderstanding and misinterpretation of the signs and prophecies given in the sacred books of these religions.

410. As mentioned above in Note No. 6, in the Bahá'í Writings, including the Writings of the Báb Himself, the Bábí religion is called the Dispensation of the Bayán and the followers of the Báb are referred to as the people of the Bayán.

411. In the writings of the Báb, the people of the Bayán besides the "Letters of the Living," are classified in groups such as Mirrors, Guides and Witnesses:

> The Bayán uses three terms in connection with the believers: "mirrors," a general term for the followers of the Bayán[107]; and "witnesses" and "guides," terms applied specifically to the scholars, the learned, and the teachers (Persian Bayán, Unit I, Chapter 1 and Unit II, Chapter 3).
> (Muḥammad Afnan, "The Báb's Bayán: An Analytical Survey," World Order, 31:4, pp. 7–16, 2000 Summer)

412. As stated by the Báb, the purpose of His Revelation was to prepare the world for the advent of Him Whom God shall make manifest, and the Bayán is replete with the Báb's wishes and admonitions to keep the people of the Bayán ready and vigilant to embrace Him Whom God shall make manifest the moment He reveals Himself. A few examples are presented here.

> I SWEAR by the most holy Essence of God—exalted and glorified be He—that in the Day of the appearance of Him Whom God shall make manifest a thousand perusals of the Bayán cannot equal the perusal of a single verse to be revealed by Him Whom God shall make manifest.
> (The Báb, *Selections from the Writings of the Báb,* p. 103)

> O congregation of the Bayán, and all who are therein! Recognize ye the limits imposed upon you, for such a One as the Point of the Bayán[108] Himself hath believed in Him Whom God shall make manifest, before all things were created. Therein, verily, do I glory before all who are in the kingdom of heaven and earth. Suffer not yourselves to be shut out as by a veil from God after He hath revealed Himself. For all that hath been exalted in the Bayán is but as a ring upon My hand, and I Myself am, verily, but a ring upon the hand of Him Whom God shall make manifest—glorified be His mention! He turneth it as He pleaseth, for

---

[107] In Bayán terminology the believers are called the mirrors because by their belief they reflect the light of the Sun of Reality (the Manifestation of God).

[108] The Báb refers to Himself as "the Point of the Bayán."

> whatsoever He pleaseth, and through whatsoever He pleaseth. He, verily, is the Help in Peril, the Most High
> (The Báb, *Selections from the Writings of the Báb,* p. 168)

> Beware, O concourse of Mirrors, lest on that Day titles make you vainglorious. Know ye of a certainty that ye, together with all those who stand above you or below you, have been created for that Day. Fear ye God and commit not that which would grieve His heart, nor be of them that have gone astray. Perchance He will appear invested with the power of Truth while ye are fast asleep on your couches, or His messengers will bring glorious and resplendent Tablets from Him while ye turn away disdainfully from Him, pronounce sentence against Him—such sentence as ye would never pass on yourselves—and say, "This is not from God, the All-Subduing, the Self-Existent."
> (The Báb, *Selections from the Writings of the Báb,* p. 166)

lest when He, Who is the Quintessence of truth,[413] the inmost Reality of all things,[414] the Source of all light,[415] is made manifest, they cling unto certain passages of the Book, and inflict upon Him that which was inflicted in the Dispensation of the Qur'án.[416]

413. All these accolades and titles have been bestowed by the Báb on Him Whom God shall make manifest in the Bayán and His other Writings. The word "Quintessence" means "the pure and concentrated essence" as in the following verse from the Kitáb-i-Asmá:

> If ye wish to distinguish truth from error, consider those who believe in Him Whom God shall make manifest and those who disbelieve Him at the time of His appearance. The former represent the essence of truth, as attested in the Book of God, while the latter the essence of error, as attested in that same Book. Fear ye God that ye may not identify yourselves with aught but the truth, inasmuch as ye have been exalted in the Bayán for being recognized as the bearers of the name of Him Who is the eternal Truth.
> (The Báb, *Selections from the Writings of the Báb,* p. 142)

On this subject Bahá'u'lláh states:

> He it is Whose praise the Bayán hath celebrated. In it His excellence hath been extolled, and His truth established, and His sovereignty proclaimed, and His Cause perfected.
> (Bahá'u'lláh, *Prayers and Meditations,* pp. 85—86)

The following verse from the Bayán is confirmation of the above statement:

> IT is not permissible to ask questions from Him Whom God will make manifest, except that which well beseemeth Him. For His station is that of the Essence of divine Revelation. . . . Whatever evidence of bounty is witnessed in the world, is but an image of His bounty; and every thing owes its existence to His Being . . . The Bayán is, from beginning to end, the repository of all of His attributes, and the treasury of both His fire and His light.
> (The Báb, *Selections from the Writings of the Báb,* p. 101)

414. The inmost Reality of all things, is another attribute of Him Whom God will make manifest:

> SAY, ye will be unable to recognize the One True God or to discern clearly the words of divine guidance, inasmuch as ye seek and tread a path other than His. Whenever ye learn that a new Cause hath appeared, ye must seek the presence of its author and must delve into his writings that haply ye may not be debarred from attaining unto Him Whom God shall make manifest at the hour of His manifestation. Wert thou to walk in the way of truth as handed down by them that are endowed with the knowledge of the inmost reality, God, thy Lord, will surely redeem thee on the Day of Resurrection. Verily He is potent over all things.
> (The Báb, *Selections from the Writings of the Báb,* p. 144)

415. The Báb praised Him Whom God will make manifest as "the Source of His divine light."

> The light of the people of the world is their knowledge and utterance; while the splendors shed from the glorious acts

> of Him Whom God shall make manifest are His Words, through whose potency He rolleth up the whole world of existence, sets it under His Own authority by relating it unto Himself, then as the Mouthpiece of God, the Source of His divine light—exalted and glorified be He—proclaimeth: "Verily, verily, I am God, no God is there but Me; in truth all others except Me are My creatures. Say, O My creatures! Me alone, therefore, should ye fear."
> (The Báb, *Selections from the Writings of the Báb,* p. 98)

416. As mentioned above in Note No. 412, the Báb in many places in His Writings warned His followers (the people of the Bayán) not to act in the same way as the followers of the previous religions by following their leaders (the Witnesses of the Bayán) and rejecting, opposing and inflicting hardship on Him Whom God will make manifest. The following verse is an example:

> O YE who are invested with the Bayán! Ye shall be put to proof, even as those unto whom the Qur'án was given. Have pity on yourselves, for ye shall witness the Day when God will have revealed Him Who is the Manifestation of His Own Self, invested with clear and irrefutable proofs, while ye will cling tenaciously to the words the Witnesses of the Bayán have uttered. On that Day ye will continue to rove distraught, even as camels, seeking a drop of the water of life. God will cause oceans of living water to stream forth from the presence of Him Whom God shall make manifest, while ye will refuse to quench your thirst therefrom, notwithstanding that ye regard yourselves as the God-fearing witnesses of your Faith. Nay, and yet again, nay! Ye will go astray far beyond the peoples unto whom the Gospel, or the Qur'án or any other Scripture was given. Take good heed to yourselves, inasmuch as the Cause of God will come upon you at a time when you will all be entreating and tearfully imploring God for the advent of the Day of His Manifestation; yet when He cometh ye will tarry and will fail to be of those who are well-assured in His Faith.
> (The Báb, *Selections from the Writings of the Báb,* p. 141)

The Báb also predicted this and admonished the people of Bayán not to cling unto certain passages of the Book (the Bayán), reject

Him Whom God will make manifest and inflict upon Him what was inflicted upon the Báb by the people of the Qur'án (Muslims).

> Thus have We firmly exhorted you—a befitting exhortation indeed—that haply ye may cleave tenaciously unto it and attain thereby salvation on the Day of Resurrection. The time is approaching when ye will be at peace with yourselves in your homes, and lo, Him Whom God shall make manifest will have appeared, and God wisheth you to return unto Him, even as God called you into being through the Primal Point. However, all of you will seek guidance while pursuing the promptings of your own desires. Some of you are filled with pride by reason of your religion, others because of your learning. Ye will, one and all, cling unto some part of the Bayán as a means of self-glorification.
> (The Báb, *Selections from the Writings of the Báb,* p. 130)

> AT the time of the manifestation of Him Whom God shall make manifest everyone should be well trained in the teachings of the Bayán, so that none of the followers may outwardly cling to the Bayán and thus forfeit their allegiance unto Him. If anyone does so, the verdict of 'disbeliever in God' shall be passed upon him.
> (The Báb, *Selections from the Writings of the Báb,* p. 85)

For, verily, powerful is He, the King of divine might,[417] to extinguish with one letter of His wondrous words, the breath of life in the whole of the Bayán and the people thereof, and with one letter bestow upon them a new and everlasting life,[418] and cause them to arise and speed out of the sepulchres of their vain and selfish desires.[419]

417. The Báb describes the station, attributes and characteristics of Whom God shall make manifest. Among them is "His absolute might."

> THE glory of Him Whom God shall make manifest is immeasurably above every other glory, and His majesty is far above every other majesty. His beauty excelleth every other embodiment of beauty, and His grandeur immensely exceedeth every other manifestation of grandeur. Every

light paleth before the radiance of His light, and every other exponent of mercy falleth short before the tokens of His mercy. Every other perfection is as naught in face of His consummate perfection, and every other display of might is as nothing before His absolute might. His names are superior to all other names. His good-pleasure taketh precedence over any other expression of good-pleasure. His pre-eminent exaltation is far above the reach of every other symbol of exaltation. The splendor of His appearance far surpasseth that of any other appearance. His divine concealment is far more profound than any other concealment. His loftiness is immeasurably above every other loftiness. His gracious favour is unequalled by any other evidence of favor. His power transcendeth every power. His sovereignty is invincible in the face of every other sovereignty. His celestial dominion is exalted far above every other dominion. His knowledge pervadeth all created things, and His consummate power extendeth over all beings.
(The Báb, *Selections from the Writings of the Báb,* pp. 156–57)

If in the Day of His manifestation a king were to make mention of his own sovereignty, this would be like unto a mirror challenging the sun, saying: "The light is in me."
(The Báb, *Selections from the Writings of the Báb,* p. 100)

418. The Báb states that Him Whom God will make manifest has the power to extinguish and restore the followers of the Bayán to a new and everlasting life:

SEND down Thy blessings, O my God, upon the Tree of the Bayán, upon its root and its branch, its boughs, its leaves, its fruits and upon whatsoever it beareth or sheltereth. Cause this Tree then to be made into a magnificent Scroll to be offered to the presence of Him Whom Thou wilt make manifest on the Day of Judgment, that He may graciously allow the entire company of the followers of the Bayán to be restored to life and that He may, through His bounty, inaugurate a new creation. Indeed all are but paupers in the face of Thy tender mercy, and lowly servants before the tokens of Thy loving-kindness. I beg of Thee, by Thy bounty, O my God, and by

> the outpourings of Thy mercy and bestowals, O my Lord, and by the evidences of Thy heavenly favors and grace, O my Best Beloved, to watch over Him Whom God shall make manifest that no trace of despondency may ever touch Him
> (The Báb, *Selections from the Writings of the Báb,* p. 172)

419. The Báb defines the meaning of arising out of sepulchers or "resurrection from the sepulchres:"

> True resurrection from the sepulchres means to be quickened in conformity with His Will, through the power of His utterance.
> (The Báb, *Selections from the Writings of the Báb,* p. 158)

Take heed, and be watchful; and remember that all things have their consummation in belief in Him, in attainment unto His day, and in the realization of His divine presence.[420]

420. Bahá'u'lláh here again refers the people of the Bayán to the utterances of the Báb regarding Him Whom God shall make manifest. The Báb defined the consummation of all religious belief as attainment unto His Day and His divine presence:

> THOU hast asked concerning the fundamentals of religion and its ordinances: Know thou that first and foremost in religion is the knowledge of God. This attaineth its consummation in the recognition of His divine unity, which in turn reacheth its fulfilment in acclaiming that His hallowed and exalted Sanctuary, the Seat of His transcendent majesty, is sanctified from all attributes. And know thou that in this world of being the knowledge of God can never be attained save through the knowledge of Him Who is the Dayspring of divine Reality.
> (The Báb, *Selections from the Writings of the Báb,* p. 117)

> For the believers of that Day are the inmates of Paradise, while the unbelievers are the inmates of the fire. And know thou of a certainty that by Paradise is meant recognition of and submission unto Him Whom God shall make manifest,

> and by the fire the company of such souls as would fail to submit unto Him or to be resigned to His good-pleasure.
> (The Báb, *Selections from the Writings of the Báb,* p. 82)
>
> There is no paradise more wondrous for any soul than to be exposed to God's Manifestation in His Day, to hear His verses and believe in them, to attain His presence, which is naught but the presence of God, to sail upon the sea of the heavenly kingdom of His good-pleasure, and to partake of the choice fruits of the paradise of His divine Oneness.
> (The Báb, *Selections from the Writings of the Báb,* p. 77)

"There is no piety in turning your faces toward the east or toward the west, but he is pious who believeth in God and the Last Day."[421]

421. This is a part of the Qur'án, Súrah of the Cow, verse 172. Turning the face toward the east and the west is a part of the rituals for performing the Islamic daily prayers. In this verse the Qur'án advises Muslims that piety is not in performing the ritualistic aspects of the prayers or other religious precepts, but in acting and living by the requirements of true belief in God and the Day of Resurrection. To emphasize the impending appearance and the exalted station of Him Whom God shall make manifest and to keep the Bábis vigilant, the Báb instructed His followers to stand up when the mention of Him Whom God shall make manifest was made, to keep a seat empty in all their meetings, lest He come in and all the seats are taken and He has to look for a seat, and not to eat onion and garlic, lest when conversing with them the odor of the onion and garlic might bother Him. In warning the people of the Bayán that more important than those ritualistic acts, was their readiness to accept and support Him Whom God shall make manifest on the Day of fruition of Bayán—the day of appearance of Him Whom God shall make manifest—the Báb states:

> Take good heed of yourselves, O people of the Bayán, lest ye perform such deeds as to weep sore for His sake night and day, to stand up at the mention of His Name, yet on this Day of fruition—a Day whereon ye should not only arise at His Name, but seek a path unto Him Who personifies that Name—ye shut yourselves out from Him as by as veil.

(The Báb, *Selections from the Writings of the Báb,* p. 84)

> O ye who are invested with the Bayán! Ye can act similarly. Take ye heed, therefore, lest ye deprive yourselves of attaining the presence of Him Who is the Manifestation of God, notwithstanding that ye have been day and night praying to behold His countenance; and be ye careful lest ye be deterred from attaining unto the ocean of His good-pleasure, when perplexed and to no avail ye roam the earth in search of a drop of water.
> (The Báb, *Selections from the Writings of the Báb,* p. 137)

Give ear, O people of the Bayán, unto the truth whereunto We have admonished you, that haply ye may seek the shelter of the shadow extended, in the Day of God, upon all mankind.[422]

422. This might be an allusion to the Báb's statement that Paradise for the people of the Bayán was the shelter under the shadow of His (Him Whom God will make manifest) affirmation.

> THE Bayán shall constitute God's unerring balance till the Day of Resurrection which is the Day of Him Whom God will make manifest. Whoso acteth in conformity with that which is revealed therein will abide in Paradise, under the shadow of His affirmation and reckoned among the most sublime Letters in the presence of God; while whoso deviateth, were it even so much as the tip of a grain of barley, will be consigned to the fire and will be assembled neath the shadow of negation. This truth hath likewise been laid bare in the Qur'án where in numerous instances God hath set down that whoever should pass judgment contrary to the bounds fixed by Him, would be deemed an infidel . .
> (The Báb, *Selections from the Writings of the Báb,* p. 102)

As stated above in Note No. 412, the primary purpose of the Revelation of the Báb was to prepare the world for the advent of Him Whom God shall make manifest, and His book the Bayán as stated by Shoghi Effendi, is a "eulogy of the Promised One."[109] The Báb wished for all His followers, the people of the Bayán, to

[109] *God Passes By,* p. 24.

be vigilantly expecting the advent of Him Whom God shall make manifest, and to accept Him and submit to His command at the time of His appearance, without a moment of hesitation. He stated:

> Indeed those who will bear allegiance unto Him Whom God shall make manifest are the ones who have grasped the meaning of that which hath been revealed in the Bayán; they are indeed the sincere ones, while those who turn away from Him at the time of His appearance will have utterly failed to comprehend a single letter of the Bayán, even though they profess belief and assurance in whatever is revealed in it or observe its precepts.
> (The Báb, *Selections from the Writings of the Báb,* p. 138)

The Báb admonished the concourse of His followers (the Mirrors of the Bayán) in most clear terms regarding their duty at the time of appearance of Him Whom God will make manifest by stating the title by which He was known:

> WHEN the Daystar of Bahá will shine resplendent above the horizon of eternity it is incumbent upon you to present yourselves before His Throne. Beware lest ye be seated in His presence or ask questions without His leave. Fear ye God, O concourse of the Mirrors.
> (The Báb, Selections from the Writings of the Báb, p. 164)

As a result of the repeated warnings and admonitions of the Báb, a majority of the people of the Bayán (Bábis) accepted Bahá'u'lláh as the Promised One of the Bayán (Him Whom God shall make manifest). But unfortunately, as predicted by the Báb, some of the Witnesses, Guides, and Mirrors, due to their ambition for leadership, greed and pride, clung to certain passages of the Book and deprived themselves of the Paradise of the Bayán, which was sheltering under the shadow of Bahá'u'lláh's affirmation. Bahá'u'lláh addressing those who followed these leaders, stated:

> Say: O people of the Bayán! We have chosen you out of the world to know and recognize Our Self. We have caused you to draw nigh unto the right side of Paradise—the Spot out of which the undying Fire crieth in manifold accents: "There is none other God besides Me, the All-Powerful, the Most High!" Take heed lest ye allow yourselves to be shut

> out as by a veil from this Day Star that shineth above the dayspring of the Will of your Lord, the All-Merciful, and whose light hath encompassed both the small and the great. Purge your sight, that ye may perceive its glory with your own eyes, and depend not on the sight of any one except your self, for God hath never burdened any soul beyond its power. Thus hath it been sent down unto the Prophets and Messengers of old, and been recorded in all the Scriptures.
> (Bahá'u'lláh, *Gleanings from the Writings of Bahá'u'lláh,* pp. 106–7)

Through this authoritative statement: "Give ear, O people of the Bayán, unto the truth whereunto We have admonished you," Bahá'u'lláh has again prior to His public declaration provided an intimation to His own exalted station (see Notes Nos. 286 and 291 above). In the words of Christ:

> He that hath ears to hear, let him hear.
> (Matthew 11:15)

Appendix I

Additional Materials, Introduction

Footnotes Nos. 20, 24 and 26

Islam and Muḥammad:

At the time of the birth of Muḥammad in the sixth century AD, the Arabian Peninsula was an area which was sparsely populated by tribal people, who, whether living as nomads or settled in towns or villages, had strong tribal identity. There were several clans within each tribe, and there was a hierarchy of clans and individuals within each tribe. These tribes were frequently at war with each other, and when one tribe's man was killed by a man from another tribe, his tribe had to avenge his death either by killing the killer or a man from the killer's tribe or by demanding blood money. Therefore, feuds could go on for generations. Sometimes two tribes would form an alliance to fight against another tribe.

The western part of the Arabian Peninsula, and especially the city of Mecca, was the site of a trade route connecting India to Syria and Byzantium, i.e., the eastern Roman Empire.

The majority of the tribal Arabs were idol worshipers, although there were several Jewish tribes and some Christians living mainly in the larger cities. The idol worshipers made their idols from stone or wood and would keep these idols in shrines, some of which became important because several tribes kept their idols in there. Every year at a certain period the tribes would gather together around their shrine in a festival. Four months out of each year were free from fighting by sanctions and customs. During this period of time when fighting was forbidden they would engage in trading and the settlement of disputes and cultural activities such as the recitation of poetry (an important aspect of Arab culture). The custodians of these shrines were important and powerful people and were respected by all.

The different settlements of Arabs, Christians, and Jews in Yemen, Mecca, and Yat͟hreb, etc. did not make a nation. The city of Mecca and its shrine, known as the Ka'bih, became very important, because it was the place that many powerful tribes were keeping their idols. Mecca was also a crossroads between the Orient and the Mediterranean world. The

Byzantines found indispensable the Arab caravans of jewels, spices from India, silk from China, skins, metals, perfumes, gums, and dates.

The Arabic word "Ka'bih" literally means cube, and it refers to the holy sanctuary (a cubical building containing a black meteorite rock) located at the heart of the structure in Mecca (called the House of Ka'bih). It is a structure fifty-five feet long, forty-five feet wide and something over fifty-five feet high. It has, since the time of Muḥammad, had a covering of cloth, which is renewed annually.

Abraham traditionally built the Ka'bih, its site being granted to Him and Ishmael for a place of worship that would be monotheistic and universal (The Qur'án 22:27). The Qur'án says of it: "The first temple that was founded for mankind, was that in Becca (the middle area of Mecca), Blessed, and a guidance to human beings. In it are evident signs, even the standing-place of Abraham: and he who entereth it is safe. And the pilgrimage to the temple, is a service due to God from those who are able to journey thither." (The Qur'án 3:90–91).

The Black Stone (Ḥajaru'l-Aswad) is set in the southeast corner of the Ka'bih wall; it is semi-circular, about six inches in height and eight inches wide, and reddish-black in color. The territory around Mecca (Haram) was and still is sacred. It was during the four months of the year spent in general amnesty and truce, that pilgrims made their journeys to Mecca and to the merchandise fairs.

In and around the Ka'bih in the time before Muḥammad—the Days of Ignorance (Jahiliyya)—were 360 idols, equaling the days of the year. Their chief idol was Ḥobal, a bearded man made of red agate, with one hand of gold and dressed in multicolored clothing. People consulted him about marriage, where to dig a well, and other problems, using divining arrows. They did acknowledge a vaguely defined supreme Deity called Alláh; but they joined partners with Him, lesser deities called al ilahat—the goddesses. Muḥammad's teaching was Lá iláha illá'lláh— There is no iláh(god) but Alláh (God).

Muḥammad was born 570–571 AD. This is the year of the "Elephant," an assault on Mecca by Ethiopians who came on elephants. Ebrahah the Ethiopian, Ruler of Yemen (as stated in the Qur'án, Súrah of Elephants) attacked Mecca, but he was defeated because a large flock of birds dropped pebbles of baked clay from a high altitude on his army.

Qusayy, Muḥammad's ancestor, seized the custodianship of Ka'bih by force and established his tribe of Quraysh, his clan, and his family as custodians of the idol house. The tribe and family of Qusayy were in charge of supplying food and water for pilgrims and were also engaged in trading and commerce. Háshim, the great grandfather of Muḥammad, was a merchant. He expanded trade with Persia and Yemen.

After Háshim came his nephew 'Abdu'l Moṭaleb, Muḥammad's grandfather. The grandfather of Muḥammad became custodian of the Ka'bih and the ruler of Mecca. He had ten sons. The youngest was 'Abdu'lláh, father of Muḥammad, who died at the age of twenty-five, within a few months of Muḥammad's birth. His mother's name was Aminah.

Muḥammad was put under the care of a woman from the nomadic tribe of Banu-Asad, called Ḥalimah. Muḥammad was raised by Ḥalimah until he was six and then was given back to His mother who took Him to Yathreb, a city 200 miles north of Mecca. After the passing of His mother and 'Abdu'l Moṭaleb when He was eight years old, He went to live with one of His uncles called Abi-Ṭáleb, the head of the Banu-Hashem clan. Muḥammad was poor and practiced several trades: He tended herds, kept a little shop, went on caravan expeditions, and to the great fairs. He became known for the purity of His life and they called Him al-Amin—the Trusted One.

Muḥammad accompanied His uncle on trade trips and in Busra (flourishing town north of Arabia). A Nestorian monk called Buheira saw Him and told His uncle to take care of Him because he saw Christ in Him.

At the age of twenty-five, Muḥammad was married to Khadijeh, a prominent woman in Mecca, who had been twice widowed and was fifteen years older than him. She was a merchant, and Muḥammad, as her agent, successfully conducted one of her caravans to Syria. They had four sons and four daughters. Only his daughters lived past childhood, and his daughter Fáṭima outlived her father by six months.

Muḥammad received His first revelation in the year 610 AD at Mount Hira, located close and to the north of Mecca, where He often went for prayer and meditation. He saw the Archangel Gabriel who appeared veiled in light, standing in front Him in the air and stated as recorded in the Qur'án:

> In the Name of God, the Compassionate, the Merciful
> Recite thou, in the name of thy Lord who created;—Created man from Clots of Blood:—Recite thou! For thy Lord is the most Beneficent, Who hath taught the use of the pen;—Hath taught Man that which he knoweth not.
> (The Qur'án 96:1–10)

There was a hiatus in revelations between 610 and 613 AD, and He thought perhaps the initial revelation was an isolated occurrence, but one day again He received revelation in the same manner. He was so shaken that He ran home and asked His wife to cover Him. He subsequently received the following revelation, which was recorded in the Qur'án:

> In the Name of God, the Compassionate, the Merciful
> O Thou, enwrapped in thy mantle! Arise and warn! Thy Lord—magnify Him! Thy raiment—purify it! The abomination—flee it! And bestow not favours that thou mayest receive again with increase; And for thy Lord wait thou patiently. For when there shall be a trump on the trumpet, That shall be a distressful day, A day, to the Infidels, devoid of ease.
> (The Qur'án 74:1–10)

In the first three years of His ministry, the number of known believers was limited to five.

1) Khadijah (His wife)
2) 'Alí (His cousin)
3) Zayd Ibn Ḥarithah
4) Abu Bakr Ibn-i-Abi Quahafah. (two years younger than Muḥammad)
5) Kháled Ibn-i-Sa'ad.

In the fourth year of His ministry, Muḥammad invited Bani Hashem (His clan in the tribe of Quraysh). But one of His uncles, Abu' Lahab, scattered them, and before He could speak and announce His mission, Abu' Lahab threw Muḥammad on the ground and put his foot on Muḥammad's neck.

> When the Verse:—"And warn your tribe of near-kindred, was revealed, the Prophet ascended the Ṣafa (mountain) and started calling, 'O Bani Fihr! O Bani 'Adi!' addressing various tribes of Quraysh till they were assembled. Those who could not come themselves, sent their messengers to see what was there. Abu Lahab and other people from Quraysh came and the Prophet then

> said, ‘Suppose I told you that there is an (enemy) cavalry in the valley intending to attack you, would you believe me?’ They said, ‘Yes, for we have not found you telling anything other than the truth.’ He then said, ‘I am a warner to you in face of a terrific punishment.’ Abu Lahab said (to the Prophet) ‘May your hands perish all this day. Is it for this purpose you have gathered us?’ Then it was revealed: ‘Perish the hands of Abu Lahab (one of the Prophet's uncles), and perish he! His wealth and his children will not profit him. . . .’” (111.1–5)
> (Ḥadith, *Bukhari, Volume 6*, Book 60, Number 293)

As Muḥammad continued to teach His Faith, the Meccans did not know what to make of Him. For a time they mocked Him:

> "Here cometh the son of 'Abdu'llah with his news from heaven." Then, as He continued to warn them, and to denounce their gods, and as He made some converts, they tried to bribe Him: "If thou wishest to acquire riches . . . we will collect a fortune larger than is possessed by any of us; if thou desirest honors . . . we shall make thee our chief . . ."
> (Ameer-‘Alí, *The Spirit of Islam*, p. 98)

> He answered, "Do ye indeed disbelieve in Him . . . do ye assign Him peers? The Lord of the worlds is He!." They appealed to His uncle and protector, the head of His clan, and this uncle begged Him to desist from teaching, as He was bringing ruin on Himself and His family. He answered, "Were the sun to come down on my right hand and the moon on my left, and the choice were offered me of abandoning my mission until God himself should reveal it, or perishing in the achievement of it, I would not abandon it."
> (T. W. Arnold, *Preaching of Islam*, pp. 13–14)

The Quraysh (Muḥammad's own tribe) pursued Him, they covered Him and His disciples with filth when they were praying, and they incited children and the rabble to follow and mock them. A woman strew thorns where He would walk. They, especially His uncle, managed to stop Him from praying in the Ka'bih. Part of Súrah 96 is in reference to this incident:

> What thinkest thou of him that holdeth back a servant of God when he prayeth? What thinkest thou? Hath he followed the true Guidance, or enjoined Piety? What thinkest thou? Hath he treated

> the truth as a lie and turned his back? What! doth he not know how that God seeth? Nay, verily, if he desist not, We shall seize him by the forelock, The lying sinful forelock! Then let him summon his associates; We too will summon the guards of Hell: Nay! obey him not; but adore, and draw nigh to God.
> (The Qur'án 96:5–10)

Muḥammad arranged for a second gathering of the house of Hashem (His own Clan within the tribe of Quraysh), during which some influential members such as 'Umar (who later became the second Caliph) accepted His claim and followed Him, but other leaders increased their opposition to Him.

For several years Muḥammad preached His new Faith, and the Meccans scoffed. They asked Him to perform different miracles such as: turning the hills to gold, making a book descend from heaven, showing them Gabriel (whom, He claimed was bringing Revelation from God to Him), causing a well of pure water to spring out in the desert, and prophesying the future price of merchandize. They wanted to know why His God could not tell Him about the market movements, if He was all-knowing. He responded in the following way:

> I am only a man like you. It is revealed to me that your God is one God: go straight then to Him, and implore his pardon. And woe to those who join gods with God.
> (The Qur'án 41:6)

He further stated that He was the:

> Announcer of glad tidings and charged with warnings! But most of them withdraw and hearken not: And they say, "Our hearts are under shelter from thy teachings, and in our ears is a deafness, and between us and thee there is a veil. Act as thou thinkest right: we verily shall act as we think right.
> (The Qur'án 41:4)

The persecutions became so intense that He sent many of His disciples to safety in Abyssinia (615 AD), where there was a pious Christian king. The king asked why they had fled, and they answered,

> O King, we were plunged . . . in ignorance and barbarism; we adored idols, we lived in unchastity; we ate dead bodies, and we

> spoke abominations . . . when God raised among us a man . . . he called us to the unity of God . . . to fly vices, and . . . abstain from evil . . . For this reason our people have risen against us . . .
> (Ameer-'Alí, *The Spirit of Islam*, p. 100)

To kill Muḥammad would have meant a civil war, and so the Meccans tortured His poor disciples. Between 617 and 619 AD, the leaders of Mecca boycotted Him and His followers and forbade the people of Mecca to have any dealings with them. They called Him crazy and mocked Him, saying that He was bringing news from heaven. His uncle Abu'Lahab took to crying out in the roadways that He was an imposter Who sought to lead the people away from the faith of their fathers, and people would tell Him that His relatives knew Him best.

> Once the Prophet fell ill and did not offer the night prayer (Tahajjud prayer) for a night or two. A woman (the wife of Abu Lahab) came to him and said, "O Muhammad ! I do not see but that your Satan has left you." Then Allah revealed (Surat-Ad-Duha):
>
> By the noon-day Brightness, And by the night when it darkeneth! Thy Lord hath not forsaken thee, neither hath he been displeased. And surely the Future shall be better for thee than the Past, And in the end shall thy Lord be bounteous to thee and thou be satisfied.
> (The Qur'án 93:1–5)
> (Ḥadith, *Bukhari, Volume 6*, Book 61, No. 506)

His wife, Khadíjih, and His kind uncle and supporter Abu'Ṭálib both died in 619 AD. Because His life became more difficult in Mecca, He went to a City called Ta'if, where He had spent some of His childhood. But the people stoned Him and threw Him out of the city.

He returned to Mecca and experienced the Night Journey (Mi'ráj or "Ascent")—a spiritual journey or experience in which He attained the presence of God. But Muslims believe that His Journey was a physical or corporeal journey in which He went from Mecca to Masjid'ul-Aqsá (the remote temple, i.e., Jerusalem) and that from there He rose through the seven heavens to the throne of God, and they relate many fantastic stories regarding what He saw and did during this journey which took a few seconds. According to some Qur'ánic commentators, when Muḥammad was leaving Mecca He pulled the door of His house closed behind Him and when He came back the door was not yet fully closed. All of this is based on a verse from Súrah 17 of the Qur'án, The Night Journey:

> Glory be to Him who carried his servant by night from the sacred temple of Mecca to the temple that is more remote, whose precinct we have blessed, that we might shew him of our signs! for He is the Hearer, the Seer.
> (The Qur'án 17:1)

In the summer of 620 AD, during the pilgrim season, Muḥammad contacted a few people from the two tribes of Aws and Khazraj in Ya<u>th</u>reb. They offered Him help and support, and the next year a few Muslims migrated to Ya<u>th</u>reb.

The pressure and persecution of the opposition was increasing day by day. He and a tiny group of His followers were encircled by men so wild they buried children alive as a point of honor, who killed casually, and who—because His teachings meant the destruction of the national religion and the loss of their own wealth and power—had for thirteen long years been waiting to shed His blood. Finally the Meccans united to murder Muḥammad. They arranged for members of all the clans to attack Him at once, so that the blood-guilt would not rest on any one of them. They waited outside His house, watching as He lay in His cloak on His bed, but when dawn came, they saw it was not Muḥammad there but 'Alí (His cousin). Muḥammad had escaped to Ya<u>th</u>reb (which later on was called "Madínat al Nabí", the City of the Prophet, or, for short, "Medina"). Muḥammad left Mecca with Abu Bakr in June or September 622. He hid for three days in a cave in Mount Thour and then arrived in Medina and resided there for the rest of His life. The Meccans were cheated of their prey.

This move, which is known as Ḥijrah or Ḥijrat (pioneering), revolutionized the fortunes of His Faith, and was later on taken as the starting point of the Islamic calendar. The year 622 AD is known as the year of Ḥijrat.

Within two years of Ḥijrat, Muḥammad became the ruler of Medina. The despised outcast, the one they had called a crazed poet, a madman, a liar, was now the head of a State. All Arabia rose against Medina; the Meccans rallied the tribes, including a "fifth column" within Medina itself. The battle was on, between idolatry and true worship, between Ḥobal [the greatest idol] and the Omnipotent Lord, between freedom and death.

The Meccan leaders gathered their forces, and during the next six years there were several battles between the Muslims and their enemies. Muḥammad did not like to fight, but He had no choice. He had to defend against the attacks in order to protect His Faith and His followers. In the autumn of 623 AD, at the Battle of Badr, the Meccans were put to flight.

In the spring of 625 AD, the Meccans rose again with an army of 3,000 strong, and attacked Muḥammad with His one thousand men at the hill of Uḥud, three miles from Medina. It was at Uḥud that the idolatrous women marched to battle, beating their tumbrels and singing: "We are the daughters of the morning star; soft are the carpets we tread . . . our necks are adorned with pearls, and our tresses are perfumed with musk. The brave who confront the foe we will clasp to our bosoms, but the bastards who flee we will spurn—not for them our embraces!" It was here that these women mutilated the dead, and that Hind, the notorious wife of Muḥammad's chief enemy, Abu Sufyan, ripped out the liver of a Muslim hero and devoured it. It was this battle that the Muslims lost, because the archers who were holding the Meccan cavalry in check disobeyed Muḥammad and left their positions to look for booty. Muḥammad was wounded in the mouth and on the temple, and it was reported that He was killed. 'Alí wept in despair when he saw Him, and brought water in his shield, saying, "Wash the blood from Thy face, O Apostle of God, that Thy men may know Thee . . . Then 'Alí raised up the Prophet's banner and rallied the defeated Muslims."

(Chronique de Abou Djafar Mohammed-ben-Jarir Ben Yazid Tabari, tr. by M.H. Zotenberg, Paris, 1871; III, 33)

Between 625 and 627 AD there were several clashes between Muslims and Idolaters. The Jewish tribe of Banu-Nazir, which resided in Medina, and was secretly in allegiance with Muḥammad's enemies, was partially destroyed and pushed out of Medina.

In April 627 AD, the Quraysh and their allies from other tribes came again, 10,000 strong, and besieged Medina. On the advice of Salmán the Persian, a stratagem previously unknown in Arabia was used: a trench was dug around the city. The Prophet Himself worked with the others at digging the trench. An account says:

> He "seized a pickaxe . . . and with it he struck a flint which had defied those who were digging; a spark came out of it, and he—peace be with him—said 'In this spark I saw the cities of Chosrau [Chosrau or Khusraw was the title of Anushirvan, King of Persia].' Then he struck another blow, and another spark came out; and he said 'In it I saw the cities of Caesar. Verily God will give them to my nation after me.'" There was a fifteen day siege, but the trench saved Madina and a Storm put the enemy to flight. Islam had conquered its strong enemies.
> (ʻAlí Tabari, *The Book of Religion and Empire*, tr. by A. Mingana, Manchester University Press, 1922, 44)

In early 628 AD, Muḥammad and the Meccans established a Truce at Al Hudaybiyyah, based on which they agreed to end wars and hostilities against each other. In March 628 AD, Muḥammad went on pilgrimage to Mecca. During these years, Muḥammad sent letters to Heraclius, the Greek Emperor, Khusraw, the King of Persia, Negus of north Africa, Magrawqris (patriarch ruler of Egypt), and some others. He also changed the Qiblih [point of adoration of Muslims] toward which Muslims all over the world stand when they say their daily prayers, from Jerusalem to Mecca.

Khusraw Anushirvan, the King of Persia, became very angry when he received Muḥammad's letter because the letter started with "from Muḥammad the Apostle of God to Khusraw, the king of Persia," which placed Muḥammad's name before his own on the letter. He tore up the letter and said that it did not deserve a response. On hearing this, Muḥammad said, "God will tear up his kingdom in the same way." Khusraw ordered his General in South Arabia, Badhan, to capture and send Muḥammad to Ctesiphon [the capital of the Persian Empire].

The old blood-tie was now replaced throughout Arabia by a new, much wider loyalty. For the first time, hundreds of hostile Arab tribes were now united under one banner—Islam.

Less than two years after the truce at Al Hudaybiyyah was made, the Meccans assisted a tribe of their allies to fight a tribe that was allied with Muslims, and broke the truce. Muḥammad, with an army of ten thousand of His followers, moved to Mecca on the first day of the month of Ramadan in the year 630. There was no resistance by the Meccans and He took Mecca without fighting. He told the Meccans: "I say to you what my brother Joseph said to his brothers:

> No blame be on you this day. God will forgive you, for He is the most merciful of those who shew mercy.
> (The Qur'án 12:92)

He struck down the 360 idols in the house of Ka'bih, reciting the following verse from the Qur'án:

> Truth is come and falsehood is vanished. Verily, falsehood is a thing that vanisheth.
> (The Qur'án 17:83)

After the fall of Mecca, the Arab tribes surrounding Mecca decided to oppose Him, and confronted the Muslims in a battle known as the Battle of Hunain. Victory in the Battle of Hunain established the undisputed rule of Muslims in Arabia. In 629–630 AD, most of the Arabian Peninsula became Muslim. Muḥammad sent a teacher to each tribe that accepted Islam. He advised them to:

> Deal gently with the people, and be not harsh; cheer them, and condemn them not . . . the key to heaven is to testify to the truth of God and to do good works."
> (Ameer-'Alí, *The Spirit of Islam*, p. 208)

In 632 AD, Muḥammad went on His last pilgrimage to Mecca, known as the "farewell pilgrimage" (Ḥajat-ul-Veda). The Shí'ahs say that on His way back when He was returning to Medina, Muḥammad stopped at a Caravan stop called Ghadir-i-Khum, and there, from an improvised pulpit said: "Of whomsoever I am Lord, then 'Alí is also his Lord. O God; be supporter of whoever supports 'Alí and the enemy of whoever opposes him."

Shortly after His return to Medina, Muḥammad fell ill. He was ill with Pneumonia, and had an intense fever.

> A disciple laid his hand on Muḥammad's forehead and said, "How fierce is the fever upon thee!" "Yea, verily," said Muḥammad, "but I have been during the night season repeating in praise of the Lord seventy Súrahs, including the seven long ones." The disciple said, "Why not rest and take thine ease, for hath not the Lord forgiven thee?" "Nay," replied Muḥammad, "wherefore should I not yet be a faithful servant unto Him?"
> (Muir, William, *The Life of Mohammad*, p. 488)

As He grew worse, He asked if there was any gold in the house; on being told there was, He insisted that His wife 'Ayishih give it away to the poor, and could not rest until she had done this. He said, "It would not have become me to meet my Lord, and this gold still in my hands." While He lay dying, He called for pen and ink to write His will, but 'Umar said, "Pain is deluding God's Messenger; we have God's Book, which is enough." They disputed at the bedside about whether to bring the pen and ink, and He sent them away. He was praying in a whisper when He ascended on June 8, 632 AD. Announcing the death of Muḥammad, 'Umar said:

> To those who believed in Muḥammad I say: Muḥammad is dead. To those who believe in God I say: He is the Eternal One who never dies.
> (Bausani, *Religion In Iran*, p. 112)

Muḥammad taught:

1). Tawhid: Divine Unity, Oneness and transcendence of God.

This is the assertion in the first half of Shaháda (Muslim declaration of the faith): "There is no god but God."

> God! there is no god but He, the Living, the Merciful!
> (The Qur'án 3:1)

God is:

All-compassionate, All-merciful, All-powerful, All-embracing.
God is the Creator of the universe, independent of time and place, well beyond the grasp of man.

2). Nubuwwa (Prophethood): Succession of Messengers of God from Adam to His person.

The prophets are the Intermediaries between God and man, Who bring God's Revelation to humanity:

> Verily we have revealed to thee as we revealed to Noah and the Prophets after him, and as we revealed to Abraham, and Isma'uel and Isaac, and Jacob, and the tribes, and Jesus, and Job, and Jonah, and Aaron, and Solomon; and to David gave we Psalms.

> Of some apostles we have told thee before: of other apostles we have not told thee—And discoursing did God discourse with Moses—Apostles charged to announce and to warn, that men, after those apostles, might have no plea against god. And God is Mighty, Wise!
>
> But God is himself witness of what He hath sent down to thee: In His knowledge hath He sent it down to thee. The angels are also its witnesses: but God is a sufficient witness!"
> (The Qur'án 4:160–63)

He also described the situation of all Prophets:

> So oft then as an apostle cometh to you with that which your souls desire not, swell ye with pride, and treat some as impostors, and slay others?
> (The Qur'án 2:81)
>
> Is it that whenever there comes to you a Messenger with what ye yourselves desire not, ye are puffed up with pride? Some ye called impostors, and others ye slay!
> (The Qur'án, Yusuf Ali tr, 2:85)
>
> Is it ever so, that, when there cometh unto you a messenger (from Allah) with that which ye yourselves desire not, ye grow arrogant, and some ye disbelieve and some ye slay ?
> (The Qur'án, Pickthall tr, 2:87)

3). Ma'ad: Advent of Day of Judgment, Resurrection, and Reckoning.

The Day of Resurrection is mentioned in more than 200 places in the Qur'án.

> O our Lord! we have indeed heard the voice of one that called. He called us to the faith—Believe ye on your Lord'—and we have believed. O our Lord! forgive us then our sin, and hide away from us our evil deeds, and cause us to die with the righteous. O our Lord! and give us what thou has promised us by thine apostles, and put us not to shame on the day of the resurrection. Verily, Thou wilt not fail thy promise.
> (The Qur'án 3:190)

> Say: Whose is all that is in the Heavens and the Earth? Say: God's. He had imposed mercy on Himself as a law. He will surely assemble you on the Resurrection day; there is no doubt of it.
> (The Qur'án 6:12)

The above three are common beliefs of all Muslims. In addition to these, Shí'ahs believe in leadership of "Imáms" (the Imámate) and 'Adl, the "Justice of God."

Imámate: The Imáms, who are the descendants of Muḥammad through His daughter Fátimah and succeed 'Alí, are the authorized spiritual leaders of the community, who understand the Qur'án and can lead the faithful.

Justice of God: The individual is responsible for his own actions, and God will subsequently judge man's actions in accordance to His justice.

Other important teachings are:

Obligatory Prayer, Fasting, Alms, One fifth Tax, Pilgrimage, Jihad, Enjoining to Do Good, Exhortation to Desist from Evil.

THE PERSON OF MUḤAMMAD

Before His declaration, Muḥammad was known as a man with religious bent. Some Muslim scholars believe that He was following the religion founded by Abraham, which was known as the Ṣabean (also spelled as Ṣabaeans or Ṣabeites) religion, as Muḥammad names the Ṣabeans as believers in God and at the same rank as Jews and Christians:

> Believers, Jews, Christians and Sabaeans—whoever believes in God and Last Day and does what is right Shall be rewarded by their Lord; they have nothing to fear or regret.
> (The Qur'án, N. J. Dawood tr, 2:62)

> Verily, they who believe, and the Jews, and the Sabeites, and the Christians—whoever of them believeth in God and in the last day, and doth what is right, on them shall come no fear, neither shall they be put to grief.
> (The Qur'án 5: 73)

Like the other Manifestations of God, He was a perfect example for humanity to follow. As stated in the Qur'án:

> A noble pattern had ye in God's Apostle, for all who hope in God, and in the latter day, and oft remember God!
> (The Qur'án 33:21)

He was a handsome and likable man. He was very stern in punishing criminals and improper behavior and those who wanted to harm His Faith, but was very forgiving on personal matters and spared His personal enemies. One of His enemies who drove his lance against the Prophet's daughter, who was pregnant, and caused her death, came and threw himself on His feet asked for His mercy and forgiveness, and Muḥammad pardoned him. He was a merciful person, because God loves merciful people.

The God of the Qur'án is compassionate and merciful. This is mentioned and repeated in many places in the Qur'án. A few examples are shown below:

> In the Name of God, the Compassionate, the Merciful.
> (The Qur'án 1:1)

> Goodly promises hath He made to all. But God hath assigned to the strenuous a rich
> recompense, above those who sit still at home, Rank of his own bestowal, and forgiveness, and mercy; for God is Indulgent, Merciful.
> (The Qur'án 4:98)

> He will vouchsafe His mercy to whom He will, for God is of great bounteousness.
> (The Qur'án 3:67)

> Say: Through the grace of God and his mercy! and in this therefore let them rejoice: better is this than all ye amass.
> (The Qur'án 10:59)

The Qur'án states that God has imposed mercy upon Himself:

> Say: Whose is all that is in the Heavens and the Earth? Say: God's. He had imposed mercy on Himself as a law.
> (The Qur'án 6:12)

> A beautiful tradition [from Muḥammad] relates that there are seven degrees of punishment, but eight of blessedness, because God's mercy exceeds His justice.
> (Teachings of Hafiz (G. L. Bell tr))

Muḥammad was always thankful. The Qur'án repeatedly directs the believers to be thankful:

> [I]f ye be thankful He will be pleased with you.
> (The Qur'án 39:9)

He was immaculate in His person, the essence of cleanliness. He liked the color green and loved fragrances, and would use musk and ambergris, and burn camphor and good smelling wood. The Qur'án states:

> Verily God loveth those who turn to Him, and loveth those who seek to be clean.
> (The Qur'án 2:222)

Many of our modern social customs are traceable to Muḥammad. He said that Muslims have six duties toward each other:

1. When you meet another Muslim, greet him.
2. When he invites you to dinner, accept with thankfulness.
3. When he asks for advice, give it with kindness.
4. When he sneezeth, say May God have mercy upon you.
5. When he is sick, visit him.
6. When he dieth, follow his bier.

He also said not to show greediness when eating with others, and not to race forward to eat before others or finish before others.

He also stated that a person should follow his guest to the door when he leaves. He advised His followers not to stay very long when they are a guest at someone's house. He also counseled them not to interfere with the management of the house and not to show up at mealtime if not specifically asked to come to dinner.

Modern societies for prevention of cruelty to animals owe a lot to His teachings and example. He taught kindness to animals, and there are a lot of stories illustrating practical ways for people to be kind to animals.

He was a very patient person, and the Qur'án enjoins patience in over seventy passages. He taught people to love the next world. He said this world was like a vapor in a desert.

He advised people to be kind to the poor and give alms. He lived very simply and modestly, even when He was the greatest leader of Arabia.

He helped His beloved wife with the housework. He kindled the fires and swept the floor, patched his garments and shoes, and milked the goats.

He taught kindness to weak and underclass people. He said he who wrongs a Jew or Christian will have me as his accuser in the next world.

In one sense, Muḥammad did not found a new religion, but renewed the one religion brought by successive holy Prophets before Him, Who were on the same plane as Muḥammad Himself:

> Say ye: "We believe in God, and that which hath been sent down to us, and that which hath been sent down to Abraham and Ismael and Isaac and Jacob and the tribes: and that which hath been given to Moses and to Jesus, and that which was given to the prophets from their Lord. No difference do we make between any of them: and to God are we resigned (Muslims)."
> (The Qur'án 2:130)

He taught that the soul is immortal and accountable for its actions. Muslims do not believe in original sin or vicarious atonement; salvation is not only for Muslims but for the followers of all previous faiths:

> Verily, they who believe, and the Jews, and the Sabeites, and the Christians—whoever of them believeth in God and in the last day, and doth what is right, on them shall come no fear, neither shall they be put to grief.
> (The Qur'án 5:73)

There is an Islamic tradition relating that a believer who had not seen Muḥammad in a few months, saw Him in a mosque and was amazed at how much He had aged. When he asked the Prophet about this, Muḥammad replied that it was the revelation of the Súrah of Húd and its sister Súrahs that had aged Him. Rodwell relates the following story:

> In later life, as Muhammad was entering the mosque, a disciple

> said, "Ah, Thou for Whom I would sacrifice father and mother, white hairs are hastening upon Thee!" And the Prophet raised up His beard with His hand and gazed at it; and the disciple's eyes filled with tears. "Yes," said Muhammad, "(the Súrih of) Húd and its sisters have hastened my white hairs."
> (Rodwell, The Qur'án, 225–26n)

The verse in the Súrah of Húd that caused Him to age is the verse that commands Him to be steadfast and perform the duties of the Messenger of God. That verse is as follows:

> And truly thy Lord will repay every one according to their works! for he is well aware of what they do.
> Go straight on then as thou hast been commanded, and he who hath turned to God with thee, and let him transgress no more. He beholdeth what ye do.
> (The Qur'án 11:113–14)

Covenant of Muḥammad and Division in Islam

Muḥammad passed away on June 8, 632 AD. H. M. Bályuzi states:

> The Prophet lay dead. As the news spread, confusion prevailed. 'Umar, in his headstrong way, refused to countenance the fact that Muḥammad had passed out of this world. With drawn sword he stood in the thoroughfare defying anyone who dared to assert the fact of the Prophet's death, until the gentle Abu-Bakr, wise and calm, arrived at the scene and pacified him. Hearing the shattering news, Abu-Bakr hurried to his daughter's house, approached the mortal remains of the Prophet, pulled aside the robe that covered Him and put his lips thrice on Muḥammad's forehead. "Greater art Thou," he said, "than the measure of praise, greater than the reach of lamentation. Were it within our power, we would have offered our lives for Thy life.' Striving to restrain his tears, he added: 'Were it not that Thou hast forbidden us to weep over the dead, streams of tears would have rained from our eyes as we wept." Then, after admonishing 'Umar, he ascended the pulpit that had been Muḥammad's, as the people, bewildered and dazed, gathered round him, and he addressed them thus:
>
> "Whoever worshipped the person of Muḥammad, let him know that Muḥammad hath died; and whoever worshipped God, let him

> know that God doth not die. Muḥammad was the Messenger of God, and other Prophets too, before Him, left this world. Muḥammad has gone from our midst; but keep your faith in Him and worship God. Should you rebel and break your faith, the loser will not be God."
>
> 'Umar submitted, and those who had gathered, understanding what had befallen them, dispersed. But dire winds of discord were already blowing.
>
> (H. M. Bályuzi, *Muḥammad and the Course of Islam*, p. 163)

Some scholars believe that it was 'Umar, who, after realizing that Muḥammad has passed away, said: "To those who believed in Muḥammad I say: Muḥammad is dead. To those who believe in God I say: He is the Eternal One who never dies." (Bausani, *Religion In Iran*, p. 112). Abu Bakr and 'Umar made an agreement to assume the leadership after Muḥammad, and they managed to set 'Alí aside.

Abu Bakr became Caliph (the successor to Muḥammad). 'Alí did not object to this selection, this was due to the fundamental necessity to prevent schism. Abu Bakr was Caliph for two years and three months. He managed to subdue the Arab tribes, who, after the death of Muḥammad, wanted to go back to their old religion and way of life. Abu Bakr died in 632. He nullified the act of the election of the Caliph by appointing 'Umar to succeed him at his death bed.

'Umar Ibn Al-Khaṭṭáb, 634–644 AD

'Umar was an expert Islamic jurist, known for his pious and just nature, which earned him the epithet *Al-Farooq* ("the one who distinguishes between right and wrong"). Under 'Umar's Caliphate, the Islamic army made great strides and the Islamic territory was greatly expanded. Heraclius' Roman army was defeated during the wars between the years 638 and 641. In the year 638, Jerusalem was surrendered, and by 641 the whole area of Syria, Lebanon, and the land that extended to the shores of the Red Sea came under Caliphate rule. The Sassanid Empire was conquered and came under the rule of Muslims after the battles of Jalúlá and Nahavand in 641. The vast territory of the Persian Empire, which extended to the north of India and west of China was gradually joined to the Islamic Empire. 'Umar was assassinated by a Persian man who was captured in the war and was sold as a slave. ‘Umar died in 644. On his death bed, ‘Umar arranged for ‘Uthmán to be selected as the Caliph.

‘Uthmán, 644–656

‘Uthmạn was from the Ummayyad clan and is the person who was responsible for bringing that clan to power. He was a weak person, and appointed his relatives to important posts. He appointed Mu‘aviyyih, the son of Abu Sufyán and Hind, the arch-enemy of Muḥammad, (who became Muslim when he faced death, and was forgiven by Muḥammad) as the Governor of Syria. He was eventually killed by people from Egypt.

‘Alí, 656–661

After the death of ‘Uthmán, people asked ‘Alí to be the Caliph. ‘Alí, who was adamant to accept, warned them that he would be just and tough. Mu‘aviyyih accused ‘Alí of being the instigator of ‘Uthmán’s killing and asked for revenge. He displayed ‘Uthman’s blood-soaked shirt in Damascus (in Shí‘ah culture, the phrase “Uthman’s shirt” has been historically used as proverbial for vain pretext).

Muḥammad’s widow, ‘Ayishih, who hated ‘Alí, together with two other prominent people, Ṭalheh and Zubayr, gathered an army and came to fight with ‘Alí. In that battle ‘Ayishih rode a camel, and the battle became known as the Battle of the Camel. ‘Alí won the battle and Ṭalheh and Zubayr were killed. ‘Alí pardoned ‘Ayishih and escorted her to Medina. A year later, Mu‘aviyyih, who was deposed by ‘Alí from his post, came back with his army to fight ‘Alí. In the Battle of Ṣaffain in July 657, when Mu‘aviyyih and his Vizier ‘Amr-ibn-al-‘Aws realized that they are being defeated they had their soldiers adorn the tips of their swords with the pages of the Qur’án, and the war ended with both sides agreeing to arbitration. The arbitrator from ‘Alí’s side, Abu Musa Ash‘ari, Governor of Kufah, was deceived by ‘Amr-ibn-al-‘Aws. This caused some of ‘Alí’s supporters to feel that ‘Alí had betrayed them by accepting arbitration. They left ‘Alí’s camp and decided to oppose the Caliphate of both ‘Alí and Mu‘aviyyih. These people were called Kharejities. ‘Alí fought with the Kharejities in the Battle of Nahrawan and defeated them. Only three decades after the Prophet’s death, men who served him side by side were fighting each other. ‘Alí changed the capital from Medina to Kufah. ‘Alí was assassinated by the Kharejities in revenge for their defeat in the Battle of Nahrawan, and died on January 27, 661. He was most courageous, and a just, compassionate, knowledgeable, and eloquent companion of Muḥammad.

The above four people: Abu-Bakr, ‘Umar, ‘Uthman, and ‘Alí, are called the Rightly Guided Caliphs by the majority of Muslims (Sunnis).

After ‘Alí, his oldest son, Ḥassan, abdicated his claims to Mu‘aviyyih, who established the ‘Umayyad Dynasty and himself as Caliph. The majority of Muslims accepted this and the Caliphate became a hereditary institution. A group of Muslims regarded ‘Alí as the rightful successor to Muḥammad, and after ‘Alí, his sons Ḥassan and á and their descendants (whom they call Imáms). These are the Shí‘ahs—a very small minority at the time. The Imámate continued until the death of the eleventh Imám and the disappearance of the twelfth, who Shí‘ahs believed was in occultation until the day of Resurrection. In the early sixteenth century, when the Safavid Dynasty was established in Iran, Shí‘ah Islam was adopted as the official religion and they formed the majority in that area.

‘Ummayyad Caliph Abdul Malik took parts of North Africa, and built the Mosque of ‘Umar and Aqsa in the year 705 AD. The Arab general Abu-Musa conquered all North Africa. His freed man Ṭáriq landed in Gibraltar in 711 AD, and within two years they took Spain. In 732 AD, Charles Martle defeated the Muslims at Tours and stopped their move toward the rest of Europe. Abdul-Rahman, the sole remnant of the ‘Ummayyads, ruled Spain.
(Based in part on *Six Lessons on Islam* by Marzih Gail and H. M. Bályuzi, *Muḥammad and the Course of Islam*)

The Qur’án

The Qur’án, pronounced "Qoor-Ann," is the Holy Book of the religion of Islam. Muslims believe that it is a Message from God (Alláh) to humanity, which was transmitted to Prophet Muḥammad through the angel Gabriel. The Qur’án was revealed in parts and segments during a period of approximately twenty-three years (610 AD to 632 AD). Prophet Muḥammad was forty years old when the Qur’án began to be revealed to Him, and He was sixty-three when the revelation was completed. The Qur’án was revealed in the Arabic language and is considered the most unique, and the best and highest standard of literary work in that language. It has been translated into many other languages.

At the time of the revelation of the Qur'án, every word that was uttered by the Prophet Muḥammad was recorded by scribes, selected by the Prophet. These scribes recorded the revealed words on any suitable object that was available to them. These included the leaves of Palm trees, pieces of wood, parchment or leather, flat stones, and even camel's shoulder blade bones. Scribes included 'Alí Ibn-i-Abi Ṭalib (Muḥammad's Cousin and son-in-law), Mu'awiyah Ibn-i-Abi Sufyán, Ubey Ibn-i-Ka'ab, Zayd Ibn-i-Thabit. Some of the people who had sharp memories and were present would memorize it and recite it for others.

After the passing of the Prophet Muḥammad, His successors (Caliphs) decided to put all of the Qur'án's parts together. At the time of the first Caliph (Abu Bakr), all the written records were gathered in one place (in the residence of one of the Prophet's wives, Ḥafsah, daughter of 'Umar (the second Caliph)). Zayd Ibn-i-Thabit, one of the main scribes and memorizers of the Qur'án, was assigned to compile the work into one book. He completed this task with the help of other memorizers and reciters, and prepared the Book. During the period of 'Uthman's Caliphate (the third Caliph, 644–656 AD), several copies of the Qur'án were made and sent to different parts of the Islamic Empire. The original was kept at the house of Ḥafsah, and all the drafts and records were destroyed.

The Qur'án has 114 chapters, which are called Sura or Súrah. They are different in length, some have a few verses and some more than two hundred. Each Súrah has a name, which was selected by the early compilers based on the theme or the subject, such as the Súrah of the Cow, Súrah of the Spider, Súrah of Women, or the Súrah of Mary. A part of the Qur'án was revealed while the Prophet was residing in Mecca and a part in Medina after He moved to that City, and therefore, the Súrahs have the designation of being revealed in Mecca or Medina. The original compilation of the Qur'án was not arranged chronologically, and except for the opening chapter, all chapters are arranged in order of length, the longer ones at the beginning and shorter ones toward the end. Some Islamic scholars and translators have rearranged the order of Súrahs chronologically, an example is the Rodwell translation.

The Qur'án has been translated into many languages. There is no official translation, or one that is accepted by the majority of Muslims. There are more than a dozen famous English translations, which often differ significantly in the translation of the same verse.

The verses in each chapter contain moral or social teachings, laws and ordinances, and stories of the past prophets, peoples, or events. There are similarities between some of the stories, personalities, and events mentioned in the Qur'án and the Old Testament, but there are also significant differences in their portrayals of certain historical figures and events.

Ḥadi<u>th</u> (Tradition)

The religion of Islam is supported by two pillars, one is the Qur'án and the other is the Sunnah (the words and deeds or the living example) of Prophet Muḥammad, which were heard or observed by His close followers, and recorded for posterity. Customarily, the word Tradition (Ḥadi<u>th</u>) is used in reference to the words or sayings of the Prophet (the verbal part of Sunnah).
What makes the Qur'án different from the Sunnah is primarily its form and nature. Unlike the Sunnah, the Qur'án is considered literally the Words of God (Alláh), whereas the Sunnah was inspired by Alláh but the wording and actions are the Prophet's. Muslims believe that the Qur'án was expressed using any human's words. Its wording is, letter-for-letter, fixed by no one but Alláh.

The Qur'án is the more important pillar of the two, although the second pillar, the Sunnah of the Prophet is also considered authoritative. Its authority is derived from certain Qur'ánic verses that made the sayings of the Prophet complementary to the words of the Qur'án and declared them to be authoritative like the the Qur'án:

> And to thee have we sent down this Book of Monition that thou mayest make clear to men what hath been sent down to them, and that they may ponder it.
> (The Qur'án 16:44)

> And We have sent down unto thee (also) the Message; that thou mayest explain clearly to men what is sent for them, and that they may give thought.
> (The Qur'án, Yusuf 'Alí tr, 16:44)

> And We have revealed unto thee the Remembrance that thou mayest explain to mankind that which hath been revealed for them.
> (The Qur'án, New revised translation, 16:44)

> It is He Who has sent amongst the Unlettered a messenger from among themselves, to rehearse to them His Signs, to sanctify them, and to instruct them in Scripture and Wisdom—although they had been, before, in manifest error.
> (The Qur'án, Yusuf 'Alí tr, 62:2)

> It is He who hath sent to the pagan folk (Arabs) an Apostle from among themselves, to rehearse His signs to them, and to purify them, and to impart to them a knowledge of "the Book" and wisdom; for aforetime were they in manifest error.
> (The Qur'án 62:2)

> He it is who hath sent among the unlettered ones a messenger of their own, to recite unto them His revelations and to make them grow, and to teach them the scripture and Wisdom.
> (The Qur'án, New revised translation, 62:2)

Reports on the sayings and the traditions of Prophet Muḥammad, or what He witnessed and approved, are believed by Muslims to be the real explanation, interpretation, and the living example of the Prophet for the teachings of the Qur'án. As mentioned above, the Sunnah has a high authority in Islam; and God in the Qur'án orders Muslims to follow the teachings and the example of Prophet Muḥammad.

> A noble pattern had ye in God's Apostle, for all who hope in God, and in the latter day, and oft remember God!
> (The Qur'án 33:21)

> Ye have indeed in the Messenger of Allah a beautiful pattern of (conduct) for anyone whose hope is in Allah and the Final Day, and who engages much in the praise of Allah.
> (The Qur'án, Yusuf 'Alí tr, 33:21)

His sayings are found in books called the Ḥadith books. In general, the word Sunnah means habit, practice, customary procedure, or action, norm, and usage sanctioned by tradition. In Sunni Islam specifically, any time the word Sunnah is mentioned, it is to refer to Prophet Muḥammad. Here it means His sayings, practices, living habits.

The Qur'án and Sunnah are also the two major legal sources of Islamic jurisprudence. The Sunnah may confirm what is mentioned in the Qur'án, interpret and explain it, specify what is meant by some general verses, limit and restrict the meaning of some verse in it, or may explain something that has been revealed in it.

Traditions (Aḥadith, plural for Ḥadith) are generally of three kinds:

- Ḥadith-i-Qudsi (Holy Traditions), are traditions (the sayings of the Prophet) in which the Prophet speaks on behalf of God, i.e. says that Alláh says so and so. In this type of Tradition, the meaning of the Tradition was revealed by God to the Prophet, but He put them in His own words, unlike the Qur'án which is the word of God, and the Prophet conveyed it exactly as it was revealed to Him.
- Ḥadith-i-Nabavi (the Prophetic Traditions), are the words or sayings of the Prophet that are His views or ideas and have been transmitted verbatim through several people and recorded as His words.
- Ḥadith-i-Marvy (the Transmitted Traditions), are the words of some of the companions of the Prophet Muḥammad regarding His words and His actions.

The followers of the Shí'ah sect of Islam believe that an authentic and reliable tradition from the Prophet Muḥammad states: "I leave two things of value amidst you in trust which if you hold on to, you will never go astray: the Qur'án and Etrat (the members of my household). These will never be separated until the Day of Judgment." They believe that the word "Etrat" (members of my household) means Imám 'Alí Ibn-i-Abi Ṭaleb (the cousin and son-in-law of the Prophet) and His male descendants (those who were accepted by the Shí'ah as Imáms (the inspired religious leaders)). The Shí'ah accept the authority of those whom they call the "Fourteen Sinless or Inerrant." These are the Prophet Muḥammad, Imám 'Alí, his wife Fátimah, the daughter of the Prophet, and their accepted male descendants or Imáms (eleven that followed 'Alí).

Based on this belief, the Shí'ah hold that the words and deeds of the Imáms form a corpus that is complementary to the Prophetic Sunnah and Traditions. These Imáms have authority in religious sciences and are inerrant in the explanation of the teachings and injunctions of Islam. Their sayings, received orally or through reliable transmission, are reliable and authoritative. To Shí'ah the source of religious thought and practice of Islam, consists of two parts: The Book (the Qur'án) and the Sunnah, and by the Sunnah, they mean traditions received from the Prophet and the accepted Imáms.

After the passing of the Prophet Muḥammad and throughout the years, hundreds of thousands of traditions were related by His companions and followers, some of which were contrary to each other, and even contrary to the text of the Qur'án. There was also suspicion that some of the traditions were fabricated by different people to either promote their point of view and their interpretations of the holy text, or were politically motivated to promote certain people's agendas or to denounce their enemies. On occasions, traditions were fabricated for financial gain. For example, there is a belief among some Muslim scholars, that one of the companions of the Prophet Muḥammad, and a very important narrator of ḥadith called Abû Huraira, fabricated more than 5000 false traditions. The Shí'ah sect was doubly affected by this forgery problem, because there were some people who fabricated traditions from different Imáms.

This damaged the reliability and utility of this major pillar of the Islamic religious practice and the source of jurisprudence. Therefore, throughout the centuries, a very complicated system for verification of the authenticity, accuracy, and reliability of the Aḥadith (Traditions) was developed, which was gradually accepted as a major part of the Islamic religious science. This system, among other things, was concerned with the biography of the learned men who cited the traditions and the chain of transmission of each tradition in order to be able to discriminate between the true and false traditions. The experts in this science were called Muhadeth, and some of the famous ones enjoyed great recognition and positions of leadership and authority in their community.
(Based on materials from the following Books: Marzieh Gail, *Six Lessons on Islam*; H. M. Bályuzi, *Muḥammad and the Course of Islam*; Moojan Momen, *An Introduction to Shí'i Islam*, and *Islam and the Bahá'í Faith*; Alessandro Bausani, *Religion in Iran*; Ira M. Lapidus, *A History of Islamic Societies*; Roy Mottahedeh, *The Mantle of the Prophet: Religion and Politics in Iran.*)

Footnote Nos. 29, 31, 32, and 33:

The Twelfth Imám, His Occultation and Return

Perhaps no aspect of the history of Shí'ah Islam is as confused as the stories relating to the Twelfth Imám, and this is not surprising as this is the point in Shí'ah history where the events related become of a miraculous, extraordinary nature and the non-believer may be unwilling to go along with the facts as related by Shí'ahs. But even for the committed believer, it is difficult to decide which of the many and often contradictory versions presented in the Traditions to follow. The following version is the one that is usually presented in the books published for popular reading.

The mother of the Twelfth Imám was a Byzantine slave-girl named Narjis Khátún (or Ṣaqíl or Sawsan or Rayhána). In the more fully elaborated versions of the story she becomes the Byzantine Emperor's daughter who was informed in a vision that she would be the mother of the Mahdí. She was bought by the Tenth Imám, 'Alí al-Hádí, for his son the Eleventh Imám, Hasan al-Askarí.

The Twelfth Imám was born in 255/868 (some sources vary by as much as five years from this date) in Sámarrá. He was given the same name as the Prophet, Abu'l-Qásim Muḥammad. The usual miraculous accounts of his talking from the womb, etc., may be passed over to the only occasion on which he is said to have made a public appearance. This was in 260/874 when the Eleventh Imám died. It appears that none of the Shí'ah notables knew of the birth of Muḥammad and so they went to the Eleventh Imám's brother, Ja'far, assuming that he was now the Imám. Ja'far seemed prepared to take on this mantel and entered the house of the deceased Imám in order to lead the funeral prayers. At this juncture a young boy came forward and said: "Uncle, stand back! For it is more fitting for me to lead the prayers for my father than for you." After the funeral, Ja'far was asked about the boy and said he did not know who the boy was. For this reason, Ja'far has been vilified by generations of Shí'ahs as *Kadhdháb*, the liar.

The boy was seen no more, and Shí'ah tradition states that from that year he went into occultation. At Sámarrá, beside the gold-domed Shrine of the Imáms 'Alí al-Hádí and Hasan al-'Askarí, is a mosque under which there is a cave. The end of one of the rooms of the cave is partitioned off by a gate which is called Báb al-Ghayba (Gate of the Occultation) and was built on the instructions of the Caliph an-Násir in 606/1209. The area behind the gate is called Hujrat al-Ghayba (Chamber of the Occultation) and in the corner of this is a well, the Bi'r al-Ghayba (Well of the Occultation) down which the Imám Mahdí is said to have disappeared. Shí'ahs gather in the rooms of the cave and pray for his return.

The Lesser Occultation

Those Shí'ahs who followed the line of the Imáms were thrown into confusion by the death of Hasan al-'Askarí. Ja'far remained unshakeable in his assertion that his brother had no progeny and some gathered around him as the Imám. Others asserted that the Twelfth Imám had not yet been born but would be born in the Last Days just before the Day of Judgment. Others asserted that it was the Eleventh Imám, Hasan al-'Askarí, who had gone into occultation. Thus the Shí'ah were fragmented into several factions. . . . It is difficult to assess at this distance in history and with the bias of the sources available what proportion of the Twelver Shí'ahs of the time accepted the position of 'Uthmán al-'Amrí, which was to become the orthodox Twelver position. Al-'Amrí claimed that Muḥammad, the son of Hasan al-'Askarí, did exist and was in occultation and that he, 'Uthmán, was the intermediary between the Hidden Imám and the Shí'ah.

But it should not necessarily be assumed that 'Uthmán al'-'Amrí's assertion was perceived by the Shí'ahs of the time as a radical change. For, after all, the Tenth and Eleventh Imáms, as far as the generality of their followers were concerned, had also been in effective occultation. Because of the vigilant and hostile surveillance of the 'Abbásids, they had rarely shown themselves to their followers and are even said to have spoken to some of those who met them from behind a curtain. Their contact with their followers was through a network of Shí'ah agents called the *Wikála* which had been responsible for communicating the messages of the Imáms and collecting the monies offered by the Shí'ah. This network of agents was in contact with one or two special agents of the Tenth and Eleventh Imám who in turn were in direct contact with the Imám. 'Uthmán al-'Amrí had been the secretary and special agent of the Tenth and Eleventh Imáms, and thus effectively controlled the *Wikála*. With the death of the Eleventh Imám, all that al-'Amrí was saying was that the Twelfth Imám was also in hiding due to the threat against his life from the 'Abbásids and that he, 'Uthmán, had been appointed to continue the position that he had held under the previous Imáms. For the majority of the Shí'ah it must have seemed that nothing much had changed. It is probably only after about seventy years (i.e. the normal lifespan of a man) had passed that the question of the

Occultation became problematic and began to require doctrinal exposition. Thus al-Kulayní, who completed his book less than seventy years after the start of the Occultation has little or no discussion of the Occultation itself or of the position of al-'Amrí and his successors as intermediaries, and neither do any of the extant Shí'ah books preceding it. A few decades later, however, it is a topic of major importance to most Shí'ah writers and entire books are devoted to the issue.

'Uthmán nominated his son, Abú Ja'far Muḥammad ibn 'Uthmán, as his successor. For forty-five years these two laid claim to the position of being the agents of the Hidden Imám. They would take messages and questions from the Shí'ah to the Hidden Imám and would return with answers, usually verbal but sometimes written. They would also receive the monies offered by the Shí'ah to the Imám as *khums* and *zakát*. They were involved in bitter disputes with Ja'far and his followers who denied the existence of the Eleventh Imám's son and laid claim to his brother's estate—a legal battle that took seven years and was finally decided by the Caliph al-Mu'tamid. Narjis, the supposed mother of the Twelfth Imám, was also the subject of much wrangling that went on over twenty years.

The third person to be nominated as the agent of the Hidden Imám was Abu'l-Qásim Ḥusayn ibn Rúh an-Nawbakhtí. He came to this position in 305/917, after the death of Muḥammad al-'Amrí. Conditions had changed considerably by this time. The Caliph Muqtadir (reigned from 907 to 932 AD) was favorable to the Shí'ah and the Nawbakhtí family, who were Shí'ahs and wielded considerable power at his court as ministers. However, even at this late date there were disputes among the Shí'ah over the question of the Occultation. Abú Ja'far Muhammed ibn 'Alí ash-Shalmaghání (executed in 322/933), who had been a close confidant of Ḥusayn ibn Rúh and his agent in Baghdád, suddenly turned against the latter and at first laid claim to the position of being the rightful agent of the Imám and later denounced the whole concept of the Occultation as a lie. Another who fell out with what was rapidly becoming the Twelver Shí'ahs orthodoxy was Ḥusayn ibn Mansúr al-Halláj (c. 244/858 – executed 309/922). Exactly what it was that Shalmaghání and Halláj said or did which brought upon them the anger of the Shí'ah and eventually, through the power of the

Nawbakhtí family, death at the hands of the state cannot now easily be discerned among the mass of gratuitous accusations and disinformation piled upon them by later writers. It has been suggested, however, that their open avocation of extremist claims (*ghuluww*) threatened the delicate balance that allowed Shí'ah families such as the Nawbakhtís and the Ál al-Furát to hold power and authority in a Sunni state, which allowed Shí'ahs to enjoy unprecedented freedom. It is clear that whatever differences there may have been among the Shí'ah following the death of the Eleventh Imám in 874, by the third and fourth decades of the tenth century (i.e. the closing years of the Lesser Occultation), the majority of the Shí'ahs agreed about the line of Twelve Imáms. There was still confusion and doubt over the question of the Occultation and this was to continue for a further hundred years. It was also during this period that the first of the four "canonical" collections of *hadíth, al-Káfí fí Ilm ad-Dín*, was being completed by al-Kulayní, thus helping to bring about a convergence and consolidation of views among the Twelver Shí'ahs.

The fourth and last agent of the Hidden Imám was Abúl-Ḥusayn 'Alí ibn Muḥammad as-Samarrí. He held office for only three years and died in 329/941. These four successive agents of the Hidden Imám are each called by the Shí'ahs the *Báb* (Gate, plural *Abwáb*), the *Safír* (Ambassador, plural *Sufará*), or the *Náib* (Deputy, plural *Nuwwáb*) of the Twelfth Imám.

At the time of his death, as-Samarrí brought the following written message from the Hidden Imám:

> In the name of God the Merciful, The Compassionate! O 'Alí ibn Muḥammad as-Samarrí, may God magnify the reward of your brethren upon you! There are but six days separating you from death. So therefore arrange your affairs but do not appoint anyone to your position after you. For the second occultation has come and there will not now be a manifestation except by the permission of God and that after a long time has passed, and hearts have hardened and the earth become filled with tyranny. And there will come to my Shi'a those who claim to have seen me, but he who claims to have seen me before the emergence of the Sufyání and the Cry (from the heavens) is assuredly a lying

> imposter. And there is no power nor strength save in God the Almighty, the All-High.

And so the Shí'ahs passed, in 329/941, into what is known as the Greater Occultation, the period of time when there is no agent of the Hidden Imám on earth.

One final historical point is that although the history of the four agents of the Hidden Imám has been given above as it is to be found in the Shí'ah histories, there is some considerable evidence that this was a later superimposition of interpretation on the facts of history. In the early works there is no indication that the number of agents was limited to four, and several others are mentioned. It seems likely, then, that after the death of the Eleventh Imám, for the duration of a natural lifespan (i.e. seventy years), the former system of the *Wikála* had continued to operate. But then the Shí'ahs began to be thrown into confusion and doubt over the matter of the Occultation. And so the scholars of the early Buyid period spent a great deal of time writing books explaining and proving the doctrine of the Occultation of the Twelfth Imám. It was probably also at about the end of the Lesser Occultation that the Twelfth Imám came to be identified with the figure of the Mahdí.

The Doctrine of Occultation

In its simplest form, the doctrine of the Occultation (*Ghayba*) declares that Muḥammad ibn Hasan, the Twelfth Imám, did not die but has been concealed by God from the eyes of men. His life has been miraculously prolonged until the day when he will manifest himself again by God's permission. During his Lesser Occultation, he remained in contact with his followers through the four *Bábs (al-Abwáb al-Araba'a).* During the Greater Occultation, which extends to the present day, he is still in control of the affairs of men and is the Lord of The Age *(Sáhib az-Zamán)* but there is no longer a direct route of communication. However, it is popularly believed that the Hidden Imám does still occasionally manifest himself to the pious either when awake or more commonly in dreams and visions. It is believed that written messages left at the tombs of the Imáms can reach him. The Hidden Imám was popularly supposed to be resident in the far-off cities of Jábulsá and Jábulqá, and in former times books were written about persons who had succeeded in traveling to these places. Less has been made of this particular tradition in recent times when modern geographical knowledge permeated the Shí'ahs masses and it became generally realized that no such places existed. There are also accounts of persons who have seen the Imám in person, in visions or dreams.

The occurrence of the Occultation is considered to have been due to the hostility of the Imám's enemies and the danger to his life. He remains in occultation because of the continuance of this threat. The severance of communication with the Hidden Imám is not considered to contradict the dictum that "the earth is not left without an Imám," for, say the Shí'ah writers, the sun still gives light and warmth to the earth even when hidden behind a cloud.

The Hidden Imám has a large number of titles including the following: Sáhib az-Zamán (Lord of the Age), Sáhib al-Amr (Lord of Command), al-Mahdí (the Rightly-Guided One), al-Qá'im (He who will arise), al-Imám al-Muntazar (the Awaited Imám) and the Baqiyyat Alláh (Remnant of God).

The Doctrine of Return (Raj'a)

The Hidden Imám, the Imám Mahdí, is in occultation awaiting the time that God has decreed for his return. This return is envisaged as occurring shortly before the final Day of Judgment. The Hidden Imám will then return as the Mahdí with a company of his chosen ones and there will also return his enemies led by the one-eyed Dajjál and the Sufyání. The Imám Mahdí will lead the forces of righteousness against the forces of evil in one final apocalyptic battle in which the enemies of the Imám will be defeated.

The Imám Mahdí will rule for a number of years and after him will come the return of Christ, the Imám Ḥusayn and also the other Imám, prophets, and saints. Strictly speaking, the term *raj'a* only applies to the return to life of figures who have died such as the Imám Ḥusayn. It is more correct to refer to the *zuhúr* (appearance) of *qiyám* (arising) of the Twelfth Imám who did not die and is in occultation. Return is envisaged by Shí'ahs as involving only the Imám, their supporters, and their enemies. Those who were neutral in, or unaffected by, the struggle will remain in their graves until the Day of Resurrection.

Signs of the Return of the Imám Mahdí

Eschatological expectation in relation to the Twelfth Imám plays a very important part in the popular religion of Twelver <u>Sh</u>í'ahs. In the Traditions relating to the advent of the Mahdí, there are numerous signs that are held to herald his advent. Some of these are related to the general condition of the world when the Mahdí will appear while others give specific signs of his return.

Perhaps the best known of the general signs, a Tradition that is related in both <u>Sh</u>í'ah and Sunni sources, states that the Mahdí will fill the earth with justice after is has been filled with injustice and tyranny.

Some modern <u>Sh</u>í'ahs, such as the scholar az-Zanjání, claim that some of the conditions of the world that have been related as accompanying the advent of the Mahdí appear to have been fulfilled by modern scientific inventions. Thus one of these Traditions seems to be referring to television:

"I heard Abú'Abdu'lláh [the Sixth Imám] saying: the believer, in the time of the Qá'im, while in the east, will be able to see his brother in the west and he who is in the west will be able to see his brother in the east."

Other prophecies are seen as referring to the radio and airplane. The following is a lengthy Tradition quoted from the Sixth Imám, Ja'far as-Sádiq, by Kulayní which describes the moral degradation at the time of the coming of the Mahdí and is seen as referring to several modern phenomena such as the secularization of society, the appearance of women in national parliaments and other consultative assemblies, and the advent of the "permissive society":

> When you see that truth has died and people of truth have disappeared, and you see that injustice prevails through the land; and the Qur'an has become despised and things are introduced into it that are not in it and it is turned towards

men's desires; and you see the people of error having mastery over the people of truth; and you see evil out in the open and that doers of evil are not prevented nor do they excuse themselves; and you see moral depravity openly manifest and men being content with men and women satisfied by women; and you see the believer silent, his word not being accepted; and you see the sinful lying and he is not refuted nor does his deceit redound upon him, and you see the lowly despising the great; and you see the wombs cut open; and you see he who boasts of moral depravity is laughed at and is not spurned; and you see young men being handed over like women and women co-habiting with women and their numbers increasing; and you see men spending their wealth on things other than pious deeds and no-one opposes or hinders them; and you see the onlooker turn his back on the efforts of the believer; and you see one person molesting his neighbor and no-one prevents it; and you see the unbeliever joyful because he does not see gladness in the believer when he sees corruption in the world; and you see alcoholic drinks being drunk openly . . . and you see women occupying places in the assemblies just as men do and usury is carried out openly and adultery is praised . . . and you see the forbidden thing made legal and the legal thing forbidden; and you see that religion becomes a matter of opinion and the Book and its laws fall into disuse; and you see the leaders drawing close to the unbelievers and away from good people; and you see the leaders corrupt in their rule; . . . and you see men eating what their wives have obtained as a result of their immorality and knowing this and persisting in it; . . . and you see places of entertainment appearing which no-one who passes them forbids them and no-one is bold enough to put an end to them; and you see a worshipper only praying in order that the people may see him; and you see the experts in religious law devoting themselves to things other than religion, seeking the world and leadership; and you see the people living together like animals; and you see the pulpit from which fear of God is enjoined but the speaker does not act in the manner he has enjoined others to act; . . . and when you see the tokens of

> truth that I have taught, then be aware [of the advent of the Mahdí] and seek salvation from God.
> (*An Introduction to Shí'i Islam*, pp. 161–67)

There are several similar prophecies from the Imám 'Ali concerning the coming of the Imam Mahdí, one concerning the degraded state of Islam at the time of his advent is:

> The Apostle of God said: There will come a time for my people when there will remain nothing of Qur'an except its outward form and nothing of Islam except its name and they will call themselves by this name even though they are the people furthest from it. Their mosques will be full of people but they will be empty of right guidance. The religious leaders (fuqahá) of that day will be most evil religious leaders under the heavens; sedition and dissension will go out from them and to them will it return."
> (*An Introduction to Shí'i Islam*, p. 168)

Footnote No. 37:

The International Archives

> Before proceeding to the momentous decision of building the new International Archives, I should like to mention an episode which further demonstrates the eager interest of Shoghi Effendi in collecting information and facts pertaining to the Sacred Writings and the history of the Cause. One evening, as I entered the dining-room, the Guardian was already seated at his place at the table, his face shining with an inner jubilation which he could neither control nor conceal. At his side, upon the table, stood a small bundle, an object wrapped in a coloured silk handkerchief, typical of the East and of Iran in particular. As soon as we were all seated and attentive, even before dinner was served, he said that a pilgrim had that day arrived from Tihrán, bringing with him one of the most precious documents to be placed in the archives. He united the handkerchief and with great reverence lifted out a manuscript in book form, and, placing it in a position that every one could see, added that it contained two original Tablets in the handwriting of 'Abdu'l-Bahá. One was the *Íqán* and the other was a Tablet the name of which I do not now remember.

These manuscripts, Shoghi Effendi stated, were transcribed by ‘Abdu’l-Bahá in His beautiful calligraphy, when He was about eighteen years old, and bore some additions in the Hand of Bahá’u’lláh, insertions which He had written on the margins of many pages in reviewing the manuscripts. Shoghi Effendi had never before seen the original of the *Íqán* and was deeply astonished to discover that the phrase he had chosen from this book and placed on the title page of his translation of Nabil’s Narrative, *The Dawn-Breakers*, was an after-reflection of Bahá’u’lláh’s, written by Himself, on the margin of one page. The phrase in question is the one stating: “I stand, life in hand, ready; that perchance . . .”[25]

The Guardian, that evening, was not only astonished but overjoyed as well, because he was conscious that through a mysterious process he had been inspired to adopt that phrase as an eternal testimonial to Bahá’u’lláh’s yearning to sacrifice His life for the Báb, the Primal Point. All of us who were seated at the table were awed and profoundly stirred, and I, in particular, felt that the existence of a spiritual link between our Guardian and the invisible world of God was something that no one should ever doubt.”
(Hugo Giachery, *Shoghi Effendi: Recollections*, p. 149)

Appendix II

Additional Materials, Main Text

Note No. 2

Mysticism

Mysticism and the mystical way of life have existed in the world for thousands of years, but, beginning in the middle of the nineteenth century, an ever-increasing number of scholars in the West have become interested in the subject, and an extensive body of literature covering all aspects of the nature and practice of mysticism has been generated. There are many definitions offered for mysticism and mystics, a few of which include:

- immediate consciousness of the transcendent or ultimate reality or God
- belief in the existence of realities beyond perceptual or intellectual apprehension that is central to being and directly accessible by subjective experience
- pursuit of communion with ultimate reality through direct experience, intuition, or insight
- engagement in practices that nurture direct experience
- pursuit of inner awakening and enlightenment

Evelyn Underhill, claimed by some to be the foremost authority on mysticism in the English-speaking world, in her 500-page book on mysticism, defined mysticism as the methodology and practice for "transition from the life of sense to the life of spirit." She states:

> Mysticism is seen to be a highly specialized form of that search for reality, for heightened and completed life, which we have found to be a constant characteristic of human consciousness. It is largely prosecuted by that "spiritual spark," that transcendental faculty which, though the life of our life, remains below the threshold in ordinary man. Emerging from its hiddenness in the mystic, it gradually becomes the dominant factor in his life.
> (Evelyn Underhill, *Mysticism: A Study in Nature and Development of Spiritual Consciousness,* pp. 82–93)

Note No. 3

Detachment:

Three barriers between God and man are delineated by Bahá'u'lláh in a Tablet cited by Adib Taherzadeh in the *Revelation of Bahá'u'lláh,* Vol. 2, p. 35:

> In another Tablet (Bahá'u'lláh, *Ma'idiy-i-Asmani,* vol. VIII, p. 29) Bahá'u'lláh states that there are three barriers between God and man. He exhorts the believers to pass beyond them so that they may be enabled to attain His presence. The first one . . . is attachment to the mortal world. The second attachment to the next world and all that is destined for man in the life hereafter. And the third is attachment to the "Kingdom of Names."

1. Attachment to the world in the Writings of Bahá'u'lláh,

    a. Say: Should your conduct, O people, contradict your professions, how think ye, then, to be able to distinguish yourselves from them who, though professing their faith in the Lord, their God, have, as soon as He came unto them in the cloud of holiness, refused to acknowledge Him, and have repudiated His truth? Disencumber yourselves of all the attachments to this world and the vanities thereof. Beware that ye approach them not, in as much as they prompt you to walk after your own lusts and covetous desires, and hinder you from entering the straight and glorious Path.

    Know ye that by "the world" is meant your unawareness of Him Who is your Maker, and your absorption in aught else but Him. The "life to come," on the other hand, signifieth the things that give you a safe approach to God, the All-Glorious, the Incomparable. Whatsoever deterreth you, in this Day, from loving God is nothing but the world. Flee it, that ye may be numbered with the blest. Should a man wish to adorn himself with the ornaments of the earth, to wear its apparels, or partake of its benefits, no harm can befall him, if he alloweth nothing whatever to intervene between him and God, for God hath ordained

every good thing, whether created in the heavens or in earth, for such of His servants that truly believe in Him. Eat ye, O people, of the good things which God hath allowed you, and deprive not yourselves of His wondrous bounties . . .
(*Gleanings from the Writings of Bahá'u'lláh,* pp. 275–76)

b. In his second Tablet to Napoleon III, Bahá'u'lláh makes clear that detachment from the world differs from renouncing the world:

O Concourse of monks! Seclude not yourselves in churches and cloisters. Come forth by My leave, and occupy yourselves with that which will profit your souls and the souls of men! Thus biddeth you the King of the Day of Reckoning. Seclude yourselves in the stronghold of My love. This verily, is a befitting seclusion, were ye of them that perceive it. He that shuteth himself up in a house is indeed as one dead. It behooveth man to show forth that which will profit all created things, and he that bright forth no fruit that is fit for fire.
(Bahá'u'lláh, quoted in Shoghi Effendi, *The Proclamation of Bahá'u'lláh,* p. 95)

2. Detachment from the next world:

a. In past religions: The rewards of worship and a virtuous life were often emphasized by religious leaders. The following is the description of Paradise in the Qur'án in the Súrah of the Inevitable for which many a believer has given his life:

> And they who were foremost on earth—the foremost still these are they that shall be brought nigh unto God, in the gardens of delight; a crowd of the former and a few of the latter generations; on inwrought couches reclining on them face to face; aye-blooming youths go round about to them; with goblets and ewers and a cup of flowing wine; their brows ache not from it, nor fails the sense: and with such fruits as shall please them best, and with flesh of such birds as they long for: and their shall be the

> Houris, with large dark eyes, like pearls hidden in their shells, in recompense of their labors past. No vain discourse shall they hear therein, nor charge of sin, but only the cry, "Peace! Peace!"
> And the people of the right hand—Oh! How happy shall be the people of the right hand! Amid the thornless sidrahs and talh trees clad with fruit, and in the extended shade, by flowing waters, and with abundant fruits, unfailing, unforbidden, and on lofty couches. Of a rare creation we have created the Houris, and we have made them ever virgins, dear to their spouses, of equal age with them, For the people of the right hand, a crowd of the former, and a crowd of the latter generations.
> (The Qur'án 61:10–39)

Similarly, the same Súrah lists the misery of those who go against the Will of God:

> But the people of the left hand-oh! How wretched shall be the people of the left hand! Amid pestilential winds and in scalding water, and in the shadow of a black smoke, not cool, and horrid to behold. For truly, ere this, were blessed with worldly goods, but persisted in heinous sin, and were wont to say, "What! After we have died, and become dust and bones, shall be raised? And our fathers, the men of yore?
> (The Qur'án 61:40–48)

b. By contrast, in this Revelation, worship is viewed in light of detachment from the next life. The notion of the worship of God motivated by the love one feels for Him rather than by the anticipation of reward and punishment in the next life was explained by both the Báb and by Bahá'u'lláh.

> Worship God in such wise that if Thy worship lead thee to the fire, no alteration in thine adoration would be produced, and so likewise should thy recompense be paradise. Thus and thus alone should

be the worship that befitteth the one True God. Shouldst thou worship him because of fear, this would be unseemly in the sanctified court of His presence, and could not be regarded as an act by thee dedicated to the Oneness of His Being. Or if thy gaze should be on paradise, and Thou shouldst worship Him while cherishing such a hope, thou wouldst make God's creation a partner with Him, notwithstanding the fact that paradise is desired by men. Fire and Paradise both bow down and prostrated themselves before God. That which is worthy of His Essence is to worship Him for His sake, without fear of fire, or hope of paradise.

Although when true worship is offered, the worshipper is delivered from the fire, and entereth the paradise of God's good-pleasure, yet such is not the motive of his act. However, God's favor and grace ever flow in accordance with the exigencies of His inscrutable wisdom.
(The Báb, *Selections from the Writings of the Báb,* pp. 77–8)

2). Bahá'u'lláh in the Kitáb-i-Aqdas states:

The tongue of My power hath, from the heaven of My omnipotent glory, addressed to My creation these words: "Observe My commandments, for the love of My beauty." Happy is the lover which hath inhaled the divine fragrance of his Best Beloved from these words, laden with the perfume of a grace which no tongue can describe.
(Bahá'u'lláh, The Kitáb-i-Aqdas, ¶4)

3. Attachment to the "Kingdom of Names"

a. Regarding the Kingdom of Names Bahá'u'lláh states:

The Pen of the Most High is unceasingly calling; and yet how few are those that have inclined their ears to its voice! The dwellers of the kingdom of names have busied themselves with the gay livery of the world,

forgetful that every man hath eyes to perceive and ears to hear cannot but readily recognize how evanescent are its colors.
(Bahá'u'lláh in *Gleanings from the Writings of Bahá'u'lláh,* pp. 195–96)

b. Examples of attachment to the "Kingdom of Names" in the Writings of Bahá'u'lláh are discussed by Adib Taherzadeh in the *Revelation of Bahá'u'lláh*, vol. 2, pp. 39–40:

> In the Láwḥ-i-Naṣr (For a further history of this Tablet, see *The Revelation of Bahá'u'lláh,* pp. 245–47), speaking with the voice of God, Bahá'u'lláh states that a name from among His names which He had created with one Word and into which He hath breathed a new life, rose up against him and opposed his authority. Because of attachment to this name, He testifies that some of the people of the Bayán rejected His Cause and deprived themselves of His glory. Here Bahá'u'lláh is alluding to the name "Azal" (Eternity), the title of Mírzá Yaḥyá. Indeed, this name, which is one of the attributes of God, became a barrier for many who followed him because of their attachment to an exalted title. Mírzá Yaḥyá himself was also misled by this name. He extolled its virtues and remained attached to it until the end of his life.
>
> In many of His Tablets Bahá'u'lláh exhorts His followers not to become bond-slaves of the Kingdom of Names. The well-known Islamic saying, "The Names come down from Heaven" has many significances. In this world every one of God's attributes is clad with a name, and every such name reveals the characteristic of its attribute. For instance, generosity is an attribute of God, and it manifests itself in human beings. However, a person who has this attribute often becomes proud of it and loves to be referred to as generous. When this generosity is acknowledged by other people he becomes happy, and when it is ignored, unhappy. This is one form of attachment to the Kingdom of Names.

Although this example concerns the name "generosity", the same is true of all the names and attributes of God manifested within the individual. Usually, man ascribes these attributed to his own person rather than to God and employs them to exalt his own ego. For instance, a learned man uses the attribute of knowledge to become famous and feels gratified and uplifted when his name is publicized far and wide. Or there is an individual whose heart leaps with feelings of pride and satisfaction when he hears his name mentioned and finds himself admired. These are examples of attachment to the Kingdom of Names.

c. 'Abdu'l-Bahá, our Exemplar, also exemplified detachment from the "Kingdom of Names":

'Abdu'l-Bahá, the true Exemplar of the teachings of Bahá'u'lláh, demonstrated this form of detachment by His actions. Throughout His life, He never wished to exalt His name nor did He seek publicity for Himself. . The exalted titles that were conferred upon him by Bahá'u'lláh were indicative of 'Abdu'l-Bahá's lofty station. Yet, 'Abdu'l-Bahá never applied them to himself. Instead, after the ascension of Bahá'u'lláh, He took the title of 'Abdu'l-Bahá (Servant of Bahá) and urged the believers to call Him only by this name. True servitude at the threshold of Bahá'u'lláh was all he prized. These are some of His words as he describes with utter self-effacement the reality of His station:

My name is 'Abdu'l-Bahá. My qualification is 'Abdu'l-Bahá. My reality is 'Abdu'l-Bahá. My praise is 'Abdu'l-Bahá. Thralldom to the Blessed Perfection is my glorious and refulgent diadem, and servitude to all the human race my perpetual religion. . . . No name, no title, no mention, no commendation have I, nor will I ever have, except 'Abdu'l-Bahá. This is my longing. This is my yearning. This is my eternal life. This is my everlasting glory.

('Abdu'l-Bahá, quoted by Shoghi Effendi, *The World Order of Bahá'u'lláh*, pp. 138–39).

Bahá'u'lláh defines the "essence of detachment" in Words of Wisdom:

> The essence of detachment is for man to turn his face toward the courts of the Lord, to enter His presence, behold His Countenance, to stand as witness before Him.
> (*Tablets of Bahá'u'lláh*, p. 155)

Note No. 11

Ode titled "O Cupbearer" revealed by Bahá'u'lláh:

These two lines are from the ode (ghazál) titled "Sáqí az Ghayb-i-Baqá," which was revealed by Bahá'u'lláh during the period in which He lived in Sulaymaníyyih under the name Dervish Muḥammad, and was composed under the sobriquet "Dervish." This is a beautiful and spiritually charged Ode that contains many allusions to the exalted station of Bahá'u'lláh and to His mission for reviving and vivifying the world. In order to allow readers to experience the spiritual beauty of this ode, this author's provisional translation, although severely inadequate, is presented below. In preparing this provisional translation, the present author benefited significantly from the translation of some lines of this ode by other authors, particularly the provisional translation of Franklin D. Lewis (published in *Lights of Irfán*, Book II, pp. 83–91):

O Cupbearer from the unseen immortal realm, cast aside the veil from your countenance
That I may drink the eternal wine from the beauty of the Divine Providence

What thou have in the Wine Cellar will not break the bile of love*
From that wine of inner meaning, Cupbearer, bring forth an ocean

That this veiled, love-frenzied one may begin to roar
That this divinely drunk one may be aroused from stupor

Kindle the fire of love and burn away all things,
Then set thy foot into the land of the lovers.

If thou are not detached from all attributes of existence, O' man of the path
Thou will not taste the wine of eternal life from the succulent ruby lips of the beloved

Step on the apex of the worldly dominion, then come under Poverty's sheltering shade
That now thou mayest see the Eternal dominion on every side

If the concern for life is in thy heart, do not come here
But if thou hast a heart and a soul to sacrifice, bring them and come

This is the custom of the path if thou desire union with Bahá
If thou are not the man for this path, be gone and burden us not

If thou wishest to be apprised of the mysteries of love
Open the eye of admonition and close the path to pride

That thou mayest observe that Sinai of Moses came to circumambulate here
That thou mayest observe the spirit of Jesus restless in his love for Him

That thou mayest find the book of Divine unity within the two braids of the Friend
That thou mayest read the scroll of Divine sanctity on the two cheeks of the Beloved

Now take the wine of joy from the vivifying spring of love
That thou mayest happily cast your head at the feet of the Beloved

All are dead in this assemblage, but for the sake of the Friend
O' messiah of the age, blow your warm and reviving breath

That the birds of existence fly out of the prison of the body
Up into the infinite expanse of heaven, beneath the sheltering-shade of the Lord of the Might

Dervish! The world is burned by this divine soul-burning flame
The time has come to quicken it with this lamenting melody

* This might be an allusion to a practice in traditional Middle Eastern medicine. Those who suffered from sickness caused by excessive secretion of bile would drink old wine to cure themselves of their affliction. In Persian literary traditions the love-frenzied people who were depressed and deeply affected by separation from their beloved and had a sickly and yellowish countenance, were depicted like those who suffered from excessive secretion of bile, which would cause the same effect.

The last few lines of this Ode contain intimations to His own station and His upcoming declaration. In this line: "That you see the Sinai of Moses came to circumambulate here. That you see the spirit of Jesus restless in its love for Him" there are allusions to the Revelation that Moses received in Sinai and to the passion of Jesus.

Note No. 68, Imám Ja'fár-i-Ṣádiq:

Abú 'Abdu'lláh Ja'fár, known by the title as-Ṣádiq (the truthful), is the sixth Imám of the Twelver Shí'ah sect. After Imám 'Alí Ibn-i-Abí-Ṭáleb and Imám Ḥusayn, he is the most well-known Imám, known for his piety, Islamic religious knowledge, theology, jurisprudence, and Qur'ánic exegeses and interpretation. He is also well-known for his expertise in transmission and evaluation of the authenticity of the Islamic Traditions (Aḥadi<u>th</u>). He had a great number of students and a number of the famous Islamic jurists—such as Abú Ḥanífa, the founder of the Ḥanafí school of Islamic jurisprudence and Málik Ibn-i-Anas, the founder of the Málikí school of Islamic jurisprudence in the Sunní sect—are regarded as his students.

Note No. 107

Ba<u>gh</u>dád

Ba<u>gh</u>dád, also known as Dar-al-salám (the abode of peace), is located on the banks of the Tigris River. The city dates back to at least the eighth century, and probably to pre-Islamic times. Once the center of the Muslim world, it was the site of the largest university in the world.

Although there is dispute over its Persian origin, there have been several rival proposals as to its specific etymology. The most reliable and most widely accepted among these is that the name is a Middle Persian compound of *Bhaga* "god" + *dād* "given", translating to "God-given" or "God's gift." Other leading proposals are that the name comes from Middle Persian *Bāgh-dād,* in which *Bāgh* means garden and *dād* means justice, "the Garden of Justice" or *dād* meaning "given," "The Given Garden," or the heavenly or "the God given Garden."

The city of Baghdád is often said to have been founded on the west bank of the Tigris on 30 July 762 by the 'Abbásid Dynasty, led by Caliph al-Mansur, replacing Harran as the seat of the Caliphate (Capital City); however, a city of Baghdád is mentioned in pre-Islamic texts, including the Talmud, and the Abbásid city was likely built on the site of this earlier settlement.

Baghdád eclipsed Ctesiphon, the capital of the Persian Empire, which was located some thirty km (twenty miles) to the southeast, which had been under Muslim control since 637, and which became quickly deserted after the foundation of Baghdád. The site of Babylon, which had been deserted since the second century BC, lies some ninety km (fifty-five miles) to the south.

The city was designed as a circle about two km in diameter, leading it to be known as the "Round City." The original design shows a ring of residential and commercial structures along the inside of the city walls, but the final construction added another ring inside the first. In the center of the city lay the mosque, as well as headquarters for guards. The purpose or use of the remaining space in the center is unknown. The circular design of the city was a direct reflection of the traditional Persian Sasanian urban design. The ancient Sasanian city of Gur/Firouzabad is nearly identical in its general circular design, radiating avenues, and the government buildings and temples at the center of the city.

The roundness points to the fact that it was based on Persian precedents such as Firouzabad in Persia. The two designers who were hired by al-Mansur to plan the city's design were Naubakht, a former Persian Zoroastrian who also determined that the date of the foundation of the city would be astrologically auspicious, and Mashallah, a Jew from Khorasan, an area in the northeast of Persia, present-day Iran.

Within a generation of its founding, Baghdád became a hub of learning and commerce. The House of Wisdom or House of Knowledge was an establishment dedicated to the translation of Greek, Middle Persian, and Syriac works. The Barmakids (a family of Persian origin, administrators of the courts of the 'Abbásid Dynasty) were influential in bringing scholars from the nearby Academy of Gundishapur (a City in western Persia), facilitating the introduction of Greek and Indian science into the Arabic world. Baghdád was likely the largest city in the world from shortly after its foundation until the 930s, when it was tied by Córdoba (in Spain). Several estimates suggest that the city contained over a million inhabitants at its peak. A portion of the population of Baghdád originated in Persia, especially from Khorasan. Many of Scheherazade's tales in *One Thousand and One Nights* (a classical story book) are set in Baghdád during this period.

By the tenth century, the city's population was between 300,000 and 500,000. Baghdád's early meteoric growth slowed due to troubles within the Caliphate, including relocations of the capital to Samarra (during 808–819 and 836–892), the loss of the western and easternmost provinces, and periods of political domination by the Persian/Iranian Buwayhids (a post Islamic-invasion Persian dynasty, AD 945–1055) and Seljuk Turks (AD 1055–1135). Nevertheless, the city remained one of the cultural and commercial hubs of the Islamic world until February 10, 1258, when it was sacked by the Mongols under Hulagu Khán during the sack of Baghdád. The Mongols massacred most of the city's inhabitants, including the 'Abbásid Caliph Al-Musta'sim, and destroyed large sections of the city. The canals and dykes forming the city's irrigation system were also destroyed. The sack of Baghdád put an end to the 'Abbásid Caliphate, a blow from which the Islamic civilization never fully recovered.

At this point Baghdád was ruled by the Il-Khánids, the Mongol emperors of Persia/Iran. In 1401, Baghdád was again sacked, by Timur ("Tamerlane"). It became a provincial capital controlled by the Jalayirid (another post Islamic-invasion Persian dynasty, AD 1400–1411), Qara Quyunlu (1411–1469), Aq Quyunlu (1469–1508), and Ṣafavid (the most powerful post Islamic-invasion Persian dynasty, AD 1508–1534) dynasties.

In 1534, Baghdád was conquered by the Ottoman Turks. Under the Ottomans, Baghdád fell into a period of decline, partially as a result of the enmity between its rulers and Persia. For a time, Baghdád had been the largest city in the Middle East before being overtaken by Constantinople in the sixteenth century. The city saw relative revival in the latter part of the eighteenth century under the Mamluk rule.

(Based partly on information provided in Wikipedia, The free Encyclopedia, with some modifications)

Note No. 278

Djinns

In Islamic traditions the Djinns are said to be creatures made from "smokeless fire" by Alláh (God) in the same way humans were made of dust or earth. According to the Qur'án, Djinns have free will, and Iblis (Shaitan, in English, Devil or Satan) was a Djinn who used this freedom in front of Alláh by refusing to bow to Adam when Alláh told Iblis to do so. By refusing to obey Alláh's order he was thrown out of Paradise and called "Shaitan." Djinns are frequently mentioned in the Qur'án. Súrah 72 of the Qur'án (named Al-Jinn) is mostly about them. Another Súrah (Al-Naas) mentions the Djinn in the last verse. It is also mentioned in the Qur'án that Muḥammad was sent as a Prophet to both "humanity and the Djinn." Islamic traditions hold that there are three main creatures besides the various animals in the world: angels, humans, and djinns.

Angels: Angels are made from light (Noor). In Islamic traditions they are described as the slaves of God who have no free will. They do not commit any sin nor disobey God, and they always worship him.

Humans: Humans are created from earth and are given free will to do good or bad in their lives. Because of their free will, they will be held accountable for their choices in this life on the Day of Judgment. Those who follow and obey God (Alláh), will be rewarded with paradise/heaven.

Djinns: Similar to humanity, Djinns have free will allowing them to follow any religion they choose to, such as Islam, Christianity, Judaism, Hinduism, etc. The only difference is that they are made of smokeless fire and therefore are not visible to humans. There are more Djinns than humans, in terms of population. Djinns have the power to fly and fit into any space so they live in remote areas, mountains, seas, trees, and in the air, in their own communities. Similar to the humans, Djinns will also be judged on the Day of Judgment and will be sent to Jannat (heaven) or Nar (hell) according to the life they lead.

Every person is assigned a special Djinn to be with him all the time, also called a qareen (companion), they are the Djinns that whisper into your soul and tell you to give in to your evil desires. Some Islamic commentators hold that the Prophet Muḥammad's Djinn turned into a Muslim Djinn at the time of the recitation of the Qur'án, as the Djinn found it most beautiful.

In many places in the Old Testament, reference is made to a "familiar spirit," a person possessed by which would be rejected from the community or killed. The same entities were referenced in the New Testament as "unclean spirits," "spirits that were cast out of people," or "devils that possessed people" and were cast out by Jesus or His disciples. These familiar spirits, evil spirits, or unclean spirits could take over the body and soul of people and make them act or live improperly or disturb their physical wellbeing. A few examples of these references are cited below:

> Regard not them that have familiar spirits, neither seek after wizards, to be defiled by them: I am the LORD your God.
> (Leviticus 19:31)

> A man also or woman that hath a familiar spirit, or that is a wizard, shall surely be put to death: they shall stone them with stones: their blood shall be upon them.
> (Leviticus 20:27)

> There shall not be found among you any one that maketh his son or his daughter to pass through the fire, or that useth divination, or an observer of times, or an enchanter, or a witch. Or a charmer, or a consulter with familiar spirits, or a wizard, or a necromancer.
> (Deuteronomy 18:10–11)

> When the event was come, they brought unto him many that were possessed with devils: and he cast out the spirits with his word, and healed all that were sick.
> (Matthew 8:16)

> And when he had called unto him his twelve disciples, he gave them power against unclean spirits, to cast them out, and to heal all manner of sickness and all manner of disease.
> (Matthew 10:1)

> And when he was come to the other side into the country of the Gergesenes, there met him two possessed with devils, coming out of the tombs, exceeding fierce, so that no man might pass by that way. And, behold, they cried out, saying, What have we to do with thee, Jesus, thou Son of God? art thou come hither to torment us before the time? And there was a good way off from them an herd of many swine feeding. So the devils besought him, saying, If thou cast us out, suffer us to go away into the herd of swine.
> (Matthew 8:28–31)

In the old Arabic and Persian translations of the Bible, the word Djinn or Jenn is used for "familiar spirit" or "unclean Spirit" and devils that possess people, as the characteristics of these entities matches those of the Djinns.
(Based partly on information provided in Wikipedia, The free Encyclopedia)

Note No. 318

The Great Advent Awakening.

The following is a brief history of the Adventist movement. In the mid-1700s and the early 1800s, independent of one another, people throughout the world began to study the prophecies of the Old Testament book of Daniel and the New Testament book of Revelation and the Apocalyptic prophecies became the topic of biblical scholarship and personal devotion. In the mid-1700s Johann Bengel, in Germany, and in the early 1800s, Manuel de Lacunza, a Catholic priest in South America who wrote under the pen name of Juan Josafa Ben-Ezra, Edward Irving, Joseph Wolf, Heinrich Kelber, William Davis of South Carolina, Alexander Campbell and William Miller, simultaneously came to the same conclusion that Jesus was coming very, very soon. These biblical scholars who were concerned with and made predictions regarding the time of the Second Advent are called Adventists. Among the Adventists William Miller who made very specific predictions for the time (the year) of the advent, became a preacher of the Second Coming and found a great following. A brief history of the Adventist movement based on materials from Seventh-Day Adventists and other sources is presented below.

Johhan Bengel

Bengel was a classically trained, extremely careful interpreter of the biblical text. He is possibly best known as a biblical commentator: he wrote extensive notes on every book of the New Testament, exploring grammatical, historical, and interpretive issues at length, in expositions that were clear and compelling—and still worth reading today. At the heart of this work of exegesis was a trust in the words of scripture. This trust went so far that it took Bengel in directions that today might seem a shade bizarre. Thinking that all the words of scripture were inspired—including the words of the prophets and the book of Revelation—Bengel became convinced that God's great involvement with human affairs was nearing a climax, and that biblical prophecy indicated that his own generation was living near the end of days. He, in fact, believed he knew when the end would come: it would be about a century in the future, in 1836.

Bengel was not taken aback by verses such as Matt. 24:36, which says that "of that day and hour no one know, not the angels in heaven, nor even the Son, but the Father only." Careful interpreter that he was, Bengel points out that here Jesus speaks in the present tense: in his own *day* Jesus could say "no one knows," but that doesn't mean that at a later time no one would know . . . and the end was but a century away (he was writing in the 1730s).

> The Great Tribulation, which the primitive church looked for from the future Antichrist, is not arrived, but is very near; for the predictions of the Apocalypse, from the tenth to the fourteenth chapter, have been fulfilling for many centuries; and the principal point stands clearer and clearer in view, that within another hundred years, the great expected change of things may take place . . . . Still, let the remainder stand, especially the great termination which I anticipate for 1836.
> (Bart Ehrman, *Misquoting Jesus*, pp. 109–110)

Edward Irving

Edward Irving (4 August 1792–7 December 1834) was a Scottish clergyman, generally regarded as the main figure behind the foundation of the Catholic Apostolic Church. . . . For years the subject of prophecy had occupied much of his thoughts, and his belief in the near approach of the second advent had received such wonderful corroboration by the perusal

of the work of a Jesuit priest, Manuel Lacunza, writing under the assumed Jewish name of Juan Josafat Ben-Ezra, that in 1827 he published a translation of it, accompanied with an eloquent preface. The religious opinions of Irving concerning unfulfilled prophecy followed by an almost exclusive study of the prophetical books and especially the Apocalypse. His apocalyptic lectures in 1828 was crowding the largest churches of Edinburgh on summer morning.
(Source: Wikipedia, The Free Encyclopedia)

Dr. Joseph Wolf

Around this same time, Dr. Joseph Wolf, a Jew converted to Christianity, believed that Christ was coming in the early 1800s. As Joseph had learned about Jesus, he knew that this was no ordinary man. He read the fifty third chapter of Isaiah which told of Christ's coming as a "lamb to the slaughter." When he asked his father about it, he was told to never read it again. That was not good enough for Joseph. He later became a Christian. He then became a "missionary to the world" and traveled throughout Asia proclaiming the Second Coming of Jesus.

Others

Three hundred ministers in the Church of England and six hundred nonconformist ministers preached the Second Coming in England. In Sweden, Denmark, and Norway, the public preaching of the word was outlawed just after eighteen hundreds of child preachers also proclaimed the soon coming of Jesus. So at the end of the 1260 years of Daniel 12:7, a renewed interest in the Second Coming of Christ swept Europe and was felt in the farthest missionary outposts in Asia and Africa.

William Miller

William Miller had studied the prophecies of Daniel from 1816 to 1831. He began proclaiming that Jesus was coming soon. Miller was born in 1782 in Pittsfield, Massachusetts and grew up in Hampton, N.Y. His parents were Baptists but, through his reading in the local library, he gradually drifted toward Deism.[110]

---

1. [110] Belief in the existence of a supreme being, specifically of a creator who does not intervene in the universe. The term is used chiefly of an intellectual movement of the 17th and 18th centuries that accepted the existence of a creator on the basis of reason but rejected belief in a supernatural deity who interacts with humankind.

In the Battle of Plattsburg during the war of 1812, William Miller witnessed what he perceived to be supernatural intervention by a Higher Power on behalf of the beleaguered and greatly outnumbered U.S. forces. That challenged his Deistic notions that God was a distant Being who cared not for humans and did not involve Himself in their affairs. He also saw a number of his friends killed. Following the war, he settled down as a farmer and began to reevaluate his belief system. As he pondered the Deist's belief of no hope after death, he became terribly disheartened. He recorded his thought in his book, Great Controversy, pages 318, 319.

> Annihilation was a cold and chilling thought, and accountability was sure destruction to all. The heavens were as brass over my head, and the earth as iron under my feet. Eternity-what was it? And death- why was it? The more I reasoned, the further I was from demonstration. The more I thought, the more scattered were my conclusions. I tried to stop thinking, but my thoughts would not be controlled. I was truly wretched, but did not understand the cause. I murmured and complained, but knew not how or where to find the right. I mourned, but without hope. . . . Suddenly . . . the character of a Saviour was vividly impressed upon my mind.

William Miller reverted back to Christianity. He then set out to challenge his skeptical friends. He was driven to study the Bible with a scientific zeal. His study took him on a fifteen-year course of study. Miller thought it best to dispense with commentaries. Reading verse by verse with the Bible as its own interpreter (like Lacunza, Bengel, Edward Irving, and Joseph Wolf), he discovered that the end was at hand. The impact of his discovery would soon shake the religious world. . . . Unto two thousand and three hundred days, then shall the sanctuary be cleansed.

What Is The Sanctuary?

Miller had accepted the popular assumption that the sanctuary was the world. So, he deduced that the cleansing of the sanctuary must be the cleansing of the world by fire at the Second Coming. As he traced the 2300 day/year prophecy, he saw certain events that would take place along the way. He discovered the prediction of the Christ's baptism in A.D. 27, his crucifixion in A.D. 31, and the gospel to the Gentiles in A.D. 34. As he extended the 2300 years down through the ages, he eventually concluded

---

(https://www.google.com/#q=deism+definition)

that 2300 day/year prophecy ended in 1844. He reasoned that since Jesus was baptized in A.D. 27 and died in A.D. 31, exactly fulfilling the prophecy, then the sanctuary's cleansing must also be fulfilled literally in 1844. So, accepting the popular view of the sanctuary, he believed the earth would be cleansed by fire in 1844 with the Second Coming of Christ.

Others all over the world like Joseph Wolf, William Davis of South Carolina, and Alexander Campbell, almost simultaneously reached the same conclusion on their own. As Miller came to his conclusion, the thought pressed upon his mind again and again "Go tell it to the world." But he was a farmer and he thought, "I can't tell it. I'm not eloquent. I can't preach." But the weighty sense of responsibility kept coming to his mind, "Go tell it to the world."

Sharing with Friends

At first Miller shared it with a few friends, but for the most part kept it to himself. However, he had no peace as the Scriptural injunction kept coming to his mind, "If you do not tell it, you are accountable. Their blood will be on your head. Watchman, give the message." Miller was overwhelmed. As he related later in his writings, one day as this conviction was heavy upon him, Miller went to a grove to pray. In prayer, he made a sort of deal with God. "Oh, God," he prayed, "I am but a farmer. I have no desire to preach, yet I sense Your convicting power. I am surrendered to Your will. If you open the opportunity, I am willing." Relieved, he returned to the house thinking that, since no one would approach him, he was off the proverbial hook. He was quite certain the matter was now settled.

The Millerite Movement: The Farmer Begins To Preach

A short time later, however, he heard a knock on the door. "Uncle Bill! Uncle Bill! Dad wants you to come to Dresden to preach." Miller was shocked but true to his word, Miller went. In this first meeting, thirteen families accepted his ideas. From 1831-1844, Miller preached to thousands of people in the United States. The Advent movement grew like wild fire. Methodists, Baptists, Episcopalians, Catholics, and Lutherans accepted the message. In the vilest cities and the smallest villages the call went out, "Jesus is coming! The sanctuary is to be cleansed! Christ is coming in 1844!" The skeptics and scoffers said, "No man knows the day or the hour." Miller answered, "I'm not announcing the day or the hour. On the basis of prophecy we are pointing out the year." So it was that the second advent movement continued to grow.

Great Meetings

As the Millerites were forced out of the popular churches of the day, they decided to meet in tents. In the years shortly before 1844, as many as 500,000 attended 125 Millerites meetings in tents. As they saw the widespread opposition to the teaching of the Bible and the Second Coming of Jesus, the Millerites began to preach for the first time that the popular churches were Babylon (Revelation 18:4)

Date Setting

At first, based on the Jewish calendar, the Millerites believed that Jesus would come between the spring of 1843 and 1844. That time came and went. Many cast aside their faith in the Bible and prophecy. At an Exeter, N.H. camp meeting on August 12, 1844, many studied anew the prophecies and the ancient sanctuary service. A man by the name of Samuel Snow discovered that the cleansing of the sanctuary occurred on the tenth day of the seventh Jewish month. Using the ancient Jewish calendar, he discovered that the Jewish religious year began in April. He also discovered that the tenth day of the seventh month would occur on October 22, 1844. This new insight spread and 50,000 new converts joined the ranks of the Millerites. Miller himself was reluctant to accept such a precise date; but shortly before October 22, he too accepted it.

The Adventists literature state that "although we know that Miller was wrong about the event, we do know he was right about the date. Imagine that little group of Millerites on the evening of October 22. Their all-consuming passion was to meet Jesus in peace. "Jesus is coming! Jesus is coming!" the message echoed and reechoed through New England and the world. Hundreds and thousands believed that Jesus would return that day. The message was so powerful that saloons were turned into meeting halls. People who had wronged their neighbors made things right. On the microfilm record of the Providence, Rhode Island Journal an amazing add appeared on the front page.

"If I owe anybody any money as a result of my business dealings and if I've not been faithful in paying it, please let me know so I can pay up my debts, because Jesus is coming October 22, 1844, and I want to ascend in the cloud and go with Him."

The Great Disappointment

So that night many gathered in the groves and fields in prayer to await the return of their Lord. The hours ticked by. At last midnight came, but Jesus didn't come. What was sweet at first suddenly became bitter. The sweet prophecy of Daniel's little book was now the source of a great disappointment. Many had sold their homes and failed to bring in the harvest from the fields. Every hope was centered in the soon return of Jesus. That night, many spent the entire night in bitter weeping and returned the next morning to their villages to meet the jeers and laughter of their neighbors. Hiram Edson wrote recalling the experience:

> Our fondest hopes and expectations were blasted, and such a spirit of weeping came over us as I never experienced before. It seemed that the loss of all earthly friends could have been no comparison. We wept, and wept, till the day dawn. I mused in my own heart, saying, My advent experience has been the richest and brightest of all my Christian experiences. If this had proved a failure, what was the rest of my Christian experiences worth? Has the Bible proved a failure? Is there no God, no heaven, no golden home city, no paradise? Is all this but a cunningly devised fable? Is there no reality to our fondest hope and expectation of these things? And thus we had something to grieve and weep over, if all our fond hopes were lost.
> (Incomplete Manuscript of Hiram Edson.)

The Heavenly Sanctuary Recognized In the Corn field

The following morning, Edson and a few others went to a barn to pray. After prayer, he was walking home through a corn field with O.R.L Crosier when he looked up and suddenly realized that the sanctuary to be cleansed was not the earthly, but the heavenly sanctuary. He saw that on October 22, 1844 Jesus left the Holy Place in the heavenly sanctuary and entered the Most Holy Place to begin his second and last phase of ministry. Suddenly the prophecies came into sharp focus in his mind. He wrote, "It has been vividly impressed upon my mind that the sanctuary to be cleansed by fire is not the earth, but it is the heavenly sanctuary."

How many sanctuaries?

They went home and studied their Bibles again. They now studied the subject of the sanctuary. How many sanctuaries are there? Two - one on earth and the other in the heaven. They discovered that the earthly is a kind of model of the heavenly. And since the earthly sanctuary was destroyed in 70 A.D. by Titus, the only sanctuary that could be cleansed in 1844 is in heaven. They discovered that the cleansing of the sanctuary prefigured a special work of judgment in heaven to determine the reward of the righteous and to remove the record of sins from the heavenly records. They discovered that they were living in the time called by John the Revelator "the hour of God's judgment."

Disappointment

The Great Disappointment of 1844 was very much like the previous great disappointment of A.D. 31. Jesus' followers thought He would set up His kingdom on earth. Instead, He was killed. That night after the crucifixion, they were utterly disappointed. Then Jesus arose and their false views were corrected. Arising from the ashes of disappointment after Christ's ascension, the New Testament church pointed men and women to the heavenly sanctuary where Jesus Christ entered the Holy Place to minister on their behalf. Likewise, after the persecution of the little horn, they started an end-time movement from the ashes of the disappointment of 1844. Correcting their misconceptions, they discovered that Jesus had entered the Most Holy Place in the heavenly sanctuary. They also discovered that, like the New Testament church, they must point men and women to the heavenly sanctuary where Jesus Christ had begun another phase of ministry in the heavenly judgment.

A Bitter Sweet Experience Prophesied

As they read the tenth chapter of Revelation, they were amazed to discover that this chapter perfectly marked their experience. Just as John had said, the experience was "sweet" at first then "bitter." They were certainly disappointed when Jesus didn't come. Now, they wondered, was the movement based on the prophecies of Daniel and pointing to the Second Coming going to die? Was it to become fragmented? What would happen to those Lutherans, Methodists, Baptists, Catholics, and Episcopalians who had expected Jesus' Second Coming in 1844."
(Based partially on the Seventh-Day Adventists source materials posted at: http://www.teachinghearts.org/dre04histadventist.html)

Note No. 347

Láwḥ-i-Shikkar-Shikan-Shavand.

This Tablet is one of the most beautiful Tablets of Bahá'u'lláh. Translation of a part of this tablet published in the compilation "Fire and Light" [*Nár va Nur*] is quoted below:

> They that yearn for the abode of the Beloved, they that circle round the sanctuary of the desired One, are not apprehensive of trials and adversities, nor do they flee away from that which is ordained by God. They receive their portion from the ocean of resignation and drink their fill from the soft flowing stream of His mercy. They would not surrender the good pleasure of the Friend in exchange for the kingdom of both worlds, nor would they barter that which the Well-Beloved hath decreed in return for dominion over the realms of the infinite. They would eagerly drink the venom of woe as if it were the water of life and would drain deadly poison to its bitter dregs just as a sweet and life-giving draught. In the arid wastes of desolation they are stirred with enthusiasm through the remembrance of the Friend, and in the dreary wilds of adversity they are eager and impatient to offer themselves as a sacrifice. Unhesitatingly have they renounced their lives and directed their steps towards the abode of the Best Beloved. They have closed their eyes to the world and fixed their gaze upon the beauteous countenance of the Friend, cherishing no desire but the presence of the loved One and seeking no attainment save reunion with Him. They fly with the feathers of trust in God, and soar with the wings of adherence unto His Will. In their estimation a blood-shedding blade is more desirable than finest silk and a piercing dart more acceptable than mother's milk.
>
> *"High-spirited souls by myriad are deemed necessary in this path,*
> *To lay down a hundred lives with every fleeting breath"*
>
> It behoveth us to kiss the hand of the would-be assassin and to set out, dancing, on our way to the habitation of the Friend. How indescribably pleasant is that hour, how immeasurably sweet that moment when the inmost spirit is intent upon sacrificing itself, when the tabernacle of fidelity is hastening to attain the heights of self-surrender! With necks laid bare, we yearn for the stroke of the ruthless sword wielded by the

hand of the beloved. With breasts aglow with light, we eagerly await the dart of His decree. Contemptuous of name, we have detached ourselves from all else but Him, we shall not run away, we shall not endeavour to repel the stranger, we pray for calamity, that thereby we may soar unto the sublime heights of the spirit, seek shelter beneath the shade of the tree of reunion, attain the highest stations of love, and drink our fill from the wondrous wine of everlasting communion with Him. Surely we will not forfeit this imperishable dominion, nor will we forgo this incomparable blessing. If hidden beneath the dust, we shall rear our heads from the bosom of the tender mercy of the Lord of the mankind. No trial can suppress these companions, no mortal feet can traverse this journey, nor can any veil obscure this countenance.

Yea, it is clear and evident that in view of the multitudes of internal and external opponents who have raised the standards of opposition, who have girded the loins of endeavour to eliminate these poor creatures, it standeth to reason that one should turn away from them and flee from this land, nay, from the face of the earth. However, through the loving-kindness of God and by the aid of His invisible confirmations, we are as radiant as the sun and as shining as the moon. We are established upon the throne of tranquillity and seated upon the couch of fortitude. Of what importance is the shipwreck to the fish of the spirit? What doth a soul celestial care if the physical frame is destroyed? Indeed this body is for it a prison; and the ship but a place of confinement to the fish. What else but a nightingale can understand a Nightingale's melody and who else but the intimate friend can recognize the familiar voice of the Friend?
(*The Bahá'í World,* Vol. XVIII: 1979–83, p. 9, a translation by Mr. Habib Taherzadeh, with the assistance of a Committee at the Bahá'í World Center, from the "Fire and Light" [*Nár va Nur*] (a compilation from the Writings of Bahá'u'lláh, 'Abdu'l-Bahá and Shoghi Effendi), Bahá'í Verlag GMBH, D-6238 Hofheim-Langenhain, 1982-139, p. 11)

The provisional translation of the rest of the Tablet, Láwḥ-i-Shikkar-Shikan-Shavand, incorporating the above excerpt, translated by Shahrokh Monjazeb, is available at:
http://bahai-library.com/?-file=bahaullah_-shikkar_shikan_monjazeb.

Appendix III

Story of Joseph

Note No. 35

The Old Testament and Qur'án both use the medium of storytelling as a means for the spiritual education of humanity, just as Jesus also used parables for the same purpose. The story of Joseph is covered in both the Old Testament and the Qur'án. It is the most important, next to the story of Abraham in the Old Testament, and forms the last fourteen chapters of the Book of Genesis.

Like stories about other personalities such as Abraham and Noah, and events such as the creation of Adam and the Flood that are related in both books, there are many similarities but also some differences in the way the story is conveyed in the two books. In most instances, the variations that appear in Qur'ánic versions have great spiritual, educational, and social significance.

The saga of Joseph is also the most important one in the Qur'án. It is related in the Súrah of Joseph and is called the *Aḥsan'ul-Qiṣaṣ,* meaning the most beautiful of narratives or the best of stories. It is the only subject in the Qur'án that occupies a whole Súrah or chapter (Súrah 12); no Súrah besides this one is entirely devoted to one subject.

Because of the many references to this story that are found in the Bahá'í Writings, brief accounts of it from both the Old Testament and the Qur'án are presented here.

The story according to the Book of Genesis in the Old Testament is this:

Joseph was the eleventh son of Jacob's twelve sons, and his father loved him more than his older brothers. Once he had a dream that the sun, the moon, and eleven stars made obeisance to him. The special attention of his father caused the older brothers to hate him and they decided to kill him. They arranged for him to go to the fields with them, but before they killed him, one of them said it would be better to sell Joseph to travelers who would take him to a faraway land. Joseph was thrown into a well, and Midianites in a passing caravan traveling to Egypt pulled him out and he was sold for twenty pieces of silver to the caravan people. The brothers returned to their father and told him that a wolf had devoured Joseph, and Jacob grieved for him.

Joseph was sold in Egypt to a minister from the court of the Pharaoh, who took him into his house. Joseph was a very wise and competent person and he was put in charge of his master's household and properties. The minister's wife wanted to have an affair with him, but Joseph was a righteous man and did not agree to this. Once, when he was alone with her in the house, she caught him by his garment, but he ran away and his garment was left with her. She then showed Joseph's garment to her husband and accused Joseph of misbehavior. Joseph was cast into prison and, while he was there, he interpreted people's dreams. One of the people who was in prison with him was the Pharaoh's ex-chief butler. The butler had a dream, and when he related the dream to Joseph, Joseph interpreted it to mean that he would be released from prison in three days and would be restored to his previous position. Joseph asked the butler to remember him when he was back in the court of Pharaoh and to arrange for his release from prison.

The butler was released and subsequently became the Pharaoh's butler again. However, he forgot about Joseph, who remained in prison until approximately two years later when the Pharaoh had a dream, which no one in his court could interpret. The butler remembered Joseph and recommended that the Pharaoh bring Joseph out of prison to interpret his dream. In the dream Pharaoh was standing by the river and he saw seven healthy well favored and fat-fleshed kine (cows) come out and graze in the meadow. Then seven ill-favored and lean-fleshed kine came out and ate the seven well-favored and fat kine. He also had a similar dream in which seven rank and good ears of corn came up upon one stalk and then seven thin ears blasted with east wind sprung up after them, and the seven thin ears devoured the seven good ears.

Joseph interpreted the Pharaoh's dream to indicate that Egypt would have seven years of good weather and ample rainfall, in which it would have great harvests and plenty, followed by seven years of drought and famine. He recommended that food and grain be stored during the first seven years to help manage the time of the drought and poor harvests. Pharaoh was very impressed by Joseph and appointed him the official in charge of resource management of his empire. During the years of plenty, Joseph managed the resources with great competence, such that when the years of drought and poor harvest arrived, the people of Egypt were well prepared and did not suffer.

During these years Jacob and his sons were suffering from the drought and famine in Canaan (present-day Israel), and Jacob decided to send his sons (except Benjamin, Joseph's younger brother) to Egypt to purchase food and grain to bring back to Canaan, their homeland. When the brothers arrived in Egypt, they were brought to Joseph's presence and he recognized them, but he did not immediately reveal his own identity to them. Through a series of dramatic events, he revealed his identity to his brothers and sent food, grain, and other gifts to his father, who at first did not believe the story he was told— that Joseph was alive and was the most important official in Egypt. But when he saw all the food and gifts, he rejoiced. Joseph eventually moved his father, brothers, and their families to Egypt, and they settled in an area that was provided to them by the Pharaoh.

As mentioned above, the Qur'ánic story is similar to the Old Testament story with a few variations, the most notable of which are that when Jacob was told that Joseph was killed, he grieved so much for Joseph that he lost his eyesight. He said:

> "Oh! how I am grieved for Joseph!" and his eyes became white with grief, for he bore a silent sorrow.
> (The Qur'án 12:84)

In addition, God protected Joseph from being deceived by the wife of the prince, and it is indicated that he would have been deceived if God had not aided and protected him by showing him a sign:

> But she longed for him; and he had longed for her had he not seen a token from his lord.* Thus we averted evil and defilement from him, for he was one of our sincere servants.
> (The Qur'án 12:24)

* He saw the apparition of his father advising him not to act improperly.

Joseph was extraordinarily handsome and had heavenly beauty.

> And in the city, the women said, "The wife of the Prince hath solicited her servant: he hath fired her with his love: but we clearly see her manifest error."
> And when she heard of their cabal, she sent to them and got ready a banquet for them, and gave each one of them a knife, and said, "Joseph shew thyself to them." And when they saw him they were amazed at him, and cut their hands, and said, "God keep us! This is no man! This is no other than a noble angel!"
>
> She said, "This is he about whom ye blamed me. I wished him to yield to my desires, but he stood firm. But if he obey not my command, he shall surely be cast into prison, and become one of the despised."
>
> He said, "O my Lord! I prefer the prison to compliance with their bidding: but unless thou turn away their snares from me, I shall play the youth with them, and become one of the unwise."
>
> And his Lord heard him and turned aside their snares from him: for he is the Hearer, the Knower.
> (The Qur'án 12:30–34)

Although Joseph proved his innocence, they still cast him in prison:

> Yet resolved they, even after they had seen the signs of his innocence, to imprison him for a time.
> (The Qur'án 12:35)

When Joseph was sending his brothers back to Canaan with food, grain, and gifts, he also gave them his shirt to take to his father and told them:

> Go ye with this my shirt and throw it on my father's face, and he shall recover his sight: and bring me all your family.
> (The Qur'án 12:93)

As the brothers approached Canaan, from a far distance, Jacob perceived the smell of Joseph and thus found the truth that Joseph was alive. When Joseph's garment was placed on his face, he regained his eyesight.

> And when the caravan departed, their father said, "I surely perceive the smell of Joseph: think ye that I dote?"
> They said, "By God, it is thy old mistake."
> And when the bearer of good tidings came, he cast it on his face, and Jacob's eyesight returned.
> (The Qur'án 12:94–96)

References to different aspects of the story of Joseph abound in Jewish, Christian, and Islamic religious literature and in commentaries on their holy books. This subject has a very special place in Persian poetry and mystical literature, and some have turned it into a romantic love story. Even in the twentieth century and up to present time, Joseph remains a popular subject of books, plays, and other creative works.

There are many allusions to this story in the Writings of the Central Figures of the Bahá'í Faith. On the first night he met the Báb, Mullá Ḥusayn, known as Báb'u'l-Báb ("the Gate of the Gate" and the Báb's first believer), requested the Báb to reveal a commentary on the Qur'án's Súrah of Joseph. The beloved Guardian describes the Book revealed by the Báb:

> Already in Shíráz, at the earliest stage of His ministry, He had revealed what Bahá'u'lláh has characterized as "the first, the greatest, and mightiest of all books" in the Bábí Dispensation, the celebrated commentary on the Súrih of Joseph entitled the Qayyúmu'l-Asmá', whose fundamental purpose was to forecast what the true Joseph (Bahá'u'lláh) would, in a succeeding Dispensation, endure at the hands of one who was at once His arch-enemy and blood brother. This work, comprising above nine thousand three hundred verses, [is] divided into one hundred and eleven chapters, each chapter a commentary on one verse of the above-mentioned súrih . . .
> (*God Passes By*, p. 23)

Qayyúm, which means self-subsisting and everlasting, is numerically equivalent to "Joseph" according to numerology or Abjad[111] numerals.

---

[111] Numerology is an ancient technique that assigns a number to every letter of an alphabet. It is called *Gematria* in Hebrew and *Abjad* in Arabic. In these systems, the numerical value of "a" is 1, that of "b" is 2, and so forth. The serial arrangement of the letters and their equivalent numbers are based on ancient alphabetical arrangements.

Because of the abundance of allegorical references to this story in the Bahá'í Writings, it seems that all Manifestations of God, especially the Báb and Bahá'u'lláh, are likened unto Joseph, and the story of Joseph is an allegory of all Manifestations of God. All Manifestations possess extraordinary and amazing spiritual beauty as exemplified by Joseph. The brothers could represent the religious leaders of the time and the unbelieving masses of people who refuse to recognize the ascendancy of the Manifestations, and sell Them for a paltry sum. The wife of Joseph's master can be seen as representing the world and its material attractions, which attempt to seduce Them and distract Them from Their mission (an example of such an attempt would be the New Testament story of Satan trying to seduce Jesus with the pleasures and riches of the world), and when They do not submit to the world the world wrongs Them and casts Them into prison. However, because of their divine power and spiritual might, in the course of time Their cause prevails and They become the Beloveds of the world.

Bahá'u'lláh describes Himself as the "Divine Joseph" Who has been "bartered away" by the heedless "for the most paltry of prices":

> Say: O people! Dust fill your mouths, and ashes blind your eyes, for having bartered away the Divine Joseph for the most paltry of prices. Oh, the misery that resteth upon you, ye that are far astray! Have ye imagined in your hearts that ye possess the power to outstrip Him and His Cause? Far from it! To this He, Himself, the All-Powerful, the Most Exalted, the Most Great, doth testify.
> (*Gleanings from the Writings of Bahá'u'lláh*, p. 208)

The Báb, in the Qayyúmu'l-Asmá', identifies Bahá'u'lláh as the "true Joseph" and forecasts the ordeals that He would endure at the hands of His treacherous brother (The Kitáb-i-Aqdas, note 190, pp. 248–49). Likewise, Shoghi Effendi draws a parallel between the intense jealousy that the preeminence of 'Abdu'l-Bahá had aroused in His half-brother, Mírzá Muḥammad-'Alí, and the deadly envy "which the superior excellence of Joseph had kindled in the hearts of his brothers." (The Kitáb-i-Aqdas, note 1, p. 165)

Bahá'u'lláh makes a reference to the story of Joseph when foretelling the future ascendancy of His Cause, the phenomenon of entry by troops, and the recognition of His own station by the people of the world:

> For now, however, they have hidden Me behind a veil of darkness, whose fabric they have woven with the hands of idle fancy and vain imagination. Erelong shall the snow-white hand of God rend an opening through the darkness of this night and unlock a mighty portal unto His City. On that Day shall the people enter therein by troops, uttering what the blamers aforetime exclaimed, that there shall be made manifest in the end that which appeared in the beginning.
> (*The Summons of the Lord of Hosts*, p. 135)

It seems that "the blamers aforetime" is a reference to the women blamers, who saw Joseph and exclaimed,

> God keep us! This is no man! This is no other than a noble angel! She said, "This is he about whom ye blamed me."
> (The Qur'án 12:31)

When in future the progress of the Cause of Bahá'u'lláh will rend the veil of darkness asander and ascendancy of Bahá'u'lláh is established, people will exclaim "This is no man! This is no other than a noble angel!"

Appendix IV

Olivet Discourse

Note No. 121 & 122, The Olivet Discourse in Synoptic Gospels:

Table 1: Comparative Review of the Olivet Discourse in Synoptic Gospels

Matthew Chapter 24	Mark Chapter 13	Luke Chapter 21
Prophecy Regarding the Destruction of the Temple In Jerusalem	**Prophecy Regarding the Destruction of the Temple In Jerusalem**	**Prophecy Regarding the Destruction of the Temple In Jerusalem**
1 And Jesus went out, and departed from the temple: and his disciples came to him for to shew him the buildings of the temple. 2 And Jesus said unto them, See ye not all these things? verily I say unto you, There shall not be left here one stone upon another, that shall not be thrown down.	13:1 And as he went out of the temple, one of his disciples saith unto him, Master, see what manner of stones and what buildings are here! And Jesus answering said unto him, Seest thou these great buildings? there shall not be left one stone upon another, that shall not be thrown down.	21:5 And as some spake of the temple, how it was adorned with goodly stones and gifts, he said, 21:6 As for these things which ye behold, the days will come, in the which there shall not be left one stone upon another, that shall not be thrown down.
Disciples Enquire Regarding the Time and Signs of These Events	**Disciples Enquire Regarding the Time and Signs of These Events**	**Disciples Enquire Regarding the Time and Signs of These Events**
3 And as he sat upon the mount of Olives, the disciples came	13:3 And as he sat upon the mount of Olives over against the	21:7 And they asked him, saying, Master, but when shall these

unto him privately, saying, Tell us, when shall these things be? and what shall be the sign of thy coming, and of the end of the world?	temple, Peter and James and John and Andrew asked him privately, 4 Tell us, when shall these things be? and what shall be the sign when all these things shall be fulfilled?	things be? and what sign will there be when these things shall come to pass?
Jesus Responds, Stating the Signs of the Destruction of the Temple in Jerusalem	**Jesus Responds, Stating the Signs of the Destruction of the Temple in Jerusalem**	**Jesus Responds, Stating the Signs of the Destruction of the Temple in Jerusalem**
24:4 And Jesus answered and said unto them, Take heed that no man deceive you. 5 For many shall come in my name, saying, I am Christ; and shall deceive many. 6 And ye shall hear of wars and rumours of wars: see that ye be not troubled: for all these things must come to pass, but the end is not yet. 7 For nation shall rise against nation, and kingdom against kingdom: and there shall be famines, and pestilences, and earthquakes, in divers places. 8 All these are the beginning of sorrows.	13:5 And Jesus answering them began to say, Take heed lest any man deceive you: 6 For many shall come in my name, saying, I am Christ; and shall deceive many. 13:7 And when ye shall hear of wars and rumours of wars, be ye not troubled: for such things must needs be; but the end shall not be yet. 13:8 For nation shall rise against nation, and kingdom against kingdom: and there shall be earthquakes in divers places, and there shall be famines and troubles: these are the beginnings of sorrows. 13:9 But take heed to yourselves: for they	21:8 And he said, Take heed that ye be not deceived: for many shall come in my name, saying, I am Christ; and the time draweth near: go ye not therefore after them. 21:9 But when ye shall hear of wars and commotions, be not terrified: for these things must first come to pass; but the end is not by and by. 21:10 Then said he unto them, Nation shall rise against nation, and kingdom against kingdom: 21:11 And great earthquakes shall be in divers places, and famines, and pestilences; and fearful sights and great signs

9 Then shall they deliver you up to be afflicted, and shall kill you: and ye shall be hated of all nations for my name's sake. 10 And then shall many be offended, and shall betray one another, and shall hate one another. 11 And many false prophets shall rise, and shall deceive many. 12 And because iniquity shall abound, the love of many shall wax cold. 13 But he that shall endure unto the end, the same shall be saved. 14 And this gospel of the kingdom shall be preached in all the world for a witness unto all nations; and then shall the end come. 15 When ye therefore shall see the abomination of desolation, spoken of by Daniel the prophet, stand in the holy place, (whoso readeth, let him understand:) 16 Then let them which be in Judaea flee into the mountains:	shall deliver you up to councils; and in the synagogues ye shall be beaten: and ye shall be brought before rulers and kings for my sake, for a testimony against them. 13:10 And the gospel must first be published among all nations. 13:11 But when they shall lead you, and deliver you up, take no thought beforehand what ye shall speak, neither do ye premeditate: but whatsoever shall be given you in that hour, that speak ye: for it is not ye that speak, but the Holy Ghost. 13:12 Now the brother shall betray the brother to death, and the father the son; and children shall rise up against their parents, and shall cause them to be put to death. 13:13 And ye shall be hated of all men for my name's sake: but he that shall endure unto the end, the same shall be saved. 13:14 But when ye shall see the abomination of desolation, spoken of	shall there be from heaven. 21:12 But before all these, they shall lay their hands on you, and persecute you, delivering you up to the synagogues, and into prisons, being brought before kings and rulers for my name's sake. 21:13 And it shall turn to you for a testimony. 21:14 Settle it therefore in your hearts, not to meditate before what ye shall answer: 21:15 For I will give you a mouth and wisdom, which all your adversaries shall not be able to gainsay nor resist. 21:16 And ye shall be betrayed both by parents, and brethren, and kinsfolks, and friends; and some of you shall they cause to be put to death. 21:17 And ye shall be hated of all men for my name's sake. 21:18 But there shall not an hair of your head perish. 21:19 In your patience possess ye your souls. 21:20 And when ye shall see Jerusalem

17 Let him which is on the housetop not come down to take any thing out of his house: 18 Neither let him which is in the field return back to take his clothes. 19 And woe unto them that are with child, and to them that give suck in those days! 20 But pray ye that your flight be not in the winter, neither on the sabbath day: 21 For then shall be great tribulation, such as was not since the beginning of the world to this time, no, nor ever shall be. 22 And except those days should be shortened, there should no flesh be saved: but for the elect's sake those days shall be shortened. 23 Then if any man shall say unto you, Lo, here is Christ, or there; believe it not. 24 For there shall arise false Christs, and false prophets, and shall shew great signs and wonders; insomuch that, if it were possible, they shall deceive the very elect.	by Daniel the prophet, standing where it ought not, (let him that readeth understand,) then let them that be in Judaea flee to the mountains: 13:15 And let him that is on the housetop not go down into the house, neither enter therein, to take any thing out of his house: 16 And let him that is in the field not turn back again for to take up his garment. 13:17 But woe to them that are with child, and to them that give suck in those days! 13:18 And pray ye that your flight be not in the winter. 13:19 For in those days shall be affliction, such as was not from the beginning of the creation which God created unto this time, neither shall be. 13:20 And except that the Lord had shortened those days, no flesh should be saved: but for the elect's sake, whom he hath chosen, he hath shortened the days. 13:21 And then if any man shall say to you,	compassed with armies, then know that the desolation thereof is nigh. 21:21 Then let them which are in Judaea flee to the mountains; and let them which are in the midst of it depart out; and let not them that are in the countries enter thereinto. 21:22 For these be the days of vengeance, that all things which are written may be fulfilled. 21:23 But woe unto them that are with child, and to them that give suck, in those days! for there shall be great distress in the land, and wrath upon this people. 21:24 And they shall fall by the edge of the sword, and shall be led away captive into all nations: and Jerusalem shall be trodden down of the Gentiles, until the times of the Gentiles be fulfilled.

25 Behold, I have told you before. 26 Wherefore if they shall say unto you, Behold, he is in the desert; go not forth: behold, he is in the secret chambers; believe it not.	Lo, here is Christ; or, lo, he is there; believe him not: 13:22 For false Christs and false prophets shall rise, and shall shew signs and wonders, to seduce, if it were possible, even the elect. 13:23 But take ye heed: behold, I have foretold you all things.	
Christ Provides the Signs of His Second Coming.	**Christ Provides the Signs of His Second Coming.**	**Christ Provides the Signs of His Second Coming.**
27 For as the lightning cometh out of the east, and shineth even unto the west; so shall also the coming of the Son of man be. 28 For wheresoever the carcase is, there will the eagles be gathered together. 29 Immediately after the tribulation of those days shall the sun be darkened, and the moon shall not give her light, and the stars shall fall from heaven, and the powers of the heavens shall be shaken: 30 And then shall appear the sign of the Son of man in heaven:	13:24 But in those days, after that tribulation, the sun shall be darkened, and the moon shall not give her light, 13:25 And the stars of heaven shall fall, and the powers that are in heaven shall be shaken. 13:26 And then shall they see the Son of man coming in the clouds with great power and glory. 13:27 And then shall he send his angels, and shall gather together his elect from the four winds, from the uttermost part of the earth to the uttermost part of heaven.	21:25 And there shall be signs in the sun, and in the moon, and in the stars; and upon the earth distress of nations, with perplexity; the sea and the waves roaring; 21:26 Men's hearts failing them for fear, and for looking after those things which are coming on the earth: for the powers of heaven shall be shaken. 21:27 And then shall they see the Son of man coming in a cloud with power and great glory. 21:28 And when these things begin to come to pass, then look up, and

and then shall all the tribes of the earth mourn, and they shall see the Son of man coming in the clouds of heaven with power and great glory. 31 And he shall send his angels with a great sound of a trumpet, and they shall gather together his elect from the four winds, from one end of heaven to the other. 32 Now learn a parable of the fig tree; When his branch is yet tender, and putteth forth leaves, ye know that summer is nigh: 33 So likewise ye, when ye shall see all these things, know that it is near, even at the doors. 34 Verily I say unto you, This generation shall not pass, till all these things be fulfilled. 35 Heaven and earth shall pass away, but my words shall not pass away. 36 But of that day and hour knoweth no man, no, not the angels of heaven, but my Father only. 37 But as the days of	13:28 Now learn a parable of the fig tree; When her branch is yet tender, and putteth forth leaves, ye know that summer is near: 13:29 So ye in like manner, when ye shall see these things come to pass, know that it is nigh, even at the doors. 13:30 Verily I say unto you, that this generation shall not pass, till all these things be done. 13:31 Heaven and earth shall pass away: but my words shall not pass away. 13:32 But of that day and that hour knoweth no man, no, not the angels which are in heaven, neither the Son, but the Father. 13:33 Take ye heed, watch and pray: for ye know not when the time is. 13:34 For the Son of man is as a man taking a far journey, who left his house, and gave authority to his servants, and to every man his work, and commanded the porter to watch. 13:35 Watch ye therefore: for ye know	lift up your heads; for your redemption draweth nigh. 21:29 And he spake to them a parable; Behold the fig tree, and all the trees; 21:30 When they now shoot forth, ye see and know of your own selves that summer is now nigh at hand. 21:31 So likewise ye, when ye see these things come to pass, know ye that the kingdom of God is nigh at hand. 21:32 Verily I say unto you, This generation shall not pass away, till all be fulfilled. 21:33 Heaven and earth shall pass away: but my words shall not pass away. 21:34 And take heed to yourselves, lest at any time your hearts be overcharged with surfeiting, and drunkenness, and cares of this life, and so that day come upon you unawares. 21:35 For as a snare shall it come on all them that dwell on the face of the whole earth. 21:36 Watch ye therefore, and pray always, that ye may be

Noe were, so shall also the coming of the Son of man be. 38 For as in the days that were before the flood they were eating and drinking, marrying and giving in marriage, until the day that Noe entered into the ark, 39 And knew not until the flood came, and took them all away; so shall also the coming of the Son of man be. 40 Then shall two be in the field; the one shall be taken, and the other left. 41 Two women shall be grinding at the mill; the one shall be taken, and the other left. 42 Watch therefore: for ye know not what hour your Lord doth come. 43 But know this, that if the goodman of the house had known in what watch the thief would come, he would have watched, and would not have suffered his house to be broken up. 44 Therefore be ye also ready: for in such an hour as ye think not the Son of man	not when the master of the house cometh, at even, or at midnight, or at the cockcrowing, or in the morning: 13:36 Lest coming suddenly he find you sleeping. 13:37 And what I say unto you I say unto all, Watch.	accounted worthy to escape all these things that shall come to pass, and to stand before the Son of man. 21:37 And in the day time he was teaching in the temple; and at night he went out, and abode in the mount that is called the mount of Olives. 21:38 And all the people came early in the morning to him in the temple, for to hear him.

cometh. 45 Who then is a faithful and wise servant, whom his lord hath made ruler over his household, to give them meat in due season? 46 Blessed is that servant, whom his lord when he cometh shall find so doing. 47 Verily I say unto you, That he shall make him ruler over all his goods. 48 But and if that evil servant shall say in his heart, My lord delayeth his coming; 49 And shall begin to smite his fellow servants, and to eat and drink with the drunken; 50 The lord of that servant shall come in a day when he looketh not for him, and in an hour that he is not aware of, 24:51 And shall cut him asunder, and appoint him his portion with the hypocrites: there shall be weeping and gnashing of teeth.		

Appendix V

Messengers and Prophets

Note No. 192

The Qur'án names and describes two classes of divine intermediaries, the revealers and the promoters of the words of God, namely the Messenger (Rasoul) and the Prophet (Nabí). The Qur'án in many verses indicates that Messengers and Prophets are not the same, and that the Messengers have a higher station or rank. They are Those Who receive Revelation, are endowed with a Book, and inaugurate a Dispensation. In Bahá'í terminology They are designated as "Manifestations of God." The Prophets, on the other hand, are the promoters of the Faith of God and helpers of the Messengers. The following Qur'ánic verses confirm this difference in station and function:

> And raise up in their midst a messenger from among them who shall recite unto them Thy revelations, and shall instruct them in the Scripture and in wisdom and shall make them grow. Lo! Thou, only Thou, art the Mighty, Wise
> (The Qur'án, Pickthall tr, 2:129)

> Even as We have sent unto you a messenger from among you, who reciteth unto you Our revelations and causeth you to grow, and teacheth you the Scripture and wisdom, and teacheth you that which ye knew not.
> (The Qur'án, Pickthall tr, 2:151)

The following verses indicate the difference between the rank of the messengers/apostles and prophets:

> Never sent We a messenger or a prophet before thee but when He recited (the message) Satan proposed (opposition) in respect of that which he recited thereof. But Allah abolisheth that which Satan proposeth. Then Allah establisheth His revelations. Allah is Knower, Wise;
> (The Qur'án, Pickthall tr, Súrah 22:52)

> We have not sent any apostle or prophet before thee, among whose desires Satan injected not some wrong desire, but God shall bring

> to nought that which Satan had suggested. Thus shall God affirm His revelations for God is Knowing, Wise!
> (The Qur'án 22:51)

> When Allah made (His) covenant with the prophets, (He said): Behold that which I have given you of the Scripture and knowledge. And afterward there will come unto you a messenger, confirming that which ye possess. Ye shall believe in him and ye shall help him. He said: Do ye agree, and will ye take up My burden (which I lay upon you) in this (matter)? They answered: We agree. He said: Then bear ye witness. I will be a witness with you.
> (The Qur'án, Pickthall tr, 3:81)

As stated in the above verse, prophets are sent to help the messengers. When Moses was ready to go to pharaoh, He asked God to send His brother Aaron along to help Him:

> My brother Aaron is clearer of speech than I. Send him, therefore, with me as a help, and to make good my cause, for I fear lest they treat me as an imposter.
> (The Qur'án 28:34)

God accepted Moses' request and sent Aaron along as a helper/prophet:

> And we bestowed on him in our mercy his brother Aaron, a Prophet.
> (The Qur'án 19:54)

The messengers are sent to bring revelation to mankind.

> Allah verily hath shown grace to the believers by sending unto them a messenger of their own who reciteth unto them His revelations, and causeth them to grow, and teacheth them the Scripture and wisdom; although before (he came to them) they were in flagrant error.
> (The Qur'án, Pickthall tr, 3:164)

> O sons of Adam! verily, there will come to you apostles from amongst you, narrating unto you my signs[112]; then whoso fears

[112] The word sign here is a translation of the Arabic word "Áyát," which also means verses, revelations, and miracles (as the Qur'ánic verses are each considered miracles).

> God and does what is right, there is no fear for them, nor shall they grieve.
> (The Qur'án, E.H. Palmer tr, 7:33)

> O children of Adam! there shall come to Apostles from among yourselves, rehearsing my signs to you; and whoso shall fear God and do good works, no fear shall be upon them, neither shall they be put to grief.
> (The Qur'án 7:33)

Another example is when Zachariah the father of John the Baptist was given the glad tiding that he will have a son, it was stated that he will be a prophet.

> God announceth John (Yahia) to thee, who shall be a verifier of the word from God, and a greater one, chaste, and a prophet of the number of the just.
> (The Qur'án 3:35)

But when mentioning Christ in the same Súrah, He is referred to as an apostle/messenger:

> And he will teach him the Book, and the Wisdom, and the Law, and the Evangel; and he shall be an apostle to the children of Israel.
> (The Qur'án 3:43)

It seems that the distinction between the station of the Major Prophets or Messengers and Prophets was clearly understood by the Jews and Christians as well.

The statement in Deuteronomy regarding a Prophet "like unto Moses" that God put words in his mouth (giving Him direct Revelation) distinguishes between the station of Moses and other Prophets of Israel who were inspired through dreams or visions.

> And the LORD said unto me, They have well spoken that which they have spoken. I will raise them up a Prophet from among their brethren, like unto thee, and will put my words in his mouth; and he shall speak unto them all that I shall command him. And it shall

> come to pass, that whosoever will not hearken unto my words which he shall speak in my name, I will require it of him.
> (Deuteronomy 18:17–19)

When elucidating the station of John the Baptist, Jesus stated:

> Jesus began to say unto the multitudes concerning John, What went ye out into the wilderness to see? A reed shaken with the wind? But what went ye out for to see? A man clothed in soft raiment? behold, they that wear soft clothing are in kings' houses. But what went ye out for to see? A prophet? yea, I say unto you, and more than a prophet. For this is he, of whom it is written, Behold, I send my messenger before thy face, which shall prepare thy way before thee.
> (Matthew 11:7–12)

Bibliography

Works of Bahá'u'lláh

Epistle to the Son of the Wolf. 1st pocket-size ed. Translated by Shoghi Effendi. Wilmette, IL: Bahá'í Publishing Trust, 1988.

Gems of Divine Mysteries. Haifa, Israel: Bahá'í World Centre, 2002.

Gleanings from the Writings of Bahá'u'lláh. Translated by Shoghi Effendi. Wilmette, IL: Bahá'í Publishing, 2005.

The Hidden Words. Translated by Shoghi Effendi. Wilmette, IL: Bahá'í Publishing, 2002.

The Kitáb-i-Aqdas: The Most Holy Book. Haifa, Israel: Bahá'í World Centre, 1992.

The Kitáb-i-Íqán: The Book of Certitude. Translated by Shoghi Effendi. Wilmette, IL: Bahá'í Publishing, 2003.

Prayers and Meditations. Translated by Shoghi Effendi. Wilmette, IL: Bahá'í Publishing Trust, 1987.

The Proclamation of Bahá'u'lláh to the Kings and Leaders of the World. Haifa: Bahá'í World Centre, 1967.

Seven Valleys and the Four Valleys. Translated by Ali-Kuli Khan and Marzieh Gail. Wilmette, IL: Bahá'í Publishing Trust, 1991.

The Summons of the Lord of Hosts: Tablets of Bahá'u'lláh. Haifa, Israel: Bahá'í World Centre, 2002.

Tablets of Bahá'u'lláh revealed after the Kitáb-i-Aqdas. Compiled by the Research Department of the Universal House of Justice. Translated by Habib Taherzadeh et al. Wilmette, IL: 1988.

Writings of Bahá'u'lláh: A Compilation. New Delhi: Bahá'í Publishing Trust, 1986.

ÁTHÁR-I-QALAM-I-A'ALÁ (Tablets Revealed by Bahá'u'lláh) Volume I, Kitáb-i-Mubín, Third Edition, Institute for Bahá'í Studies in Persian, P.O. Box 65600, Dundas, Ontario, L9H 6Y6 Canada.

ÁSÁR-E-QALAM-E-Á'LÁ, (Reprinted from Writings of *Bahá'u'lláh)*, Vol. III, Printed in Iran 121 B.E., Baha'i Publishing Trust, Post Box No. 19 New Delhi (India)

Works of the Báb

Selections from the Writings of the Báb. Compiled by the Research Department of the Universal House of Justice. Translated by Habib Taherzadeh et al. Wilmette, IL: Bahá'í Publishing Trust, 2006.

Works of 'Abdu'l-Bahá

'Abdu'l-Bahá in London: Addresses and Notes of Conversations. London: Bahá'í Publishing Trust, 1982.

'Abdú'l-Bahá Tablet to August Forel. Oxford: George Ronald Publishers, 1978.

A Traveler's Narrative Written to Illustrate the Episode of the Báb. Translated by Edward G. Browne. New and corrected ed. Wilmette, IL: Bahá'í Publishing Trust, 1980.

Foundations of World Unity. Wilmette, IL: Bahá'í Publishing Trust, 1972.

Paris Talks: Addresses Given By 'Abdu'l-Bahá in Paris in 1911. 12th ed. London: Bahá'í Publishing, 2011.

Promulgation of Universal Peace: Talks Delivered by 'Abdu'l-Bahá during His Visit to the United States and Canada in 1912. Compiled by Howard MacNutt. 2d ed. Wilmette, IL: Bahá'í Publishing, 2012.

The Secret of Divine Civilization. Translated from the Persian by Marzieh Gail in consultation with Ali-Kuli Khan. Wilmette, IL: Bahá'í Publishing Trust, 1990.

Selections from the Writings of 'Abdu'l-Bahá. Compiled by the Research Department of the Universal House of Justice. Translated by a Committee at the Bahá'í World Center and Marzieh Gail. Wilmette, IL: Bahá'í Publishing, 2010.

Some Answered Questions. Compiled and translated from the Persian by Laura Clifford Barney, Newly Revised by a Committee at the Bahá'í World Center. Haifa, Israel: Bahá'í World Centre, 2014.

Tablets of Abdul-Baha Abbas. 3 vols. New York: Bahai Publishing Society, 1909–16.

Tablets of the Divine Plan. Wilmette, IL: Bahá'í Publishing Trust, 1993.

Will and Testament of 'Abdu'l-Bahá. Wilmette, IL: Bahá'í Publishing Trust, 1944.

Works of Shoghi Effendi

Advent of Divine Justice. Wilmette, IL: Bahá'í Publishing Trust, 1990.
Arohanui: *Letters from Shoghi Effendi to New Zealand.* Suva, Fiji: Bahá'í Publishing Trust, 1982.

Bahá'í Administration: Selected Messages 1922–1932. Wilmette, IL: Bahá'í Publishing Trust, 1974.

Directives from the Guardian. New Delhi: Bahá'í Publishing Trust, 1973.
God Passes By. New ed. Wilmette, IL: Bahá'í Publishing Trust, 1974.

The Light of Divine Guidance: The Messages from the Guardian of the Bahá'í Faith to the Bahá'ís of Germany and Austria. Hofheim-Langenhain, Germany: Bahá'í-Verlag, 1982.

The Promised Day Is Come. Wilmette, IL: Bahá'í Publishing Trust, 1996.
The Unfolding Destiny of the British Bahá'í Community: The Messages from the Guardian of the Bahá'í Faith to the Bahá'ís of the British Isles. London: Bahá'í Publishing Trust, 1981.

The World Order of Bahá'u'lláh: Selected Letters. Wilmette, IL: Bahá'í Publishing Trust, 1991.

CALL TO THE NATIONS. Extracts from the writings of Shoghi Effendi, Bahá'í World Center, 1977.

Bahá'í Compilations

Bahá'u'lláh, 'Abdu'l-Bahá, Shoghi Effendi and the Universal House of Justice.*The Compilation of Compilations: Prepared by the Universal House of Justice.* 3 vols. Australia: Bahá'í Publications Australia, 1991.

———. *Lights of Guidance.* Compiled by Helen Hornby. New ed. New Delhi, India: Bahá'í Publishing Trust, 1994.

Bahá'u'lláh, the Báb and 'Abdu'l-Bahá. *Bahá'í Prayers: A Selection of Prayers Revealed by Bahá'u'lláh, the Báb, and 'Abdu'l-Bahá.* Wilmette, IL: Bahá'í Publishing Trust, 2002.

Other Scripture

The Holy Bible, King James Version. Nashville, Tennessee: Thomas Nelson Publishers, 1982.

The Koran. Translated by N. J. Dawood. Baltimore: Penguin, 1968.

The Koran. Translated by J. M. Rodwell. London: Everyman, 1994.

The Glorious Qur'án. An Explanatory Translation by Marmaduke Pickthall. New York: Tahrike Tarsile Qur'an, Inc., 2001.

The Holy Qur'án. Translated by Abdullah Yusuf Ali. Elmhurst, New York: Tahrike Tarsile Qur'an, Inc., 2001.

Other Works

1000 Qudsi Hadiths: An Encyclopedia of Divine Sayings, New York, Arabic Virtual Translation Center, LLC., 2012.

Abu'l-Faḍl, Mírzá. *The Brilliant Proof.* Los Angeles: Kalimat Press, 1998.

Afnan, Muḥammad. "The Báb's Bayán: An Analytical Survey," *World Order,* 31:4, 2000 Summer.

Ameer Ali, Syed. *The Spirit of Islam.* Kessinger, 2010.

Arnold, T. W. *Preaching of Islam: A History of the Propagation of the Muslim Faith.* Low Price Publications, 2001.

Balyuzi, H. M. *'Abdu'l-Bahá: The Centre of the Covenant of Bahá'u'lláh.* Oxford: George Ronald, 1971.

———. *Bahá'u'lláh: The King of Glory*. Oxford: George Ronald, 1980.
———. *Muḥammad and the Course of Islam.* Oxford: George Ronald, 1976.

Barnstone, Willis. *The Other Bible.* New York: HarperOne, 2005.

Bausani, Alessandro. *Religion in Iran from Zoroaster to Bahá'u'lláh.* New Yok, Bibliotheca Persica Press, 2000.

Brodie, Fawn M. *No Man Knows My History, the life of Joseph Smith.* Vintage Books, a division of Random House, Inc., New York, 1971

Clarke, Adam. Commentary on the Whole Bible. http://www.preteristarchive.com/Books/1810_clarke_commentary.html

Dunbar, Hooper C. *A Companion to the Study of The Kitáb-i-Íqán.* Oxford: George Ronald, 1997.

Ehrman, Bart. *Misquoting Jesus: The Story Behind Who Changed the Bible and Why.* New York: HarperOne, 2007.
Gail, Marzieh. *Six Lessons on Islam.* Wilmette, IL: Bahá'í Publishing Trust, 1953.

Giachery, Hugo. *Shoghi Effendi: Recollections.* Oxford: George Ronald, 1973.

Gorlin, Daniel. *Jesus and Early Christians in the Gospels.* Oxford: George Ronald, 2002.

Is͟hráq-K͟hávari. 'Abdu'l-Ḥamíd. *Qámus-i-Íqán,* Vols. 1–4. Muassesseh Mellí-i-Maṭbuát-i-Amrí, Iran, 128 B.E.

Kourosh, Sohrab. *Self Study Notes for The Seven Valleys of Bahá'u'lláh,* New Delhi, India: Bahá'í Publishing Trust, 2014.

Lambden, Stephen. "Prophecy in Johannine Farewell Discourse," in *Scripture & Revelation,* Bahá'í Studies, Vol. III, (Moojan Momen ed.)

Lapidus, Ira M. *A History of Islamic Societies.* Cambridge: Cambridge University Press, 2002.

Lights of 'Irfán: Papers Presented at the 'Irfán Colloquia and Seminars, Book Eleven. Haj Mehdi Arjmand Memorial Fund, Fund, 'Asr-i-Jadíd Publisher, Darmstadt, Germany 2010.

McBride Pèrigord, Emily. *Translation of French Foot-Notes of The Dawn-Breakers,* Wilmette, IL: Bahá'í Publishing Trust, 1996.

Merriam-Webster Collegiate Dictionary. Springfield, Mass: Merriam-Webster, Incorporated, 11th edition, 2003.

Momen, Moojan. *An Introduction to Shí'i Islam.* Oxford: George Ronald, 1985.

Momen, Wendi. *A Basic Bahá'í Dictionary.* Oxford: George Ronald, 1996.

Mottahedeh, Roy. *The Mantle of the Prophet: Religion and Politics in Iran.* Oxford: Oneworld, 2008.

Muir, William. *The Life of Mohammad from Original Sources.* Admant Media, 2001.

Mullá Hádí Sabzivárí. *The Metaphysics of Sabzavárí* (trans. T. Izutsu and M. Mohaghegh). New York, 1977.

Nábil-i-A'zam [Muḥammad-i-Zarandí]. *The Dawn-Breakers: Nabíl's Narrative of the Early Days of the Bahá'í Revelation.* Translated and edited by Shoghi Effendi. Wilmette, IL: Bahá'í Publishing Trust, 1932.

Rabbaní, Rúḥíyyih. *The Priceless Pearl.* London: Bahá'í Publishing Trust, 1969.

Safínih-i-'Irfán: A Collection of Papers Presented at Irfán Colloquia, Vol. 2. Haj Mehdi Arjmand Memorial Fund, 'Asr-i-Jadíd Publisher, Darmstadt, Germany 1999

Schimmel, Annemarie. *As Through a Veil.* London: Oneworld, 2001.

Summarized Sahíh Al-Bukhári: Arabic-English, Translated by Dr.

Muhammad Muhsin Khan. Islamic University, Al-Madinah Al-Munawwarah, Darussalam, Publishers & Distributors, Riyadh-Saudi Arabia, 1996.

Tabari, Ali. *The Book of Religion and Empire.* A. Mingana, trans. Manchester University Press, 1922, 44.

Taherzadeh, Adib. *Child of the Covenant: A study Guide to the Will and Testament of 'Abdu'l-Bahá.* Oxford: George Ronald, 2000.

———. *The Revelation of Bahá'u'lláh: Adrianople 1863–68.* Oxford: George Ronald, 1977.

———. *The Revelation of Bahá'u'lláh, Volume Three: 'Akká, The Early Years 1868–77.* Oxford: George Ronald, 1983.

———. *The Revelation of Bahá'u'lláh, Volume One: Baghdád 1853–63.* Rev. ed. Oxford: George Ronald, 1976.

———. *The Revelation of Bahá'u'lláh, Volume Four: Mazra'ih & Bahjí 1877–1892.* Oxford: George Ronald, 1987.

Tai-Seale, Thomas. *Thy Kingdom Come.* Los Angeles: Kalimat Press, 1992.

Underhill, Evelyn. *Mysticism: A Study in Nature and Development of Spiritual Consciousness.* Dover Publications, 2002.

INDEX

‘

‘Abbássids, 392
‘Abdu’l Moṭaleb, 497
‘Abdú’l Qádir Gilaní, 397
‘Abdú’l-Bahá, ii
‘Abdu’l-Ḥamíd Ishráq-Khávari, iii
‘Abdu’lláh, 497
‘Abdu'l-Majíd-i-Shírází, xvii
‘Akká, 147, 259, 263, 289, 434, 584
‘Alí, xix, xxii, 1, 138, 211, 219, 263, 321, 329, 358, 360, 363, 391, 392, 393, 449, 498, 499, 501, 502, 503, 504, 505, 508, 513, 514, 515, 516, 517, 518, 519, 521, 523, 524, 540, 560
‘Alí-Kuli Khán, xxii
'Alí-Muḥammad, 126
‘Ali'u’l-A‘lá, 1
‘Ayn al-Yaqín, 245
‘Ilm al-yaqín, 245
‘Ilm علم, 389
‘Irfán, 1
‘Izrá’íl, 282
‘Ulama علما, 390
‘Umar, 350, 395, 500, 513, 515, 516
‘Umar ibn al Khaṭṭáb, 350
'Umar Khayám, 14
‘Umayyads, 392
‘Urvatu'l-Vuthqá, 207

A

A. L. M. Nicolas, 365, 391, 392
Aaron, 6, 24, 34, 35, 81, 117, 298, 300, 310, 311, 312, 313, 342, 351, 390, 404, 506, 572
Abhá Beauty, 147
Abhá Paradise, 39
Abi-Ṭáleb, 497
Abjad, 366
ablution, 231, 233
abode of peace, 150, 151, 540
abomination of desolation, 167, 171
Abraham, 30, 45, 56, 57, 58, 60, 61, 62, 63, 64, 65, 66, 67, 68, 69, 70, 71, 72, 75, 80, 81, 137, 193, 258, 283, 284, 285, 288, 289, 301, 320, 340, 342, 411, 412, 413, 447, 465, 496, 506, 508, 511, 555
Abram, 58

abrogation, 201, 401, 402, 432
absolute nothingness, 11
Abu Bakr, 220, 498, 502, 512, 513, 516
Abû Huraira, 520
Abu Lahab, 262, 407
Abu Sufyan, 503
Abu’l- Ḥikam, 101
Abu’l-Jahl, 101
Abu’l-Qásim, xix
Abyssinia, 500
Adam, 30
Adamic Cycle, 237
Ádhirbáyján, xiv, 262, 294, 322
Adib Taherzadeh, iii, xii, 5
Adrianople, 147, 243, 264, 366, 584
adultery, 18, 84, 114, 115, 287, 310, 457, 460, 528
Adventists, 181, 371, 372, 373, 545, 550, 552
aei-parthenos, 16
Afnán, xv
Afnán-i-Kabír, xvi
Aḥadith, 136, 138, 390, 519, 520, 540
Aḥmad, 134, 135, 360, 363, 364, 365, 366, 367, 368, 369, 370, 454, 455
Ajal, 466
Al Hudaybiyyah, 504
Albrecht Bengal, 181
alchemy, 441
Aleppo, 69
Alexander Campbell, 371
Al-Ḥudaybíyyah, 428
Allah, 109, 110, 152, 236, 284, 303, 409, 461, 462, 501, 507, 518, 571, 572
allegoric, 48
allegorical, 431
allegory, 54
Al-Madá’in, 359
Almighty, 38
Amalekites, 461
ambiguous, 110

amillennial, 180
Amos, 224
Amram, 298, 299, 300
anachronism, 312
Ancient of days, 335
angels, 28, 40, 43, 88, 168, 172, 173, 219, 246, 247, 248, 282, 300, 334, 371, 390, 419, 421, 429, 439, 440, 443, 446, 450, 507, 543, 546, 567
Annas, 101
Annemarie Schimmel, 105
annulment, 114, 115, 116, 401, 402
Ansár, 358
anthropomorphists, 218
Antipas, 348
Apocalypse, 168, 546, 547
Apocrypha, 140, 312
apocryphal, 312
Apostle, 96, 134, 138, 143, 184, 292, 319, 401, 411, 412, 451, 454, 465, 469, 470, 472, 503, 504, 509, 518, 529
apostles, 31
appellations, 21
Áqá Mírzá Núru'd-Dín, xv
Arabia, 30
Arabian Peninsula, 505
Arabic, v
Arabic Bayán, 9
Arabisation, 108
Arám, 30
Ararat, 48
archangels, 282
archeologists, 48
aristocracy, 101
Ark, 44
Aron Kodesh, 229, 277
ascendancy, 18
atonement, 173, 177, 229, 404, 511
Azal, xii

Á

Áud, 30, 55
Áyát, 237, 466, 482, 572
Áyatu'l-Kursi, 367
Ázar, 69

B

Báb, xiii
Babel, 341
Bábí, xii
Bábí Faith, xii
Bábí religion, 9
Babylon, 461, 541, 550
Badá, 52
Badí, 326
Baghdád, xii, 18
Bahá, 493
Bahá'í Literature, x
Bahá'u'lláh, i
Bahá'í Revelation, x
Baḥrain, 360
Balyuzi, 18
Bani Hashem, 407, 498
banners of light, 435
baptism, 351, 352, 353, 356, 449, 548
Baptism, 118, 284
Bar Kokhba, 350
bar mitzvah, 230
Barjesus, 175
Barnabas, 194
bat mitzvah, 230
Baṭḥá, 279
Battle of Badr, 503
Bayán, xii, xv, 8, 9, 53, 128, 274, 278, 293, 321, 322, 355, 362, 366, 411, 442, 451, 453, 483, 484, 485, 486, 487, 488, 489, 490, 491, 492, 493, 494, 536, 580
Beelzebub, 121, 316
Beer-sheba, 63
beetle, 327
Beirut, xvi
Best-Beloved, 54
Bethlehem, 138, 287, 288, 307, 308, 309, 344, 345, 346, 350
bewilderment, 11
Bible, vii
Biblical, 48
birthright, 72
bishops, 223
blaspheme, 66
blasphemy, 27
Blessed Beauty, xv, 67, 147, 199
Blessed Perfection, 260, 537
Bombay, xvi, xxii

Book of Acts, 106
Book of Revelation, 43
bread, 5, 34, 35, 36, 37, 38, 39, 42, 49, 59, 63, 79, 97, 152, 153, 154, 155, 156, 210, 231, 232, 267, 286, 287, 385, 386, 404, 414, 433, 459
bread of heaven, 37
Buddha, 214
Buheira, 497
Burning Bush, 75
burnt offering, 117, 118, 403
But for Thee, 411
Byzantine, xix

C

Caesar, 504
Caiaphas, 27, 101, 171, 224, 297, 405
Caliph, xx, 78, 220, 393, 500, 513, 514, 515, 516, 521, 523, 541, 542
calumniate, 98
Camphor, 240, 241
Canaan, 58, 60, 61, 433, 461, 557, 558
canonical Gospels, 139
canonization, 463
Capernaum, 37, 154, 287
Capricorn, 345
carpenter, 15
Caspian Sea, 367
Catholics, 16
celestial City, 476
celestial dominion, 82
Celsus, 312
Chaldees, 57, 58, 69, 70, 320
chalice, 14, 101
chariot, 93, 377
cherubims, 440
Cherubims, 43
Chihríq, xiii
children of negation, 32
chosen ones of God, 474
Chosrau, 504
Christians, 28
circumambulate, 399
circumambulation, 143
circumcise, 61
circumcision, 63, 79, 80, 191, 193, 229, 404
city of faith, 99
City of Faith, 248
City of God, 100
cleaving of Heaven, 251
Codex Sinaticus, 463
Codex Vaticanous, 463
Codex Vaticanus, 135
collyrium, 209
Comforter, 132, 133
commandment, 24
commandments, 18, 53, 84, 118, 129, 189, 191, 231, 254, 302, 394, 467, 535
commentaries, 50
Commentators, 31
comprehend, 11, 21
concourse, 99, 102, 148, 184, 197, 222, 223, 248, 293, 423, 450, 485, 493
Concourse, 125, 304, 339, 533
confound, 57
congregation, 34
conjunction, 345
connotation, 14
Constantine, 179, 350
Constantinople, 69, 147, 543
contentment, 11
contradictory, 16
Copt, 108
Countenance, 24
Covenant, 32
Creator, 11
crimson, 77, 159, 219
Crimson Ark, 50
Crimson Pillar, 397
crown of thorns, 414
crucifixion, 28, 175, 177, 178, 179, 191, 277, 348, 415, 471, 473, 548, 552
Crusaders, 350
Ctesiphon, 359
Cupbearer, 19
Cup-bearer, 14
Cycle of Fulfillment, 238

D

Dajjál, xx, xxi, 446, 526
Dalá'il-i-Sab'ih, 365
Daniel, x, 149, 167, 169, 170, 171, 181, 240, 335, 370, 447, 465, 545, 547, 551, 552, 564, 582
Dante, 431
Dár-al-salám, 150, 151

daughters of men, 44
David, 51, 114, 116, 117, 120, 121, 122, 140, 142, 176, 229, 287, 288, 289, 290, 307, 308, 309, 316, 324, 350, 403, 405, 406, 410, 433, 461, 506
Dawning-Place, 21
Day of Atonement, 5
Day of Resurrection, xviii
Days of Concealment, 437
Dayspring, 2
Daystar, 10, 87, 162, 222, 233, 258, 315, 321, 338, 472, 478, 479, 493
Daystars, 52, 213, 218, 421, 481
deity, 108
Delay, 437
demonstrate, 30
detachment, 4
Devil, 43
Dhimmeh, 102
disciples, xii
disobedience, 49
Dispensation, 7, 8, 9, 13, 21, 52, 113, 136, 143, 148, 185, 197, 199, 201, 214, 228, 236, 237, 239, 242, 253, 258, 282, 290, 294, 318, 319, 320, 327, 388, 395, 405, 411, 442, 453, 456, 483, 485, 559, 571
Dispensation of Jesus Christ, 8
Dispensation of the Bayán, 9
Dispensation of the Qur'án, 8
divine Assayer, 448
Divine Being, 21
Divine Comedy, 431
Divine Cupbearer, 158
divine grace, 99
Divine inspiration, 13
Divine Lote Tree, 34
Divine Plan, 39
divine promise, 49
Divine Revelation, xi
divine springtime, 161
Divine Tree, 34
Divine unity, 203, 296, 539
Divine Unity, 38
Divine Youth, 221
divorce, 114, 115, 202, 299, 348, 402
Djinn, 324, 543, 544, 545
Dositheus, 175
dove, 45
Dove, 158, 160
dragon, 43

E

Eblis, 40
Ebrahah, 496
ecclesiastical, 257, 262, 322, 391
Edict of Milan, 179
Edward Irving, 371
effulgent, 19, 33
Egypt, xvi, 5, 34
Elam, 59
Elias, 7, 23, 24, 25, 92, 95, 96, 129, 130, 131, 355, 377, 378, 379, 415
Elijah, 7, 24, 25, 28, 92, 95, 96, 120, 129, 201, 231, 299, 351, 354, 375, 377, 378, 379, 388, 445
Elisha, 92
elixir, 441
Elizabeth, 96
Eloi, 415
emanating, 20
Emmanuel, 307
encyclopedia, 50
Encyclopedia, 74
enlightenment, 10
enrapture, 54
Epistle, ix, xxi, 26, 55, 66, 67, 103, 128, 147, 159, 189, 224, 243, 244, 274, 289, 293, 318, 323, 367, 383, 393, 412, 469, 575
Esaias, 95
Esau, 72
eschatological, 169, 170, 172, 180, 354, 425, 428
eschatology, 170, 171, 172, 180, 185
eschaton, 428
essence, 10
Essenes, 352
eternity, 34
Etrat, 519
etymology, 150
Eucharist, 155
Euphrates, 60
evanescent, 14
Evangel, 137, 138, 139, 453, 454, 455, 456, 457, 464, 469, 471, 472, 573
Evangelist, 267, 404
Eve, 40
Ever-Abiding, 12

evil-doers, 31
exalted, 11
exegesis, 451
exile, 67
Exodus, 34
Exposition, 8
eye of God, 103
Ezekiel, 289

F

Fadak, 457
famine, 58, 210, 277, 556, 557
fancy, 11
fantastical, 16
Farewell Discourse, 133
Fárs, 357
Farsi, 127
Fársi, xxii
Fashioner, 271
fasting, 110, 193, 228, 229, 230, 231, 232, 233, 234, 239, 240, 318, 326, 353, 450
Fath-'Ali Sháh, 363
Fátima, 219
Fáṭima, 497
fig tree, 168, 188, 272, 406, 410, 567
figurative, xii, 106, 109, 110, 111, 123, 170, 240
firmament, 8
fluidity, 104
forbidden fruit, 40
forefathers, 17
Fountain, 13
fragrances, 53
France, 259
friendliness, 17
fulfillment, 49
Furkan, 137
Fus'ha, 127

G

Gabriel, 71, 282, 284, 308, 351, 408, 417, 420, 497, 500, 515
Galilee, 114, 256, 308, 309, 347, 349, 353
garment, 51
generation, 32, 84, 86, 168, 171, 172, 178, 224, 255, 259, 340, 352, 421, 542, 546, 567
Genesis, 41
genocide, 74
Gentile, 141, 142, 193, 352
Gentiles, 142, 176, 191, 192, 193, 194, 195, 196, 202, 385, 405, 413, 445, 548, 564
geocentric cosmology, 472
Ghadir-i-Khum, 505
Ghawth-i-A'ẓam, 397
ghayb-i-baghá, 19
ghazál, 19
Godhead, 13, 22, 26, 203, 323, 427, 428, 475
Golgotha, 414
Gomorrah, 58
Gospels, 23
grace, 20
Great Comet of 1819, 359
great disappointment, 181, 551, 552
Greek Orthodox, 350
Guardian, 48

Ḥ

ḥadíth, 105, 411, 479
Ḥadíth, xvii
Ḥadith-i-Marvy, 519
Ḥadith-i-Nabavi, 519
Ḥadith-i-Qudsi, 519
Ḥafiz, 14
Hagar, 60
Háhút, 382
Haifa, xxii
Ḥajaru'l-Aswad, 496
Ḥájí, xiii
Ḥájí Mírzá Kamálu'd-Dín, 380
Ḥaq, 245, 478
Ḥaq al Yaqín, 245
Ḥazrat-i-A'lá, 1
Ḥijáz, 125, 279
Ḥijrah, 279, 502
Ḥobal, 503
ḥúrí, 397, 398
ḥúrís, 397, 398, 399, 431
Ḥusayn, 18, 22, 220, 422, 424, 425, 523, 524, 526, 540, 559

H

habitation, 12, 33
Hadrian, 350
Hakim Hezghil Hayem, 67
halo, 28
handiwork, 11
Haran, 58
Haykal, 22
hearken, 14
heaven of
Certitude, 387
Command, 386
divine knowledge, 387
immutable purpose, 387
Revelation, 388
Utterance, 387
Will, 386
heavenly muse, 43
heavens will clive asunder, 465
Hebrew, 72, 80, 114, 212, 229, 287, 307, 312, 350, 415, 416, 441, 559
Hebron, 59
heedlessness, 33, 127
heifer, 60
Heinrich Kelber,, 371
Hellenistic, 142
hemaj-i-ṛeá'a, 257
Heraclius, 504
Herod Antipas, 351
Herod Antipater, 346, 347
Herod I, 346
Hidden Treasure, 18
Hidden Words, 33
Him Whom God shall make manifest, 493
Him Whom God will make manifest, 9
Hin, 365
holiness, 33
holy bread, 5
Holy Ghost, 132, 194, 307, 308, 314, 353, 564
Holy Land, 68
Holy Mariner, 50
Holy of Holies, 5, 25
Holy Spirit, 122, 137, 139, 155, 159, 249, 267, 276, 282, 313, 327, 328, 332, 351, 356, 376, 401, 404, 414, 479
Holy Tradition, 105
Holy Traditions, 519
honour, 15
Howard MacNutt, xxii
Húd, 29
humiliations, 29
Husbán, 226
hypocrites, 101, 168, 187, 223, 232, 447, 567

I

I'tiżád-al-Salṭanah, 392
i'nná, 476
Ibn-i-Fáriḍ, 395, 396
Ibn-i-Ṣúríyá, 457, 458, 461
idol sculptor, 69
idol worship, 45
idolaters, 102
illumination, 3
Imám, xiv, xviii, xix, xx, xxii, 16, 22, 50, 111, 207, 211, 220, 226, 262, 360, 361, 362, 363, 367, 391, 392, 393, 441, 449, 515, 519, 520, 521, 522, 523, 524, 525, 526, 527, 529, 540
Imám Ja'fár-i-Ṣádiq, 111
Imám Músáy-i-Káẓim, xiv
Imám, Ḥasan al-'Askarí, xix
Imáms, xvii, xix, xx, 50, 62, 63, 110, 136, 206, 211, 219, 220, 226, 233, 439, 468, 508, 515, 519, 520, 521, 522, 524, 525
immaculate conception, 311, 312
immaculate Souls, 219
immemorial, 10
immortal, 14
immutable, 59
impetus, 20
Imran, 102, 298, 312
inaccessible, 11
incumbent, 17
India, xvi, xxii
infancy gospels, 140, 142
Infancy Gospels, 139
infidel, 15
infidels, 45, 46, 430, 442, 453, 454
inscrutable, 28
inspiration, 43
International Archives, xxii, 529
intoxicating, 14

Iraq, xii
iron, 104
Isaac, 64
Isaac Newton, 370
Isaiah, 83, 95, 111, 112, 190, 240, 252, 256, 266, 272, 289, 307, 334, 447, 465, 547
Iṣfahán, 329, 357, 359
Iṣfáhán, 391
Ishmael, 60
Islam, xviii
Islamic, 31
Islamic Empire, 63
Israel, xxii, 5, 7, 24, 28, 34, 35, 58, 63, 68, 71, 72, 73, 74, 76, 79, 82, 83, 84, 92, 93, 95, 107, 108, 114, 117, 118, 119, 120, 122, 123, 134, 139, 173, 175, 188, 189, 191, 193, 224, 231, 254, 255, 277, 287, 288, 289, 290, 300, 301, 335, 336, 342, 346, 350, 352, 377, 380, 381, 385, 403, 416, 433, 447, 454, 458, 459, 460, 461, 465, 470, 557, 573, 575, 576, 578
Israelites, 5, 63, 72, 74, 75, 80, 82, 88, 108, 114, 173, 193, 299, 305, 459, 461, 464
Isráfíl, 185, 282

J

Ja'far al-Ṣádiq, 441
Jabarút, 383
Jacob, 64
James, 15
Jehovah, 114, 372
Jericho, 93
Jerusalem, 59, 94, 95, 106, 131, 145, 173, 178, 179, 180, 182, 188, 192, 193, 194, 220, 228, 229, 230, 277, 278, 281, 282, 284, 288, 290, 291, 313, 344, 345, 346, 349, 350, 401, 460, 461, 501, 504, 513, 563, 564
Jesus
  brothers, 255
Jēth'rō, 75
Jewish, 64, 67, 83, 96, 101, 114, 115, 120, 129, 141, 169, 171, 173, 174, 175, 178, 179, 187, 190, 191, 195, 197, 206, 228, 229, 230, 231, 246, 258, 288, 291, 299, 308, 309, 312, 328, 346, 347, 352, 357, 381, 400, 445, 453, 457, 458, 461, 462, 468, 470, 495, 503, 547, 550, 559
Jibra'íl, 282
Johann Bengel, 371
John Milton, 43
John the Baptist, 25, 96, 130, 131, 170, 171, 308, 348, 351, 352, 353, 354, 355, 357, 378, 379, 384, 573, 574
Joseph, 15
Joseph Smith, 372
Joseph Wolf, 371
Josephus, 174, 175, 347, 354
Jou'al, 327
Judaism, xviii, 25, 80, 92, 120, 142, 174, 193, 228, 230, 231, 277, 291, 312, 352, 431, 543
Judas, 15
Judea, 346
Judeo-Christian, 43, 108
Jupiter, 345

K

Ka'bah, 18
Ka'bih, 233, 278, 279, 283, 399, 407, 495, 496, 497
Ka'bah, 143
káfur, 241
Kalím'u'lláh, 342
Karbilá, xvii, 19, 126, 360, 361, 364, 368, 370, 423
Karbílá, 29
Káshán, 345
Kaw<u>th</u>ar, 188
Káẓimayn, 423
Keturah, 64
<u>Kh</u>adijah, 498
<u>Kh</u>adíjih Bigum, xv
<u>Kh</u>ál-i-A'ẓam, xii
<u>Kh</u>alil'u'lláh, 56
<u>Kh</u>án-i-<u>Sh</u>ávirdí, 264
<u>Kh</u>aybar, 457, 458
<u>Kh</u>urásán, xiv, 363, 391
Khusraw, 504
King James, vii
kingdom, 23, 28, 65, 90, 96, 101, 108, 112, 119, 122, 157, 166, 170, 171, 180, 189, 191, 213, 216, 221, 223, 231, 232, 266, 287, 288, 308, 320,

327, 335, 341, 342, 346, 347, 348, 352, 355, 357, 374, 378, 380, 382, 384, 385, 413, 447, 475, 484, 491, 504, 535, 552,553, 564, 567
kingdom of God, 119, 170, 352, 567
Kingdom of Names, 5
Kirmánsháh, 363
Kitáb-i-Aqdas, x, 2
Kitáb-i-Badi‘, 366
knowledge, 11
Kosher, 191

L

Láḥíjí, 10
Láhút, 382
lapwing, 325
Latter-Day Saints, 372
Law, 137
Láwḥ Basít al-Haqíqa, 78
Lawḥ-i-Dunyá, xvi
Láwḥ-i-Shikkar-Shikan, 425, 553, 554
Lawḥ-i-Sulṭán, 423
Lawlák, 411
leprous, 81
Letters of the Living, xiii
Levi, 71
Leviathan, 332
light of guidance, 304
literal interpretation, 48
Lord of hosts, 123
Lord of Hosts, 440
lost sheep, 191, 385, 433
Lot, 68
Lote-Tree, 88, 128
love, 11
luminosity, 104

M

mad poet, 409
Magi, 344, 350
magicians, 82
Magnum Opus, 441
Mahdi, 465
Máh-Kú, 8
Majlisí, 50
Malachi, 24
Malakút, 383
manifest, 21
manna, 34, 35, 36, 97, 153, 154, 286, 287, 385, 458, 459
Mansúr-i-Ḥalláj, 78
mantle, 51
Manúchihr Khán, 359, 391, 393
Marcion, 119
martyrdom, 102
Martyrdom, xiii
Martyrs, 4, 66
Mary, 15
Mashhad, 362
Masjid’ul-Aqsá, 501
Masjid-al-Aqsá, 278
Massacre of Innocents, 346
matchless, 14
materialization, 120
Mázindarán, 147
Mecca, xiv, 18, 29, 125, 138, 143, 219, 233, 262, 278, 279, 281, 283, 284, 320, 357, 358, 362, 365, 399, 407, 409, 417, 419, 428, 433, 434, 463, 465, 495, 496, 497, 501, 502, 504, 505, 516
Medina, 125, 278, 279, 280, 281, 284, 320, 358, 363, 368, 391, 393, 457, 458, 463, 502, 503, 505, 514, 516
Mēl-chĭśe-dēc, 59
Mēl-chĭźe-dēk, 59
Memphis, 108
Mesopotami, 64
Messengers, 10
Messiah, 15, 22, 24, 27, 28, 96, 114, 120, 121, 122, 123, 124, 129, 131, 137, 149, 163, 172, 176, 182, 183, 187, 190, 191, 196, 201, 202, 255, 287, 288, 308, 316, 351, 352, 375, 377, 378, 379, 388, 400, 405, 406, 407, 410, 413, 415, 416, 419, 425, 443, 444, 445, 472
metaphor, 89
Mi‘ráj, 501
Michael, 282
Midian, 301, 302
Mĭdí-ans, 75
Midrash, 342
Mihdí, 126
Míká’íl, 282
millennium, 170, 179, 188, 431
Millerites, 371, 550
ministry, 48

miracle, 97, 139, 141, 142, 237, 349, 391, 392, 393, 414, 417, 424, 437
miracles, 82
Miriam, 298
Mírzá, xiii
Mírzá Abu'l-Faḍl, 91
Mírzá Áqá Ján, xvii
Mírzá Buzurg Khán, 422
Mírzá Ḥasan-'Alí, xvi
Mírzá Haydar 'Alí, 329
Mírzá Muḥiṭ, 18
Mírzá Sa'íd Khán, 424
Mírzá Siyyid 'Alí, xii
Mírzá Siyyid Ḥasan, xvi
Mírzá Siyyid Muḥammad, xiv
Mírzá Yaḥyá, xii
monk, 497
monotheism, 64
monotheistic, 419
moon, 65
Mormon, 372
Mosaic Dispensation, 8
Mosaic law, 114
mosque, 31
Most Great Prison, 434
Most Sublime Pen, 221, 222
Mother Book, 198
mother city, 434
Mount Carmel, xxii
Mount Hira, 497
Mount Horeb, 302
Mount Olive, 146, 165
Mount Sinai, 75, 86, 302, 303, 304, 467
Mountain of Mákú, 452
mouthpiece, 21
Mu 'Tamidu'd-Dawlih, 359
Muftí, 264
Muh'kamát, 110
Muhajerun, 358
Muḥammad Sháh, 22, 261
Muḥyi'd-Dín-i-'Arabí, 395
Mullá Hádí Sabzivárí, 78
Mullá Ḥasan-i-'Ammú, 423
Mulla Jafar, 328
musk, x
Muslim, 22
Muslims, xiv, xviii, 16, 134, 137, 180, 185, 197, 207, 220, 232, 233, 236, 251, 257, 283, 284, 291, 312, 358, 359, 377, 381, 386, 389, 398, 399, 411, 417, 431, 439, 443, 446, 454, 463, 464, 465, 470, 473, 488, 491, 501, 502, 503, 504, 505, 508, 510, 511, 513, 515, 516, 517, 518
Mutashábihát, 110
mystic, 4
Mystical, 3
mysticism, 4
Mysticism, 3

N

Nabi, 446, 465
Nabíl, xv, 19, 264, 326, 530, 583
Nabil-i-A'zam, 361, 363, 367, 368, 370
Nabilu'd-Dawlih, xxii
Nag Ḥammadi, 139
Najaf, 360, 361, 364, 423
Naráq, 381
Násiri'd-Dín Sháh, 326
Násút, 384
naváfil, 105
Naw-Ruz, 231
Nazarene, 114
Nazareth, 51, 107, 114, 121, 169, 176, 307, 308, 309, 316, 350, 375, 376, 406, 418
Nebuchadnezzar, 460, 461
Neo-Babylonian, 460
Nero, 175
Nesr, 46
Nestorian, 497
new bottles, 13
new wine, 13
New-Testament, xi
niche, 303, 474
Night Journey, 88, 501
nightingale, 33
Nightingale, 107, 158, 159, 160, 162, 554
Nile, 60
Nimrod, 28, 340, 341, 342
Noah, 30, 44
Nudbih, 220
Núr, 264, 363
Nura, 127

O

obligatory prayers, 450

occultation, xix, xx, xxii, 50, 207, 515, 521, 522, 524, 526
ocean, 34
ode, 19
Ode, 19, 158, 395, 538, 540
Odoric of Pordenone, 345
Olivet Discourse, 163, 166, 168, 169, 170, 172, 173, 176, 178, 179, 181, 336, 425, 444, 563
Omniscient, 271
oppression, 76, 101, 148, 182, 210, 212, 213, 222, 300, 433
Oriental, v
orphan, 241, 256
orthodoxy, 257, 523
Ottoman Empire, xii, 350, 424

P

pagans, 102
Panthera, 140, 310
papal court, 67
papal government, 390
parable, 80, 111, 112, 168, 188, 200, 208, 212, 265, 266, 270, 303, 426, 567
Paraclete, 132, 134, 135, 176
Paradise, 40
Paran, 83, 464
Parousia, 336
path, 11
Paul, 119, 176, 191, 194, 195, 196, 278, 328, 418
peerless, 21
Pen of Glory, 126, 388
pentateuch, 402
Pentateuch, 118, 190, 231, 456, 459, 460, 463, 464
Penuel, 73
People of the Book, 102
perfect Balance, 100
Perfect Man, 374
perpetual, 11
perpetual virginity, 16, 141, 449
persecution, 31
Persian, iii, v, vi, xi, xxi, xxii, 1, 3, 8, 9, 14, 19, 33, 34, 48, 53, 65, 78, 86, 126, 127, 150, 159, 183, 227, 248, 294, 295, 323, 324, 325, 326, 344, 345, 356, 357, 358, 359, 360, 361, 366, 389, 398, 422, 424, 448, 477, 478, 481, 484, 503, 504, 513, 540, 541,542, 545, 559, 577, 578
Persian Bayán, 8
perspicuous, 109
Peter, 7, 23, 129
Pharaoh, 28, 58, 433
Pharisees, 13, 27, 28, 95, 96, 98, 101, 114, 116, 117, 170, 187, 194, 206, 223, 297, 403, 407, 410, 421, 447
Philip, 256
Philistines, 63
Phillip, 26
philosopher, 78, 119, 180, 309, 441
Phoenix, 332, 333
phylacteries, 254
physical, 15
pilgrimage, xvi
Point of the Bayán, 484
polysemic, 478
ponder, 28
Pontius Pilate, 348
postulate, 16
potentialities, 11
Prayer of Fasting, 11
priest, 59
priesthood, 59
Primal Point, xxi, 103
Primal Will, 8
profligate, 15
progenitor, 72
progressive revelation, 99
prophecy, 9
Prophet Muḥammad, xvii, xix
prophetic cycle, 237, 239
Prophetic Cycle, 238
Prophetic Traditions, 519
Prophets, 10
Providence, 98
Psalms, 229, 255, 273, 287, 288, 289, 334, 335, 506
Ptolemaic, 472
publicans, 407

Q

Qá'f, 333
Qádiríyyih, 397

Qá'im, xiv, xviii, xix, xx, 16, 22, 30, 50, 143, 319, 360, 431, 446, 452, 465, 526, 527
Qámus-i-Íqán, iii
Qaṣídiy-i-Tá'íyyih, 395
Qaṣídiy-i-Varqá'íyyih, 396
Qayyúmu'l-Asmá, 102
Qiblih, 233, 276, 277, 278, 282, 284, 291, 292, 399, 504
Quadricep, 74
Qumran, 352
Quraysh, 279, 407, 428, 497, 498, 499, 500, 503

R

Rabbi, 175, 457
Rabbinic, 80, 287, 291, 299, 300
Rabbinical, 342
radiant, 19
Rā-gū'el, 77
ráji'ún, 476
rak'ahs, 283
Ramaḍán, 110, 232
Raphael, 185, 282
Rasoul, 236, 446, 465, 571
raven, 45
Rebekah, 64
Redemptive scheme, x
rejection, 43
Remembrance, 77
resplendent, 20
resurrection, xviii, xx, 157, 176, 180, 185, 186, 265, 272, 428, 429, 430, 431, 450, 452, 490, 507
Resurrection, xviii, xxiv, 126, 169, 182, 184, 223, 243, 251, 252, 272, 377, 429, 430, 431, 435, 436, 443, 444, 451, 452, 453, 465, 486, 488, 491, 492, 507, 508, 515, 527
Reū'el, 77
Riḍá, 226, 362
Riḍván, xii, 55, 128, 158, 161, 163, 186, 227, 248, 323, 437
Rik'ats, 283
Risálíy-i-Khál, xxi
ritualistic, 33
rival, 26
River Jordan, 24
robe, 51
Rod of Moses, 82
Rose Garden, 160
Rumelia, 69
Rúz-bih, 357

Ṣ

ṣabá, 323
Ṣabean, 508
Ṣáḥib az-Zamán, xx
ṣalát, 228
Ṣáliḥ, 30, 55
Ṣeráṭ, 431, 450, 451, 453
Ṣúfísm, 397

S

sabá, 323
sabachthani, 415
Sabbath, 114, 115, 116, 117, 143, 187, 190, 202, 229, 230, 255, 267, 402, 403, 404, 410
sacred Mosque, 282, 283, 285
sacred Tree, 89, 149, 437
sacrifice, 100
Sa'dí, 14
Sadratu'l-Muntahá, 88
Sadratu'l-Muntahá, 88, 198, 199
Sadrih, 436, 437
Saladin, 350
Sale, vii
Salem, 59
Sálik, 9
Salmán, 357, 358, 359, 503
Salmán-i-Fársí, 357
Salome, 354
Salsabil, 305, 306, 343
Sam, 30
Samaria, 124, 175, 194
sanctification, 20
sanctuary, 5
Sáqí, 19
Sarah, 61
Sarai, 58
Satan, xx, 39, 40, 41, 43, 263, 427, 429, 501, 543, 560, 571
satanic, 122, 211, 227, 319, 390, 393
Saudi Arabia, 125, 279, 283, 584

Saul, 328
scenarios, 52
science, 20
scorn, 47
scout, 45
scribes, 25
scriptures, i, xi, 21, 48, 53, 88, 98, 108, 116, 117, 139, 142, 146, 149, 186, 206, 207, 214, 215, 221, 228, 234, 235, 239, 240, 241, 242, 312, 372, 380, 403, 433, 457
Seal of Prophets, 236
seal of the prophets, 412, 465
search, 11
Second Advent, 170, 171, 172, 181, 188, 371, 372, 545
seeker, xxiv, 11
Seir, 464
Self, i, xxiii, xxiv, 11, 87, 159, 218, 219, 225, 243, 250, 320, 382, 420, 421, 481, 482, 483, 485, 487, 493, 582
self-abnegation, 12
self-subsisting, 10
self-surrender, 11
seminaries, 269, 270, 469
Semitic, 135
Sephora, 75
Sept, 108
sepulchres, 186, 187, 223, 328, 488, 490
Sermon on the Mount, 114
serpent, 41, 82
Seven Valleys, 11
Shabestari, 78
Shah, 102, 209, 363
Shakespeare, 276
Shaykh, 11
Shaykh 'Abdu'l-Ḥusayn, 422
Shaykh Aḥmad-i-Aḥsá'i, 360
Shaykh Murtaḍáy-i-Anṣárí, 423
Shaykhí, 18, 262, 360, 367
Shaykhu'l-Islám, 262
Sheba, 323, 324, 325, 326, 341
she-camel, 55
shewbread, 116, 403
Shí'ah, xvii, 111
Shinar, 57
shining hands, 82
Shíráz, xiii, xv, xvi, xx, 322, 362, 559
Shoaib, 301
Shoghi Effendi, i
Shu'aib, 30
Shuaibe, 77
Siddur, 229
Siddurim, 229
sifter of wheat, 328
Simon, 15
Simon bar Kokhba, 175
Simon Magus, 175
Sinai, 5, 342
sinew, 73
sires, 17
Síyáh-Chál, 366, 437
Siyyid 'Alí Muḥammad, 1
Siyyid 'Alí, xiii
Siyyid Javád, xiii
Siyyid Javá'd-i-Karbilá'í, xvii
Siyyid Káẓim, 18, 360, 363, 364, 365, 367, 368, 369, 370, 373
Siyyid Káẓim-i-Rashtí, 360
Siyyid-i-Lawlák, 411
slavery, 102
snow-white Path, 397
Sodom, 58
solar years, 49
Solomon, 120, 122, 176, 288, 289, 290, 324, 325, 506
Son of God, 27, 60, 173, 261, 309, 336, 338, 412, 413, 414, 416, 545
Son of man, 21, 25, 27, 32, 36, 97, 116, 130, 154, 167, 171, 172, 178, 182, 261, 286, 287, 334, 335, 336, 337, 338, 355, 374, 375, 378, 379, 384, 386, 400, 403, 405, 407, 412, 415, 416, 426, 434, 443, 444, 567
Son of Mary, 16, 137, 139, 152, 163
sons of God, 44
Sonship, 63, 314, 414
sorcerers, 82
sorrowful, 18
sovereignty, xxiv, 52
Sowah, 46
sower, 111, 112, 212, 265, 266, 270
sparrows, 143
speech of birds, 324
Spirit of God, 4, 113, 121, 123, 163, 258, 314, 315, 337, 356
Spirit of truth, 132, 249
splendour, 12
St. Augustine of Hippo, 180

St. John, 62
staff, 82
standards, 20
star, 65
Star of Jesus, 345
Stephen, 418
subaḥát-i-Jalál, 14
sublimity, 4
subtil, 41
Sufyání, 446, 524, 526
Sulaymáníyyih, 19, 395
Sulṭán, 263
Suluk, 9
Sunnah, xvii
Sunni, 111, 225, 232, 257, 518, 524, 527
supererogative, 105
superhuman, 16
superior, 15
supernatural, 30
superstition, 100
Súrah of Húd, 29, 30, 31, 32, 47, 56, 58, 409, 511, 512
Súriy-i-Múlúk, 264
swoon, 86
symbolism, 56
synagogue, 15, 37, 154, 287, 418
synoptic Gospels, 114, 129, 146, 163
Syria, 69

T

tabernacle, 5, 6, 9, 25, 189, 474, 475, 553
Tabernacle, 5, 9, 173, 290
Tablet of Kullu'ṭ-Ṭa'ám, 381
Tablet of Visitation, 52
Tabríz, 262, 322
Taḥríf, 455, 456, 457, 462, 465, 467, 469, 470, 471
Ta'if, 280
tajalíyát, 19
Talmud, 80, 299, 456, 541
Taymour-i-Kháwrazmi, 359
Tehran, 363, 392, 437
Temple, 22, 38, 142, 146, 163, 165, 169, 170, 172, 173, 177, 178, 179, 199, 228, 229, 230, 277, 278, 288, 290, 291, 313, 351, 461, 563, 564
temptation, 43
Ten Commandments, 83
Tetrarch, 347
Thagout, 207
Thamud, 55
the Báb, ii, 8
the Great Disappointment, 371, 372
The Letters of Living, 370
theologian, 119, 180
theological, i, 133, 140, 169, 173, 214, 234, 299, 449
theology, 20
Theudas, 175
thief in the night, 252, 426
thlipsis, 212
Thummim, 7
thunderstruck, 10
Tigris River, 150, 540
Tisha B'Av, 230
tithes, 59
Tiyyu'l-Arḍ, 391
Torah, 24, 80, 102, 113, 121, 122, 123, 134, 191, 196, 229, 230, 255, 277, 291, 316, 454, 455, 456, 457, 464, 469, 471, 472
Touchstone, 447
Tower of Bable, 341
traditions, xi, xviii
transcendent, 4
transcendent glory, 13
transfiguration, 7, 23, 25, 299
Transfiguration, 378
transgress, 31
transient, 33
Transliteration, v
Transmitted Traditions, 519
transmute, 89
traverse, 11
Tree of divine Reality, 436
tribulation, 71, 112, 167, 170, 179, 181, 212, 259, 266, 338, 374, 400, 443, 564, 567
true liberty, 54
true poverty, 11
trumpet, 84, 168, 185, 186, 187, 243, 252, 328, 400, 440, 443, 498, 567
Turkey, 260
Tús, 391, 393
twin luminous lights, 367

Ṭ

Ṭihrán, xiii

U

Uḥud, 503
ulamás, 362
Umat, 466
Umayyad dynasty, 63
Unapproachable, 22
Uncompounded Reality, 78
unerring, 20
unity, 11
universal, 214, 217, 237, 239, 267, 289, 304, 305, 330, 374, 432, 496
Universal House of Justice, iii
Universal Manifestations of God, 214
universality, xi
unknowable, 11
Unseen, 22, 52
Ur, 57, 58, 69, 320
Urim, 7
utterance, 8, 23
Utterances, 332

V

váḥid, 8
Vaḥíd Dárábí, 209
vain imaginations, 476
vain imagining, 15
Vain imaginings, 14
Valí-'Ahd, 262
Vehicle, 21
veils of glory, 14
Venus, 345
victory, 52, 53, 295, 365, 434
vinegar, 414, 415, 416
Vineyard of God, 372
vipers, 32, 224, 352
Virgin Birth, 315
Virgin Mary, 312, 313, 314
vituperative, 448

W

Wadd, 46
wayfarer, 12
whirlwind, 92
white hand, 82
wicked, 46
wilderness, 35
wilds of remoteness, 99, 248
William Davis, 371
William Miller, 181, 371, 373, 545, 547, 548
Wolf, 55
wonderment, 11
Word of God, 53, 66, 121, 123, 163, 170, 212, 274, 275, 276, 287, 289, 315, 316, 317, 318, 356, 388, 405, 422, 428, 446, 461, 467
worldly-wise, 54
wrath of God, 473
Wronged One, 67, 146, 147, 148, 274, 295, 469

Y

Yaghuth, 46
Yahuk, 46
Yaḥyá, 351, 356, 366, 380, 536
Ya<u>th</u>reb, 358, 495, 497, 502
Ya<u>th</u>rib, 279, 280
Yazd, xvi, 363, 367
Yemen, 496
Yom Kippur, 229, 230
Youth, xiii, 261, 263, 391

Z

Zachariah, 351, 355, 573
Zacharias, 96
Zion, 106, 174, 182, 252, 289, 400, 401
Zĭp-pórah, 75
Zoroaster, 214
Zoroastrianism, xviii, 431
Zoroastrians, 230

www.ingramcontent.com/pod-product-compliance
Lightning Source LLC
Chambersburg PA
CBHW080718300426
44114CB00019B/2414